TAX CRIMES

TAX CRIMES

Second Edition

JOHN A. TOWNSEND, ESQ.
Townsend & Jones
Adjunct Professor
University of Houston Law Center

LARRY A. CAMPAGNA, ESQ.
Chamberlain, Hdrlicka, White, Williams & Aughtry
Adjunct Professor
University of Houston Law Center

STEVE JOHNSON
University Professor of Law
Florida State University College of Law

SCOTT A. SCHUMACHER
Professor of Law
Director, Graduate Program in Taxation
University of Washington School of Law

CAROLINA ACADEMIC PRESS
Durham, North Carolina

Print ISBN: 978-1-6304-3075-7
eBook ISBN: 978-1-6304-3089-4
Paperback ISBN: 978-1-5310-3617-1

Library of Congress Cataloging-in-Publication Data

Townsend, John A., 1942- author.

Tax crimes / John A. Townsend, Esq., Townsend & Jones, Adjunct Professor, University of Houston Law Center; Larry A. Campagna, Esq., Chamberlain, Hdrlicka, White, Williams & Aughtry, Adjunct Professor, University of Houston Law Center; Steve Johnson, University Professor of Law, Florida State University College of Law; Scott A. Schumacher, Professor of Law, Director, Graduate Program in Taxation, University of Washington School of Law. — Second edition.

pages cm.

Includes index.

ISBN 978-1-63043-075-7 (hardbound) — ISBN 978-1-63043-089-4 (eBook)

1. Tax evasion—United States I. Campagna, Larry A., author. II. Johnson, Steve R., 1949- author. III. Schumacher, Scott A., author. IV. Title.

KF6334.T69 2015
345.73'0233--dc23 2015003706

Carolina Academic Press
700 Kent Street
Durham, NC 27701
(919) 489-7486
www.caplaw.com

Printed in the United States of America
2026 Printing

Preface

For many years, LL.M. programs in taxation offered courses that covered criminal tax issues. Criminal tax procedure often was included in survey courses of tax procedure, and sometimes the criminal tax penalties were covered in a separate course. However, until we offered the original version of this book, no casebook included both the substantive and procedural issues involved in the investigation, prosecution, and defense of criminal tax cases. We believe that this book is the only published book covering those subjects.

The book begins with an overview of the criminal tax system, the personnel involved, and an introduction to some of the issues that will be addressed in more detail in later chapters. We then discuss the elements of the numerous crimes for which a defendant may be charged, focusing on key aspects such as willfulness. Next, the book covers how tax cases are investigated, including the most common steps from a civil tax examination through indictment. In these chapters we will examine the tools the Government has at its disposal to obtain information, as well as the defenses a person under investigation may assert. We then turn to trial and sentencing issues, and we examine the ethical issues and collateral consequences that arise in the investigation and litigation of criminal tax cases. Finally, the book provides a review of the criminal tax system, allowing the reader to put all the foregoing concepts together, with a special emphasis on practical tips for handling these complex and exciting cases.

Each chapter closes with a practical problem designed to highlight some of the key issues addressed in the cases and materials. The problems are based on situations encountered in practice or found in decided cases. Although some of the problems either state or disclose the issues and even the applicable statutes, many of them require analysis of a given set of facts to first determine and then resolve the critical issues.

Books in the Graduate Tax Series are designed to be read with, and complement, the study of the Code and Regulations. LL.M. programs build on, and significantly expand, students' knowledge of the Code, Regulations, and judicial doctrines. But this casebook should be accessible to J.D. students as well as LL.M. candidates, as long as they have had exposure to a basic federal income tax course and some introduction to federal civil, criminal, or tax procedure.

The focus of this book is primarily on criminal tax matters. However, many criminal tax cases begin as civil audits, and most criminal tax cases end with the IRS attempting to assess and collect the taxes it alleges are due and owing. Thus, we will examine civil tax procedure as it relates to criminal tax cases in some detail. For additional information on civil tax procedure, we recommend David M. Richardson, Jerome Borison, and Steve Johnson's *Civil Tax Procedure*, another book in the LexisNexis Graduate Tax Series.

In the original version of this book, we thanked many people who have helped and inspired us in the journey that led to the first version. Their contributions are still with us and present in this version of the book. Others we unintentionally failed to name also contributed. And since the publication, others have contributed to our understanding, practicing, teaching and writing on the subject of tax crimes (as well as living a better life). Rather than attempting again to name those contributors, we just state here that we greatly appreciate contributions. We are indebted to them to pass the torch that they lit. We are reminded of Thomas Jefferson's great quote:

> He who receives an idea from me, receives instruction himself without lessening mine; as he who lights his taper at mine, receives light without darkening me.

We hope that others will light their tapers from ours and pass the instruction so generously entrusted to us.

Table of Contents

Chapter 1

OVERVIEW OF THE CRIMINAL TAX SYSTEM

IRC: §§ 7201, 7202, 7203, 7204, 7205, 7206, 7207, 7208, 7209, 7210, 7211, 7212, 7213, 7213A, 7214, 7215, 7216, 7217 (skim all these sections)

I. INTRODUCTION

"What's the worst that could happen?" One cannot prudently embark on any endeavor without having analyzed that question. In tax practice, the worst that can happen to your client (or to you) is criminal prosecution. The table below lists some people prominent in their respective fields. From our context, you can guess what they have in common. That's right. They all were convicted of federal tax crimes.

Government

Spiro Agnew, Vice President of the United States

Robert B. Anderson, Secretary of the Treasury

Joseph D. Nunan, Jr., Commissioner of Internal Revenue

Mario Biaggi, Congressman & most decorated officer in history of NYC Police

George H. Ryan, Sr., Governor of Illinois

Jack Abramoff, Washington Superlobbyist

Entertainment

Lauryn Hill, Grammy-winning rapper/songwriter

Jeffrey Atkins a/k/a rapper Ja Rule

Joe Francis, founder of "Girls Gone Wild"

Harry Reems, co-star of "Deep Throat" and other porn films

Chuck Berry, rock and roll legend

Ron Isley of the Isley Brothers, R&B singer

Sports

Jim Thorpe, professional golfer

Baseball stars Pete Rose, Duke Snider & Willie McCovey

Business

Peter Madoff, managing director of Bernie Madoff's Ponzi scheme

Moses Annenberg, founder of "TV Guide"

Victor Posner, prominent industrialist

Walter Anderson, telecommunications entrepreneur and venture capitalist

Leona Helmsley, New York hotel queen ("Only little people pay taxes.")

H. Ty Warner, creator of "Beanie Babies" and other plush toys

Andreas Bachmann, Bradley Birkenfeld and David Parse, Swiss bankers helping Americans hide income

"Business"

Alphonse "Scar Face" Capone, Chicago entrepreneur

Jake "Greasy Thumb" Guzik, Capone's CFO

Frank "the Enforcer" Nitti, Capone's successor

John "the 'Teflon Don' " Gotti, head of Gambino Mafia family

Frank Locascio, Gotti's underboss

Dave Beck, "mobbed up" President of the Teamster's Union

Lawyers

Webster Hubbell, Associate Attorney General of the United States

William Campbell, federal judge

Sam Currin, United States Attorney and state chair of a major political party

Stanley Cohen, activist lawyer who represented Osama bin Laden's son-in-law

Paul Daugerdas and Donna Guerin, creators of bogus tax shelters

Edgar Paltzer, Swiss attorney helping Americans hide income

This course is an important part of your training as a tax lawyer. Many attorneys have found criminal tax to be a fulfilling area, either full time or as part of a combined civil or criminal controversy practice. Moreover, no tax lawyer — even one whose practice is wholly civil — can afford to be ignorant of criminal tax rules and procedures. What begins as a civil matter can become criminal. The tax practitioner must be able to read the warning signs that a matter has or may become criminal. In addition, the tax practitioner must know what to do to prevent or to contain the damage in criminal tax investigations and prosecutions. The lawyer who lacks these skills is dangerous to his or her clients and perhaps to him or herself.

This chapter sets the stage for the course and identifies the actors. Below, we consider four topics: (1) scope of the book, (2) introduction to the criminal tax system, (3) policy issues, and (4) plan of the book.

II. SCOPE OF THE BOOK

This book focuses principally upon the interface of our federal tax system with the criminal justice system. The focus is upon federal tax crimes enumerated in the Internal Revenue Code of 1986 (the "Code").[1] The materials also deal with tax crimes' frequent companions, such as Title 18 U.S.C. offenses for aiding and abetting (section 2), conspiracy (section 371), and false statements (section 1001). These crimes are often charged with or in lieu of the traditional tax crimes and, in the tax context, support the goals of the criminal tax enforcement system.

The book also deals with crimes arising from the Government's War on Crime. Reacting to concerns about drug trafficking and organized crime, Congress enacted laws — illustrated by the money laundering provisions — to attack the profit in that type of criminal conduct. Money laundering is the process by which criminals disguise and use the proceeds of crime. Thus, for example, they may push drug profits (usually in the form of cash) through a legitimate business in order to provide a seemingly legitimate source for the fund. Typically, critical components of these laundering attempts will involve financial institutions. The money laundering laws impose reporting requirements for cash transactions, establish criminal penalties for non-filing or avoiding reporting, and criminalize financial transactions in the proceeds of the types of criminal conduct that concerned Congress. The focus of these crimes is not tax enforcement, but other criminal priorities such as drug trafficking and organized crime.

However, there is a connection between these crimes and tax crimes. When there are illegal sources (particularly for drug trafficking and organized crime), the participants often desire not only to hide their criminal conduct but also to avoid paying tax on their profits. The IRS considers money laundering to be "tax evasion in progress."[2] Hence, the federal tax system has an interest in the major non-tax crimes.

The IRS has historically been the chief enforcer of the criminal tax laws. The IRS has developed unique financial skills in investigating sophisticated tax crimes. These skills also are particularly suited for investigating the financial schemes that attend money laundering and other financial crimes related to illegal source income. With the IRS's skills and with its revenue interest in large sums of untaxed illegal profits, the IRS was a logical player in the enforcement of the money laundering laws. By a Memorandum of Understanding among the IRS, the Attorney General, and the Postmaster General, the IRS has been allocated jurisdiction to investigate violations of 18 U.S.C. section 1956 and 1957 when the underlying conduct is subject to

---

[1] Through this book, references to sections will be to the Internal Revenue Code (26 U.S.C.) unless otherwise noted. The United States has largely abolished common-law crimes. Certainly, we have no common-law tax crimes. Thus, tax behavior is criminal only if it violates one or another of the crimes set out in statute, whether in the Code or another body of federal statutes.

[2] Quoted by Treasury Inspector General for Tax Administration, The Criminal Investigation Function Provides Adequate Guidance to Field Officers for Money Laundering Investigations, Report No. 2002-10-150 (Aug. 21, 2002); *see also* Jeremiah Coder, *IRS CI Division to Stay "Aggressive" Under New Chief*, TAX NOTES, May 21, 2007, at 705 (quoting Eileen Mayer, Chief of CI, describing money laundering as "tax evasion in progress").

investigation under the Code or the Bank Secrecy Act ("BSA").[3] Pursuant to this agreement, the IRS plays a key role in enforcement of the money laundering statutes. In its enforcement efforts focused on money laundering, IRS agents may act independently or by assignment to organized crime or drug task forces where these skills are deployed with the skills of other enforcement agencies, such as the FBI and Customs.[4] Accordingly, this book treats both tax crimes, the general related crimes (such as conspiracy), and money laundering.

III. INTRODUCTION TO THE CRIMINAL TAX SYSTEM

The ensuing chapters of this book describe the criminal tax system in detail. By way of introduction, we address below four foundational matters: (1) the purpose of the criminal tax system, (2) the mens rea requirement (willfulness) common to the principal tax crimes, (3) an overview of the procedural aspects of criminal tax, and (4) policy issues.

A. Purpose of the Criminal Tax System

The criminal tax system must be understood in the context of the role it plays in the overall tax system.[5] Although many other considerations influence the design and content of our tax laws, the fundamental purpose of our, indeed any, tax system is to raise money for the Government. "That collection of taxes is vital to the functioning, indeed existence, of government cannot be denied."[6] Thus, to paraphrase Justice Holmes, taxes are the price we pay for civilized society.[7]

Criminal and civil sanctions exist to fortify the better instincts of taxpayers, in order to safeguard the revenues essential to government. The Department of Justice's Criminal Tax Manual ("CTM")[8] explains the role of criminal tax enforcement thusly:

> The Government helps to preserve the integrity of this Nation's self-assessment tax system through vigorous and uniform criminal enforcement of the internal revenue laws. Criminal prosecutions punish tax law violators and deter other persons who would violate those laws. To achieve maximum deterrence, the Government must pursue broad, balanced, and uniform

---

[3] The Memorandum is included in the Internal Revenue Manual ("IRM") at Exhibit 31.8.1–3.

[4] Currently, U.S. Customs and Border Protection.

[5] For review of the history of criminal tax enforcement in the United States, see 1 Ian M. Comisky, Lawrence S. Feld & Steven M. Harris, *Tax Fraud & Evasion* ch. 1 (6th ed. 2007).

[6] United States v. Kimbell Foods, Inc., 440 U.S. 715 (1979); *see also* Bull v. United States, 295 U.S. 247, 259 (1935) ("taxes are the life-blood of government, and their prompt and certain availability an imperious necessity"); Edmund Burke, *quoted in* State Tax Notes, Jan. 15, 2007, at 149 ("The revenue of the state is the state.").

[7] Compania General de Tabacos de Filipinas v. Collector of Internal Revenue, 275 U.S. 87, 100 (1927) (dissenting opinion).

[8] The CTM is cited frequently in this book. The CTM is an indispensable tool to understanding federal criminal tax enforcement priorities and policies. The current version of the CTM is 2012. In prior versions, such as the 2008 and 2001 versions, material was sometimes arranged differently. In this book, references to the CTM are to the 2012 version unless specifically indicated.

> criminal tax enforcement. Uniformity in tax cases is necessary because tax enforcement potentially affects more individuals than any other areas of criminal enforcement. Broad and balanced enforcement is essential to effectively deter persons of varying economic and vocational status, violators in different geographic areas, and different types of tax law violations.[9]

So, the prosecution of any particular tax crime has the purpose of not only punishing the offender, but more importantly of sending a message to the entire population of taxpayers (or those who should be taxpayers), to give them the incentive to get right on their taxes.

As an example of criminal tax enforcement priorities, consider the protestor genre of cases.[10] Tax protestors seize on (or are sold or conjure up) a variety of "arguments" — constitutional, statutory, natural law, or otherwise — the net effect of which, they urge, is to deny the Government's right to tax and, more specifically, excuse their failure to pay taxes.[11] The courts uniformly reject these arguments. Taxpayers nevertheless continue to assert them often on the theory or hope that, so long as they can convince a court that they sincerely held the beliefs, they can play the audit lottery without being subject to criminal penalties.[12] If allowed to proceed undisturbed, these movements can result in a significant loss of revenue as unwitting and witting participants join the schemes. The IRS must act and does so both civilly and criminally. The Government will criminally prosecute the more egregious offenders and publicize their conviction and sentencing in order to warn others already involved or contemplating becoming involved in such schemes.

B. Mens Rea; the Guilty Mind; Willfulness

In Anglo-American jurisprudence, crimes generally (though not invariably) have required a culpable mental state — often called *mens rea*. *Mens rea* is a broad concept that is far too complex to develop fully in this course.[13] Instead, we will focus on the specific implementation of the concept for tax crimes and related crimes.

The *mens rea* standard typically encountered as to tax and related crimes is willfulness: the taxpayer-defendant must have acted "willfully" in order to have committed a tax crime.[14] In *Bishop*, a leading case, the Supreme Court said:

> The Court's consistent interpretation of the word "willfully" to require an element of *mens rea* implements the pervasive intent of Congress to

[9] CTM 2.00 (incorporating U.S. Attorney's Manual ¶ 6-4.010).

[10] Protestor cases constitute only a small fraction of criminal tax prosecutions, but they are usually highly visible.

[11] The various schemes are too numerous to mention. The IRS has identified at least 40 frivolous protestor arguments. Some of the more common protestor arguments are rebutted at the IRS's website, www.irs.gov.

[12] This defense is explored in connection with the *Cheek* case excerpted in Chapter 2A.

[13] For a useful discussion of *mens rea* in criminal law generally, see Joshua Dressler, Understanding Criminal Law 10 (4th ed. 2006).

[14] For example, as developed in greater detail in Chapter 2A, the most important of the tax crimes (section 7201) applies to those who "willfully attempt" to evade federal tax.

construct penalties that separate the purposeful tax violator from the well-meaning, but easily confused, mass of taxpayers. Until Congress speaks otherwise, we therefore shall continue to require, in both tax felonies and tax misdemeanors that must be done "willfully," the bad purpose or evil motive described in *Murdock*, [290 U.S. 389 (1933)].[15]

BRYAN v. UNITED STATES

United States Supreme Court
524 U.S. 184 (1998)

[Authors' note: "Willfulness" is the *mens rea* standard for many federal non-tax crimes also. In defining that standard, the courts often have looked to tax crime definitions in non-tax cases and non-tax crime definitions in tax cases. In *Bryan*, the Court interpreted a federal statute which criminalized "willfully" dealing in firearms without a federal license. In the excerpt below, the Court adverted to four cases that you will encounter again later in this book.]

The word "willfully" is sometimes said to be "a word of many meanings" whose construction is often dependent on the context in which it appears. *See, e.g., Spies v. United States*, 317 U.S. 492, 497 (1943). Most obviously, it differentiates between deliberate and unwitting conduct, but in the criminal law, it also typically refers to a culpable state of mind. As we explained in *United States v. Murdock*, 290 U.S. 389 (1933), a variety of phrases have been used to describe that concept.[16] As a general matter, when used in the criminal context, a "willful" act is one undertaken with a "bad purpose." In other words, in order to establish a "willful" violation of a statute, "the Government must prove that the defendant acted with knowledge that his conduct was unlawful." *Ratzlaf v. United States*, 510 U.S. 135, 137 (1994).

[Authors' note: In response to the defendant's argument that "willfully" should be interpreted consistently with the interpretation of the term in the federal tax laws, the Court said:] In certain cases involving willful violations of the tax laws, we have concluded that the jury must find that the defendant was aware of the specific provision of the tax code that he was charged with violating. *See, e.g., Cheek v. United States*, 498 U.S. 192 (1991).[17] Similarly, in order to satisfy a willful violation in *Ratzlaf*, we concluded that the jury had to find that the defendant knew that his structuring of cash transactions to avoid a reporting requirement was unlawful. *See* 510 U.S. at 138, 149. Those cases, however, are readily distinguishable. Both the tax

---

[15] United States v. Bishop, 412 U.S. 346, 361 (1973).

[16] [12] The word often denotes an act which is intentional, or knowing, or voluntary, as distinguished from accidental. But when used in a criminal statute, it generally means an act done with a bad purpose; without justifiable excuse; stubbornly, obstinately, perversely. The word is also employed to characterize a thing done without ground for believing it is lawful, or conduct marked by careless disregard whether or not one has the right so to act.

[17] [17] Even in tax cases, we have not always required this heightened *mens rea*. In *United States v. Pomponio*, 429 U.S. 10 (1976) (per curiam), for example, the jury was instructed that a willful act is one done "with [the] bad purpose either to disobey or to disregard the law." *Pomponio*, 429 U.S. at 11. We approved of this instruction, concluding that "the trial judge . . . adequately instructed the jury on willfulness." *Pomponio*, 429 U.S. at 13.

cases[18] and *Ratzlaf*[19] involved highly technical statutes that presented the danger of ensnaring individuals engaged in apparently innocent conduct.[20] As a result, we held that these statutes "carve out an exception to the traditional rule" that ignorance of the law is no excuse[21] and require that the defendant have knowledge of the law.[22] The danger of convicting individuals engaged in apparently innocent activity that motivated our decisions in the tax cases and *Ratzlaf* is not present here because the jury found that this petitioner knew that his conduct was unlawful.[23]

Return to the statement in *Bryan*: "In certain cases involving willful violations of the tax laws, we have concluded that the jury must find that the defendant was

---

[18] [18] As we stated in *Cheek v. United States*, 498 U.S. 192, 199–200 (1991),

"The proliferation of statutes and regulations has sometimes made it difficult for the average citizen to know and comprehend the extent of the duties and obligations imposed by the tax laws. Congress has accordingly softened the impact of the common-law presumption by making specific intent to violate the law an element of certain federal criminal tax offenses. Thus, the Court, almost 60 years ago, interpreted the statutory term 'willfully' as used in the federal criminal tax statutes as carving out an exception to the traditional rule [that every person is presumed to know the law]. This special treatment of criminal tax offenses is largely due to the complexity of the tax laws."

[19] [19] *See Bates v. United States*, 522 U.S. 23, 31 n.6 (1997) (slip op., at 7 n.6) (noting that *Ratzlaf's* holding was based on the "particular statutory context of currency structuring"); *Ratzlaf*, 510 U.S. at 149 (Court's holding based on "particular context" of currency structuring statute).

[20] [20] 510 U.S. at 144–145 ("Currency structuring is not inevitably nefarious . . . . Nor is a person who structures a currency transaction invariably motivated by a desire to keep the Government in the dark"; Government's construction of the statute would criminalize apparently innocent activity.); *Cheek*, 498 U.S. at 205 ("In our complex tax system, uncertainty often arises even among taxpayers who earnestly wish to follow the law, and it is not the purpose of the law to penalize frank difference of opinion or innocent errors made despite the exercise of reasonable care. *United States v. Bishop*, 412 U.S. 346, 360–361 (1973) (*quoting Spies v. United States*, 317 U.S. 492, 496 (1943))"); *Murdock*, 290 U.S. at 396 ("Congress did not intend that a person, by reason of a bona fide misunderstanding as to his liability for the tax, as to his duty to make a return, or as to the adequacy of the records he maintained, should become a criminal by his mere failure to measure up to the prescribed standard of conduct.").

[21] [21] *Cheek*, 498 U.S. at 200; *see also Ratzlaf*, 510 U.S. at 149 (noting the "venerable principle that ignorance of the law generally is no defense to a criminal charge," but concluding that Congress intended otherwise in the "particular context" of the currency structuring statute).

[22] [22] Even before *Ratzlaf* was decided, then Chief Judge Breyer explained why there was a need for specificity under those statutes that is inapplicable when there is no danger of conviction of a defendant with an innocent state of mind. He wrote:

> "I believe that criminal prosecutions for 'currency law' violations, of the sort at issue here, very much resemble criminal prosecutions for tax law violations. *Compare* 26 U.S.C. §§ 6050I, 7203 with 31 U.S.C. §§ 5322, 5324. Both sets of laws are technical; and both sets of laws sometimes criminalize conduct that would not strike an ordinary citizen as immoral or likely unlawful. Thus, both sets of laws may lead to the unfair result of criminally prosecuting individuals who subjectively and honestly believe they have not acted criminally. *Cheek v. United States*, 498 U.S. 192 (1991), sets forth a legal standard that, by requiring proof that the defendant was subjectively aware of the duty at issue, would avoid such unfair results." *United States v. Aversa*, 984 F.2d 493, 502 (1st Cir. 1993) (concurring opinion).

He therefore concluded that the "same standards should apply in both" the tax cases and in cases such as *Ratzlaf*. 984 F.2d at 503.

[23] [23] Moreover, requiring only knowledge that the conduct is unlawful is fully consistent with the purpose of [the Firearms Owners' Protection Act (FOPA)], as FOPA was enacted to protect law-abiding citizens who might inadvertently violate the law.

aware of the specific provision of the tax code that he was charged with violating." Do not read these words literally. It is the rare tax cheat who really knows the Code provisions, and the courts do not condition conviction on proof of such knowledge.[24] As the Seventh Circuit said pungently: "Knowledge of the law's demands does not depend on knowing the citation any more than ability to watch a program on television depends on knowing the frequency on which the signal is broadcast."[25]

We will revisit the willfulness element in more detail in Chapter 2A. The foregoing is intended as an introduction to the issue and not as a definitive test of how the term "willfully" as used in tax and related crimes will be interpreted.

C. Overview of the Procedural Aspects of the System

Chapter 6 describes in detail how criminal cases are processed from initial investigation through sentencing. It is appropriate here, however, to give a brief and highly simplified overview of the system and the players.

1. IRS Phase

The IRS is the chief investigator of tax crimes. The IRS branch that investigates tax crimes is Criminal Investigation ("CI"), sometimes referred to by experienced practitioners as "CID," an acronym for its prior name (Criminal Investigation Division). CI agents are referred to as "Special Agents."[26] Special Agents are law enforcement officers, with many of the powers accorded to law enforcement officers generally, such as making arrests and carrying firearms.[27] CI sometimes conducts investigations internally, without any other law enforcement agency's involvement. Such investigations are called "administrative investigations." By contrast, CI agents may be assigned to assist a federal grand jury conducting a criminal tax investigation, but such investigations are not CI investigations.

In administrative investigations, Special Agents may use the IRS administrative summons to compel testimony and the production of documents.[28] They also may use other investigative techniques, including clandestine observations, informants, stings, and the like. Special Agents may also seek search warrants, with the assistance of the local United States Attorney, when they can show need and

---

24 *See, e.g.*, United States v. Mousavi, 604 F.3d 1084, 1092 (9th Cir. 2010).

25 United States v. Patridge, 507 F.3d 1092, 1094 (7th Cir. 2007), *cert. denied*, 552 U.S. 1228 (2008).

26 Thus, if a client tells her lawyer that she has been contacted by an "IRS agent," one of the first questions the lawyer should ask is "what was the Agent's exact title?" A visit from a Special Agent is quite a different thing from a visit from a Revenue Agent or Revenue Officer.

27 For example, section 7608(a) specifically grants authority to agents enforcing the criminal, forfeiture or seizure provisions laws related to liquor, tobacco, and firearms taxes and reporting to carry firearms, execute and serve search warrants and arrest warrants, and to arrest person in certain cases. Section 7608(b) specifically grants authority to agents enforcing other criminal tax provisions to execute and serve search and arrest warrants and to make arrests. Although section 7806(b) does not specifically grant authority for Special Agents to carry firearms (as section 7608(a) does in the case of liquor, tobacco, and firearms taxes), the Treasury Department and the IRS take the position that the authority of Special Agents to carry firearms in enforcing the general criminal tax laws is implied. IRM 9.1.2.4.1. Hence, Special Agents will often carry firearms in carrying out their duties.

28 IRC § 7608(b)(2)(A). Administrative summonses are discussed in greater detail in Chapter 7.

probable cause to believe that a crime has been committed.

CI's significant resources include IRS counsel who are assigned to CI, like "in-house counsel." The Special Agent has this legal advice readily available in all phases of the investigation. Previously, IRS counsel were in a separate office under the supervision of IRS Chief Counsel which serviced all of the IRS, including CI. By analogy, this was sort of like "outside counsel." Being part of a separate office, counsel was then usually less involved at key stages of the investigation. Under the new structure, counsel is expected to be actively involved on an as-needed basis and thus assist Special Agents in avoiding some of the procedural and strategic problems previously encountered because of lack of easy access to counsel.

CI investigations are typically thorough and time-consuming, depending upon statute-of-limitations considerations. The statute of limitations for most tax crimes is six years.[29]

CI concludes an investigation by either: (1) declining to pursue the matter further (referred to as a declination) or (2) forwarding the matter to the Department of Justice Tax Division ("DOJ Tax") for criminal prosecution or for further investigation by a grand jury. If the IRS declines the case, it will be referred back to the IRS civil or collection agents for further processing as appropriate. Forwarding to DOJ Tax is called a "referral."

The case will be referred to DOJ Tax via a Criminal Reference Letter ("CRL").[30] A key component of the referral package will be the Special Agent's Report ("SAR"),[31] in which the Special Agent develops all known considerations relevant to prosecution and sentencing. The SAR is usually extremely thorough, reflecting the careful development of the case during the IRS phase of the criminal process. IRS counsel will review the SAR critically and encourage revisions where appropriate.

2. DOJ Tax Approval Phase

DOJ Tax authorizes all criminal tax prosecutions and sets national prosecution standards and priorities that further overall compliance with the federal tax system. In addition to its criminal tax role, DOJ Tax has principal authority for virtually all civil tax litigation except in the United States Tax Court. DOJ Tax handles all tax trials in the District Courts, Bankruptcy Courts, and the Court of Federal Claims. DOJ Tax handles all appeals (including appeals from the Tax Court) and all tax cases in the Supreme Court. Thus, DOJ Tax is well situated to coordinate national priorities in authorizing criminal tax prosecutions. It has authority to approve all tax-related indictments.

DOJ Tax is headed by an Assistant Attorney General ("AAG"). The AAG has a deputy with principal responsibility for criminal tax matters. Criminal tax matters are handled by one of DOJ Tax's sections — the Criminal Enforcement Section

---

[29] IRC § 6531. Statutes of limitations are discussed in detail in Chapter 5.

[30] The CRL is referenced often in the Part 31 of the IRM dealing with criminal tax. IRM 31.4.7 states the purpose, content, and style of the CRL.

[31] SAR also is the acronym for Suspicious Activity Reports, useful leads originating outside the IRS. Both types of SARs are discussed more fully in Chapter 6.

("CES"). CES's attorneys are based in Washington. CES divides its jurisdiction geographically. For example, the general southern area of the U.S. is handled by a subsection called Southern, often referred to as CES — Southern. There also are Northern and Western subsections plus offices in a few large cities, including New York, Los Angeles, and San Francisco. Although CES's attorneys are generally based in Washington, they may be assigned to longer term details on task forces located elsewhere.

The criminal tax enforcement system has limited resources. Coordination and prioritizing are essential to get the maximum bang for the enforcement dollar. CES marshals and applies its investigative and prosecutorial resources so as to support our tax system. CES does that by prosecuting relatively few cases each year (some 2,000 to 3,000), focusing on the strongest cases in which conviction is highly likely and picking targets with a sufficiently high profile (for whatever reason) that the conviction might be publicized and encourage compliance by persons who become aware of the convictions.

Upon receipt of the referral from CI (via the CRL), CES determines whether the case is within its prosecution enforcement priorities. CES can decline to accept the IRS's recommendation and return the matter to the IRS either for further investigation or with instructions to close out the criminal investigation. If, however, CES approves further processing, it will usually forward the matter to the United States Attorney's Office ("USAO") for the district where venue for criminal prosecution lies.

3. Grand Jury and Prosecution Phase

a. The Prosecutor

The USAO will assign the case to an Assistant United States Attorney ("AUSA") who will present the case to the grand jury and conduct such further investigation and prosecution as necessary. If for any reason the USAO is not interested in pursuing the matter or is too busy to do so efficiently and timely, the USAO may request assistance from CES which may take the form of co-counsel to an AUSA for the case or even the lead prosecuting attorney position, often by making the CES attorney a Special Assistant United States Attorney ("SAUSA") for the district.[32] Consider the following from the perspective of the USAO:

> The USAO can also request litigation assistance from the Tax Division. This assistance may be requested in a variety of forms. Some USAOs refer most, or all, of their tax cases to the Tax Division, which conserves the resources of the USAO for other priority cases in the district. Other USAOs request that a Tax Division attorney be assigned to work with an AUSA and to provide a second chair attorney with technical experience and expertise in tax cases. Still other USAOs mix these methods by farming some cases in their entirety out to the Tax Division, and by using the Tax Division to assist AUSAs at other trials and investigations.

---

32 *See* USAM 6-4.245.

> To an AUSA, the benefit from assigning a tax case in its entirety to the Tax Division is obvious: assign the Tax Division attorney the case, show him or her the file, introduce him or her to the court, and go back to your office. There can also be benefits, however, from a joint trial.
>
> First, as with the grand jury investigation, the Tax Division attorney brings technical expertise from criminal tax trials. Second, since the Tax Division is likely to have addressed many of the standard motions and pleadings in tax cases, the Tax Division attorney can handle pretrial motion work and document preparation. Third, the Tax Division attorney can bring fresh and different perspectives to the trial. Since the Tax Division litigates tax cases all over the country, its attorneys can bring helpful suggestions for presenting and framing tax issues, presenting tax case documents as exhibits, and handling certain types of tax case witnesses. Clearly, on occasion I have told the Tax Division attorney, "That's all well and good, but it won't work here with our judge." On the other hand, it is important to consider the fresh ideas brought from the Tax Division's experience in other jurisdictions. As with the joint grand jury investigation, to guarantee success in a joint trial, it is most important to delineate the roles and tasks clearly at the start and to take time to develop a sound working relationship between the attorneys.[33]

Some judicial districts are blessed or cursed with AUSAs who have substantial tax prosecution experience and U.S. Attorneys who believe that tax cases are consistent with local criminal enforcement priorities. In such districts, an AUSA will usually handle tax prosecutions from the grand jury through the sentencing.

b. The Grand Jury Investigation

If the CI investigation was thorough, there may be no need for further investigation. In that case, the prosecutor will simply present the evidence to the grand jury without further investigation and the indictment will then (usually) be forthcoming upon the prosecutor's request.

There may, however, be a need for further investigation. This occurs when CES or the prosecutor feels the need for investigation, often to fill in gaps perceived in the IRS's CRL or SAR.

Moreover, increasingly, although the initial CI investigation is still the norm in tax crime prosecutions, tax crimes are being investigated from the inception by grand juries. For example, grand juries may investigate other federal crimes and uncover tax violations that should be prosecuted as an adjunct to the other crimes that are investigated and prosecuted. This often occurs in investigating money laundering and organized crimes when, from a criminal enforcement priority standpoint, the other crimes are the real focus but the tax crimes may substantially further the overall investigation. For example, Al Capone was targeted for a host of heinous crimes but was ultimately nailed for a tax crime. Moreover, increasingly, criminal tax investigations are being instituted as grand jury investigations before

---

[33] John W. Vandreuil, *An AUSA's Perspective on Working with the Tax Division*, 46/3 USA Bulletin 11 (Apr. 1998).

a CI administrative investigation is started or completed because, as will be discussed in Chapter 6, grand jury investigations in some cases can be far more efficient than CI administrative investigations. For example, grand jury investigations appear to be the vehicle of choice for investigating potential tax crimes in the round of abusive tax shelters proliferating in the late 1990s and early 2000s; these cases could have been investigated by CI, but the perception (and often the reality) was that the grand jury is the superior investigation tool.

When the grand jury is the preferred investigative tool, one or more CI Special Agents are typically assigned to assist the grand jury. Then, if the prosecutor wants to indict for a tax crime, the Special Agent(s) will prepare an SAR to be used to obtain CI's recommendation and CES's approval. Since the policy decision has been made that tax crimes generally should support the overall revenue function of Government, it is important that indictment for tax crimes be consistent with — or at least not in conflict with — overall tax enforcement goals, thus requiring the IRS's review and recommendation and CES's approval.

c. Indictment and Trial

If the grand jury indicts, the case is then prosecuted. Usually, because of the high standards in seeking an indictment in the first place, the Government has a very good case and pre-trial negotiations will result in a plea.[34] If no plea is negotiated, the trial goes forward. The trial is simply a criminal trial, with some nuances driven by the tax setting. But the standard criminal trappings are there — trial pursuant to the Federal Rules of Criminal Procedure, Federal Rules of Evidence, and various local rules and practices applying to general criminal proceedings.

4. Sentencing Phase

If the defendant is convicted, the defendant will be sentenced. The Code provisions defining tax crimes set forth the maximum incarceration and fines for the crimes. However, there are two other key influences on the punishments that are actually meted out to convicted tax defendants.

First, except in the most egregious cases, the maximum incarceration and fines set out in the Code provisions are not imposed. Rather, some lesser sentence is imposed under the sentencing factors identified in 28 U.S.C. section 3553(a), the most prominent of which involve the United States Sentencing Guidelines. The guidelines provide a general framework for sentencing but have certain features uniquely tailored to tax crimes. In short, the Code provisions provide the maximum incarceration and fine, but the Sentencing Guidelines are the principal factor in setting the actual incarceration and fine.[35] Knowing how the Guidelines will play out

---

[34] Federal judges are prohibited from involving themselves in plea discussions. Fed. R. Crim. Proc. 11. Violation of that prohibition does not necessarily require vacatur of a guilty plea. Such cases are subject to the harmless error rule. United States v. Davila, 133 S. Ct. 2139 (2013) (involving guilty plea to conspiracy to defraud the United States by filing false income tax returns).

[35] The Guidelines are no longer mandatory, as a result of the Supreme Court's decision in United

permits the lawyer to massage the earlier stages in the process for maximum client advantage.

Second, 18 U.S.C. section 3571 (sometimes referred to as the Criminal Fine Enforcement Act of 1984) ("CFEA")[36] increases the maximum permissible fines for both misdemeanors and felonies. Thus, for example, the Code provision for tax evasion (section 7201) provides for (in addition to incarceration) maximum fines of $100,000 for individuals and $500,000 for corporations. Section 3571, however, provides that the maximum permissible fine for a felony conviction is at least $250,000 for individuals and $500,000 for corporations and may exceed even those amounts based on doubling the pecuniary loss to the victim.[37] These maximums, however, are also subject to the caveat noted that actual sentencing is pursuant to the Guidelines which result in sentences below the maximums in all except the most egregious of tax cases.

5. Judicial Appeals

The taxpayer may appeal his conviction and/or sentence, provided that the taxpayer has not waived his right to appeal. Most tax indictments result in plea agreements in which the taxpayer generally has no right to appeal unless he has preserved some issue for appeal. The Government usually will insist upon an express statement in the plea agreement that the right to appeal is waived.

IV. SOME POLICY ISSUES

The succeeding chapters of this book will identify numerous policy issues with respect to particular Code and non-Code sections. Below, we introduce some policy issues of more general character, specifically: (1) causes of criminal behavior, (2) purposes of the criminal justice system, (3) interface of tax and non-tax enforcement, (4) extent of criminal tax enforcement, and (5) federal tax amnesty.

A. Causes of Criminal Behavior

As one might infer from the variety of behavior reflected in the cases in this book, there is no single reason for criminal tax behavior. Yet policymakers must ask and try to answer the question of whether there are larger reasons for criminal tax behavior that can be addressed or at least recognized. Below, Kim M. Bloomquist explores one set of hypotheses.

> Socrates: Here, then, is a discovery of new evils against which the guardians will have to watch, or they will creep into the city unobserved.
>
> Adeimantus: What evils?
>
> Socrates: Wealth and poverty; the one is the parent of luxury and indolence, and the other of meanness and viciousness, and both of

---

States v. Booker, 543 U.S. 220 (2005). However, the Guidelines remain important. Sentencing is discussed in detail in Chapter 10.

[36] Pub. L. No. 98-596, 98 Stat. 3134.

[37] *See* 18 U.S.C. § 3571(b)(3) & (c)(3).

discontent. — PLATO, THE REPUBLIC, Book IV.

A satisfactory explanation of the Cox Paradox [the paradox, based on empirical data, of a U-shaped curve whereby tax noncompliance is greatest at the upper and lower income levels, an inverted U-shaped distribution of compliance behavior] would provide an important key to understanding the causes of income tax evasion. The two main competing theoretical explanations for the Cox Paradox indirectly point to income inequality as a contributing factor. Economists emphasize the greater opportunities to evade among both the rich and poor, while behaviorists would interpret rising economic disparity as a cause of taxpayer stress and increasing evasion propensity. This paper tests the hypothesis that income inequality is a determinant of income tax evasion.

Empirical results show a statistically significant relationship between a measure of income inequality (Gini coefficient) and U.S. wage and salary reporting noncompliance for the period 1947 to 1999. It must be stressed that this finding is not proof of causation in the same sense that mathematical laws describe the motions of the physical universe. Simply put, human beings are not robots, they possess free will and can choose to obey the law or do otherwise. However, this paper has argued that the observed positive correlation between the level of inequality and underreporting rate is consistent with prevailing behavioral and economic theories of tax evasion.

Although not conclusive evidence of causation, this result suggests that a continuation of the global trend of widening economic disparity will make the job of tax enforcement a more challenging one in the years to come. Policy makers have a variety of options to improve compliance. Particular emphasis should be placed on increasing the visibility of transactions by extending third-party reporting of income where possible. Enhanced customer service and a simplified tax code should make it easier for many taxpayers to comply. Reducing the time between an act of evasion and its detection would make evasion less attractive as an alternative to a short-term, high-interest loan. While the audit rate was not found to have a statistically significant influence on wage and salary underreporting, this was not too surprising given the already high probability of detection from information documents. Taxpayer audits likely are a more effective enforcement tool when applied to income not covered by third-party reporting, such as business net profits and capital gains.

On the other hand, tax compliance programs that negatively affect taxpayers' financial status may have the unintended consequence of increasing, rather than reducing, evasion. For example, if the adoption of a single flat rate tax system shifts more of the total tax burden onto low-income households, evasion by this group of taxpayers may increase. Alternatively, relying on the wealthy to pay for an ever-increasing share of public goods and services may eventually provoke a "Revolt of the Haves" (Citrin, 1979; Graetz, 1999). If the results reported here are an indication, then macroeconomic policies or the lack thereof that result in a shrinking

> middle class will inevitably bring about increased tax evasion.
>
> Clearly, a topic of such importance for the design of tax policy merits further investigation. Ideas for follow-on studies include extending this approach to other categories of income, such as business and investment income, and substituting a wealth-based measure of inequality for the Census Bureau's Gini coefficient. Andreoni, Erard, and Feinstein (1998) have called for more empirical studies in countries outside the United States. Schneider and Enste (2000) provide a good summary of the available data to begin this work. However, their study highlights the lack of reliable evasion data. In particular, there is a need for additional time-series measures of evasion to identify trends that persist over several decades. Finally, a more realistic theoretical framework would admit interdependencies among variables. This topic seems particularly suited for carefully designed experimental studies.[38]

There is an immense and growing literature on the causes of tax compliance and tax evasion, both in the United States and abroad.[39] The conclusions in the literature often are tentative, and the cross-cultural applications of research are hazardous. For all of its inherent difficulty, however, research into the causes of tax criminality is worthwhile, especially if policymakers base their actions and decisions on firm empirical foundations rather than supposition or political expediency.

B. Purposes of the Criminal Justice System

Broader societal issues of criminal law are worthy of study and important to understanding the criminal system and criminal tax system we have. Students may recall from their first years in law school casebook readings and class discussions about the theories of and rationales for criminal punishment.[40] This criminal tax coursebook assumes some student familiarity with the general contours of criminal law and policy.

Our criminal justice system is multi-faceted. At its most basic level, it punishes conduct that violates norms imposed by society through criminal laws. But the criminal justice system has significant goals other than punishment. In the federal system, these various goals are reflected in the United States Sentencing Guidelines which summarize the goals of criminal punishment as "deterrence,

---

[38] U.S. Income Inequality and Tax Evasion: A Synthesis, *reproduced at* 2003 WTD 144-9 (July 28, 2003).

[39] *E.g.*, Leslie Book, *Study of the Role of Preparers in Relation to Taxpayer Compliance with Internal Revenue Laws, in* 2 National Taxpayer Advocate 2007 Ann. Rep. 44; Marjorie E. Kornhauser, *Normative and Cognitive Aspects of Tax Compliance: Literature Review and Recommendations for the IRS Regarding Individual Taxpayers, in id.* at 138; Leandra Lederman, *The Interplay Between Norms and Enforcement in Tax Compliance*, 64 Ohio St. L. J. 1453 (2003); Thomas J. Stuhldreher & Wendy L. Stuhldreher, *Taxes and Ethics: Taxpayer Attitudes over Time*, J. Tax Prac. & Proc., June–July 2007, at 29.

[40] For a summary of the theories and rationales, see Joshua Dressler, Understanding Criminal Law ch. 2 (4th ed. 2006).

incapacitation, just punishment, and rehabilitation."[41] We do not enter here the debate of the goals of a criminal system and their relative priorities, but take the lay of the land as we find it. We focus here principally upon the punishment aspect, the type of conduct that attracts punishment, and the ways the practitioner can be of assistance to clients caught up in the enforcement system. Chapter 10 will discuss the Sentencing Guidelines in some detail and will thus deal with these issues in understanding sentencing policies.

C. Interface of Tax and Non-Tax Enforcement

Because of their skills as financial investigators, IRS Special Agents have become heavily involved in the federal government's War on Crime. So much so that many worried that CI's original and traditional role in buttressing tax compliance was being compromised.

In April 1999, the Criminal Investigation Review Task Force headed by former federal judge and former FBI Director William Webster issued a report on the state of the IRS's criminal enforcement division ("the Webster Report"). The report made recommendations for improving CI. The IRS has implemented or is in the process of implementing many of the recommendations and otherwise refocusing its mission.

The Webster Report recommended that CI refocus its efforts on its "central mission" — which is "to act as the Internal Revenue Service's criminal investigative component in support of the administration of the federal internal revenue laws." The Webster Report recommended that much of the resources of CI that had been diverted to non-tax crimes be shifted back to general tax enforcement. CI can continue to be involved in these other areas that can effectively use its financial skills, but the principal focus must be on tax administration.

Prosecutions for tax crimes as adjuncts to other law enforcement initiatives to nail the really bad guys — Mafia, drug traffickers, etc. — were unlikely to offer incentives to most Americans to comply with the tax laws, nor is it even likely to offer many really bad guys the incentive to comply with the tax laws. It was simply a convenient way to get some of the really bad guys without any significant contribution to the administration of the tax laws. That is not to say that these really bad guys should not be prosecuted, but the concern addressed in the Webster Report is diverting the IRS's criminal resources away from the central mission to support the tax system. Most of the taxes that are not reported and paid voluntarily are not owed by this category of really bad guys. Hence, in terms of its overall tax administration mission, CI's efforts need to be focused on the broader area of tax noncompliance. As the IRS refocuses its efforts, there may be more criminal tax cases brought against ordinary Americans where the goal is not only to punish the particular offender but to strike fear (or at least compliance) in other persons considering tax crimes.

---

[41] U.S.S.G. ch. 1, subpt. A.1.2; *see also* 18 U.S.C. § 3553(a)(2). The Sentencing Guidelines are revised frequently, often every one or two years.

In the years since it was issued, there has been some movement in the direction suggested by the Webster Report.[42] However, the ground hardly shakes as a result of a stampede by CI in that direction. For example, in 2007, the head of CI stated that approximately 59% of the cases started by CI have a tax component.[43] For fiscal year 2013, of the 5,314 investigations initiated, 2,570 involved legal source tax crimes while 1,753 involved illegal source financial crimes and 991 involved narcotics-related financial crimes.[44] Thus, substantial amounts of Special Agent time and effort remain committed to non-tax enforcement.

D. Extent of Criminal Tax Enforcement

Benjamin Disraeli once mused that "there are lies, damned lies, and statistics."[45] Here are statistics from the IRS web page:[46]

	2008	2009	2010	2011	Average
Investigations Initiated					
Tax Investigations	2283	2612	2889	2682	2617
Other Financial Crimes	1466	1509	1817	2038	1708
Total	3749	4121	4706	4720	4325
Prosecution Recommendations					
Tax Investigations	1297	1278	1507	1610	1423
Other Financial Crimes	1488	1292	1527	1800	1527
Total	2785	2570	3034	3410	2950
Indictments/Informations					
Tax Investigations	1171	1141	1250	1325	1222
Other Financial Crimes	1376	1194	1395	1673	1410
Total	2547	2335	2645	2998	2632
Sentenced					
Tax Investigations	1016	1113	1054	1162	1086
Other Financial Crimes	941	1116	1118	1044	1055
Total	1957	2229	2172	2206	2141

The conviction rate is quite high. The data are not presented for convictions but are for sentencing. Since convictions result in sentencing, the data indicate a four-

[42] Ironically, increased attention to traditional tax crimes, particularly so-called "legal source income cases," can cause CI's enforcement statistics to drop since such cases "have always been both time and resource intensive because they are generally more complex and require rigorous documentation and corroboration to meet the government's burden of proof." Eileen Mayer (chief of CI), *quoted by* Allen Kenney, *TIGTA Finds Downturn in Criminal Investigation Enforcement Statistics*, Tax Notes, June 18, 2007, at 1108.

[43] Remarks of Eileen Mayer reported by Jeremiah Coder, *IRS CI Division to Stay "Aggressive" Under New Chief*, Tax Notes, May 21, 2007, p. 705.

[44] *IRS Data Book 2013*, tbl 18, at 44.

[45] This quote is sometimes attributed to Mark Twain.

[46] The web page is entitled "Enforcement Statistics — Criminal Investigation (CI) Enforcement Strategy" (as of Sept. 18, 2012).

year conviction rate on Tax Investigations (not including Other Financial Crimes) of 89%. However, DOJ prosecutes more tax and tax-related crimes than those referred by the IRS. As recently as 2007, DOJ Tax claimed a 97% conviction rate on the whole subset (although the data are inconclusive as to that claim).

Other good statistical analyses of the IRS CI function appear in periodic reports from the Treasury Inspector General for Tax Administration (TIGTA). TIGTA's July 2011 study reported that CI:

- Completed more than 4,300 criminal investigations — an increase of 12.4%.
- Maintained a Department of Justice case acceptance rate of 93.9% and a United States Attorney case acceptance rate of 91.8% — increases of 2.2% and 3.1%, respectively.
- Achieved a conviction rate of 90.2% — an increase of 3%.
- Obtained 2,184 convictions — an increase of 3.8%.[47]

According to the IRS, criminal enforcement jumped sharply in fiscal year 2013 over the previous year, including increases of 12.5% in criminal tax investigations, nearly 18% in prosecutions recommended, and over 25% in total convictions. The IRS reported a 93% conviction rate for the year. One explanation for the increases is greater enforcement against identity theft and relates fraudulent refunds, which comprised about a quarter of the total cases. The average sentence imposed upon conviction was reported to be 31 months.[48]

Criminal tax cases arise in a wide variety of contexts, including individual and corporate fraud employment tax underpayment, abusive trusts and tax shelters, money laundering, counterterrorism, and tax defiers (protestors). Areas of emphasis change. Among particularly "hot" areas in recent years are cross-border tax evasion (including undeclared foreign bank accounts)[49] and refund fraud associated with identity theft.[50]

Because statistics are a matter of interpretation, one should draw conclusions from the foregoing statistics with care. For example, TIGTA sometimes has drawn somewhat less optimistic conclusions from IRS statistics than CI has. Analyzing CI's statistics, TIGTA determined that: (i) investigations initiated by CI fell 8.5% in 2006 compared to 2005, (ii) prosecution referrals by CI decreased by 5% in 2006

---

[47] TIGTA, *Trends in Criminal Investigation's Enforcement Activities Showed Improvements for Fiscal Year 2010, With Gains in Most Performance Indicators* (2011) (2011-30-068); *see also* TIGTA, *Actions Are Needed to Accurately Reflect Criminal Investigation's Fraud Referral Evaluation Period and Improve the Criminal Fraud Referral Process* 6 (May 24, 2013) (2013-3-051).

[48] IRS Information Release IR-2014-18 (Feb. 24, 2014) (reporting 5,314 investigations initiated, 4,364 prosecutions recommended, and 3,865 informations and indictments).

[49] *See, e.g.*, Steven Toscher, *Update on the Department of Justice's and Internal Revenue Service's Criminal and Civil International Enforcement Program: Don't Let the Statistics on Sentencing Fool You*, 55/3 TAX MANAGEMENT MEMO. (CBNA) 39 (Feb. 10, 2014).

[50] In 2013, the IRS "protected $17.8 billion from refund fraud, we initiated 1400 investigations, and we obtained over 1000 indictments and 400 convictions" related to refund fraud and identity theft. Prepared Remarks of Commissioner of Internal Revenue John Koskinen before the National Press Club (Washington, D.C.), Apr. 2, 2014, at 7.

compared to 2005, (iii) convictions of the targets of CI investigations decreased by 6% in 2006, and (iv) the rate at which DOJ declined CI referrals increased in 2006. These findings, if correct, show some erosion of gains achieved earlier in the decade. The erosion may result from flat staffing patterns (*i.e.*, little or no growth in CI field agents since 2000) and from CI's increased attention to "legal source income cases," which take more time and consume more resources because they are more complex and require more rigorous documentation.[51]

A good source for alternative statistics and conclusions is the Syracuse University Transaction Access Records Clearinghouse ("TRAC") web site.[52] In any event, all of the statistical analyses (including TRAC) permit some fair conclusions for present purposes. First, relative to the number of taxpayers and the number of tax returns filed or required to be filed, the prosecution rate is low — very low. Second, relative to the number of indictments, the conviction rate is very high. Third, relative to the number of convictions, the incarceration rate is high.

Policy questions that come easily to mind are: What is the incentive for taxpayers to comply "voluntarily" with such a low rate of criminal prosecutions? How can the Government maximize the incentive value of such a low rate of actual prosecutions? Can taxpayers assume that, since the Government pursues so few tax evaders, the Government will focus on the worst tax offenders and will leave marginal tax cheats (our clients) alone? These and related issues will be addressed in this book.

The types and proportions of cases represented in enforcement statistics change as enforcement priorities evolve. According to a chief of CI, international tax evasion has been and will continue to be a "huge priority," perhaps CI's top priority. Identity theft has emerged in recent years as a major problem. The IRS has identified nearly 500,000 taxpayers who were victims of identity theft between 2008 and 2012, and the IRS may lose as much as $26 billion over five years in fraudulent refunds associated with identity theft. Money laundering, suspicious activity reports, and cybercrimes are often priority areas.[53]

E. Federal Tax Amnesty

Nearly all U.S. states and many foreign countries have declared amnesties with respect to their tax scofflaws[54]; some have done so more than once. Details of the programs differ. In general, such a program declares that, within a defined window of time, taxpayers who failed to file or pay may bring their accounts current. As an

---

[51] *See* Allen Kenney, *TIGTA Finds Downturn in Criminal Investigation Enforcement Statistics*, Tax Notes, June 18, 2007, at 1108; Allen Kenney, *TIGTA Expresses Concern over New Fraud Program's Effectiveness*, Tax Notes, June 18, 2007, at 1108.

[52] http://trac.syr.edu/.

[53] Eric Kroh, *IRS Criminal Investigation Division Chief Outlines Priorities*, Tax Notes, June 25, 2012, at 1569 (quoting remarks of Richard Weber).

[54] *See, e.g.*, Craig M. Boise, *Breaking Open Offshore Piggybanks: Deferral and the Utility of Amnesty*, 14 Geo. Mason L. Rev. 667 (2007); Leo P. Martinez, *Federal Tax Amnesty: Crime and Punishment Revisited*, 10 Va. Tax Rev. 535 (1991); Gerald P. Moran, *Tax Amnesty: An Old Debate as Viewed from Current Public Choices*, 1 Fla. Tax Rev. 307 (1992).

incentive, taxpayers who take advantage of the program are assured that no criminal penalties (and sometimes no civil penalties) will be imposed upon them.

From the state's perspective, the idea is to get tax delinquents "back into the system," hoping that the redeemed tax sinners will remain compliant in the future.[55] The state also looks forward to a revenue bounce for the years of delinquency since the likelihood is small that the state revenue authority would have caught the tax delinquents in the ordinary course and extracted payment from them. Amnesties are designed to appeal to taxpayers like those described by a commentator: "Many of these taxpayers have been subjected to the snowball effect; that is, they may stop filing for one year, not receive any IRS queries, be scared by the proposition of re-filing or of filing delinquent returns due to imagined penalties and criminal liability, and then begin a career of non-filing going forward."[56]

On the other hand, the objection to such programs is that they will cause compliance to drop in the long run. When a state has shown its willingness to cut such deals, risk-taking taxpayers may become even more aggressive in the future, hoping or expecting that another round of amnesty will be available to them later if needed.[57]

Suggestions that the federal government implement a tax amnesty have never gotten very far. Below, a congressional staff report sets out the concerns:

- The staff of the Joint Committee on Taxation estimates that a Federal tax amnesty would result in a net revenue loss to the Federal Government. This net revenue loss occurs primarily because a Federal tax amnesty is estimated to have the long-run effect of reducing overall taxpayer compliance with Federal tax laws. However, a form of amnesty could be designed to contain the amount of the revenue loss to relatively modest levels.
- Present law contains certain features that are similar to elements of tax amnesty programs. These features include the voluntary disclosure policies discussed in later chapters of this book, the installment agreement provisions, and offers in compromise.[58] In contrast to a tax amnesty program, however, the present-law provisions are tailored to the situations of specific taxpayers, rather than providing broad relief from past taxes for noncompliant taxpayers. The Internal Revenue Service has substantially increased the use of these provisions in recent years.
- A taxpayer's decision whether to evade taxes depends in part on the

[55] About 60,000 taxpayers using offshore accounts to evade taxes accepted a partial amnesty offered by the United Kingdom. This number far exceeds the 1,300 taxpayers who responded to the IRS's Offshore Voluntary Compliance Initiative in 2003. *See* Martin A. Sullivan, *Keeping Score on Offshore: U.K. 60,000, U.S. 1,300*, TAX NOTES, July 2, 2007, at 23.

[56] Theodore M. David, *The Tax Non-Filer: Public Enemy Number One?*, PRACTICAL TAX LAWYER, Spring 2007, at 7, 8.

[57] *See, e.g.*, Parker Sinclair, *The Case Against Tax Amnesties*, 2010 STT 118-5 (June 21, 2010).

[58] For discussion of installment agreements and offers in compromise, see DAVID M. RICHARDSON, JEROME BORISON & STEVE R. JOHNSON, CIVIL TAX PROCEDURE ch. 13 (2d ed. 2007).

resources and efforts that the Government expends on the enforcement of existing laws. While an amnesty may be one way to obtain taxes that have not been paid and to bring new taxpayers into the tax system, increasing resources devoted to enforcement and increasing the penalties for failure to comply with the tax laws are other ways to achieve the same objectives.

- Economists generally believe that taxpayers choose a level of compliance with the tax laws by weighing the tradeoff between compliance and evasion and choosing the level of compliance that will lead to the highest expected level of net benefits. Among the factors that will influence a taxpayer's decision between compliance and evasion are the probability of the evasion being detected through audit, the back taxes and civil and criminal penalties that will be imposed if evasion is detected, the taxpayer's ethics or degree of honesty, damage to the reputation of the taxpayer if the evasion is detected, the taxpayer's level of "risk aversion," and the perceived benefits derived from a successful evasion of taxes.
- In the standard economic model of tax evasion, the creation of an amnesty program alone would have no effect on taxpayer behavior because the taxpayer has chosen a level of compliance based on a rational weighing of the benefits and costs of evasion. If these costs and benefits are not changed, the taxpayer's behavior will not change. If, however, the penalties for evasion are increased or the likelihood of detection through audit increases, then the rational taxpayer may choose to take advantage of the amnesty since the expected costs of previous evasion have been increased.
- State experience with tax amnesty will not necessarily parallel the experience that could be expected at the Federal level. First, many sources of State tax revenues do not have Federal counterparts. Second, pre-amnesty State tax enforcement efforts have generally been less rigorous than efforts at the Federal level. Thus, State amnesties that are coupled with increased enforcement efforts might be expected to be relatively more successful than a Federal amnesty because past evasion is likely to have been more common with respect to State taxes and taxpayers will view the increased enforcement efforts of the States as increasing the costs of State tax evasion. Further, many State amnesties included accounts receivable in their amnesties, which could be viewed as revenues that the State was likely to collect in any event.
- The experience of foreign governments with amnesty programs cannot generally be compared to the experience that might be expected in the United States. In most foreign countries, a larger portion of the national economy escapes the tax system than in the United States. Most foreign countries have larger underground economies. In addition, many countries exempt transactions occurring outside the country from taxation, creating an incentive to move untaxed profits outside the country. Few foreign countries have the level of tax enforcement that the United States has at the Federal level, especially with regard to the use of computer technology

and requirements of withholding and information reporting.[59]

Calls for a federal tax amnesty will surely be heard from time to time from those unpersuaded by the above reasoning. Although there is no general, formal amnesty program, the IRS and DOJ Tax have a voluntary disclosure policy. Under this policy, a tax delinquent who "comes clean" before the Government gets on his trail usually will not be criminally prosecuted. In a way, this policy operates as a sort of administrative amnesty program.[60]

V. PLAN OF THE BOOK

A. Chapters

The remaining chapters of this book divide into five clusters. The first cluster consists of Chapters 2A, 2B, and 3. These chapters contain the substantive elements of the crimes covered by this course. Chapter 2 addresses the tax crimes in the Internal Revenue Code, and Chapter 3 addresses the non-tax crimes that often are changed along with tax crimes. Chapter 2 is divided into Chapters 2A and 2B. Chapter 2A explores the most important of the tax crimes: tax evasion under section 7201. Chapter 2B describes the other significant tax crimes.

The second cluster consists of Chapters 4 through 10. They deal with the procedures governing criminal tax investigations and prosecutions. Specifically, these chapters address modes of proof; prosecution policies and affirmative defenses; case investigation and development; information gathering by the Government; pre-trial; and trial and post-trial.

The third cluster is Chapter 10. That chapter examines the crucial area of sentencing. Since the Government usually establishes the existence of a crime (via guilty plea or conviction at trial), sentencing sometimes is the stage at which criminal tax defense counsel can be of greatest help to the client.

The fourth cluster consists of Chapters 11 through 13. These chapters delve into constraints and ancillary considerations. Specifically, these chapters take up ethical considerations in criminal tax practice, major collateral consequences of being prosecuted and of being convicted, and civil tax liabilities and penalties.

Finally, the fifth cluster is Chapter 14. That chapter summarizes the course, weaving together the many strands that make for effective practice in this challenging and rewarding area of law.

B. Terms and Methodology

We have taken some stylistic liberties with the excerpts from cases and other materials in this book. We often omit citations, punctuation marks, footnotes, and the like, and we often omit portions of text that distract from the key points we are

---

[59] Staff of the Joint Committee on Taxation, Tax Amnesty, Summary of Findings (JCS-2-98) (Jan. 30, 1998).

[60] The voluntary disclosure policy is discussed in Chapter 6.

trying to make through the excerpt. To enhance readability, omissions usually are not flagged. Thus, if in your practice you want to quote one or another of the authorities excerpted in this book, you should always go to the original source to be sure you render the quotation completely accurately.

Acronyms are common in criminal tax work, as they are in law practice generally. We use and abuse acronyms frequently in this book. Typically, we define an acronym the first time it is used in this book but use it without definition subsequently. Included in this book as Appendix A is a Glossary of Acronyms relevant to criminal tax practice.

C. Additional Resources

There are a number of other materials, both in print and electronic, that you may find useful in criminal tax practice. Some of these are identified in Appendix B included in this book.

PROBLEM

Please read Appendix C, Appendix D, Appendix E, and Appendix F as part of this Problem. Appendices C, D, and E are the indictments in three prominent criminal tax cases. Appendix C is the indictment of Richard Hatch, the first winner of the "Survivor" television program. In 2006, Hatch was convicted of three counts of tax evasion but acquitted of non-tax charges. He was sentenced to 51 months in prison. His conviction and sentence were upheld on appeal, and his motions to vacate or correct the sentence were denied. *United States v. Hatch*, 514 F.3d 145 (1st Cir. 2008), *cert. denied*, 555 U.S. 820 (2008); *United States v. Hatch*, 2011 U.S. Dist. LEXIS 49944 (1st Cir. May 9, 2011).

Appendix D is the indictment of actor Wesley Snipes, star of more than 50 movies, including the "Blade" series. In 2008, Snipes was acquitted of conspiracy and false claims charges but found guilty of willful failure to file tax returns for three of the six years charged. He was sentenced to 36 months of imprisonment followed by one year of supervised release, the conditions of which are set out in Appendix F. His conviction and sentence were upheld on appeal, and his motions for new trial, leave to interview jurors, and bail pending certiorari were denied. *United States v. Snipes*, 611 F.3d 855 (11th Cir. 2010), *rehearing en banc denied*, 131 S. Ct. 2962 (2011); *United States v. Snipes*, 751 F. Supp. 2d 1279 (M.D. Fla. 2010), *aff'd*, 2011 U.S. App. LEXIS 18491 (11th Cir. Sept. 6, 2011). Snipes' co-defendants were convicted on the conspiracy and false claim charges.

Appendix E is the indictment of 19 individuals who worked for or cooperated with KPMG, a major international accounting and business services firm. KPMG itself entered into a Deferred Prosecution Agreement with the Government, acknowledging its guilt in connection with a number of illegal tax shelter schemes it promoted and paying a $456 million fine. The 19 individuals were separately indicted. Two pleaded guilty, three were convicted at trial, one was acquitted at trial, and 13 had their cases dismissed because excessive prosecutorial pressure on KPMG resulted in denial of the defendants' Sixth Amendment right to counsel.

United States v. Stein, 495 F. Supp. 2d 390 (S.D.N.Y. 2007), *aff'd*, 541 F.3d 130 (2d Cir. 2008).

Appendices C, D, and E reflect the diversity of conduct that can give rise to criminal tax prosecution, the diversity of statutes under which prosecution may occur, and the diversity of styles in writing indictments that exist among the various DOJ offices. At this early point in this course, you will not be familiar with the elements of the various crimes that are alleged in the three indictments.

Thus, read the three indictments with focus on their content and structure. Be prepared to discuss in class: (1) the types of conduct that the Government asserts were criminal, (2) the blend of tax and non-tax crimes alleged in the three cases, (3) how the indictments were organized, (4) the levels of specificity or generality with which the indictments describe the charges, and (5) any other noteworthy features of the indictments.

Further Note on Appendix C

The *Hatch* indictment mixes tax and non-tax counts. Federal Rule of Criminal Procedure 8(a) allows such joinder "if the offenses charged . . . are of the same or similar character, or are based on the same act or transaction, or are connected with or constitute parts of a common scheme or plan." Tax convictions sometimes have been overturned for improper joinder with insufficiently related non-tax charges. *E.g., United States v. Litwok*, 678 F.3d 208 (2d Cir. 2012); *United States v. Rubenstein*, 507 F.3d 82 (2d Cir. 2007). The courts attempt to balance judicial efficiency against the risk of prejudice.

Further Notes on Appendix D

(1) The *Snipes* indictment embraces three defendants: Snipes, Kahn, and Rosile. Federal Rule of Criminal Procedure 8(b) allows such joinder if the multiple defendants "are alleged to have participated in the same act or transaction, or in the same series of acts or transactions, constituting an offense or offenses." The interactions of these three defendants easily met this standard.

(2) Chapter 8 addresses venue issues. The Eleventh Circuit's decision in *Snipes* contains an instructive analysis of venue. *Snipes, supra*, 611 F.3d at 865–67.

(3) *Snipes* is part of a long train of cases in which the Government — with mixed success — has prosecuted tax protestors. Among the numerous examples, in 2006, inveterate tax protester Irwin ("Some People Never Learn") Schiff was sentenced to 151 months imprisonment and three years of supervised release following his most recent conviction for conspiracy and tax fraud. *United States v. Schiff*, 2012 U.S. Dist. LEXIS 135934 (D. Nev. Sept. 21, 2012). In 2012, Troy Beam (former CPA and Pennsylvania state auditor turned tax defier) was sentenced to 74 months in prison upon conviction for tax evasion, obstructing the IRS, and willful failure to file returns. 2012 TNT 70-30 (Apr. 11, 2012).

Further Notes on Appendix E

(1) The *Stein* indictment involves an even more extensive network of defendants than *Snipes*. Especially since multiple tax shelters were involved, the case for joinder is somewhat more attenuated but is strong enough.

(2) Chapter 2A discusses situations in which the state of the substantive tax law is so uncertain that willfulness (an element of most tax crimes) cannot, as a matter of law, exist. For an argument that the economic substance doctrine — a prime weapon the Government uses against tax shelters — is highly obscure and uncertain, see Jasper L. Cummings, Jr., *Economic Substance Doctrine Felonies*, TAX NOTES, May 30, 2011, at 977.

(3) The Government has continued to aggressively pursue entities and individuals associated with the more egregious tax shelters. For example, in 2007, the Jenkins & Gilchrist law firm signed a Deferred Prosecution Agreement, paid a $76 million penalty to the Government and $85 million to settle a class action suit by former clients, and went out of business. In 2012, the accounting firm BDO USA LLP entered into a Deferred Prosecution Agreement and paid a $50 million penalty.

The Government has had mixed success in prosecutions of individuals responsible for creating, marketing, and concealing illegal tax shelters. For example, prosecution of seven BDO and Jenkins & Gilchrist associated lawyers and accountants resulted in three guilty pleas, one acquittal, and three convictions (including major target Paul Daugerdas). Some of the convictions were overturned because a juror lied during voir dire. *E.g.*, *United States v. Daugerdas*, 2013 U.S. Dist. LEXIS 87335 (S.D.N.Y. May 22, 2013); *United States v. Daugerdas*, 915 F. Supp. 2d 493 (S.D.N.Y. 2013); *United States v. Daugerdas*, 2012 U.S. Dist. LEXIS 167631 (S.D.N.Y. Nov. 7, 2012). The principal defendant, Paul Daugerdas, was convicted at retrial. He was sentenced to 15 years in prison and was ordered to forfeit around $165,000,000 in proceeds of the offenses and to pay around $371,000,000 in restitution.

Prosecution of six lawyers and accountants associated with tax shelters created by the Ernst & Young accounting firm resulted in one guilty plea, one defendant becoming a fugitive, and four convictions at trial, two of which were affirmed and two of which were reversed in part or whole on appeal. *United States v. Coplan*, 703 F.3d 46 (2d Cir. 2012).

In 2013, Michael Parker, a KPMG-associated CPA and attorney who also ran a tax shelter boutique, received 54 months of prison time and three years of supervised release after pleading guilty to conspiracy to defraud the United States. He also testified against two others accused of conspiracy, but they were acquitted.

Chapter 2A

CRIMES UNDER THE INTERNAL REVENUE CODE — TAX EVASION

IRC: § 7201

I. INTRODUCTION

Chapters 2A and 2B deal with tax crimes under the Code, the crimes reflecting solely tax priorities. This Chapter 2A deals with the most frequently charged tax crime: tax evasion under section 7201. Chapter 2B deals with the other Title 26 offenses.

Tax evasion under section 7201 is the "capstone" of the traditional tax crimes.[1] This is the worst the taxpayer can do in terms of punishment for offending the tax system. However, as described in Chapter 3, money laundering — a non-tax offense often charged along with tax offenses — can carry greater penalties.

Section 7201 applies to two types of evasion. The first, and the more commonly charged, is evasion of assessment. This is an attempt by the taxpayer to prevent the IRS from knowing that additional tax is due. Evasion can be attempted through failing to file a return, but filing a false return is the more common method. The return may be false because it understates income, overstates deductions or credits, or both. Filing a false return may be accompanied by other acts of evasion of assessment, such as making false statements to IRS agents, keeping multiple sets of books, and the like.

The second type of evasion is evasion of payment. This occurs when the IRS knows of and usually has assessed the tax liability, but the taxpayer takes affirmative steps to prevent the IRS from collecting the tax. A classic example of evasion of payment is the movement of one's resources offshore beyond the IRS's means of collection. More subtle forms of evasion of payment can occur if the taxpayer deliberately spends or wastes all assets in order to avoid having any source from which the IRS could collect the tax.

There is some semantical dispute as to whether section 7201 describes two separate offenses or simply describes one offense — tax evasion — that is committed by attempting to evade assessment or attempting to evade payment.[2] It

---

[1] Spies v. United States, 317 U.S. 492, 497 (1943).

[2] *See, e.g.*, United States v. McLaughlin, 126 F.3d 130, 136 (3d Cir. 1997), *cert. denied*, 524 U.S. 951 (1998) ("Section 7201 includes two distinct offenses: evading assessment and evading payment . . . . These offenses require different elements of proof."). In *McLaughlin*, the indictment charged the

is unnecessary to enter this semantical fray here since it does not affect the outcomes of actual cases.

Section 7201 provides that violators "shall be fined not more than $100,000 ($500,000 in the case of a corporation), or imprisoned not more than 5 years, or both, together with the costs of prosecution." And that is per count. Each tax year potentially is a separate count, and the Government usually brings multi-year section 7201 charges. Thus, theoretically, a defendant convicted of violating section 7201 for three years could be sentenced to 15 years of incarceration.[3]

Sometimes, for tactical reasons, the Government chooses to prosecute conduct over several years as a single section 7201 charge. Defendants may challenge this choice as involving duplicity, the improper joinder of distinct and separate offenses in a single count.[4] However, the courts have held that "tax evasion covering several years may be charged in a single count as a course of conduct . . . where the underlying basis of the indictment is an allegedly consistent, long-term pattern of conduct directed at the evasion of taxes for [those] years."[5]

The elements of tax evasion of the false return variety are described by the following jury instruction:

> To establish the offense of attempting to evade and defeat a tax, the government is required to prove beyond a reasonable doubt the following three elements:
>
> First, a substantial . . . tax was due and owing from the defendant in addition to that declared in his [her] . . . tax return;
>
> Second, the defendant made an affirmative attempt, in any manner, to evade or defeat . . . tax; and
>
> Third, the defendant willfully attempted to evade and defeat the tax.[6]

---

defendant with evasion of payment, but the case was tried as an evasion of assessment case. The court held that this might be a variance — even though section 7201 is arguably a single crime — but that the conviction should not be reversed because the defendant had not been prejudiced. The defendant was aware that the case was tried as an evasion of assessment case and actually addressed that issue at trial.

[3] Actual sentences imposed are rarely this long. As described in Chapter 10, many considerations influence sentencing. Sentences imposed in tax cases vary widely — from as little as probation or brief home detention to as much as over 20 years — depending on the circumstances. The average length of incarceration in section 7201 cases is in the vicinity of 24 to 30 months. *E.g.*, Theodore M. David, *The Tax Non-Filer: Public Enemy Number One?*, Practical Tax Law., Spring 2001, at 7, 8.

[4] United States v. Haddy, 134 F.3d 542, 548 (3d Cir. 1998).

[5] United States v. Shorter, 809 F.2d 54, 56 (D.C. Cir. 1987) (permitting the Government to charge one count of tax evasion for conduct occurring over 12 tax years); *see also* United States v. Root, 585 F.3d 145, 150–51 (3d Cir. 2009).

[6] CTM Government Proposed Jury Instr. No. 26.7201-3 (2008 ed.) (footnote omitted). Sometimes the CTM's proposed instructions carry a pro-prosecution spin. For tax evasion, however, the CTM instruction is straightforward. *See also* United States v. Miller, 588 F.3d 897, 907 (5th Cir. 2009) ("The elements of a violation of 26 U.S.C. § 7201 are: (1) existence of a tax deficiency; (2) an affirmative act constituting an evasion or an attempted evasion of the tax; and (3) willfulness.").

In *United States v. Maggert*, 2011 U.S. App. LEXIS 10976 (11th Cir. May 31, 2011), the district court

Another jury instruction adds:

> The proof need not show the precise amount or all of the additional tax due as alleged in the indictment, but the government must prove beyond a reasonable doubt that the defendant attempted to evade or defeat payment of some substantial portion of the additional tax he knew he was required by law to pay.[7]

Below, we examine more closely the elements of tax evasion, specifically requirements as to affirmative act, willfulness, and tax underpayment. Thereafter, we explore of how a taxpayer may attempt to undo tax fraud after having committed it.

II. AFFIRMATIVE ACT

There must be an affirmative attempt to evade or defeat the tax due and owing. The statute uses the term "attempts." The courts have added the "affirmative" spin to the statute in recognition of the seriousness of the crime and to distinguish tax evasion from other, lesser tax crimes. For example, a taxpayer may intend to evade tax by failing to file his tax return. But a mere failure to do something is not an affirmative attempt to evade tax. Hence, the failure to file alone — without some other affirmative conduct to attempt to evade — will not support a tax-evasion charge. (It will, however, support the lesser, misdemeanor offense of failure to file under section 7203.)

SPIES v. UNITED STATES

United States Supreme Court
317 U.S. 492 (1943)

[Authors' note: In this case, the Court interpreted sections 145(a) and 145(b) of 1936 legislation. These provisions were predecessors of current sections 7203 and 7201, respectively.]

Petitioner has been convicted of attempting to defeat and evade income tax, in violation of § 145(b) of the Revenue Act of 1936. Petitioner admitted at the opening of the trial that he had sufficient income during the year in question to place him under a statutory duty to file a return and to pay a tax, and that he failed to do either. The evidence during nearly two weeks of trial was directed principally toward establishing the exact amount of the tax and the manner of receiving and handling income and accounting, which the Government contends shows an intent to evade or defeat the tax. Petitioner's testimony related to his good character, his physical illness at the time the return became due, and lack of willfulness in his defaults, chiefly because of a psychological disturbance, amounting to something more than worry but something less than insanity.

---

modified the circuit pattern instruction, resulting in omission of the affirmative act element. The circuit court nonetheless upheld the conviction. The defendant did not object at trial. He also failed to establish "plain error" on appeal, in part because there was overwhelming evidence that Maggert committed numerous affirmative acts of evasion." *Id.* at 879.

[7] Fifth Circuit Pattern Jury Instruction 2.96.

Section 145(a) makes, among other things, willful failure to pay a tax or make a return by one having petitioner's income at the time or times required by law a misdemeanor. Section 145(b) makes a willful attempt in any manner to evade or defeat any tax such as this a felony. Petitioner was not indicted for either misdemeanor. The indictment contained a single count setting forth the felony charge of willfully attempting to defeat and evade the tax, and recited willful failure to file a return and willful failure to pay the tax as the means to the felonious end.

The petitioner requested an instruction that "You may not find the defendant guilty of a willful attempt to defeat and evade the income tax, if you find only that he had willfully failed to make a return of taxable income and has willfully failed to pay the tax on that income." This was refused, and the Court charged that "If you find that the defendant had a net income for 1936 upon which some income tax was due, and I believe that is conceded, if you find that the defendant willfully failed to file an income tax return for that year, if you find that the defendant willfully failed to pay the tax due on his income for that year, you may, if you find that the facts and circumstances warrant it find that the defendant willfully attempted to evade or defeat the tax." The Court refused a request to instruct that an affirmative act was necessary to constitute a willful attempt, and charged that "Attempt means to try to do or accomplish. In order to find an attempt it is not necessary to find affirmative steps to accomplish the prohibited purpose. An attempt may be found on the basis of inactivity or on refraining to act, as well."

It is the Government's contention that a willful failure to file a return, together with a willful failure to pay the tax, may, without more, constitute an attempt to defeat or evade a tax within § 145(b). Petitioner claims that such proof establishes only two misdemeanors under § 145(a), and that it takes more than the sum of two such misdemeanors to make the felony under § 145(b). The legislative history of the section contains nothing helpful on the question here at issue, and we must find the answer from the section itself and its context in the revenue laws.

The United States has relied for the collection of its income tax largely upon the taxpayer's own disclosures rather than upon a system of withholding the tax from him by those from whom income may be received. This system can function successfully only if those within and near taxable income keep and render true accounts. In many ways, taxpayers' neglect or deceit may prejudice the orderly and punctual administration of the system as well as the revenues themselves. Congress has imposed a variety of sanctions for the protection of the system and the revenues. The relation of the offense of which this petitioner has been convicted to other and lesser revenue offenses appears more clearly from its position in this structure of sanctions. The penalties imposed by Congress to enforce the tax laws embrace both civil and criminal sanctions. The former consist of additions to the tax upon determinations of fact made by an administrative agency and with no burden on the Government to prove its case beyond a reasonable doubt. The latter consist of penal offenses enforced by the criminal process in the familiar manner. Invocation of one does not exclude resort to the other.

The failure in a duty to make a timely return, unless it is shown that such failure is due to reasonable cause and not due to willful neglect, is punishable by an addition to the tax of 5 to 25 per cent thereof, depending on the duration of the default. But a duty may exist even when there is no tax liability to serve as a base for application of a percentage delinquency penalty; the default may relate to matters not identifiable with tax for a particular period; and the offense may be more grievous than a case for civil penalty. Hence the willful failure to make a return, keep records, or supply information when required, is made a misdemeanor, without regard to existence of a tax liability. § 145(a). Punctuality is important to the fiscal system, and these are sanctions to assure punctual as well as faithful performance of these duties.

Sanctions to insure payment of the tax are even more varied to meet the variety of causes of default. It is the right as well as the interest of the taxpayer to limit his admission of liability to the amount he actually owes. But the law is complicated, accounting treatment of various items raises problems of great complexity, and innocent errors are numerous, as appears from the number who make overpayments. It is not the purpose of the law to penalize frank difference of opinion or innocent errors made despite the exercise of reasonable care. Such errors are corrected by the assessment of the deficiency of tax and its collection with interest for the delay. If any part of the deficiency is due to negligence or intentional disregard of rules and regulations, but without intent to defraud, five per cent of such deficiency is added thereto; and if any part of any deficiency is due to fraud with intent to evade tax, the addition is 50 per cent thereof. Willful failure to pay the tax when due is punishable as a misdemeanor. § 145(a). The climax of this variety of sanctions is the serious and inclusive felony defined to consist of willful attempt in any manner to evade or defeat the tax. § 145(b). The question here is whether there is a distinction between the acts necessary to make out the felony and those which may make out the misdemeanor.

A felony may, and frequently does, include lesser offenses in combination either with each other or with other elements. We think it clear that this felony may include one or several of the other offenses against the revenue laws. But it would be unusual and we would not readily assume that Congress by the felony defined in § 145(b) meant no more than the same derelictions it had just defined in § 145(a) as a misdemeanor. Such an interpretation becomes even more difficult to accept when we consider this felony as the capstone of a system of sanctions which singly or in combination were calculated to induce prompt and forthright fulfillment of every duty under the income tax law and to provide a penalty suitable to every degree of delinquency. The difference between willful failure to pay a tax when due, which is made a misdemeanor, and willful attempt to defeat and evade one, which is made a felony, is not easy to detect or define. Both must be willful, and willful, as we have said, is a word of many meanings, its construction often being influenced by its context. It may well mean something more as applied to nonpayment of a tax than when applied to failure to make a return. Mere voluntary and purposeful, as distinguished from accidental, omission to make a timely return might meet the test of willfulness. But in view of our traditional aversion to imprisonment for debt, we would not without the clearest manifestation of Congressional intent assume that mere knowing and intentional default in payment of a tax, where there had been no willful failure to disclose the liability, is intended to constitute a criminal offense of any degree. We would expect willfulness in such a case to include some element of evil motive and want of justification in view of all the financial circumstances of the taxpayer.

Had § 145(a) not included willful failure to pay a tax, it would have defined as misdemeanors generally a failure to observe statutory duties to make timely returns, keep records, or supply information — duties imposed to facilitate administration of the Act even if, because of insufficient net income, there were no duty to pay a tax. It would then be a permissible and perhaps an appropriate construction of § 145(b) that it made felonies of the same willful omissions when there was the added element of duty to pay a tax. The definition of such nonpayment as a misdemeanor, we think, argues strongly against such an interpretation.

The difference between the two offenses, it seems to us, is found in the affirmative action implied from the term "attempt,"as used in the felony subsection. It is not necessary to involve this subject with the complexities of the common-law "attempt." The attempt made criminal by this statute does not consist of conduct that would culminate in a more serious crime but for some impossibility of completion or interruption or frustration. This is an independent crime, complete in its most serious form when the attempt is complete, and nothing is added to its criminality by success or consummation, as would be the case, say, of attempted murder. Although the attempt succeeds in evading tax, there is no criminal offense of that kind, and the prosecution can be only for the attempt. We think that in employing the terminology of attempt to embrace the gravest of offenses against the revenues, Congress intended some willful commission in addition to the willful omissions that make up the list of misdemeanors. Willful but passive neglect of the statutory duty may constitute the lesser offense, but to combine with it a willful and positive attempt to evade tax in any manner or to defeat it by any means lifts the offense to the degree of felony.

Congress did not define or limit the methods by which a willful attempt to defeat and evade might be accomplished and perhaps did not define lest its effort to do so result in some unexpected limitation. Nor would we by definition constrict the scope of the Congressional provision that it may be accomplished "in any manner." By way of illustration, and not by way of limitation, we would think affirmative willful attempt may be inferred from conduct such as keeping a double set of books, making false entries or alterations, or false invoices or documents, destruction of books or records, concealment of assets or covering up sources of income, handling of one's affairs to avoid making the records usual in transactions of the kind, and any conduct, the likely effect of which would be to mislead or to conceal. If the tax-evasion motive plays any part in such conduct the offense may be made out even though the conduct may also serve other purposes such as concealment of other crime.

In this case there are several items of evidence apart from the default in filing the return and paying the tax which the Government claims will support an inference of willful attempt to evade or defeat the tax. These go to establish that petitioner insisted that certain income be paid to him in cash, transferred it to his own bank by armored car, deposited it, not in his own name but in the names of others of his family, and kept inadequate and misleading records. Petitioner claims other motives animated him in these matters. We intimate no opinion. Such inferences are for the jury. If on proper submission the jury found these acts, taken together with willful failure to file a return and willful failure to pay the tax, to constitute a willful attempt to evade or defeat the tax, we would consider conviction of a felony sustainable. But we think a defendant is entitled to a charge which will point out the necessity for such an inference of willful attempt to defeat or evade the tax from some proof in the case other than that necessary to make out the misdemeanors; and if the evidence fails to afford such an inference, the defendant should be acquitted.

The Government argues against this construction, contending that the milder punishment of a misdemeanor and the benefits of a short statute of limitation should not be extended to violators of the income tax laws such as political grafters, gamblers, racketeers, and gangsters. We doubt that this construction will handicap prosecution for felony of such flagrant violators. Few of them, we think, in their efforts to escape tax, stop with mere omission of the duties put upon them by the statute, but if such there be, they are entitled to be convicted only of the offense which they have committed.

Reversed.

Spies establishes that evasion requires some affirmative act, not the mere failure to file or pay. Nonetheless, the Government sometimes charges under section 7201 taxpayers who have failed to file. How does a failure to file turn into tax evasion in the real world? This occurs, for example, if the taxpayer files W-4's claiming an outrageous number of exemptions so that no income tax is withheld and then files no return.[8] It can also occur if the taxpayer fails to file and then, upon inquiry by the IRS as to why he did not file, the taxpayer advises that he had no income when he did in fact have sufficient income to require that he file a return.[9] The lie is the affirmative act.[10] (As we shall see below, the lie can be a key element for the crime of tax evasion and can also be the key element in other crimes such as false statements under 18 U.S.C. § 1001.[11])

The battleground anticipated by the *Spies* Court was just how minimal an affirmative act must be to meet the *Spies* spin on the "attempt" requirement. *Spies* provided examples. The Department of Justice adds:

> Even an activity that would otherwise be legal can constitute an affirmative act supporting a section 7201 conviction, so long as the defendant commits the act with the intent to evade tax. *See United States v. Voigt*, 89 F.3d 1050, 1090 (3d Cir. 1996); *United States v. Jungles*, 903 F.2d 468, 474 (7th Cir. 1990) (taxpayer's entry into an "independent contractor agreement," although a legal activity in and of itself, satisfied "affirmative act" element of section 7201); *United States v. Conley*, 826 F.2d 551 (7th Cir.

---

[8] *E.g.*, United States v. King, 126 F.3d 987 (7th Cir. 1997); United States v. Williams, 928 F.2d 145 (5th Cir.), *cert. denied*, 502 U.S. 811 (1991).

[9] United States v. Goodyear, 649 F.2d 226 (4th Cir. 1981).

[10] *E.g.*, United States v. Beacon Brass Co., Inc., 344 U.S. 43 (1952).

[11] *See* Chapter 3.

1987) (use of nominees and cash done with intent to evade payment of taxes).[12]

Consider the following additional areas. (i) Would the filing of a false W-4 in a year well beyond the statute of limitations support a criminal conviction for failure to file in a later year if the employer continued to withhold through the later year based upon the earlier W-4? The answer is yes, but why?[13]

(ii) Would a taxpayer's regular practice of spending all of his money, thus rendering himself unable to pay tax, be sufficient to meet the attempt requirement for evasion? Or, is that just a mere failure to pay, which is a separate and lesser crime as discussed in Chapter 2B? The Department of Justice admits that even obstinate refusal to pay a tax even if coupled with the open, non-secret assignment of income is not tax evasion.[14] But, Justice also cautions that other affirmative actions such as using secret bank accounts, using nominees, and even paying other creditors ahead of the IRS may be tax evasion. So, not surprisingly, Justice cites cases for the proposition that maintaining a "cash lifestyle" so as not to have assets the IRS can readily seize can be an act of evasion.[15]

UNITED STATES v. McGILL

United States Court of Appeals, Third Circuit
964 F.2d 222 (1992)

[Authors' note: The taxpayer-defendant was a lawyer.[16] He failed to pay income taxes that he reported on his return. Among other collection efforts, the IRS levied on the taxpayer's bank accounts. The taxpayer then stopped using the accounts and began using accounts held by his wife or business associates. He also opened up a new account (that the IRS did not know about) in his own name. The court held that funneling money through others' accounts supplied the affirmative act, but that using his own new account was not an act of evasion.]

[U]nless a taxpayer is in the situation of giving voluntary admissions during an investigation or a forced response to a subpoena, the failure of the taxpayer to report the opening of an account in his or her own name in his or her own locale cannot amount to an affirmative act of evasion. Omissions, including failures to report, do not satisfy the requirements of § 7201; the Government must prove a specific act to mislead or conceal. McGill testified that he opened the account on the advice of counsel in response to IRS criticism for banking under the names of

---

[12] CTM 8.06.

[13] *See* United States v. King, 126 F.3d 987 (7th Cir. 1997) (upholding section 7201 conviction of a tax protester who just did not "get it").

[14] CTM 8.06[2].

[15] CTM 8.06[2] (citing, among others, United States v. Shorter, 809 F.2d 54, 57 (D.C. Cir.), *cert. denied*, 484 U.S. 817 (1987)); *see also* Steve R. Johnson, *The Financial Inability Defense to Tax Crimes*, 23/3 ABA Sec. Tax'n NewsQuarterly 6 (2004).

[16] [Authors' note: To our discredit, lawyers and accountants are not highly tax compliant groups. Numerous lawyers and accountants throughout the United States have been convicted of tax crimes. The IRS has issued an audit technique guide to help its Revenue Agents and other personnel audit the tax returns of attorneys. *IRS Releases Audit Technique Guide for Attorneys' Returns*, 2011 TNT 138-13 (July 19, 2011).]

others. There is no evidence that McGill concealed this new account from the IRS apart from the fact that he did not inform the IRS of its existence.[17]

[Authors' note: The concurring opinion, although agreeing to the result, took the majority to task over the breadth of its language regarding the act of setting up a new bank account unknown to the IRS.]

In *Spies v. United States*, the Supreme Court said that an "affirmative willful attempt [of tax evasion] may be inferred from . . . any conduct, the likely effect of which would be to mislead or to conceal." This is an expansive definition, one which takes into account that not "all tax payment evaders approach their problem in the same way." Where there is sufficient evidence, the question whether conduct supports a legitimate inference of willful attempt to evade taxes is for the jury, *see Spies*, 317 U.S. at 500, whose findings we must accord deference.

At the time McGill opened the [new] account in August 1988, he was the target of a criminal investigation for tax evasion and had been the subject of five years of civil collection efforts by the IRS. The $9,000 the Government alleges he deposited in the account consisted of legal fees which had escaped an IRS levy. Although McGill was aware these funds were subject to levy, he admitted expending them on personal and business items. Nevertheless, he claims to have reported them on his income tax return for that year.

I agree that, in the ordinary case, opening a personal banking account and depositing funds in it will not by itself amount to an affirmative act of tax evasion. But it seems to me that under the proper circumstances, this conduct may support a legitimate inference that a taxpayer has attempted to evade payment of federal tax liabilities. *Cf. United States v. White*, 417 F.2d 89, 92 (2d Cir. 1969), *cert. denied*, 397 U.S. 912 (1970) (allowing jury to infer affirmative act of tax evasion from fact that defendant had "maintained a separate personal banking account in a neighboring town in which he deposited large amounts of [unreported] currency from unidentified sources").

Assuming McGill deposited the $9,000 in legal fees subject to levy in the account, I would find these circumstances present here. Even though McGill claims to have reported the $9,000 on his tax return, because he was aware these funds were subject to levy and was the target of a criminal investigation for tax evasion at the time, I would hold that his deposit and expenditure of the $9,000 without first notifying the IRS supports a legitimate inference that he committed an affirmative act of tax evasion under § 7201. *See United States v. Eley*, 314 F.2d 127, 132 (7th Cir. 1963) (upholding jury instruction which listed as an "affirmative, willful attempt" to evade taxes the "failure during the course of an investigation to supply any information for purposes of a computation, assessment or collection of income tax when such failure is found . . . to be unjustified").

However, because I agree with the majority that the Government has failed to meet its burden in establishing that McGill in fact deposited the $9,000 which had escaped the IRS levy in the account in August 1988, I concur in the result on Counts 7 and 8.

---

[17] [Authors' note: 964 F.2d at 233–34 (record citations omitted).]

[Authors' note: Returning to the majority opinion (as to which all judges concurred on the balance of the case, in addressing the taxpayer's willfulness defense on the counts for which it was prepared to affirm), the court said as follows.]

Further, the judge told the jury that McGill's inability to pay his taxes had no bearing on willfulness. McGill vehemently asserts that he never raised inability to pay as a defense to the evasion of payment charge, though he did assert inability to pay as a defense to the charge of willful failure to pay. We decline to resolve the apparent split of authority as to whether a taxpayer's inability to pay should bear on the willfulness of his violations. Even if the inability to pay were relevant, the defense is unavailing to McGill, who could have altered his lifestyle and thus, freed the money required to pay his tax obligations.[18]

UNITED STATES v. BEACON BRASS CO., INC.

United States Supreme Court
344 U.S. 43 (1952)

On March 16, 1951, a one-count indictment was returned in the United States District Court for the District of Massachusetts against the appellees, Beacon Brass Company, a corporation, and Maurice Feinberg, its president and treasurer. The indictment charged that in violation of § 145(b) [tax evasion], the appellees have willfully attempted to evade taxes by making false statements to Treasury representatives on October 24, 1945, "for the purpose of supporting, ratifying, confirming and concealing the fraudulent, and incorrect statements and representations made in the corporate tax return of said Beacon Brass Co., Inc., for the fiscal period ending October 31, 1944, filed on or about January 5, 1945."

The six-year limitation period, applicable to offenses under this statute, had expired on a charge for filing a false tax return in January 1945, but it had not expired on a charge of making false statements to Treasury employees in October 1945. The District Court viewed the indictment as charging the separate crimes of filing a false return and making subsequent false statements to Treasury representatives, and dismissed the indictment as duplicitous.

On September 14, 1951, a second indictment was returned against the appellees which repeated the charge that in violation of § 145(b) they "did willfully and knowingly attempt to defeat and evade a large part of the taxes due and owing by the said corporation . . . by making certain false and fraudulent statements and representations, at a hearing and conference before representatives and employees of the United States Treasury Department, on or about October 24, 1945." Reference to the allegedly false return filed in January 1945 was omitted, and instead it was charged that the false statements were made "for the purpose of concealing additional unreported net income."

Section 35(A) of the Criminal Code, 18 U.S.C. (1946 ed.) § 80 [now 18 U.S.C. § 1001] makes it unlawful to "knowingly and willfully . . . make . . . any false or fraudulent statements or representations . . . in any matter within the jurisdiction of any department or agency of the United States." Obviously, at the times of the

---

[18] [Authors' note: 964 F.2d at 238.]

indictments here, the three-year limitation period for violations of this statute had expired as to statements made in October 1945. The District Court concluded that since § 35(A) deals specifically with false statements, Congress must be presumed to have intended that the making of false statements should be punishable only under § 35(A). Therefore, the District Court dismissed the indictment on the ground that it failed to charge an offense under 26 U.S.C. § 145(b).

We have before us two statutes, each of which proscribes conduct not covered by the other, but which overlap in a narrow area illustrated by the instant case. At least where different proof is required for each offense, a single act or transaction may violate more than one criminal statute. Unlike § 35(A), § 145(b) requires proof that the false statements were made in a willful effort to evade taxes. The purpose to evade taxes is crucial under this section. The language of § 145(b) which outlaws willful attempts to evade taxes "in any manner" is clearly broad enough to include false statements made to Treasury representatives for the purpose of concealing unreported income. *Cf. Spies v. United States*, 317 U.S. 492, 499. The question raised by the decision below is whether by enacting a statute specifically outlawing all false statements in matters under the jurisdiction of agencies of the United States, Congress intended thereby to exclude the making of false statements from the scope of § 145(b).

We do not believe that Congress intended to require the tax-enforcement authorities to deal differently with false statements than with other methods of tax evasion. By providing that the sanctions of § 145(b) should be "in addition to other penalties provided by law," Congress recognized that some methods of attempting to evade taxes would violate other statutes as well. Moreover, since no distinction is made in § 35(A) between written and oral statements, the reasoning of the court below would be equally applicable to false tax returns which are, of course, false written statements. But the Courts of Appeals have uniformly applied § 145(b) to attempts to evade taxes by filing false returns. Further support for our conclusion can be found in *United States v. Noveck*, where this Court rejected the contention that the enactment of § 145(b) impliedly repealed the general perjury statute insofar as that statute applied to false tax returns made under oath. Finally, the enactment of other statutes expressly outlawing false statements in particular contexts negates the assumption — which was the foundation of the decision of the court below — that Congress intended the making of false statements to be punishable only under § 35(A). The appellees contend that the acts charged constitute only one crime of tax evasion which was complete when the allegedly false tax return was filed. On the basis of this contention, appellees seek to sustain the decision below on the grounds that the six-year statute of limitations had run, and that the dismissal of the first indictment is res judicata and a bar to the second indictment for the same offense. We do not consider these questions because our jurisdiction on this appeal is limited to review of the District Court's construction of the statute in the light of the facts alleged in the indictment.

The judgment of the District Court is reversed, and the cause is remanded for further proceedings not inconsistent with this opinion.

How far can we take *Beacon Brass*? Assume that a taxpayer filed a fraudulent

1999 return in 2000 falsely claiming large net operating losses that not only wiped out his tax liability for 1999 but also are carried forward to wipe out tax liabilities in 2008 (the return for which was filed in April 2009). By claiming the false net operating losses on his 2008 return filed after the criminal statute of limitations on 1999 had expired, the taxpayer has committed a separate act of evasion — evading his 2008 taxes.[19]

What if, however, the taxpayer did not claim the net operating losses on his 2008 return, realizing that he would thereby be committing a felony? He is just happy that the criminal statute of limitations has expired on 1999. His falsely claimed net operating losses did save him taxes in 1999, so his civil statute of limitations is still open.[20] During the course of the audit of the 2008 return (on which he did not claim the carryforward losses), the IRS agent asks the taxpayer for retained copies of prior returns. The taxpayer supplies him the returns for 1995 through 2008. The agent notices the large 1999 net operating loss and asks the taxpayer about it. Then, realizing that the agent may focus on the 1999 taxes saved and assert a civil tax liability, along with penalties and interest, for 1999 under the unlimited civil statute, the taxpayer tries to fade the heat by lying. The taxpayer has then committed felony tax evasion with respect to his 1999 income tax liability even though the criminal statute of limitations for the 1999 tax year was not otherwise open. He has just refreshed an otherwise closed criminal statute of limitations.

III. WILLFULNESS

A. Generally

The *mens rea* element, although implicit in the attempt requirement, is supplied specifically by the willfulness requirement. The willfulness element of tax crimes generally is the "voluntary, intentional violation of a known legal duty."[21] The taxpayer must know that he has a duty to pay the tax and must knowingly intend not to meet that duty. The taxpayer does not have to be an evil person, nor does the taxpayer have to have acted with evil motive or in bad faith. All that is required is that he knew of the duty and intended to violate it.

UNITED STATES v. POMPONIO

United States Supreme Court
429 U.S. 10 (1976) (per curiam)

[Authors' note: *Pomponio* involves the substantive offense under § 7206(1), which is commonly referred to as "tax perjury" because it requires a materially false statement willfully made on a return filed under penalty of perjury. The focus here

[19] *Cf.* Gandy Nursery, Inc. v. United States, 318 F.3d 631, 638–39 (5th Cir. 2003) (holding that tax fraud conviction in the net operating loss year — 1999 in the above example — collaterally estops the taxpayer from denying civil fraud in the carryover year — 2008 in the above example). See Part III of Chapter 13 for discussion of collateral estoppel.

[20] I.R.C. § 6501(c)(1) (unlimited statute of limitations for assessment as to fraudulent returns). See Part IV of Chapter 13 for discussion of the civil statute of limitations.

[21] United States v. Pomponio, 429 U.S. 10, 13 (1976).

is on the willfulness requirement which is common to tax evasion under section 7201 and tax perjury under section 7206(1).]

After a jury trial, respondents were convicted of willfully filing false income tax returns in violation of 26 U.S.C. § 7206(1). Based on its reading of *United States v. Bishop*, 412 U.S. 346 (1973), the Court of Appeals held that the jury was incorrectly instructed concerning willfulness, and remanded for a new trial. The United States petitioned for certiorari. We reverse.

The respondents were charged with falsifying tax returns in two principal ways: (1) they allegedly caused corporations they controlled to report payments to them as loans, when they knew the payments were really taxable dividends; and (2) they allegedly claimed partnership losses as deductions knowing that the losses were properly attributable to a corporation. Their defense was that these transactions were correctly reported, or at least that they thought so at the time. The jury was instructed that respondents were not guilty of violating § 7206(1) unless they had signed the tax returns knowing them to be false, and had done so willfully. A willful act was defined in the instructions as one done "voluntarily and intentionally and with the specific intent to do something which the law forbids, that is to say with [the] bad purpose either to disobey or to disregard the law." Finally, the jury was instructed that "[g]ood motive alone is never a defense where the act done or omitted is a crime," and that consequently motive was irrelevant except as it bore on intent. The Court of Appeals held this final instruction improper because "the statute at hand requires a finding of a bad purpose or evil motive." In so holding, the Court of Appeals incorrectly assumed that the reference to an "evil motive" in *United States v. Bishop* and prior cases meant something more than the specific intent to violate the law described in the trial judge's instruction.

In *Bishop*, we held that the term "willfully" has the same meaning in the misdemeanor and felony sections of the Revenue Code, and that it requires more than a showing of careless disregard for the truth. We did not, however, hold that the term requires proof of any motive other than an intentional violation of a known legal duty. We explained the meaning of willfulness in § 7206 and related statutes:

> The Court, in fact, has recognized that the word "willfully" in these statutes generally connotes a voluntary, intentional violation of a known legal duty. It has formulated the requirement of willfulness as "bad faith or evil intent," or "evil motive and want of justification in view of all the financial circumstances of the taxpayer," *Spies*, 317 U.S. 498, or knowledge that the taxpayer "should have reported more income than he did." *Sansone*, 380 U.S. [343,] 353. See *James v. United States*, 366 U.S. 213, 2216 L. Ed. 2d 246, 81 S. Ct. 1052 (1961).

Our references to other formulations of the standard did not modify the standard set forth in the first sentence of the quoted paragraph. On the contrary, as the other Courts of Appeals that have considered the question have recognized, willfulness in this context simply means a voluntary, intentional violation of a known legal duty. The trial judge in the instant case adequately instructed the jury on willfulness. An additional instruction on good faith was unnecessary. As an alternative ground for ordering a new trial, the Court of Appeals held that respondents were entitled to instructions exonerating them if they believed that the payments to them were loans and that the losses belonged to the partnership. Our inspection of the record indicates that such instructions were given and that they were adequate.

The respondents' other allegations of error which the Court of Appeals found it unnecessary to reach should be considered by that court in the first instance.

The petition for certiorari is granted, the judgment of the Court of Appeals is reversed, and the case is remanded for further proceedings consistent with this opinion.

CHEEK v. UNITED STATES

United States Supreme Court
498 U.S. 192 (1991)

JUSTICE WHITE delivered the opinion of the Court.

This case turns on the meaning of the word "willfully" as used in §§ 7201 and 7203. Petitioner John L. Cheek has been a pilot for American Airlines since 1973. He filed federal income tax returns through 1979 but thereafter ceased to file returns. He also claimed an increasing number of withholding allowances — eventually claiming 60 allowances by mid-1980 — and for the years 1981 to 1984 indicated on his W-4 forms that he was exempt from federal income taxes. In 1983, petitioner unsuccessfully sought a refund of all tax withheld by his employer in 1982. Petitioner's income during this period at all times far exceeded the minimum necessary to trigger the statutory filing requirement.

As a result of his activities, petitioner was indicted for 10 violations of federal law. He was charged with six counts of willfully failing to file a federal income tax return for the years 1980, 1981, and 1983 through 1986, in violation of 26 U.S.C. § 7203. He was further charged with three counts of willfully attempting to evade his income taxes for the years 1980, 1981, and 1983 in violation of § 7201. In those years, American Airlines withheld substantially less than the amount of tax petitioner owed because of the numerous allowances and exempt status he claimed on his W-4 forms. The tax offenses with which petitioner was charged are specific intent crimes that require the defendant to have acted willfully.

At trial, the evidence established that between 1982 and 1986, petitioner was involved in at least four civil cases that challenged various aspects of the federal income tax system. In all four of those cases, the plaintiffs were informed by the courts that many of their arguments, including that they were not taxpayers within the meaning of the tax laws, that wages are not income, that the Sixteenth Amendment does not authorize the imposition of an income tax on individuals, and that the Sixteenth Amendment is unenforceable, were frivolous or had been repeatedly rejected by the courts. During this time period, petitioner also attended at least two criminal trials of persons charged with tax offenses. In addition, there was evidence that in 1980 or 1981 an attorney had advised Cheek that the courts had rejected as frivolous the claim that wages are not income.

Cheek represented himself at trial and testified in his defense. He admitted that he had not filed personal income tax returns during the years in question. He testified that as early as 1978, he had begun attending seminars sponsored by, and following the advice of, a group that believes, among other things, that the federal tax system is unconstitutional. Some of the speakers at these meetings were lawyers who purported to give professional opinions about the invalidity of the federal income tax laws. Cheek produced a letter from an attorney stating that the Sixteenth Amendment did not authorize a tax on wages and salaries but only on gain or profit. Petitioner's defense was that, based on the indoctrination he received from this group and from his own study, he sincerely believed that the tax laws were being unconstitutionally enforced and that his actions during the 1980–1986 period were lawful. He therefore argued that he had acted without the willfulness required for conviction of the various offenses with which he was charged.

In the course of its instructions, the trial court advised the jury that to prove "willfulness" the Government must prove the voluntary and intentional violation of a known legal duty, a burden that could not be proved by showing mistake, ignorance, or negligence. The court further advised the jury that an objectively reasonable good-faith misunderstanding of the law would negate willfulness, but mere disagreement with the law would not. The court described Cheek's beliefs about the income tax system and instructed the jury that if it found that Cheek "honestly and reasonably believed that he was not required to pay income taxes or to file tax returns," a not guilty verdict should be returned.

After several hours of deliberation, the jury sent a note to the judge that stated in part:

> We have a basic disagreement between some of us as to if Mr. Cheek honestly & reasonably believed that he was not required to pay income taxes.
>
> Page 32 [the relevant jury instruction] discusses good faith misunderstanding & disagreement. Is there any additional clarification you can give us on this point?

The District Judge responded with a supplemental instruction containing the following statements:

> [A] person's opinion that the tax laws violate his constitutional rights does not constitute a good faith misunderstanding of the law. Furthermore, a person's disagreement with the government's tax collection systems and policies does not constitute a good faith misunderstanding of the law.

At the end of the first day of deliberation, the jury sent out another note saying that it still could not reach a verdict because "we are divided on the issue as to if Mr. Cheek honestly & reasonably believed that he was not required to pay income tax." When the jury resumed its deliberations, the District Judge gave the jury an additional instruction. This instruction stated in part that "an honest but unreasonable belief is not a defense and does not negate willfulness," and that "advice or research resulting in the conclusion that wages of a privately employed person are not income or that the tax laws are unconstitutional is not objectively reasonable and cannot serve as the basis for a good faith misunderstanding of the law defense." The court also instructed the jury that "persistent refusal to acknowledge the law does not constitute a good faith misunderstanding of the law." Approximately two hours later, the jury returned a verdict finding petitioner guilty on all counts.[22]

Petitioner appealed his convictions, arguing that the District Court erred by instructing the jury that only an objectively reasonable misunderstanding of the law negates the statutory willfulness requirement. The United States Court of Appeals for the Seventh Circuit rejected that contention and affirmed the convictions. In prior cases, the Seventh Circuit had made clear that good-faith misunderstanding of the law negates willfulness only if the defendant's beliefs are objectively reasonable; in the Seventh Circuit, even actual ignorance is not a defense unless the defendant's ignorance was itself objectively reasonable. In its opinion in this case, the court noted that several specified beliefs, including the beliefs that the tax laws are unconstitutional and that wages are not income, would not be objectively reasonable. Because the Seventh Circuit's interpretation of "willfully" as used in these statutes conflicts with the decisions of several other Courts of Appeals, we granted certiorari.

The general rule that ignorance of the law or a mistake of law is no defense to criminal prosecution is deeply rooted in the American legal system. Based on the notion that the law is definite and knowable, the common law presumed that every person knew the law. This common-law rule has been applied by the Court in numerous cases construing criminal statutes. The proliferation of statutes and regulations has sometimes made it difficult for the average citizen to know and comprehend the extent of the duties and obligations imposed by the tax laws. Congress has accordingly softened the impact of the common-law presumption by making specific intent to violate the law an element of certain federal criminal tax offenses. Thus, the Court almost 60 years ago interpreted the statutory term "willfully" as used in the federal criminal tax statutes as carving out an exception to the traditional rule. This special treatment of criminal tax offenses is largely due to the complexity of the tax laws. In *United States v. Murdock*, 290 U.S. 389 (1933), the Court recognized that:

> "Congress did not intend that a person, by reason of a bona fide misunderstanding as to his liability for the tax, as to his duty to make a return, or as to the adequacy of the records he maintained, should become a criminal by his mere failure to measure up to the prescribed standard of conduct."

The Court held that the defendant was entitled to an instruction with respect to whether he acted in good faith based on his actual belief. In *Murdock*, the Court interpreted the term "willfully" as used in the criminal tax statutes generally to mean "an act done with a bad purpose," or with "an evil motive."

Subsequent decisions have refined this proposition. In *United States v. Bishop*, we described the term "willfully" as connoting "a voluntary, intentional violation of a known legal duty," and did so with specific reference to the "bad faith or evil

---

[22] [Authors' note: Footnote 6 on page 198 of the *Cheek* opinion describes jury notes that were sent to the judge during deliberations. They included "[a]t least two notes from individual jurors [that] expressed the opinion that [Cheek] sincerely believed in his cause even though his beliefs might have been unreasonable." These notes demonstrate the prejudice created by the instruction given by the trial court.]

intent" language employed in *Murdock*. Still later, *United States v. Pomponio* addressed a situation in which several defendants had been charged with willfully filing false tax returns. The jury was given an instruction on willfulness similar to the standard set forth in *Bishop*. In addition, it was instructed that "good motive alone is never a defense where the act done or omitted is a crime." The defendants were convicted but the Court of Appeals reversed, concluding that the latter instruction was improper because the statute required a finding of bad purpose or evil motive.

We reversed the Court of Appeals, stating that "the Court of Appeals incorrectly assumed that the reference to an 'evil motive' in *United States v. Bishop*, and prior cases requires proof of any motive other than an intentional violation of a known legal duty." As "the other Courts of Appeals that have considered the question have recognized, willfulness in this context simply means a voluntary, intentional violation of a known legal duty." We concluded that after instructing the jury on willfulness, "an additional instruction on good faith was unnecessary." Taken together, *Bishop* and *Pomponio* conclusively establish that the standard for the statutory willfulness requirement is the "voluntary, intentional violation of a known legal duty."

Cheek accepts the *Pomponio* definition of willfulness, but asserts that the District Court's instructions and the Court of Appeals' opinion departed from that definition. In particular, he challenges the ruling that a good-faith misunderstanding of the law or a good-faith belief that one is not violating the law, if it is to negate willfulness, must be objectively reasonable. We agree that the Court of Appeals and the District Court erred in this respect.

Willfulness, as construed by our prior decisions in criminal tax cases, requires the Government to prove that the law imposed a duty on the defendant, that the defendant knew of this duty, and that he voluntarily and intentionally violated that duty. We deal first with the case where the issue is whether the defendant knew of the duty purportedly imposed by the provision of the statute or regulation he is accused of violating, a case in which there is no claim that the provision at issue is invalid. In such a case, if the Government proves actual knowledge of the pertinent legal duty, the prosecution, without more, has satisfied the knowledge component of the willfulness requirement. But carrying this burden requires negating a defendant's claim of ignorance of the law or a claim that because of a misunderstanding of the law, he had a good-faith belief that he was not violating any of the provisions of the tax laws. This is so because one cannot be aware that the law imposes a duty upon him and yet be ignorant of it, misunderstand the law, or believe that the duty does not exist. In the end, the issue is whether, based on all the evidence, the Government has proved that the defendant was aware of the duty at issue, which cannot be true if the jury credits a good-faith misunderstanding and belief submission, whether or not the claimed belief or misunderstanding is objectively reasonable. In this case, if Cheek asserted that he truly believed that the Internal Revenue Code did not purport to treat wages as income, and the jury believed him, the Government would not have carried its burden to prove willfulness, however unreasonable a court might deem such a belief. Of course, in deciding whether to credit Cheek's good-faith belief claim, the jury would be free to consider any admissible evidence from any source showing that Cheek was aware of his duty to file a return and to treat wages as income, including evidence showing his awareness of the relevant provisions of the Code or regulations, of court decisions rejecting his interpretation of the tax law, of authoritative rulings of the Internal Revenue Service, or of any contents of the personal income tax return forms and accompanying instructions that made it plain that wages should be returned as income.

We thus, disagree with the Court of Appeals' requirement that a claimed good-faith belief must be objectively reasonable if it is to be considered as possibly negating the Government's evidence purporting to show a defendant's awareness of the legal duty at issue. Knowledge and belief are characteristically questions for the fact finder, in this case the jury. Characterizing a particular belief as not objectively reasonable transforms the inquiry into a legal one and would prevent the jury from considering it. It would of course be proper to exclude evidence having no relevance or probative value with respect to willfulness; but it is not contrary to common sense, let alone impossible, for a defendant to be ignorant of his duty based on an irrational belief that he has no duty, and forbidding the jury to consider evidence that might negate willfulness would raise a serious question under the Sixth Amendment's jury trial provision. It is common ground that this Court, where possible, interprets congressional enactments so as to avoid raising serious constitutional questions. It was therefore error to instruct the jury to disregard evidence of Cheek's understanding that, within the meaning of the tax laws, he was not a person required to file a return or to pay income taxes and that wages are not taxable income, as incredible as such misunderstandings of and beliefs about the law might be. Of course, the more unreasonable the asserted beliefs or misunderstandings are, the more likely the jury will consider them to be nothing more than simple disagreement with known legal duties imposed by the tax laws and will find that the Government has carried its burden of proving knowledge.

Cheek asserted in the trial court that he should be acquitted because he believed in good faith that the income tax law is unconstitutional as applied to him and thus, could not legally impose any duty upon him of which he should have been aware. Such a submission is unsound, not because Cheek's constitutional arguments are not objectively reasonable or frivolous, which they surely are, but because the *Murdock-Pomponio* line of cases does not support such a position. Those cases construed the willfulness requirement in the criminal provisions of the Internal Revenue Code to require proof of knowledge of the law. This was because in "our complex tax system, uncertainty often arises even among taxpayers who earnestly wish to follow the law," and " 'it is not the purpose of the law to penalize frank difference of opinion or innocent errors made despite the exercise of reasonable care.' " *United States v. Bishop*, 412 U.S. 346, 360–361 (1973) (quoting *Spies v. United States*, 317 U.S. 492 (1943)).

Claims that some of the provisions of the tax code are unconstitutional are submissions of a different order. They do not arise from innocent mistakes caused by the complexity of the Internal Revenue Code. Rather, they reveal full knowledge of the provisions at issue and a studied conclusion, however wrong, that those provisions are invalid and unenforceable. Thus, in this case, Cheek paid his taxes for years, but after attending various seminars and based on his own study, he concluded that the income tax laws could not constitutionally require him to pay a tax.

We do not believe that Congress contemplated that such a taxpayer, without risking criminal prosecution, could ignore the duties imposed upon him by the Internal Revenue Code and refuse to utilize the mechanisms provided by Congress to present his claims of invalidity to the courts and to abide by their decisions. There is no doubt that Cheek, from year to year, was free to pay the tax that the law purported to require, file for a refund and, if denied, present his claims of invalidity, constitutional or otherwise, to the courts. Also, without paying the tax, he could have challenged claims of tax deficiencies in the Tax Court, with the right to appeal to a higher court if unsuccessful. Cheek took neither course in some years, and when he did was unwilling to accept the outcome. As we see it, he is in no position to claim that his good-faith belief about the validity of the Internal Revenue Code negates willfulness or provides a defense to criminal prosecution under §§ 7201 and 7203. Of course, Cheek was free in this very case to present his claims of invalidity and have them adjudicated, but like defendants in criminal cases in other contexts, who "willfully" refuse to comply with the duties placed upon them by the law, he must take the risk of being wrong.

We thus hold that, in a case like this, a defendant's views about the validity of the tax statutes are irrelevant to the issue of willfulness and need not be heard by the jury, and, if they are, an instruction to disregard them would be proper. For this purpose, it makes no difference whether the claims of invalidity are frivolous or have substance. It was therefore not error in this case for the District Judge to instruct the jury not to consider Cheek's claims that the tax laws were unconstitutional. However, it was error for the court to instruct the jury that petitioner's asserted beliefs that wages are not income and that he was not a taxpayer within the meaning of the Internal Revenue Code should not be considered by the jury in determining whether Cheek had acted willfully.

For the reasons set forth in the opinion above, the judgment of the Court of Appeals is vacated, and the case is remanded for further proceedings consistent with this opinion.

Justice Scalia, concurring in the judgment.

I concur in the judgment of the Court because our cases have consistently held that the failure to pay a tax in the good-faith belief that it is not legally owing is not "willful." I do not join the Court's opinion because I do not agree with the test for willfulness that it directs the Court of Appeals to apply on remand.

As the Court acknowledges, our opinions from the 1930's to the 1970's have interpreted the word "willfully" in the criminal tax statutes as requiring the "bad purpose" or "evil motive" of "intentionally violating a known legal duty." *See, e.g., United States v. Pomponio; United States v. Murdock.* It seems to me that today's opinion squarely reverses that long-established statutory construction when it says that a good-faith erroneous belief in the unconstitutionality of a tax law is no defense. It is quite impossible to say that a statute which one believes unconstitutional represents a "known legal duty." *See Marbury v. Madison*, 5 U.S. 137 (1803).

Although the facts of the present case involve erroneous reliance upon the Constitution in ignoring the otherwise "known legal duty" imposed by the tax statutes, the Court's new interpretation applies also to erroneous reliance upon a tax statute in ignoring the otherwise "known legal duty" of a regulation, and to erroneous reliance upon a regulation in ignoring the otherwise "known legal duty" of a tax assessment. These situations as well meet the opinion's crucial test of "revealing full knowledge of the provisions at issue and a studied conclusion, however wrong, that those provisions are invalid and unenforceable." There is, moreover, no rational basis for saying that a "willful" violation is established by full knowledge of a statutory requirement, but is not established by full knowledge of a requirement explicitly imposed by regulation or order. Thus, today's opinion works a revolution in past practice, subjecting to criminal penalties taxpayers who do not comply with Treasury Regulations that are in their view contrary to the Internal Revenue Code, Treasury Rulings that are in their view contrary to the regulations, and even IRS auditor pronouncements that are in their view contrary to Treasury Rulings. The law already provides considerable incentive for taxpayers to be careful in ignoring any official assertion of tax liability, since it contains civil penalties that apply even in the event of a good-faith mistake. To impose in addition criminal penalties for misinterpretation of such a complex body of law is a startling innovation indeed.

I find it impossible to understand how one can derive from the lonesome word "willfully" the proposition that belief in the nonexistence of a textual prohibition excuses liability, but belief in the invalidity (*i.e.*, the legal nonexistence) of a textual prohibition does not. One may say, as the law does in many contexts, that "willfully" refers to consciousness of the act but not to consciousness that the act is unlawful. Or alternatively, one may say, as we have said until today with respect to the tax statutes, that "willfully" refers to consciousness of both the act and its illegality. But it seems to me impossible to say that the word refers to consciousness that some legal text exists, without consciousness that that legal text is binding, *i.e.*, with the good-faith belief that it is not a valid law. Perhaps such a test for criminal liability would make sense (though in a field as complicated as federal tax law, I doubt it), but some text other than the mere word "willfully" would have to be employed to describe it — and that text is not ours to write.

Because today's opinion abandons clear and longstanding precedent to impose criminal liability where taxpayers have had no reason to expect it, because the new contours of criminal liability have no basis in the statutory text, and because I strongly suspect that those new contours make no sense even as a policy matter, I concur only in the judgment of the Court.

Justice Blackmun, with whom Justice Marshall joins, dissenting.

It seems to me that we are concerned in this case not with "the complexity of the tax laws," but with the income tax law in its most elementary and basic aspect: Is a wage earner a taxpayer and are wages income?

The Court acknowledges that the conclusively established standard for willfulness under the applicable statutes is the "voluntary, intentional violation of a known legal duty." That being so, it is incomprehensible to me how, in this day, more than 70 years after the institution of our present federal income tax system with the passage of the Income Tax Act of 1913, any taxpayer of competent mentality can assert as his defense to charges of statutory willfulness the proposition that the wage he receives for his labor is not income, irrespective of a cult that says otherwise and advises the gullible to resist income tax collections. One might note in passing that this particular taxpayer, after all, was a licensed pilot for one of our major commercial airlines; he presumably was a person of at least minimum intellectual competence.

The District Court's instruction that an objectively reasonable and good-faith misunderstanding of the law negates willfulness lends further, rather than less, protection to this defendant, for it adds an additional hurdle for the prosecution to overcome. Petitioner should be grateful for this further protection, rather than be opposed to it.

This Court's opinion today, I fear, will encourage taxpayers to cling to frivolous views of the law in the hope of convincing a jury of their sincerity. If that ensues, I suspect we have gone beyond the limits of common sense.

While I may not agree with every word the Court of Appeals has enunciated in its opinion, I would affirm its judgment in this case. I therefore dissent.

Mr. Cheek won the above battle, but he lost the war. After remand, Cheek received a second jury trial, presided over by a different district court judge. He was again convicted on all counts. He was sentenced to jail for a year and a day and was fined $62,000. On appeal, this second conviction was upheld in all respects.[23]

The *Cheek* majority drew a distinction between good faith misunderstanding about what tax statutes mean and good faith misunderstanding about whether such statutes are constitutional. Justice Scalia's concurrence criticized that distinction, and students and others sometimes fail to grasp it. Thus, some examples are in order.

"Tax protesters" has a special meaning. It does not refer to people who complain about tax rates being too high, tax statutes being too complicated, distinctions in the Code being unfair, or the like. The First Amendment guarantees everyone the right to hold such views in private and to articulate them in public. Instead, "tax protesters" refers to people who underpay their tax liabilities, justifying such behavior through any of a variety of cockamamie "arguments" that have been universally rejected by the courts (often with the imposition of section 6673 or other penalties for asserting frivolous arguments).

There are dozens of stock tax protester arguments. They have prompted the IRS to devote part of its website (www.irs.gov) to identifying and refuting the arguments. You may wish to locate and skim that portion of the website.

To illustrate the *Cheek* distinction, one common protester approach is to scrutinize the records of state ratifying conventions, uncovering perceived irregularities on the basis of which the protesters claim that the Sixteenth Amendment

---

[23] United States v. Cheek, 3 F.3d 1057 (7th Cir. 1993), *cert. denied*, 510 U.S. 1112 (1994). Mr. Cheek was a frequent visitor to the federal courts. To review his various brushes with the civil and criminal tax laws, see 3 F.3d at 1059 & n.1.

was not properly ratified by the requisite number of states, thus that the federal income tax is unconstitutional. A defendant who refuses to pay income tax based on a sincere (though erroneous) belief in this argument could be convicted under section 7201. Under *Cheek*, such a belief would not be a defense.

In contrast, another common protester argument is that, under section 3401(c), "employee" includes only federal and state governmental officials and employees, thus that wages paid to private sector employees are not taxable.[24] A defendant (who is a private sector employee) could be found not guilty under section 7201 if the jury concludes that the defendant sincerely (though erroneously) believed this argument. Such an argument is statutory, not constitutional, thus can give rise to a defense under *Cheek*.

The so-called good faith defense — sometimes called the *Cheek* good faith defense — technically is not a defense. The Government must prove willfulness. Willfulness does not exist if the defendant acted in good faith. Does that mean that, in order to prove willfulness, the Government must disprove good faith?

The general parameters are established. If the defense goes to an element of the offense, then the Government must prove the element beyond a reasonable doubt — which means negating the defense beyond a reasonable doubt. If, however, the defense does not negate an element of the crime, the defendant bears the burden of proving the defense by a preponderance of the evidence.[25] As noted, the defense of good faith goes to an element of the crime — willfulness — and hence the Government must negate the defense beyond a reasonable doubt.

Almost invariably, the Government's proof of willfulness will be sufficient to permit the jury to infer beyond a reasonable doubt that the defendant lacked good faith. But defendants who want to emphasize their good faith will want the judge to specifically instruct that good faith negates willfulness. Generally, courts will give the good faith instruction only if the evidence affirmatively puts good faith in play — makes it a real issue for the jury.

How does the defendant do that? The most direct way would be testimony by the defendant. But that would make the defendant subject to cross-examination. Often, the defense would conclude that the potential benefits of the defendant testifying are less than the risks of the defendant testifying. Courts reject the notion that the defendant's testimony is the only way good faith can be put in play.[26] Circumstantial evidence, including perhaps lay opinion evidence as to the defendant's mental state, may suffice to put the issue in play. If so, the trial judge should give the instruction.[27]

---

[24] This argument is wrong because it ignores the fact that section 7701(c) defines "includes" and "including" expansively, not restrictively.

[25] Smith v. United States, 133 S. Ct. 714 (2013).

[26] *E.g.*, United States v. Kokenis, 662 F.3d 919, 927 (7th Cir. 2011).

[27] Lay opinion testimony as to the defendant's mental state including presumably good faith, might be admissible under Fed. R. Evid. 701. *See, e.g.*, United States v. Goodman, 633 F.3d 963, 968 (10th Cir. 2011); United States v. Abramson-Schmeiler, 2011 U.S. App. LEXIS 23789 (10th Cir. Nov. 29, 2011). A good case on this opportunity for lay opinion testimony on the ultimate intent issue is United States v. Rea, 958 F.2d 1206 (2d Cir. 1992).

B. Willfulness and Tax Protesters

Consider the following from the Government's perspective.

The often patently frivolous arguments routinely made by illegal tax protesters are not confined to oral representations. Illegal tax protesters are renowned for their penchant to inundate prosecutors with paper — frivolous motion after frivolous motion. Illegal tax protesters often represent themselves, making motion practice even more difficult. As a result, trying to figure out what their arguments are can be a difficult task.

Most of the common tactics and defenses used by illegal tax protesters have been routinely dismissed by the courts. Illegal tax protesters, however, ignore these decisions and claim that no one from the Government will answer their questions. Some of the more common tactics and defenses that have been raised by illegal tax protesters and rejected by the courts are: (1) the income tax is voluntary, (2) wages are not income, (3) the Sixteenth Amendment was never properly ratified, and (4) the IRS has the duty to prepare tax returns for the taxpayer.

One defense that must be carefully handled is the "good faith" defense, which is used to refute willfulness. Illegal tax protesters routinely attempt to prove that they "believed" they did not have to file tax returns or pay taxes. Many of the reasons they use, such as the ones mentioned above, may seem unbelievable. Nevertheless, this is an issue that must go to the jury. In the seminal case of *Cheek v. United States*, 498 U.S. 192, 201, 111 S. Ct. 604, 112 L. Ed. 2d 617 (1991), the Supreme Court held that a taxpayer's "belief" that he or she was not required to file a tax return, however, incredible such a misunderstanding of and beliefs about the law might be, does not have to be objectively reasonable! Rather, the standard is a subjective one. Still, this defense is not insurmountable.

In an attempt to present a good faith defense, most illegal tax protesters will attempt to introduce copies of the Constitution, the IRS Special Agents' Handbook, various court decisions, protester publications, as well as other documents. The admissibility of these documents is generally left to the discretion of the court. To limit or prevent an illegal tax protester from introducing these documents into evidence, consider arguing that: (1) the contents of these documents are more prejudicial than probative; and (2) the admissibility of these documents invades the province of the court to instruct the jury on the law. The key is to distinguish between a misunderstanding of the law versus a disagreement with the law. Whether to object to the admission of these protester documents, however, is a trial strategy that varies from case to case and circuit to circuit.

Whether or not the documents themselves are admitted into evidence, a defendant will generally be allowed to testify about his or her beliefs during the prosecution period and what he or she relied on to form those beliefs. Evidence about what the law is or should be may be excluded. However, evidence that is relevant to a jury's determination of what a defendant thought the law was may not be excluded. A defendant who testifies that he or she knew the law, but disagrees with — or does not like — the law, is not entitled to a good faith instruction.

If legal documents, protester publications or similar protester-type documents are introduced or if the defendant is allowed to testify about what the law is, ask for a limiting instruction. Such an instruction should remind the jury that: the document or statement is the defendant's understanding of what the law was; that the jury is the judge of the facts, not the law; and that the document or statement was admitted solely for the purpose of showing the defendant's state of mind and not to prove the actual requirements of the law. If the document or statement is a misstatement of the law, ask the court to instruct the jury with a correct statement of the law.

Finally, because illegal tax protesters do not limit their illegal schemes to the Federal arena, do not forget to look for documents that may be on file with a state or county government, such as state tax returns or property tax filings. These records, or the lack thereof, may serve as evidence of willfulness in the Federal case.[28]

C. Willful Blindness or Deliberate Ignorance

Willfulness requires specific intent. The taxpayer must know the legal obligation. Does this foreclose prosecution if the best the Government can prove is that the taxpayer kept himself deliberately ignorant so that there was no specific intent? There is a concept of willful blindness — a taxpayer who deliberately determines to be ignorant of the law or his obligations under the law. This concept is referred to as conscious avoidance, willful blindness, willful ignorance, deliberate ignorance, or some variation thereof.[29] The Supreme Court observed in a civil case as follows:

> The doctrine of willful blindness is well established in criminal law. Many criminal statutes require proof that a defendant acted knowingly or willfully, and courts applying the doctrine of willful blindness hold that defendants cannot escape the reach of these statutes by deliberately shielding themselves from clear evidence of critical facts that are strongly suggested by the circumstances. The traditional rationale for this doctrine is that defendants who behave in this manner are just as culpable as those who have actual knowledge. Edwards, *Criminal Degrees of Knowledge*, 17 Mod. L. Rev. 294, 302 (1954) (observing on the basis of English authorities that "up to the present day, no real doubt has been cast on the proposition that [willful blindness] is as culpable as actual knowledge"). It is also said that persons who know enough to blind themselves to direct proof of critical facts in effect have actual knowledge of those facts.

---

[28] Jennifer E. Ihlo, *The Gold Fringed Flag: Prosecution of the Illegal Tax Protestor*, 46/3 USA Bull. 15 (April 1998).

[29] CTM 8.08[4] n.9.

> This Court's opinion more than a century ago in *Spurr v. United States*, 174 U.S. 728 (1899), while not using the term "willful blindness," endorsed a similar concept. The case involved a criminal statute that prohibited a bank officer from "willfully" certifying a check drawn against insufficient funds. We said that a willful violation would occur "if the [bank] officer purposely keeps himself in ignorance of whether the drawer has money in the bank." Id., at 735. Following our decision in *Spurr*, several federal prosecutions in the first half of the 20th century invoked the doctrine of willful blindness. Later, a 1962 proposed draft of the Model Penal Code, which has since become official, attempted to incorporate the doctrine by defining "knowledge of the existence of a particular fact" to include a situation in which "a person is aware of a high probability of [the fact's] existence, unless he actually believes that it does not exist." ALI, Model Penal Code § 2.02(7) (Proposed Official Draft 1962). Our Court has used the Code's definition as a guide in analyzing whether certain statutory presumptions of knowledge comported with due process. And every Court of Appeals — with the possible exception of the District of Columbia Circuit — has fully embraced willful blindness, applying the doctrine to a wide range of criminal statutes.[30]

To this, Justice Kennedy objected in dissent:

> Having interpreted the statue to require a showing of knowledge, the Court holds that willful blindness will suffice. This is a mistaken step. Willful blindness is not knowledge; and judges should not broaden a legislative proscription by analogy.
>
> * * * *
>
> The Court appears to endorse the willful blindness doctrine here for all federal criminal cases involving knowledge. It does so in a civil case where it has received no briefing or argument from the criminal defense bar, which might have provided important counsel on this difficult issue.[31]

So, at least for the time being, the critical mass favors instructing the jury that conscious avoidance equates to knowledge and willfulness.[32]

The following is a discussion of the willful blindness concept from the Department of Justice's perspective:

> It is a defense to a finding of willfulness that the defendant was ignorant of the law or of facts which made the conduct illegal, since willfulness requires a voluntary and intentional violation of a known legal duty. However, if the defendant deliberately avoided acquiring knowledge of a fact or the law, then the jury may infer that he actually knew it and that he

[30] Global Tech Appliances, Inc. v. SEB S.A., 131 S. Ct. 2060, 2068–69 (2011).

[31] *Id.* at 2072–73.

[32] *E.g.*, United States v. Stadtmauer, 620 F.3d 238, 252–60 (3d Cir. 2010) (in the context of convictions for conspiracy and violation of section 7206(2), upholding a willful blindness instruction against various challenges, including that it is inconsistent with *Cheek*).

was merely trying to avoid giving the appearance (and incurring the consequences) of knowledge.

In such a case, the use of an "ostrich instruction" — also known as a deliberate ignorance, conscious avoidance, willful blindness, or a *Jewell* instruction[33] — may be appropriate.

A number of courts have approved the use of such instructions under proper circumstances. However, it has also been said that the use of such instructions is "rarely appropriate." Thus, it is advisable not to request such an instruction unless it is clearly warranted by the evidence in a particular case. Furthermore, the language of any deliberate ignorance instruction in a criminal tax case must comport with the Government's obligation to prove the voluntary, intentional violation of a known legal duty. The deliberate ignorance instruction set forth in *United States v. Fingado*, 934 F.2d at 1166, appears to be suitable for a criminal tax case. Further, to avoid potential confusion with the meaning of "willfulness" as it relates to the defendant's intent, it may be wise to avoid use of the phrase "willful blindness," using instead such phrases as "deliberate ignorance" or "conscious avoidance." [34]

Faced with such facts, the Government will request a jury charge as follows:

> The government may prove that the Defendant . . . acted "knowingly" by proving, beyond a reasonable doubt, that this defendant deliberately closed [his] [her] eyes to what would otherwise have been obvious to [him] [her]. No one can avoid responsibility for a crime by deliberately ignoring what is obvious. A finding beyond reasonable doubt of an intent of the defendant to avoid knowledge or enlightenment would permit the jury to infer knowledge. Stated another way, a defendant's knowledge of a particular fact may be inferred from a deliberate or intentional ignorance or deliberate or intentional blindness to the existence of that fact.
>
> It is, of course, entirely up to you as to whether you find any deliberate ignorance or deliberate closing of the eyes and the inferences to be drawn from any such evidence.
>
> You may not infer that a defendant had knowledge, however, from proof of a mistake, negligence, carelessness, or a belief in an inaccurate proposition.[35]

The Fifth Circuit pattern jury instruction couples the instruction with the definition of knowingly and is more succinct:

---

[33] *See* United States v. Jewell, 532 F.2d 697 (9th Cir.), *cert. denied*, 426 U.S. 951 (1976).

[34] CTM 8.06[4] (2001). The 2012 version, CTM 8.08[4], does not differ materially in substance. The same discussion contains the suggestion "that any time a deliberate ignorance or conscious avoidance instruction is given, the prosecutor should also insure that the jury is expressly directed not to convict for negligence or mistake." CTM 8.06[4] (2001); *See also* CTM 8.08[4].

[35] CTM 8.06[4] (2001); *see also* 1A Kevin F. O'Malley, Jay E. Grenig & William C. Lee, Federal Jury Practice and Instructions: Criminal § 17.09 (5th ed. 2000); Pamela H. Bucy, *Criminal Tax Fraud: The Downfall of Murderers, Madams and Thieves*, 29 Ariz. St. L.J. 639, 662–64 (1997).

> The word "knowingly," as that term has been used from time to time in these instructions, means that the act was done voluntarily and intentionally, not because of mistake or accident.
>
> [You may find that a defendant had knowledge of a fact if you find that the defendant deliberately closed his eyes to what would otherwise have been obvious to him. While knowledge on the part of the defendant cannot be established merely by demonstrating that the defendant was negligent, careless, or foolish, knowledge can be inferred if the defendant deliberately blinded himself to the existence of a fact.][36]

However, the instruction is appropriate only "when defendant claims lack of guilty knowledge and the proof at trial supports an inference of deliberate indifference."[37] The evidence must show: "(1) subjective awareness of a high probability of the existence of illegal conduct; and (2) purposeful contrivance to avoid learning of the illegal conduct."[38] In view of the *Pomponio-Cheek* insistence upon violation of a known duty, it has not yet been definitively resolved whether the "intentional disregard" instruction is appropriate in a tax case requiring willfulness.[39]

Finally, Judge Posner delivered a pungent discussion of the dangers inherent in the deliberate ignorance instruction as follows:

> The most powerful criticism of the ostrich instruction is, precisely, that its tendency is to allow juries to convict upon a finding of negligence for crimes that require intent. The criticism can be deflected by thinking carefully about just what it is that real ostriches do (or at least are popularly supposed to do). They do not just fail to follow through on their suspicions of bad things. They are not merely careless birds. They bury their heads in the sand so that they will not see or hear bad things.[40] They

---

[36] Fifth Circuit Pattern Jury Instruction 1.37 (2001 edition).

[37] United States v. Threadgill, 172 F.3d 357, 358 (5th Cir.), *cert. denied*, 528 U.S. 871 (1999).

[38] United States v. Threadgill, 172 F.3d 357, 358 (5th Cir.), *cert. denied*, 528 U.S. 871 (1999).

[39] *Compare* United States v. London, 66 F.3d 1227, 1239–42 (1st Cir. 1995) (instruction appropriate), *with* United States v. Retos, 25 F.3d 1220, 1229–30 (3d Cir. 1994) (instruction not appropriate). *See also* United States v. Mapelli, 971 F.2d 284 (9th Cir. 1992) (holding that a "deliberate ignorance" instruction improperly diluted the Government's burden of proof).

The Second Circuit requires that "a conscious avoidance charge must communicate two points: (1) that a jury may infer knowledge of the existence of a particular fact if the defendant is aware of a high probability of its existence, (2) unless the defendant actually believes that it does not exist." United States v. Kaiser, 609 F.3d 556, 566 (2d Cir. 2010) (citing cases) (punctuation and citations omitted). To reinforce its insistence on these charges, the Second Circuit ordered that its statement of these requirements be circulated to all AUSAs engaged in criminal prosecutions in the circuit.

[40] [Authors' note: In United States v. Black, 530 F.3d 596, 604 (7th Cir. 2009), *vacated and remanded*, 130 S. Ct. 2963 (2010), Judge Posner later defended the ostrich as follows:

> The reference of course is to the legend that ostriches when frightened bury their head in the sand. It is pure legend and a canard on a very distinguished bird. Zoological Society of San Diego, Birds: Ostrich, www.sandiegozoo.org/animalbytes/t-ostrich.html (visited June 12, 2008) ("When an ostrich senses danger and cannot run away, it flops to the ground and remains still, with its head and neck flat on the ground in front of it. Because the head and neck are lightly colored, they blend in with the color of the soil. From a distance, it just looks like the ostrich

> deliberately avoid acquiring unpleasant knowledge. The ostrich instruction is designed for cases in which there is evidence that the defendant, knowing or strongly suspecting that he is involved in shady dealings, takes steps to make sure that he does not acquire full or exact knowledge of the nature and extent of those dealings. A deliberate effort to avoid guilty knowledge is all the guilty knowledge the law requires. "To know, and to want not to know because one suspects, may be, if not the same state of mind, the same degree of fault." A good example of a case in which the ostrich instruction was properly given is *United States v. Diaz*, 864 F.2d 544, 550 (7th Cir. 1988). The defendant, a drug trafficker, sought "to insulate himself from the actual drug transaction so that he could deny knowledge of it," which he did sometimes by absenting himself from the scene of the actual delivery and sometimes by pretending to be fussing under the hood of his car.
>
> The critical question so far as his guilt or innocence was concerned is simple (to pose, not necessarily to answer): what did he know? Did he know that he was renting his house for use as a wire-room, or did he believe that he was renting his house to the Orlando crew for some private purpose of theirs unconnected with gambling? (Even criminals have private lives.) The ostrich instruction did not advance this inquiry; it confused it, by pointing the jury to circumstances of deliberate avoidance of knowledge that did not exist. As we said in *United States v. Bigelow*, 914 F.2d 966, 971 (7th Cir. 1990), when the facts require the jury to make a "binary choice" between "actual knowledge" and "complete innocence," the ostrich instruction should not-be given.
>
> The true intermediate case between a clearly proper giving of the ostrich instruction because the defendant did physical acts to insulate himself from knowledge, as in *Diaz*, and the clearly improper giving of the instruction because the only issue is the defendant's actual knowledge or complete ignorance, is the case of purely psychological avoidance. *Josefik* was such a case. "It is inconceivable that Josefik did not believe that the scotch was stolen, and in context all the challenged instruction [the ostrich instruction] meant is that he could not get off the hook simply by resolutely refusing to find out for sure whether it was stolen." In other words, the deliberate effort to avoid guilty knowledge that we said is all the guilty knowledge the law requires can be a mental, as well as a physical, effort — a cutting off of one's normal curiosity by an effort of will. There is no evidence of either sort of effort here.[41]

Finally, the Supreme Court's discussion of the concept of conscious avoidance relates to avoidance of knowledge of facts. The CTM discussion says that the concept can apply to avoidance of knowledge of "a fact or the law."[42] This would seem to follow from the concept, because intentional violation of a known legal duty necessarily requires knowledge of the facts and the law. In a sense, every *Cheek*

---

has buried its head in the sand, because only the body is visible"). It is too late, however, to correct this injustice.]

[41] United States v. Giovannetti, 919 F.2d 1223, 1228–29 (7th Cir. 1990).

[42] CTM 8.08[4].

good faith defense presents the issue of conscious avoidance because, if the defendant consciously avoided knowing the law's mandate, he or she has not acted in good faith. However, the *Cheek* good faith defense is usually not addressed with a conscious avoidance instruction, although conceivably it could be. That would not be a defendant-friendly outcome.

D. Willfulness — Reliance on Professional

A defendant will frequently assert that he or she lacked willfulness because he or she relied upon a tax professional. This is a *Cheek* argument. It technically is not a defense per se but rather an argument that the Government failed to meet its burden of proof. The Government thus has to show that the defendant did not rely upon the tax professional in order to show willfulness. But, as in *Cheek*, the defendant has to put the "defense" in play by introducing some evidence of reliance on the tax professional. Once the defendant does that, it is then the Government's burden to show that the taxpayer did not rely.

One way the Government can do that is through the tax professional. The Government may rely upon the tax professional — usually the accountant or other non-lawyer professional who has no privilege to assert[43] — in order to build its case in chief. For example, if the defendant affirmatively misrepresented matters to the tax professional, that can establish the willfulness element.

More often, when the defendant asserts reliance on the tax professional as negating willfulness, the defendant will have not made an affirmative misrepresentation to the tax professional. Rather he or she will have failed to advise the tax professional as to the matters that would affect the tax reporting on the return. The usual setting for this type of omission is failure to tell the accountant preparing the return of some fact or facts that would increase the tax liability reported. It is often stated in such omission cases that the defendant must show that he or she made full disclosure to the accountant.[44] Reading these statements literally would mean that the defendant's failure to disclose precludes the defense whether the failure was intentional or unintentional. Can that be the case under *Cheek*? The tax laws are complex, and the facts necessary to resolve a tax issue may not be known to a taxpayer. A defendant may thus have failed to advise the accountant of a fact or facts simply from ignorance rather than an attempt to mislead the accountant into reporting a tax liability that is less than the amount properly due. It can be argued that *Cheek* requires that, in failing to make full disclosure to the accountant, the taxpayer knew that he was failing to make full disclosure, thus using the accountant as an unwitting tool to effect the tax crime.

Finally, even if the return preparer on the information given by the defendant arguably should have smoked out the problem, the return preparer's negligence is still no defense if the Government can otherwise prove the defendant's intentional violation of a known legal duty. In one case,[45] the defendant sought to introduce

---

[43] The "federally authorized tax practitioner" privilege created in 1998 does not apply in criminal tax investigations and proceedings. I.R.C. § 7525(a)(2).

[44] *E.g.*, United States v. Bishop, 291 F.3d 1100, 1107 (9th Cir. 2002), *cert. denied*, 537 U.S. 1176 (2003).

[45] United States v. St. Pierre, 599 F.3d 19 (1st Cir. 2010).

expert testimony that the return preparer knew or should have known of the omission of income, but the trial judge sustained the Government's objection to the evidence. The First Circuit held that, even if the return preparer's conduct were negligent, the mere failure to discover and properly treat the undisclosed income would not be a defense in a case where the evidence showed beyond a reasonable doubt that the defendant willfully omitted the income. The First Circuit did acknowledge that, in cases where the preparer's neglect could be relevant (presumably where the evidence is not overwhelming as to the defendant's intent), such expert evidence might be admissible at trial. So, for a defendant asserting a "reliance on professional" defense, the defendant should focus on this case as a roadmap for convincing the trial judge to admit the evidence as reasonably bearing on defendant's reliance.

E. Willfulness — Complexities and Uncertainties in the Law

Since criminal conduct requires the violation of a known legal duty, one cannot be guilty of a crime if the legal duty is not certain. Hence, one defense to a tax crime is that the duty upon which the criminal allegation is based is not sufficiently certain to put the taxpayer or other person charged upon notice that failure to honor the uncertain duty could subject him or her to criminal charges.

The Supreme Court addressed this concept in *James v. United States.*[46] The issue was whether the taxpayer could be prosecuted under section 7201 for failing to report and pay tax on embezzled income. In order to resolve that issue the Court had to determine whether embezzled funds were income taxable under the Code and, if so, whether the taxpayer could be prosecuted for failure to report the income. This sets up the issue quite nicely, for the fact that the Court had to resolve the substantive issue — *i.e.*, whether embezzled funds are taxable — meant that the issue was not without doubt. Indeed, the reason it was in doubt was because the Supreme Court, in the earlier *Wilcox* case, had held that embezzled funds were not income for federal tax purposes. In *Rutkin*, an intervening case (after *Wilcox* and before *James*), the Supreme Court held that extorted funds were income. Although the Court in the intervening case had not overruled *Wilcox*, the intervening decision seemed to undercut the rationale for *Wilcox*. Yet, *Wilcox* stood unreversed, so there was a strong argument based on *Wilcox* that embezzled funds were not income.

The *James* Court started its analysis by holding that embezzled funds are income, thus overruling *Wilcox*. The dissenting opinions took the Court to task on that issue, but the important point for our purposes is that, because *Wilcox* had not yet been overruled, at the time of the taxpayer's embezzlement in *James*, the taxpayer could not have known that he had a legal duty to report the embezzled funds as income. So, after holding that embezzled funds were, after all, income, the Court in *James* addressed whether the taxpayer could be prosecuted for failing to report that income while *Wilcox*'s holding was still unreversed precedent. The Court said:

---

[46] 366 U.S. 213 (1961), *overruling* Commissioner v. Wilcox, 327 U.S. 404 (1946).

> We believe that *Wilcox* was wrongly decided and we find nothing in congressional history since then to persuade us that Congress intended to legislate the rule. Thus, we believe that we should now correct the error and the confusion resulting from it, certainly if we do so in a manner that will not prejudice those who might have relied on it. We should not continue to confound confusion, particularly when the result would be to perpetuate the injustice of relieving embezzlers of the duty of paying income taxes on the money they enrich themselves with through theft while honest people pay their taxes on every conceivable type of income.
>
> But, we are dealing here with a felony conviction under statutes which apply to any person who "willfully" fails to account for his tax or who "willfully" attempts to evade his obligation. In *Spies v. United States*, 317 U.S. 492, 499, 63 S. Ct. 364, 87 L. Ed. 418 (1943), the Court said that § 145(b) of the 1939 Code embodied "the gravest of offenses against the revenues," and stated that willfulness must therefore include an evil motive and want of justification in view of all the circumstances. 317 U.S. at 498. Willfulness "involves a specific intent which must be proven by independent evidence and which cannot be inferred from the mere understatement of income." *Holland v. United States*, 348 U.S. 121, 139 (1954).
>
> We believe that the element of willfulness could not be proven in a criminal prosecution for failing to include embezzled funds in gross income in the year of misappropriation so long as the statute contained the gloss placed upon it by Wilcox at the time the alleged crime was committed. Therefore, we feel that petitioner's conviction may not stand and that the indictment against him must be dismissed."[47]

Since *James* made it clear that willfulness cannot be present if the underlying legal duty is uncertain, one line of defense to tax crimes is that the underlying legal duty is sufficiently uncertain in the *James* sense. Some key cases illustrate this defense. One of the most controversial is the *Garber* case below.

UNITED STATES v. GARBER

United States Court of Appeals, Fifth Circuit
607 F.2d 92 (1979) (en banc)

[Authors' note: The taxpayer had a rare form of blood, the periodic sale of the plasma from which drew high compensation. The taxpayer did not report the income. The Government charged her under section 7201 with evading income taxes. The taxpayer urged, consistent with *James*, that uncertainty as to taxability of blood prevented her prosecution for tax evasion. The plurality opinion in that case agreed as follows.]

A tax return is not criminally fraudulent simply because it is erroneous. Willfulness is an essential element of the crime charged. As such, the government must prove beyond a reasonable doubt that the defendant willfully and intentionally attempted to evade and defeat income taxes for each year in question by filing with

---

[47] 366 U.S. at 221–22.

the IRS tax returns which she knew were false. [Citing *Pomponio* and *Bishop*.] It is not enough to show merely that a lesser tax was paid than was due. Nor is a negligent, careless, or unintentional understatement of income sufficient. [Citing *Holland* and *Murdock*.] The government must demonstrate that the defendant willfully concealed and omitted from her return income which she knew was taxable.

When the taxability of unreported income is problematical as a matter of law, the unresolved nature of the law is relevant to show that defendant may not have been aware of a tax liability or may have simply made an error in judgment. Furthermore, the relevance of a dispute in the law does not depend on whether the defendant actually knew of the conflict. In *United States v. Critzer*, 498 F.2d 1160 (4th Cir. 1974), the Fourth Circuit reversed a criminal tax fraud conviction against an Eastern Cherokee Indian who failed to report a portion of her income derived from land held by the United States in trust for the Eastern Cherokee Band. The evidence clearly established that the underreporting was intentional. Whether the income was taxable, however, was a disputed question dependent on the interpretation of certain land allotment statutes, which the court did not resolve. Instead, it reversed the conviction because of the absence of authority definitively governing the situation. The court's language is particularly apt here:

> As a matter of law, defendant cannot be guilty of willfully evading and defeating income taxes on income, the taxability of which is so uncertain that even co-ordinate branches of the United States Government plausibly reach directly opposing conclusions. As a matter of law, the requisite intent to evade and defeat income taxes is missing. The obligation to pay is so problematical that defendant's actual intent is irrelevant. Even if she had consulted the law and sought to guide herself accordingly, she could have had no certainty as to what the law required.

Critzer differs from this case in that the defendant there had been advised by the Bureau of Indian Affairs that the income received from the transactions on the Reservation was exempt from taxation. The fact that Garber did not have the benefit of such official advice does not persuade us that the result here should be different. The *Critzer* court did not so limit its holding:

> It is settled that when the law is vague or highly debatable, a defendant actually or imputedly lacks the requisite intent to violate it.

To hold otherwise would advocate convicting an unsophisticated taxpayer who failed to seek expert advice as to whether certain income was taxable while setting free a wise taxpayer who could find advice that taxes were not due on the identical type of debatably taxable income.

That *Critzer* was not decided on the basis of the defendant's actual intent is further evidenced by the reasoning of the court and its reliance on *James v. United States*, 366 U.S. 213 (1961). In *James*, the Supreme Court put to rest a dispute over the taxability of embezzled funds. Fifteen years before *James*, the Court had held such funds non-taxable. *CIR v. Wilcox*, 327 U.S. 404 (1946). Subsequently a realigned Court undermined the viability of *Wilcox* by deciding that extortion money was taxable, distinguishing *Wilcox* on tenuous grounds. *Rutkin v. United States*, 343 U.S. 130 (1952). When the taxability of embezzled funds again reached the Court in *James*, it decided that *Rutkin* had in effect overruled *Wilcox* and that embezzled monies were taxable. Nevertheless, the court reversed James' conviction for willfully failing to report embezzled funds in violation of section 7201 because of the uncertainty of the law created by *Wilcox*. Significantly, neither *James*, nor the cases following *James* required actual reliance on *Wilcox*, to negate willful intent. As noted in *Critzer*:

> [T]he uncertainty created by *Wilcox* as a matter of law precluded a demonstration of "willfulness," without regard to the defendant's actual state of mind with respect to his knowledge or reliance on *Wilcox*.

498 F.2d at 1163.

Both *Critzer* and *James* involved disagreements among recognized authorities which were more clearly documented than the theories presented here. *James* involved conflicting Supreme Court decisions, and in *Critzer*, the Bureau of Indian Affairs and the Internal Revenue Service strongly disagreed on the taxability of the income. In the case presently before us, as conceded by all the experts who testified, there is a dearth of authority directly supporting either argument. However, the fact that the question has never before evoked anything more than theories on either side adds to rather than detracts from the critical conflict upon which defendant's criminal liability hinges. Neither position is frivolous, and the fact that both are urged without clear precedential support in law demonstrates that the court should not have restricted the evidence or instructed as it did.

The tax treatment of earnings from the sale of blood plasma or other parts of the human body is an uncharted area in tax law. The parties in this case presented divergent opinions as to the ultimate taxability by analogy to two legitimate theories in tax law. The trial court should not have withheld this fact, and its powerful impact on the issue of Garber's willfulness, from the jury. In a case such as this where the element of willfulness is critical to the defense, the defendant is entitled to wide latitude in the introduction of evidence tending to show lack of intent.[48]

Concerned about the line of cases exemplified by *Garber*, the Government attempts to limit the damage through the following analysis.

> Care should be taken to distinguish a case such as *Garber*, which is based on "unique, indeed near bizarre, facts." In *Burton*, the [Fifth Circuit] explained and limited its opinion in *Garber*. The court stated that "apart from those few cases where the legal duty pointed to is so uncertain as to approach the level of vagueness, the abstract question of legal uncertainty of which a defendant was unaware is of marginal relevance," explaining that "[e]vidence of legal uncertainty, except as it relates to defendant's effort to show the source of his state of mind, need not be received, at least where . . . the claimed uncertainty does not approach vagueness and is neither

[48] [Authors' note: 607 F.2d at 97–99; *see also* United States v. Harris, 942 F.2d 1125, 1132 (7th Cir. 1991) (holding that, since willfulness entails voluntary, intentional violation of a known — and therefore knowable — legal duty, if the tax liability is sufficiently in doubt willfulness is impossible as a matter of law, and the defendant's actual intent is irrelevant).]

> widely recognized nor related to a novel or unusual application of the law." And, in *United States v. Curtis*, 782 F.2d 593, 599–600 (6th Cir. 1986), the Sixth Circuit rejected *Garber* for the following reasons: (1) *Garber* allows juries to find that uncertainty in the law negates willfulness even if the defendant was unaware of the uncertainty; (2) it distorts the expert's role and intrudes upon the judge's duty to inform the jury about the law; and, (3) requires the jury to assume the judge's "responsibility to rule on questions of law."
>
> In those few courts which recognize uncertainty in the law as a potential defense, the court must find that the law clearly prohibited the defendant's alleged conduct. *United States v. Dahlstrom*, 713 F.2d 1423, 1428 (9th Cir. 1983), *cert. denied*, 466 U.S. 980, 104 S. Ct. 2363, 80 L. Ed. 2d 835 (1984). In *Dahlstrom*, the court reversed the convictions of the defendants, who had instructed investors on creating and carrying out abusive tax shelters, because the legality of the shelters was "completely unsettled." *Dahlstrom*, 713 F.2d at 1428. Taxpayers have fair notice of a scheme's illegality if it is clear that it is illegal under established principles of tax law, regardless of whether an appellate court has so ruled.
>
> To aid in establishing willfulness at trial, items turning on reasonably debatable interpretations of the Tax Code and questionable items of income should be eliminated from the case, and, whenever possible, complicated facts should be simplified. This is advantageous both for purposes of presentation to the jury and to strengthen the government's argument that there is no doubt that this was a criminal act to evade taxes, because the taxability and tax consequences were known to the taxpayer.[49]

Given the fact that the "uncertainty of law" defense is firmly grounded on the Supreme Court's *James* decision, is the Government right in suggesting that only a "few courts" recognize the defense? Given *James*, all courts must recognize the defense. The battlefield is over what level of uncertainty is required for the defense to apply.

UNITED STATES v. HARRIS

United States Court of Appeals, Seventh Circuit
942 F.2d 1125 (1991)

David Kritzik, now deceased, was a wealthy widower partial to the company of young women. Two of these women were Leigh Ann Conley and Lynnette Harris, twin sisters. Directly or indirectly, Kritzik gave Conley and Harris each more than half a million dollars over the course of several years. For our purposes, either Kritzik had to pay gift tax on this money or Harris and Conley had to pay income tax. The United States alleges that, beyond reasonable doubt, the obligation was Harris and Conley's. In separate criminal trials, Harris and Conley were convicted of willfully evading their income tax obligations regarding the money, and they now appeal.

[49] CTM 8.06[2] (2001) (most case citations omitted). To similar effect, see CTM 8.08[2].

Under *Commissioner v. Duberstein*, 363 U.S. 278, 285 (1960), the donor's intent is the "critical consideration" in distinguishing between gifts and income. We reverse Conley's conviction and remand with instructions to dismiss the indictment against her because the government failed to present sufficient evidence of Kritzik's intent regarding the money he gave her. We also reverse Harris' conviction. The district court excluded as hearsay letters in which Kritzik wrote that he loved Harris and enjoyed giving things to her. These letters were central to Harris' defense that she believed in good faith that the money she received was a non-taxable gift, and they were not hearsay for this purpose.

We do not remand Harris' case for retrial, however, because Harris had no fair warning that her conduct might subject her to criminal tax liability. Neither the tax code, the Treasury Regulations, or Supreme Court or appellate cases provide a clear answer to whether Harris owed any taxes or not. The closest authority lies in a series of Tax Court decisions — but these cases *favor* Harris' position that the money she received was not income to her. Under this state of the law, Harris could not have formed a "willful" intent to violate the statutes at issue. For this reason, we remand with instructions that the indictment against Harris be dismissed. The same conclusion applies to Conley, and provides an alternative basis for reversing her conviction and remanding with instructions to dismiss the indictment.

F. Proving Willfulness

Willfulness is a state of mind. There are no witnesses and only in a rare case would a defendant admit the required state of mind. State of mind is thus usually provable only through circumstantial evidence — proof of acts from which the state of mind can be inferred.

UNITED STATES v. YTEM

United States Court of Appeals, Seventh Circuit
255 F.3d 394 (2001)

Posner, Circuit Judge.

The defendant, an accountant who worked in Illinois, embezzled funds of his employer by writing, without authorization, three checks to himself aggregating more than $135,000 during a two-month period and depositing them in his personal account in a Maryland bank that happens to have offices only in that state and in Virginia. The locations of his place of work and of his bank are relevant because he was charged not only with willful failure to report his embezzled income on his federal income tax return for the year in which he received that income, 26 U.S.C. sec. 7206(1), but also with having transported money obtained by fraud across state lines. 18 U.S.C. sec. 2314. He was convicted of both crimes, was sentenced to a total of 27 months in prison, and appeals, challenging only the sufficiency of the evidence to convict him.

The appeal bespeaks a deep or perhaps desperate misunderstanding of the law of evidence, especially with regard to the second charge. It is conceded that all the government had to show was that the defendant had caused the checks to be transported across state lines. It is also conceded that the checks indeed ended up in either a Maryland or a Virginia office of the bank in which they were deposited and that one of the checks was accompanied by a note to the bank in the defendant's handwriting telling the bank what to do with the check. Presumably the defendant mailed the checks (and the accompanying note) to the bank but there is no direct evidence of this; that is, no one testified to having seen the defendant mail these items and he does not admit having mailed them. He argues that therefore he cannot be proved guilty beyond a reasonable doubt of having caused them to be transported across state lines.

He admits that certainty is not required to establish guilt beyond a reasonable doubt, that a conviction based on fingerprint evidence for example cannot be overturned by pointing out that there is some minute probability of erroneous fingerprint identification. But he insists that a conviction can survive remote doubts about its correctness only when it is based on computed probabilities; common sense probabilities will not do. That is wrong. Common sense as well as science is a source of justified true beliefs, including warranted confidence that certain probabilities though unquantified are so slight that they do not create reasonable doubt. Often this confidence is formed by comparing hypotheses and sensibly adjudging one to be vastly more probable than the others, even taken all together. This case illustrates that routine and unexceptionable reasoning process nicely. While it is conceivable that the defendant did not cause the checks to end up in Maryland or Virginia — maybe after writing them and the accompanying note he changed his mind and threw them in the wastepaper basket in his office and the cleaning people picked them up after hours and mailed them to the defendant's bank — this hypothesis is so unlikely to be true that in the absence of any evidence in support of it (and there is none) a rational jury would be entirely justified in dismissing the probability of its being true as minute in relation to the probability that the defendant himself caused the checks to end up where they did; indeed a jury would be irrational to conclude otherwise.

The situation is a little more doubtful with respect to the defendant's conviction for willfully filing a false return. To be convicted of that offense he had to be proved to have known (at least if he made an issue of his knowledge) that illegal income is taxable and so his income from embezzlement should have been reported, 26 U.S.C. sec. 7206(l); *Cheek v. United States*, 498 U.S. 192, 201–02 (1991); [other citations omitted], since otherwise the return though false would not be willfully so; and again there is no direct evidence that he knew — evidence that could only have taken the form of an admission by him, for that is the only form that direct evidence of a person's state of mind can take. (There are no eyewitnesses to the mental contents of a person's head, as opposed to external phenomena, such as the placing of a letter in a mailbox.) But the circumstantial evidence was convincing, and the absence of direct evidence therefore, no bar to conviction. We are, however, doubtful about the validity of the government's argument that the defendant's efforts (which incidentally were rather feeble) to conceal the embezzlement was evidence that he knew that embezzled income is taxable. For he would have had an incentive to conceal the embezzlement in order to save his job and avoid prosecution for embezzlement, even if embezzled income were tax-free. But there is plenty of other circumstantial evidence of the defendant's intent to avoid tax. The defendant was an accountant, moreover an experienced one; he personally prepared the fraudulent tax return; the sums taken were large (they amounted to 75 percent of his total income during the period of the embezzlement), and (the weakest bit of evidence) he used the money for ordinary expenses, the sort of thing people usually defray from taxable income. Furthermore, the fact that illegal income is taxable is widely known, even among lay people. Everyone knows that Al Capone, for example, was nailed for income-tax evasion, not for the bootlegging, loan-sharking, extortion, and prostitution that generated the income. Accountants know better than anyone except tax lawyers that illegal income is taxable.

It is possible nevertheless that this experienced accountant who prepared his own tax return thought that illegal income was tax exempt, but it is too remote a possibility to compel an acquittal, at least in the absence of any evidence that might make it plausible, such as that the defendant suffered from some psychiatric disorder that had deranged his knowledge of elementary tax law or his ability to use that knowledge in filling out his income tax return. Anything is possible; there are no metaphysical certainties accessible to human reason; but a merely metaphysical doubt (for example, doubt whether the external world is real, rather than being merely a dream) is not a reasonable doubt for purposes of the criminal law. If it were, no one could be convicted. As with the transportation of the checks, so with the charge of willfully filing a false return, the jury had to choose between two hypotheses. One was that the defendant knew that embezzled income is taxable. The other was that he thought embezzled income tax-free — a token of the government's affection for embezzlers and other thieves. The former hypothesis was, in the circumstances, far more likely than the latter. That is enough to compel affirmance. There is no suggestion that the jury was improperly instructed or that it might have been misled by any error committed at the trial.

Affirmed.

IV. TAX DUE AND OWING

A. No Tax, No Tax Evasion

Where there is no tax due and owing, there is no tax evasion.[50] Arguments have been made that this defense is not necessarily commanded by the statute.[51] However, consistent interpretation over the years makes it a solid defense.[52] Thus,

---

[50] *E.g.*, Boulware v. United States, 128 S. Ct. 1168, 1178 (2008). *But see* United States v. Kayser, 488 F.3d 1070 (9th Cir. 2007) (pre-*Boulware* case holding that it was error to refuse a jury instruction, properly grounded in the evidence, that unclaimed deductions can eliminate tax due from omitted income but noting that the defendant bears the burden of proving the deductions).

For this purpose, "tax" does not include penalties or interest. *E.g.*, United States v. Wright, 211 F.3d 233 (5th Cir. 2000) (noting that the Sentencing Guidelines also do not consider penalties and interest). See Chapter 10 for discussion of the Sentencing Guidelines.

[51] *See* Robert H. Jensen, *Reflections on United States v. Leona Helmsley: Should "Impossibility" Be*

one of the first lines of defense to explore is whether the taxpayer really owes the tax the Government alleges as an essential element of its tax evasion count. In her infamous criminal trial,[53] Leona Helmsley ("only little people pay taxes") asserted this defense by claiming that her husband's real estate empire generated far more depreciation deductions than they had claimed on their returns. Indeed, she urged, the unclaimed deductions were more than sufficient to eliminate the "tax due" element despite omission of large sums of income. This did not work for Ms. Helmsley, but it is an avenue that the experienced practitioner will explore. As one court noted:

> The government must demonstrate the existence of a deficiency beyond a reasonable doubt, but need not prove the extent of the deficiency with mathematical certainty. There is no deficiency in the absence of a showing that the government is actually due a tax in excess of that reported. Therefore, undeclared deductions, credits, losses carried over from prior years, and so on, should be considered when calculating the . . . deficiency.[54]

The tax attorney will typically hire a seasoned tax accountant to recalculate the tax liability to see if indeed the taxpayer owes no taxes or the amount of taxes owed are not material. This defense is often intertwined with the issue noted above that the Government cannot bring a tax charge where the underlying legal duty is not certain and is thus, as a matter of law, not a known legal duty. Often, the taxpayer will have taken aggressive reporting positions on several or even many items on the return. The accountant will first exclude from his or her calculations any items as to which there is a *James*-type uncertainty defense. The Government should have excluded all such items in its calculations upon which the charge is based, but it may not have done so and the taxpayer may be able to argue, as in *James* and *Gerber*, that the legal duty is uncertain. Moreover, as in *Helmsley*, the taxpayer may assert that she was entitled to additional tax benefits which she did not claim.

---

a Defense to Attempted Income Tax Evasion?, 12 VA. TAX REV. 335 (1993). Jensen is principally concerned about the person with fraudulent intent who misreports some item but is "saved" by some offsetting but unknown other item in her favor. However, section 7206(1), the tax perjury statute discussed in Chapter 2B, covers that situation, so the "problem" may not be grave.

[52] *E.g.*, Sansone v. United States, 380 U.S. 343, 352–53 (1965); United States v. Kayser, 488 F.3d 1070 (9th Cir. 2007).

[53] *See* United States v. Helmsley, 941 F.2d 71 (2d Cir. 1991), *cert. denied*, 502 U.S. 1091 (1992). Some read *Helmsley* as not allowing the unclaimed deduction defense, but close reading will disclose that the case did not so hold. Moreover, in the *Sansone* case, the Supreme Court explained that section 7201 has an element that section 7207, a lesser offense, lacks: tax due and owing. The Court reasoned that the defendant would be entitled to a lesser included offense instruction "if the jury believed that an understatement of deductible expenses had offset the understatement of gross receipts," which would preclude conviction under section 7201 but not conviction under section 7207. Sansone v. United States, 380 U.S. 343, 353 (1965); *see also* United States v. Kayser, 488 F.3d 1070 (9th Cir. 2007).

[54] United States v. Bishop, 264 F.3d 535, 550 (5th Cir. 2001) (citations omitted).

UNITED STATES v. CRUZ

United States Court of Appeals, Eleventh Circuit
698 F.2d 1148 (1983)

[Authors' note: The taxpayer, a Dominican citizen who was a U.S. resident, was subject to tax in the Dominican Republic and in the United States. The taxpayer had not filed a Dominican return for years. He did file a U.S. return. The Government charged under section 7201 that he had not reported all of his income. The taxpayer urged that, even if he did have the additional income the Government alleged, he still was not subject to U.S. tax because he would be entitled to a foreign tax credit under section 901. Section 905(a) allows a U.S. taxpayer to elect to claim the FTC when (1) accrued or (2) paid. The election can be made within ten years. At or shortly before the trial, the taxpayer elected to accrue the tax for the FTC. The taxpayer then urged that, based on the Dominican taxes that he accrued for the year, he was entitled to a credit that would wipe out his U.S. tax. With no U.S. tax liability, he could not be charged with violating section 7201. The taxpayer urged that it was not relevant to his liability for that year that he ultimately did not ever pay the Dominican tax. The Code's fix for a taxpayer who claims the FTC by accruing a foreign tax but then does not ultimately pay the foreign tax within a ten-year window is to retroactively increase the tax for the year. However, that ten-year time period would lapse only after the criminal statute of limitations (six years) had expired. The Court held that the taxpayer could nevertheless be prosecuted, reasoning as follows.]

In construing the requirements of section 905, we will not be constrained by intricate technicalities which would create a haven for federal tax evasion. When interpreting statutes, we are required to give a practical interpretation which will not produce an absurd result.[55] If we accept Cruz's interpretation of section 905, an accused taxpayer will always avoid successful prosecution. For example, under Cruz's interpretation, a taxpayer in his position could wait and pay no tax, either to the United States or the Dominican Republic until the United States authorities became aware of an irregularity in his tax return. Once discovered, he could either pay or immediately admit the foreign tax and claim the retroactive United States tax credit under section 6511(d)(3), as an absolute defense. Thus, he could fix the amount of the foreign tax liability which would automatically entitle him to the foreign tax credit. If the fraudulent omission is overlooked, both the United States and the Dominican Republic are cheated of taxes. In short, the taxpayer is able to gamble that neither government will become aware of his tax liability. Additionally, if the United States waits for the ten years allowed by statute for the taxpayer to fix the amount of the foreign tax liability, then the six-year statute of limitations on the section 7201 prosecution lapses. Against this background, we must approach this case from a practical viewpoint.

The determination of criminal liability is the real issue at stake, not merely the question of Cruz's right, as in a civil case, to a foreign tax credit. Since this is a criminal matter, the government need only establish that Cruz received unreported

---

[55] [Authors' note: *See generally*, Steve R. Johnson, *The "Absurd Results" Doctrine in State and Local Tax Cases*, State Tax Notes, Oct. 19, 2009, at 195.]

income, and that his nondisclosure resulted in a tax deficiency. The record reveals that the government provided these elements. At this point, Cruz had the burden of negating the deficiency by showing that it was either wrongly computed, cancelled by another deduction or, in this instance, a credit not yet allowed. Cruz sought to prove that the deficiency was negated by showing a credit not yet allowed.

Cruz presented, primarily by expert testimony, four items of evidence as proof of his right to a foreign tax credit: (1) that he was a resident of the Dominican Republic, (2) that he had determined his Dominican tax liability, (3) that the Dominican Republic's statute of limitations had not expired for the collection of taxes, and (4) that his Dominican Republic tax liability for the respective years were final. No proof, however, was offered which indicated that Cruz fixed the amount of his foreign tax liability prior to trial. Only after the discovery of the deficiency and trial did Cruz fix the amount of his foreign tax liability. His after trial payment of the foreign tax liability cannot be used on appeal to overturn the conviction. In this respect, the jury instruction given by the district court was correct. The instruction required that there be a firmly established taxable amount owed the foreign government and determined by it before the taxpayer would be entitled to a foreign tax credit. The practical effect of this decision means the tax evader can no longer play one government against the other to defeat an evasion prosecution.

Cruz shows the importance for the defense counsel in a criminal case to bring to the task an understanding of the intricacies of substantive tax law. That may be done by engaging appropriate experts. Indeed, one of the first orders of business in a tax evasion representation is to marshal the resources to determine if the taxpayer has this type of defense. In an appropriate case, it can make the difference. It did not in *Cruz*, but it can be argued that the court wrongly decided the case. The Government cannot prosecute where there is doubt as to the tax liability. Where the Code unequivocally gives the taxpayer the right to claim the credit, even ex post facto, by accrual rather than payment, it cannot be said that there is no doubt as to the tax liability.[56] It is true, as the court noted, this would mean that it would be difficult to bring a tax evasion prosecution against a person who is subject to a foreign tax that will substantially wipe out his U.S. tax liability, but if there is to be a fix for the criminal warp, Congress arguably should legislate the fix rather than have the courts simply ignore the glitch in a criminal case.[57]

---

[56] The *Cruz* issue has not surfaced again as to the "tax due and owing" element, but it has arisen in the context of determining the tax loss for sentencing. In United States v. Tilga, 824 F. Supp. 2d 1295 (D.N.M. 2011), the court allowed the accrual of the foreign tax credit for determining the tax loss. The *Tilga* court questioned *Cruz*, as have commentators. *See* Sheldon I. Banoff & Richard M. Lipton, *Using Extended FTC S/L to Defend Against Tax Evasion Charges*, 115 J. TAX'N 358 (2011); Jeffrey L. Rubinger & Andrew H. Weinstein, *Foreign Tax Credits: Can a Deficiency Be Retroactively Wiped out for Criminal Tax Evasion Purposes?*, 112 J. TAX'N 116 (2010).

Indeed, although the Department of Justice maintains the position it took in *Cruz*, the IRS has acknowledged that accrued foreign tax credits can be a valid defense to tax evasion. IRS Office of Chief Counsel, Criminal Tax Division, TAX CRIMES HANDBOOK § 1.03[3][g]5 (2009).

[57] Arguably, Congress has legislated. Section 905(c)(2) provides that, in general, no credit is available for accrued taxes not paid within two years after the close of the year. That would eliminate *Cruz* defenses in at least some potential cases.

B. Substantiality and Materiality

If the statute were read literally, a taxpayer evading $1 of tax could be convicted. It is doubtful that a jury would convict on that proof, however. Some courts add a nonstatutory spin on the "tax due" element by requiring that the tax due be substantial.[58] One recent case explicitly rejected the argument that the tax due must be substantial. In *United States v. Daniels*,[59] the court stated that the statute does not contain a substantiality requirement and held "the government need not charge a substantial tax deficiency to indict or convict under 26 U.S.C. § 7201." The court's reasons were as follows:

> To hold otherwise would contradict the clear language of the statute and lead to an absurd result. Requiring the government to charge and prove that a defendant's tax deficiency is substantial in order to prosecute her for tax evasion would prevent the prosecution and punishment of those who willfully cheat the government out of small or "insubstantial" amounts of money. A substantiality element would invite taxpayers to cheat on their taxes in small amounts without fear of prosecution. We cannot countenance such a result. Although evidence of a large or substantial tax deficiency may aid the government in proving willfulness, it is not itself an element of the offense.[60]

However, this debate is largely academic. There can be no question that in the exercise of prosecutorial discretion — a discretion also influenced by what juries will actually do in a case where the tax evaded is "insubstantial" — a tax prosecution will not be brought where the tax evaded is not substantial in some sense we (and a jury) can recognize. Even in *Daniels*, the court noted: "Defendants do not propose an amount at which a tax deficiency becomes 'substantial,' or how we could set a threshold. In any event, defendants did not contest substantiality at trial, and at sentencing they conceded a tax loss of over $69,000. Certainly, this amount is substantial under any rubric."[61]

The Department of Justice and the IRS accept that there is a substantiality requirement.[62] In general, the IRS will recommend criminal prosecution under section 7201 only if the average yearly additional tax for criminal purposes is at least $2,500 in "specific items" cases with uncomplicated facts or at least $10,000 for the prosecution period in "indirect method" cases or cases with complicated facts.[63]

---

[58] *E.g.*, United States v. Helmsley, 941 F.2d 71, 83–84 (2d Cir. 1991).

[59] 387 F.3d 636 (7th Cir. 2004), *cert. denied*, 544 U.S. 911 (2005); *see* Keith J. Benes, David Gallai, Louisa J. McGruder & Anne M. Petersen, *Tax Violations*, 35 Am. Crim. L. Rev. 1219, 1230 (1968) (noting a split in the circuits on this issue).

[60] 387 F.3d at 641.

[61] 387 F.3d at 641, n.3.

[62] *See, e.g.*, CTM 8.07[3].

[63] LGM CT-1, Text 131.1 (1992), *revised by* LGM CT-1 (1995). See Chapter 4 for discussion of the "specific items" and "indirect methods" modes of proof.

C. Criminal Tax Numbers

The tax due that the Government will use to support its tax evasion prosecution is not necessarily the tax due for civil tax purposes. To illustrate, assume that, for civil tax purposes, the taxpayer had $100,000 income that he or she failed to report. Assume that the tax liability on that omitted income is $35,000. The $100,000 of omitted income consists of two items — $60,000 of embezzlement income which the taxpayer clearly knew was taxable and chose not to report and $40,000 of personal injury income which the Government is satisfied that the taxpayer thought or could have reasonably thought was excludable under section 104(a)(2) but which for technical reasons is not properly excludable under that section. In calculating the tax due for tax evasion purposes, the Government will compute the tax only on the $60,000 of embezzlement income and will not include the $40,000 of personal injury income. This is referred to as the "criminal numbers," and it is important to get a clear fix on these numbers. Obviously, if defense counsel can get the criminal numbers down sufficiently, the Government may perceive some difficulty in trying to make a tax evasion case and may give up the prosecution.

There are thus the civil tax numbers and the criminal tax numbers. The civil numbers are never less than the criminal numbers and are usually more because of the phenomenon just mentioned — *i.e.*, some components of the tax calculation may not be items which could support a tax evasion prosecution. The other important numbers are the "tax loss numbers" used in the Sentencing Guidelines to determine the guideline sentencing range that will apply if the taxpayer is found guilty. The tax loss numbers are conceptually the same as the criminal numbers because they are the tax loss attributable to the taxpayer's fraud. But there are some nuances in the concept that will be addressed in Chapter 10 in discussing the Sentencing Guidelines.

D. Corporate Diversions

A common fact pattern with closely held C corporations is for the shareholder(s) to take money out of the corporation in a way that underreports the corporation's tax liability and underreports a shareholder's tax liability. There are many ways of implementing this type of double underreporting. A common pattern is for the shareholder of a corporation that has a lot of cash coming through its business (*e.g.*, a restaurant business) to pocket some of the cash each day, thus preventing it from being shown on the books from which the corporation and the shareholder calculate their tax liabilities. As to the shareholder, the income that results from such a diversion is dividend income. Dividends are taxable to the recipient shareholder. "Dividend" is a term of art under section 316(a). It is not just a distribution from the corporation to the shareholder but is a distribution from the earnings and profits ("E&P") of the corporation. The Code does not define E&P, and calculating E&P may be dicey.[64]

There's the rub. The conventional wisdom is that, to convict of a crime, the Government must prove each element of its case beyond a reasonable doubt. For

[64] *See generally* Boris I. Bittker & James S. Eustice, Federal Taxation of Corporations and Shareholders ¶ 8.03 (7th ed. 2006).

tax evasion, that includes proving a tax due and owing. Does the Government have to prove the E&P calculations to support the dividend treatment that in turn supports the element of the crime — a material tax due and owing?

In general, under section 301(c), distributions of money by a corporation to a shareholder are taxed in three tranches: (1) as a dividend to the extent of the corporation's accumulated or current E&P; (2) any remainder as tax-free return of basis to the extent of the shareholder's stock basis; and (3) any remainder as capital gain. For most of our modern income tax history, the first tranch (dividend) has been ordinary income. The top current individual rate is 35%.[65]

Under this regime, there is no uniform effect of diverted corporate income. Assume, for example, that Corporation X wholly owned by individual A is entitled to receive $100 from one of its customers. The customer pays corporation X in cash. Instead of putting the cash on the corporate books, A puts it in his pocket. Neither X nor A reports the $100. Whether X has taxable income depends on whether it has enough deductions to offset the $100. Whether A has income, and if so how much, depends on how much E&P X has, how much basis A has in his or her X stock, and what tax rate applies. There are myriad variations producing different levels of tax based on these factors.

To return to the question asked — what is the Government's burden, if any, to prove E&P where it must prove that the taxpayer failed to report shareholder-level tax on the diverted income? That issue is heavily dependent upon the existence of E&P so as to support a dividend in an amount sufficient to convict. Does the Government have to prove E&P, which can be one of the more murky areas of the tax law, before it may convict?[66]

The Supreme Court addressed a variation of this issue in *Bouleware v. United States*.[67] The issue the Court technically resolved is whether, in order to require the Government to prove sufficient E&P to establish tax due and owing, the defendant must at least put into play whether the defendant or the corporation "intended" the diversion to be a dividend. The Court unanimously answered "no." Regardless of intent, there can be no dividend and no tax liability absent E&P.

As in *Cheek*, so in *Boulware*: the defendant won the battle but lost the war. On remand, the Ninth Circuit upheld the trial court's refusal to present to the jury the defense that the diverted funds were a non-taxable return of capital. The appellate court concluded that the defendant's proffer was insufficient to require giving the requested instruction and that, in any event, the evidence showed the defendant's basis in his stock was millions of dollars less than the amount distributed or diverted.[68]

---

[65] As a result of 2003 legislation, however, dividends from most U.S. and some foreign corporations are taxed like long-term capital gains — thus usually at a 15% rate — for tax years 2003 through 2008.

[66] In many businesses, calculating E&P is not difficult. It is difficult, however, when the corporation has a long history or there are unusual facts. Still, whatever the difficulty of the calculation in a particular case, the question remains whether the Government has to prove E&P in order to prove tax evasion at the shareholder level.

[67] 128 S. Ct. 1168 (2008).

[68] United States v. Boulware, 558 F.3d 971 (9th Cir. 2009), *cert. denied*, 558 U.S. 1048 (2009). *See* Scott

Is the Government required from the beginning to prove up E&P as an essential part of its case? Will verdict be directed against the Government absent proof of E&P? Recognizing practicalities, the courts have generally required defendants to meet some minimal burden to put the issue in play.

UNITED STATES v. BOK

United States Court of Appeals, Second Circuit
156 F.3d 157 (1998)

[Authors' note: The taxpayer was convicted of tax evasion (§ 7201) and tax perjury (§ 7206(1)) with respect to his two tax returns. The facts reported by the court of appeals are a bit unclear. However, with respect to the evasion count as to his personal return resulting from corporate diversions, the taxpayer-defendant did attempt to make a defense that the corporate diversions were not dividends and were instead all return of capital because the corporation did not have the required E&P. The court of appeals addressed the issue as follows.]

On the morning of the last day of the government's case, one day before the trial court submitted the case to the jury, Bok presented the court with several additional requests to charge. One of them concerned the treatment for tax purposes of money withdrawn by a shareholder from a corporation. Through that proposed charge, Bok sought to characterize the money he received from Abacus for his condominium and his municipal bonds as a nontaxable return of capital that he had invested in the corporation rather than as a taxable dividend. The proposed charge read as follows:

> If a shareholder in a corporation withdraws his capital from that corporation, either all or part of that withdrawal is not income to the shareholder, and need not be reflected on that shareholder's personal income tax return. The same treatment occurs if the shareholder directs the corporation to pay to a third party for his benefit all or part of his capital contribution.

The government opposed the use of the proposed charge, arguing both that it was not legally correct as written and that there was no basis in fact for its inclusion in the charge as a whole.

After entertaining arguments from both sides, the trial court decided against including Bok's proposed charge as written. The trial judge did invite Bok to work with the government to craft a more correct statement of the law, but the two sides evidently never reached agreement on an instruction. The trial judge went on to say that, in keeping with his obligation to instruct the jury correctly on the law, he had included a charge "about a corporate distribution and how that can be income." Ultimately the relevant portion of the charge read as follows:

> Gains or profits and income derived from any source whatever are included in gross income for the purpose of taxation of income. This includes both lawful and unlawful gains.

A. Schumacher, *The Ninth Circuit Says Aloha to* Boulware — *Again*, Tax Notes, Mar. 30, 2009, at 1631.

> In order to prove that the defendant received substantial additional income omitted from his tax return, the government has introduced evidence that the defendant was the sole shareholder, or owner, of Abacus Construction Corp., a corporation, and receivéd certain funds or assets from the corporation for the purchase of an apartment and a bond.
>
> If you find that the defendant obtained such funds, or assets, or other property from Abacus Construction Corp., then you should proceed to determine whether this was income to the defendant.
>
> In this connection, the question for you to determine is whether the defendant had control over the funds, or assets, or other property from that corporation, took it as his own and treated it as his own, so that as a practical matter he derived economic value from the funds, or assets, or other property received. If you find this to be the case, then the funds, or assets, or property received by the defendant would be income; if you do not find this to be the case, then the funds or assets or other property obtained by the defendant would not be income to the defendant.

We have long recognized that under certain circumstances monies lawfully withdrawn from a corporation by one of its shareholders may constitute a nontaxable return of capital. A central condition for the application of the return of capital theory — which we have also called the "no earnings and profits, no income" rule — is that the corporation must not have earned a profit for the year in which the withdrawal was made. Under this theory, if a shareholder has invested capital in a corporation and the corporation has not earned a profit for the year at issue, any monies the shareholder removes from the corporation (up to the amount of invested capital) constitute only a return of the shareholder's basis, not dividend income.

The return of capital theory derives from the Internal Revenue Code itself, which defines the term "dividend" to mean "any distribution of property made by a corporation to its shareholders . . . out of its earnings and profits of the taxable year, . . . without regard to the amount of the earnings and profits at the time the distribution was made." 26 U.S.C. § 316(a)(2) (1994). The Code further provides that "that portion of the [corporate] distribution [of property to its shareholders] which is not a dividend shall be applied against and reduce the adjusted basis of the stock." 26 U.S.C. § 301(c)(2) (1994). The natural implication of the two provisions read together is that in the absence of earnings or profits, a shareholder may treat any distribution up to the value of capital invested in the corporation — that is, the taxpayer's basis — as a return of that capital. Both the Tax Court and the Tax Litigation Service [*sic*] of the IRS have explicitly adopted this approach in the civil enforcement context.

We have made clear that the return of capital theory applies equally in both criminal and civil cases, assuming that the diversion itself was not unlawful. In *D'Agostino*, we explicitly rejected the prevailing rule in several of our sister Circuits. These require only that the government prove that the taxpayer had "actual command" over the funds at issue in a criminal tax evasion case and do not require a showing that earnings and profits existed in a year in which the distribution was made.

Similarly, in return of capital cases, a taxpayer's intent is not determinative in defining the taxpayer's conduct. That is, the taxpayer or the corporation need not have described the distribution at issue as a dividend or a return of capital at the time it was made; rather, the realities of the transaction — including the amount of the shareholder's basis and the corporation's earnings or profits, as well as the amount of the distribution — govern its characterization for tax purposes. In this way, the court in *D'Agostino* applied the return of capital theory even though it had "little doubt the D'Agostinos acted with bad intentions" when Mrs. D'Agostino surreptitiously diverted up to $4,000 each week in large bills from the couple's solely-owned businesses to her kitchen drawer.

The fact that the return of capital theory applies in this Circuit does not, however, end our inquiry. We must also determine whether Bok established an adequate basis in the record for the proposed charge. The legal standard is generous: Generally "a criminal defendant is entitled to instructions relating to his theory of defense, for which there is some foundation in the proof, no matter how tenuous that defense may appear to the trial court." On appeal, however, "[a] conviction will not be overturned for refusal to give a requested charge . . . unless that instruction . . . represents a theory of defense with basis in the record that would lead to acquittal." In determining whether an adequate basis exists for a return of capital charge, we must first determine the extent and nature of the showing the defendant must make.

Although our earlier cases have not stated it with perfect clarity, a defendant does always bear the burden of production — under which the defendant must make an initial showing on each key element of the theory — to receive an instruction on the return of capital theory. That is, there must be some credible evidence that the corporation did not enjoy income or profits for the tax year at issue, and that the amount of the taxpayer's capital contribution exceeded the amount of the distribution from the corporation. The court in *Leonard* effectively held as much:

> In prosecutions for income tax violations, production of a rather slight amount of evidence by the Government, here the proof of receipt of what are charitably characterized as constructive dividends rather than embezzled funds, may transfer the burden of going forward to the defendant. Although the ultimate burden of persuasion remains with the Government, Leonard did not introduce sufficient evidence of an absence of earnings or profits.

Though *Leonard* used precatory language in discussing the defendant's burden of production, it did not purport to do away with the general requirement that a proposed jury instruction must have an adequate basis in fact. To the extent that *Leonard* was at all unclear on the issue, we now clarify that in order to merit a charge on the return of capital theory, a defendant must satisfy a burden of production by showing that an adequate basis in fact exists for the charge. As suggested by the cases cited in *Leonard,* this is not the only circumstance in which a taxpayer faces a burden of production once the government has come forward with evidence of tax evasion. *See, e.g., United States v. Vardine*, 305 F.2d 60, 63 (2d Cir. 1962) ("It is reasonable to require the defendant, if he wishes to disprove intent and likely source [of a net worth bulge], to bear the burden of going forward when he alleges that he had additional deductions not claimed on his income tax return."). Of course in cases involving the return of capital theory, the allocation of the burden of going forward to the taxpayer does not affect the ultimate burden of persuasion, which always remains with the government.

Like the taxpayer in *Leonard*, Bok failed to satisfy his burden of going forward and therefore did not establish an adequate basis in the record for his proposed instruction. Specifically, neither Bok nor the government produced any admissible evidence to suggest that Abacus lacked earnings or profits for 1988. Although Bok did introduce Abacus's 1988 financial statements, he made clear that they were offered only to show Bok's state of mind when he gave information to his accountant, not for the underlying truth of the figures in the statements. Even if the financial statements had been admitted for their truth, they alone would not have satisfied Bok's burden because they were based entirely on information provided by Bok, purportedly using an entirely different method of accounting than that used on Abacus's corporate return. In addition, Bok had suggested that Abacus did have net earnings for 1988. During the IRS's investigation, Bok accounted for the low figures in the gross receipts portion of Abacus's return by explaining that he had mistakenly entered the corporation's net profits in place of its gross receipts. At trial Bok referred to this explanation for the false statements on Abacus's returns in arguing that he lacked the requisite intent to be convicted. Bok continues to make the same argument on appeal, noting his contention that the numbers on the gross receipts line of Abacus's tax returns "were really net profits." Finally, Bok declined the trial court's invitation to elicit facts to support his proposed charge. Because Bok's accountant had not been qualified as an expert witness, the trial court rejected Bok's attempt to establish through the cross examination of the accountant that, as a matter of law, a return of capital was a nontaxable event. In doing so, however, the trial court expressly suggested that Bok use the witness to develop facts that Bok might later use as the basis for a jury instruction; Bok did not follow up on the trial court's suggestion.

Thus, despite our generous approach to jury instructions, under which the defendant is entitled to an instruction on his theory when "there is some foundation in the proof, no matter how tenuous," Bok did not provide sufficient facts to warrant his proposed charge. Given the lack of evidence produced by Bok on the issue of Abacus's earnings or profits, we cannot say the trial judge erred in finding no basis in the record for the return of capital theory. Because Bok failed to satisfy his burden of production, the trial court properly rejected Bok's proposed instruction.

Is it right that the Government can shift to the defendant any burden with respect to an element of the crime? The courts pay homage to the requirement that the Government prove the elements beyond a reasonable doubt and that it is not incumbent upon the defendant to do anything. Yet, as we have seen, the defendant is required to mount this defense as to an element of the Government's case because of a shifting trial burden. We return to this issue from time to time, for the defendant's counsel must be keenly aware when some burden has been shifted to the defendant.[69]

Many contexts other than corporate diversions or E&P uncertainties present the same issue as to when, despite the concept that the Government must prove each element beyond a reasonable doubt, a legal or practical burden shifts to the defendant. Does the Government make a tax evasion case simply by showing that a taxpayer omitted an item of income from his return? What if the taxpayer failed to report deductions, so that there either was not a tax due and owing or, if there was, the amount was not material? Must the Government prove not only the omitted income but also the negative, *i.e.*, that the taxpayer's other tax attributes did not wipe out the tax effect of the omitted income?[70] Is the burden shifted to the taxpayer to prove that he or she did not have a tax due and owing? This issue has rarely, if ever, been sharply defined for court decision. But the Government will certainly attempt to correctly determine the taxpayer's liability in its investigation and not even bring the case if there are offsetting deductions. How does the Government prove that there were no offsetting deductions? And, if the case gets to trial, can a taxpayer rest on the Government's failure to prove beyond a reasonable doubt that there were no offsetting deductions?

More practically, of course, if there are offsetting deductions, the taxpayer will want to try to prove them in his or her defense as Mrs. Helmsley unsuccessfully attempted. Once the taxpayer puts them in play, presumably, the Government would then have to prove beyond a reasonable doubt that the deductions were not available. Otherwise it will not have shown a tax due and owing beyond a reasonable doubt. (But, as we shall note in Chapter 13 in discussing proof issues related to the net worth method, for such items as this, as a practical matter, the burden of proof has really been shifted to the defendant.)

As discussed in Chapter 10, with respect to corporate diversions, certain conventions have arisen in the sentencing phase of the case which may permit a court to determine the sentencing tax loss without getting hung up on these technicalities. The question raised here but not answered is whether these conventions, in effect, apply to the case in chief in which the Government is required to prove the elements of the offense beyond a reasonable doubt.

V. EX POST FACTO SOLUTIONS TO TAX EVASION

After creating his criminal tax exposure, is there anything the taxpayer can do to undo the problem? Death will obviate prosecution, but this approach will not recommend itself to most clients. Are there more realistic and palatable options?

One feature of our income tax is that the rigors of annual accounting are mitigated by net operating loss carrybacks under section 172 (and by other carrybacks) that are generated in later tax years. Can a taxpayer who commits tax

---

[69] The Supreme Court recognized, but ducked, this issue in *Boulware v. United States*, 128 S. Ct. 1168, 1181 n.14 (2008).

[70] As to the (sometimes exaggerated) difficulties of "proving a negative," see Kevin W. Saunders, *The Mythic Difficulty in Proving a Negative*, 15 Seton Hall L. Rev. 276 (1985); Note, *Proving a Negative — When the Taxpayer Denies Receipt*, 70 Cornell L. Rev. 141 (1984).

evasion for Year One by filing a fraudulent return avoid a section 7201 charge for Year One by generating in a later year a net operating loss or other carryback that ex post facto wipes out the Year One liability? The answer is "no."[71]

In another vein, a taxpayer having committed tax evasion by filing a fraudulent original return might consider filing an accurate amended return. A client might ask whether doing so would purge the fraud. As a matter of law, the answer is "no."[72] However, "coming clean" before the IRS begins to examine the taxpayer's original return may influence the Government to forgo criminal prosecution. This strategy of voluntary disclosure via an amended return is often available with respect to most of the commonly encountered tax crimes. It is discussed in detail in Chapter 5.

PROBLEM

You are an attorney employed by the United States Department of Justice Tax Division in the Criminal Section. A new file has arrived on your desk. The IRS is recommending prosecution under section 7201. You skim the file before leaving the office in the evening. You discover the following:

Ronald Wolzak is the president and sole owner of Crafty Construction, a C corporation. Crafty is a contractor at various small building sites. There are six workers (Able, Baker, Charlie, Dan, Evan, and Fred) who work regularly at Crafty's job sites. They perform the activities specified by Wolzak on behalf of Crafty, and they do so at the times, in the places, and in the manner specified by Wolzak on behalf of Crafty. Crafty has always and for all purposes taken the position that the six workers are independent contractors, not employees.

Crafty compensated the six workers for their services by giving them old gold and silver coins. The coins have face values, but their face values are far below the fair market values of the coins. The coins are more valuable than their face amounts both because of current prices of gold and silver and because of the coins' vintage, giving them status as collectibles.

The IRS Special Agents who developed the case interviewed Wolzak and the six workers. They all said essentially the same thing. They claim that using and contracting to use gold and silver coins at face value as a medium of exchange is a lawful exercise of a statutory right. Moreover, they assert that the only real money is "hard money," by which they mean currency in the form of precious metals or at least fully backed by precious metals. They assert that U.S. "paper money" has been worthless since the United States went off the gold standard. They view the Federal Reserve System as being under the control and direction of the International Monetary Fund and "foreign financial interests." Their use of old gold and silver coins is part of what they describe as their "boycott of the corrupt and un-American Federal Reserve System." They also offer their view that the federal income tax is unconstitutional because the Sixteenth Amendment was not

---

71 *E.g.*, Willingham v. United States, 289 F.2d 283, 287–88 (5th Cir.), *cert. denied*, 368 U.S. 828 (1961).

72 *See* Hill v. United States, 363 F.2d 176, 180 (5th Cir. 1966) (by implication). *Cf.* Badaracco v. Commissioner, 464 U.S. 386 (1984) (filing an accurate amended return does not purge the fraud for purposes of the civil fraud penalty).

properly ratified by the requisite number of states.

Crafty and the six workers value the coins for tax purposes at their face amounts, not at their fair market values. For example, assume Able received from Crafty in a given year coins with an aggregate face amount of $100 but aggregate fair market value of $30,000. On these facts, Crafty would take the position that it had paid $100 to Able for the year, and Able would take the position that he had received $100 from Crafty for the year. As a result, none of the six workers filed federal income tax returns for the years they worked for Crafty. They maintained that their incomes (as measured by the face amounts of the coins) fell under the levels at which returns are required to be filed. *See* IRC § 6012(a)(1).

You are aware of two decisions holding that, when gold coins have a fair market value in excess of face value, taxpayers must report income at the fair market value, not the face value. California Federal Life Ins. Co. v. Commissioner, 680 F.2d 85, 86–87 (9th Cir. 1982); Cordner v. United States, 671 F.2d 367, 368–69 (9th Cir. 1982).

At this point, you leave your office, resolving to read the rest of the file tomorrow. On your commute home, you mull the case over. Specifically, you consider and form tentative conclusions about the following questions:

1. Are section 7201 charges appropriate here? Consider whether the prima facie elements of section 7201 are met, which of the actors are appropriate defendants, and all other relevant matters.

2. What defenses could the putative defendants advance? Identify all defenses — including both failure-of-proof defenses and affirmative defenses — and evaluate their strengths and weaknesses.

3. Identify relevant factual ambiguities and why they matter. What additional information will you look for in the case file when you review it more fully?

Chapter 2B

CRIMES UNDER THE INTERNAL REVENUE CODE — OTHER OFFENSES

IRC: §§ 6050I, 7202, 7203, 7206, 7207, 7212, 7512

I. INTRODUCTION

Section 7201, which was explored in Chapter 2A, is the capstone criminal tax provision in the Internal Revenue Code. However, it does not stand alone. Chapter 75 of the Code sets out a number of other tax crimes and related provisions. Sometimes — as with sections 7206(1) and 7207 for example — the other provisions cover territory that section 7201 might cover, but they are easier to prove than section 7201 is, and, as a consequence, sometimes (but not always) entail lesser punishment in the event of conviction than would ensue upon conviction under section 7201.[1] Other times — as with section 7212 for example — the other provisions cover territory that falls or arguably falls outside the ambit of section 7201.

This Chapter 2B discusses the principal Title 26 offenses other than section 7201. We discuss, in order, sections 7206(1), 7206(2), 7212(a), 7203, 7202, 7215, 7207, and 6050I.[2]

II. SECTION 7206(1) TAX PERJURY

A. The Elements Generally

Section 7206(1) is often referred to as the tax perjury statute because it criminalizes the making of a false statement under penalty of perjury. However, tax perjury is broader than perjury in the general federal criminal law[3] because, as discussed below, corporations can be guilty of tax perjury.

The elements of tax perjury are described by the following jury instruction:

---

[1] In addition to incarceration, the taxpayer-defendant and her attorney should think carefully about the collateral consequences of conviction, described in Chapter 12. These consequences may be less severe when conviction is of a misdemeanor rather than a felony.

[2] In addition to these sections, there are other tax crimes of less general significance located in various places in Title 26. *E.g.*, I.R.C. § 999(f) (fine of up to $25,000 and imprisonment of up to one year for failure to report international boycott).

[3] *See* 18 U.S.C. § 1622.

Title 26, United States Code, Section 7206(1), makes it a crime for anyone willfully to make a false material statement on an income tax return.[4]

For you to find the defendant guilty of this crime, you must be convinced that the government has proved each of the following beyond a reasonable doubt:

First: That the defendant signed an income tax return that contained a written declaration that it was made under penalties of perjury;

Second: That in this return, the defendant falsely stated that ________________________ [state material matters asserted, *e.g.*, the defendant received gross income of $________ during 20_______];

Third: That the defendant knew the statement was false;

Fourth: That the false statement was material; and

Fifth: That the defendant made the statement willfully, that is, with intent to violate a known legal duty.[5]

B. Materiality

Read literally, section 7206(1) would not require a false document as to a material matter or even a false document. All it would require is that the defendant *believed* that the document was false as to a material matter. Read that way, however, conviction would be possible under the statute for a bad intent even if the return in fact was not false as to a material matter (despite the taxpayer's intent that it be false). However, section 7206(1) is not construed literally in this respect. As shown by the pattern jury instruction above, the defendant must have made or subscribed a return, statement, or other document that was in fact false as to a material matter.

For example, one case held that substantiality of tax amounts was not required to be charged to the jury because the statute does not require it as an element, even though the indictment had alleged substantiality. The court held: "False statements about income do not have to involve substantial amounts in order to violate this statute."[6] This invites the question whether there is a difference between substantiality and materiality, for the pattern instruction above does require materiality.

What if the taxpayer overstates his income on the return and thus overstates his tax liability? Is the materiality requirement met? A district court handled this

---

[4] [Authors' note: Section 7206(1) charges usually involve filed tax returns. However, the language of the statute embraces any document "which contains or is verified by a written declaration that it is made under penalties of perjury," not just filed returns.]

[5] Fifth Circuit Pattern Jury Instruction 2.97.

[6] United States v. Helmsley, 941 F.2d 71, 92 (2d Cir. 1991), *cert. denied*, 502 U.S. 1091 (1992).

argument in a section 7206(2) prosecution of a taxpayer and his loan broker who had prepared the taxpayer's return overstating income in order to obtain a loan from an organization known as the Money Store Investment Corp. The defendant argued that giving the IRS more than it was due was not material. The court viewed the materiality requirement in section 7206(1) (taxpayer's false statement on return) and section 7206(2) (preparer's false statement on return) as being *in pari materia*. The court reasoned:

> In any event, neither case would govern over *United States v. Peters*, 153 F.3d 445, 461–62 (7th Cir. 1998), on which the government relies. There, the defendant argued that the government had to prove a tax deficiency in order to convict under section 7206(1), which argument amounted to a contention that unless there was a tax deficiency, the false statement was not material. The court rejected that argument, holding that proof of a tax deficiency was not essential to prove materiality. The court set out the elements of the offense including a definition of "material": "A false statement is 'material' when it has 'the potential for hindering the IRS's efforts to monitor and verify the tax liability' of the corporation and the taxpayer." [Q]uoting *United States v. Greenberg*, 735 F.2d 29, 32 (2d Cir. 1984); *see United States v. Di Varco*, 484 F.2d 670, 673 (7th Cir. 1973) (Even though the government did not prove understatement of income, the court held that a false statement as to source of income on a tax return was material, relying in part on the policy that the IRS is entitled to accurate information). There is, of course, no question that the amount of income on a tax return is material in that it would have the potential for hindering the IRS's efforts to monitor and verify [the defendant's] tax liability; thus, it follows that this indictment alleges a violation of section 7206(2).[7]

The application of this element of the offense has nothing to do with the intent of the maker or subscriber. The question is solely one of materiality as determined by the trier of fact. Materiality is heavily fact dependent. But the question that must be answered is: Material relative to what?

The element obviously covers a false statement that materially lowers the actual tax reported on the return. That covers much, but not all, of the ground covered by section 7201. The additional element required by section 7201 is an intent to evade, which need not be shown under section 7206(1). Moreover, as seen above, there is no requirement of tax due and owing.[8] Hence, section 7206(1) can apply when section 7201 cannot. Indeed, section 7206(1) may apply to a false statement associated with full payment of the tax liability or even material overstatement of the tax liability. For this reason, it is sometimes said that evidence that there is no tax due and owing is irrelevant in a tax perjury case. However, such a lack does bear on intent to commit tax perjury.[9]

---

[7] United States v. Bouzanis, 2003-1 U.S.T.C. ¶ 50,315, at 87,825 (N.D. Ill. 2003).

[8] *E.g.*, United States v. Johnson, 558 F.2d 744, 745, *reh'g denied*, 562 F.2d 1258 (5th Cir. 1977), *cert. denied*, 434 U.S. 1065 (1978).

[9] *See* United States v. Loe, 248 F.3d 449, *reh'g & reh'g en banc denied*, 255 F.3d 228 (5th Cir.), *cert. denied*, 534 U.S. 974 (2001).

Moreover, from a prosecutorial judgment-call standpoint, it is less likely that the Government will pursue someone for a false statement when the taxpayer has in fact correctly reported the tax liability, or even overreported and overpaid the tax liability.[10] This is unlike a tax protestor scheme intending to disrupt the system beyond the individual taxpayer involved. And, as described in Chapter 10, if the IRS really suffered no loss (or no material loss) in tax, sentencing under the Sentencing Guidelines will be minimal (almost certainly probation unless the taxpayer has a significant criminal history) and the ripple effect to other taxpayers will be almost minimal because there will be no significant publicity. Accordingly, in virtually every section 7206(1) prosecution, the Government will believe that it can establish a material tax loss and will do so at the time of sentencing.

What, then, is the standard for materiality, if it is to be something other than a gut reaction to the facts in any given case? The courts have applied two tests, only one of which seems satisfactory. Some courts have held that anything required to be disclosed on the return is material. That does not seem wholly satisfactory, for it assumes materiality merely from the IRS's choice to include the disclosure requirement on the return.

The second, more satisfying test is the so-called *Di Varco*[11] test basing the materiality determination upon whether the false item has a natural tendency to influence or impede the IRS in determining and auditing the taxpayer's liability. Under the *Di Varco* test of materiality, for example, a drug dealer who reports his drug activities on Schedule C as a law firm business and pays all taxes due can be convicted, for his statement of the nature of the business could tend to influence or impede the IRS in the determination and substantiation of his correct tax liability.

C. Declaration of Perjury

This element should be evident. The document is usually a return, which contains, just above the signature line, a printed "under penalties of perjury" declaration. This declaration is called the jurat. The section 7206(1) charge is not available if the taxpayer submits a false document without a declaration of perjury. That does not mean that submitting a false document is not a crime, as will be seen from the discussion below of section 7207 and the discussion in Chapter 3 of 18 U.S.C. section 1001. Submitting false documents might also be covered by section 7212 and in specific settings might be covered by section 7206(2) and 18 U.S.C. section 287.

The jurat contained on the Form 1040 states: "Under penalties of perjury, I declare that I have examined this return and accompanying schedules and statements, and to the best of my knowledge and belief, they are true, correct, and

---

[10] For example, assume that a taxpayer lies about having signatory authority over a foreign bank account but properly reports all income he had, including the interest from the foreign bank account that he denied signatory authority over. The Government may have a technical section 7206(1) case, although the proper reporting may put pressure on the Government's ability to prove willfulness because there is no motive to lie.

[11] United States v. Di Varco, 343 F. Supp. 101, 103 (N.D. Ill. 1972), *aff'd*, 484 F.2d 670 (7th Cir. 1973), *cert. denied*, 415 U.S. 916 (1974); *see also* United States v. Pirro, 212 F.3d 86 (2d Cir. 2000) (*quoting* United States v. Peters, 153 F.3d 445, 461 (7th Cir. 1998), *cert. denied*, 525 U.S. 1070 (1999)).

complete." The schedules and statements are thus included in the jurat.

Occasionally, taxpayers will submit false documents with the jurat stricken. If that occurs, the false statements therein cannot be prosecuted under section 7206(1), but, as developed below, the Government has ample alternative criminal prosecution options — for example, section 7203 (failure to file) and 18 U.S.C. section 1001 (false statements) — with respect to this type of conduct. In addition, striking out the jurat has unpleasant civil consequence. Submitting a Form 1040 with an excised jurat does not constitute the filing of a return.[12] Accordingly, section 6651(a)(1) delinquency penalties can be imposed, and the section 6501 statute of limitations on assessment does not begin to run. Moreover, of course, excising the jurat increases the chance that the IRS will audit the "return."

D. Belief as to Truth

In submitting the document, the defendant must believe that the document is not true as to a material matter. As discussed above, the misstatement must be material. The question is subjective. Did the defendant believe that the document was false as to a material matter (in addition to the document actually being false as to a material matter)?

What if the return was actually false as to a material matter; the taxpayer subjectively believed it to be false; but the taxpayer did not believe the matter was material? For example, assume the local thug has a protection racket in his neighborhood but wants to pay his tax. He dutifully reports his gross receipts and doesn't claim any deductions, but falsely reports that it came from a legitimate consulting business. As noted above, falsely stating the activity giving rise to the income is material. But would this local thug believe that it was material? Not being a sophisticate in the imperatives of the tax system, this thug might believe that if he correctly reports (even overreports) his income, the IRS can have no beef and any errors would not be material. Of course, the thug must know that his act of misdescribing his income source may mislead the IRS and make it less likely that the IRS will audit. But to him, that is not material since he has correctly reported his income. The thug takes the stand and testifies that the misdescription was based upon his concern that the IRS would turn it over to state or local vice authorities and that he had no idea that it would affect tax administration. Consider whether he is guilty under section 7206(1) and whether this is a jury issue.

E. Willfulness

The taxpayer must have submitted the document willfully with the intent to mislead and thus violate the law. Willfulness is the same as was discussed in Chapter 2A under section 7201 — "a voluntary, intentional violation of a known legal duty."[13]

---

[12] *E.g.*, IRC § 6065; *see, e.g.*, Beard v. Commissioner, 82 T.C. 766, 777 (1984) (court reviewed), *aff'd per curiam*, 793 F.2d 139 (6th Cir. 1986).

[13] *E.g.*, Cheek v. United States, 498 U.S. 192, 200 (1991).

This element tends to merge with prior elements. If the taxpayer submitted a document knowingly false as to a material matter, he almost certainly did so willfully — unless, of course, he can show that some compulsion negates willfulness. The devil made me do it will not be a defense, but its cousin (lack of mental capacity to commit the offense) might be.

F. Tax Due and Owing Not Required

As seen above, a tax due and owing is not an element of section 7206(1) as it is with section 7201. Since the Government sometimes encounters difficulty in proving a material tax due and owing, it will often charge the taxpayer under section 7206(1) when it could have charged the taxpayer under section 7201. This eases the Government's burden at trial. And, as will be seen in Chapter 10 under the Sentencing Guidelines discussion, the punishment is generally the same for a conviction under section 7206(1) as it would have been under section 7201. Hence, in order to lighten its burden and get the maximum bang for its prosecutorial buck, the Government may charge under section 7206(1).

G. Required Documents

The Fifth Circuit has limited section 7206(1) to situations involving documents required by statute or regulation.[14] However, other circuits have rejected this limitation,[15] and even the Fifth Circuit has limited its holding.[16]

In a variation of this theme, taxpayers have argued that, if the document is not required to be filed, then the filing of a false document cannot be prosecuted under section 7206(1) or its companion section 7206(2). In one case,[17] the defendants filed false Forms 8300 (currency transaction reports) naming individuals they desired to harass and they incited others to do likewise. In each of the instances, the persons named had not paid cash in excess of $10,000. The IRS prosecuted the defendants under sections 7206(1) and 7206(2). The defendants argued that, if there is no duty to file a return — as there would not be if they had not received cash in excess of $10,000 — they could not be prosecuted for filing a form with false information. They argued that either such conduct cannot be a willful violation or the falsity cannot be material. The court handily rejected the argument because, even if the defendants had no duty to file the return, once they did so, they had an obligation to file a true and correct return. Filing a return with knowingly false information is, therefore, willful and material if, as noted earlier, the false information would have a tendency to influence the operations of the IRS. Obviously, the defendant's intent with respect to the false CTRs was to cause the IRS to expend resources dealing with the named individuals — thus harassing them.

---

[14] United States v. Levy, 533 F.2d 969 (5th Cir. 1976).

[15] *E.g.*, United States v. Holroyd, 732 F.2d 1122 (2d Cir. 1984).

[16] *See* United States v. Damon, 676 F.2d 1060 (5th Cir. 1982) (holding that schedules attached to the signed return are part of the document required to be signed).

[17] United States v. Anderson, 353 F.3d 490 (6th Cir. 2003), *cert. denied*, 541 U.S. 1068 (2004).

H. *Ingredient Technology*

A key section 7206(1) case is *United States v. Ingredient Technology Corp.*[18] The Government prosecuted a corporation and some of its officers for conspiracy (a concept discussed below) and for section 7206(1) violation, for a scheme to avoid invading the corporate taxpayer's LIFO base level, which would have resulted in significant tax. The LIFO method of accounting treats the last purchased inventory as the first out. (By contrast, the FIFO method treats the first purchased inventory as the first out.) In a period in which the cost of inventory is rising, the taxpayer gets a benefit (higher cost of goods sold and less taxable income) so long as the year-end inventory level is sustained. The benefit is that tax attributable to the economic activity is deferred. (It operates somewhat like a tax shelter, at least as compared to its FIFO counterpart.) The deferral, however, begins to end as and when the inventory level decreases. The LIFO base is said to be eroded or invaded. In effect, what happens as inventory declines is that the historical low cost of the inventory items paid many years ago gets assigned as cost of goods sold. Since the historic cost is so low, much larger amounts of taxable income are generated.

The corporation wanted to avoid invading its LIFO base, *i.e.*, decreasing its inventory relative to prior periods. But the corporation also wanted to enhance profits by better managing inventory. This meant, generally, keeping the minimum inventory possible for its business operations.[19] Recognizing that this business imperative would, if sustained through the end of the year, cause its LIFO base to be eroded, thus generating the deferred taxes, the officers of the corporation entered into contracts whereby the corporation purchased inventory (raw sugar) at year-end (thus increasing inventory so that the LIFO base was not invaded) and immediately after year-end sold the sugar back to the company from which it had purchased it. Physical storage of the underlying sugar did not change hands; only raw title changed hands for the short period. There was no profit on the transaction, and it was done solely to show a large amount of inventory on hand at the end of the year.

Two other significant facts were *sub rosa*. First, the officers of the corporation and the putative seller or re-purchaser of the sugar entered into a secret agreement as to the resale of the sugar. Second, evidencing that the seller or re-purchaser considered it a sham from the inception, the seller or re-purchaser declared title to the sugar to a regular customer with whom it had already entered into a contract.

As a defense to the section 7206(1) charge, the defendants argued that, as a matter of law, the corporation was entitled to include the inventory because it had legal title and risk of loss. The court rejected the argument, treating the entire arrangement as a sham, devoid of business purpose, and done solely to affect tax liability. In so holding, the court relied on Supreme Court authority for the proposition that taxation is concerned with the reality of actual command over

---

[18] 698 F.2d 88 (2d Cir.), *cert. denied*, 462 U.S. 1131 (1983).

[19] This was a rough precursor of "Just in Time" inventory concepts.

property rather than the refinements of title.[20] Here, the seller or re-purchaser had command and even sold the same sugar to one of its customers while it was purportedly owned by the corporation. The court concluded:

> We conclude that the concept of inventory from an accounting point of view and the term inventory in the applicable Treasury Regulations would be meaningless were there to be included in the term or concept property bought, agreed to be resold, never intended to be utilized in the trade or business of the taxpayer (except for tax purposes), and in fact under the corporate taxpayer's dominion, control, and at its risk about as long as the pea in the proverbial shell game is under the shell.[21]

The court also rejected a *James-Garber* type argument — which it styled a Due Process argument — that the legal defects in the planning were not sufficiently clear that it could be the subject of criminal prosecution. The defendants knew what they were doing was wrong which is why they had the secret agreement and even lied to their auditors about the pre-commitment to resell. The court also rejected the *Garber* holding that uncertainty in the law is a jury issue as to which evidence could be adduced.[22]

I. Further Notes on Materiality

Section 7206(1) requires that the false statement be material and that the taxpayer acted with the knowledge that it was material. Logically, one would think, the jury must make those findings. For many years, however, most courts of appeals held that materiality was a question for the judge to decide rather than a question that was submitted to the jury. In *United States v. Gaudin*,[23] the Supreme Court rejected that notion, stating that when materiality is part of the element of the offense, it is a mixed question of fact and law that must be decided by the jury. The Court reasoned:

> [T]he resolution of the question before us seems simple. The Constitution gives a criminal defendant the right to demand that a jury find him guilty of all the elements of the crime with which he is charged; one of the elements in the present case is materiality; respondent therefore had a right to have the jury decide materiality.[24]

The Court handily rejected the Government's attempts to avoid the force of this relatively simple syllogism (which had escaped most courts of appeals for years). *Gaudin* involved a prosecution under 18 U.S.C. section 1001, which makes it a felony to make false statements as to a material fact. This "false statement" crime in Title 18 frequently surfaces in tax prosecutions because of statements made to IRS officers, particularly revenue agents conducting audits and revenue officers trying to collect assessed taxes.

---

20 698 F.2d at 95 (quoting Corliss v. Bowers, 281 U.S. 376, 378 (1930)).

21 698 F.2d at 95.

22 *Id.* at 96–98.

23 515 U.S. 506 (1995).

24 *Id.* at 511.

Materiality is an element of many crimes, either explicitly or implicitly, and section 7206(1) is one of them. Accordingly, *Gaudin* has sweeping implications in the many criminal contexts in which materiality is either expressly required by the statute or, if it is missing from the statute, in which the statute is interpreted to include this requirement. After *Gaudin*, the defendant and the Government must make their materiality pitches to the jury, and the jury may very well be swayed by different considerations than a judge would.

The Court in *Gaudin* said as to materiality: "The parties also agree on the definition of 'materiality': The statement must have a natural tendency to influence, or [be] capable of influencing, the decision of the decision-making body to which it was addressed."[25] This is a good working definition for tax crimes as well.

Gaudin raised significant questions as to what to do about the many cases in the pipeline or already finally decided in which a defendant was convicted without this critical issue being submitted to and decided by the jury. In many of these trials, the defendant's counsel did not object to the decision of the materiality issue by the judge. Often, that was the law of the circuit, and to object would have been meaningless. After *Gaudin*, serious issues revolved around whether these defendants would get new trials. If some would and some wouldn't, how would the cut be made? At this point, concerns of managing the caseload crept into the judicial decision-making process and caused much judicial thrashing over the unknowable issue of whether the defendants' fundamental rights were violated. In *Neder v. United States*, the Supreme Court held the issue was subject to a harmless error analysis. Harmless error will be found, and thus conviction affirmed, only if it is found harmless beyond a reasonable doubt.[26]

J. True But Misleading Answers

In *United States v. Reynolds*,[27] the taxpayer skimmed money from a public project. However, he elected to file a Form 1040EZ which is supposed to be filed only by relatively low-income taxpayers. The 1040EZ requests information only for wages, salaries, tips, and interest. The taxpayer dutifully inserted all information requested on the return. The taxpayer did not include the skimmed income because it fit none of the categories on the form. The question was whether he could be prosecuted under section 7206(1). The Government's theory was that by including only the information requested on the form, he implicitly represented that he had no other income. The court responded:

> The prosecutor's argument that by filing Form 1040EZ, a taxpayer implicitly represents that he has no additional income has more substance, but this is not the theory in the indictment. It charged that line 7, specifically, was false, and line 7 is derived arithmetically from other lines.

---

25 *Id.* at 509.

26 527 U.S. 1 (1999). For an example of the application of the *Neder* test, see United States v. Foster, 229 F.3d 1196 (5th Cir. 2000), *cert. denied*, 531 U.S. 1197 (2001). *Cf.* Whorton v. Bockting, 549 U.S. 406 (2007) (discussing when a new rule constitutes a "watershed rule" of criminal procedure, such that it should be applied retroactively on collateral review).

27 919 F.2d 435 (7th Cir. 1990), *cert. denied*, 499 U.S. 942 (1991).

> Section 7206(1) is a perjury statute, and literal truth is a defense to perjury, even if the answer is highly misleading. Using the wrong form does not violate § 7206(1). If the form has an open-ended line calling for § 61 income, and the taxpayer leaves some income out, § 7206(1) applies. Form 1040EZ is anything but open-ended, however. The right charges are tax evasion (26 U.S.C. § 7201) and failure to supply information required by law (26 U.S.C. § 7203). Reynolds did not reveal his complete income (§ 7203) and evaded taxation on that income (§ 7201). Neither the indictment nor the charge to the jury set out the elements of these offenses, so the problem is deeper than a citation to the wrong statute in the indictment. We vacate Reynolds' tax convictions, without foreclosing indictment and trial for the offenses that match the prosecution's theory of the case.[28]

In *United States v. Pirro*,[29] the chairman of the board of a hospital center brought to Pirro's attention some commercial property that, if purchased, could be leased to physicians affiliated with the hospital. An S Corporation ("Properties") purchased the building and leased it to another corporation, apparently associated with the hospital. Properties was owned 90% by Pirro and 10% by another person. Properties received lease payments and paid some portion of the lease payments to another corporation wholly owned by Pirro which, in turn, paid those amounts to another corporation that was wholly owned by the chairman. S Corporation returns require the disclosure of the stockholders of the S Corporation. On the S Corporation return (Form 1120S) for the year, Pirro did not disclose that the chairman was a stockholder nor did he disclose any other ownership interest of the chairman. The indictment charged that the chairman had acquired an "ownership interest" in Properties, that Pirro failed to report that ownership interest, and that, by that failure, Pirro violated section 7206(1).

At trial, Pirro moved to dismiss on the ground that the charge related to a requirement that the law did not specify. In particular, the law requires that stockholders be identified but says nothing about a person having an "ownership interest" which was the allegation in the indictment. The district court dismissed the count.

Section 6037(a) requires that the return of an S Corporation include "the names and addresses of all persons owning stock in the corporation . . . [and] the number of shares of stock owned by each shareholder." No other ownership interests are identified or required to be disclosed by the statute or by the Form 1120S. (Of course, in a corporation, the classic paradigm is that all ownership interests are nominated stock.) The court held that there is no legal requirement that ownership interests be disclosed unless they are stock. Hence, Pirro could not have violated a known legal duty in disclosing the two stockholders without further disclosing a nonstockholder having some "ownership interest" which was the only allegation made in the indictment. In short, "[t]he tax law provided Pirro no notice that failure to report an 'ownership interest' was criminal."[30] Quoting from other appellate

---

[28] *Id.* at 437.

[29] 212 F.3d 86 (2d Cir. 2000).

[30] *Id.* at 91.

decisions, the court distinguished a civil case from a criminal case as follows:

> [C]riminal prosecutions are a different story. These must rest on a violation of a clear rule of law. If defendants [in a tax case] could not have ascertained the legal standards applicable to their conduct, criminal proceedings may not be used to define and punish an alleged failure to conform to those standards.
>
> "It is settled," this court observed in the analogous criminal tax case of *United States v. Critzer*, "that where the law is vague or highly debatable, a defendant — actually or imputedly — lacks the requisite intent to violate it." 498 F.2d 1160, 1162 (4th Cir. 1974). Criminal prosecution for the violation of an unclear duty itself violates the clear constitutional duty of the government to warn citizens whether particular conduct is legal or illegal.[31]

The court of appeals rejected the Government's attempt to rely upon cases such as *Ingredient Technology* where the court, in a section 7206(1) prosecution, declined to be bogged down by the technicalities of ownership. The court provided no analysis, and simply summarily concluded that *Ingredient Technology* did not involve the situation before the court. Are *Pirro* and *Ingredient Technology* reconcilable?

The law of perjury in its usual context under 18 U.S.C. section 1621 does not permit prosecution for literally true but misleading answers, at least in a judicial proceeding in which the cross-examiner can follow through on misleading responses.[32] *Reynolds* and *Pirro* are consistent with this general concept in a document setting. Keep in mind in this regard that the IRS can fine tune its documents to address the specific issues, thus laying the foundation for future section 7206(1) prosecutions.

III. SECTION 7206(2) AIDING AND ASSISTING FALSE RETURN

A. The Elements Generally

The general federal crimes in Title 18 of the United States Code include the offense of aiding and abetting someone else's commission of a crime: 18 U.S.C. Section 2.[33] Section 7206(2) is the Internal Revenue Code's loose parallel to the Title 18 offense, but the two are not the same.[34] As will be seen in Chapter 3, Title 18 aiding and abetting requires that the person who was aided and abetted be guilty of a crime. One person alone cannot be guilty of Title 18 aiding and abetting

---

[31] *Id.* (citations and punctuation marks omitted).

[32] *E.g.*, Bronston v. United States, 409 U.S. 352 (1973).

[33] Strictly speaking, 18 U.S.C. section 2 does not create an independent crime. Instead, it eliminates the common law distinction between principals and accessories, so that both sets of actors can be punished alike for the applicable offense.

[34] *See* United States v. Williams, 644 F.2d 696, 701 (8th Cir.), *cert. denied*, 454 U.S. 841 (1981).

without some criminal conduct of another. In contrast, section 7206(2) does not require that the person whose taxes are reduced or affected have any knowledge of the proscribed conduct. One person acting alone can be guilty of a crime under section 7206(2).

The elements of section 7206(2) aiding and assisting are described by the following jury instruction. The Fifth Circuit Pattern Jury Instructions provide:

> Title 26, United States Code, Section 7206(2), makes it a crime for anyone willfully to aid or assist in the preparation under the internal revenue laws of a document which is false or fraudulent as to any material matter.
>
> For you to find the defendant guilty of this crime, you must be convinced that the government has proved each of the following beyond a reasonable doubt:
>
> First: That the defendant aided in [assisted in] [procured] [counseled] [advised] the preparation [presentation] of a return [an affidavit] [a claim] arising under [in connection with any matter arising under] the internal revenue laws;
>
> Second: That this return [affidavit] [claim] falsely stated that ___________ [state] material matters asserted, e.g., ___________ received gross income of $________ during 20________].
>
> Third: That the defendant knew that the statement in the return [affidavit] [claim] was false;
>
> Fourth: That the false statement was material; and
>
> Fifth: That the defendant aided in [assisted in] [procured] [counseled] [advised] the preparation [presentation] of this false statement willfully, that is, with intent to violate a known legal duty.
>
> It is not necessary that the government prove that the falsity or fraud was with the knowledge or consent of the person authorized or required to present such return [claim] [affidavit] [document].
>
> A statement is "material" if it has a natural tendency to influence, or is capable of influencing, the Internal Revenue Service in investigating or auditing a tax return or in verifying or monitoring the reporting of income by a taxpayer.[35]

B. Willful Assistance

Section 7206(2) is designed to hit the person other than the taxpayer who assists in the preparation of a false document, including a false return. The prototypical target of the provision is the tax return preparer,[36] but it can sweep much broader

[35] Fifth Circuit Pattern Jury Instruction 2.98.

[36] *See* United States v. Kelley, 105 F.2d 912 (2d Cir. 1939).

than tax return preparers. The statute "has a broad sweep, and makes all forms of willful assistance in preparing a false return an offense."[37] The statute, thus, covers tax shelter promoters who prepare false documents that appear to support a false position taken on the return and preparers of Schedule K-1's or appraisals for tax issues (such as charitable contributions) who provide false information which is then incorporated by innocent taxpayers on their returns. *United States v. Crum*[38] involved a tax shelter investment in beavers (that's right!). The defendant, Crum, was the beaver raiser, normally a functionary in the overall arrangement, which had been devised by much more crafty people, but Crum did participate in some of the promotional activities and participated in backdating the contracts in order for the taxpayers to appear to qualify for tax benefits to which they were not entitled. Crum argued that section 7206 applied only to tax return preparers. The court rejected the argument because the plain language of the statute contains no such limitation.

C. Document False as to a Material Matter

The document must be false as to any material matter. The same materiality standards apply as discussed above. There is no requirement as there is for section 7206(1) that the defendant charged have signed under penalty of perjury or even have signed a document at all.

D. Willfulness

This same willfulness standards apply as discussed in Chapter 2A.

IV. SECTION 7212(a) CORRUPTLY IMPEDING TAX ADMINISTRATION

A. The Elements Generally

Section 7212(a) is violated by: (i) "corruptly or by force or threats of force" trying to impede Government tax officials from performing their duties; or (ii) "in any other way corruptly or by force or threats of force . . . obstruct[ing] or imped[ing], or endeavor[ing] to obstruct or impede, the due administration of [the Internal Revenue Code]."[39]

It should be obvious that the conduct described in portion (i) of the statute is criminal.[40] Thus, we will focus on portion (ii). Portion (ii) is commonly called the

---

[37] United States v. Hooks, 848 F.2d 785, 791 (7th Cir. 1988); *see also* United States v. Coveney, 995 F.2d 578, 588 (5th Cir. 1993).

[38] 529 F.2d 1380 (9th Cir. 1976).

[39] For the history and interpretation of section 7212(a), see John A. Townsend, *Tax Obstruction Crimes: Is Making the IRS's Job Harder Enough?*, 9 Hous. Bus. & Tax L.J. 255 (2009). The question posed by the article's title applies to section 7212 and also to conspiracies to defraud the United States by interfering with the operations of the IRS. The conspiracy aspect of the question is addressed in Chapter 3.

[40] The fact patterns presented in such cases offer virtually "slam dunk" convictions. *See, e.g.*, United

Omnibus Clause, for reasons which will become apparent. Precisely what conduct the Omnibus Clause criminalizes may be somewhat amorphous.

Section 7212's Omnibus Clause is specific to tax administration, but there is a Title 18 counterpart (18 U.S.C. § 1505) that generally covers analogous conduct before all agencies or congressional committees. In pertinent part, section 1505 provides:

> Whoever corruptly, or by threats or force, or by any threatening letter or communication influences, obstructs or impedes or endeavors to influence, obstruct, or impede the due and proper administration of the law under which any pending proceeding is being had before any department or agency of the United States, or the due and proper exercise of the power of inquiry under which any inquiry or investigation is being had by either House, or any committee of either House or any joint committee of the Congress —
>
> Shall be fined under this title or imprisoned not more than five years, or both.

Technically, conduct subject to Section 7212(a)'s Omnibus Clause might be charged under this Title 18 provision. In tax administration cases, however, the more specific crime under section 7212(a) typically is charged. Nonetheless, interpretation of section 1505 offers guidance in interpreting section 7212(a)'s Omnibus Clause.[41]

Many circuits do not have pattern jury instructions as to section 7212. Accordingly, set out below are the pattern jury instructions contained in the CTM. Care should be taken in using CTM instructions because they state the Government's best case and, thus, do not have the more objective imprimatur of judicially sanctioned pattern jury instructions. Thus, while trial courts almost routinely accept their circuit's pattern jury instructions, subject to such modifications as required by the evidence at trial, a court will adopt an instruction based on the CTM only if the court is persuaded independently that the instruction is well founded in the law and in the evidence in the case at hand. A defense counsel, thus, may have some opportunity to persuade the court to add some nuances. Still, the CTM

States v. Lovern, 293 F.3d 695 (4th Cir.), *cert. denied*, 537 U.S. 1058 (2002) (holding that, although the district court's failure to submit the element of whether the official was acting under Title 26 was error, the harmless error doctrine could be applied if the error was "harmless beyond a reasonable doubt.") The *Lovern* court cited *Neder v. United States*, 527 U.S. 1, 7 (1999), and *United States v. Gaudin*, 515 U.S. 506, 522–23 (1995) (discussed in Subpart II.I *supra*).

Similar issues can arise under state law as well. A tax preparer who sent threatening letters to the assistant district attorney who was prosecuting him was sentenced to between three and six years in prison. Noeleen G. Walder, *Tax Preparer Who Threatened Prosecution Is Sentenced to 3 to 6 Years*, available at http://www.lexis.com/research/retrieve?_m=8c1b693e68e5bb461734cc406f2f6776&csvc=bl&cform=searchForm&_fmtstr=FULL&docnum=1&_startdoc=1&wchp=dGLbVzk-zSkAl&_md5=4202eed393cd596c43d5089593bccf81 (Sept. 20, 2010).

[41] Section 1505 and a parallel Title 18 provision, section 1503 have similar language and, thus, are useful in interpreting the Omnibus Clause. *See* CTM 17.04[2] (citing United States v. Williams, 644 F.2d 696, 700–01 & n.11 (8th Cir.), *cert. denied*, 454 U.S. 841 (1981), and United States v. Martin, 747 F.2d 1404, 1409 (11th Cir. 1984), *reh'g denied*, 756 F.2d 885 (11th Cir. 1985)); United States Attorney's Resource Manual, title 9 ("Protection of Government Processes"). Title 18 obstruction is discussed in Chapter 3.

instructions offer a good point of departure for analysis. The instructions are as follows:

> In order for you to find the defendant guilty of this charge, the Government must prove each of the following elements beyond a reasonable doubt:
>
> *First*: The defendant in any way corruptly;
>
> *Second*: Endeavored to;
>
> *Third*: Obstruct or impede the due administration of the Internal Revenue Laws.
>
> Endeavor means to knowingly and intentionally act or to knowingly and intentionally make any effort which has a reasonable tendency to bring about the desired result.
>
> An endeavor is any effort or any act or attempt to effectuate an arrangement or to try to do something, the natural and probable consequences of which is to obstruct or impede the due administration of the Internal Revenue Laws.
>
> To act "corruptly" is to act with the intent to secure an unlawful advantage or benefit either for oneself or for another.
>
> To "obstruct or impede" is to hinder or prevent from progress, check, stop, also to retard the progress of, make accomplishment difficult and slow.[42]

B. Corrupt Conduct

DOJ Tax interprets this element as follows: "'Corruptly' in the context of section 7212(a) means to act with the intent to secure an unlawful advantage or benefit either for oneself or another."[43] So viewed, there is no requirement of evil intent. Acting with an intent to secure an unlawful advantage is antisocial, but it may not be evil. The CTM also justifies this broad reading by referring to the statutory phrase "in any other way."

The benefit sought need not be financial. For example, the filing of a false Form 1099 to harass perceived enemies would be an unlawful advantage.[44] And, the targets need not be IRS employees or officials, since false 1099's or other tax reports related to other taxpayers are equally disruptive of tax administration.

---

42 CTM Government's Proposed Jury Instructions Nos. 26.7212(a)-2, 3, 4, 6 & 7 (citations omitted).

43 CTM 17.04[1], *citing* United States v. Reeves, 752 F.2d 995, 998 (5th Cir.), *reh'g denied*, 757 F.2d 284 (5th Cir.), *cert. denied*, 474 U.S. 834 (1985) (cited with approval in *United States v. Popkin*, 943 F.2d 1535, 1540 (11th Cir. 1991), *cert. denied*, 503 U.S. 1004 (1992).

44 United States v. Yagow, 953 F.2d 423, 427 (8th Cir. 1992) (*relying on* United States v. Reeves, 752 F.2d 995, 998 (5th Cir.), *cert. denied*, 474 U.S. 834 (1985)); United States v. Reeves, 782 F.2d 1323, 1325–26 (5th Cir.), *cert. denied*, 479 U.S. 837 (1986); *see also* United States v. Dykstra, 991 F.2d 450, 453 (8th Cir.), *cert. denied*, 510 U.S. 880 (1993).

The Government sometimes gives the impression that it thinks that section 7212 criminalizes any conduct that just makes the IRS's job harder. It made a similar claim in *Caldwell*, a case involving a *Klein* conspiracy which, as interpreted, convers the same conduct as section 7212 (except for the *Klein* conspiracy requirement of multiple actors with a joint undertaking).[45] Judge Kozinski rejected that claim in *Caldwell*, and we think it should be rejected in the section 7212 context as well. Taxpayers and their representative take myriad actions every day with the intent to make the IRS's job harder. *Corruptly* means something far worse than merely intentional conduct. The precise demarcation may necessarily be uncertain, but it can be discerned in particular cases, and the Government's expansive claims can be reigned in.

In *Doss*, the Ninth Circuit interpreted the parallel requirement in one of the general obstruction provisions, 18 U.S.C. section 1512(b), that the defendant "corruptly persuade" with the intent to effect certain acts, including withholding testimony. The court held that merely persuading one to withhold testimony is not enough. The act of persuading must be corrupt, and "corrupt" means something wrongful.[46] *Doss* relied significantly on the Supreme Court's *Arthur Andersen* decision, which was decided after other cases which would have virtually conflated "corrupt" and "persuade," leaving only a requirement that defendant act intentionally.[47] *Doss* and *Andersen* hold that corruptly means something different from merely intentional. A similar analysis can apply to the tax obstruction requirement that the defendant "corruptly endeavor."

C. Endeavoring

The jury instruction definition in the CTM adequately describes the endeavoring element.[48] "Endeavoring" connotes somewhat the same notion as "attempts" in section 7201. There must be affirmative action taken.

D. Obstructing or Impeding

The defendant must have taken the action with the intent to impede. The actions need not have succeeded.[49] For example, disgruntled taxpayers or their allies sometimes file retaliatory liens against IRS or DOJ personnel to deter or distract them from continuing investigations or prosecutions. This object is never accomplished, but the conduct remains illegal under various statutes, including section 7212.[50]

---

[45] This is a paraphrase of Judge Kozinski's formulation of the claim for the *Klein* conspiracy. *See* United States v. Caldwell, 989 F.2d 1056, 1058 (9th Cir. 1993).

[46] United States v. Doss, 630 F.3d 1181 (9th Cir. 2011).

[47] Arthur Andersen LLP v. United States, 544 U.S. 696 (2005).

[48] For an approved jury instruction on "endeavor" similar to the one above, see *United States v. Kelly*, 147 F.3d 172, 177 (2d Cir. 1998).

[49] United States v. Rosnow, 977 F.2d 399 (8th Cir.), *reh'g denied*, 981 F.2d 970 (8th Cir. 1992), *cert. denied sub nom.* Dewey v. United States, 507 U.S. 990 (1993).

[50] *E.g.*, 2012 TNT 59-43 (Mar. 27, 2012) (Washington taxpayer sentenced to 41 months in prison for filing $20 billion in false liens against IRS revenue officer and others); 2011 TNT 138-43 (July 19, 2011)

E. Background

The expansive use of the Omnibus Clause has been a matter of discussion for some time.[51] The provision was initially enacted by Congress to deal with improper attempts to influence IRS investigations. The language of the Omnibus Clause, however, is capable of broad and uncertain construction. What is "corrupt conduct?" The statute doesn't tell us. Is it like pornography, so we'll know it when we see it?

Until fairly recently, the Government rarely used the Omnibus Clause because there were more focused crimes for the types of conduct that have historically concerned the Government. Thus, for example, if the taxpayer failed to maintain records so that the IRS would be hampered in its ability to audit, the Government could still bring a tax evasion charge under section 7201. When the Government somewhat belatedly saw the Omnibus Clause as an opportunity to expand the scope of its criminal enforcement weapons, it explained its earlier inaction as "timid."[52]

DOJ's Deputy Assistant Attorney General for Tax and a prominent practitioner squared off over the issue. First, the DOJ official:

> Tax obstruction cases under section 7212 have been increasing, Matthews said, but account for less than 5 percent of the cases. "I guess comparing where we were a few years ago, I guess you could call it an epidemic," he said.
>
> "The reason why the government is using that statute more is because it really allows us to tell us a story in the indictment, particularly when we face fact patterns where they're long and detailed, complicated courses of conduct, particularly if they're multiple years, conduct that doesn't neatly fall into tax years," Matthews said.

And the practitioner's side:

> "The children at the IRS found a new toy to play with" in using Section 7212, said Robert S. Fink, with Kostelanetz & Fink, New York.

(Florida taxpayer, currently serving five years for tax fraud, pleaded guilty to impeding the IRS and filing false liens against prosecutors, investigators, and court personnel involved in his trial).

[51] *See, e.g.*, Kathryn Kenneally, *White Collar Crime: Ill-Advised Government Theories*, 23 CHAMPION 68 (1999).

[52] In *United States v. Williams*, 644 F.2d 696, 699 (8th Cir.), *cert. denied*, 454 U.S. 841 (1981), the court said:

> Our research, however, has disclosed no case brought by the Government under the more general "omnibus clause" of section 7212. We note, therefore, that the proper interpretation of this clause presents us with an issue of first impression, and that we proceed cautiously where for over twenty-five years the Government has feared to tread.
>
> At one time the Government contended that section 7212 applied only to conduct involving force or threats of force. *See United States v. Henderson*, 386 F. Supp. 1048, 1055–56 (S.D.N.Y. 1974). The Government in the present case has characterized its position in *Henderson* as "timid."

The government is using Section 7212 in a way that the section was not intended to be used, Fink said. The most visible Section 7212 case involved National Basketball Association referees, including one who was charged with cashing in a first class ticket for a coach class ticket and pocketing the difference, he said.[53]

F. Relationship to More Specific Crimes

The CTM formerly stated:

> In general, the use of the "omnibus" provision of Section 7212(a) should be reserved for conduct occurring after a tax return has been filed — typically conduct designed to impede or obstruct an audit or criminal tax investigation, when 18 U.S.C. Section 371 charges are unavailable due to insufficient evidence of a conspiracy. However, this charge might also be appropriate when directed at parties who engage in large-scale obstructive conduct involving actual or potential tax returns of third parties. Continually assisting taxpayers in the filing of false returns or engaging in other conduct designed to make audits difficult; and other numerous, large-scale violations of 26 U.S.C. Section 7206(2) or 18 U.S.C. Section 287 (as it pertains to refund claims for other or fictitious taxpayers), are examples of situations when Section 7212(a) charges might be appropriate. Such an application of the "omnibus" clause is consistent with what we believe to be the overall purpose of Section 7212(a), which is to penalize conduct aimed directly at IRS personnel in the performance of their duties, and at general IRS administration of the federal tax enforcement program, but not to penalize tax evasion as such.
>
> The omnibus clause should not be utilized when other more specific charges are available and adequately reflect the gravamen of the offense. Section 7212(a) pleadings might be utilized to set forth allegations concerning attempted conspiracies with undercover agents to impede or impair the functions of the IRS, but no Section 7212(a) count should be predicated on such conduct alone, as that conduct by itself would rarely be sufficient to impede or impair the due administration of the Internal Revenue Code.[54]

More recently, the Government has taken a more expansive view of the role of section 7212. This is reflected in the current version of the CTM, which replaces the above with the following:

> A § 7212(a) omnibus clause charge is particularly appropriate for corrupt conduct that is intended to impede an IRS audit or investigation. Examples of such conduct include, but are not limited to, providing false information, destroying evidence, attempting to influence a witness to give false testimony, and harassing an IRS employee.

---

[53] *Level of Criminal Tax Fraud Cases Leveling Off, Justice Department Official Says*, 45 DTR G-2 (Mar. 9, 1998).

[54] CTM 3.00 (2001) (incorporating then-effective Tax Division Directive No. 77).

A § 7212(a) omnibus clause charge can also be authorized in appropriate circumstances to prosecute a person who, prior to any audit or investigation, engaged in large-scale obstructive conduct involving the tax liability of third parties. Examples include, but are not limited to, assisting in preparing or filing a large number of fraudulent returns or other tax forms, or engaging in other corrupt conduct designed to obstruct the IRS from carrying out its lawful functions.

The omnibus clause should not be used as a substitute for a charge directly related to tax liability — such as tax evasion or filing a false tax return — if such a charge is readily provable. Alleging and proving an actual or intended tax loss may result in an enhanced sentence and may estop a target from contesting application of a civil fraud penalty.

The fact that conduct that violated § 7212(a) was in furtherance of a preexisting criminal scheme — for example, an ongoing conspiracy or a continuing attempt to evade taxes — does not preclude prosecution under § 7212(a). Targets who first commit primary tax crimes and then engage in conduct designed to obstruct the IRS can be held accountable for the obstruction and punished more severely than those who do not engage in additional criminal conduct.

When the obstruction involves a grand jury investigation, obstruction of justice or perjury charges (*e.g.*, 18 U.S.C. §§ 1510, 1512 or 1623) that more specifically address the conduct are preferable to § 7212(a) charges.[55]

UNITED STATES v. KELLY

United States Court of Appeals, Second Circuit
147 F.3d 172 (1998)

[Authors' note: The taxpayer, an attorney and experienced businessman, negotiated an agreement upon leaving the employment of a corporation to be paid consulting fees aggregating to $244,200 over an 18-month period. The corporation actually paid these earlier than the consulting services were to commence and treated them as earned by the taxpayer by the time of payment. It appeared that there would really be no consulting going on. After receiving the payments, the taxpayer entered an agreement with his corporation, Condor, assigning to Condor the taxpayer's duties under the agreement and the right to the fees under the first contract. By then, the taxpayer had already received the fees, and there were no real duties under the contract. The taxpayer then wrote to the first corporation and asked that all tax reporting forms with respect to the transaction be issued to Condor. The first corporation refused and issued a Form 1099 to the taxpayer. The taxpayer reported the receipts on his Schedule C, but zeroed that reporting out with a deduction in an equivalent amount and noted that he had assigned the income to Condor.

In an ensuing audit, the taxpayer met with the agent twice. In the first meeting,

---

[55] CTM 3.00 (incorporating current Tax Division Directive No. 129, superseding former Directive No. 77).

the taxpayer advised that he had deducted the item because it had been assigned to Condor and gave the agent copies of the two agreements. The taxpayer also represented that Condor had filed no tax return for the year. In the second meeting, the taxpayer took the same position as to the reason for deducting the item, but advised the agent this time that Condor "picked up" the income, which is common parlance for, and the agent took it to mean, that Condor had reported the income on its tax return. The agent thereafter determined that Condor had in fact filed no tax return. The agent also subsequently determined that the taxpayer had not in fact actually transferred any of the monies to Condor. The agent determined that the contractual arrangement between the taxpayer and Condor was a sham.

The Government indicted the taxpayer under section 7206(1) for making a false individual return omitting the income and under section 7212(a)'s Omnibus Clause for providing the agent a false and fraudulent assignment agreement. Kelly was acquitted of the section 7206(1) charge, but convicted of the section 7212(a) Omnibus Clause charge. Kelly argued on appeal that the Omnibus Clause requires actual threats or injury to an IRS agent, but the court handily rejected that argument on the basis of the plain language of the Omnibus Clause which is not so limited. The court then moved to Kelly's other arguments as to the Omnibus Clause:]

Kelly next contends that the decision to charge him under section 7212(a) violated a policy statement issued by the Tax Division of the Department of Justice. That directive instructs officers of the Department not to utilize the omnibus clause of section 7212(a) "where other more specific charges are available and adequately reflect the gravamen of the offense." Kelly argues that there was a more specific and appropriate charge available to the Government in his case, namely tax evasion under section 7201, and that the Government should have prosecuted him under that statute rather than section 7212(a). We are not persuaded by this contention. As a general rule, noncompliance with internal departmental guidelines is not, of itself, a ground of which defendants can complain. Such guidelines provide no substantive rights to criminal defendants.[56] Moreover, the record does not support Kelly's claim of noncompliance.

Kelly characterizes his actions as "garden variety" tax evasion rather than obstruction. We disagree. Kelly's delivery of the Condor assignment agreement to Marcantonio [the IRS agent] did more than merely further a tax evasion scheme — it was designed to impede Marcantonio from uncovering a tax evasion scheme that already had been effectuated. It expanded and delayed the progress of Marcantonio's audit and investigation and, thus, can be characterized accurately as obstruction, rather than evasion.

Kelly suggests the district court's broad interpretation of the statute potentially could run afoul of the constitutional doctrines of overbreadth and vagueness. In support of his position, Kelly cites *United States v. Poindexter* in which the court held, over the strong dissent of Judge Mikva, that use of the term "corrupt" in the more general obstruction-of-proceedings statute, 18 U.S.C. section 1505, rendered that statute unconstitutionally vague as applied. However, five other circuits have

---

[56] [Authors' note: There are numerous cases to this effect. *E.g.*, United States v. Rutherford, 555 F.3d 190, 196–97 (6th Cir. 2009).]

upheld the constitutionality of section 7212(a) in the face of claims similar to that presently posed by Kelly. These decisions are cited and discussed in the well-reasoned opinion of District Judge Gertner in *United States v. Brennick*, 908 F. Supp. 1004, 1010–13 (D. Mass. 1995). Finding the analyses in these opinions both pertinent and persuasive, we reach the same result.

We also reject Kelly's contention that "willfulness" is a necessary element of section 7212(a) and that the district court should have instructed the jury accordingly. In making this argument, Kelly relies upon *Cheek v. United States* which involved 26 U.S.C. sections 7201 and 7203. Unlike section 7212(a), both of these sections specifically require proof of willfulness. There is no single, universal definition of the word "willfully." [citing *Pomponio* and *Murdock*] Usually, however, the varying definitions contain certain common general elements. When, as here, a court properly instructs a jury concerning these elements, it need not usurp the function of Congress by inserting the term "willfully" in a statute where Congress saw fit to omit it.

The key words in section 7212(a) are "corruptly" and "endeavors." The district court instructed the jury that:

> To act corruptly is to act with the intent to secure an unlawful advantage or benefit either for one's self or for another.

This is a well-accepted definition of the term "corruptly" when used in this context. The district court then defined "endeavors" as follows:

> It means to knowingly and intentionally act or to knowingly and intentionally make any effort which has a reasonable tendency to bring about the desired result.
>
> A person acts knowingly if he acts intentionally and voluntarily and not because of ignorance, mistake, accident, or carelessness.

Before you can find that the defendant acted intentionally, you must be satisfied beyond a reasonable doubt that the defendant acted deliberately and purposefully, that is, defendant's acts must have been the product of the defendant's conscious objective rather than the product of mistake or accident.

The district court's definition of the proof required for the section 7212(a) violation was as comprehensive and accurate as if the word "willfully" was incorporated in the statute. We are reluctant, therefore, to add the word "willfully" to section 7212(a), where Congress has seen fit to omit it.

G. Post-Filing Conduct Only?

Kelly mentioned a DOJ Tax policy with respect to Omnibus Clause prosecutions. Another DOJ Tax policy was as follows:

> In general, the use of the "omnibus" provision of Section 7212(a) should be reserved for conduct occurring after a tax return has been filed — typically conduct designed to impede or obstruct an audit or criminal tax investigation, when 18 U.S.C. section 371 charges are unavailable due to insufficient evidence of conspiracy. However, this charge might also be

appropriate when directed at parties who engage in large-scale obstructive conduct involving actual or potential tax returns of third parties.[57]

Focus on the last sentence ("However . . ."). [58] Go back and read the statute in full and attempt to answer from the text of the statute whether the reading in the last sentence quoted from the CTM goes beyond the text of the statute.

UNITED STATES v. KASSOUF

United States Court of Appeals, Sixth Circuit
144 F.3d 952 (1998)

[Authors' note: A court of appeals addressed this issue for the first time and curbed the DOJ Tax's expansive application of section 7212. Tucked away in a 26-count indictment, was a count that alleged the defendant had violated the section 7212(a) Omnibus Clause by conducting partnerships and corporate general partners in a way that would make audit less able to trace the defendant's activities and that the defendant affirmatively misled the IRS by filing tax returns that did not disclose these transactions and income earned with respect to them. The act of filing false tax returns would be crimes under provisions discussed above, such as sections 7201, 7206(1), and 7206(2), depending upon context. The issue raised by the use of the Omnibus Clause is what, if anything, it adds.

At the trial level and on appeal, the defendant made several arguments with respect to the Omnibus Clause. He alleged that the Government's allegations failed to state a violation of the Omnibus Clause; that the Omnibus Clause, if interpreted to state a crime in this case, was unconstitutional; and that the statute of limitations upon prosecution had expired. The trial court dismissed the count on the basis that the Omnibus Clause required a pending IRS proceeding or investigation that was impeded or obstructed. The Government appealed.

The issue as framed to the court of appeals was whether the Omnibus Clause required a pending IRS investigation or proceeding that the taxpayer's conduct was intended to affect. The court found the statutory language inconclusive on the issue. The court then looked to the interpretation of 18 U.S.C. section 1503, which has an Omnibus Clause with "almost identical language" with respect to obstruction of the due administration of justice. That provision has been interpreted to require a pending judicial proceeding and that the defendant be aware of the judicial proceeding. Section 1503 does not apply to antecedent acts even if they are designed to affect an ultimate judicial proceeding. The court found the authority limiting 18 U.S.C. section 1503 in this way to be "instructive," and specifically declined to accept the Fifth Circuit's suggestion in *United States v. Reeves*[59] that the Omnibus Clause is broader than the 18 U.S.C. section 1503's omnibus clause. The court reasoned:]

---

[57] CTM 17.00 (2001).

[58] As noted previously, the 2012 version of the CTM takes a more expansive view of section 7212 than the 2001 version did. The essence of the "However" sentence remains the Government's policy, though. The 2012 CTM states: "A charge under the omnibus charge may also be appropriate to prosecute a person who, prior to any audit or investigation, engaged in large-scale obstructive conduct involving the tax liability of third parties." CTM 17.03.

[59] 752 F.2d 995 (5th Cir. 1985).

Here, were we to permit the allegations in Count 26 to stand, we would be imposing liability for conduct with even less of a causal connection than that rejected by the Supreme Court in *Aguilar*.[60] We would be permitting the IRS to impose liability for conduct which was legal (such as failure to maintain records) and occurred long before an IRS audit, or even a tax return was filed. The speculative nature of this "obstructive" conduct is readily apparent, and we agree with the district court that the statute cannot be construed to prohibit it. Because Title 26 encompasses such routine actions as even the government points out, imposing liability for actions committed before a person knew of an investigation or proceeding, would open them up to a host of potential liability of conduct that is not specifically proscribed.

In construing section 7212(a) to require a pending IRS action under the code of which the defendant is aware, we are also mindful that courts should interpret statutes that impose criminal liability narrowly to ensure proper notice to the accused. In this day, when Congress is attempting to curb the reach of the IRS into the homes of taxpayers,[61] we cannot construe a penal law such as section 7212(a) to permit such an invasion into the activities of law-abiding citizens. As the district court noted, out of the hundreds of people who file taxes every day, there is no guarantee that a particular tax return will be audited. Therefore, it would be highly speculative to find conduct such as the destruction of records, which might or might not be needed, in an audit which might or might not ever occur, is sufficient to make out an omnibus clause violation. Were the court to find otherwise, we would be opening the statute to legitimate charges of overbreadth and vagueness, particularly where the statute may impose liability for otherwise lawful conduct. Kassouf may have had no idea that conduct such as the failing to maintain records (before his tax returns were ever filed) might obstruct IRS action because he had no specific knowledge that the IRS would ever investigate his activities. If upon hearing that the IRS was conducting an audit of his returns, however, Kassouf had begun destroying records and funneling money through various accounts to prevent detection of his illegal activities, section 7212(a) would clearly apply.

[Authors' note: Thus, the majority concluded that the Omnibus Clause did not support a charge for activity when there was no pending investigation. The dissenting judge on the three-judge panel saw things differently, reasoning from the similar but not identical language of 18 U.S.C. section 1503 as follows:]

As noted by the majority, however, courts must presume that Congress knew of the prevailing law when it enacted a statute. Section 1503 was in effect long before § 7212(a) and the "due administration of justice" wording of § 1503 has consistently been construed to require affected judicial proceedings. It is only logical, therefore, to conclude that if Congress wished 26 U.S.C. § 7212(a) to be interpreted in an identical fashion, identical language would have been inserted into that statute.

---

60 [Authors' note: United States v. Aguilar, 515 U.S. 593 (1995) (imposing a nexus requirement as to 18 U.S.C. section 1503 and supporting a strict reading of obstruction statutes generally).]

61 [Authors' note: The court's reference is to the largely manufactured hysteria about IRS abuses that led to enactment of the Internal Revenue Service Restructuring and Reform Act of 1998. For discussion, see Steve R. Johnson, *The Dangers of Symbolic Legislation: Perceptions and Realities of the New Burden-of-Proof Rules*, 84 Iowa L. Rev. 413, 446–48 (1999).]

In its wisdom, our nation's legislative body chose, however, to distinguish the requirements of the statutes by use of broader language in § 7212(a). Pursuant to those provisions, it is not only the administration of "justice" that is protected from undue obstruction, but the very administration of the myriad duties performed under the Title.

The majority unnecessarily sounds the alarm that such a reading of the plain language of the statute will result in criminal prosecutions of individuals who may, for example, innocently dispose of old tax returns and records later requested by the Internal Revenue Service for audit purposes. In light of recent revelations of abuses perpetrated by employees of the Internal Revenue Service, such concern is understandable. The comforting fact remains, however, that the statute itself still requires that any obstruction of the due administration of Title 26 be accomplished by means of corruption, force, or threats of force. If the courts of our land remain vigilant and scrupulously require government prosecutors to toe the well-defined line drawn by Congress in this legislation, I am confident the majority's fears will be allayed.

Although no federal court of appeals appears to have addressed directly the precise issue now before us, every sister circuit that has examined the reach of 26 U.S.C. § 7212(a) has accepted the principle that the provisions of that subsection do not require the government to prove the existence of an ongoing or pending tax investigation or proceeding. I see no reason for us now to rush into the breach to create an analytical split on this question. I would REVERSE the district court's dismissal of Count 26 of the indictment and REMAND this matter for further proceedings as necessary.

In *United States v. Bowman*,[62] the Sixth Circuit recognized that *Kassouf* may have painted with too broad a stroke in limiting the application of section 7212 to a pending IRS investigation. Bowman engaged in an elaborate scheme whereby he sent false IRS 1099 forms with respect to various financial institutions and individuals whom he felt had wronged him. The false 1099s indicated that those financial institutions and businesses had cancellation of indebtedness income. Bowman also filed a Form 1096 with the IRS which summarized the information in the Forms 1099 he had sent. The question presented was whether this conduct could be subject to prosecution under the Omnibus Clause. Specifically, relying upon *Kassouf*, Bowman argued that, since there was no pending IRS investigation, he could not be prosecuted under that provision. The Sixth Circuit limited *Kassouf* to its facts, reasoning:

> In determining whether Bowman's conduct violated the omnibus clause, this Court must evaluate the impact of Bowman's activities on the execution of the duties of the IRS. Bowman willfully and knowingly filed false information on his 1099 and 1096 forms, and these filings had a direct impact on the administration of this agency's duties. Moreover, the obvious purpose of his actions was to harass his creditors.

[62] 173 F.3d 595 (6th Cir. 1999).

> We hold that *Kassouf* must be limited to its precise holding and facts, and that it cannot be read to encompass the kind of activity for which Bowman was indicted. All of the reasoning in *Kassouf* supports the conclusion that an individual's deliberate filing of false forms with the IRS specifically for the purpose of causing the IRS to initiate action against a taxpayer is encompassed within § 7212(a)'s proscribed conduct. The filing of false tax forms is not legal when undertaken; it is not speculative; it is specifically designed to cause a particular action on the part of the IRS. The action it is designed to cause is not routine; rather, the intended action is one that, but for the false filing, would not be undertaken at all relative to the victimized taxpayers. Finally, unless *Kassouf* is limited to its facts, its effect would be to prevent the prosecution of actions whose sole purpose is to obstruct or impede the IRS in the administration of its duties, as those acts of obstruction only trigger or attempt to trigger investigations by the IRS. Prosecution of such acts does not offend the goal of *Kassouf*: "In this day, when Congress is attempting to curb the reach of the IRS into the homes of taxpayers, we cannot construe a penal law such as § 7212(a) to permit such an invasion into the activities of law-abiding citizens." *Kassouf*, 144 F.3d at 958. Indeed, to preclude the prosecution of such acts may tend to proliferate the very invasion *Kassouf* sought to prevent, but the law-abiding citizens whose homes will be invaded would be those of the hapless victims of Bowman and his ilk. Therefore, we conclude that Bowman's activities are proscribed by § 7212(a).[63]

V. SECTION 7203 FAILURE TO FILE, KEEP RECORDS, SUPPLY INFORMATION, OR PAY TAX

A. The Elements Generally

Upon conviction under section 7203, the maximum period of incarceration per count usually is one year. That makes this offense a misdemeanor.[64] However, the last sentence of section 7203 provides for heightened punishment for failure to file returns required under section 6050I, dealing with reporting cash transactions. This aspect of section 7203 is discussed separately below.

Section 7203 is violated by any of four failures: (1) failure to pay tax or estimated tax; (2) failure to make (that is, to file) a return; (3) failure to keep records; and (4) failure to supply information. Of these, failure to file a return is the most frequently encountered in practice. Accordingly, the bulk of the discussion below focuses on failure to file although failure to pay also is briefly addressed. Students and

---

[63] 173 F.3d at 600.

[64] In 2007, Acting IRS Commissioner Kevin Brown urged that willful non-filing be elevated from a misdemeanor to a felony. "There's symbolism there that's quite important . . . . Frankly, you cannot interest U.S. attorneys in prosecuting misdemeanors. Perhaps in the drug area, but not in the tax area." *Quoted by* Dustin Stamper, *Brown Following Everson's Lead*, TAX NOTES, May 14, 2007, at 606, 607. The Obama Administration has several times urged this change, but Congress has not yet acted on it.

practitioners, however, should remember the other types of failures covered by section 7203.

Here is the CTM's form jury instruction with respect to failure to file:

> Count ______ of the indictment [information] charges that the defendant ____________ was required by law to file a tax return for the tax year 20______, on or before the ________ day of __________, 20________, and that the defendant willfully failed to file such a return.
>
> In order to sustain its burden of proof for the crime of willful failure to file a tax return as charged in Count ______ of the indictment [information] * * *, the government must prove the following three (3) essential elements beyond a reasonable doubt:
>
> > One: The defendant ____________ was required by law or regulation to file a tax return concerning his [her] income for the taxable year ended December 31, 20______;
> >
> > Two: The defendant failed to file such a return at the time required by law; and
> >
> > Three: In failing to file the tax return, the defendant acted willfully.[65]

[As an alternative, the CTM formerly presented the elements in four parts as follows:]

> The defendant, ____________, is accused of failing to file an income tax return for the year 20______.
>
> It is against federal law to fail to file a required income tax return. For you to find ____________ guilty of this crime, you must be convinced that the government has proved each of these things beyond a reasonable doubt:
>
> > First, that ____________ received income of [state applicable dollar amount] or more between January 1 and December 31 of [year].
> >
> > Second, that ____________ failed to file an income tax return as required by [April 15, 20______].
> >
> > Third, that ____________ knew he was required to file a return.
> >
> > Fourth, that ____________ failed to file on purpose, and not as a result of carelessness.[66]

---

65 CTM Government Proposed Jury Inst. Nos. 26.7203-1 & 3.

66 CTM 124 (2001).

B. Duty to File Return

In the case of the most common returns (income tax returns), the Government's burden to prove this crime is as light as it gets. The Government must, of course, prove the minimal amount of income required to invoke the duty to file,[67] but the Government need not launch the type of case that would be required for an evasion conviction. The Government merely needs to prove a duty to file the return, failure to file, and willfulness. There is no requirement that a tax be due. However, as a practical matter, cases in which no tax is due have limited jury appeal and limited potential for incarceration under the Sentencing Guidelines.

C. Failure to File Timely

In theory, this element would be satisfied by any delinquency — even one day. However, the Government will not prosecute for a minor temporal delinquency. Indeed, as discussed more fully in Chapter 5 with respect to the Government's "voluntary disclosure" policy, a return filed much later can avoid a prosecution, and the Government is normally more than tolerant toward delinquent tax filers. But, technically speaking, the Government's forbearance on such delinquencies is not statutorily commanded.

The Government usually establishes failure to file by having someone from the Service Center testify or produce a Certificate of Assessments and Payments indicating the taxpayer's filing history and that, after dutiful search, the IRS has been unable to find a return that has been filed or record of any payment having been made. A Service Center employee will testify as to the certificate. Rule 803(10) of the Federal Rules of Evidence, an exception to the hearsay rule, permits the introduction of such a negative certificate to indicate that a return was not filed. That does not mean that a defendant is without means to attack the persuasiveness of such a record.[68] There will usually be some other indication of the failure to file.

Taxpayers sometimes mount the defense that they filed or paid and the IRS just lost the return or the payment. If the taxpayer really wants to succeed in this defense, however, the taxpayer will probably have to take the stand, thereby waiving his Fifth Amendment privilege and effectively having the case turn upon whether the jury believes him on this critical issue.

Sometimes taxpayers file documents which purport to be returns but which contain very little or no real information other than the taxpayer's name and social security number. The question frequently arising for both civil and criminal tax purposes is whether the document, although on a return form, is a return. In the criminal context, the question is whether the taxpayer can be prosecuted for failure to file. The cases generally hold that a wholly deficient "return" is not a return.[69]

---

[67] *See* IRC § 6012 and the Treasury Regulations thereunder.

[68] *See, e.g.*, United States v. Silkman, 156 F.3d 833 (8th Cir. 1998), *appeal after remand*, 220 F.3d 935 (8th Cir. 2000), *cert. denied*, 531 U.S. 1129 (2001). *Silkman* is discussed in Chapter 9.

[69] *See, e.g.*, United States v. Vance, 730 F.2d 736, 738 (11th Cir.), *reh'g denied*, 736 F.2d 1528 (11th Cir. 1984); United States v. Moore, 627 F.2d 830, 835 (7th Cir. 1980), *cert. denied*, 450 U.S. 916 (1981); United States v. Smith, 618 F.2d 280, 281 (5th Cir.), *cert. denied*, 449 U.S. 868 (1980); United States v. Rickman,

D. Willfulness

This is often the battleground in failure-to-file cases, but it is a battleground where the odds are stacked against the taxpayer who has not filed. The Government must of course establish that the taxpayer knew of his or her duty to file the return, but it is the rare citizen indeed who doesn't know that he or she has a duty to file a return or pay a tax. The jury will infer knowledge of that duty in most cases. The Government can often show that the taxpayer filed returns in earlier years, thus demolishing this defense if asserted. The taxpayer will often assert that factors beyond his or her control caused him to not file and, therefore, his failure to file was not willful. The Court in *Cheek* discussed this issue.[70]

One defense asserted in this context is that filing a return or filing an adequate return violates the Fifth Amendment privilege. This defense is discussed in Chapter 5.

E. Miscellaneous

Failure to file is the most common section 7203 offense prosecuted by the Government. That is not to say that many non-filers are prosecuted. Only a very small percentage — probably significantly less than 1% of non-filers — are prosecuted. Still, in the universe of tax crimes that get prosecuted, failure to file prosecutions are common.

This fact reflects several imperatives. First, there is a huge tax gap among non-filers.[71] By prosecuting and publicizing the convictions, the Government's thinking is that more people are encouraged to get back into the tax system. Second, it may well be that the reasonably "capturable" revenue loss from non-filers is greater than that for filers who cheat. Third, failure to file is an easy case to prove. Solid failure-to-file cases can be brought with limited resources and publicized to encourage others to file.

Many failure-to-file cases are pursued against tax protestors who can be constituents of large protest movements. One common gambit is for such protestors to file W-4 forms claiming a large number of exemptions, so as to zero out withholding payments and then fail to file. For these taxpayers, the failure-to-file gambit wouldn't work if the Government had the money as a result of withholding, so combining the failure-to-file with other forms of self-help (such as the W-4's) can step the case up to a tax evasion felony case rather than a failure-to-file misdemeanor. The Government nevertheless will usually prosecute these cases as simple failure-to-file cases.

---

638 F.2d 182, 184 (10th Cir. 1980). *But see* United States v. Long, 618 F.2d 74, 75 (9th Cir. 1980).

[70] Cheek v. United States, 498 U.S. 192 (1991). *Cheek* is discussed in Chapter 2A.

[71] Commentators interpreting IRS statistics have quantified this gap somewhat differently. *Compare* Theodore M. David, *The Tax Non-Filer: Public Enemy Number One?*, PRACTICAL TAX LAWYER, Spring 2007, at 7, 8 (putting the tax gap at about $345 billion, as much as 25% of which "may come from non-filing"), *with* Mark A. Luscombe, *Tax Protestors: Is the IRS Turning the Corner?*, TAXES, May 2007, at 3 (estimating that $30 billion of the total $353 billion tax gap comes from non-filing). *See also* Charles P. Rettig, *Non-Filers Beware: Who's That Knocking at Your Door?*, J. TAX PRAC. & PROC., Oct.–Nov. 2006, at 15.

F. Failure to Pay

As noted, section 7203 also covers failure to pay. As noted in Chapter 2A, section 7201 also covers evasion of payment. As regards failure to pay, therefore, section 7203 and section 7201 have common elements. Technically, section 7203 requires only proof of willful failure to pay, while the evasion of payment prong of section 7201 requires proof of an attempt to evade or defeat the payment of the tax. The requirements are stated differently, so section 7203 failure-to-pay may be treated as a lesser included offense to section 7201.[72]

Because of the overlap, some of the same issues arise in section 7203 failure-to-pay cases as arise in section 7201 evasion-of-payment cases. Thus, a common defense in section 7203 cases is that, despite owing the tax, the defendant did not have the wherewithal to pay the tax and, hence, his or her failure to pay the tax was not willful.[73]

VI. SECTIONS 7202 AND 7215 FAILURE TO COLLECT AND PAY OVER

A. The Elements Generally

Sections 7202 and 7215 partly cover the same ground. Section 7202 is a felony provision applicable to willful failures by persons under the duty to collect, account for, and pay over tax. Section 7215 is a misdemeanor that can apply to failures to comply with section 7512(b). Section 7512(b) requires an employer delinquent in payment obligations for withheld income tax or FICA tax from employees' compensation to pay over more promptly than would otherwise be required. Section 7215(b) creates affirmative defenses when there was reasonable doubt as to whether collection was required, there was reasonable doubt as to who was required to do the collecting, or the failure was due to circumstances beyond the defendant's control.

The CTM form jury instruction as to section 7202 is as follows:

> Count I charges that on or about the ______ day of ________, 20______, in the District of ____________, the defendant, ____________, a resident of ______________, who conducted a business as a sole proprietorship under the name and style of ____________,[74] with its principal place of business in ____________, and who, during the quarter [designate appropriate quarter] of the year 20______, ending ____________ , 20______, deducted and collected from the total taxable wages of his [her] employees federal income taxes and Federal Insurance Contributions Act taxes in the sum of $______, did willfully fail to

---

[72] *See, e.g.*, United States v. McGill, 964 F.2d 222, 226 (3d Cir.), *cert. denied*, 506 U.S. 1023 (1992).

[73] *See, e.g.*, McGill, *supra*; United States v. Tucker, 686 F.2d 230, *reh'g denied*, 690 F.2d 905 (5th Cir.), *stay denied*, 459 U.S. 1027, *cert. denied*, 459 U.S. 1071 (1982). *See generally* Steve R. Johnson, *The Financial Inability Defense to Tax Crimes*, 23/3 ABA Section of Taxation News Quarterly 6 (2004).

[74] Section 7202 is not limited to sole proprietors, but Schedule C operations are fertile breeding grounds for tax derelictions of this type.

truthfully account for and pay over to the Internal Revenue Service said federal income taxes withheld and Federal Insurance Contributions Act taxes due and owing to the United States of America for the said quarter ending ___________, 20______.

In order to establish the offense charged in the indictment, the government must prove the following three elements beyond a reasonable doubt:

First, the defendant was a person who had a duty to collect, truthfully account for, and pay over federal income and social security taxes that the defendant was required to withhold from the wages of employees for the calendar quarter ending ___________, 20______,

Second, the defendant failed to collect or truthfully account for and pay over federal income and social security taxes that the defendant was required to withhold from the wages of employees for the calendar quarter ending ___________, 20______, and

Third, the defendant acted willfully.[75]

B. The "Withhold and Pay Over" Obligation

The tax system provides for various payment agents to withhold from a payment to a taxpayer and report and pay over the amount to the IRS. The most prominent instance is the employer's obligation to withhold federal income taxes and the employee's share of FICA taxes from the gross pay of employees. Under Chapters 21 and 24 of the Code, the employer is required to withhold, report, and pay over the withholdings to the Government. As to the employees, the employer effectively collects by paying the employees net wages, *i.e.*, the gross wages net of the amounts required to be collected from the net wages. These taxes are commonly referred to as "trust fund" taxes because, upon withholding them from the employee's gross wages, the employer is deemed to hold them in trust for the Government until they are paid over.

In a technical, state law sense, the withholdings are not trust funds because the withholding agent is not required to establish a separate trust fund corpus, and the "withholdings" are usually and legally maintained in the general operating or payroll account until the withholding agent is required to pay over, which typically is some days after the "withholding."[76] Troubled businesses frequently rely upon the float from such withholdings to stay afloat and end up not being able to ultimately pay over the amount thus "withheld." Section 6672 (the responsible person or trust fund recovery penalty) imposes civil liability upon the person or persons responsible for collecting, accounting, and paying over such withheld amounts. Section 7202 provides criminal penalties.

---

[75] CTM 111, 112 (2001). The current version is essentially the same. CTM Government Proposed Jury Inst. Nos. 26.7202-1 & 3.

[76] For description of the applicable rules, see IRS Pub. 15, Circular E: Employer's Tax Guide 20–30 (2013).

C. Relationship of Sections 7202 and 7215

Initially, the Government encountered difficulty in proving willfulness in section 7202 prosecutions.[77] This is because courts and juries found it difficult to convict a felony when the withholding agent was trying to keep his business afloat and, by the time the funds were required to be paid over, they just weren't available.[78] As a result, Congress enacted section 7215, which creates a misdemeanor offense for certain conduct otherwise covered by section 7202. Section 7215 applies for violations of section 7512(b), which authorizes the IRS to notify withholding agents of their failure to comply with the withholding and pay-over requirements. Upon receipt of notice, withholding agents are required to timely withhold and deposit the withheld amounts to the IRS. Then, if the withholding agent fails to comply, the withholding agent can be prosecuted under section 7215.

Failure to collect, account for, and pay over are objective acts that the Government usually has little difficulty proving. The question that is presented in a section 7215 case is what type of objective circumstances that prevent the taxpayer from paying over are defenses. Section 7215(b) allows a defense of failure to pay because of circumstances beyond the employer's control, but it forecloses an argument that lack of funds immediately after the payment of wages (*i.e.*, a net wages payment) is beyond the employer's control. Put bluntly, the employer is supposed to not pay the employee rather than pay net wages which leave the employer without sufficient funds to pay the IRS.

The reluctance of judges and juries to convict under section 7202 — and with it the reluctance of DOJ to wield this weapon — has diminished in recent years. In the 1975 *Poll* case, the Ninth Circuit held that a defendant could introduce evidence "that the corporation lacked the liquid resources to pay the full amounts due and that he intended to make up the deficiencies later," as being relevant to the defendant's willfulness.[79] In 2008, however, the Ninth Circuit held that *Poll* had in effect been overruled by intervening Supreme Court authority.[80] In recent years, juries seem increasingly willing to convict under section 7202 and judges to impose substantial punishment.[81]

---

[77] CTM 9.03 (2001).

[78] *See* United States v. Poll, 521 F.2d 329 (9th Cir. 1975).

[79] United States v. Poll, 521 F.2d 329, 330–32 (9th Cir. 1975).

[80] United States v. Easterday, 539 F.3d 1176 (9th Cir. 2008). For an argument that some vestige of the defense remain see Steve R. Johnson, Easterday *and the "Inability to Pay" Defense for Tax Crimes*, 124 Tax Notes 787 (2009).

[81] Easterday was found guilty on 107 of 109 counts and was sentenced to 30 months imprisonment, followed by three years of supervised relief. *See also* United States v. Blanchard, 618 F.3d 562 (6th Cir. 2010) (section 7202 conviction results in 22 months of incarceration plus 36 months of supervised release).

UNITED STATES v. EVANGELISTA

United States Court of Appeals, Second Circuit
122 F.3d 112 (1997)

[Authors' note: This case demonstrates a typical fact pattern in which a taxpayer's attempt to avoid liability under section 6672 turns what would normally be a civil case into a criminal case. The defendants were father and son. They were convicted of conspiracy to defraud the IRS under section 7202 and under 18 U.S.C. section 371 (which is explored in Chapter 3). The defendants offered several arguments on appeal, one of which entailed the proper construction of section 7202.]

We affirm the Evangelistas' convictions and sentences in full. We write primarily to address their second argument, regarding the proper construction of, and the requirements for conviction under, 26 U.S.C. § 7202.

[Authors' note: The father and members of his family, including the son, owned and operated several active real estate development and related businesses. The businesses operated through several entities, one of which was a payroll company serving as centralized paymaster for the other corporations.

The businesses expanded rapidly and, by 1986, had a gross fair market value of $150–200 million. The businesses were highly leveraged and, thus, vulnerable to market fluctuations. By 1991, they had lost virtually all the properties through foreclosures and the father had a substantial negative net worth. Along with these reversals, not surprisingly, they began experiencing significant cash flow difficulties. As occurs often in these circumstances, businessmen have to decide which of the competing creditors will get paid. The businesses stopped paying over to the IRS the trust fund taxes. The total trust fund tax liability eventually reached $1.5 million. Although not paying over the taxes, the centralized paymaster consistently filed the appropriate quarterly returns — Forms 941 — showing the withheld taxes.

In 1989, the IRS initiated collection action with respect to the unpaid taxes. The IRS had a series of negotiations with the businesses in which the IRS requested financial statements in order to structure an arrangement to resolve the liability and also advised that "staying current" in the trust fund liabilities was a prerequisite to structuring an arrangement to resolve the past due trust fund taxes. No financial statements were submitted, and the businesses did not stay current on their trust fund tax liabilities. They continued to fail to pay over the withheld amounts. Furthermore, the family continued to take other actions to defeat the IRS's ability to collect the tax. As the court said:]

In the period 1989 through 1995, the Evangelistas engaged in a series of schemes that (according to the government) were designed to: (a) defeat collection of the trust funds by the IRS; and (b) prevent the IRS from seizing other family and business assets to satisfy the trust fund obligations. First, the Evangelistas repeatedly commingled personal and corporate funds, and then spent those monies on personal expenses and new businesses, thereby beggaring Monaco and the other entities that owed the trust fund payments. For example, the government showed that numerous checks payable to Evangelista, Sr. in respect of the family's businesses were deposited in personal checking accounts set up in the names of himself and his wife (jointly), and in the names of at least two of their children, including Claude Evangelista. On those personal accounts, hundreds of thousands of dollars in checks were drawn for (*inter alia*) mortgage and other expenses associated with at least two family residences; wedding expenses for Evangelista, Sr.'s two daughters; college tuition for a son and one daughter; and the lease payments and related expenses for a Mercedes Benz driven primarily by Evangelista, Sr.'s wife.

The Evangelistas frustrated seizure of other family assets by transferring ownership of those assets from family members who were personally liable for the overdue trust funds (chiefly Evangelista, Sr.) to those who were not. For example, title to Evangelista, Sr.'s personal residence was transferred to two of his children (jointly), and his $1 million partnership interest in one real estate enterprise was assigned to his son Claude. Once again, these intra-family transfers and personal expenditures took place while Monaco and other Evangelista entities owed the IRS over $1 million in past-due trust funds for which Evangelista, Sr. (at least) was personally liable.

At trial, the defendants' principally urged that they had relied on their long-time accountant who was their sole witness at trial. The defendants chose not to testify in their own behalves. The court said that the apparent thrust of the defense was that the "family businesses had suffered financial hardship, and had endeavored — in good faith, and with assistance and advice from accounting professionals — to resolve those problems as best they could." On balance, according to the court, the accountant's testimony was not helpful to them. The accountant's testimony also makes clear that he consistently advised the Evangelistas: (a) that they were personally liable for the outstanding trust funds and obligated to pay them; (b) that they had no right to use the trust funds for any purpose other than paying the IRS; and (c) that they should enter into an agreement with the IRS to begin at least partial payment of the funds. Most important, [the accountant] never told Evangelista, Sr. not to pay the trust funds that were owed, nor did he advise that payment could be put off or deferred pending negotiation of a formal payment arrangement.

As indicated at the outset, we write chiefly to address a question of statutory interpretation regarding the requirements for conviction under § 7202. That statute, entitled "Willful failure to collect or pay over tax," provides in relevant part: "Any person required under this title to collect, account for, and pay over any tax imposed by this title who willfully fails to collect or truthfully account for and pay over such tax shall . . . be guilty of a felony . . . ." 26 U.S.C. § 7202.

The Evangelistas argue that § 7202 defines two offenses, expressed schematically as follows:

[1] the willful failure to collect trust fund taxes, and

[2] the willful failure to:

  [a] truthfully account for, and

  [b] pay over such taxes.

According to the Evangelistas, the second of these offenses — the only one at issue here — requires proof of two discrete elements: both a willful failure to "truthfully account for" trust funds, and a willful failure to "pay over" those funds.

Appellant's Brief at 36 (quoting 26 U.S.C. § 7202). The Evangelistas argue that because they consistently filed the required Forms 941 tax returns — as the government apparently concedes — they did "truthfully account for" the trust funds that they owed; and, therefore, the government failed as a matter of law to prove both elements of the crime under § 7202.

The government counters that under "[a] fair reading of the statute and the legislative history" of § 7202, "Congress intended that an employer . . . perform all three duties, namely: (1) collection of trust fund taxes; (2) truthful accounting for trust fund taxes; and (3) paying over to the government trust fund taxes." Appellee's Brief at 33. In the government's view, the "account for and pay over" provision of § 7202 — even assuming that the statute defines two separate offenses — is, therefore, violated by the willful failure to perform either the duty to account or the duty to pay.

These competing interpretations of § 7202 raise a question of first impression in this Circuit. We agree with the government that the plain language of the disputed passage in § 7202 creates a dual obligation — to "truthfully account for and pay over" trust fund taxes — that is satisfied only by fulfilling both separate requirements. Accordingly, the command of the statute is violated by one "who willfully fails" either to "account for" or to "pay over" the necessary funds.

We find support for our view in one of the few published decisions to consider this issue. The argument raised here by the Evangelistas was also presented in *United States v. Brennick*, 908 F. Supp. 1004 (D. Mass. 1995), and was rejected in persuasive terms by that court. Preliminarily, the *Brennick* court read § 7202 much the same as we do: "The phrase 'truthfully account for and pay over' is . . . unambiguously conjunctive. Somebody who was required to 'truthfully account for and pay over' a tax would be required to do both things to satisfy the requirement"; therefore, "any intentional failure to complete the required task (to truthfully account for and pay over the tax) constitutes a crime." *Id.* at 1016.

We agree as well with the *Brennick* court's conclusion that:

> [T]he only plausible reading of the plain language of the statute penalizes the failure to complete the duty imposed by law: truthfully accounting for and paying over the withholding tax collected by an employer. The alternative reading is inconsistent with any reasonable understanding of the purposes of the statute. It would result in a greater penalty for one who simply failed to collect trust fund taxes than for one who collected them and, as is charged here, used them for his own selfish purposes . . . , so long as he notified the IRS that he had collected the tax. That Congress intended to make such a distinction is simply inconceivable.

Id. at 1017.

In arguing the contrary position, the Evangelistas rely on two opinions by panels of the Ninth Circuit, *United States v. Poll*, 521 F.2d 329 (9th Cir. 1975) (following *Wilson v. United States*, 250 F.2d 312 (9th Cir. 1957)). We are aware of no other authority that even remotely supports the Evangelistas' interpretation of § 7202. The Ninth Circuit in *Poll* stated, in the last line of a long footnote appended to the last sentence of the opinion, "We continue to regard the crime [under § 7202] as requiring two failures to act, willful failure to truthfully account and willful failure to pay over." *See* 521 F.2d at 335 n.3 (emphasis in original). As *Brennick* points out, this statement is dicta. *See Brennick*, 908 F. Supp. at 1015. *Poll* was not concerned with whether proof of two elements (failure to "account for and pay over") was required; the only issues in *Poll* were how to define "willfulness" under § 7202, and what evidence could be adduced to show it. *See, e.g., Poll*, 521 F.2d at 331. The most that can be said is that *Poll* (and *Wilson*) assume without analysis that § 7202 (and its predecessor statute in *Wilson*) require both a willful failure to account for and a willful failure to pay over.

The Evangelistas' final argument is based on a comparison between § 7202 and 26 U.S.C. §§ 7215 and 7512. Section 7215 provides that it is a misdemeanor to fail to comply with § 7512, which in turn penalizes anyone who "fails to collect, truthfully account for, or pay over such tax." 26 U.S.C. § 7512(a)(1). The Evangelistas argue that the use of the disjunctive ("or") in § 7512, violation of which is punished as a misdemeanor, demonstrates that Congress used the conjunctive ("and") in § 7202 for the purpose of adding an element to an offense that is punished as a felony. No such labored analysis is needed to account for the distinction in penalty, which can be attributed to the fact that the felony offense under § 7202 entails the element of "willfulness," while the misdemeanor under §§ 7215 and 7512 does not.

In sum, we hold that the government satisfies the requirements for conviction under § 7202 when it proves beyond a reasonable doubt that the defendant willfully failed either to "truthfully account for" or to "pay over" the required trust fund taxes.

Could the Evangelistas have been charged on this fact pattern with a violation of section 7201, which historically is considered the more serious offense? Probably. But, as will be apparent when we discuss the Sentencing Guidelines in Chapter 10, there is little incentive for the Government to take on the extra burdens required for a section 7201 prosecution because the sentencing would be basically the same anyway.

Those who enter a tax controversy practice will encounter the basic fact pattern in *Evangelista* although that case is an extreme one. It is not uncommon for the persons running businesses to use the Government as the unknowing lender of last resort, by taking monies that they have collected (or are deemed to have collected) for the Government through the payroll and using them for other business needs. This often occurs because the business' financial condition makes alternative lending sources unavailable. Usually, but not always, the responsible persons will view the failure to pay trust fund taxes as a temporary expedient, hoping that the business will work through the cash flow shortage, so as to permit the full payment of the taxes, penalties, and interest. Then, the business fails, with trust fund taxes unpaid. Usually, in such cases, the Government will limit itself to asserting only the civil penalty under section 6672. That penalty seeks to recoup the unpaid trust fund taxes from those persons within the organization who were responsible for nonpayment, the persons who had the authority and power to determine which creditors would get paid and thus who made or participated in the decision to pay others rather than the IRS.

Only in egregious circumstances does the Government pursue the criminal sanctions. What brought the Evangelistas to their woe was a persistent and long-running pattern of delaying the IRS and using the monies for other purposes even after they were fully aware of the gravity of the problem. Of course, the Evangelistas were always subject to the civil penalty under section 6672, and that would be bad enough.[82] But, through their egregious conduct, they subjected themselves to the Government instituting criminal proceedings and obtaining a conviction.

VII. SECTION 7207 FRAUDULENT RETURNS, STATEMENTS, OR OTHER DOCUMENTS

A. Elements Generally

The CTM form jury instructions as to section 7207 are as follows: The first instruction is for the presentation of a false document to the IRS.

> Count I charges that on or about the ______ day of ________, 20______, in the District of ___________,[83] the defendant, ___________, a resident of ___________ did willfully file a document with the Internal Revenue Service, United States Treasury Department, at ___________, which the defendant knew to be false as to an important matter.
>
> In order to sustain its burden of proof for the crime of filing a false document as charged in Count ______ of the indictment [information], the government must prove the following three elements beyond a reasonable doubt:
>
> One: The defendant ___________ filed a document with the Internal Revenue Service that contained false information as, detailed in the indictment [information], as to a material matter;
>
> Two: The defendant ___________ knew that this information contained in this document was false; and
>
> Three: In filing this false document, the defendant ___________ acted willfully.[84]

---

[82] In addition, the related persons and entities to whom assets were wrongfully transferred could be civilly liable under either fraudulent conveyance or transferee liability theories. *See* David M. Richardson, Jerome Borison & Steve Johnson, Civil Tax Procedure ch. 15 (2d ed. 2007). In theory, the Government might also try to criminally prosecute the transferees other than the son (who was prosecuted), but such prosecution would be unlikely as a practical matter unless the other transferees were deeply and egregiously involved in the machinations.

[83] As is discussed in greater detail in Chapter 8, where the offense was committed bears on the question of venue.

[84] CTM Government Proposed Jury Inst. Nos. 26.7207-1 & 3.

B. Overlap with Other Tax Crimes

Section 7207 is a misdemeanor. Crimes that meet the elements of section 7207 usually also meet the elements of a felony tax crime — section 7201, section 7206(1), or a tax conspiracy, commonly referred to as a *Klein* conspiracy under 18 U.S.C. section 371. Thus, given such a set of acts, the Government has a choice as to whether to go felony or to go misdemeanor. All other things being equal, the Government would rather go felony, because a felony conviction has the maximum systemic impact to support the tax system through the ripple effect of general deterrence.

Because of the Sentencing Guidelines, the actual sentence for a multi-year pattern of evasion via false returns might be the same whether the taxpayer is convicted for a felony (under either section 7201 or section 7206(1)) or a misdemeanor under section 7207. When that is the case, there may be some collateral non-sentencing differences between the felony and the misdemeanor. This will be covered in more detail in Chapter 10, the Sentencing Guidelines.

C. DOJ Tax Charging Policy for Section 7207

DOJ Tax policy used to use section 7207 only in a limited number of cases as follows:

> (1) Altered document cases involving "the submission to the Internal Revenue Service of checks containing amounts which had been altered (usually, increased) after the checks had cleared the bank ("raised canceled checks"), altered invoices, and similar altered documents as support for overstated deductions." This did not include altered federal tax returns. Furthermore, even in this limited class of cases, section 7207 was "restricted to those cases where the Tax Division determined that the circumstances did not warrant a felony prosecution."
>
> (2) Other cases where the subject is, or promises to be a cooperating witness if the tax charges are satisfactorily resolved, approval of a section 7207 plea may be given if: (a) the Tax Division has not previously authorized charges under sections 7206(1), 7201, or a tax (*Klein*) conspiracy; (b) the subject has agreed to cooperate in the criminal investigation and prosecution and in the civil side of the case; and (c) the underpayment of taxes does not exceed $2,500 (if it does so, the plea must be to a felony). There are some additional administrative requirements.[85]

Current DOJ Tax policy is not so restricted. The 2012 CTM states: "The usual situation [for use of section 7207] will involve an IRS audit and the submission to the [IRS] auditor of altered canceled checks, altered invoices, or altered receipts to support overstated deductions."[86] It also provides: "The Tax Division generally will not authorize a prosecution or plea agreement under Section 7207 where the allegedly false document forming the basis for a charge under Section 7207 is a tax

---

[85] CTM 16.02 (2001).

[86] CTM 16.03.

return."[87] Apart from these considerations, however, "there is no limit on the type of document that can be the subject of a violation of [section] 7207."[88]

D. Government Choice

It is the Government's choice whether to pursue the misdemeanor section 7207 charge or a felony charge under section 7201 or section 7206(1). The courts have rejected any argument that a taxpayer must be prosecuted under the misdemeanor charge rather than the felony charge. Thus, one court said:

> This Court has long recognized that when an act violates more than one criminal statute, the Government may prosecute under either so long as it does not discriminate against any class of defendants.[89] Whether to prosecute and what charge to file or bring before a grand jury are decisions that generally rest in the prosecutor's discretion.[90]

As noted, DOJ Tax policy is to forgo the felony in favor of the misdemeanor only in rare cases. Thus, a practitioner concerned about not only the immediate criminal case but collateral effects of a felony conviction,[91] might make strenuous efforts to get the Government to accept a plea to one or more section 7207 misdemeanors with the argument that the defendant will get the same penalty anyway. The Government rarely agrees to this. However, because of the special circumstances of the plea bargaining with Andrew Fastow of Enron infamy and his wife, Lea Fastow, the Government did agree to this gambit as a way of limiting the judge's discretion in sentencing Lea Fastow.

VIII. SECTION 6050I CURRENCY TRANSACTION REPORTING

A. Generally

Section 6050I requires persons engaged in a trade or business who "receive $10,000 in cash in one transaction (or two or more related transactions)" to make a return. The return (on IRS Form 8300) must include the name, address, and TIN of the person from whom the cash was received; the amount of cash; the date and nature of the transaction; and certain other information prescribed by the IRS. There are exceptions and many nuances. The statute also criminalizes structuring transactions to evade the reporting requirements.

In addition, section 7203, the failure to file provision, provides in its final sentence that willful violation of any part of section 6050I renders the offense a

---

[87] CTM 16.03[1].

[88] CTM 16.03.

[89] [Authors' note: For discussion of discriminatory prosecution, see Steve R. Johnson, *The Selective Enforcement Defense in Civil and Criminal Tax Cases*, 27/2 ABA SECTION TAX'N NEWS Q. 14 (Winter 2008).]

[90] United States v. Fern, 696 F.2d 1269, 1274 (11th Cir. 1983).

[91] *See* Chapters 12 and 13.

felony (not a misdemeanor) which is punishable for each count by as many as five years (not one year) of imprisonment.

Section 6050I has four criminal aspects. They are described below in subparts B, C, D, and E.

B. Failure to File

The duty to file is in section 6050I. The prosecution is under section 7203 (failure to file). The elements under section 7203 are set forth and discussed above. To summarize, they are: (1) a duty to file, (2) a failure to file, and (3) willfulness.

C. Filing a False Return

The prosecution is under section 7206(1) (tax perjury). The elements under section 7206(1) are discussed above, and may be summarized as follows: (1) a false return was submitted; (2) the return contained a jurat; (3) the defendant did not believe the return to be true and correct as to a material matter; and (4) the defendant's signing was willful.

D. Assisting in Filing False Forms 8300

The prosecution is under section 7206(2). The elements under section 7206(2) are discussed above, and may be summarized as follows: (1) the defendant aided or assisted in the preparation of a false return or other document with tax consequences; and (2) the defendant did so willfully.

E. Structuring

Structuring is done to avoid the filing requirement. This is typically effected through breaking down a large amount of cash into separate deposits or other transactions so as to cause each amount to fall under $10,000.[92]

F. Additional Considerations

There is no section 7201 evasion prosecution for failure to file the CTR or filing a false CTR because there is no tax due and owing. However, the failure-to-file criminal offense (section 7203), which is normally a misdemeanor (maximum one-year sentence), ups the ante for failure to file the CTR to five years.

Civil penalties apply to failing to file the CTR and to filing a false or inadequate CTR.[93] These penalties are particularly important to lawyers who must struggle with the Fifth Amendment implications of the information required to be disclosed.[94]

---

[92] 31 U.S.C. § 5324(d). See Chapter 3 for additional discussion of structuring.

[93] IRC § 6721.

[94] These implications are discussed more fully in Chapter 11.

PROBLEMS

Problem 1

The *Kelly* case is excerpted in Subpart IV.F above. The case presents interesting questions involving the relationship of section 7212 to other criminal provisions. Consider the following questions:

(a) Could Kelly's conduct have supported a conviction under section 7201? For some unarticulated reason, the jury acquitted Kelly as to the section 7206(1) charge, which suggests that the jury might also have acquitted under section 7201. But set aside any concern about what the jury did. Do the facts of *Kelly* support a charge under section 7201? In answering this question, consider the following:

(i) Would the creating of the agreement with Condor have met the "affirmative act" requirement of section 7201? See the *Spies* case excerpted in Chapter 2A.

(ii) Would the mere filing of Kelly's Form 1040 zeroing out the income based on a sham agreement meet the requirement for an affirmative act, especially if (as occurred in *Kelly*) the taxpayer disclosed the zeroing out? Again see *Spies*.

(iii) Was Kelly's statement to the IRS agent that Condor had "picked up" the payments an act of tax evasion, or at least did it refresh the statute of limitations as in the *Beacon Brass* case also excerpted in Chapter 2A?

(b) In light of your answer to Question (a) above, did the Government have an option as to the statute under which to charge Kelly? Could the Government have charged Kelly under both section 7201 and section 7212? You will be in a better position to analyze such matters after you read the lesser-included-offense materials included in Chapter 5. At this stage, though, you can profitably consider why the Government did not charge Kelly under section 7201. Can you articulate some reasons based on the materials thus far?

(c) Section 7212(a) does not specifically require that the defendant have acted "willfully." However, it does require that the defendant have acted "corruptly." Does "willfully" inhere in "corruptly"? Can one act corruptly without acting willfully? Can one endeavor without acting willfully?

Problem 2

You are an IRS Special Agent in the Tampa (Pinellas County), Florida office. You are contacted by Maria Pavon, an IRS Revenue Agent. Pavon is thinking of making a criminal referral, and she seeks your advice. During your discussions, Pavon provides the following information:

For many years, Edgar Moten has owned and operated an automotive garage and repair shop in Tampa. He is 35 years of age and unmarried. He has never filed federal income tax returns or forms extending the due dates for such returns. The IRS Examination Division became aware of Moten in late 2011 when he was arrested for illegal drug trafficking. As a result of the ensuing newspaper stories and discussion with the arresting DEA agents, the IRS began an income tax audit of Moten. Pavon's inquiries into Moten's bank accounts, property, and life style suggest that Moten had substantial income, probably from narcotics trafficking.

For about a decade, Moten has had an intimate relationship with Barbara Gorice. Moten and Gorice have never lived together. Gorice has been employed throughout this time as a hair stylist. In December 2011, shortly after his arrest, Moten executed quitclaim deeds transferring all of his real property to Gorice. Six parcels were so transferred, with an aggregate value of approximately $1,000,000. The deeds recited that the transfers were in consideration for "$1 plus other good and valuable consideration."

In June 2012, the IRS sent a letter to Moten stating that the IRS was auditing Moten's 2011 tax year and requesting that Moten appear for an interview at the IRS's offices in Tampa at a designated time. Moten did not appear, and he has not responded to either that letter or follow-up letters. In October 2012, the IRS prepared a substitute-for-return under section 6020(b) and issued to Moten a statutory notice of deficiency based on it. The deficiency notice determined that Moten had income tax liability of $50,000 for 2011 based on unreported income and also determined that Moten was liable for a 75% penalty under sections 6651(a)(1) and 6651(f). Moten did not file a Tax Court petition contesting these determinations, and the IRS assessed the determined liabilities in March 2013. No payment has yet been made on the assessed liabilities.

Subsequently, the IRS went through a similar process (all the same steps) as to Moten's 2012 tax year. The IRS determined a $60,000 income tax deficiency for 2012 as well as a 75% section 6651 penalty. Again, Moten filed no Tax Court petition; the determined liabilities were assessed; and no payment has been made as to the liabilities.

In July 2012, Revenue Agent Pavon was driving past the largest and most valuable of the six parcels transferred in December 2011 from Moten to Gorice. Pavon noticed that there was a "for sale" sign on the property. Upon further investigation, Pavon discovered that one of the other parcels already had been sold and that the remaining parcels were up for sale.

Based on this information, in August 2012, the IRS took the following steps: The IRS determined that Gorice was liable as a transferee under section 6901 for Moten's 2011 income tax liabilities. The IRS determined that the sale and prospective sale of the parcels created peril to the collection of Gorice's transferee liability. Accordingly, it made a jeopardy assessment of that liability under section 6861. The IRS timely sent to Gorice the notices required by section 7429 and also timely sent to her a statutory notice of transferee liability.

Gorice timely exercised her section 7429(a) right to expedited administrative review of the jeopardy assessment, but the Appeals Office (Appeals Officer Marcy Singleton) upheld the assessment. Thereupon, Gorice timely exercised her section 7429(b) right to expedited judicial review, but the District Court (Judge Lydia Thurston) upheld the assessment. In the District Court action, the United States was represented by AUSA Paul Sanders.

For tax years before 2012, Gorice had filed Forms 1040 that were facially complete, reporting income and deductions. The IRS had never audited any of those returns. In 2012, her anger, fears, and frustration with her tax woes drove Gorice to seek help from a local tax protester organization: the Every Person His Own Sovereign Society ("EPHOS"). The head of EPHOS, Tom Carly, explained to Gorice various "legal" tactics and theories she could use in opposing the IRS.

Gorice continued to be employed. In April 2013, she mailed to the IRS Service Center a Form 1040 for 2012. The label area of the 1040 stated Gorice's name and social security number, but it gave her business address instead of her home address. On every substantive line on the form, Gorice wrote a symbol. An attachment to the form stated that the symbol means "Refuse to answer, based on my Fifth Amendment Right Against Self Incrimination." The form bore Gorice's signature, and the jurat was unaltered. For your convenience, a blank Form 1040 for 2012 is appended to this Problem as Exhibit A.

In May 2013, a document was filed in the Pinellas County Recorder's Office and Courthouse. Copies of the document were mailed to the organizations listed under "cc" after the first thumbprint. The document is appended to this Problem as Exhibit B.

1. Evaluate what, if any, tax crimes the Government might assert have been committed on the above facts. Consider all possible defendants. Also, consider all possible tax crimes, including both those discussed in this Chapter 2B and section 7201 discussed in Chapter 2A.

2. Consider what additional information you would need in order to evaluate the applicability of the various tax crimes. What additional information should the file contain before CID recommends any prosecution(s)?

Note 1: Subsequent chapters of this book will develop in detail matters of policy and procedure that would bear on how the Government would handle a situation such as this. At this point, you are not expected to know those matters, so the emphasis in this Problem is on the technical elements of the Code crimes and whether those elements are, or depending on additional factual development might be, satisfied here.

Note 2: Exhibit B was adapted from a document actually filed against some Government employees and officials. Much of it is rambling, nonsensical, and incoherent. Thus, you need not (indeed, for your happiness and sanity, should not) attempt to read and understand it fully. It is possible, though, to fairly easily grasp what the document is intended to be and to do. Once you have grasped that, you will be able to appreciate the significance of the document to the Problem.

PROBLEM 2 — EXHIBIT A

Form **1040** Department of the Treasury—Internal Revenue Service (99) **U.S. Individual Income Tax Return** **2013** OMB No. 1545-0074 IRS Use Only—Do not write or staple in this space.

For the year Jan. 1–Dec. 31, 2013, or other tax year beginning , 2013, ending , 20 See separate instructions.

Your first name and initial	Last name	Your social security number
If a joint return, spouse's first name and initial	Last name	Spouse's social security number
Home address (number and street). If you have a P.O. box, see instructions.	Apt. no.	▲ Make sure the SSN(s) above and on line 6c are correct.
City, town or post office, state, and ZIP code. If you have a foreign address, also complete spaces below (see instructions).		**Presidential Election Campaign** Check here if you, or your spouse if filing jointly, want $3 to go to this fund. Checking a box below will not change your tax or refund. ☐ You ☐ Spouse
Foreign country name	Foreign province/state/county	Foreign postal code

Filing Status

Check only one box.

1 ☐ Single
2 ☐ Married filing jointly (even if only one had income)
3 ☐ Married filing separately. Enter spouse's SSN above and full name here. ▶
4 ☐ Head of household (with qualifying person). (See instructions.) If the qualifying person is a child but not your dependent, enter this child's name here. ▶
5 ☐ Qualifying widow(er) with dependent child

Exemptions

6a ☐ **Yourself.** If someone can claim you as a dependent, **do not** check box 6a
b ☐ **Spouse**

Boxes checked on 6a and 6b ____

c **Dependents:** (1) First name Last name	(2) Dependent's social security number	(3) Dependent's relationship to you	(4) ✓ if child under age 17 qualifying for child tax credit (see instructions)
			☐
			☐
			☐
			☐

If more than four dependents, see instructions and check here ▶ ☐

No. of children on 6c who:
• lived with you ____
• did not live with you due to divorce or separation (see instructions) ____
Dependents on 6c not entered above ____

d Total number of exemptions claimed

Add numbers on lines above ▶ ☐

Income

Attach Form(s) W-2 here. Also attach Forms W-2G and 1099-R if tax was withheld.

If you did not get a W-2, see instructions.

7	Wages, salaries, tips, etc. Attach Form(s) W-2	7	
8a	**Taxable** interest. Attach Schedule B if required	8a	
b	**Tax-exempt** interest. **Do not** include on line 8a — 8b		
9a	Ordinary dividends. Attach Schedule B if required	9a	
b	Qualified dividends — 9b		
10	Taxable refunds, credits, or offsets of state and local income taxes	10	
11	Alimony received	11	
12	Business income or (loss). Attach Schedule C or C-EZ	12	
13	Capital gain or (loss). Attach Schedule D if required. If not required, check here ▶ ☐	13	
14	Other gains or (losses). Attach Form 4797	14	
15a	IRA distributions — 15a — b Taxable amount	15b	
16a	Pensions and annuities — 16a — b Taxable amount	16b	
17	Rental real estate, royalties, partnerships, S corporations, trusts, etc. Attach Schedule E	17	
18	Farm income or (loss). Attach Schedule F	18	
19	Unemployment compensation	19	
20a	Social security benefits — 20a — b Taxable amount	20b	
21	Other income. List type and amount	21	
22	Combine the amounts in the far right column for lines 7 through 21. This is your **total income** ▶	22	

Adjusted Gross Income

23	Educator expenses	23	
24	Certain business expenses of reservists, performing artists, and fee-basis government officials. Attach Form 2106 or 2106-EZ	24	
25	Health savings account deduction. Attach Form 8889	25	
26	Moving expenses. Attach Form 3903	26	
27	Deductible part of self-employment tax. Attach Schedule SE	27	
28	Self-employed SEP, SIMPLE, and qualified plans	28	
29	Self-employed health insurance deduction	29	
30	Penalty on early withdrawal of savings	30	
31a	Alimony paid b Recipient's SSN ▶	31a	
32	IRA deduction	32	
33	Student loan interest deduction	33	
34	Tuition and fees. Attach Form 8917	34	
35	Domestic production activities deduction. Attach Form 8903	35	
36	Add lines 23 through 35	36	
37	Subtract line 36 from line 22. This is your **adjusted gross income** ▶	37	

For Disclosure, Privacy Act, and Paperwork Reduction Act Notice, see separate instructions. Cat. No. 11320B Form **1040** (2013)

Form 1040 (2013) Page **2**

Tax and Credits

38 Amount from line 37 (adjusted gross income) . . . 38

39a Check if: { ☐ **You** were born before January 2, 1949, ☐ Blind. } **Total boxes**
☐ **Spouse** was born before January 2, 1949, ☐ Blind. } **checked ▶ 39a** ☐

b If your spouse itemizes on a separate return or you were a dual-status alien, check here ▶ 39b ☐

Standard Deduction for—
- People who check any box on line 39a or 39b or who can be claimed as a dependent, see instructions.
- All others:

Single or Married filing separately, $6,100

Married filing jointly or Qualifying widow(er), $12,200

Head of household, $8,950

40 **Itemized deductions** (from Schedule A) **or** your **standard deduction** (see left margin) . . 40

41 Subtract line 40 from line 38 . . . 41

42 **Exemptions.** If line 38 is $150,000 or less, multiply $3,900 by the number on line 6d. Otherwise, see instructions 42

43 **Taxable income.** Subtract line 42 from line 41. If line 42 is more than line 41, enter -0- . . 43

44 **Tax** (see instructions). Check if any from: **a** ☐ Form(s) 8814 **b** ☐ Form 4972 **c** ☐ ______ 44

45 **Alternative minimum tax** (see instructions). Attach Form 6251 . . . 45

46 Add lines 44 and 45 . . . ▶ 46

47 Foreign tax credit. Attach Form 1116 if required . . . 47

48 Credit for child and dependent care expenses. Attach Form 2441 48

49 Education credits from Form 8863, line 19 . . . 49

50 Retirement savings contributions credit. Attach Form 8880 50

51 Child tax credit. Attach Schedule 8812, if required . . . 51

52 Residential energy credits. Attach Form 5695 . . . 52

53 Other credits from Form: **a** ☐ 3800 **b** ☐ 8801 **c** ☐ ______ 53

54 Add lines 47 through 53. These are your **total credits** . . . 54

55 Subtract line 54 from line 46. If line 54 is more than line 46, enter -0- . . . ▶ 55

Other Taxes

56 Self-employment tax. Attach Schedule SE . . . 56

57 Unreported social security and Medicare tax from Form: **a** ☐ 4137 **b** ☐ 8919 . . 57

58 Additional tax on IRAs, other qualified retirement plans, etc. Attach Form 5329 if required . . 58

59a Household employment taxes from Schedule H . . . 59a

b First-time homebuyer credit repayment. Attach Form 5405 if required . . . 59b

60 Taxes from: **a** ☐ Form 8959 **b** ☐ Form 8960 **c** ☐ Instructions; enter code(s) ______ 60

61 Add lines 55 through 60. This is your **total tax** . . . ▶ 61

Payments

62 Federal income tax withheld from Forms W-2 and 1099 . . 62

63 2013 estimated tax payments and amount applied from 2012 return 63

If you have a qualifying child, attach Schedule EIC.

64a **Earned income credit (EIC)** . . . 64a

b Nontaxable combat pay election 64b

65 Additional child tax credit. Attach Schedule 8812 . . . 65

66 American opportunity credit from Form 8863, line 8 . . . 66

67 Reserved . . . 67

68 Amount paid with request for extension to file . . . 68

69 Excess social security and tier 1 RRTA tax withheld . . . 69

70 Credit for federal tax on fuels. Attach Form 4136 . . . 70

71 Credits from Form: **a** ☐ 2439 **b** ☐ Reserved **c** ☐ 8885 **d** ☐ 71

72 Add lines 62, 63, 64a, and 65 through 71. These are your **total payments** . . . ▶ 72

Refund

73 If line 72 is more than line 61, subtract line 61 from line 72. This is the amount you **overpaid** 73

74a Amount of line 73 you want **refunded to you.** If Form 8888 is attached, check here . ▶ ☐ 74a

Direct deposit? See instructions.

▶ b Routing number ▶ c Type: ☐ Checking ☐ Savings

▶ d Account number

75 Amount of line 73 you want **applied to your 2014 estimated tax** ▶ 75

Amount You Owe

76 **Amount you owe.** Subtract line 72 from line 61. For details on how to pay, see instructions ▶ 76

77 Estimated tax penalty (see instructions) . . . 77

Third Party Designee

Do you want to allow another person to discuss this return with the IRS (see instructions)? ☐ **Yes.** Complete below. ☐ **No**

Designee's name ▶ Phone no. ▶ Personal identification number (PIN) ▶

Sign Here

Under penalties of perjury, I declare that I have examined this return and accompanying schedules and statements, and to the best of my knowledge and belief, they are true, correct, and complete. Declaration of preparer (other than taxpayer) is based on all information of which preparer has any knowledge.

Joint return? See instructions. Keep a copy for your records.

Your signature	Date	Your occupation	Daytime phone number
Spouse's signature. If a joint return, **both** must sign.	Date	Spouse's occupation	If the IRS sent you an Identity Protection PIN, enter it here (see inst.)

Paid Preparer Use Only

Print/Type preparer's name	Preparer's signature	Date	Check ☐ if self-employed	PTIN
Firm's name ▶		Firm's EIN ▶		
Firm's address ▶		Phone no.		

Form **1040** (2013)

PROBLEM 2 — EXHIBIT B

Commercial/Common Law Lien Filing Date: May 19, 2013

FILED BY CERTIFIED MAIL # ________ "Without prejudice UCC 1-207 non assumsit"

IN THE DISTRICT COURT OF CLAIMS IN THE UNITED STATES OF THE 5TH JUDICIAL DISTRICT FOR THE UNITED STATES OF AMERICA, AND LIENED ON THE SUMTER COUNTY SHERIFF AND LIENED ON THE PINELLAS COUNTY SHERIFF

John Doe Public

Lien Claimant

VS.

De Facto Courts, ALL Judges in Equity, ALLnregistered foreign agents, A/K/A/ Maria Pavon, Marcy Singleton, Lydia Thurston, and Paul Sanders, Officials, those as Individuals and ALL SPOUSES of those named collectively and individually, the various Branches, Agencies, Depts., ALL IRS agents, commissioner of IRS, the federal reserve bank, ALL supreme court justices, ALL U.S. attorney generals in office since 1938, 100 senators, treasury department agents, 434 congressmen, ALL federal judges, U.S. postal inspectors/agents, equity judges, bar members, all sheriffs, court bailiffs as Customs officers, ALL U.S. marshals, (Interpol agents), dept. of justice — judiciary committee officials, Head of Interpol/U.S. attorney generals officials Genocide, aiding/ abetting within Our Lands. Bar Members of "THE CLUB," members who signed the unlawful treaties and declarations of Interdependence, Members of ILLUMINATI, Satanic Masonic Secret York & Scottish Rites Society Law Enforcement "hired guns" in America, Priory de Sion, Skull and Bones-Bohemian Club Members, Council of Foreign Relations, Trilateralists Members, and most importantly each and Every SPOUSE of those listed above named on this lien for without their support much of this would not have been able to be accomplished or profited to them or their heirs, and other unknown Agents/officials.

Plaintiffs, Lien Debtors

FILING OF A DEBT "SECURITY CLAIM OF COMMERCIAL/COMMON LAW LIEN AND SWORN AFFIDAVIT," DEMAND FOR AN INDEMNITY BOND, FILING A HABEAS CORPUS, A BILL OF SERVICE ATTACHED, ON THE PROPERTY LOCATED IN PINELLAS COUNTY AND ON THE BOND(S) AND SIGNATURES OF THE OFFICIALS AND AGENCIES AND FEDERAL RESERVE NOTES FOR ONE MILLION DOLLARS IN VALUE EACH PER AGENT, JUDGE, IRS OFFICIAL/AGENT, U.S. MARSHAL FOR: MISPRISION OF TREASON, MISPRISION OF FELONY, SEDITION, ABUSE

OF OFFICE &TRUST, CAUSING "IRREPARABLE HARM OF THE ADMINISTRATION OF JUSTICE" UNDER COLOR OF LAW, VIOLATING OUR NATIONAL CONSTITUTION, MALICIOUS PROSECUTION, HARASSMENT, ABSENCE OF ANY JURISDICTION IN REM OR PERSONAM, FELONY THEFT, SIGNING ILLEGAL AND UNLAWFUL TREATIES, PLEDGING OUR NATIONAL & STATE PARKS (OUR HUMAN & NATURAL RESOURCES & AGRICULTURAL PRODUCTS) ALONG WITH ALL BIRTH CERTIFICATES & LABOR INTO INVOLUNTARY SERVITUDE FOREVER TO THE INTERNATIONAL BANKERS UNDER FICTION, FRAUD AND DECEIT IN LIEU OF PAYMENT FOR A DEBIT ENTRY WHILE THEY COLLAPSE AMERICA THROUGH FALSE ECONOMIC PERIL, DENIAL OF PROPER STANDING & "DUE PROCESS," SUPPRESSION OF FACTS, DENIAL OF CIVIL RIGHTS, UNLAWFUL ACTS, "SELLING US OUT," "DOMESTIC ENEMIES," CRUEL & UNUSUAL PUNISHMENT, VIOLATING "LACK OF GOOD FAITH" DOCTRINE, HAVING "UNCLEAN HANDS," AND "FAILURE TO DISCLOSE," COMMITTING ACTS OF GENOCIDE BY INJURY AND DIRECT HARM KNOWINGLY UPON ME AS A MEMBER OF THE POSTERITY OF "WE THE PEOPLE" AND CLEARLY GOING AGAINST THE ORGANIC CONSTITUTION OF OUR NATION, ACTS OF WAR AGAINST THE PEOPLE, THIS LIEN IS ON THEIR PERFORMANCE BOND & DEBT SINCE THEY ARE OF FOREIGN STATUS AND SURRENDERED THEIR BIRTHRIGHTS, DEMAND FOR AN ARTICLE III COMMON LAW COURT AS IS MY RIGHT AND DEMAND. ATTACHED IS A HABEAS CORPUS WITH A BILL FOR THEIR CLAIMS AGAINST ME WHEN I JUDGE THEIR JURISDICTION, WITH A DEMAND FOR AN INDEMNITY BOND TO THIS LIEN THUS MAKING A BINDING CLASS "A" BOND TO THE SHERIFF AS INDIVIDUALS AND DEBTORS WITH THEIR SPOUSES.

SWORN AFFIDAVIT

COMES NOW, Claimant as John Doe Public Sui Juris, being of free natural born Sovereign of the Republic of the Union of States of the United States of America.

I am domiciled in the Florida Republic and hereby challenge any Jurisdiction in writing and the court must provide proof in writing. This Lien is upon your Bonds for a maximum of One Million dollars in value per official/agent/judge, marshal(s) and bailiff-being a Customs Agent to the Court. (Hagens v. Lavine, 415 US 533, Note 3, and "No sanction can be imposed absent proof of Jurisdiction" Standard v. Olsen, 74 S. Ct. 768. "I challenge your jurisdiction and grant NO Jurisdiction at any time." Thus, documenting crimes against John Doe Public for which all shall be held accountable. Malfeasance of Public Officials, violating the Federal R.I.C.O. act, Christianity is custom and custom is Law. I demand a Common Law Court by the Seventh Amendment. Be it known that I am under the Common Law as was my Great Grandfather. As a member of the "posterity" for which the National Constitution was written demands to know how I was being tried, as a non-white citizen under the 14th Amendment or as a member of the "posterity" are there two types of citizens? I also make known that the Judge(s) are biased and prejudiced see reference to Sei Fujii v. California and Atkens et al vs. US where they are paid by the International Monetary Fund (IMF) and are "Members of the Club" come with "unclean hands doctrine," in lack of "good faith" doctrine, and have "failed to disclose" the fact that the IRS represents a Foreign Principal and are unregistered agents of a foreign principal thus considered "Foreign or Domestic Enemies" if allowed to violate Sovereign Members through abuse of Office, color of Law, having no Corpus Delecti which the Sheriff can present. I demand that a "verified Complaint" must be presented: 1. signed before and witnessed by a Judicial Branch officer; 2. signed under sworn oath; 3. signed under penalties of perjury; and 4. signed waiving any immunity from prosecution for perjury to be valid, otherwise, there is a contempt of court with no injured party. My Bill is submitted at this time. Thus, the Sheriff is bound under a Class "A" Bond and is a debtor now liened. Application for Foreign Status has been applied for each offending official, IRS Agent, and each offending Judge A/K/A Maria Pavon, Marcy Singleton, Lydia Thurston, and Paul Sanders, and their signature is not required UCC 9-305. The Court has a negative pregnant situation. The Sheriff is commanded to preset the damaged party — the Corpus Delecti immediately "Federal courts being courts of limited jurisdiction, the presumption is that it is without jurisdiction unless the contrary affirmatively appears." Grace v. American Central INS Co., 109 U.S. 278. My sincere Religious Convictions do not allow me to participate in Fraud and Deceit with which the court approaches. Deuteronomy 25:13. Filed is my copy of Revocation of Signature and Power of Attorney, Assertion of Fourth Article rights against illegal search seizure and dispossession. These officials are in danger of Misprision of Sedition, Misprision of Treason, collusion, conspiracy, impersonating a Judicial Branch when in fact they are an Equity Court which cannot hear Law. AM 4/WPC and AM 14/DP. Any action taken against me must be fully described to me in writing and is to be immediately challenged in writing, Issued by a Court of LAW not an agency like the IRS who is in co-hoots with the Judge paid by the IMF, signed by a Judge representing a Foreign Tribunal by "Secret Democratic Oath" sworn to search, fine, and seize the people out of existence, not an agent-like the IRS and sworn on Oath. Codes are not Law. In the case of John B. Daly v. Minnesota, there is no lawful money. Appearing specially and not generally and do hereby claim and exercise All Rights, Immunities, Privileges and Liberties, enumerated and not enumerated, and serve Notice, in conjunction with the statements as follows:

DENIAL OF WAIVER AND CONSENT TO LEGISLATIVE OR FOREIGN TRIBUNALS/PRINCIPALS, IRS

1.) This IS A DENIAL of Waiver and Consent to Legislative/Foreign Tribunals. By what authority do they have to represent a Foreign Principal.

2.) Tribunals under Title 13 of the Revised Statutes and/or United States Code are Legislative Tribunals of the De Facto F.E.M.A. Emergency, Democratic, Florida Republic, as Corporator and/or under direction of International control, over the "Democratic States of the United States of America," and are operating under pretenses and colors of law and/or Federal Rules of Court Procedure in violation of the Separation of Powers Doctrine, including but not limited to Articles of the ordained Constitution of the Florida Republic, are under pretext and colors thereof, expatriating and alienating, extraditing, and

commencing actions against De Jure Preamble Free Citizens of the several States of the Union of States of the United States of America, and of the Florida Republic on whom they have no Jurisdiction and lack personal Jurisdiction.

3.) (a) These said administrative Tribunals have been and are now operating under Foreign Doctrines of Expatriation and Alienation of Jus soil, Jus sanguinis, De jure Citizenship, and impair and reduce said De Jure Citizens and posterity to "Persons." The Courts have acted in collusion & co-conspiracy to prejudice and bias the People and assume a status over the free Citizens that is not theirs. No Court of Equity can hear Our Claim. Every court case in America going back to 1938 needs to be retried.

(b) And where as also these Foreign Legislative Statutory Tribunals have and are now attempting to regulate, abrogate and expropriate Rights and Immunities and Liberties of Citizens under false pretenses and colors of Law, Abuse of Office, Foreign Law License Titles of Nobility, and Corporate Character, by bringing and commencing actions against John Doe Public, Preamble Citizens over whom they have no jurisdiction, in violation of Article IV Section 2 of the ordained and established Constitution of the Union of States of the United States of America (1787). "Where rights by the Constitution are involved, there can be no rule making or legislation which would abrogate them." "All laws which are repugnant to the Constitution are null and void." Marbury v. Madison, 5 U.S. (2 Cranch) 137, 180 (1803), and "No one is bound to obey an unconstitutional law and no courts are bound to enforce it." "Their Treaties and Pactions" are null and void and are not lawful.

Respondent Court/Tribunal produce ALL documents, Constitutions, Charters, Treaties, Arguments, Conventions, Pactions, confederations, and/or Alliances from and/or under which it usurps its delegation and promulgation of Power and Authority to enter, set, or act in any manner whatever in This or Any Other Case or Controversy, within said Free, Sovereign, Independent State and Nation, and: Where as also it is hereby COMMANDED AND ORDERED that the above named Respondent Court Tribunals which acted against me illegally, to produce ALL documents of International origin, including but not limited to ALL contracts, Agreements, and/or Pactions with Foreign Organizations such as the Bankrupt Corporations, and/or Associations, whether Artificial or contrived. All commit sedition, criminal malpractice (malfeasance), insurrection and rebellion against the U.S. Constitution. They have courts of equity and not of Law. They ignore the law and abuse the People across the land. "One cannot be punished for exercising the Constitutional Rights." "When government becomes a lawbreaker it breeds contempt for the Law."

It is further COMMANDED AND ORDERED that the above named Respondent Court/Tribunal, or the Judge/Magistrate/Commissioner thereof, produce ANY AND ALL Oaths of Office, any secret conventions, pactions with any entity, foreign or domestic, by which usurpation of Power and Authority are derived, by which the suspension of the Lawful De Jure Constitutional Courts and Offices tribunals act, whether they be formed or erected under color of law or pretense formed under direction and/or control thereof. And be it further

COMMANDED that the above named Respondent Tribunal produce ANY AND ALL Agreements, Corpus Delecti, Contracts, Compacts, Conventions, Pactions, and unlawful Treaties and Oaths taken being fully disclosed as a matter of record.

I, John Doe Public, Suis Juris, Shall amend other names of other violators.

Submitted this 19th day of May, 2013.

John Doe Public, "At Law" Sui Juris
right thumb print

Deuteronomy 19:15..."so at the mouth of two or more witnesses so shall the matter be established.

1. ________ 2. ________

cc: the Press

Bonding Companies

Equifax Credit Information

The Business & Consumer Report

Dun & Bradstreet Credit Reporting Services

Financial Institutions

Treasury Department

BILL FOR SERVICE

THE TOTAL CIVIL VALUE OF THIS COMPLAINT AT ONE MILLION FEDERAL RESERVE NOTES PER SHERIFF, BAILIFF, IRS AGENT, IRS DIRECTOR, IRS COLLECTION CHIEF, JUDGE, U.S. ATTORNEY, STATE ATTORNEY, ANY MARSHAL(S) IS NOW TABULATED FOR EACH BEING LISTED BELOW FOR PROOF OF JURISDICTION.

	AMOUNT OWED IN FEDERAL RESERVE NOTES	
1)	Maria Pavon, IRS Revenue Agent	One Million FRN's[95]
2)	Marcy Singleton, IRS Appeals Officer	One Million FRN's
3)	Lydia Thurston, U.S. District Judge	One Million FRN's
4)	Paul Sanders, U.S. Atty.	One Million FRN's

THE ATTACHED DOCUMENTS ARE A HABEAS CORPUS, A COMMERCIAL/COMMON LAW LIEN UPON THE ESCROWED PROPERTY, REAL PROPERTY, SIGNATURES, AND BONDS IN THE NORMAL COMMERCIAL SENSE AND AS SUCH IS A SECURITY REPRESENTING ACCOUNTS RECEIVABLE.

IN ADDITION, ACTUAL MONETARY COST AND LOSSES TO THE LIEN CLAIMANT CAUSED BY ACTIONS AND VIOLATIONS OF THE LIEN DEBTORS IS IN EXCESS OF 2 MILLION DOLLARS.

Until the claims of this lien are categorically responded to, point by point, to the satisfaction of the Lien Claimant, or damages to the Lien Claimant are paid, or by the verdict "duly" convened at LAW and properly conducted, this Lien will not be removed. Any Judge attempting to remove this Commercial/Common Law Lien process, without the verdict of a commercial (Seventh Article of the National Constitution) Jury Trial, will be added as a Lien Debtor. Any attempt to rescue property impounded by this Lien is pound breach, a felony. Conduct Yourself Accordingly.

THIS IS NOT A LIS PENDENS LIEN

Common Law Seal

Documenting Crimes Against the People

John Doe Public "At Law"

Right Thumb Print

Deuteronomy 19:15... "so at the mouth of two more witnesses shall the matter be established."

1. ______________________

2. ______________________

[95] [Authors' note: FRN stands for "Federal Reserve Note," in other words the paper money in our wallets. It is a standard tax defier position that FRNs are valueless since the United Stated went off the gold standard.]

Chapter 3

RELATED CRIMES OUTSIDE THE INTERNAL REVENUE CODE

18 U.S.C. §§ 2, 286, 287, 371, 1001, 1341, 1343, 1956, and 1957

31 U.S.C. §§ 5313, 5316, 5322, and 5324

I. INTRODUCTION

This chapter will focus on the most common crimes outside of Title 26 that the Government charges in tax-related cases. Given the overlap in federal criminal statutes, conduct of a taxpayer may be charged under Title 26 or under various statutes within Title 18.[1] Depending upon the conduct engaged in, the Title 18 charges may be in lieu of or in addition to Title 26 counts. While prosecutors have many options, we will only cover the few most important Title 18 crimes.[2] In addition, we will discuss the policies the Government employs in deciding whether to charge conduct under Title 26 or a statute outside the Code.

II. CONSPIRACY

A. Introduction

The most important non-Title 26 crime charged in tax cases is conspiracy. The Government frequently adds conspiracy charges in tax prosecution to increase its chances of obtaining a conviction. The mere charge of "conspiracy" connotes something sinister, and adding numerous defendants into a single case with an overarching conspiracy charge may make it difficult for the jury to assess independently the guilt or innocence of each. The Government also receives more tangible and strategic benefits from the conspiracy charge — vicarious liability for offenses committed by others in furtherance of the conspiracy,[3] ability to admit statements that would otherwise be inadmissible hearsay,[4] relaxed standard of

---

[1] For example, filing a false tax return might also be charged as mail fraud or wire fraud, see 18 U.S.C. §§ 1341, 1343, or making a false statement, *see* 18 U.S.C. § 1001.

[2] Some of the other Title 18 charges available to federal prosecutors include perjury, 18 U.S.C. §§ 1621, 1622, and 1623, and obstruction of justice, 18 U.S.C. §§ 1505, 1512, 1519, and 1520.

[3] *See, e.g.*, Pinkerton v. United States, 328 U.S. 640 (1946).

[4] *See* Fed. R. Evid. 801(d)(2)(E): "A statement is not hearsay if . . . the statement is offered against a party and is . . . a statement by a coconspirator of a party during the course and in furtherance of the

proof and relevancy,[5] tolling or refreshing of the statute of limitations,[6] and venue in judicial districts of the Government's choosing.[7] It is therefore not surprising that the Government charges conspiracy whenever it can imagine more than one bad guy behind the tree — it is so easy to do (just some extra words in the indictment), the benefits are great, and there is little downside for the Government. This means, of course, that the Government's power to tack on conspiracy charges can be abused. As the Supreme Court noted: "We agree that indictments under the broad language of the general conspiracy statute must be scrutinized carefully as to each of the charged defendants because of the possibility, inherent in a criminal conspiracy charge, that its wide net may ensnare the innocent as well as the culpable."[8]

The Internal Revenue Code does not contain a conspiracy statute.[9] Instead, conspiracy to commit a crime under the Code is charged under 18 U.S.C. section 371, the general federal conspiracy statute. Section 371 sets out two types of conspiracies: (1) conspiracy to commit an offense against the United States and (2) conspiracy to defraud the United States.[10] If a tax case is charged as a conspiracy to commit an offense against the U.S., the offense is generally a Title 26 offense like tax evasion or filing a false return. If a tax case is charged under the conspiracy to defraud clause, it is charged as a so-called "*Klein* conspiracy," where the Government alleges the defendant conspired to defraud the United States for the purpose of "impeding, impairing, obstructing and defeating the lawful [government] functions of the [Internal Revenue Service of the] Department of the Treasury in the [ascertainment, computation, assessment, and] collection of the revenue: to wit, income taxes."[11]

B. The Elements

Regardless of the clause under which it is brought, the elements of a conspiracy case are:

1. The existence of an agreement by two or more persons to commit an offense against the United States or to defraud the United States;
2. The defendant's knowing and voluntary participation in the conspiracy; and
3. The commission of an overt act in furtherance of the conspiracy.[12]

---

conspiracy." Thus, charging a conspiracy may permit the Government to introduce evidence that it could not have otherwise introduced.

[5] Blumenthal v. United States, 332 U.S. 539, 557 (1947).

[6] *See* Grunewald v. United States, 353 U.S. 391, 396–97 (1957).

[7] Hyde v. United States, 225 U.S. 347, 362–63 (1912).

[8] Dennis v. United States, 384 U.S. 855, 860 (1966).

[9] Conduct that could be charged as a conspiracy can, however, be charged under the omnibus clause of section 7212.

[10] While section 371 lists two types of violations, the courts have generally held that there is only one offense under that section. *See, e.g.*, United States v. Hope, 861 F.2d 1574, 1578 n.8 (11th Cir. 1988).

[11] United States v. Klein, 247 F.2d 908, 915 (2d Cir. 1957).

[12] CTM 23.03.

Tax conspiracy cases have their own unique flavor. Nonetheless, since they are charged under the general conspiracy statute, they are seasoned by nearly a century of conspiracy law, and the lawyer should become familiar with non-tax conspiracy cases.[13]

1. The Agreement

The essence of a conspiracy is the agreement itself. As Justice Jackson noted:

> The modern crime of conspiracy is so vague that it almost defies definition. Despite certain elementary and essential elements, it also, chameleon-like, takes on a special coloration from each of the many independent offenses on which it may be overlaid. It is always 'predominantly mental in composition' because it consists primarily of a meeting of minds and an intent.[14]

Like the tango, a conspiracy requires (at least) two people — a defendant cannot conspire with himself.[15] In order to establish the existence of an agreement, the Government must show that the defendant and at least one other person reached an understanding or agreement to carry out the objective of the conspiracy.[16] As long as a defendant understands the unlawful nature of the scheme and knowingly and intentionally joins in that scheme, that is sufficient to convict him for conspiracy. Even though a conspiracy requires two people, the Government need not name the other defendant in the indictment.[17] In fact, the Criminal Tax Manual provides:

> Prosecutors should be aware that it is the position of the Department of Justice that, in the absence of some sound reason, it is not desirable to identify unindicted coconspirators in conspiracy indictments. United States Attorneys' Manual (USAM) 9-11.130 (June 2008). The recommended practice in such cases is to merely allege that the defendant "conspired with another person or persons known to the grand jury" and supply the identity, if requested, in a bill of particulars. The above policy does not apply, however, where the person "has been officially charged with the misconduct at issue." USAM 9-27.760.[18]

A defendant cannot, however, conspire with undercover agents. Since the prosecution must prove that at least two culpable parties reached an agreement, proof of an agreement solely between a defendant and a government agent or informer will not support a conspiracy conviction.[19] Surprisingly, a corporation can be part of a conspiracy with one or more its own employees or shareholders, and it

---

[13] The classic dissertation on conspiracy law is Abraham S. Goldstein, *Conspiracy to Defraud the United States*, 68 Yale L.J. 405 (1959). A more current treatment is John A. Townsend, *Is Making the IRS's Job Harder Enough?*, 9 Hous. & Bus. Tax L.J. 260 (2009).

[14] Krulewitch v. United States, 336 U.S. 440, 446–448 (1949) (concurring).

[15] Morrison v. California, 291 U.S. 82, 92 (1934).

[16] *See, e.g.*, United States v. Barnes, 604 F.2d 121, 161 (2d Cir. 1979).

[17] Rogers v. United States, 340 U.S. 367, 375 (1951) ("identity of the other members of the conspiracy is not needed, inasmuch as one person can be convicted of conspiring with persons whose names are unknown").

[18] CTM 23.04[2][a].

[19] United States v. Pennell, 737 F.2d 521, 536 (6th Cir. 1984), *cert. denied*, 469 U.S. 1158.

can be held criminally liable under section 371, even though it is not a sentient being able to enter into an agreement.[20] However, there generally must be more than one human actor involved in the conspiracy for a corporation to be charged with conspiracy.[21]

The Government need not prove that the alleged conspirators entered into any formal agreement, that they directly stated between themselves all the details of the scheme, or that the agreement was in writing. The Government need not prove that all of the details of the scheme alleged in the indictment were actually agreed upon or carried out. Nor must it prove that all of the persons alleged to have been members of the conspiracy were actually members, or that the alleged conspirators actually succeeded in accomplishing their unlawful objectives.

The traditional rule was that, although the Government must prove that a defendant was a member of a conspiracy, this requirement may be satisfied by a showing of only a "slight connection" to the conspiracy or "slight evidence" of the defendant's participation, so long as the connection is proven beyond a reasonable doubt.[22] However, this is now the minority rule. The trend in the courts directly addressing the issue is that the use of "slight evidence" or any similar formulation raises the unacceptable potential for impairing the requirement that the Government prove the elements of the crime, including the defendant's agreement to participate and his participation in the conspiracy. As Judge Easterbrook has noted:

> "Conspiracy" is a net in which prosecutors catch many little fish. We should not go out of our way to tighten the mesh. Prosecutors have many legitimate advantages in the criminal process. Defendants' great counterweight is the requirement that the prosecution establish guilt beyond a reasonable doubt. [The slight evidence rule] reduces the power of that requirement.[23]

The Second Circuit, following Judge Easterbrook's lead, held that the various formulations of the slight evidence notion "do not accurately describe the government's burden of proof in conspiracy cases, and the use of these formulations should be discontinued."[24] The modern cases recognize that because of the very broad nature of the conspiracy statute and the ability to reach even peripheral players,

---

[20] *See, e.g.*, United States v. Ames Sintering Co., 927 F.2d 232, 236 (6th Cir. 1990); United States v. Hartley, 678 F.2d 961, 972 (11th Cir.), *rehearing denied*, 688 F.2d 852 (11th Cir. 1982), *cert. denied*, 459 U.S. 1170 (1983).

[21] *See, e.g.*, United States v. Stevens, 909 F.2d, 431, 432–34 (11th Cir. 1990).

[22] United States v. Boone, 951 F.2d 1526, 1543 (9th Cir. 1991).

[23] United States v. Martinez de Ortiz, 883 F.2d 515, 524–25 (7th Cir. 1989) (Easterbrook, concurring) (citations omitted).

[24] United States v. Huezo, 546 F.3d 174, 180 n.2 (2d Cir. 2008), *cert. denied*, 558 U.S. 936 (2009). In the authors' judgment, the objections to the use of these "slight" formulations have carried the day. *See also* United States v. Pflueger, 2013 U.S. Dist. LEXIS 58088 (D. Haw. Mar. 20, 2013) (Eighty-seven-year-old defendant acquitted of conspiracy to defraud IRS because government failed to establish beyond a reasonable doubt the intent element. "The crime of conspiracy includes an intent element which requires the Government to show that each member of the conspiracy had knowledge of the object of the conspiracy and joined the conspiracy intending to achieve that object.")

there is a danger that individuals who were not part of "the agreement" might be charged and convicted of the conspiracy.

2. Knowing and Voluntary Participation in the Conspiracy

The second element the Government must prove is that the defendant knowingly and voluntarily participated in the conspiracy and that he or she intended to join it and to accomplish the object of the conspiracy.[25] A defendant need not know all of the details of the conspiracy or know all of the members to be considered part of a conspiracy.[26] Similarly, a defendant may become a member of a conspiracy even if that person agrees to play a minor role in the conspiracy, so long as he or she understands the essential nature of the scheme and intentionally joins in it.[27] The Government is not required to prove that each defendant specifically agreed to commit the offense or knew that the offense would be committed.[28] Rather, it is sufficient if the Government establishes that the offense was in furtherance of the conspiracy or was reasonably foreseen as a necessary or natural consequence of the unlawful agreement. The Government is, however, required to prove that the defendant knowingly participated in the conspiracy that is charged in the indictment. The Ninth Circuit's decision in *United States v. Krasovich* illustrates that issue.

UNITED STATES v. KRASOVICH
United States Court of Appeals, Ninth Circuit
819 F.2d 253 (1987)

The dispositive issue in this appeal is the sufficiency of the evidence underlying the appellant's conviction of conspiracy to defraud the United States in violation of 18 U.S.C. § 371. Appellant Krasovich was convicted on one count (Count Eight) of a multi-count, multi-defendant indictment. That count charged Krasovich with conspiracy to defraud the Internal Revenue Service "in the ascertainment, computation, assessment, and collection of . . . the personal income taxes of John Thomas Drummond."

The underlying facts are not now disputed. John Drummond and his wife Andrea Drummond were in the cocaine business. Krasovich was their mechanic, servicing and repairing various vehicles for them. In December of 1984, the government arrested the Drummonds and instituted civil forfeiture proceedings against vehicles and earth moving equipment they allegedly owned. The vehicle that was the subject of Count Eight of the indictment was a used pickup truck purchased several months later, in April, 1985. Krasovich paid for the truck with money provided by Andrea Drummond. Krasovich registered the truck in his name and later confessed to a

---

[25] *See, e.g.*, United States v. Berger, 224 F.3d 107, 114–15 (2d Cir. 2000); United States v. Esparza, 876 F.2d 1390, 1392 (9th Cir. 1989).

[26] *See, e.g.*, Blumenthal v. United States, 332 U.S. 539, 557 (1947); United States v. Horn, 946 F.2d 738, 741 (10th Cir. 1991).

[27] United States v. Andrews, 953 F.2d 1312, 1318 (11th Cir. 1992); United States v. Medina, 940 F.2d 1247, 1250 (9th Cir. 1991); United States v. Warner, 690 F.2d 545, 550 (6th Cir. 1982).

[28] United States v. Etheridge, 424 F.2d 951, 965 (6th Cir. 1970).

drug enforcement agent that he did this so that the truck would not be registered in Andrea's name.

The evidence at trial showed that Krasovich knew that the Drummonds were involved in the drug trade. It also showed that Krasovich had filed false statements with the government claiming ownership of other vehicles and equipment belonging to the Drummonds. There was evidence showing that an Internal Revenue Service agent had previously told Krasovich in connection with those false claims, but not in connection with the pickup truck, that it could be illegal to claim another's property as his own.

As explained more fully below, there was no evidence, direct or circumstantial, to indicate that when Krasovich purchased the truck in April of 1985, he intended or agreed with anyone else to impede the Internal Revenue Service in its collection of taxes, as charged in the indictment. The appellant therefore argues, and we hold, that the evidence was insufficient to permit a jury reasonably to find Krasovich guilty of the crime charged in the indictment. The conviction must be reversed.

The principal purpose of an indictment is to "provide the defendant with a description of the charges against him in sufficient detail to enable him to prepare his defense and plead double jeopardy at a later prosecution." *United States v. Lane*, 765 F.2d 1376, 1380 (9th Cir. 1985). The indictment must contain the elements of the offense charged and apprise the defendant of what he must be prepared to meet. "An indictment charging a conspiracy under 18 U.S.C. § 371 should allege an agreement, the unlawful object toward which the agreement is directed, and an overt act in furtherance of the conspiracy." *Lane*, 765 F.2d at 1380. The indictment in this case charged an agreement with Andrea Drummond, the object of which was to impede the collection of federal income taxes owed by Andrea's husband John.

The existence of a conspiratorial agreement or common purpose may be inferred from the evidence. "[W]e view the evidence and all inferences reasonably drawn from the evidence in the light most favorable to the government." *United States v. Ramirez*, 710 F.2d 535, 548 (9th Cir. 1983). Knowledge of the objective of the conspiracy is an essential element of any conspiracy conviction.

It therefore follows that where, as here, the objective is alleged to be interference with "the ascertainment, computation, assessment, and collection of . . . the personal income taxes of John Thomas Drummond," the government must prove knowledge of that objective. Thus, in *Ingram*, the defendants were charged with a conspiracy to evade federal wagering tax. The Supreme Court reversed the convictions of two lower-level functionaries because of the absence of any proof that they were aware of the tax liability. Cautioning that the crime of conspiracy must not become a dragnet for every substantive offense, the Court found the proof insufficient, even though the defendants were involved in concealing a gambling operation. 360 U.S. at 679–80. This case is similar in all material respects. The government did not show that the defendant knew the alleged objective of the conspiracy.

Not only must the government prove knowledge of the illegal objective, it must also prove an agreement with a co-conspirator to pursue that objective as a common one. Thus, a conviction has been held improper where one alleged conspirator, in enlisting another, told him the operation's objective was tax evasion when in fact it was cashing fraudulent checks. There the court held that although both alleged co-conspirators agreed to commit offenses against the United States, they had not agreed on the same offense. Thus, in the absence of any proof that the defendant knew of the tax objective of an alleged co-conspirator, there can be no adequate proof of an agreement to pursue that objective.

An extensive discussion of the requirements for proof involving an indictment under § 371 for revenue fraud is found in recent decisions of the Eleventh and Fifth Circuits in *United States v. Browning*, 723 F.2d 1544 (11th Cir. 1984), and *United States v. Enstam*, 622 F.2d 857 (5th Cir. 1980), *cert. denied*, 450 U.S. 912 (1984). In *Enstam*, the court said that the government's burden is not met if it shows only that the object of a conspiracy was to hide the source of money rather than specifically to impede the collection or assessment of income taxes. The court emphasized later in *Browning*, where the indictment charged impairing the IRS in its function of identifying revenue and collecting taxes, that the evidence must demonstrate that the conspirators knew of that objective. This ruling comports with the general principle that although a defendant may be found guilty of conspiracy even if he did not know all of the details of the scheme, the evidence must demonstrate that he knew the conspiracy's essential objectives.

In this case, there may well have been ample evidence that Andrea Drummond intended to use Krasovich to hide true ownership of property in order to evade income taxes. There is, however, no basis on which a reasonable jury could conclude that the defendant Krasovich had the same objective with respect to the transaction alleged in Count Eight. Nothing in the circumstances of the transaction suggests that Krasovich knew that the purpose of the concealment was to evade taxes.

Andrea Drummond may have wished to conceal ownership of the truck because she wanted to use it in illegal activities, or because she wanted to avoid drawing attention to herself or her finances, or because she feared seizure of the truck under the forfeiture statute if her ownership became known. "This is not a case where efforts at concealment would be reasonably explainable only in terms of motivation to evade taxation." *Ingram*, 360 U.S. at 679; *see also id.* at 678–80. Indeed, the only link between the defendant and the tax laws on the evidence before the jury was a conversation between Krasovich and the IRS agent approximately a month before Krasovich claimed ownership of the pickup truck. In sum, the evidence is not sufficient to show that Krasovich conspired with Andrea Drummond with the objective of interfering with the Internal Revenue Service's collection of John Drummond's taxes, Andrea Drummond's taxes, or any other taxes.

3. Overt Act

The third element the Government must prove is that a member of the conspiracy committed an "overt act" in furtherance of the conspiracy. The function of the overt act requirement is to show that the conspiracy is actually proceeding and is not simply an agreement existing solely in the minds of the conspirators.[29] An overt act is any act done by a member of the conspiracy for the purpose of carrying

---

[29] Yates v. United States, 354 U.S. 298, 334 (1957).

out or accomplishing the object of the conspiracy.[30] The overt act need not necessarily be criminal in character, and the act itself may be totally legal in itself.[31] However, the act must be in furtherance of an illegal scheme or plan. For example, it is perfectly legal to rent a car. However, if a person rents a car to be used as the getaway car in a bank robbery conspiracy, the renting of the car will suffice as an overt act. While the Government must allege overt acts in the indictment, it is not required to prove all of the overt acts alleged in an indictment. Proof of at least one overt act committed in furtherance of the conspiracy is sufficient.[32]

A particularly important issue for tax conspiracy centers around whether a so-called "act of concealment" may constitute an overt act. Generally, an act of concealment can be an overt act, but the act may only be considered if it was committed prior to the object of the conspiracy being accomplished. Once accomplished, the conspiracy is over and subsequent overt acts are not part of or in furtherance of the conspiracy. In *Grunewald v. United States*,[33] the Supreme Court was concerned with the Government's attempts to lengthen indefinitely the duration of a conspiracy by simply showing that the conspirators took steps to cover their tracks in order to avoid detection and punishment after the central purpose of the conspiracy had been accomplished. The Court stressed that a "distinction must be made between acts of concealment done in furtherance of the main criminal objectives of the conspiracy, and acts of concealment done after these central objectives have been obtained, for the purpose only of covering up after the crime."[34]

The problem with tax conspiracies, however, is that the object of the crime is usually to conceal income from the IRS. Indeed, the very definition of an affirmative act of evasion in a tax evasion case is "any conduct, the likely effect of which would be to mislead or . . . conceal."[35] In addition, overt acts in furtherance of conspiracies to defraud the United States in connection with tax assessment and collection or to commit tax offenses generally involve acts which mislead or conceal. Thus, criminal tax conspiracies usually contemplate acts of concealment to further the crime and these acts may be admissible as overt acts.[36] The Criminal Tax Manual urges prosecutors to be careful in how they draft indictments to avoid the *Grunewald* problem: "Note that care must be taken when drafting an indictment charging a conspiracy contemplating concealment. If the indictment is not properly drafted to include concealment as an object of the conspiracy, *Grunewald* might preclude the admission into evidence of certain acts of concealment."[37]

---

30 United States v. Falcone, 311 U.S. 205, 210 (1940).

31 This issue is discussed at length in the context of the *Caldwell* case below.

32 *See, e.g.*, United States v. Lewis, 759 F.2d 1316, 1344 (8th Cir. 1985).

33 353 U.S. 391 (1957).

34 *Id.* at 405.

35 Spies v. United States, 317 U.S. 492, 499 (1943).

36 *See, e.g.*, United States v. Vogt, 910 F.2d 1184, 1201–02 (4th Cir. 1990), *rehearing denied*, 1990 U.S. App. LEXIS 16473 (4th Cir. 1990), *cert. denied*, 498 U.S. 1083 (1991); United States v. Pinto, 838 F.2d 426, 435 (10th Cir. 1988).

37 CTM 23.06[2].

C. *Pinkerton* Liability

The crime of conspiracy is an independent crime separate from the substantive offense that may be the object of the conspiracy, and the conspiracy statute does not require that any substantive offense actually have even been committed. Significantly, even if the substantive offense that is the object of the conspiracy is committed, the conspiracy does not merge into that the substantive offense. The substantive offense and the conspiracy to commit the offense can be charged independently or together. Indeed, the Government may obtain a conviction on a conspiracy charge even if at the time of the agreement and overt act the Government has defeated the criminal object of the conspiracy.[38] For both the substantive crime and the conspiracy to be tried, the Government must prove (i) as to the conspiracy, the agreement and at least one overt act in furtherance that was reasonably foreseeable within the scope of the agreement and (ii) as to the substantive offense for one who did not commit the offense and thus can only be liable because of the conspiracy, that the offense was committed and that the offense committed was reasonably foreseeable in furtherance of the conspiracy. The latter point may be stated in the negative: A person may be a member of the conspiracy but will not be charged with respect to a substantive offense that "was not in fact done in furtherance of the conspiracy, did not fall within the scope of the unlawful project, or was merely a part of . . . the plan which could not be reasonably foreseen as a necessary or natural consequence of the unlawful agreement."[39]

In *Pinkerton*, the Court held that a conspirator can be found guilty of both the crime of conspiracy, as well as any separate offense committed within the scope of the conspiracy, even if the conspirator did not commit the substantive offense and did nothing more than join the conspiracy. *Pinkerton* thus imposes vicarious liability upon conspirators. The principle established in *Pinkerton* is often referred to as *Pinkerton* liability for the substantive offense. *Pinkerton* liability is a term of art that practitioners simply must know.

D. Conspiracy to Commit a Substantive Offense

As discussed above, the first of the two types of conspiracy described in section 371 is a conspiracy to commit an offense against the United States (what we will call offense conspiracy). In tax cases, the offense that was the object of an alleged conspiracy would usually be a tax crime, such as sections 7201, 7206(1), and 7206(2). Often the person charged with the conspiracy is not the person liable for the tax but is one who conspired with others to understate the tax liability of another by filing a false return or other acts. What mental state must the Government prove in order to convict the person of the offense conspiracy? In Chapter 2A, we discussed that in tax cases the Government is generally required to prove that the defendant acted willfully, *i.e.*, an intentional violation of a known legal duty.[40] Section 371 does not itself contain a willfulness requirement. However, the Supreme Court in

---

[38] *See* United States v. Jimenez Recio, 537 U.S. 270 (2003).

[39] Pinkerton v. United States, 328 U.S. 640, 647–8 (1946).

[40] *See, e.g.*, Cheek v. United States, 498 U.S. 192 (1991).

Ingram v. United States,[41] held that willfulness is required for conviction of an offense conspiracy involving tax charges where the mental state required to commit the offense is willfulness. Thus, in order for the Government to obtain a conviction of an offense conspiracy, it must prove that the defendant knew that the agreement was to commit an act that would intentionally violate a known legal duty. In *Ingram*, the four defendants — two owners (Ingram and Jenkins) and two employees (Smith and Law) — participated in the conduct and concealment of lottery operations that were illegal under state law. The two owners failed to pay the federal wagering taxes that they owed by virtue of the illegal lottery. The other two, as employees, were not liable for the taxes. The Government indicted and convicted all four of conspiracy to evade the taxes. In addressing the conspiracy charges against the two employees, the Court held:[42]

> Conspiracy to commit a particular substantive offense cannot exist without at least the degree of criminal intent necessary for the substantive offense itself. The substantive offense which Smith and Law were accused of conspiring to commit was the willful evasion of federal taxes, an offense which, even presuming knowledge of the tax law, obviously cannot be committed in the absence of knowledge of willfulness.
>
> Indulging, as of course we must, in that view of the evidence most favorable to the Government, we simply cannot discern adequate foundation in the present record for a finding that Smith and Law had such knowledge of Ingram's and Jenkins' wagering tax liability. The record is completely barren of any direct evidence of such knowledge. It was not shown, for example, that any reference had ever been made by any of the petitioners to possible tax liability, or that they had filed a return or paid a tax in previous years. The Government relied instead upon evidence which, it asserts, circumstantially proved the requisite knowledge on the part of Smith and Law. These circumstances were simply the intimate connection of Smith and Law with the operation of the lottery itself, their cooperation in conducting it secretly, and their apparent knowledge that it was conducted at a profit. The Government points out that not only would payment of the taxes have decreased the profits to be derived from operation of the lottery, but in addition would have required registration, including the names and addresses of the bankers and writers, with the local internal revenue office and the posting of a wagering tax stamp at the place of business. 26 U.S.C. (Supp. V) §§ 4412, 6806(c). The information contained in the registration would have been available to local law enforcement officials. 26 U.S.C. (Supp. V) § 6107.
>
> Yet these circumstances actually are colorless as to the vital issue of knowledge on the part of Smith and Law that their superiors owed federal wagering taxes. Certainly the secrecy of the operation did not go to show that knowledge.

---

[41] 360 U.S. 672, 678 (1959).

[42] *Id.* at 678–680.

This is not a case where efforts at concealment would be reasonably explainable only in terms of motivation to evade taxation. Here, the criminality of the enterprise under local law provided more than sufficient reason for the secrecy in which it was conducted. A conspiracy, to be sure, may have multiple objectives, and if one of its objectives, even a minor one, be the evasion of federal taxes, the offense is made out, though the primary objective may be concealment of another crime. But the fact that payment of the federal taxes by Ingram and Jenkins might have resulted in disclosure of the lottery and subsequent prosecution of Smith and Law by local authorities would permit an inference that concealment of the lottery was motivated by a purpose to evade payment of federal taxes only if, independently, there were proof that Smith and Law knew of the tax liability. Evidence that Smith and Law might have wanted the taxes to be evaded if they had known of them, and that they engaged in conduct which could have been in furtherance of a plan to evade the taxes if they had known of them, is not evidence that they did know of them. What was said in *Direct Sales Co. v. United States* on behalf of a unanimous [Supreme] Court is of particular relevance here:

> "Without the knowledge, the intent cannot exist. . . . Furthermore, to establish the intent, the evidence of knowledge must be clear, not equivocal. . . . This, because charges of conspiracy are not to be made out by piling inference upon inference, thus fashioning . . . a dragnet to draw in all substantive crimes." 319 U.S., at 711.

Smith and Law were not liable for the wagering tax. They could not, therefore, have been convicted of the crime which they were charged with having conspired to commit. To sustain their conviction on this record would make of the crime of conspiracy just that "dragnet to draw in all substantive crimes" against which the Court warned in Direct Sales.

The Court in *Ingram* reversed the conviction of the employees because of lack of proof of their knowledge of the tax liability but sustained the conviction of the two owners of the business because there was sufficient proof of their knowledge.

E. Conspiracy to Defraud the United States

The other type of conspiracy contained in section 371 is a conspiracy to defraud. The defraud clause is extremely broad and can include a variety of acts, including conduct that would not otherwise constitute a crime under federal law.[43] The case that set the parameters of the defraud clause is *Hammerschmidt v. United States*,[44] in which the Supreme Court held that the phrase "conspiracy to defraud the United States" means:

> To conspire to defraud the United States means primarily to cheat the Government out of property or money, but it also means to interfere with

---

[43] *See, e.g.*, United States v. Tuohey, 867 F.2d 534, 537 (9th Cir. 1989); CTM 23.07[1][b].

[44] 265 U.S. 182, 188 (1924).

> or obstruct one of its lawful governmental functions by deceit, craft or trickery, or at least by means that are dishonest. It is not necessary that the Government shall be subjected to property or pecuniary loss by the fraud, but only that its legitimate official action and purpose shall be defeated by misrepresentation, chicane or the overreaching of those charged with carrying out the governmental intention.

Thus, a defendant may commit a conspiracy to defraud by (1) cheating the Government out of money or property, or (2) interfering with or obstructing one of its lawful governmental functions (for our purposes the IRS) by deceit, craft, trickery, or at least by dishonest means. Because the two means are in the disjunctive, the Government need not establish a pecuniary loss to the United States, that the scheme to defraud was a success, or that the Government was actually harmed.[45] That being said, at least one court has begun to question whether the expansive reading of section 371 in *Hammerschmidt*, holding that no pecuniary loss is required, is supported by the statute.[46]

From a prosecutor's perspective, the defraud clause is a powerful tool because the Government is not required to show that the scheme was actually a crime. Thus, the prosecutor does not have to establish all of the elements of an underlying offense or prove what is usually the most difficult element of a tax case — willfulness. All the prosecutor is required to prove is that the members agreed to cheat the Government out of money or property or to interfere with or obstruct one of the Government's lawful functions "by deceit, craft[, or] trickery, or at least by means that are dishonest."[47]

Because a conspiracy to defraud charge is such a powerful and nimble tool, the courts scrutinize defraud indictments even more closely:

> When the government proceeds under the conspiracy-to-defraud clause, in cases that could as easily have been brought under the "offense" clause, the courts must be alert to subtle "attempts to broaden the already pervasive and wide-sweeping nets of conspiracy prosecutions." *Grunewald v. United States*, 353 U.S. 391, 404 (1957) . . . . The terms "conspiracy" and "defraud," when used together, have a "peculiar susceptibility to a kind of tactical manipulation which shields from view very real infringements on basic values of our criminal law." . . . Accordingly, conspiracy-to-defraud prosecutions are "scrutinized carefully." *Dennis v. United States*, 384 U.S. 855, 860 (1966).[48]

As a result, the Government must plead the "essential nature" of the alleged fraudulent scheme. It is not sufficient for the indictment to simply repeat the language in the statute; rather, it must allege the fraudulent scheme in its

---

[45] *Id.*; United States v. Rosengarten, 857 F.2d 76, 79 (2d Cir. 1988), *cert. denied*, 488 U.S. 1011 (1989).

[46] United States v. Coplan, 703 F.3d 46, 60–62 (2d Cir. 2012). Nevertheless, the panel held that it was bound by the holdings of *Hammerschmidt* and *Klein*.

[47] Hammerschmidt, 265 U.S. at 188; United States v. Goldberg, 105 F.3d 770, 773 (1st Cir. 1997).

[48] United States v. Rosenblatt, 554 F.2d 36, 40 (2d Cir. 1977).

particulars.[49] The Criminal Tax Manual instructs prosecutors that: "a defraud clause indictment should include: (1) the name of the agency impeded; (2) what functions of the agency were impeded; (3) what means were used to impede the agency; and (4) the identity of those charged with impeding the agency."[50]

F. *Klein* Conspiracy

A conspiracy to defraud the IRS is commonly referred to as a "*Klein* conspiracy," after the leading case in this area.[51] The general description of a *Klein* conspiracy is "to defraud the United States by impeding, impairing, obstructing and defeating the lawful functions of the Internal Revenue Service of the Department of the Treasury in the ascertainment, computation, assessment, and collection of the revenue: to wit, income taxes.[52] In *Klein*, the Second Circuit upheld the conspiracy conviction and in so doing listed 20 acts of concealment that qualify as efforts to impede the functions of the IRS. The Criminal Tax Manual summarizes these acts into eight general courses of conduct:[53]

1. Alteration of the books to make liquidating dividends appear as commissions;
2. Alteration of the books to make a gratuitous payment of $1,500,000 appear as a repayment of a loan;
3. A false entry in the books disguising as commissions what was actually a dividend, which in turn was diverted to corporate nominees;
4. A false statement in Klein's personal income tax return regarding the payment for a stock purchase;
5. Klein's false answer to Treasury interrogatories seeking to identify the owners of various Cuban corporations;
6. A return falsely reporting that stock was sold in 1950 for an immense profit;
7. The evasive affidavit of Klein's secretary denying that he remembered altering certain books; and
8. Income tax returns which falsely claimed a sale of stock.

The CTM then gives numerous examples as to conduct that has been held to qualify as a Klein conspiracy, including:[54] *United States v. Goldberg*, 105 F.3d 770, 772 (1st Cir. 1997) (scheme to conceal payments to individuals through use of "straw employees" and benefits to third parties); *United States v. Hurley*, 957 F.2d 1 (1st Cir. 1992) (money laundering scheme using front companies set up in Panama and the Bahamas, and unconventional business practices such as $100,000 transactions in currency and checks made out in names of third parties); *United*

---

[49] *Id.* at 40–42; *cf.* FRCP 9(b) (requiring pleading fraud with particularity in civil cases).

[50] CTM 23.07[1][c].

[51] United States v. Klein, 247 F.2d 908 (2d Cir. 1957).

[52] *Id.* at 915.

[53] CTM 23.07[2][a].

[54] CTM 23.07[2][b].

States v. Macchia, 35 F.3d 662, 666 (2d Cir. 1994) (gasoline excise tax scheme using daisy chain of fictitious transactions to make it appear that the insolvent "burn" company had been the first entity to engage in a sale requiring payment of the fuel excise tax); *United States v. Rosengarten*, 857 F.2d 76 (2d Cir. 1988) (creation of false tax deductions by backdating documents relating to a real estate tax shelter investment); *United States v. Nersesian*, 824 F.2d 1294 (2d Cir. 1987) (converting $117,000 in cash into money orders and traveler's checks in amounts less than $10,000 increments to avoid CTR filings); *United States v. Fleschner*, 98 F.3d 155 (4th Cir. 1996) (defendants, associated with a tax protestor group the Hickory Carolina Patriots, advised others to claim excess allowances on W-4 forms, not to file tax returns, to hide income from the banking system, and to deal in cash); *United States v. Schmidt*, 935 F.2d 1440 (4th Cir. 1991) (scheme to sell trusts known as Unincorporated Business Organizations (UBOs) where participants could assign income and assets to the trusts and take false business deductions on personal expenses, as well as hide their income in financial institutions in the Marshall Islands); *United States v. Aubin*, 87 F.3d 141 (5th Cir. 1996) (land flip, purchase, and simultaneous resale devised to obtain cash without identifying parties). *United States v. Kraig*, 99 F.3d 1361 (6th Cir. 1996) (attorney aided client in concealing assets, mainly real estate, through foreign shell corporations); *United States v. Huebner*, 48 F.3d 376, 378 (9th Cir. 1994) (defendants created sham debts and advised clients to file bankruptcy to impede IRS collection activity); and *United States v. Scott*, 37 F.3d 1564 (10th Cir. 1994) (promotion of trusts and unincorporated business organizations to eliminate income tax liability without losing control of money or assets).

Thus, the conduct that may constitute a conspiracy to defraud the IRS is exceedingly broad and may include seemingly innocuous conduct. While, as we have seen, the fraudulent conduct is not required to be an illegal act, is *any* conduct by two or more people that "impedes and impairs" the IRS an illegal conspiracy? This question should give any tax lawyer pause, since the role of a tax lawyers is arguably to make the IRS's job more difficult. The leading case on the outer borders of a conspiracy to defraud charge is the Ninth Circuit's opinion in *Caldwell.*

UNITED STATES v. CALDWELL

United States Court of Appeals, Ninth Circuit
989 F.2d 1056 (1993)

We consider whether conspiring to make the government's job harder is, without more, a federal crime.

Patricia Caldwell was a bookkeeper for the Northwest Community Exchange. The Exchange was a "warehouse bank," a device people use to keep their financial transactions secret. It used numbered accounts, promised to keep no records of clients' transactions and vowed not to disclose information about the accounts to third parties. The Exchange's ostensible goal was maintaining client privacy, but this privacy also helped the Exchange's customers avoid paying taxes.

When you mess with the IRS, the IRS messes back. The government eventually shut down NCE and arrested several of its customers and employees, including

Caldwell. Caldwell was convicted by a jury of conspiring to defraud the United States in violation of 18 U.S.C. § 371, and she now appeals. She was not charged with aiding and abetting tax avoidance or conspiring to avoid taxes.

The "defraud clause" of 18 U.S.C. § 371 prohibits all conspiracies "to defraud the United States, or any agency thereof in any manner or for any purpose." While this seems to cover only defrauding in the normal sense of the word — acquiring another's property by intentional misrepresentations — the word "defraud" has been read much more broadly. "Defrauding" the government under section 371 means obstructing the operation of any government agency by any "deceit, craft or trickery, or at least by means that are dishonest." *Hammerschmidt v. United States*, 265 U.S. 182, 188 (1924). The conspiracy need not aim to deprive the government of property. It need not involve any detrimental reliance by the government. Neither the conspiracy's goal nor the means used to achieve it need to be independently illegal. To convict someone under 18 U.S.C. § 371 the government need only show (1) he entered into an agreement (2) to obstruct a lawful function of the government (3) by deceitful or dishonest means and (4) at least one overt act in furtherance of the conspiracy. This is a very broad provision, which subjects a wide range of activity to potential criminal penalties.

Yet the government proposes an even broader reading of section 371, one that eliminates element (3) altogether. It contends *any* conspiracy to obstruct a government function is illegal, even if the obstruction is not done deceitfully or dishonestly. Under this reading, the government argues, people have a duty "not to conduct their business affairs in such a manner that the IRS would be impeded and impaired in its . . . collection of revenue. Or, as government counsel candidly asserted at oral argument, "if what you're doing, legal or illegal, is intended to impede and impair the Internal Revenue Service, . . . that constitutes a crime under section 371."

We think not. The Supreme Court has made it clear that "defraud" is limited only to wrongs done "by deceit, craft or trickery, or at least by means that are dishonest." *Hammerschmidt*, 265 U.S. at 188. Obstructing government functions in other ways — for example, by violence, robbery or advocacy of illegal action — can't constitute "defrauding."

And surely this is the sensible reading of section 371. Under the government's theory, a husband who asks his wife to buy him a radar detector would be a felon — punishable by up to five years in prison and a fine of $10,000 — because their actions would obstruct the government function of catching speeders. So would a person who witnesses a crime and suggests to another witness (with no hint of threat) that they not tell the police anything unless specifically asked about it. So would the executives of a business that competes with a government-run enterprise and lowers its prices to siphon off the government's customers. So would co-owners of land who refuse to sell it for use as a military base, forcing the government to go to the extra trouble of condemning it. So would have Elliot Richardson and William Ruckelshaus, had they agreed with each other to quit if asked by President Nixon to fire Archibald Cox.

The federal government does lots of things, more and more every year, and many things private parties do can get in the government's way. It can't be that each such action is automatically a felony. The government may, if it wants to, explicitly outlaw conduct it thinks unduly obstructs its functions; in fact, in 1987, it enacted a regulation, 31 C.F.R. § 103.37, prohibiting the very conduct at issue in this case. But we're unwilling to conclude Congress meant to make it a federal crime to do *anything*, even that which is otherwise permitted, with the goal of making the government's job more difficult.

The instruction given to the jury reflected the government's spurious theory. The district court told the jury it should find Caldwell guilty if she merely agreed

> to defraud the United States by impeding, impairing, obstructing and defeating the Internal Revenue Service in ascertaining, computing, assessing and collecting taxes. The law relating to [this] element[ ] is as follows: You must find beyond a reasonable doubt that there was a joint plan to obstruct, impede, impair and defeat [the IRS].

The district court didn't tell the jurors they had to find Caldwell agreed to do this by deceitful or dishonest means.

Failing to instruct jurors about an essential element of a crime is constitutional error because it lets them convict without finding the defendant guilty of that element. Maybe the jury did think Caldwell meant to obstruct the government in a deceitful or dishonest way, perhaps by failing to file required reports, or by making false statements to the government. But it's also possible the jury took the same view the government urged us to take, and found Caldwell guilty just because she agreed to help obstruct the IRS, even if she didn't agree to do so deceitfully or dishonestly. And because the Sixth Amendment requires that all elements of the crime be found by the jury — not just by appellate judges reviewing the record — we can't say the error was harmless.

Making it easy for people to cheat on their taxes hardly deserves a good conduct medal. And Caldwell might indeed have conspired to obstruct the government by deceitful or dishonest means; the government may still try to prove this by retrying her before a properly instructed jury. But what the government actually did prove — that Caldwell conspired to make the IRS's job harder — just isn't illegal.

There are places where, until recently, "everything which [was] not permitted [was] forbidden. . . . [W]hatever [was] permitted [was] mandatory. . . . Citizens were shackled in their actions by the universal passion for banning things." *Yeltsin Addresses RSFSR Congress of People's Deputies*, BBC Summary of World Broadcasts, Apr. 1, 1991, *available in* LEXIS, Nexis Library, OMNI file. Fortunately, the United States is not such a place, and we plan to keep it that way. If the government wants to forbid certain conduct, it may forbid it. If it wants to mandate it, it may mandate it. But we won't lightly infer that in enacting 18 U.S.C. § 371 Congress meant to forbid all things that obstruct the government, or require citizens to do all those things that could make the government's job easier. So long as they don't act dishonestly or deceitfully, and so long as they don't violate some specific law, people living in our society are still free to conduct their affairs any which way they please.

G. Indictments: Offense or Defraud Conspiracy or Both?

If the conduct violates both the offense clause and the defraud clause, can the Government charge either offense? Can it charge both? In one sense it does not matter because the courts hold that the conspiracy statute establishes a single offense. Thus, even if the Government were to charge both types of conspiracy, the defendant is a subject to only a single five-year maximum sentence. In *United States v. Minarik*,[55] the Sixth Circuit held that in order to properly alert defendants of the charges against them, prosecutors must use the offense clause, rather than the defraud clause, when the conduct charged constitutes a conspiracy to violate a specific statute. However, other circuits reject the holding in *Minarik* and allow the Government to charge the defraud clause when the fraud constitutes a separate federal criminal offense,[56] and the Sixth Circuit itself has restricted *Minarik* to its facts.[57]

Assuming the Government can charge either an offense or defraud conspiracy, may it throw both up against the wall and see what sticks? The risk (to defendants at least) is that if both an offense conspiracy and a defraud conspiracy are charged in the same count of an indictment, the jury may become confused and a defendant could be convicted by a nonunanimous jury. For example, the Ninth Circuit reversed a defendant's conviction and held:

> Because Count I charged two conspiracies, there was a distinct possibility of a nonunanimous jury verdict. Some jurors could have voted to convict Gordon and Loeswick on Count I believing the appellants guilty of conspiracy to obstruct justice but innocent of conspiracy to defraud (or vice versa). When there is such a genuine possibility of jury confusion or that a conviction may occur as the result of different jurors concluding that the defendant committed different acts, the trial judge is obligated to give curative instructions or submit special interrogatories to ensure a unanimous verdict.[58]

However, the Second Circuit affirmed the conviction of Leona Helmsley on a conspiracy count that charged both offense conspiracy and conspiracy to defraud, because the court found that the judge's instructions prevented any possible jury confusion that might result from the duplicitous indictment.[59] If both types of conspiracy are charged in the same indictment, it is imperative that counsel object to the indictment prior to trial and, if the objection is overruled, request an instruction that would mitigate any confusion.

---

[55] 875 F.2d 1186, 1187 (6th Cir. 1989), *rehearing denied*, 1989 U.S. App. LEXIS 12381 (6th Cir 1989).

[56] *See, e.g.*, United States v. Arch Trading Co., 987 F.2d 1087, 1092 (4th Cir. 1993); United States v. Harmas, 974 F.2d 1262, 1266–67 (11th Cir. 1992); United States v. Bilzerian, 926 F.2d 1285, 1301–02 (2d Cir.), *cert. denied*, 502 U.S. 813 (1991).

[57] United States v. Sturman, 951 F.2d 1466, 1473–74 (6th Cir. 1991), *rehearing denied en banc*, 1992 U.S. App. LEXIS 531 (6th Cir.), *cert. denied*, 504 U.S. 985 (1992).

[58] United States v. Gordon, 844 F.2d 1397, 1401–1402 (9th Cir. 1988).

[59] United States v. Helmsley, 941 F.2d 71, 90 (2d Cir. 1991), *cert. denied*, 502 U.S. 1091 (1992).

H. The Withdrawal Defense

If defendants knowingly join a conspiracy, are they forever part of the scheme or is possible to obtain a divorce, or at least a legal separation? The general rule is that once the Government shows members joined the conspiracy, their continued participation in the conspiracy is presumed to continue until the object of the conspiracy has been achieved.[60] However, if members of a conspiracy can show that they actually withdrew from the conspiracy, this may sever their liability.[61] Moreover, if the evidence shows that the defendant withdrew from the conspiracy before the applicable limitations period (*i.e.*, more than six years prior to the indictment when the limitations period is six years), withdrawal is a complete defense to a conspiracy charge. If members wish to withdraw, they must do more than just stop taking an active role: "Mere cessation of activity is not enough to start the running of the statute; there must also be affirmative action, either the making of a clean breast to the authorities, or communication of the abandonment in a manner reasonably calculated to reach co-conspirators."[62] However, even if the defendant completely severs his or her ties with the enterprise, "the defendant still may remain a part of the conspiracy if he or she continues to do acts in furtherance of the conspiracy and continues to receive benefits from the conspiracy's operations."[63]

Who bears the burden of proving the withdrawal, the defendant as an affirmative defense, or the Government as part of proving all of the elements of its case? This question used to vary by circuit. However, the Supreme Court addressed this issue and held:

> Allocating to a defendant the burden of proving withdrawal does not violate the Due Process Clause. While the Government must prove beyond a reasonable doubt every fact necessary to constitute the crime with which the defendant is charged, . . . proof of the nonexistence of all affirmative defenses has never been constitutionally required. . . . The State is foreclosed from shifting the burden of proof to the defendant only when an affirmative defense *does* negate an element of the crime. . . . Where instead it excuses conduct that would otherwise be punishable, but does not controvert any of the elements of the offense itself, the Government has no constitutional duty to overcome the defense beyond a reasonable doubt.
>
> Withdrawal does not negate an element of the conspiracy crimes charged here. The essence of conspiracy is the combination of minds in an unlawful purpose. . . . To convict a defendant of narcotics or RICO conspiracy, the Government must prove beyond a reasonable doubt that two or more people agreed to commit a crime covered by the specific conspiracy statute (that a conspiracy existed) and that the defendant knowingly and willfully participated in the agreement (that he was a

---

[60] *See, e.g.*, United States v. Barsanti, 943 F.2d 428, 437 (4th Cir. 1991).

[61] *See, e.g.*, United States v. United States Gypsum Co., 438 U.S. 422, 464–65 (1978).

[62] United States v. Borelli, 336 F.2d 376, 388 (2d Cir. 1964) (internal quotation marks and citation omitted).

[63] United States v. Antar, 53 F.3d 568, 583 (3d Cir. 1995).

member of the conspiracy). Far from contradicting an element of the offense, withdrawal presupposes that the defendant committed the offense.[64]

III. AIDING AND ABETTING

A. Introduction

A statute that is similar to, yet fundamentally different from, conspiracy is the aiding and abetting statute of 18 U.S.C. section 2. As we have seen, the conspiracy statute establishes a crime independent of the criminal offense that was the object or aim of the conspiracy. By contrast, section 2 is not itself an offense statute — it makes the person who aids and abets liable as a principal. The offense of conviction is the criminal statute itself — *e.g.* filing a false claim for refund (section 7206(1)). Thus, an underlying criminal offense must be pled and proved in order for liability to attach under 18 U.S.C. section 2.[65] Section 2 provides:

(a) Whoever commits an offense against the United States or aids, abets, counsels, commands, induces or procures its commission, is punishable as a principal.

(b) Whoever willfully causes an act to be done which if directly performed by him or another would be an offense against the United States, is punishable as a principal.

Section 2 "makes punishable as a principal one who aids or abets another in the commission of a substantive offense."[66] Section 2 covers two types of aiding and abetting. Under section 2(a), the Government must prove that someone other than the defendant committed the substantive crime.[67] Ironically, however, the Government need not obtain a conviction or even prosecute the other person in order to bring a prosecution against the aider and abettor.[68] In effect, section 2(a) treats the person who aids and abets a crime, but whose actions do not rise to actually committing the crime itself, as a co-principal with the person who takes the final step and violates a criminal statute.[69]

---

[64] Smith v. United States, 133 S. Ct. 714, 719 (2013) (internal quotation marks and citation omitted). By contrast, the good faith defense to a crime requiring that the defendant acted willfully goes to an element of the offense of tax evasion. Thus, assuming the issue of good faith is in play based on the evidence, the Government must prove beyond a reasonable doubt that the defendant lacked of good faith. *See* Chapter 2A.

[65] *See, e.g.*, United States v. Roan Eagle, 867 F.2d 436, 445 (8th Cir.), *cert. denied*, 490 U.S. 1028 (1989); United States v. Martin, 747 F.2d 1404, 1407 (11th Cir. 1984), *rehearing denied en banc*, 756 F.2d 885 (11th Cir. 1985).

[66] Londono-Gomez v. INS, 699 F.2d 475, 476 (9th Cir. 1983).

[67] *But see* IRC § 7206(2), where proof of the underlying offense is unnecessary. As a result, in false return cases, the Criminal Tax Manual directs that section 7206(2) should be charged rather than section 2(a). CTM 21.05[1].

[68] United States v. Ruffin, 613 F.2d 408, 412 (2d Cir. 1979).

[69] United States v. Causey, 835 F.2d 1289, 1291–92 (9th Cir. 1987).

Under section 2(b), however, the Government need not prove that someone other than the defendant was guilty of the substantive crime. Indeed, if the someone other than the defendant was guilty, the defendant would be charged under section 2(a) as an aider and abettor, rather than a causer. A person who causes the commission of an offense is punishable as a principal, even though the person who completes the wrongful act violates no criminal statute due to lack of criminal intent or capacity. Section 2(b) punishes the individual who *causes* a criminal act, because no crime would take place without his or her participation.[70] According to one court, the reviser's note to section 2 indicates that subsection (b) was added in 1948 to "remove[ ] all doubt that one who puts in motion or assists in the illegal enterprise but causes the commission of an indispensable element of the offense by an *innocent* agent or instrumentality, is guilty as a principal."[71]

B. The Elements

In order to obtain a conviction under 18 U.S.C. section 2, the Government must prove each of the following elements beyond a reasonable doubt:

1. The defendant associated with the criminal venture;
2. The defendant knowingly participated in the venture; and,
3. The defendant sought by his or her actions to make the venture succeed.[72]

1. Associated with the Criminal Venture

Association with the criminal venture has been interpreted to mean that the defendant "shared in the criminal intent of the principal."[73] In prosecutions under subsection 2(a), this means that the Government must show that: (1) the perpetrator of the underlying crime had the requisite criminal intent to commit that offense and (2) the aider and abettor had the same requisite intent.[74] Under subsection 2(b), the Government need only prove that the defendant who caused the commission of the illegal act had the requisite criminal intent to commit the underlying offense; the intent of the actor who committed the criminal act is irrelevant.[75]

2. Participation and Success of Venture

In order to aid and abet, a person must do more than merely be present at the scene of a crime and have knowledge of its commission. The element of participation requires the Government to show some active participation or encouragement, or

---

70 *Id.* at 1292.

71 *Id.*

72 Nye & Nissen v. United States, 336 U.S. 613, 619 (1949); CTM 21.03.

73 United States v. Roan Eagle, 867 F.2d 436, 445 n.15 (8th Cir. 1989).

74 United States v. Lindell, 881 F.2d 1313, 1323 (5th Cir. 1989), *rehearing denied*, 1989 U.S. App. LEXIS 15201 (5th Cir. Sept. 20, 1989), *cert. denied*, 496 U.S. 926 (1990); United States v. Gaskins, 849 F.2d 454, 459 (9th Cir. 1988).

75 United States v. Laurins, 857 F.2d 529, 535 (9th Cir. 1988), *cert. denied*, 492 U.S. 906 (1989); United States v. Rucker, 586 F.2d 899, 905 (2d Cir. 1978).

some affirmative act designed to further the crime, by the defendant.[76]

3. Knowing Participation in the Venture

As we have discussed, the Government must show that some underlying criminal offense was committed by the perpetrator, but the Government need not show that the principal was convicted, indicted, or even identified. In order to satisfy the third element of the crime the Government must only show that the defendant knowingly participated in the furtherance of the venture. The Government must show that the defendant actively participated in some affirmative act designed to further the crime.

C. Further Analysis

We have discussed above certain provisions that create derivative liability for an actor who does not actually commit the crime. These may be *Pinkerton* liability, accomplice liability for aiding and abetting under section 2(a), and "causer" liability under section 2(b). These provisions are not applicable to the person who actually commits the crime and is therefore a principal in that crime, and punishable for that reason alone. For example, assume that two persons promote a tax shelter but, owing to its complexity, the taxpayer investing in the shelter is not guilty of the crime of tax evasion. Tax evasion is not a status crime — *i.e.*, it can be committed by persons other than the taxpayer. Hence, even in the absence of the taxpayer's guilt, the promoters can be guilty of the crime of tax evasion if their actions meet the elements of the crime. In such a case, it is at least questionable whether the jury should be presented those theories of derivative liability. We hope the readers will see the conceptual reason for the issue. Derivative liability is designed to punish as principals those who are not principals. But, for the crime of tax evasion, the actions that would otherwise invoke derivative liability would invoke direct principal liability, thus mooting derivative liability.

IV. FILING FALSE CLAIMS (18 U.S.C. SECTIONS 286 AND 287)

A. Introduction

18 U.S.C. sections 286 and 287 are designed to protect the Government from false, fictitious, or fraudulent claims.[77] Section 287 makes it a crime to file false claims against the Government, while section 286 covers conspiracies to file false claims. Cases brought under sections 286 and 287 could be brought under section 7206(1) and (2), and 18 U.S.C. sections 371 and 1001. However, the majority of false claim charges in tax cases are brought against individuals who file multiple false income tax returns claiming refunds of income tax within the same year. The introduction of electronic filing of income tax returns has led to a proliferation of

---

[76] United States v. Morrow, 923 F.2d 427, 436 (6th Cir. 1991); United States v. Perez, 922 F.2d 782, 785 (11th Cir.), *cert. denied*, 501 U.S. 1223 (1991).

[77] CTM 22.03, *citing* United States v. Montoya, 716 F.2d 1340, 1344 (10th Cir. 1983).

multiple defendant, multiple return cases, many of which are filed under sections 286 and 287. The CTM advises prosecutors that sections 286 and 287 are the preferred charges when one or more false claims for refund are made on false or fictitious income tax returns.[78]

In an example of the kind of case charged under section 286 and 287, the Fifth Circuit upheld the convictions against five defendants, each of whom were involved in a conspiracy to file false electronic tax returns. The court described the conduct of the defendants as follows:

> All five were convicted for their role in a sizeable conspiracy to file false income tax returns with the United States government. Members of this conspiracy would recruit people to file tax returns and assist them in filling out fraudulent returns. Typically, these returns would claim that the filer was in the transportation business and had bought an enormous amount of fuel, entitling the person to a huge fuel excise tax credit and, consequently, a hefty tax refund. These returns were usually filed electronically through the rapid refund system at an office called Tax Sense. When the refund check arrived, one of the conspirators would drive the filer to the bank to cash it, then collect the conspiracy's share of the refund. The conspirators were not generous: ordinarily, a filer would get to keep only $200 out of a $3000 refund.[79]

The Government could have charged those cases as false return cases under section 7206(2) or conspiracy to file false returns, in violation of 18 U.S.C. section 371. The Government chose instead, in keeping with its advice in the CTM, to charge the conduct under sections 286 and 287.

B. False Claims for Refund (Section 287)

In order to obtain a conviction under 18 U.S.C. section 287, the Government must prove the following elements:

1. The defendant made or presented a claim to a department or agency of the United States for money or property;
2. The claim was false, fictitious or fraudulent; and
3. The defendant knew at the time that the claim was false, fictitious or fraudulent.[80]

For purposes of section 287, a tax return seeking a refund is considered to be a "claim against the United States."[81] A claim must actually be made or presented to the Government to fall within section 287. This means that for paper returns, the Government must show that the return was filed with the IRS. For electronic

---

[78] *Id.*

[79] United States v. Okoronkwo, 46 F.3d 426, 429–30 (5th Cir.), *cert. denied*, 516 U.S. 833 (1995) and 516 U.S. 1134 (1996).

[80] CTM 22.03; Johnson v. United States, 410 F.2d 38, 46 (8th Cir.), *cert. denied*, 396 U.S. 822 (1969).

[81] *See, e.g.*, United States v. Drape, 668 F.2d 22, 26 (1st Cir. 1982).

returns, a section 287 violation is complete when the electronic portion of the return is received by the IRS.[82]

The second element of § 287 is phrased in the disjunctive. Thus, charges under the statute may be based on proof that a claim submitted to the Government is either false, fictitious, *or* fraudulent.[83] In explaining this element of the offense, the Tenth Circuit stated:

> A claim is false or fictitious within the meaning of § 287 "if untrue when made, and then known to be untrue by the person making it or causing it to be made." A claim is fraudulent "if known to be untrue, and made or caused to be made with the intent to deceive the Government agency to whom submitted."[84]

A claim for refund may be false, fictitious, or fraudulent, even though the defendant might be entitled to a refund if an accurate return were filed.[85] All that is required is that the return filed is false and that the defendant is not entitled to the refund on the facts represented on that return. Similarly, a return may be false under the statute if the defendant files a correct return in the name of another taxpayer in an attempt to obtain the refund that is due the other taxpayer.[86]

The third element under section 287 requires the Government to prove that a false claim against the Government was made, "knowing such claim to be false, fictitious or fraudulent." It is not necessary for the Government to prove willfulness in the indictment, which often makes section 287 an attractive alternative to section 7206(2). The requisite knowledge can be "proved by either a showing that the defendant was aware he was doing something wrong or that he acted with a specific intent to violate the law."[87]

C. Conspiracy to File False Claims (Section 286)

This chapter has already covered at some length the law of conspiracy in the context of 18 U.S.C. section 371. A conspiracy under section 286 is, in essence, a conspiracy to defraud "as applied." In order to establish a violation of 18 U.S.C. section 286, the following elements must be proved beyond a reasonable doubt:

1. An agreement, combination, or conspiracy to defraud the United States;
2. By obtaining or aiding to obtain the payment of any false, fictitious or fraudulent claim.[88]

---

[82] CTM 22.03[1].

[83] United States v. Murph, 707 F.2d 895, 897 (6th Cir. 1983) ("the government may prove and the trial judge may instruct in the disjunctive form used in the statute"), *cert. denied*, 464 U.S. 844 (1983).

[84] United States v. Irwin, 654 F.2d 671, 683 n.15 (10th Cir. 1981), *cert. denied*, 455 U.S. 1016 (1982), (*citing* United States v. Milton, *supra*, 602 F.2d at 233 & n.6, quoting 2 E. Devitt & Blackmar, Federal Jury Practice and Instructions § 28.04 (3d ed. 1977)).

[85] *See* United States v. Gieger, 190 F.3d 661, 666 (5th Cir. 1999), *rehearing denied en banc*, 207 F.3d 660 (5th Cir. 2000).

[86] *See, e.g.*, Kercher v. United States, 409 F.2d 814, 818 (8th Cir. 1969).

[87] United States v. Maher, 582 F.2d 842, 847 (4th Cir. 1978), *cert. denied*, 439 U.S. 1115 (1979).

[88] CTM 22.04.

In order to obtain a conviction under section 286, the Government must prove that the defendants agreed to engage in a scheme to defraud the Government and knew that the objective of the scheme was illegal. Unlike section 371, proving that an overt act was made by one of the conspirators is not an element of a section 286 conspiracy.[89] Instead, the Government must prove that the conspirators agreed to defraud the Government by obtaining the payment of false claims against the Government. There is no requirement that the coconspirators actually obtained the payment or that the Government prove that any steps were taken to consummate the filing of a false claim, so long as the existence of the agreement can be proved. However, as the Criminal Tax Manual notes: "As a practical matter, the proof in section 286 cases generally does not differ from proof in section 371 tax cases, because in most false claims conspiracy cases the existence of the agreement will be proved by acts that were undertaken in furthering the conspiracy or in consummating the attempt to obtain payment of the claim."[90]

V. FALSE STATEMENTS (18 U.S.C. SECTION 1001)

A. Introduction

18 U.S.C. section 1001 is predicated on the Government's right to ask questions and receive honest answers so that it can somewhat efficiently go about the business of governing. As the Supreme Court said: "Our legal system provides methods for challenging the Government's right to ask questions — lying is not one of them. A citizen may decline to answer the question, or answer it honestly, but he cannot with impunity knowingly and willfully answer with a falsehood."[91] The sweep of section 1001 is quite broad — it goes beyond the general perjury and the tax perjury statutes because it requires no oath or statement under penalty of perjury. All it requires is a false statement as to a material matter to a Government officer in the course of his conducting the Government's business.

B. The Elements

The Government must prove the following elements beyond a reasonable doubt to establish a violation of section 1001:

1. The defendant made a false statement or representation, or made or used a false document;
2. In a matter within the jurisdiction of the executive, legislature or judicial branch of the Government of the United States;
3. The false statement or representation, or false document related to a material matter; and

---

[89] United States v. Lanier, 920 F.2d 887, 892 (11th Cir.), *rehearing denied en banc*, 931 F.2d 901 (11th Cir. 1991).

[90] CTM 22.05.

[91] Bryson v. United States, 396 U.S. 64, 72 (1969).

4. The defendant acted willfully and with knowledge of the falsity.[92]

As to the first element, the Supreme Court has recognized that the term "false statement . . . or representation" includes both oral and written statements.[93] There is no requirement that the statement be under oath. The statute applies to unsworn, as well as sworn, statements.[94] In the criminal tax context, section 1001 is normally used in connection with false documents or statements submitted to an IRS agent during the course of an audit or investigation. It is not normally used in the case of a false statement on a return, since returns are generally signed under the penalties of perjury, and section 7206(1) would be the more appropriate charge.[95]

The second element requires the Government to prove that the false statement was made in a matter within the jurisdiction of the executive, legislature or judicial branch of the Government of the United States. Not surprisingly, the courts have uniformly found that the IRS is a "department or agency of the United States" within the meaning of section 1001.[96] Congress amended section 1001 in 1996 in response to the Supreme Court's decision in *Hubbard v. United States*,[97] which held that the predecessor to section 1001 did not apply to judicial proceedings. The statute now provides that false statements include false statements to the judicial branch. However, Congress also clarified the reach of revised subsection (a) by adding subsection (b), which creates an exception for judicial proceedings: "Subsection (a) does not apply to a party to a judicial proceeding, or that party's counsel, for statements, representations, writings, or documents submitted by such party or counsel to a judge or magistrate in that proceeding." The Ninth Circuit has held that, in order to qualify for this exception from liability, a defendant must show that (1) he was a party to a judicial proceeding; (2) his statements were submitted to a judge or magistrate; and (3) his statements were made "in that proceeding."[98] Thus, section 1001 applies only to more "housekeeping" functions of the judiciary, and it does not apply to false statements made during a court proceeding.

---

[92] United States v. Gaudin, 515 U.S. 506 (1995); CTM 24.03.

[93] United States v. Beacon Brass Co., 344 U.S. 43, 46 (1952).

[94] Neely v. United States, 300 F.2d 67, 70 (9th Cir.), *cert. denied*, 369 U.S. 864 (1962).

[95] There is, of course, a relationship between perjury and false statements in terms of punishing the falsehood. In the perjury context, *Bronston v. United States*, 409 U.S. 352 (1973), is often cited for the proposition that literal truth is a defense to a perjury charge. Whether or not that is precisely *Bronston*'s holding — or the holding is more nuanced — is beyond the scope of this footnote. The question addressed here is the relevance of *Bronston* — whatever its holding — to the crime of false statements, the key difference between them being whether the statement is made under oath in a proceeding or not. The cases that brush up against this issue usually — but not always — treat *Bronston* as setting the standard for a false statements charge. *See, e.g.*, United States v. Good, 326 F.3d 589, 592 (4th Cir. 2003). In any event, it is unlikely that a real world case would arise where a false statement would be prosecuted under § 1001 where, had it been in a sworn testimony setting, perjury would not.

[96] *See, e.g.*, United States v. Morris, 741 F.2d 188, 190–91 (8th Cir. 1984).

[97] 514 U.S. 695 (1995).

[98] United States v. McNeil, 362 F.3d 570, 572 (9th Cir. 2004).

The false statement need not be made directly to or even received by the executive, legislative or judicial branch of the government.[99] Significantly, false statements made to state, local, or even private entities who either receive federal funds or are subject to federal supervision can form the basis of a section 1001 violation.[100] An example in the Criminal Tax Manual illustrates the potential reach of section 1001:

> Because the false statements or documents need not actually be received by the executive, legislative or judicial branch, the Tax Division has authorized prosecution pursuant to section 1001 for false claims which have been prepared, but have yet to be filed with the IRS. This scenario occurs, for example, in electronic filing prosecutions where the filer has been apprehended either after or at the time of the presentation of his false claim to a tax filing service, but before transmission is effectuated. Because the false claim has not been submitted to the Service, the commonly used 18 U.S.C. § 287 charge is unavailable. Section 1001 provides a mechanism by which these false claims can be prosecuted.[101]

The third element requires that the statement be false as to a material matter. Chapter 2B contains an extensive discussion of materiality in the context of a section 7206(1) violation, and we won't repeat that material here. For purposes of section 1001, almost anything that is said to an IRS agent regarding an audit or investigation has a risk of being material. In the 1996 revision to section 1001, Congress also clarified that materiality was an element under each of the separate prongs of section 1001(a). Prior to that time there had been some confusion regarding the issue, although the Supreme Court had based its *Gaudin* decision on the assumption that materiality was required.[102]

The final element of a section 1001 violation requires the Government to prove that the defendant acted knowingly and willfully. As used in section 1001, the term "willful" simply means that the defendant did the forbidden act (*e.g.*, made a false, fictitious, or fraudulent statement) deliberately and with knowledge.[103] The Government need not prove an intent to deceive, nor need the Government prove that the defendant had actual knowledge of federal agency jurisdiction — *i.e.*, knowledge that the statements were made within federal agency jurisdiction.[104]

However, the fourth element raises an issue that arises in tax and financial crimes as to precisely what "knowingly and willfully" means. As we noted earlier, "willfully" is a nuanced word. Certainly, in a tax crimes context, willfully means at a minimum knowing that the conduct is illegal. Does the speaker commit the crime by making a knowingly false statement to a federal agent or must the speaker also know that making a knowingly false statement to a federal agent is a crime? The CTM says cryptically on this issue: "As used in § 1001, the term "willful" simply

[99] United States v. Oren, 893 F.2d 1057, 1064 (9th Cir. 1990).

[100] United States v. Gibson, 881 F.2d 318, 322 (6th Cir. 1989).

[101] CTM 24.06.

[102] United States v. Gaudin, 515 U.S. 506 (1995).

[103] United States v. Hildebrandt, 961 F.2d 116, 118 (8th Cir.), *cert. denied*, 506 U.S. 878 (1992).

[104] United States v. Yermian, 468 U.S. 63, 69–70 (1984).

means that the defendant did the forbidden act (e.g., made a false, fictitious, or fraudulent statement) deliberately and with knowledge."[105] With knowledge of what — the falsity or the falsity and its criminality? We think the CTM, fairly read, intends the former rather than the latter.[106]

C. The "Exculpatory No" Doctrine

Because of the broad language of section 1001 and the potential for prosecutorial abuse, many courts had created an exception to prosecution which was commonly referred to as the "exculpatory no" doctrine. Under this doctrine the Government was barred from prosecuting individuals who had done nothing more than falsely answer "no" in response to questions asked of them during the course of a federal criminal investigation. However, the Supreme Court resolved a split amongst the circuits and eliminated this defense for potential defendants.[107] Given the demise of the "exculpatory no" doctrine, the best course of action remains, now more than ever, for lawyers to keep their clients away from investigators. It is often easier to prove a cover up than to prove the underlying crime, and even "just saying no," if said to the wrong person, can constitute a crime.

VI. MONEY LAUNDERING (18 U.S.C. SECTIONS 1956 AND 1957)

A. Introduction

The money laundering statutes in 18 U.S.C. sections 1956 and 1957 punish certain financial transactions that involve illegal income. Not all illegally-derived income falls within the reach of sections 1956 and 1957. Rather, only certain crimes, known as "specified unlawful activity" (or SUA) can be a predicate crime to money laundering. In essence, money laundering refers to an attempt to conceal the existence, illegal source, or illegal application of income, and to disguise that illegal income to make it appear legitimate. Money laundering is among the highest national criminal enforcement priorities such as organized crime and drug dealing. The Government's hope is that substantial penalties for this conduct will not only punish but will also deter the underlying criminal conduct. Money laundering is also designed to prevent the use of the ill-gotten gains by criminals, thereby attempting make it so that crime does not pay. In most cases, the focus of the money laundering statutes are not on taxes. But tax crimes frequently travel with money laundering, and money laundering is often part of the tax crime or a *Klein* conspiracy. Sections 1956 and 1957 set forth four criminal offenses which may arise from participation in certain transactions involving the proceeds of specified unlawful activities: financial transactions, transportation, financial institutions, and

[105] CTM 24.08.

[106] For more nuance on this issue, see Judge Kavanagh's concurring opinion in United States v. Moore, 612 F.3d 698, 702 (D.C. Cir. 2010).

[107] Brogan v. United States, 522 U.S. 398 (1998).

monetary transactions. The provisions are very complex, and we will only summarize them here.

B. Section 1956 Money Laundering

1. Transaction Money Laundering

Section 1956(a)(1), the subsection that is of particular relevance to tax crimes, sets forth the crime of "transaction money laundering." The elements of that offense are:

1. The defendant conducted or attempted to conduct a financial transaction;
2. The defendant knew that the property involved in the transaction represented the proceeds of some unlawful activity (but not necessarily an SUA);
3. The property did, in fact, represent the proceeds of an SUA; and
4. The defendant took part in the transaction with the intent to
   (a) Promote an SUA, or
   (b) commit a violation of 7201 (evasion) or 7206 (tax perjury), or
   (c) conceal the location, the source, the ownership, or the control of the proceeds of an SUA, or
   (d) avoid currency transaction reporting.[108]

Under section 1956(a)(1), it is the financial transaction itself that is the conduct punished. Section 1956 defines "financial transaction" very broadly. The term "transaction" includes a purchase, sale, loan, pledge, gift, transfer, delivery, or other disposition of property.[109] When involving a financial institution, "transaction" covers nearly all common banking transactions and includes a deposit, withdrawal, transfer between accounts, exchange of currency, loan, extension of credit, purchase or sale of any stock, bond, certificate of deposit, or other monetary instrument, or any other payment, transfer, or delivery by, through, or to a financial institution.[110]

The knowledge element requires that the defendant must have known that the property involved in the transaction included the proceeds of some form of activity which constitutes a felony under state, federal, or foreign law.[111] It is not necessary to show that the defendant knew the proceeds were derived from a particular federal, state, or foreign offense, or that it was from a "specified unlawful activity" — the Government need only show that the defendant knew the property was the proceeds of some unlawful conduct. "Proceeds" means gross revenue, not profit.[112] In a controversial decision, the Third Circuit held with respect to Virgin Islands tax: "[u]npaid taxes, which are unlawfully disguised and retained by means of the filing of false tax returns through the U.S. mail, constitute 'proceeds' of mail fraud for

---

108 18 U.S.C. § 1956(a)(1)(A) & (B).

109 18 U.S.C. § 1956(c)(3).

110 18 U.S.C. § 1956(c)(2).

111 18 U.S.C. § 1956(a)(1).

112 18 U.S.C. § 1956(c)(9).

purposes of supporting a charge of federal money laundering."[113] Does this mean that every false tax return and resulting underpayment could be considered money laundering?

The next element the Government must prove is that the actual source of the funds or property involved in the transaction must be one or more of the statute's "specified unlawful activities" enumerated in section 1956(c)(7). The list of SUAs is comprised of both state and federal offenses which either generate substantial economic proceeds or require substantial funds to commit. The list includes all federal offenses which are currently RICO predicates (other than Title 31 violations), all federal and foreign felony drug offenses, and an assortment of bribery, white collar, environmental, export control, and espionage crimes. Tax crimes, however, are not among the crimes listed in the statute as "specified unlawful activity."[114]

Although tax crimes are not an SUA, the steps in pursuing tax crimes almost invariably include some aspect of mail or wire fraud, which is an SUA.[115] DOJ policy requires that DOJ Tax approve all criminal charges against a defendant "in connection with conduct arising under the internal revenue laws, regardless of which criminal statutes the United States Attorney proposes to use in charging the defendant." DOJ Tax approval will not be given "where the effect would merely be to convert routine tax prosecutions into money laundering prosecutions, as the statute was not intended to provide a substitute for traditional Title 18 and Title 26 charges related to tax evasion, filing of false returns, or tax fraud conspiracy."[116] However, as we will discuss in the wire fraud section below, tax crimes may in limited circumstances be charged as mail fraud or wire fraud, and those crimes are listed as SUAs.[117]

It does not matter that the Government is barred from prosecuting the underlying SUA. The Government will have to prove the SUA occurred in order to prevail in the money laundering charge, but it need not prosecute the putative

---

[113] United States v. Yusuf, 536 F.3d 178 (3d Cir. 2008), *cert. denied* 549 U.S. 1338 (2007); *see also* CTM 25.03[1] (2008 ed.) (noting that "*Yusuf* created a conflict with United States v. Khanani, 502 F.3d 1281, 1296–97 (11th Cir. 2007), in which the Eleventh Circuit held that the definition of 'proceeds' is limited to 'something which is obtained in exchange for the sale of something else,' and thus does not include retained taxes.")

[114] Moreover, United States Attorneys Manual § 9-105.750 explains that § 1956(a)(1) exists to facilitate prosecution of money launderers, not to displace the appropriate use of traditional Title 18 and Title 26 charges in criminal tax cases.

[115] *See, e.g.*, United States v. Yusuf, *supra*.

[116] CTM 25.01. DOJ Tax approval is not required where the gravamen of the offenses for which criminal charges are warranted are consistent with the serious offense of money laundering and not just tax offenses leveraged into money laundering. Specifically, DOJ Tax approval is not required where:

> (1) the principal purpose of the financial transaction was to accomplish some other covered purpose, such as carrying on a specified unlawful activity like drug trafficking; (2) the circumstances do not warrant the filing of substantive tax or tax fraud conspiracy charges; and (3) the existence of a secondary tax evasion or false return motivation for the transaction is one that is readily apparent from the nature of the money laundering transaction itself. USAM § 9-105.750

[117] *See* Tax Division Directive 128.

offender for the SUA. This has dramatic implications with respect to the statute of limitations, which re-starts every time the defendant or a co-conspirator does something with the proceeds that constitutes a financial transaction. Under these circumstances the defendant may not be prosecuted for the underlying offense itself because of the statute of limitations, but he or she may be prosecuted for conducting a financial transaction with the proceeds from that offense.

Finally, to establish a violation under 18 U.S.C. section 1956(a)(1), the prosecution must prove that the defendant took part in the financial transaction with the intent to engage in conduct that would (a) promote an SUA, (b) constitute a violation of sections 7201 or 7206, (c) conceal the location, the source, the ownership, the control of the proceeds of an SUA, *or* (d) avoid currency transaction reporting.[118] If the Government is going to rely upon the second condition (*i.e.*, that the defendant conducted the financial transaction with the intent to commit the specified tax crime), the Government must prove willfulness with respect to the intended tax crime. Thus, the Government will have to prove that the defendant knew that his conduct relative to the tax obligation was a crime.[119] The statute requires only that the person must "intend" to commit the prescribed tax crime, not that he or she actually committed the crime. Moreover, the mere concealment of proceeds or other actions which might, in other contexts be some proof of a tax crime (e.g., *Spies* affirmative acts), may not be indicative of a tax crime because they may simply be acts to conceal the SUA rather than the tax crime.[120]

2. Transportation Money Laundering

There is a separate offense under section 1956 for so-called transportation money laundering. In order to prove that crime, the Government must show: (1) The defendant transported monetary instrument or funds into, outside of, or through the United States; and (2) that this was done with the intent to promote SUA, *or* that the defendant knew that that funds represent proceeds of some form of unlawful activity and the defendant intended to conceal the location, source, or ownership funds or to avoid a transaction reporting requirement.[121]

C. Section 1957 Money Laundering

Section 1957 sanctions one who knowingly engages, or attempts to engage, in a monetary transaction in criminally derived property that has a value greater than $10,000 and is derived from an SUA. It is not required that the recipient actually exchange or launder the funds or that he have any specific intent to further or conceal unlawful activity. In enacting section 1957, Congress intended to dissuade people from conducting even ordinary commercial transactions with people suspected to be involved in criminal activity. However, section 1957 does require that the violator "knowingly" engage in a transaction involving criminally-derived

---

118 18 U.S.C. § 1956(a)(1)(A) & (B).

119 CTM 25.03[2][a].

120 *Id.*

121 18 U.S.C. § 1956(a)(2).

property. In order to prove a violation of section 1957, the Government must prove the following elements:

1. The person knowingly engaged or attempt to engage in a Monetary Transaction;
2. Involving "Criminally Derived Property," which is actually derived from SUA.[122]

Section 1957 is much simpler in terms of elements and more straightforward than section 1956. Consider an example: assume Dave has committed wire fraud, which is an SUA under either section 1956 or section 1957. The proceeds of the wire fraud are deposited in a tax haven bank account. Dave did not commit the fraud so that he could park the money in the tax haven bank account; Dave committed the crime so that he could enjoy the money. The bank account is simply a resting place until he enjoys the money. Assume that he then has the money wire transferred to his U.S. bank account so that he can buy a fancy residence. Can he be prosecuted for the wire transfer under section 1956 or section 1957? He cannot be prosecuted for the wire transfer under section 1956 because there is no intent to conceal in the transaction, a required element for section 1956. The wire transfer is into individual Dave's personal bank account and easily on the radar screen of the IRS and anyone else with access to U.S. bank information. However, intent to conceal is not a required element under section 1957, so he can be prosecuted under section 1957.

D. Tax Division Control of Tax and Money Laundering Crimes

As we discussed in Chapter 6, tax investigations are normally subject to elaborate procedures, requiring many levels of review within the IRS and the Tax Division. These procedures are designed to insure that tax prosecutions are consistent with tax enforcement priorities. However, these procedures do not apply in money laundering investigations by the IRS. The IRS may therefore make a direct referral of money laundering charges to the United States Attorney, rather than proceeding through the Tax Division for review and approval of the indictment. When the IRS recommends prosecution for both tax crimes and money laundering, the case will proceed through the normal review process. Then, provided the Tax Division approves, the defendant may be charged in a single indictment with tax crimes and money laundering crimes. In the following section dealing with mail and wire fraud, we will discuss Tax Division Directive No. 128, which is also relevant to money laundering. As you will see, the directive states a general policy to charge mainstream tax crimes as tax crimes rather than as Title 18 crimes such as mail fraud or wire fraud, or as an SUA under the money laundering laws. This is because mail fraud and wire fraud are almost always part of an offense under section 7201 and section 7206, since the tax return that is the subject of the offense was almost invariably sent via mail or filed electronically (i.e., mail fraud or wire fraud). In the Tax Division's view, charging garden-variety tax offenses as mail fraud or wire fraud just to be able to also charge money laundering

[122] *See* United States v. Wilson, 249 F.3d 366, 379 (5th Cir. 2001).

would subvert traditional tax enforcement.

VII. FINANCIAL REPORTING CRIMES (31 U.S.C. SECTIONS 5322 AND 5324)

A. Introduction

In an effort to battle non-tax crimes, including in recent years international terrorism, Congress enacted the Bank Secrecy Act (BSA).[123] First enacted in 1970, the rationale behind the BSA is similar to the money laundering statutes — illegal enterprises tend to deal heavily in cash, and the Government would benefit from knowing who is dealing in large amounts of cash. The BSA is enormously complicated, and we will only give you a brief overview of some of the relevant provisions.[124] In a nutshell, the BSA and the regulations promulgated pursuant to the Act's authority require financial institutions to file reports on cash transactions and other suspicious activities. It also requires persons who have foreign bank accounts to file reports regarding those accounts. Finally, the BSA contains criminal penalties for failure to file the reports and for structuring transactions to avoid the filing of those reports.

B. Reporting Requirements

The BSA and the regulations generally require certain financial institutions to report currency transactions that involve the payment, receipt, or transfer currency or other monetary instruments of more than $10,000, the transportation of currency across U.S. borders and suspicious transactions relevant to possible violations of the law.[125] Financial institutions covered by the significant reporting provisions of the BSA include not only banks and savings and loans, but broad categories of financial institutions including securities and commodity brokers, investment banking companies, currency exchanges, "money service businesses," telegraph companies, certain issuers of travelers checks and money orders, casinos, insurance companies, and operators of credit card systems.[126] The covered financial institutions are required to maintain certain records and file reports on domestic and foreign transactions involving cash or monetary amounts in excess of $10,000. As you might imagine, the IRS is the most frequent user of the financial information produced by BSA's reporting requirements.

The principal reporting requirement is the Currency Transaction Report ("CTR"). CTRs are required for all cash transactions or series of related

---

[123] Originally entitled the Bank Records and Foreign Transactions Act of 1970, as amended these sections, commonly referred to as the Bank Secrecy Act are now codified at 31 U.S.C. §§ 5311 to 5322 and are entitled Records and Reports on Monetary Instruments Transactions, with applicable regulations at 31 C.F.R. § 103.11 *et seq.*

[124] For a more detailed exposition on the BSA and all of its requirements, *see* Robert S. Fink, *Tax Controversies* section 17.01–17.02[5] (2006).

[125] 31 U.S.C. §§ 5313 and 5316; 31 C.F.R. § 103.22.

[126] 31 U.S.C. § 5312(a)(2); *see also* 31 C.F.R. § 103.11(n).

transactions that exceed $10,000. This form is similar to, but in addition to, the Form 8300 that is discussed in Chapter 2B. Depending upon the circumstances of the transaction, the financial institution may be required to prepare a report called a Suspicious Activity Report.[127] A Suspicious Activity Report is required if the transaction involves or aggregates at least $5,000, and the financial institution knows, suspects or has reason to suspect that (i) the transaction involves funds derived from illegal activities or is intended or conducted in order to hide or disguise funds or assets derived from illegal activities as part of a plan to violate or evade any federal law or regulation; (ii) the transaction is designed to evade any requirements law or other regulations promulgated under the BSA; or (iii) "the transaction has no business or apparent lawful purpose or is not the sort in which the particular customer would normally be expected to engage, and the bank knows of no reasonable explanation for the transaction after examining the available facts, including the background and possible purpose of the transaction."[128]

The BSA also requires that any person who transports or has someone else transport United States currency or other monetary instruments in excess of $10,000 into or out of the United States, or who receives monetary instruments in the United States from abroad, to report the transaction. This report is made on FinCEN Form 105 ("Report of International Transportation of Currency or Monetary Instruments," commonly known as a CMIR). The form must be filed with the United States Customs Service at the time of entry into the United States or at the time of departure, mailing, or shipping from the United States.

Finally, the BSA and regulations require the filing of a Report of Foreign Bank and Financial Accounts (known as an "FBAR"), which must be filed by United States persons having a beneficial or signatory interest in a foreign financial account.[129] The requirement to file an FBAR is independent of the requirement to answer the question on the Schedule B of the Form 1040, which asks about foreign financial accounts. Thus, not only does a false answer on the question on the Schedule B carry the prospect of a tax perjury charge, but failure to file the FBAR can result in an independent felony criminal action, which is subject to potentially harsher penalties noted later in this section. The required form is a Treasury Form TD F 90-22.1, "Report of Foreign Bank and Financial Accounts."

C. Criminal Provisions

The BSA makes it a crime to willfully fail to file a CTR, CMIR, or FBAR. The penalties for violating the reporting requirements are stiff — five years' imprisonment and a $250,000 fine.[130] Those penalties are doubled if the person

---

127 31 U.S.C. § 5318(g).

128 31 C.F.R. § 103.18(a)(2).

129 31 U.S.C. § 5314; 31 C.F.R. § 103.24.

130 31 U.S.C. § 5322(a). There are also civil penalties for failure to file FBARs, which get more severe with the gravity of the offense: (i) if negligent alone, up to $500 per incident; (ii) if there is a pattern of negligent activity, up to $50,000; (iii) if more culpable than just negligent but not willful, up to $10,000 per incident but with a reasonable cause exception; and (iv) if willful, up to the greater of $100,000 or 50%

violated the reporting requirements "while violating another law of the United States or as part of a pattern of any illegal activity involving more than $100,000 in a 12-month period."[131]

Another key criminal provision in the financial reporting regime involves the crime of "structuring." As discussed in Chapter 2B, structuring is done to avoid the filing requirement of a CTR or other similar form. Many individuals know that a CTR or other form will have to be filed by a business if a cash transaction involves more than $10,000. Clever individuals will break down a large amount of cash into separate deposits or other transactions so as to cause each amount to fall under $10,000. Structuring transactions to evade the reporting requirements is felony, and the penalties for structuring parallel the reporting penalties — five years' imprisonment and fine determined under Title 18.[132] The penalties are doubled if the person structured "while violating another law of the United States or as part of a pattern of any illegal activity involving more than $100,000 in a 12-month period."[133]

Prior to 1994, the BSA required that the structuring be done "willfully." In *Ratzlaf v. United States*,[134] the Supreme Court held that the element of willfulness required the Government to prove not only that the defendant acted to evade the reporting requirements but also that he acted with the knowledge that evading the reporting requirements was illegal. Congress quickly changed the statute, which now provides "Whoever violates this section," and criminal liability can now be imposed only upon a showing that the defendant acted to evade the reporting requirement.[135] Whether a defendant knew that the structuring was illegal is now irrelevant.

As with other criminal statutes discussed in this chapter, the Government could charge the Title 31 violations under other criminal statutes or add Title 31 charges to an indictment. The USAM instructs prosecutors that 18 U.S.C. section 1001 "can be used both in cases involving the filing of a false CTR, CMIR, or FBAR. Other possible Title 18 charges for currency offenses include 18 U.S.C. § 371 (for a conspiracy to avoid filing the currency transaction reports), 18 U.S.C. § 1341 (mail fraud), and 18 U.S.C. § 1343 (wire fraud). A false response on an income tax return or on IRS Form 4683 may involve perjury under 26 U.S.C. § 7206."[136] It is not clear whether these charges should be used in addition to or instead of Title 31 charges. However, the USAM also provides: "In determining the appropriate prohibitions to use in a prosecution for money laundering, serious consideration should be given to using this section as well as the appropriate subsection in Title 18, Sections 1956

---

of the balance in the account(s) at the time of the violation. 31 U.S.C. § 5321. In addition, section 7203, discussed in Chapter 2B, makes it a felony to file a Form 8300 for cash transactions in excess of $10,000.

[131] 31 U.S.C. § 5322(b).

[132] 31 U.S.C. § 5324(d)(1).

[133] 31 U.S.C. § 5324(d)(2).

[134] 510 U.S. 135 (1994).

[135] 31 U.S.C. § 5324(d)(1).

[136] USAM Criminal Resource Manual 2035.

and 1957 whenever any of these are applicable."[137] Nevertheless, given the complexity of the law surrounding Title 31 offenses, prosecutors may be more inclined to charge these cases as Title 18 offenses.

D. Offshore Voluntary Disclosure Initiative and FBARs

We noted above the civil reporting requirements for foreign financial accounts and the civil and criminal penalties backing up those reporting requirements. One of the most significant IRS compliance initiatives has been with respect to U.S. depositors who hid assets in foreign financial accounts. Everyone has known for many years that Swiss banks were the iconic means of hiding assets from the IRS, as well as other law enforcement agencies. However, in 2008, the Government became aware of the methods and means by which the Swiss bank UBS contributed to tax evasion by its wealthy U.S. clients. Initially, DOJ Tax CES brought John Doe summons proceedings against UBS in the Southern District of Florida to obtain the names of UBS's U.S. depositors. After much high level intrigue and negotiation: (1) UBS entered a deferred prosecution agreement and paid a fine of $780 million; (2) UBS delivered around 250 names of U.S. depositors and perhaps information and documents related to them, although it is unclear as to precisely the authority for UBS to do so; (3) UBS, with the "blessing" of the Swiss Government agreed to deliver up to 4,500 names, information and documents of U.S. depositors, pursuant to the United States' request under the U.S./Swiss Double Tax Treaty (as reinterpreted to permit the disclosures); and (4) upon compliance with these obligations, the deferred prosecution agreement and John Doe summons cases were dismissed. The Government also opened investigations against numerous other Swiss Banks, and prosecuted Switzerland's oldest private bank, Wegelin.

At the same time, the IRS began a series of special versions of its Voluntary Disclosure Practice under the IRM.[138] Under what is known as the Offshore Voluntary Disclosure Initiative (OVDI), a taxpayer must deliver to the IRS amended or delinquent original U.S. tax returns for the eight most recent years correcting any underreporting, pay the resulting tax and interest, and file delinquent or amended FBARs. With respect to the amended returns, the taxpayer must pay a 20% accuracy-related penalty under § 6662 and interest on the tax and the penalty since the due date of the respective returns; with respect to delinquent returns, the taxpayer must pay the nonfraud delinquency penalty under § 6651 plus interest. Finally, the taxpayer is subject to an additional IRS miscellaneous penalty equal to 27.5%[139] of the highest aggregate values of the foreign accounts and certain foreign assets relating to U.S. tax noncompliance (*i.e.*, the income from the foreign asset or the income used to buy the foreign asset was not previously

---

[137] USAM Criminal Resource Manual 2029.

[138] The garden-variety Voluntary Disclosure Program is set for at IRM § 9.5.11.9, and is discussed in Chapter 6.

[139] The penalty was initially 20%, but has increased to 25% and then to 27.5% with each new OVDI. The penalty is increased to 50% if the foreign bank where the taxpayer's account resides is being investigated by the IRS or DOJ, is cooperating with the Government, or has received a John Doe summons.

reported).[140] This IRS miscellaneous penalty is "in lieu of" any other penalty that could apply.[141] The IRS also offers a "streamlined disclosure" program for taxpayers who can show their failure to disclose the offshore account was not willful. If accepted into the streamlined disclosure program, the taxpayer will only have to file tax returns the previous three years and will be subject to a substantially reduced, or zero, miscellaneous penalty. Unfortunately, the IRS has provided little guidance on what constitutes willful (or non-willful) failure to file. And, significantly, there is no guarantee of non-prosecution if the IRS disagrees with the taxpayer's willfulness certification. The OVDI is buttressed by a major criminal prosecution initiative. This initiative includes prosecutions of both taxpayers and persons and entities who enabled taxpayers, including foreign banks, the bank's employees and persons, as well as lawyers and other professionals.

VIII. MAIL FRAUD AND WIRE FRAUD (18 U.S.C. SECTIONS 1341 AND 1343)

A. Introduction

Two of the older federal criminal statutes are mail fraud and wire fraud, which criminalize any scheme to defraud, as long as the mails or wires are used.[142] As we will see, the elements of these offenses are quite simple and straightforward, and the fraud statutes can cover a broad array of conduct. As a result, mail and wire fraud have become favorite criminal statutes for prosecutors.

> To federal prosecutors of white collar crime, the mail fraud statute is our Stradivarius, our Colt 45, our Louisville Slugger, our Cuisinart — and our true love. We may flirt with RICO, show off with 10b-5, and call the conspiracy law "darling," but we always come home to the virtues of 18 U.S.C. § 1341, with its simplicity, adaptability, and comfortable familiarity. It understands us and, like many a foolish spouse, we like to think we understand it.[143]

Federal prosecutors have long followed the maxim, "When in doubt, charge mail fraud."[144] This can be troubling, given that mail fraud and wire fraud are predicate crimes or SUAs for RICO and money laundering, thereby turning what would

---

[140] The IRS closed 10,439 OVDI cases in 2009. The average offshore penalty assessed on these cases was approximately $376,000. United States Government Accountability Office, *Offshore Tax Evasion, IRS Has Collected Billions of Dollars, May Be Missing Continued Evasion*, GAO-13-318 at p. 12 (Mar. 2008).

[141] Most prominently, the other penalty that could apply is the FBAR penalty, but other penalties could include the failure to file Forms 5471 with respect to ownership in foreign corporations and 3520 with respect to transfers to foreign trusts.

[142] The use mail and/or wire turns what would otherwise be a state or local crime into a federal crime, since the defendant used means of interstate commerce.

[143] Jed S. Rakoff, *The Federal Mail Fraud Statute (Part I)*, 18 Duq. L. Rev. 771, 771 (1980) (footnotes omitted).

[144] Paul Mogin, *Reining in the Mail Fraud Statute*, 26 Champion 12 (2002).

otherwise be garden-variety fraud into a much more serious offense carrying the prospect of asset forfeiture.

B. The Elements

Mail fraud and wire fraud each have three elements that the Government must prove beyond a reasonable doubt. The first two elements that the Government must prove for both crimes are:

1. the defendant knowingly created a scheme to defraud or to obtain money or property by false or fraudulent pretenses;[145] and
2. the defendant acted with a specific intent to commit fraud.[146]

Only the third element is different. For mail fraud, the Government must prove that the defendant used the mails in executing the scheme or attempting to do so,[147] while for wire fraud, the Government must prove that the defendant used interstate wire communications facilities for the purpose of carrying out the scheme.[148] In a nod to the modern world, the mail fraud statute now includes fraud effected by commercial delivery services which, of course, have the required nexus to interstate commerce[149] and thus are within the federal government's power to legislate.[150]

For many years, the courts were inclined to give a broad reading to the statutory language "scheme or artifice to defraud, or for obtaining money or property." The Fifth Circuit, for example, said that the statute punished "any conduct which fails to match the reflection of moral uprightness, of fundamental honesty, fair play and right dealing in the general and business life of members of society."[151] Such broad and rather quaint statements were not limited to common law definitions of fraud. The expansive interpretation has been summarized as follows:

> In the 1980s, as Sections 1341 and 1343 swept more and more conduct within their reach, some panels and individual judges warned that the expansion had gone too far. In an opinion by Judge Richard Posner, a Seventh Circuit panel criticized the moral-uprightness/fundamental-

---

[145] The Supreme Court in McNally v. United States, 483 U.S. 350, 360 (1987) held that the "or" should be interpreted as "and" and that as a result, § 1341 is "limited in scope to the protection of property rights."

[146] United States v. Mueffelman 470 F.3d 33, 36 (1st Cir. 2006); United States v. St. Gelais, 952 F.2d 90, 95 (5th Cir.), *cert. denied*, 506 U.S. 965 (1992).

[147] Use of the mails need not contribute directly to the fraudulent scheme. It is sufficient that the mailing be incident to an essential part of the scheme or a step in the plot. Schmuck v. United States, 489 U.S. 705, 710–11 (1989) (internal quotes omitted), *quoting* Badders v. United States, 240 U.S. 391, 394 (1916).

[148] Mueffelman, *supra*; St. Gelais, *supra*.

[149] 18 U.S.C. § 1341.

[150] The nexus is present even if the specific item does not in fact cross a state line. United States v. Photogrammetric Data Services., Inc., 259 F.3d 229 (4th Cir. 2001) *cert. denied*, 535 U.S. 926 (2002).

[151] United States v. Curry, 681 F.2d 406, 410 (5th Cir. 1982) (internal quotes omitted), *quoting* Blachly v. United States, 380 F.2d 665, 671 (5th Cir. 1967).

> honesty/fair-play/right-dealing formulation as "much too broad." Judge Ralph Winter of the Second Circuit protested that the courts had brought about the "extension of mail fraud by judicial fiat," and had left juries "free to apply a legal standard which amounts to little more than the rhetoric of sixth grade civics classes." And in 1985, four Supreme Court Justices declared that the lower courts had permitted "an extraordinary expansion" of Sections 1341 and 1343 "to permit federal prosecution for conduct that some had thought was subject only to state criminal and civil law."[152]

In *Neder v. United States*,[153] the Supreme Court, however, retreated from an expansive definition of fraud and anchored its analysis on the common law meaning of fraud. The Court has declined further expansion of the mail fraud statute in *Cleveland v. United States*[154] and *Skilling v. United States*,[155] where the Court imposed rather vague limitations on so-called "honest services fraud."[156]

C. Materiality

The Supreme Court in *Neder* also held that, although the language of mail and wire fraud statutes did not specifically contain materiality as an element of the crime, materiality of falsehood is nevertheless an element of the federal mail fraud, wire fraud, and bank fraud statutes. The Court held:

> The Government does not dispute that both at the time of the mail fraud statute's original enactment in 1872, and later when Congress enacted the wire fraud and bank fraud statutes, actionable "fraud" had a well-settled meaning at common law. Nor does it dispute that the well-settled meaning of "fraud" required a misrepresentation or concealment of *material* fact. Indeed, as the sources we are aware of demonstrate, the common law could not have conceived of "fraud" without proof of materiality. Thus, under the rule that Congress intends to incorporate the well-settled meaning of the common-law terms it uses, we cannot infer from the absence of an express reference to materiality that Congress intended to drop that element from the fraud statutes. On the contrary, we must *presume* that Congress intended to incorporate materiality " 'unless the statute otherwise dictates.' "[157]

The importation of a materiality requirement is broader than the mail fraud and wire fraud statutes. Neither of those statutes contain an explicit materiality requirement. In *Neder*, the Court held that the materiality element was implied in the use of the word "fraud," a common law concept used by Congress in defining the crimes. The Court reasoned that "the common law could not have conceived of 'fraud' without proof of materiality." Hence, the crime defined using the common law

---

[152] Paul Mogin, *supra* note 145, at 16 (footnotes omitted).

[153] 527 U.S. 1 (1999).

[154] 531 U.S. 12 (2000).

[155] 561 U.S. 358 (2010).

[156] *See* 18 U.S.C. § 1346.

[157] 527 U.S. at 22–23 (citations omitted) (emphasis in original).

word "fraud" implies the requirement of materiality. Thus, wherever the text of a criminal statute does not have an explicit requirement of materiality, one may be imported from an external source, such as the common law. By contrast, if the criminal statute does not have such an internal explicit requirement or an external referrant from which the requirement will be inferred, the crime will not require materiality.[158]

D. Overlap with More Specific Criminal Provisions

As we have seen, an act criminalized specifically by a particular statute may often violate other more general or even more specific statutes. The question then becomes whether the more particular criminal sanction should be applied exclusively or whether it is the prosecutor's option to charge either or even two or more crimes. In the mail fraud context, the crimes covered by sections 7201 and 7206(1) could also be charged as mail fraud, since virtually all tax returns are mailed to the IRS.[159] Can the Government therefore add a mail fraud charge when charging tax evasion or tax perjury? As we will see in the Sentencing Guidelines discussion of Chapter 10, adding counts may not ultimately add to the defendant's sentence. However, in the trial phase adding crimes certainly can add pizzazz to an otherwise weak case. More importantly, charging a tax crime as mail fraud can allow the Government to bring a charge money laundering, since mail fraud and wire fraud are SUAs, and Title 26 crimes are not. Charging the conduct as mail fraud or wire fraud might also allow the Government to secure a forfeiture of the proceeds.

The Tax Division has developed policies to deal with this charging question. Previously, the Tax Division's policy preferred the specific tax crimes rather than more general crimes, and thus generally disapproved the charging of more general crimes when the tax crimes seemed more appropriate.[160] The Tax Division, however, superseded this policy directive with a new directive, No. 128, adopted October 2004. That directive provides as follows:

> **CHARGING MAIL FRAUD, WIRE FRAUD OR BANK FRAUD ALONE OR AS PREDICATE OFFENSES IN CASES INVOLVING TAX ADMINISTRATION**
>
> Tax Division approval is required for any criminal charge if the conduct at issue arises under the internal revenue laws, regardless of the criminal statute(s) used to charge the defendant. Tax Division authorization is required before charging mail fraud, wire fraud or bank fraud alone or as the predicate to a RICO or money laundering charge for any conduct

---

[158] *See, e.g.*, United States v. Wells, 519 U.S. 482, 491 (1997) (holding that the crime of false statement in 18 U.S.C. § 1014 does not include a materiality requirement because the text does not require it, the legislative history does not support it and there is no external referrant in the common law to imply that Congress intended a materiality requirement).

[159] Most of the returns that are not mailed are sent electronically and therefore could be charged as wire fraud.

[160] CTM 3.00, Tax Division Directive No. 99.

arising under the internal revenue laws, including any charge based on the submission of a document or information to the IRS. Tax Division approval also is required for any charge based on a state tax violation if the case involves parallel federal tax violations.

The Tax Division may approve mail fraud, wire fraud or bank fraud charges in tax-related cases involving schemes to defraud the government or other persons if there was a large fraud loss or a substantial pattern of conduct and there is a significant benefit to bringing the charges instead of or in addition to Title 26 violations. See generally United States Attorneys' Manual (U.S.A.M.) § 9-43.100. Absent unusual circumstances, however, the Tax Division will not approve mail or wire fraud charges in cases involving only one person's tax liability, or when all submissions to the IRS were truthful.

Fraud charges should be considered if there is a significant benefit at the charging stage (e.g., supporting forfeiture of the proceeds of a fraud scheme; allowing the government to describe the entire scheme in the indictment); at trial (e.g., ensuring that the court will admit all relevant evidence of the scheme; permitting flexibility in choosing witnesses); or at sentencing (e.g., ensuring that the court can order full restitution). *See id.* § 9-27 320(B)(3) ("If the evidence is available, it is proper to consider the tactical advantages of bringing certain charges.").

For example, mail fraud (18 U.S.C. § 1341) or wire fraud (18 U.S.C. § 1343) charges may be appropriate if the target filed multiple fraudulent returns seeking tax refunds using fictitious names, or using the names of real taxpayers without their knowledge. Fraud charges also may be considered if the target promoted a fraudulent tax scheme.

Bank fraud charges (18 U.S.C. § 1344) can be appropriate in the case of a tax fraud scheme that victimized a financial institution. Example: the defendant filed false claims for tax refund and induced a financial institution to approve refund anticipation loans on the basis of the fraudulent information submitted to the IRS.

Racketeering and Money Laundering Charges Based on Tax Offenses

The Tax Division will not authorize the use of mail, wire or bank fraud charges to convert routine tax prosecutions into RICO or money laundering cases. The Tax Division will authorize prosecution of tax-related RICO and money laundering offenses, however, when unusual circumstances warrant it. A United States Attorney who wishes to charge a RICO violation (18 U.S.C. § 1962) in any criminal matter arising under the internal revenue laws, including a predicate act based on a state tax violation, in the case of a parallel federal tax violation, must obtain the authorization of the Tax Division and the Criminal Division's Organized Crime and Racketeering Section. U.S.A.M. 9-110.101. A United States Attorney who wishes to bring a money laundering charge (18 U.S.C. § 1956) based on conduct arising under the internal revenue laws must obtain the authorization of the Tax Division and, if necessary, the Criminal Division's Asset Forfeiture and

Money Laundering Section. U.S.A.M. § 9-105.300.

Directive No. 128 is the latest chapter in the Tax Division's efforts to maintain control over tax prosecutions, thereby helping to ensure a more uniform application of the criminal tax laws.

PROBLEM

Daniel owns a series of high-profile nightclubs in several cities called *Guys.* Daniel owns these clubs through a wholly-owned corporation, Guys Industries, Inc. While *Guys* clubs are quite successful, Daniel was in need of some additional cash, both to fund the expansion of his empire and to settle with his soon-to-be ex-wife, Jennifer. Like many before him, Daniel has decided to fund these enterprises with pre-tax dollars. Daniel contacted his longtime friend and business advisor Jack to find a solution. The strategy that Jack and Daniel devised is as follows: (1) They will set up a corporation in the Bahamas that is owned, at least on paper, by a colleague of Jack, but in reality the corporation is just a name and a bank account; (2) the Bahamian corporation will submit phony invoices to Guys Industries for "consulting services," which Guys Industries will pay and claim a deduction for tax purposes; and (3) the funds will be repatriated via a "loan" from the Bahamian corporation to Daniel via a wire transfer into Daniel's personal bank account. Jack and Daniel told the bookkeeper, Susan, about the plan so that she would pay invoices, but they told her that this was part of an asset protection plan and as a way to keep Jennifer (who none of them like) from getting all of Daniel's money. At Daniel's direction, Susan paid the invoices and prepared corporate tax returns for Guys Industries claiming the consulting fees as a deduction, which zeroed-out the corporation's tax liability. Daniel signed the returns as president of the corporation and Susan mailed the returns to the IRS. Daniel did not report any of the "loan" proceeds as income on his personal return.

1. Should all of the above facts come to light, what are the crimes that the government could charge and against whom could those charges be brought?

2. What crimes is the government likely to charge, given its prosecution policies?

3. Would your answer to question 1 change if Daniel claimed a refund on his personal returns?

4. Assume that Jack and Daniel's strategy goes undetected for six years. In year seven,[161] the three most recent years of Guys Industries' returns are subject to a routine civil audit by an IRS Revenue Agent, who meets with Susan. When the Agent asks about the consulting fee payments, Susan (not wanting to get Daniel in trouble with his ex-wife) invents an elaborate story about what the fees are for. After looking further into the deductions, the Agent learns that the Bahamian corporation is bogus and he refers the case criminally. What crimes can the government bring at this point, and against whom?

---

[161] Reminder: the statute of limitations for tax crimes, including conspiracy, is six years.

Chapter 4

MODES OF PROOF

IRC: §§ 280E, 6064

I. INTRODUCTION

Tax crimes present several recurring themes regarding proof. This chapter examines many of those themes. Among them are matters related to proof of the defendant's taxable income. This bears on elements of several offenses. For example:

- Such proof bears directly on the "tax due and owing" element of section 7201 tax evasion. It also bears indirectly on that section's willfulness requirement since it is easier to convince a jury that the defendant's conduct was willful when the understatements are large.
- Such proof also matters with respect to section 7203 failure to file since having enough income to meet the required filing threshold is an element of the offense.
- "Tax due and owing" is not an element of section 7206(1) tax perjury. Nonetheless, understatement of income is one type of material inaccuracy that may support such a charge.
- Proof that a client's true income was considerably higher than reported may be part of a section 7602(2) prosecution of the client's adviser or return preparer.

This chapter examines four topics: (1) the burden and standard of proof; (2) direct, indirect, and hybrid methods of proof; (3) Government employees as witnesses; and (4) presumptions.

II. BURDEN AND STANDARD OF PROOF

A. Generally

Our adversary system depends on the parties to the case to develop and present the relevant facts. Essential to such a system are identifying which party bears the burden of proof and fixing the level of confidence the trier of fact must have before concluding that the party with the burden has satisfied it. In criminal tax prosecutions, just as in other types of criminal prosecution in the United States, the burden of proof is on the Government and the standard of proof is "beyond a reasonable doubt."[1] This burden is explained in lay terms in the instructions given by the judge to jurors. For example:

> The indictment or formal charge against a defendant is not evidence of guilt. Indeed, the defendant is presumed by the law to be innocent. The law does not require a defendant to prove his innocence or produce any evidence at all [and no inference whatever may be drawn from the election of a defendant not to testify]. The government has the burden of proving the defendant guilty beyond a reasonable doubt, and if it fails to do so, you must acquit the defendant.
>
> While the government's burden of proof is a strict or heavy one, it is not necessary that the defendant's guilt be proved beyond all possible doubt. It is only required that the government's proof exclude any "reasonable doubt" concerning the defendant's guilt.
>
> A "reasonable doubt" is a doubt based upon reason and common sense after careful and impartial consideration of all the evidence in the case. Proof beyond a reasonable doubt, therefore, is proof of such a convincing character that you would be willing to rely and act upon it without hesitation in the most important of your own affairs.[2]

In a non-lay sense, it is necessary to distinguish between two aspects of the burden of proof: the duty of bringing forward evidence (also known as the burden of production and the risk of nonproduction) and the risk of nonpersuasion (also known as the burden of persuasion).[3] Courts and commentators often are less than precise in how they use these terms. Nonetheless, the unelaborated term "burden of proof" usually connotes only the burden of persuasion — as it does in the jury instruction above.

B. Standard of Proof

Trial lawyers love to describe burdens in percentage terms. In the ordinary civil case, the party bearing the burden of persuasion must prove by a preponderance of the evidence, which is quantified as evidence which the trier assesses as proving the key fact to be more likely than not — *i.e.*, in excess of 50%. If you were going to state the percentage for beyond a reasonable doubt, what would it be? One author states the inquiry as follows:

> Consider what "proof beyond a reasonable doubt" actually mandates that the jury do. Surely it requires more proof than the preponderance of the evidence standard, which governs in civil cases. As commonly explained to civil juries, the preponderance standard is quantified as any amount of certainty greater than 50%, and proof beyond a reasonable doubt must

---

1 *E.g.*, Holland v. United States, 348 U.S. 121, 126 (1954).

2 Fifth Circuit Pattern Jury Instruction 1.05 (Presumption of Innocence, Burden of Proof, Reasonable Doubt). The bracketed material is deleted in cases in which the defendant testifies.

3 *See, e.g.*, Steve R. Johnson, *The Dangers of Symbolic Legislation: Perceptions and Realities of the New Burden-of-Proof Rules*, 84 Iowa L. Rev. 413, 415–16 (1999); John A. Townsend, *Burden of Proof in Tax Cases: Valuation and Ranges*, Tax Notes, Oct. 1, 2001, at 101.

> mean more than that. But how much more proof than a preponderance is needed in a criminal case? The quantity of certainty is never quantified; instead, it is kept quite vague. Is 90% certainty required? 95%? 99%? Or could the amount of certainty be much lower, say perhaps 75%?[4]

Whatever the "percentage" level of certainty imagined to be inherent in the standard, "research has consistently shown that the jurors in criminal cases will be satisfied with much less certainty than is conventionally assumed."[5] Indeed, "[j]udges, when asked to express beyond a reasonable doubt as a probability of guilt, generally pick a number between .75 and .90 . . . , and jury quantifications are similar. These may seem shockingly low figures, implying that as many as a quarter of people convicted of crime are innocent."[6]

Other studies suggest that judges and jurors are all over the lot on the issue. In one study of judges in the Eastern District of New York, "one [judge] gave a probability of 76%, one gave 80%, four gave 85%, two gave 90%, and one gave 95%. In other words, the probabilities hovered around 85%–90%."[7] In a larger survey of federal judges throughout the country:

> Of the 171 judges who responded, 126 had thresholds that were 90% or higher. Eleven judges had thresholds of 75% or below, one of whom was satisfied with a 50% probability. The other study was conducted among Illinois state court judges. On a scale of 1 to 10, the mean level of certainty in this study was 8.9, with a median of 8.8; 63% of the judges responded with a level of 9.0 or higher. Most (but not all) judges, then, tend to see the government's burden much the way Blackstone did [about 90%].[8]

According to some of these studies, judges and jurors in 20 or 25% doubt could return a guilty verdict. One might feel concern about that. However, prosecutorial selectivity in picking cases to prosecute substantially mitigates the risk that the innocent will be convicted. Moreover, as we have seen, there are unique prosecutorial mitigating factors in tax cases that virtually require the Government to choose only very strong cases to prosecute. This further mitigates the possibility of convicting innocent tax defendants.

---

[4] Evik Lillquist, *Recasting Reasonable Doubt: Decision Theory and the Virtues of Variability*, 36 U.C. Davis L. Rev. 85, 86 (2002).

[5] *Id.* at 88. For good discussion of the difficulty of making the concept meaningful to jurors, see Thomas Lundy, *Comparison of Standards: A Strategy for Explaining Proof Beyond a Reasonable Doubt*, 27 Champion 61 (2003).

[6] Richard A. Posner, *An Economic Approach to the Law of Evidence*, 51 Stan. L. Rev. 1477, 1506 (1999); *see* Dan Simon, *A Third View of the Black Box: Cognitive Coherence in Legal Decision Making*, 71 U. Chi. L. Rev. 511, 557 n.147 (2004) (Empirical "[r]esearch that monitors perceptions of the standard reveals that while assessments vary with the methodology of elicitation, the responses tend to converge in the range of 80 to 90 percent certainty satisfying the standard.") (citing Reid Hastie, *Algebraic Models of Juror Decision Processes*, *in* Inside the Juror: The Psychology of Juror Decision Making 84,102 (Reid Hastie, ed. 1993).

[7] Lawrence Solan, *Refocusing the Burden of Proof in Criminal Cases: Some Doubt About Reasonable Doubt*, 78 Tex. L. Rev. 105, 126–27 (1999) (reporting survey by Judge Weinstein).

[8] *Id.* at 127.

C. Shifting Burden of Production

The burden of persuasion always remains on the Government, but the burden of going forward can shift. More specifically, the burden to prove beyond a reasonable doubt each element of the crime charged is on the Government from the beginning of the trial until guilt or innocence is determined. However, in some instances, the net effect of the Government's case is so strong that the Government does not have to prove the negative of propositions that are really essential to its case — unless and until the defendant puts the issue in play.

For example, if the Government shows that Abel omitted $100,000 of taxable receipts from his return, does that prove beyond a reasonable doubt that Abel owed tax on an additional $100,000 of income and thus committed tax evasion? Not necessarily since the taxpayer could have had unreported deductible expenses — perhaps even directly related to the omitted income — that either completely offset the omitted income or offset it enough that the resulting tax is not material and so is insufficient to sustain a tax evasion charge.

However, it would be unreasonable and inefficient to require the Government to show that there were no more deductions without at least requiring Abel to suggest what additional deductions there might have been.[9] In other words, once the Government proves substantial omitted income, the burden shifts to the defendant to identify additional, offsetting deductions. If the defendant does so, the burden shifts back to the Government to negative the asserted additional deductions.

By way of illustration, in one case, the taxpayer argued that, based on the type of business operations involved, the omitted, legal-source business income[10] in the magnitude asserted by the Government would have required the taxpayer to have had employees and that the costs of paying those employees would have been deductible expenses offsetting at least part of the alleged unreported income. (The taxpayer had not previously claimed deductions for such costs.) The taxpayer urged, in essence, that the Government must prove that the omitted income was not offset by associated expenses. The court rejected the argument, holding that "[t]he applicable rule here is that uniformly applied in tax evasion cases — that evidence of unexplained receipts shifts to the taxpayer the burden of coming forward with evidence as to the amount of offsetting expenses, if any."[11]

In some cases, it is not easy to draw the line between what is part of the Government's prima facie case as opposed to what is merely a defense that the Government must negate only if raised by the defendant. Consider the following case.

---

[9] As to the "difficulty of proving a negative," see Kevin W. Saunders, *The Mythic Difficulty in Proving a Negative*, 15 SETON HALL L. REV. 276 (1985); Note, *Proving a Negative — When the Taxpayer Denies Receipt*, 70 CORNELL L. REV. 141 (1984).

[10] Had the business been illegal narcotics trafficking, additional expenses — even if incurred — would have been nondeductible because of section 280E.

[11] Siravo v. United States, 377 F.2d 469, 473 (1st Cir. 1967) (citations omitted).

UNITED STATES v. TARWATER

United States Court of Appeals, Sixth Circuit
308 F.3d 494 (2002)

[Authors' note: The defendant, an accountant for a hospital, received payments that the hospital thought were being passed by the defendant to a third party (Davis) that the hospital thought was providing services to the hospital. Of course, if the defendant were merely a conduit to pass the monies from the hospital, the payments in question would not be his income and the defendant would not need to report the payments anywhere on his returns. Upon investigation, however, the IRS found some evidence that the defendant was keeping the bulk of the money and using it for his personal purposes, rather than passing it on to Davis. The defendant was indicted for tax perjury under section § 7206(1) for filing returns that omitted the portion that the Government's investigation determined the defendant had kept for himself. At trial, the Government clearly met its burden of showing that the taxpayer received the payments from the hospital and deposited them into various accounts belonging to defendant. The evidence was arguably equivocal as to whether the defendant had passed equal amounts on to Davis, in which case, as noted, it would not be the defendant's income and his failure to include any of the payments in income would have been entirely proper. The Government's bank deposits analysis suggested that the defendant did not pass most of the money on to Davis, but that was only circumstantial evidence. Since neither party called Davis to testify as to whether he received the payments in question and the defendant did not testify, the Government clearly did not directly establish that the entire amounts had not been paid over to Davis, thus being income to defendant. Over the defendant's objection, the trial court gave the following instruction to the jury:

> While the government has the burden to prove beyond a reasonable doubt that the defendant understated the amount of gross receipts or total income reported on his 1992 Federal Income Tax Return and the amount of his total income reported on his 1993 and 1994 Federal Income Tax Returns, the government is not required to prove the non-existence of alleged payments by [Tarwater] to or on behalf of Mr. Davis.

[The defendant was convicted. On appeal, the defendant challenged the instruction as impermissibly relieving the Government of a burden it bore in order to prove an essential element — to prove that the defendant had income *ab initio* that must be reported on the return. The Court of Appeals rejected the argument.]

Tarwater contends that the district court impermissibly shifted the burden of proof when it instructed the jury that "the government is not required to prove the non-existence of alleged payments by [Tarwater] to or on behalf of Mr. Davis." As Tarwater correctly suggests, the government carries the burden of proving each and every element of a criminal offense beyond a reasonable doubt, and any jury instruction that shifts that burden to a defendant constitutes a violation of due process. Whether a jury instruction violates a defendant's due process rights is reviewed *de novo*.

We do not agree that the district court impermissibly shifted the burden of proof when it instructed the jury that "the government is not required to prove the non-existence of alleged payments by [Tarwater] to or on behalf of Mr. Davis." Indeed, our review of the relevant case law convinces us that the district court's instruction was a correct statement of the law.

As suggested in numerous cases, including *Ballard, Davis, Orlowski,* and *Holland,* the government was not required to prove the absence of pass-through payments to Davis, particularly where, as here, Tarwater provided the government no help in identifying the form or source of those payments. We accordingly conclude that the district court in no way shifted the burden of proof when it instructed the jury.

Tarwater also argues that the district court erred by not giving a good faith instruction and by not giving Tarwater's proposed instruction that "a transfer of funds does not have any reporting requirements under the Internal Revenue Code." We review for abuse of discretion the district court's choice of instructions. We must consider the instructions as a whole to determine whether they fairly and adequately submitted the issues and applicable law to the jury. Generally, a defendant is entitled to an instruction on defense theories that are supported by law and raised by the evidence presented. However, we will reverse a district court's refusal to give a requested instruction only when (1) the requested instruction is a correct statement of the law; (2) the requested instruction is not substantially covered by other instructions actually delivered; and (3) the failure to give the requested instruction impairs the defendant's theory of the case.

Initially, we question whether Tarwater presented any evidence to support his good faith defense. Assuming *arguendo* that he did, however, we nonetheless find that the instructions, viewed as a whole, adequately encompassed his theory of defense.

Having found no merit to any of Tarwater's arguments on appeal, we AFFIRM.

MOORE, CIRCUIT JUDGE, dissenting.

The instruction at issue had the effect of negating the government's burden to prove the second element of § 7206(1). Tarwater contends, and the testimony of an IRS agent confirms, that: (1) the payments from Jefferson Memorial Hospital ("JMH") were income reportable either to Tarwater or Davis, but not both; and (2) if Tarwater passed through to David the payments by JMH for Davis, those payments were not income to Tarwater. Thus, if the payments were passed through, Tarwater did not knowingly file materially incorrect or illegal tax returns. In a similar situation, where the characterization of an increase in wealth as income was disputed, we held that, "[i]f the money were truly a loan, [the defendant] would have been under no duty to report it as income, and he would not be guilty of the predicate offense of filing a false tax return." *United States v. Parrott*, 148 F.3d 629, 634 (6th Cir. 1998). Because the existence of Tarwater's alleged payments to Davis was a fact necessary to establish whether Tarwater knowingly submitted false returns for 1992, 1993, and 1994, the government was required to prove beyond a reasonable doubt that he did not pass through to Davis payments by JMH for Davis.

In other words, the government was required to prove beyond a reasonable doubt that the payments by JMH were income to Tarwater. If the payments by JMH were for Davis and were passed through Tarwater to Davis, however, they were *not* income to Tarwater. The majority suggests that Tarwater's payments to Davis are analogous to offsetting expenses, relying on cases stating that the government need not come forward with evidence negating all possible offsetting expenses and nontaxable gains to make a case that a taxpayer failed to report his gross income. In the instant case, however, Tarwater does not argue that the government should have a burden to produce this evidence. Rather, in claiming that the jury instruction shifted the government's burden of proof, Tarwater rightly asserts that the government had a burden to show that the only alleged source of income in this case — payments from JMH — actually constituted income to Tarwater. By concluding that the government does not have this burden, the majority improperly extends the law of other circuits to suggest that the government is not only excused from producing evidence to negate all possible offsetting expenses or nontaxable gains, but that the government is further excused from proving beyond a reasonable doubt that a defendant received income that he knowingly failed to report. Therefore, the jury instruction at issue impermissibly shifted the burden of proof from the government to the taxpayer.

III. DIRECT, INDIRECT, AND HYBRID METHODS OF PROOF

This part addresses the means or theories by which the Government can attempt to prove the "tax due and owing" element of section 7201. These methods may be used either at the trial in chief or in sentencing. The Government may use — and in various cases has used — direct methods, indirect methods, and combinations or hybrids of direct and indirect methods.

A. Direct Method

Throughout our modern tax history, the majority of criminal tax cases have used the direct method — also known as the specific items method — of proof. In recent years, the great majority of such cases have been direct method cases.

The income tax is a tax due on net taxable income for the year. There are a host of components of income, deduction, and credit that enter the bottom-line determination of tax due. The specific items method may involve direct evidence of omitted income, overstated deductions, overstated credits, or any combination of them.[12]

Prosecutions based on false or overstated deductions are much less frequent than prosecutions based on omitted income. In part, this is because proof problems often are greater in deduction cases since the Government would have to prove a negative (that the expense was not incurred or, if incurred, was not deductible). Fraudulent deduction prosecutions usually involve taxpayers or return preparers

---

[12] *E.g.*, United States v. Potts, 321 F. Supp. 717 (E.D. Wis. 1971), *aff'd*, 459 F.2d 412 (7th Cir. 1972) (overstated deductions and unreported income used conjunctively to establish guilt).

who falsify personal exemptions, falsify itemized deductions, or claim personal expenses as business deductions.[13]

Criminal tax trials rarely deal with direct proof of every item of income, deduction, or credit. Usually, the starting point is the taxpayer's return as filed. The return is deemed the taxpayer's admission as to the items included on the return, at least as to the items the Government does not question.[14]

The Government will contest specific deductions or credits or assert additional specific items of income, calculate the income as thus adjusted and apply the appropriate rates, yielding the tax due and owing for criminal purposes. In this drill, the Government will assert only the items that, given the circumstances of the case, it can establish beyond a reasonable doubt were willfully misreported. The Government may be aware of other items that will affect the final civil tax bill, but which are insufficient to indicate evasion and therefore are omitted from the criminal calculations.

B. Indirect Methods

In many cases, the Government may not be able to assemble proof from direct methods. For those cases, the Government has developed methodologies of circumstantial proof. An indirect method may be used to corroborate amounts suggested by a specific items approach,[15] or conjunctively with another indirect method,[16] or in a multi-year case to establish income for one or more years with other years' income being established by another method.[17]

All indirect methods are based on logic: from the facts proven can the further inference be made, beyond a reasonable doubt, that a substantial amount of taxable income was omitted? It is the force of that logic — and that force alone — that justifies the use of these methods.

In order to use an indirect method, the Government should establish that a direct method either is not available or is unreliable under the circumstances. For example, the Government should show that the taxpayer's books and records are unavailable (*e.g.*, because the taxpayer never kept them or lost or destroyed them) or, if they are available, that they are not reliable (*e.g.*, because they contain substantial provable irregularities). The methodology itself may suffice to show, for example, that large cash flows are not reflected on the books and records, thus, that the books and records are unreliable. The Government usually also must establish either that there is a "likely taxable source" for the unreported income or that it has reasonably negated nontaxable sources of income.[18]

---

13 *E.g.*, United States v. Damon, 676 F.2d 1060 (5th Cir. 1982).

14 *E.g.*, United States v. Burkhart, 501 F.2d 993, 995 (6th Cir. 1974), *cert. denied*, 420 U.S. 946 (1975); *see* Warszower v. United States, 312 U.S. 342, 347 (1941).

15 *E.g.*, Heasley v. United States, 218 F.2d 86, 90 (8th Cir. 1955), *cert. denied*, 350 U.S. 882 (1955).

16 *E.g.*, United States v. Doyle, 234 F.2d 788, 793–94 (7th Cir.), *cert. denied*, 352 U.S. 893 (1956).

17 *E.g.*, United States v. Dawson, 400 F.2d 194, 203 (2d Cir. 1968), *cert. denied*, 393 U.S. 1023 (1969).

18 *E.g.*, United States v. Caswell, 825 F.2d 1228, 1231 (8th Cir. 1987); United States v. Marshall, 557

The following discussion provides only a summary of the indirect methods. These methods are heavily fact dependent and can be complex in their application. There are numerous principles in properly applying the methods, and many of them involve details beyond the scope of this book. The Department of Justice's Criminal Tax Manual and the Internal Revenue Manual contain good and substantially more detailed discussions of the indirect methods.

1. Net Worth Method

The net worth method assumes income from unexplained increases in the defendant's net worth over a given time frame — usually several consecutive years. The following is a good description of the formula and its logic:

> The Government makes out a prima facie case under the net worth method of proof if it establishes the defendant's opening net worth (computed as assets at cost basis less liabilities) with reasonable certainty and then shows increases in his net worth for each year in question which, added to his nondeductible expenditures and excluding his known nontaxable receipts for the year, exceed his reported taxable income by a substantial amount. The jury may infer that the defendant's excess net worth increases represent unreported taxable income if the Government either shows a likely source, or negates all possible nontaxable sources. [T]he jury may further infer willfulness from the fact of underreporting coupled with evidence of conduct by the defendant tending to mislead or conceal.[19]

Under this statement, the Government merely makes out a prima facie case — one that the jury, based on all the evidence, may accept but need not accept. A more mechanical statement of the method is as follows:

> The government established its case through the "net worth" approach, a method of circumstantial proof which basically consists of five steps: (1) calculation of net worth at the end of a taxable year, (2) subtraction of net worth at the beginning of the same taxable year, (3) addition of non-deductible expenditures for personal, including living, expenditures, (4) subtraction of receipts from income sources that are non-taxable, and (5) comparison of the resultant figure with the amount of taxable income reported by the taxpayer to determine the amount, if any, of underreporting.[20]

The formula is a logical one that really is a bit more sophisticated than a mere change in net worth. This is also a standard formulation:

Increase in net worth over the period

Plus nondeductible expenditures

F.2d 527, 529 (5th Cir. 1977) (the Government must prove "directly or inferentially, that the expenditures were made from taxable income").

[19] United States v. Sorrentino, 726 F.2d 876, 879–80 (1st Cir. 1984).

[20] United States v. Schafer, 580 F.2d 774, 775 (5th Cir.), *cert. denied*, 439 U.S. 970 (1978).

Less nontaxable receipts

Less exemptions

Yields taxable income

Here is a simple example using a two-year time frame and round figures to illustrate the methodology:

Net worth Dec. 31 of year 2:	$50,000
Less: Net worth Jan. 1 of year 1:	(10,000)
Increase in net worth:	40,000
Plus nondeductible expenditures (living)	50,000
Less nontaxable receipt — gift	(10,000)
Less exemptions (2 years)	(6,000)
Yields Taxable Income	$77,000
Less Taxable Income as Reported	(20,000)
Unreported Taxable Income	$57,000

This example includes a complicating factor. The formula clearly shows that, over the two-year period, the taxpayer had substantial unreported income. But the Government must be able to attribute a material amount of tax to each year it chooses to charge. Depending upon the facts, this might be quite difficult. Perhaps the Government could urge that, without some explanation from the taxpayer, the taxable income can be allocated ratably over the number of years involved (here two years, so 50% to each year). Depending upon the facts, the court might accept that argument, but it might not also. But the facts might also negate that type of mechanical allocation, in which case the Government must find some rational allocation based on the facts.

Logically, net worth must be computed for noncash assets at cost basis. If a taxpayer has appreciation in value of an asset before a "realizable" event — such as sale of the asset — the taxpayer does not have income. Thus, in the above example where the taxpayer had apparently $57,000 of unreported income, if that entire amount were attributable to the fact that an unsold asset had risen in value by $57,000 during the year, the increase in net worth would not prove any additional taxable income. Just as gifts received are not taxable income, so unrealized appreciation is not taxable income. The logic of the net worth method must be rigorously applied.

The net worth method is fraught with other dangers, as the Supreme Court noted in the leading case of *Holland v. United States*.[21] Because of these dangers, the net worth method must be prepared by the Government painstakingly, at great expense and effort. For this reason, net worth cases are uncommon because in most cases where the method might be used, there may be a more directly provable tax crime which, under the sentencing guidelines, is likely to attract the same punishment. The following discussion from the seminal net worth case addresses some of the larger issues raised by the method:

---

[21] 348 U.S. 121 (1954). See also the companion case, *Friedberg v. United States*, 348 U.S. 142 (1954).

HOLLAND v. UNITED STATES

United States Supreme Court
348 U.S. 121 (1954)

Before proceeding with a discussion of these cases, we believe it important to outline the general problems implicit in this type of litigation. In this consideration we assume, as we must in view of its widespread use, that the Government deems the net worth method useful in the enforcement of the criminal sanctions of our income tax laws. Nevertheless, careful study indicates that it is so fraught with danger for the innocent that the courts must closely scrutinize its use.

One basic assumption in establishing guilt by this method is that most assets derive from a taxable source, and that when this is not true the taxpayer is in a position to explain the discrepancy. The application of such an assumption raises serious legal problems in the administration of the criminal law. Unlike civil actions for the recovery of deficiencies, where the determinations of the Commissioner have prima facie validity, the prosecution must always prove the criminal charge beyond a reasonable doubt. This has led many of our courts to be disturbed by the use of the net worth method, particularly in its scope and the latitude which it allows prosecutors.

But the net worth method has not grown up overnight. It was first utilized in such cases as *Capone v. United States*, 51 F.2d 609 (1931) and *Guzik v. United States*, 54 F.2d 618 (1931), to corroborate direct proof of specific unreported income. In *United States v. Johnson*, [319 U.S. 503 (1943)], this Court approved of its use to support the inference that the taxpayer, owner of a vast and elaborately concealed network of gambling houses upon which he declared no income, had indeed received unreported income in a "substantial amount." It was a potent weapon in establishing taxable income from undisclosed sources when all other efforts failed. Since the *Johnson* case, however, its horizons have been widened. Until now it is used in run-of-the-mine cases, regardless of the amount of tax deficiency involved. In each of the four cases decided today, the allegedly unreported income comes from the same disclosed sources as produced the taxpayer's reported income and in none is the tax deficiency anything like the deficiencies in *Johnson*, *Capone*, or *Guzik*. The net worth method, it seems, has evolved from the final volley to the first shot in the Government's battle for revenue, and its use in the ordinary income-bracket cases greatly increases the chances for error. This leads us to point out the dangers that must be consciously kept in mind in order to assure adequate appraisal of the specific facts in individual cases.

1. Among the defenses often asserted is the taxpayer's claim that the net worth increase shown by the Government's statement is in reality not an increase at all because of the existence of substantial cash on hand at the starting point. This favorite defense asserts that the cache is made up of many years' savings which for various reasons were hidden and not expended until the prosecution period. Obviously, the Government has great difficulty in refuting such a contention. However, taxpayers too encounter many obstacles in convincing the jury of the existence of such hoards. This is particularly so when the emergence of the hidden savings also uncovers a fraud on the taxpayer's creditors.

In this connection, the taxpayer frequently gives "leads" to the Government agents indicating the specific sources from which his cash on hand has come, such as prior earnings, stock transactions, real estate profits, inheritances, gifts, etc. Sometimes these "leads" point back to old transactions far removed from the prosecution period. Were the Government required to run down all such leads it would face grave investigative difficulties; still its failure to do so might jeopardize the position of the taxpayer.

2. As we have said, the method requires assumptions, among which is the equation of unexplained increases in net worth with unreported taxable income. Obviously, such an assumption has many weaknesses. It may be that gifts, inheritances, loans, and the like account for the newly-acquired wealth. There is great danger that the jury may assume that once the Government has established the figures in its net worth computations, the crime of tax evasion automatically follows. The possibility of this increases where the jury, without guarding instructions, is allowed to take into the jury room the various charts summarizing the computations; bare figures have a way of acquiring an existence of their own, independent of the evidence which gave rise to them.

3. Although it may sound fair to say that the taxpayer can explain the "bulge" in his net worth, he may be entirely honest and yet unable to recount his financial history. In addition, such a rule would tend to shift the burden of proof. Were the taxpayer compelled to come forward with evidence, he might risk lending support to the Government's case by showing loose business methods or losing the jury through his apparent evasiveness. Of course, in other criminal prosecutions, juries may disbelieve and convict the innocent. But the courts must minimize this danger.

4. When there are no books and records, willfulness may be inferred by the jury from that fact coupled with proof of an understatement of income. But when the Government uses the net worth method, and the books and records of the taxpayer appear correct on their face, an inference of willfulness from net worth increases alone might be unjustified, especially where the circumstances surrounding the deficiency are as consistent with innocent mistake as with willful violation. On the other hand, the very failure of the books to disclose a proved deficiency might indicate deliberate falsification.

5. In many cases of this type, the prosecution relies on the taxpayer's statements, made to revenue agents in the course of their investigation, to establish vital links in the Government's proof. But when a revenue agent confronts the taxpayer with an apparent deficiency, the latter may be more concerned with a quick settlement than an honest search for the truth. Moreover, the prosecution may pick and choose from the taxpayer's statement, relying on the favorable portion and throwing aside that which does not bolster its position. The problem of corroboration, dealt with in the companion cases of *Smith v. United States* and *United States v. Calderon*, therefore becomes crucial.

6. The statute defines the offense here involved by individual years. While the Government may be able to prove with reasonable accuracy an increase in net worth over a period of years, it often has great difficulty in relating that income sufficiently to any specific prosecution year. While a steadily increasing net worth may justify an inference of additional earnings, unless that increase can be reasonably allocated

to the appropriate tax year the taxpayer may be convicted on counts of which he is innocent. While we cannot say that these pitfalls inherent in the net worth method foreclose its use, they do require the exercise of great care and restraint. The complexity of the problem is such that it cannot be met merely by the application of general rules. Trial courts should approach these cases in the full realization that the taxpayer may be ensnared in a system which, though difficult for the prosecution to utilize, is equally hard for the defendant to refute. Charges should be especially clear, including, in addition to the formal instructions, a summary of the nature of the net worth method, the assumptions on which it rests, and the inferences available both for and against the accused. Appellate courts should review the cases, bearing constantly in mind the difficulties that arise when circumstantial evidence as to guilt is the chief weapon of a method that is itself only an approximation.

The Burden of Proof Remains on the Government. Nor does this rule shift the burden of proof. The Government must still prove every element of the offense beyond a reasonable doubt though not to a mathematical certainty. The settled standards of the criminal law are applicable to net worth cases just as to prosecutions for other crimes. Once the Government has established its case, the defendant remains quiet at his peril. The practical disadvantages to the taxpayer are lessened by the pressures on the Government to check and negate relevant leads.

Circumstantial evidence in this respect is intrinsically no different from testimonial evidence. Admittedly, circumstantial evidence may in some cases point to a wholly incorrect result. Yet, this is equally true of testimonial evidence. In both instances, a jury is asked to weigh the chances that the evidence correctly points to guilt against the possibility of inaccuracy or ambiguous inference. In both, the jury must use its experience with people and events in weighing the probabilities. If the jury is convinced beyond a reasonable doubt, we can require no more. Even more insistent is the petitioners' attack, not made below, on the charge of the trial judge as to reasonable doubt. He defined it as "the kind of doubt . . . which you folks in the more serious and important affairs of your own lives might be willing to act upon." We think this section of the charge should have been in terms of the kind of doubt that would make a person hesitate to act, rather than the kind on which he would be willing to act. But we believe that the instruction as given-was not of the type that could mislead the jury into finding no reasonable doubt when in fact there was some. A definition of a doubt as something the jury would act upon would seem to create confusion rather than misapprehension. Attempts to explain the term "reasonable doubt" do not usually result in making it any clearer to the minds of the jury, and we feel that, taken as a whole, the instructions correctly conveyed the concept of reasonable doubt to the jury.

The taxpayer-defendant will have an opportunity to poke holes in the Government's net worth case. How does the taxpayer do that? Of course, such cases are fact dependent, but three approaches are common: (1) attacking the accuracy of the Government's opening or closing net worth figure, sometimes by arguing that the Government failed to prove the defendant's cash on hand at the start of the prosecution period; (2) alleging that the net worth increase is attributable to some nontaxable source(s) or that the Government has not identified a likely taxable source; or (3) maintaining that the apparent net worth increases in the prosecution years resulted from spending cash in those years that had been accumulated in prior years (an argument related to argument (1) above).

The last of these approaches is usually called the "cash hoard defense." The cash hoard — cash buried in the back yard, hidden in a mattress, or the like — is either from nontaxable sources (such as gifts or inheritances) or from taxable sources in years as to which the section 6531 statute of limitations has already expired.

The Government attempts to rebut cash hoards in various ways. They include admissions made by the taxpayer;[22] financial statements given by the taxpayer to federal or state agencies or to others (such as banks);[23] reconstruction of the taxpayer's income from pre-prosecution years using tax returns and other information to show low amounts of prior income;[24] and establishing a history that casts doubt on the idea that the taxpayer had cash lying around, such as the taxpayer filing bankruptcy, borrowing money, or not paying debts.[25]

What are the dynamics of this type of case as it goes to the jury? The defendants argue that they had an opening cash hoard which they had built up over pre-prosecution years. The defendants properly put that issue in play with their testimony — if they are so bold as to testify — or otherwise. The Government presents evidence along one or more of the lines of attack above, evidence which, if believed, would cast doubt on the existence of a cash hoard. But, should merely casting doubt be enough?

In many cases, one suspects, defendants lose because the jury simply doubts that a cash hoard existed. For example, in a companion case to *Holland*, all the jury verdict established was that the jury did not believe the taxpayer had a cash hoard large enough to explain his net worth.[26] This reveals a truism in criminal trials: the truth is one thing while what the jury believes may be another.[27] The everlasting hope of our system is that the procedural safeguards will insure that the truth and the jury's belief are the same in the overwhelming number of cases.

The problem with mere doubt or suspicion is the burden of proof. A key element of the net worth method is that the Government has accurately accounted for the opening net worth, which of course it had not if there were a cash hoard. If the Government really did not disprove the cash hoard beyond a reasonable doubt, can it be said that the Government established opening net worth beyond a reasonable doubt?

The Government's failure to investigate leads as to nontaxable sources can

---

22 *E.g.*, Smith v. United States, 348 U.S. 147 (1954).

23 *E.g.*, United States v. Mastropieri, 685 F.2d 776 (2d Cir.), *cert. denied*, 459 U.S. 945 (1982).

24 *E.g.*, United States v. Mackey, 345 F.2d 499 (7th Cir.), *cert. denied*, 382 U.S. 824 (1965).

25 *E.g.*, United States v. Hallman, 594 F.2d 198 (9th Cir.), *cert. denied*, 444 U.S. 828 (1979).

26 Friedberg v. United States, 348 U.S. 142 (1954).

27 For this reason, experienced trial lawyers define "facts" as what the jury will believe, not what is true in some cosmic sense. *E.g.*, HERBERT STEIN, TRYING CASES TO WIN 164 (1991).

seriously undermine the effectiveness of the net worth method. Thus, one strategy that a practitioner should consider during the investigation is whether to advise the IRS of leads. Most practitioners would rather spring their evidence at trial, particularly where there is little hope of avoiding the prosecution. Thus, they may not be overly inclined to supply leads during the investigation. A commentator noted:

> The leads doctrine nevertheless presents a serious dilemma to taxpayers and their counsel. If a lead is given, the government may be able to prove that the lead is inadequate or insufficient to destroy the prosecution's case. On the other hand, if a lead is not provided, the government is relieved of the obligation to investigate the lead altogether.[28]

Our previous example illustrates how the leads doctrine and trial strategy may intersect. In that example, the IRS's investigation showed that the taxpayer had opening year net worth of $50,000. Assume that the taxpayer had a checking account with $50,000 which was the only asset the IRS could locate. The IRS identifies no debt on the opening date. With that critical assumption of opening net worth and the other components developed by the IRS, the conclusion arising from the net worth method is that the taxpayer had $57,000 of unreported income in the two-year period. As indicated above, the taxpayer may assert that the method, as presented by the IRS, is flawed because he had opening net worth in the form of cash that the IRS did not identify or verify. Assume that one month before the opening date of the two-year period, the taxpayer as the sole beneficiary from a remote uncle in a different state had received a $50,000 check from the estate representing all of the estate assets. (For an estate of that size, no federal estate tax return likely would have to have been filed.) The taxpayer immediately went to Las Vegas, check in hand, cashed it there, and lost it all within days. Had he retained the $50,000 past day one of the two-year period, the $50,000 might have accounted for enough of the indicated income that the Government would not have pursued an evasion case on the $7,000 that remained, the taxpayer did not in fact retain the cash and the net worth method correctly indicates that, during the two-year period, the taxpayer had $57,000 of unreported income.

Is the taxpayer out of luck in defending against the use of the net worth method? Stated alternatively, can the taxpayer use the inheritance to throw sand in the Government's face as to the validity of the application of the method? Assume that, even if the Government could show that he cashed the inheritance check in Las Vegas, it is not likely that the IRS could discover proof beyond a reasonable doubt that he lost the $50,000 and thus, could not exclude the possibility that he held some or all of it in cash on the critical opening date of the period. Can the taxpayer — or his attorney — affirmatively advise the IRS during the investigation that the inheritance accounts for $50,000 otherwise unaccounted for cash on the opening date, thereby eliminating the net worth analysis as a means to obtain a conviction? Obviously, an affirmative misrepresentation of a known untrue fact would be unethical and would violate 18 U.S.C. section 1001, so neither the taxpayer nor his attorney would want to do that. But, could the attorney for the taxpayer (who remains silent throughout the period), ask the IRS Special Agent whether the

---

[28] Michael I. Saltzman, IRS Practice and Procedure ¶ 7A.02[1][b][iii] (2d ed. 1991).

inheritance, just three months before the opening date, had been considered? The implication from merely asking the question is that the money might account for some significant portion of the otherwise indicated unreported income, and the attorney knows that it in fact represents no portion of the unreported income otherwise indicated by the net worth methodology. Is that misleading enough to be unethical or to invoke 18 U.S.C. section 1001, although it would not constitute perjury if under oath because it is literally true that he received $50,000?

Assume that the attorney for some reason (perhaps his own sense of propriety or perhaps out of concern that the Special Agent with properly propounded summonses to the casinos could find out that the defendant had lost the bulk of the $50,000), does not play that game during the investigation, and the Government proceeds to indict based upon the net worth analysis. The attorney at trial has the right to test the methodology, and part of the methodology is that the Government has correctly identified opening net worth. Could the attorney then ask the question as to whether the IRS Special Agent (the Government's summary expert in presenting the methodology to the jury) had considered the inheritance just three months before? Could the attorney justify asking the question — which he knows will imply an incorrect conclusion — on the theory that he is entitled and even required by the ethics of his profession in representing an indicted defendant to test the methodology and ask whether some significant item that should have been considered but was not considered could bear upon the reasonableness of the Government's application of the methodology? Is this quibbling with no material distinction between questioning the methodology and giving a misleading impression? There is no easy answer to these questions, but you should struggle with the ethics of this type of situation before you proceed down a path that, in hindsight, someone may think crossed the line.

2. Expenditures Method

United States v. Johnson[29] was discussed in the above excerpt from the *Holland* case. There, the Supreme Court gave the impression that *Johnson* was a net worth case. However, the method used in *Johnson* is better characterized as the expenditures method, sometimes called the "source and application of funds" method. The following case compares the net worth method and the expenditures method.

TAGLIANETTI v. UNITED STATES

United States Court of Appeals, First Circuit
398 F.2d 558 (1968), *aff'd*, 394 U.S. 316 (1969)

This is an appeal from a conviction under 26 U.S.C. § 7201 for income tax evasion during the calendar years 1956, 1957, and 1958. Appellant alleges failure of proof of an essential element of the government's prosecution under the "cash expenditure" method of establishing unreported taxable income. Appellant filed joint tax returns with his wife for the years in prosecution, showing income from two sources: his

---

[29] 319 U.S. 503 (1943).

employment as a "locations" man for a cigarette vending machine company and his net winnings from parimutuel betting.

The government proceeded on a "cash expenditure" theory. This is a variant of the net worth method of establishing unreported taxable income. Both proceed by indirection to overcome the absence of direct proof. The net worth method involves the ascertaining of a taxpayer's net worth positions at the beginning and end of a tax period, and deriving that part of any increase not attributable to reported income. This method, while effective against taxpayers who channel their income into investment or durable property, is unavailing against the taxpayer who consumes his self-determined tax-free dollars during the year and winds up no wealthier than before. The cash expenditure method is devised to reach such a taxpayer by establishing the amount of his purchases of goods and services which are not attributable to the resources at hand at the beginning of the year or to non-taxable receipts during the year. The beginning and ending net worth positions must be identified with sufficient particularity to rule out or account for the use of a taxpayer's capital to pay for his purchases. If the end-of-year net worth position is equal to that at the beginning of the year, and if there are no nontaxable sources of income during the year, such as gifts or inheritances, the totality of the year's expenditures reflects total taxable income. If ending net worth shows an increase, the increase reflects an added component of income. If ending net worth shows a diminution, the decrease reduces pro tanto the extent to which expenditures reflect income.

In this case, the government's evidence, based on appellant's admissions at several interviews and its own independent investigation, tended to establish that appellant and his wife owned very little property. As for cash on hand, appellant during the taxable years would have about $10,000, borrowed from several banks or loan companies at eight percent interest for financing his pari-mutuel betting. Appellant's contention that there was a failure of proof in the government's case is that even assuming, *arguendo*, that the evidence adduced shows he spent more money during the indictment years than his reported gross income, there is not one scintilla of evidence to show that said expenditures came out of current receipts only and not out of available assets acquired in prior years. This is so because there is absolutely no competent evidence which, in any way suffices to clearly and accurately establish the extent of defendant's prior assets at the beginning of any or all the indictment years; i.e., there is no opening net worth for January 1, 1956, 1957 or 1958. Appellant mistakes form for substance. In this case, the prosecution presented evidence to support the conclusion that the assets owned by appellant and his wife either remained at a static level, or instead increased over the taxable years, and in any event made no contribution to the expenditures shown.

This state of the proof fully satisfies the requirement in *Holland v. United States*. In a typical net worth case, as *Holland*, precise figures would have to be attached to opening and closing net worth positions for each of the taxable years to provide a basis for the critical subtraction. In a cash expenditures case, reasonable certainty may be established without such a presentation, as long as the proof — as in this case — makes clear the extent of any contribution which beginning resources or a diminution of resources over time could have made to expenditures. We recognize that courts occasionally blur the distinction between the two approaches and use language implying that they are subject not only to the same principle of excluding the availability of nontaxable resources but also to the same method of implementing that principle, i.e., establishing net worth figures. Appellant has cited several cash expenditure cases for the latter proposition. A careful review of the language used and the problems addressed in these opinions indicates that they cannot be fairly read as embracing such an inflexible formal requirement.

3. Bank Deposits and Cash Expenditures Method

The bank deposits or cash expenditures method is also built on logic. It assumes that deposits into the defendant's bank accounts and expenditures made by the defendant are taxable income unless they came from a nontaxable source. The IRS must analyze the deposits and expenditures and track down leads that may indicate a nontaxable source. The formulation is basically as follows, subject to such nuances as the facts of an individual case require.[30]

Total bank deposits

Plus: Payments the taxpayer made in cash (including for capital assets)

Less: Deposits of nontaxable items

Less: Payments made from nontaxable sources

Yields Total Receipts (or Gross Income)

Less: Deductions (including Business Deductions)

Less: Exemptions

Yields: Taxable Income

This methodology is based on the notion that cash movement from the taxpayer either into a bank account or as payment for some good or service or as a gift or other transfer, came from a taxable source unless there is some indicated nontaxable source. In an important expenditures method case, the court stated:

> [T]he bare fact, standing alone, that a [person] has deposited a sum of money in a bank would not prove that he owned income tax on the amount; nor would the bare fact that he received and cashed a check for a large amount, in and of itself, suffice to establish that income tax was due on account of it. On the other hand, if it be shown that a [person] has a business or calling of a lucrative nature and is constantly, day by day and month by month, receiving moneys and depositing them to his account and checking against them for his own uses, there is most potent testimony that he has income, and, if the amount exceeds exemptions and deductions, that the income is taxable.[31]

This method has some advantages for the Government compared to other methods. No showing of opening or closing net worth is required,[32] and the

---

30 *See* Saltzman, *supra*, ¶ 7A.02[1][d].

31 Gleckman v. United States, 80 F.2d 394, 399 (8th Cir. 1935), *cert. denied*, 297 U.S. 709 (1936).

32 *E.g.*, United States v. Abodeely, 801 F.2d 1020, 1024 (8th Cir. 1986).

Government need not disprove the accuracy of the taxpayer's books and records as a prerequisite to using the method.[33]

The "bank deposits and expenditures" method is necessarily rough. Whether the judge in the first instance or the jury as final arbiter will accept its use will depend on the skill and diligence of the IRS agents in employing the method and of the Department of Justice prosecutors in explaining it at trial. In one prominent case, the Government attempted at trial to prove the purpose of checks drawn by the taxpayer through conclusory statements by a special agent. The agent's analysis was based on his discussions with payees and others, but none of them were called to testify. Accordingly, the evidence was rejected as hearsay.[34] However, if the agents and prosecutors do their jobs, the method can be used and will be approved.

Other than lack of willfulness, the most common defense in "bank deposits and expenditures" cases is that the deposits represent income attributable to prior years or nontaxable items. The latter contention is most plausible if the deposits are irregular in frequency or widely varying in amounts. Defendants may suggest that deposits represent loans, gifts, inheritances, political contributions, transfers between accounts, redeposits of withdrawn cash, checks cashed for customers, rebates, amounts received as an agent, other people's funds, or previously accumulated funds.

UNITED STATES v. ESSER

United States Court of Appeals, Seventh Circuit
520 F.2d 213 (1975)

Appellant-defendant, Dr. Charles Esser, a veterinarian, was indicted on three counts of willful evasion of income taxes for the years 1967, 1968, and 1969 in violation of 26 U.S.C. [section] 7201. Appellant argues that the trial court should have granted motions for judgment of acquittal based upon the government's failure to conduct a thorough examination and analysis of defendant's bank deposits. We do not accept appellant's argument and find that the trial judge had sufficient grounds for denial of the motion for acquittal.

I.R.S. Agent Hoak testified that deposit slips and underlying items of deposit are customarily introduced to demonstrate the nature of the deposits. However, in this instance, it was virtually impossible to introduce the deposit slips due to their poor quality, unreliability, and unavailability. The government introduced the bank statements and pass books as the most reliable evidence available. Though appellant attempted on cross-examination to establish that the slips and items were capable of retrieval, the question was left as one of fact for the jury.

Defendant argues also that the bank deposits theory requires an analysis of the bank deposit items themselves. He contends that the government's duty to specifically identify and analyze the defendant's deposit slips and the underlying items is mandated by the "bank deposits cases;" and that failure to do so is fatal to the government's case. On examination, the authorities reveal no such duty.

---

[33] *E.g.*, Bostwick v. United States, 218 F.2d 790 (5th Cir. 1955).

[34] Greenberg v. United States, 280 F.2d 472 (1st Cir. 1960).

These cases establish that the bank deposits theory requires the government to prove that the defendant was engaged in an income-producing business and that regular deposits of funds having the appearance of income were in fact made to bank accounts during the course of business. The total deposits figure serves as the starting point for further analysis of the taxpayer's accounts. The government must do everything that is reasonable and fair under the circumstances to identify any non-income transactions and deduct them from total deposits. Further, all proper deductions and credits must be subtracted. However, the government's investigators are not obliged to track down every conceivable lead offered by the taxpayer to justify the non-income designation of a particular item.

After the government proves that deposits having the appearance of income were made, the defendant has the burden to explain as far as possible the deposits. With this done, the jury is entitled to infer that the difference between the balance of deposited items and reported income constitutes unreported income.

The record herein supports the conclusion that a full investigation of various transactions underlying defendant's deposits was conducted, and that all reasonable steps were taken to identify and deduct non-income items such as interbank transfers and repayment of loans. The evidence showed that defendant admitted to the agents that he deposited his business receipts into his bank accounts. Further, the bank statements introduced into evidence, particularly the statements from the business checking account, showed regular deposits having the appearance of business receipts. The record is replete with testimony regarding the determination and crediting of non-income items to the total deposits. In our opinion, the evidence was more than sufficient to support the verdict below.

Appellant's argument that the government failed to prove an essential part of the charge, i.e., willfulness, lacks merit. Admittedly there was no evidence in this case of the classic indicia of fraud, e.g., duplicate books and hidden accounts. The government, however, did in our opinion present evidence sufficient to allow the jury to find that defendant engaged in a pattern of understating income for three consecutive years.

Willfulness may be inferred from conduct which would have the effect of misleading or concealing such as a continual pattern of under-reporting income. Defendant argues that there must be some type of independent evidence, i.e., dual bookkeeping, secret accounts, testimony as to intent, to prove willfulness and that it cannot be inferred from the defendant's conduct. In general, we agree that in almost every case, there must be some independent evidence to corroborate the willful intent that is either inferred or shown by the defendant's actions. However, in a case such as this wherein the facts demonstrate a clear intent to mislead over a period of years, where the evidence is overwhelming, we think the jury could reasonably infer that the defendant's actions were willful.

4. Percentage Mark-Up Method

This method is used to ascertain profits from a business. The quantity of merchandise sold is multiplied by the taxpayer's profit percentage. Brief reflection will bring to mind many possibilities for imprecision in such an approach, and those possibilities constrict the useful range of the method. As examples,

- The amount of goods sold is essential to the multiplication, and the taxpayer's records may not be accurate. (Normally, taxpayers fully report the materials or goods they buy for resale, in order to be able to deduct the costs. However, when a business person is underreporting income, he or she often will *understate* inventory costs on his or her tax returns, in order to conceal the unreported sales.) Thus, the IRS usually will want to be able to independently corroborate the taxpayer's materials or inventory costs. Thus, the percentage mark-up method is best used when the taxpayer has only one or a few suppliers.
- Compound and complex calculations are hard to perform and hard to explain to juries. Thus, the method is better used when the taxpayer sells a limited number or types of goods or when there are well established industrial or commercial averages for businesses of the kind in question. Ideal are businesses in a regulated-price environment, such as liquor retailing. Similarly, the method is better applied when the prices of goods bought and sold are relatively stable over the prosecution period than when they are highly volatile.

Taxpayers usually attack the results of the percentage mark-up method by arguing that the IRS agent incorrectly determined profit percentages in the relevant industry or that the taxpayer's business underperformed the industry's average because of lower sales, higher costs, or both.

Because of the considerable potential for inaccuracy, this method is rarely used as the sole or even principal method of proof in a criminal tax prosecution. However, it may be deployed in support or corroboration of another method of proof. It also is used in civil cases in which the IRS alleges underreporting of business income.[35]

5. Indirect Methods to Prove Overstated Deductions

As seen above, the main use of indirect methods is to establish underreporting of income. However, on rare occasions, the Government deploys an indirect method to attempt to establish overstatement of deductions. For example, in one case, the Government used what has been dubbed a "reverse net worth method"[36] in a section 7206(1) prosecution to try to show that the taxpayer overstated employee business expenses ("EBE") claimed on the taxpayer's return for one year (1974). IRS agents testified that they had reviewed the taxpayer's financial records, analyzing all receipts and disbursements made by the taxpayer during the year to determine how much cash he had available. The agents concluded that the taxpayer had only about $11,000 of cash on hand, so could not have defrayed the over $16,000 of EBE claimed on the return.

At the conclusion of the Government's case, the defense moved for a judgment of acquittal, which the court took under advisement. The jury returned a guilty

---

[35] *E.g.*, Kikalos v. United States, 408 F.3d 900 (7th Cir. 2005) (in a case in which the IRS determined deficiencies based on the percentage mark-up method, remanding the case to allow the taxpayer to present evidence based on other indirect methods of income reconstruction). The *Kikalos* opinion is critiqued in John A. Townsend, *Judge Posner's Opinion in Kikalos*, Tax Notes, Aug. 1, 2005, at 593.

[36] Robert S. Fink, 1 Tax Controversies — Audits, Investigations, Trials 19–31 (2006).

verdict. Thereafter, the court granted the motion for acquittal. Although acknowledging that the specifics of the methods in the two cases differed, the court held that the careful scrutiny counseled by *Holland* applied here as well. Despite analyzing the evidence in the light most favorable to the Government,[37] the court held that the Government's method was not sufficiently reliable to sustain conviction. The court said:

> The question which confronts us is, stated narrowly: "Does evidence of Gibson's 1974 financial transactions alone tend to negate his ability to accumulate a cash hoard which could have been used for the expenditures claimed on the 2106 form?" Our answer is that as a matter of law it does not. While this evidence tends to negate Gibson's ability to accumulate cash during 1974, it shows nothing about his ability to accumulate cash prior to 1974. Without an accurate cash on hand figure or proof of inability to accumulate cash prior to 1974, the jury has no basis for a finding that no significant amount of cash, other than that calculated, existed. Sufficient assurances of the trustworthiness of the static cash on hand contention are not present, and there is no support for a finding that Gibson's cash on hand was established with reasonable certainty. Evidence from which a jury can find guilt beyond a reasonable doubt thus does not appear in this record.
>
> The lack of evidence going to Gibson's ability to accumulate cash prior to the indictment year is particularly significant in this case because the only point of contention was cash available during 1974. By limiting the scope of inquiry to a single item, the government sharpens the need for accuracy. Against this background it is clear that the approach used by the prosecution does not provide sufficient assurances of trustworthiness.[38]

6. Defense Strategies in Indirect Method Cases

Each of the above indirect methods produces rough calculations of tax due and owing. Each is only as reliable as the IRS agent conducting the investigation is skillful and diligent. Of course, defense counsel will take pot-shots at the methodologies as opportunities present themselves. In addition, as suggested previously, a critical defense strategy will be to show that the IRS failed to pursue reasonable leads. This approach can put the taxpayer at some risk in disclosing leads and thus, potential defenses prior to trial. But providing the IRS agents leads or hints of leads can potentially set the stage for attack on the basis that the agents passed up reasonable leads.[39] Of course, the lead must suggest some potential relief to the target so that it is fair to reject the methodology for failure to pursue the lead.[40]

In one case, the Government successfully established that it had followed the leads offered. The taxpayer was a politician who attempted to rebut the Govern-

---

[37] Evidence must be reviewed in the light most favorable to the party for whom the jury gave its verdict. *E.g.*, Glasser v. United States, 315 U.S. 60, 80 (1942).

[38] United States v. Gibson, 486 F. Supp. 1230, 1238–39 (S.D. Ohio 1980).

[39] *See, e.g.*, United States v. Keller, 523 F.2d 1009, 1011 (9th Cir. 1975).

[40] *See* Scanlon v. United States, 223 F.2d 382, 388–89 (1st Cir. 1955); United States v. Anderson, 642 F.2d 281, 285 (9th Cir. 1981).

ment's net worth method by arguing that he had received gifts from up to 100 persons, thus accounting for his increase in net worth. The defendant gave the Department of Justice a list of the persons. The Government introduced a memorandum indicating that the agent had contacted the people on the list and that 75 reported that they gave only nominal amounts.[41] This was not hearsay since the memorandum was introduced in conjunction with the agent's testimony to show the reasonableness of the investigation of leads, not the truth of the statements the putative donors made to the agent. (The fiction, as with hearsay generally, is that the jury would be able to understand any limiting instruction as to the use of the testimony and use it only for that limited purpose.)

C. Hybrid Methods

The term "hybrid method" is used when the Government's case consists of components of several different theories of proof or when the method does not conform to any traditional theory of proof. Despite being unusual, a hybrid method may be situationally logical and acceptable.

For example, in one case, the Government reconstructed the defendant's income using bank deposit, expenditure, and specific item evidence. None of them, standing alone, could have given a complete picture of the defendant's total income. Specifically, the Government's case had the following components. (1) All deposits into the defendant's accounts were analyzed to identify deposits constituting current income. (2) To this total were added all identifiable specific items of income which had not been deposited into one of the accounts. (3) Also added were all cash expenditures which were not accounted for by the prior steps. The court of appeals held that the specific items were sufficient to establish a *prima facie* case and that the various components of proof were admissible even without full reconstruction of income under any single method.[42]

D. Direct Method and Indirect Methods Contrasted

Although some direct method cases are fairly simple in terms of the proof required, the evidence needed in some cases can present problems as challenging as those encountered in indirect method cases. In some cases — particularly when there is a full reconciliation of the taxpayer's records to the return — the Government can show complete omission of a particular taxable receipt or category of receipts. Proof will be more challenging when the details of the reported return entries cannot be established. In such cases, the Government will have to focus on the total amount, not on individual receipts or categories. For example, the Government may be able to establish that the taxpayer had $100,000 or more of taxable receipts for the year when the return reported only $60,000.[43] From the Government's perspective, an advantage of the direct method over indirect methods is that the Government's duty to follow up as to possible nontaxable

---

[41] United States v. Scott, 660 F.2d 1145 (7th Cir. 1981).

[42] United States v. Nunan, 236 F.2d 576 (2d Cir. 1956), *cert. denied*, 353 U.S. 912 (1957).

[43] *E.g.*, United States v. Marabelles, 724 F.2d 1374 (9th Cir. 1984).

sources of income[44] applies only in indirect method cases, not direct method cases.[45] The following case explores differences between the direct method and some indirect methods.

UNITED STATES v. BLACK

United States Court of Appeals, District of Columbia Circuit
843 F.2d 1456 (1988)

This is an appeal from a conviction of income tax evasion. Black was indicted and prosecuted on numerous counts, including a RICO Act violation, one count of conspiracy, seven counts of concealment of material facts, seven counts of causing a failure to file currency transaction reports, five counts of Travel Act violations, mail and wire fraud counts, and four counts of tax evasion. After a forty-day trial, Black was convicted on three counts of tax evasion. The Government charged that although Black received $65,827 of taxable income in 1978, $109,251 of taxable income in 1979, and $174,755 of taxable income in 1981, he failed to file a return for any of those years.

The resolution of Black's claims concerning sufficiency of evidence and adequacy of the jury charge turns entirely upon the proper characterization of the actual method used by the Government to prove Black's tax evasion. The Government contends it employed the "specific items" method of proof, a direct method of demonstrating tax evasion in which the Government produces evidence of the receipt of specific items of reportable income by the defendant that do not appear on his income tax return. Black claims, however, that the Government used the "bank deposits/cash expenditures" method. When using that indirect method of proof, the Government shows, either through increases in net worth, increases in bank deposits, or the presence of cash expenditures, that the taxpayer's wealth grew during a tax year beyond what could be attributed to the taxpayer's reported income, thereby raising the inference of unreported income.

In any indirect method case, the Government must prove that the increased wealth did not come from nontaxable sources. Otherwise, the evidence will be insufficient for there is always the possibility that the taxpayer deposited cash that he received from a non-taxable source or from income taxed in a prior year but kept on hand as cash or even from unreported income from a prior year kept on hand in cash. Such events are common human occurrences, and this possibility may of itself create reasonable doubt. Therefore, the government must establish in some fashion the amount of cash the taxpayer had on hand at the start of the period. This is part of the government's duty to negate the possibility that the bank deposits or cash expenditures in the year under investigation originated from non-taxable sources.

On the other hand, where the Government's case is based on evidence showing *specific items* of unreported income, the safeguards required for indirect methods of proof are not necessary, as the possibility that the defendant may be convicted because nontaxable income is mistakenly presumed to be taxable income, or

---

[44] *See* Holland v. United States, 348 U.S. 121, 135 (1954).

[45] *E.g.*, United States v. Lawhon, 499 F.2d 352, 356–57 (5th Cir. 1974), *cert. denied*, 419 U.S. 1121 (1975).

because cash expenditures are mistakenly assumed to be made from taxable income, is not present.

Black claims that the Government relied on a bank deposits/cash expenditures method of proof, but utterly failed to rebut the possibility that his expenditures originated from nontaxable sources, and therefore the evidence was insufficient to sustain a conviction. In particular, Black maintains that the Government was obliged to negate the possibility that his bank deposits and cash expenditures were from non-income sources, and to establish his opening net worth for the years in question. Black, moreover, argues that the jury instructions omitted necessary explanations of the assumptions inherent in indirect methods of proof, and of the inferences that may properly be made by the jury.

The Government's response is that since it introduced evidence of *specific items of income* received by Black, it was not required to disprove the likelihood of a cash hoard or a nontaxable source of income. From approximately 1975 to the time of the trial, Black was subject to an IRS lien of approximately three million dollars. During this time, Black created two corporations, Dunbar and Machine-A-Rama, portrayed by the Government as dummy corporations which had neither paid employees nor offices. At trial, Black disputed the bogus nature of these entities, claiming the corporations were involved in developing a casino in Atlantic City — a project which never materialized — and he also insisted that any money he took from these corporations was in the form of loans which he felt obligated to repay. Nevertheless, it was uncontroverted that during the period covered by the indictment, Black had no personal bank accounts and that many of Black's personal expenses were paid by checks drawn on accounts of these two corporations. Black further conceded that he created Dunbar because he did not want to put property in his own name and because he wished to conceal from the IRS money he was spending.

In the Government's view, Black received taxable income each time he wrote a check on the accounts of Dunbar and Machine-A-Rama to cover his personal expenses. Evidence that Black paid for personal expenses with checks drawn on corporate accounts and that Black never truly considered the checks to be loans would be sufficient for conviction.

Black, by focusing on isolated remarks at trial, argues that the Government presented only a cash expenditures case against him. We disagree. If the statements by the prosecutor, the testimony of the Government's tax witness, and the trial judge's instructions to the jury, are each considered in light of the evidence actually submitted, it is clear that the Government presented direct proof that Black received specific items of taxable income and did not pay tax on that income.

While there were several explicit references to the "personal expenditures method" by the prosecutor, the Government's expert witness, and the trial judge in his instructions, at no point in the trial was it suggested to the jury that evidence of personal expenditures, without more, would be sufficient to convict Black of tax evasion. Evidence of personal expenditures was relevant only because the Government contended that the very writing of the checks created income to Black. Thus, the danger encountered in a classic "cash expenditure" case — that the defendant could be convicted for spending nontaxable income — is not at all present here. In this case, the use of the phrase "personal expenditures method" was not associated at all with the "cash expenditures method" of proving tax evasion; the phrase was used solely to distinguish Black's business expenditures from his personal expenditures.

During the trial, moreover, Black's counsel undoubtedly understood the Government was not presenting a cash expenditures case, for no objection was made to the jury instructions given by the trial judge, and yet those instructions would have been inadequate had the Government relied on a cash expenditures method of proof.

Black also challenges the adequacy of the trial judge's instructions. But because no objection was made to the instructions at trial, we may reverse only if we find plain error. Fed. R. Crim. P. 30, 52(b). It is true that the trial judge's reference to the "bank deposits/expenditures method" was misconceived, but nevertheless the instructions did direct the jury to that part of the Government's case concerning the checks written by Black on the accounts of Dunbar and Machine-A-Rama, and the stipulations that the checks were written for Black's personal use and benefit. In addition, Black's counsel, in his closing argument, reiterated Black's claim that these checks were actually loans. We think, therefore, the jury was properly apprised of the issue to be resolved. Considering the strength of the Government's evidence against Black, the uncontested personal nature of the expenditures, and the incredibility of Black's claim that he considered the transactions to be loans, we do not believe any shortcomings in the instructions rose to the level of plain error affecting substantial rights.

We thus reject Black's argument that under the reasoning of *United States v. Meriwether*, 440 F.2d 753 (5th Cir. 1971), we should reverse because the jury might have convicted Black merely because he spent money. In *Meriwether*, the jury was instructed on both a specific items and net worth method of proof, with the emphasis placed on the net worth method. The court of appeals reversed because the instructions on the net worth method were flawed and there was "no way to be certain upon which method of proof the jury based its verdict of guilty." In this case, however, the jury was never instructed on the cash expenditures method, nor was it ever argued to the jury that Black could be convicted on the theory that cash expenditures were circumstantial evidence of taxable income. Ironically, a tax lawyer sitting in the courtroom could perhaps have been confused by the use of the phrase "personal expenditures method," for it might well have suggested the cash expenditures method, but the slight possibility that a jury never instructed on the cash expenditures method would have been confused is so insignificant that it cannot justify a reversal on grounds of plain error.

IV. GOVERNMENT EMPLOYEES AS WITNESSES

A. Differentiating the Roles

Frequently in tax prosecutions, the Government calls one of the special agents involved in the investigation or another IRS agent as a witness. Except in the case of a false statement prosecution or perhaps an obstruction prosecution, the IRS agent (either special or otherwise) will not have direct evidence. The IRS agent will be called as a summary witness or an expert witness or in both capacities.

As a summary witness, the IRS agent will summarize the evidence from the Government's standpoint in order to assist the jury in understanding the evidence. Thus, to use a simple example, if the evidence showed a series of 150 checks from ten different payors representing income to the defendant, an IRS agent could be called to break down the checks and check sums by payor, with a chart of the compiled results. A summary witness often is needed in situations far more complex than this simple example, but the IRS agent as summary witness can only summarize the evidence that has been admitted. The agent will identify the underlying evidence which he or she summarizes so that it is clear to the jury that, if the underlying evidence is not proved beyond a reasonable doubt, the agent's summary of the evidence is moot.

As an expert witness, an IRS agent offers expert testimony which must meet the requirements for expert testimony under Federal Rules of Evidence 701–705.[46] Often, for example, the agent will be qualified to offer expertise in the computation of a tax liability.

Sometimes, the IRS agent will serve in both capacities. Indeed, his or her testimony may blend. In the following case, the defendant on appeal complained that an IRS agent called as a summary witness had impermissibly provided expert testimony.

UNITED STATES v. PREE

United States Court of Appeals, Seventh Circuit
384 F.3d 378 (2004)

Ms. Pree contends that Agent Welch exceeded his role as a summary witness and provided inadmissible expert testimony in the guise of a summary witness. We believe Agent Welch primarily testified within his role as a summary witness. However, we acknowledge that, in such a case as the present, where an IRS Revenue Agent summarizes the evidence for purposes of establishing the tax consequences, the line between summary testimony and expert testimony is indistinct. Given the assistance such an individual can provide to the jury, it has not been unusual in previous cases for an IRS agent to testify as an "expert summary witness." *See* United States v. Benson, 941 F.2d 598, 615 (7th Cir. 1991) (Kanne, J., dissenting) ("A summary witness need not necessarily be an expert, but experts in accounting and other disciplines regularly give summary evidence of the sort envisioned by Federal Rule of Evidence 1006."), mandate recalled & amended by 957 F.2d 301 (7th Cir. 1992). As a summary witness, an IRS agent may testify as to the agent's analysis of the transaction which may necessarily stem from the testimony of other witnesses. The agent may also explain his analysis of the facts based on his special expertise. As an expert witness, an IRS agent's opinion as to the proper tax consequences of a transaction is admissible evidence. Similarly, an IRS expert's analysis of the transaction itself, which necessarily precedes his or her

---

[46] *See generally* Michael Louis Minns, *Cross-Examination of the Government's Witnesses in a Criminal Tax Defense Case*, 64 Tax Law. 125 (2010).

evaluation of the tax consequences, is also admissible evidence.

Here, Agent Welch analyzed the stock sales and described the income tax consequences. Although he was not proffered as an expert witness,[47] his qualifications were in evidence. Those qualifications included eighteen years of service with the IRS as a revenue agent, a bachelor's degree in accounting and a master's degree in taxation. While employed by the IRS, he completed additional classes in taxation, specialized training and continuing professional education. At the time of trial, he had conducted approximately two hundred tax audits and had reviewed several thousand audits of other revenue agents. Agent Welch was therefore qualified to express an opinion as to the proper tax consequences of a transaction and of the transaction itself, which necessarily precedes his . . . evaluation of the tax consequences.

Ms. Pree further contends that Agent Welch's testimony was inadmissible to the extent that he stepped into the role of an expert because he failed to use a recognized means of valuation of restricted stock. Agent Welch testified that the stock had no fair market value by virtue of the restriction because it could not be sold in a brokerage house. Admittedly, Agent Welch's statements to this effect were somewhat imprecise. Restricted stock does not lack value, per se, because it cannot be sold on the public market. Had Ms. Pree raised an objection to Agent Welch's testimony, on the ground that it constituted unreliable expert testimony, the district court would have undertaken the gatekeeping analysis Ms. Pree now recommends to this court. *See Daubert v. Merrell Dow Pharms., Inc.*, 509 U.S. 579 (1993); *see also United States v. Conn*, 297 F.3d 548, 557 (7th Cir. 2002) (indicating, in reference to a witness who was not proffered as an expert but testified in that role, that "[h]ad the defense had other concerns about the quality of [the agent's] training, the quantity of his experience, or the methodology that he employed in reaching his assessment of [the defendant's] firearms, it could have raised those questions during voir dire").

In the absence of an objection by Ms. Pree to Agent Welch's testimony as unreliable expert testimony, however, we do not perceive plain error. The conclusion that Ms. Pree's basis in the stock should be treated as zero was supported by sufficient evidence. Moreover, Ms. Pree's counsel had an opportunity to cross-examine Agent Welch as to his conclusions regarding the value of the stock. *See United States v. Gonzalez*, 933 F.2d 417, 429 (7th Cir. 1991) (indicating that "any questions or problems concerning the expert's opinion and testimony may be thoroughly explored during the cross-examination of the expert witness").

B. The Summary Witness

As noted above, a summary witness merely summarizes evidence otherwise in the record. The role of summary witnesses is explored in the following two circuit court cases.

---

[47] Authors' Note: It once was the practice to formally proffer a witness as an expert. This practice has largely been dispensed with.

UNITED STATES v. SABINO

United States Court of Appeals, Sixth Circuit
274 F.3d 1053 (2001)

Testimony summarizing evidence is admissible in income tax prosecutions when the judge charges the jury as to all the elements necessary for conviction, where the summary is intended to aid the jury in organizing proof, and where the summary is not inflammatory or prejudicially worded.

While a summary witness may give an opinion that events assumed in a question would trigger tax liability or whether particular payments under assumed circumstances would be taxable, he or she may not give a legal opinion that necessarily determines the guilt of a defendant or instructs the jury on controlling legal principles. Therefore, in a tax case, the summary witness is allowed to summarize and analyze the facts indicating willful tax evasion so long as [she does] not directly embrace the ultimate question of whether [the defendants] did in fact intend to evade income taxes.

The testimony of a summary witness should be accompanied by a limiting instruction which informs the jury of the summary's purpose and that the summary itself does not constitute evidence.

UNITED STATES v. BISHOP

United States Court of Appeals, Fifth Circuit
264 F.3d 535 (2001)

The use of summary testimony and documents is governed by Rule 1006 of the Federal Rules of Evidence, which is broadly interpreted. Rule 1006 allows admission of summaries when (1) the evidence previously admitted is voluminous, and (2) review by the jury would be inconvenient. A summary may include only evidence favoring one party, so long as the witness does not represent to the jury that he is summarizing all the evidence in the case.

Summary evidence must have an adequate foundation in evidence that is already admitted, and should be accompanied by a cautionary jury instruction. Full cross-examination and admonitions to the jury minimize the risk of prejudice.

We previously approved a cautionary instruction that summaries do not, of themselves, constitute evidence in the case but only purport to summarize the documented and detailed evidence already submitted, and an instruction that a witness's summary is not the evidence, the evidence is the documents themselves that he has been referring to.

Summary charts in particular are admissible when (1) they are based on competent evidence already before the jury, (2) the primary evidence used to construct the charts is available to the other side for comparison so that the correctness of the summary may be tested, (3) the chart preparer is available for cross-examination, and (4) the jury is properly instructed concerning use of the charts. Summaries may accompany the jury to the jury room.

Because of the limited role of the summary witness and any summary charts or other exhibits explaining the summary, a limiting instruction should be given to the jury. The court in the *Sabino* case above specifically justified the use of the summary witnesses because the district court gave a limiting instruction and the defense had a full opportunity to cross-examine the witness.[48] Similarly, in the *Pree* case above, the court observed:

> Ms. Pree also challenges the admission of Government Exhibits 101 and 102 without a limiting instruction as plainly erroneous. Other courts have held that a cautionary instruction should be given when summary evidence is admitted. *See, e.g., United States v. Bishop*, 264 F.3d 535, 547 (5th Cir. 2001) (noting previously approved instructions that "summaries do not, of themselves, constitute evidence in the case but only purport to summarize the documented and detailed evidence already submitted," and a witness' summary "is not the evidence, the evidence is the documents themselves that he has been referring to"). We ourselves have indicated that, when summary charts are introduced into evidence as a teaching device rather than as substantive evidence, the preferred practice is to give a limiting instruction regarding this purpose.
>
> No such instructions were given here; rather, a pattern instruction was given with regard to the summary evidence that stated that the summaries "truly and accurately summarize the content of voluminous books, records or documents, and should be considered together with and in the same way as all other evidence in the case." R.39. The Committee on Federal Criminal Jury Instructions for the Seventh Circuit advises that this instruction "should only be given when the accuracy and authenticity of the exhibits are not in question." PATTERN CRIMINAL FEDERAL JURY INSTRUCTIONS 3.15 (1998). The accuracy of Government Exhibits 101 and 102 were not challenged at trial. Although the "preferred practice" with respect to summary evidence is to issue an appropriate cautionary instruction, under the circumstances here, the admission of the summary evidence without such a limiting instruction was not plain error. *See also Swanquist*, 161 F.3d at 1072–73 (indicating that the defendant had an opportunity during cross examination to elicit facts suggesting the inaccuracy of summary charts and noting that a "party is not obligated . . . to include within its charts or summaries its opponent's version of the facts").[49]

C. The Expert Witness

Some aspects of the *Tarwater* case were excerpted above. The case also contained a good discussion of the expert witness issues that can arise when IRS agents testify in criminal tax cases.

[48] 274 F.3d at 1067.

[49] 384 F.3d at 394.

UNITED STATES v. TARWATER

United States Court of Appeals, Sixth Circuit

308 F.3d 494 (2002)

[Authors' Note: Earlier in this chapter, we saw another part of the *Tarwater* opinion. As relevant to present purposes, the defendant claimed that, although he received some payments, those payments were not income to him because he was merely a conduit for transferring those payments to a third party (Davis). At trial, the Government used two IRS agents (Jackson and Barton) to summarize the paper trail of deposits of the payments into the defendant's bank accounts, the amounts of checks written to the third party, and cash withdrawals. After going through the details, the Agents testified in summary:

> For each of the relevant tax years, Jackson reviewed both the monies deposited into as well as the monies drawn out of each of Tarwater's bank accounts. Jackson found that, for each year, Tarwater deposited a great deal more of the monies allegedly intended for Davis than he paid out through checks written to Davis. Even when Jackson added Tarwater's cash withdrawals and cash taken out of deposits to the checks written to Davis, giving Tarwater the benefit of an assumption that the cash was sent to Davis, Jackson still found that the monies taken in for Davis exceeded the monies sent out to Davis. According to Jackson, the excess of monies taken in for Davis over monies distributed out to Davis should have been retained in Tarwater's accounts if those monies were, in fact, meant as income for Davis. Tarwater's monthly ending bank balances demonstrated, however, that Tarwater did not retain the undistributed monies intended for Davis but, instead, spent those monies.

[The Government's expert witness, Barton, opined that Tarwater did not state the true amount of either his gross receipts or his net income for the years 1992 through 1994. Specifically, as to income, she said that (1) in 1992, Tarwater understated his income by $52,233; (2) in 1993, he understated his income by $35,950; and (3) in 1994, he understated his income by $120,945. In 1992, Tarwater's understatement of income was in part explained by his failure to report over $30,000 in gross receipts for the eight months that he operated as a Cole proprietorship. Barton explained that a correct report of gross receipts and income is necessary to a correct computation of tax liability and that a false report of income is capable of influencing the IRS in the audit of tax returns.

[Tarwater objected to Barton's testimony. The court approved the testimony, addressing Tarwater's objections as follows.]

A.

Tarwater argues that the district court should not have admitted Agent Barton's expert opinion testimony that Tarwater under-reported his income. According to Tarwater, Barton's opinion was unreliable "because it was based upon facts or assumptions about which she had no knowledge, let alone the 'specialized knowledge' required by Rule 702." Tarwater suggests that the magistrate judge who conducted the *Daubert* hearing "focused on Barton's qualifications and expressly abandoned the gate keeping function of *Daubert*." We review a district court's decision to admit expert testimony for abuse of discretion.

The magistrate judge held a *Daubert* hearing on January 18, 2001. Based on the evidence and argument presented, the judge ruled that Barton's testimony was "both relevant and reliable pursuant to Rule 702, Federal Rules of Evidence, and should be admissible at trial." In particular, the magistrate judge found that it was "clear from the evidence presented during the *Daubert* hearing that Ms. Barton is qualified to express an expert opinion on whether defendant understated his taxable income for the years 1991–1994." In concluding its twenty-five page memorandum and order, the court wrote:

> Ms. Barton is a qualified expert in her field who possesses technical knowledge that will assist the trier of fact to understand and determine the issues in this case. Her testimony is based upon sufficient facts and/or data, the testimony is the product of reliable principles and methods, and it appears that Ms. Barton has applied the principles and methods reliably to the facts of this case.

After reviewing the magistrate judge's memorandum and order, the transcript of the *Daubert* hearing, and the pleadings filed by the parties, the district court overruled Tarwater's objections and appeal of the magistrate judge's ruling on the admissibility of Barton's opinions.

In *Daubert v. Merrell Dow Pharmaceuticals, Inc.*, 509 U.S. 579 (1993), the Supreme Court held that Federal Rule of Evidence 702 requires district courts to ensure that an expert's scientific testimony "both rests on a reliable foundation and is relevant to the task at hand." *Daubert*, 509 U.S. at 597. The Court suggested a non-exclusive list of factors for courts to consider when deciding whether proposed scientific expert testimony is sufficiently "reliable." Such factors include: (1) whether a theory or technique has been or can be tested; (2) whether the theory or technique has been subjected to peer review and publication; (3) the known or potential rate of error; and (4) whether the technique has been accepted by a relevant scientific community. *Daubert*, 509 U.S. at 593–94.

In *Kumho Tire Co. v. Carmichael*, 526 U.S. 137 (1999), the Court extended *Daubert* to include any expert testimony based on "technical" and "other specialized knowledge." *Kumho Tire Co.*, 526 U.S. at 152. With respect to the individual factors enumerated in *Daubert*, the *Kumho* Court held that, while trial courts may consider such factors when assessing the reliability of all types of expert testimony, "*Daubert*'s list of specific factors neither necessarily nor exclusively applies to all experts or in every case." *Kumho*, 526 U. S. at 141. "Whether *Daubert*'s specific factors are, or are not, reasonable measures of reliability in a particular case is a matter that the law grants the trial judge broad latitude to determine." *Kumho*, 526 U.S. at 153.

After reviewing Barton's trial testimony, we cannot say that the district court abused its discretion by allowing her to testify as an expert witness. We find no merit to Tarwater's argument that the district court abandoned its *Daubert* gate-keeping function by failing to consider the *Daubert* factors. To be sure, the court concluded — and we agree — that the *Daubert* factors were of limited value here, but the court nonetheless carefully considered whether Barton's testimony was reliable and relevant. The court summarized its findings as follows:

> Ms. Barton's testimony is the product of well-established principles of bookkeeping and accounting as those areas of expertise are applied to the Internal Revenue Code. Ms. Barton demonstrated an understanding of the rules and regulations of the IRS Code that require the reporting of all taxable income. The methods employed by Ms. Barton in reaching her expert opinion were the application of her education, training, knowledge and experience to analyze defendant's tax returns and business records to determine whether the defendant complied with the requirements of the Internal Revenue Code to report all his income.

Given such findings, we are confident that the district court had an adequate basis for concluding that Barton's testimony was both reliable and relevant.

Moreover, we reject Tarwater's assertion that Barton's testimony was unreliable because "based upon facts or assumptions about which she had no knowledge." Indeed, the record refutes any such assertion. As stated by the district court:

> Ms. Barton testified that her computations were based upon Defendant's bank records and business records, and her expert opinion that Defendant under reported his income is based upon her examination of Defendant's record, her ability to trace the flow of income and the disbursement of same as viewed by a Revenue Agent with twenty-five years of experience and training, and from her analysis of Defendant's bank records and business records. It appears to the Court that Ms. Barton has applied the principles and methods of her technical expertise to the facts of this case.

At trial, Barton reiterated that her opinions were based upon her review of Tarwater's records — books, bank statements, and checks — and tax returns. Tarwater's suggestion that Barton's opinion involved a determination of the credibility of two non-testifying taxpayers is without merit.

B.

As an expert witness, Agent Barton was permitted to testify — over Tarwater's objection — regarding her opinion that Tarwater understated his income for the years 1992–1994. On direct examination, the government elicited testimony from Barton regarding her review of the documentary evidence, including Tarwater's personal and business financial records, income tax returns, bank records, and JMH records. On cross-examination, defense counsel asked Barton whether she had talked with Willie Davis (she had not), whether she knew if Tarwater had made any cash payments to Willie Davis (she knew only what was recorded in the books and records), and whether she did or did not answer "yes" when she was asked in the earlier *Daubert* hearing if she would want to talk with Willie Davis to determine whether cash payments were made to him (she answered "yes"). Tarwater contends that, by opining that Tarwater understated his income, Barton necessarily communicated her opinion that Tarwater did not make sufficient payments to or on behalf of Willie Davis. He contends that Barton thus improperly "vouched" for the credibility of Davis's alleged out-of-court statement to the effect that he had not received any cash payments from Tarwater.

We are not persuaded by Tarwater's "vouching" argument. Barton was asked by the government to review the documentary evidence, and she rendered an opinion about the accuracy of Tarwater's tax returns based on that evidence. The jury was capable of determining that, if Tarwater failed to document the alleged cash transfers to Davis, those cash transfers would not be reflected in Barton's calculations. That she did not consider undocumented transfers in no way suggests that she "vouched" for an alleged out-of-court statement by Davis that he did not receive any cash payments from Tarwater.

C.

On September 15, 2000, approximately seven months before trial, the government provided Tarwater with a written summary of Agent Barton's proposed testimony. As required by Federal Rule of Criminal Procedure 16(a)(1)(E), the summary described Barton's opinions, the bases and reasons for those opinions, and Barton's qualifications. The summary also disclosed that Barton's opinions were based on her examination of Tarwater's income tax returns, bank records, business records, and records from JMH. The government supplemented Barton's summary on September 20, 2000, disclosing to Tarwater that Barton would also testify that a taxpayer's failure to include all income on a tax return can influence the correct computation of tax liability and can impede the IRS's verification and/or audit of the tax return.

On October 3, 2000, in response to Tarwater's motion to strike Barton's testimony, the government again supplemented Barton's summary, disclosing to Tarwater the specific details of Barton's computations. The magistrate judge denied Tarwater's motion to strike Barton's testimony on January 4, 2001, ruling that the government's disclosures were sufficient and did not constitute a violation of Rule 16(a)(1)(E).

On January 18, 2001, at the *Daubert* hearing, Barton testified as to Tarwater's understatement of income for the years 1991 through 1994, giving complete details of her computations. Following the *Daubert* hearing, the magistrate denied Tarwater's renewed motion to strike Barton's testimony, again ruling that the government had complied with Rule 16(a)(1)(E). The court stated:

> The "summary" required by Rule 16(a)(1)(E) is only required to describe the witness' opinions, the bases and the reasons for those opinions, and the witness' qualifications. It does not require the expert to set forth a detailed justification for her expert opinion. That is an area which may be explored by counsel on cross-examination at trial.[50]

---

[50] Authors' Note: Rule 16(a)(1)(E)'s disclosure requirement for criminal purposes is less demanding than the Tax Court's rule for civil purposes. Tax Court Rule 143(g) requires that the complete report of an intended expert witness be submitted to the Tax Court and served on the other party not less than 30 days before the call of the calendar containing the case. That report constitutes the expert's direct examination, with minor exceptions. Failure to so disclose can preclude calling the intended expert as a witness.

The evening before Barton was scheduled to testify at trial, the government produced a report entitled "Explanation of Items." Prepared by Barton, the report revealed that, at an early stage in her investigation, Barton estimated that Tarwater was entitled to credits of $3,276.00 per year for payments to rental car companies on behalf of Davis. Barton later eliminated those credits from her computations.

Also, the evening before Barton was scheduled to testify, the government produced a copy of Barton's revised computations of Tarwater's understatement of income. Interestingly, the revisions in Barton's computations represented a net effect of approximately $18,000 in Tarwater's favor.

Based on the government's last minute production of Barton's "Explanation of Items" and revised reports, Tarwater moved to strike Barton's testimony. Claiming *Brady* and Rule 16(a)(1)(E) violations, Tarwater also moved to dismiss or to continue trial. The district court denied Tarwater's motions.

Tarwater now contends that the district court erred by denying Tarwater's motions to strike and/or to dismiss. This court reviews a district court's rulings on Rule 16(a)(1)(E) issues for abuse of discretion. We review de novo the issue of whether evidence withheld by the prosecution constitutes *Brady* material. A district court's denial of a *Brady* claim is reviewed by this court de novo to determine whether the suppressed *Brady* evidence undermines confidence in the outcome of the defendant's trial.

To establish a violation under *Brady v. Maryland*, 373 U.S. 83 (1963), a defendant has the burden of establishing that the prosecutor suppressed evidence that was unknown to the defendant. *See United States v. Agurs*, 427 U.S. 97 (1976) (explaining that the *Brady* rule applies to "the discovery, after trial, of information which had been known to the prosecution but unknown to the defense"); *United States v. Mullins*, 22 F.3d 1365, 1371 (6th Cir. 1994) (explaining that "*Brady* is concerned only with cases in which the government possesses information which the defendant does not"); *Coe v. Bell*, 161 F.3d 320, 344 (6th Cir. 1998) (explaining that there is no *Brady* violation if the defendant knew or should have known the essential facts permitting him to take advantage of the information in question, or if the information was available to him from another source).

Tarwater claims that the government violated *Brady* when it disclosed — before Barton testified — that Barton at one time gave him credit for car rental payments that Tarwater himself supposedly made on behalf of Davis. Obviously, Tarwater knew whether he did or did not make such payments on behalf of Davis. Because the information about which he complains was not unknown to him, and because the information was disclosed to him before Barton testified, permitting him to take advantage of the information during his cross-examination of Barton, we find no *Brady* violation whatsoever.

Furthermore, we find that the district court did not abuse its discretion when it denied Tarwater's motion to dismiss and/or strike on the grounds that the government violated Rule 16(a)(1)(E) by producing Barton's revised reports the day before Barton testified. Tarwater's counsel was able to review the revised reports before extensively cross-examining Barton about the changes reflected in those reports. As explained by Barton at trial, the changes were necessitated by information that Barton acquired from Tarwater's own records not long before trial. The changes, moreover, were largely in Tarwater's favor. For example, the revised reports reflected no change in the understatement of income for 1992, a $19,000 reduction in the understatement of income for 1993, and an $810 increase in the understatement of income for 1994. Because Tarwater did not suffer any surprise and because he does not suggest how the outcome of the case would have been different if he had learned about Barton's revised computations earlier, we will not disturb the decision of the district court.

V. PRESUMPTIONS

Presumptions that satisfy or lighten the burden that the Government prove each element of the offense beyond a reasonable doubt are a problem in the criminal law.[51] In criminal cases, conclusive presumptions of fact *usually* are not allowed. Such a presumption would be, for example, proof of fact X, not an element of the offense, conclusively establishing fact Y, an element of the offense.

Presumptions are encountered throughout the law. Consider a common presumption in civil cases — the mailing presumption. Proof of the fact that a document is deposited in the U.S. mail properly addressed and postmarked gives rise to a presumption that the addressee received the document via the mail. That presumption permits (but does not necessarily require) the trier of fact to conclude that the addressee received the document and effectively shifts the burden of proof or at least a burden of production from the party bearing the burden of persuasion on the fact of receipt to the opposing party.

How do presumptions apply in criminal cases where there is a constitutionally mandated requirement that the Government prove each element of the offense beyond a reasonable doubt? For example, in tax evasion cases involving false returns under section 7201 and tax perjury cases involving false returns under section 7206(1), the Government must prove that the defendant signed the return. This is usually done through some actual evidence — a person familiar with the defendant's handwriting identifies the signature on the return or a handwriting expert using exemplars or some other control signatures from the defendant identifies the handwriting on the return.

Section 6064, however, creates a presumption that a taxpayer's signature on the return is authentic. Can the Government use this presumption to, in effect, meet its burden and/or shift the burden of production on the issue to the defendant so as to potentially require the defendant to waive his Fifth Amendment privilege in order to rebut the presumption? The Fifth Circuit has so held, reasoning that (1) there is a rational connection between the name signed on the return and the presumption

---

[51] For a good survey of the range of problems created by presumptions, see Kevin W. Robinson, *Thirty-First Annual Review of Criminal Procedure: III. Trial: Proof Issues*, 90 GEO. L.J. 1740, 1747–51 (2002). This survey discussion is updated annually in the Georgetown Law Journal so the most recent survey should be consulted.

In *Boulware v. United States*, 128 S. Ct. 1168, 1181 n.14 (2008), the Supreme Court recognized, but ducked, the problem that presumptions can effectively shift to the defendant the burden of disproving what should be a part of the Government's obligation to prove all the elements of a crime.

that the person bearing that name signed the name on the return and (2) there are ways other than having the defendant testify, thus waiving the Fifth Amendment privilege, to disprove the authenticity of the signature.[52] Is this holding correct? And what does it mean in other areas in which a presumption or some equivalent might arise?

In a section 7201 tax evasion case, one element of the offense is that there is a material amount of tax due and owing. The following decision considers whether the Government can establish that element simply by introducing an IRS certificate of assessment.

UNITED STATES v. SILKMAN

United States Court of Appeals, Eighth Circuit
156 F.3d 833 (1998)

[Authors' note: The IRS had assessed the tax, and the taxpayer took various actions to avoid payment. The taxpayer was indicted for evasion of payment. The Government's proof of tax due consisted of the March 1991 notice of deficiency plus five certificates evidencing the September 1991 assessments. At the Government's urging, the district court excluded evidence offered by the defense to prove that the defendant had no taxable income for the tax years in question. The court then instructed the jury that the assessment for each year established the tax liability. The taxpayer was convicted and appealed. The court of appeals framed the issue — one of first impression — as "whether an IRS tax assessment that is administratively final for purposes of the agency's civil collection remedies is also conclusive proof of the tax deficiency in a tax evasion prosecution."]

Here, the IRS assessments were offered as conclusive proof of an underlying fact that is an element of the crime — that taxes were in fact owed. In this type of case, the overriding principle is that one charged with the commission of a felony has an absolute right to a jury determination upon all essential elements of the offense.

The government has no authority for its startling contention that an IRS assessment is conclusive proof in a criminal trial that taxes were in fact owing. We agree with the analysis in *Voorhies* — a formal tax assessment that has become administratively final is prima facie evidence of the asserted tax deficiency, and if unchallenged, it may suffice to prove this element of the crime. But the assessment is only prima facie proof of a deficiency. The assessed deficiency may be challenged by the defendant accused of tax evasion, and the issue is one for the jury. As the Supreme Court said in *United States v. Martin Linen Supply Co.*, 430 U.S. 564, 572–73 (1977), the jury's

> overriding responsibility is to stand between the accused and a potentially arbitrary or abusive government that is in command of the criminal sanction. For this reason, a trial judge is prohibited from entering a

---

[52] United States v. Kim, 884 F.2d 189 (5th Cir. 1989); *see also* United States v. Anderson, 353 F.3d 490 (6th Cir. 2003) (holding that the section 6064 presumption, in conjunction with the Government's limited and uncertain testimony, satisfied the sufficiency-of-the evidence appellate standard on the issue). *Anderson* referred to the presumption as rebuttable while at least one commentator reads *Kim* as treating the presumption as irrebuttable, *see* Robinson, *supra*, at 1747–49 n.1978.

judgment of conviction or directing a jury to come forward with such a verdict, regardless of how overwhelmingly the evidence may point in that direction.

This conclusion is consistent with *United States v. England*, where the government conceded that proof of a valid assessment was essential to its evasion case, and the court held it was error to instruct the jury the assessment was valid as a matter of law. *England* was followed in *United States v. Goetz*, 746 F.2d 705, 708–10 (11th Cir. 1984). Our conclusion is also consistent with decisions that the taxpayer may defend a charge of willfully evading the assessment of taxes by proving there was no tax due and owing, for example, by evidence of unclaimed deductions and expenses. *See, e.g.*, *Clark v. United States*, 211 F.2d 100, 103 (8th Cir. 1954); *see also Sansone*, 380 U.S. at 354 (the crime of tax evasion is complete when a false return is filed "assuming, of course, that there was in fact a deficiency").

We find further support for this conclusion in the Supreme Court's cases dealing with the validity of presumptions in criminal cases. The government argues, in effect, that the alleged tax deficiency may be conclusively presumed from an administratively final assessment. But conclusive presumptions are invalid in criminal cases because they "conflict with the overriding presumption of innocence with which the law endows the accused and which extends to every element of the crime, and would invade the fact-finding function which in a criminal case the law assigns solely to the jury." *Sandstrom v. Montana*, 442 U.S. 510, 523 (1979). The court's approach in *Voorhies*, on the other hand, creates in effect only a permissive presumption, one that "merely allows an inference to be drawn and is constitutional so long as the inference would not be irrational." *Yates v. Evatt*, 500 U.S. 391, 402 n.7 (1991). It is rational to infer that an assessment which the taxpayer chose not to contest is prima facie evidence of the asserted deficiency. But it is not rational to make the assessment conclusive proof of the deficiency, particularly because in the absence of a tax return an assessment is based upon a "substitute" return prepared by the IRS without the benefit of factual input from the taxpayer.[53]

For the foregoing reasons, we conclude that one accused of tax evasion must have the opportunity to prove, however unlikely the proposition may be, that an administratively final tax assessment does not accurately reflect the existence of a tax deficiency. Therefore, Silkman is entitled to a new trial at which he may introduce evidence relevant to whether there was in fact a tax deficiency in one or more of the tax years in question.

Silkman raises . . . additional issues on appeal that require little discussion. [H]e argues he is entitled to a judgment of acquittal because the government failed to prove tax deficiencies. We disagree. The formal assessments were prima facie evidence of tax deficiencies. When combined with the other evidence that Silkman consciously refused to file returns, ignored numerous IRS inquiries, evasively responded to the notice of deficiency, and then purposefully concealed his assets overseas, we think the trial record was more than sufficient to permit the jury to

---

[53] [Authors' note: There are two types of substitutes for returns. One is prepared by the IRS from available information but is presented to, and is signed by, the taxpayer. IRC § 6020(a). The other is prepared by the IRS but is not signed by the taxpayer. IRC § 6020(b). The *Silkman* court appears to be referring to the second type.]

find tax deficiencies and the other elements of tax evasion beyond a reasonable doubt.

Does analysis of the certificate of assessment in *Silkman* strike you as correct? Any tax expert or even IRS agent will admit, if properly questioned, that the assessment does not prove that a tax was due and owing. Tax assessments are frequently contested in tax refund and collection suits and often found to be excessive. How then can the Government simply introduce a tax assessment to show that a tax is due and owing? Shouldn't the Government have to show that the assessment was not only validly made (*i.e.*, with appropriate procedural regularity, which is historically the sole function of the certificate of assessments), but also that it properly reflected the underlying tax liability? Is this an example of the phenomenon noted above, *i.e.*, a shift of at least a production burden to the defendant to introduce some evidence that the amount assessed is excessive? Should it happen? Should the Government be permitted to meet its substantial burden to show a tax due and owing simply by introducing a certificate of an assessment?

This issue does not usually arise in evasion of assessment cases. In those cases, the IRS investigates and prosecutes before making an assessment. The Government usually will put the civil audit and assessment process on hold and will not make the assessment until after the case is prosecuted. This issue is thus practically limited to evasion of payment cases.

PROBLEM

You are an IRS Chief Counsel's office attorney doing criminal tax work. You are asked to render advice and assistance to IRS Special Agent Sara Aguilar. You and Aguilar meet, and she gives you the following information.

Aguilar is investigating the 2012 and 2013 years of Horace and Wanda Tanner. The investigation began as a result of a referral from IRS Revenue Agent Pauline Corcoran, who had been examining the Tanners' income tax returns for those years.

Horace and Wanda are married to each other. They were 33 and 29 years of age respectively in 2012. They have three minor children. Horace's formal education ended with completion of his junior year of high school. Wanda's formal education ended when she graduated from high school. Horace was arrested for aggravated assault when he was 24 although the charge was bargained down to misdemeanor assault. Wanda has no criminal record.

Since 2009, Horace and Wanda have operated an unincorporated business under the name Tanner Sod and Garden Center. According to an interview with Horace's father, they acquired the assets of the business in the following fashion. The father had been operating a business under the name of Sunnydale Sod Center. One morning in 2009, the father arrived at his business to find all of its movable assets gone. Horace and Wanda had taken them. They moved them to a new location and set up their business using those assets. The assets had a total value of approximately $50,000 at the time. Horace's father decided not to pursue legal recourse against Horace and Wanda because he was afraid of Horace and because Sunnydale Sod Center had been only marginally profitable throughout its existence. The father essentially retired in 2009 upon the theft of the assets.

Horace's father later had a conversation with Horace in which he asked Horace why Horace essentially took the business from him, especially since it was making little profit. Horace responded that he and Wanda knew a way to make the business more profitable although he did not elaborate on this statement.

Horace and Wanda have filed joint federal income tax returns since 2010. Neither filed any federal income tax returns for prior years. Their 2012 and 2013 returns reported the following:

	Net Business Income	Adjusted Gross Income	Taxable Income	Tax
2012	$18,000	$10,000	0	$2,000
2013	$16,000	$8,000	0	$1,400

Although they reported zero taxable income in each of 2012 and 2013, their returns actually showed itemized deductions in excess of their adjusted gross incomes for each year. The $2,000 and $1,400 reported tax liabilities were for self-employment tax, not regular income tax, and these liabilities were paid along with the timely filed 2012 and 2013 returns.

Horace and Wanda do not maintain separate, formal books and records for their business. The receipts items on their returns were calculated from information Horace and Wanda provided to their accountant. For the years in question, Horace and Wanda's returns were prepared by the accounting firm of J.C. Rawls & Associates. Horace and (more usually) Wanda furnished information on their income to Adele Smythe of that firm. Whenever Ms. Smythe had a question about an item, she would check it with Horace or Wanda. The owner of the firm, Jared Rawls, prepared the returns in question from Ms. Smythe's work.

After preparation, Rawls reviewed the returns line-by-line with Horace and Wanda. He asked whether there was any additional income or were any additional expenses not listed on the returns. Horace and Wanda then reviewed the returns, signed them, and mailed them.

Based on her investigation thus far, Special Agent Aguilar has tentatively concluded the following:

(1) The Rawls firm calculated Horace and Wanda's business income from deposits into three accounts (Accounts A, B, and C) they maintained at Wells Fargo Bank. However, Horace and Wanda also maintained two accounts (Accounts D and E) at Bank of America. Total deposits into and withdrawals from Accounts D and E in 2012 and 2013 were as follows:

	Account D	Account E
2012 deposits	15,000	3,000
2012 withdrawals	8,000	2,000
	7,000	1,000
2013 deposits	25,000	4,000
2013 withdrawals	5,000	6,000
	20,000	(2,000)

(2) In 2012, Horace received dividends of $2,000 on stock he owned in a publicly traded United States corporation. The 2012 return did not report any dividend income.

(3) In 2013, Horace received $40,000 as a result of selling the stock referred to in (2) above. The 2013 return did not report any capital gains.

(4) In 2012, Horace and Wanda purchased a new home for $200,000. In 2013, they added a pool and a satellite television dish to their residence. In March 2013, they took a seven-day vacation trip to Las Vegas.

(5) Adding up the individual Schedule C expenses claimed on the 2013 return, one obtains a total of $18,000. However, the figure appearing on the total line for such expenses was $22,000, and $22,000 was the figure that was subtracted from receipts to obtain 2013 net Schedule C income.

(6) Aguilar has interviewed Horace and Wanda. They told her that at the start of 2012, they had $16,000 in cash which they kept in their home. They kept such a large amount of cash at home, they said, because they don't trust banks.

At your meeting with Special Agent Aguilar, she states that she realizes that more work remains to be done but that she has "a strong gut feeling that there's a good criminal case here." She asks for your advice as to (1) what might be the appropriate criminal tax charge or charges to recommend, assuming further development of the case proves to be successful, (2) what theory or theories of proof should be pursued, (3) what "holes" you perceive in the case as it currently stands and how you think she should attempt to fill them, (4) what affirmative defenses Horace and Wanda might assert, and (5) anything else you think relevant. How would you respond to Aguilar's inquiries?

Chapter 5

PROSECUTION POLICIES AND AFFIRMATIVE DEFENSES

IRC: §§ 6330(e), 6513, 6531, 7201, 7502, 7609(e)

I. INTRODUCTION

In Chapters 2A, 2B, and 3, we discussed the various crimes defendants may be charged with and the elements of each of those offenses. Much of the Government's investigative and administrative efforts are spent determining whether a prosecutor could prove each of the elements beyond a reasonable doubt. However, even when prosecutors may be able to establish all the elements required to prove a tax crime, they may nevertheless decline to prosecute the defendant due to Department of Justice guidelines and policies. The decision as to which crimes to charge is shaped by these same policies. This chapter will discuss those administrative guidelines and policies. In addition, a defendant may avoid prosecution or foil a conviction by asserting a meritorious affirmative defense. This chapter will also explore these defenses, with principal emphasis on statutes of limitations.

II. DECLINING PROSECUTION: GETTING PROSECUTORS TO JUST SAY NO

A. Prosecutorial Discretion in General

Federal prosecutors enjoy an enormous amount of discretion in deciding whether to charge a crime, whom to charge, and what crimes to charge. And, unlike most of the rest of our criminal justice system, those decisions are made out of public view and virtually unchecked by the other branches of government.[1] As one scholar has observed, "There is a broad and rather casual acceptance of the fact that prosecutors often exercise greater control over the administration of criminal justice than do other officials."[2] The Supreme Court has articulated the reasons behind this *laissez faire* policy:

> In our criminal justice system, the Government retains "broad discretion" as to whom to prosecute. "[S]o long as the prosecutor has probable cause

[1] Courts generally decline to review prosecutorial decisions citing separation-of-powers concerns. *See, e.g.*, United States v. Cox, 342 F.2d 167 (5th Cir.), *cert. denied*, 381 U.S. 935 (1965).

[2] James Vorenberg, *Decent Restraint of Prosecutorial Power*, 94 HARV. L. REV. 1521, 1525 (1981); *see also* Michael Edmund O'Neill, *When Prosecutors Don't: Trends in Federal Prosecutorial Declinations*, 79 NOTRE DAME L. REV. 221 (2003).

> to believe that the accused committed an offense defined by statute, the decision whether or not to prosecute, and what charge to file or bring before a grand jury, generally rests entirely in his discretion." This broad discretion rests largely on the recognition that the decision to prosecute is particularly ill-suited to judicial review. Such factors as the strength of the case, the prosecution's general deterrence value, the Government's enforcement priorities, and the case's relationship to the Government's overall enforcement plan are not readily susceptible to the kind of analysis the courts are competent to undertake. Judicial supervision in this area, moreover, entails systemic costs of particular concern. Examining the basis of a prosecution delays the criminal proceeding, threatens to chill law enforcement by subjecting the prosecutor's motives and decisionmaking to outside inquiry, and may undermine prosecutorial effectiveness by revealing the Government's enforcement policy. All these are substantial concerns that make the courts properly hesitant to examine the decision whether to prosecute.[3]

The exceptions to this general rule are selective prosecution and vindictive prosecution, both of which have been held to violate constitutional protections of due process and equal protection.[4]

The gravity of the decision to charge cannot be underestimated, for once a taxpayer is charged and becomes a defendant, his life will never be the same again:

> The decision whether or not to charge affects a prospective defendant in three ways. First, it determines whether he must undergo the expense, anxiety, and embarrassment of criminal proceedings. Second, in those cases in which clear evidence of guilt exists or can be obtained by whatever resources and effort the prosecutor wishes to invest, the decision to charge determines whether or not there will be a conviction. Third, depending on the scope of judicial discretion in sentencing and, to a lesser extent, on the degree to which dispensing power is held by parole or corrections authorities, the charge decision may have a major effect on the penalty. A single lenient charge usually will result in milder punishment than will heavier or multiple charges for the same conduct.[5]

B. Deciding Whether and Whom to Prosecute

The decisions regarding whether, whom, and what to charge in tax cases are governed in part by the U.S. Attorney's Manual and the Criminal Tax Manual.[6] These decisions are based on many factors, including the Government's desire to apply the tax laws and the criminal tax laws uniformly, as well as its desire to get the maximum general deterrence from each case. The general provisions governing all prosecutors are contained in the US Attorney's Manual's "Principles

---

[3] Wayte v. United States, 470 U.S. 598, 607–608 (1985) (internal citations omitted).

[4] *See, e.g.*, Wayte, *supra*, at 608; Blackledge v. Perry, 417 U.S. 21, 28–29 (1974).

[5] Vorenberg, *supra*, at 1525–1526.

[6] As we will discuss in Chapter 6, the IRS's Law Enforcement Manuals also govern these decisions during the investigatory stage.

of Federal Prosecution."[7] The stated goal of these guidelines is to "contribute to the fair, evenhanded administration of the Federal criminal laws."

The threshold determination that a prosecutor must make is that the defendant's conduct constitutes a federal offense and that the admissible evidence will "probably be sufficient" for the Government to obtain a conviction.[8] Even if this threshold determination is made, the prosecutor may nevertheless decline to prosecute if (1) a substantial federal interest would not be served by prosecution; (2) the person is subject to effective prosecution in another jurisdiction; or (3) an adequate non-criminal alternative to prosecution exists.[9] In addition, as we discuss below, prosecutors may decline to prosecute in light of the Government's dual prosecution policy, also known as the "Petite Policy." These factors recognize that federal prosecutorial resources are limited and not every federal offense can be charged. Prosecutors are instructed to look at the conduct, circumstances, and culpability of the defendant, as well as the impact the crime had on the community.[10] However, in making this determination, the prosecutor may not take into account the person's race, religion, sex, national origin, or political association, activities or beliefs. Nor may the prosecutor take into account the impact the case will have on his or her career.[11]

The degree of discretion conferred on prosecutors in criminal tax cases is no different. Chapter 6 discusses at length the process criminal tax cases go through from investigation through indictment and prosecution. For purposes of this chapter it is sufficient to know that, after referral from the IRS, the Assistant Attorney General in charge of the Tax Division is responsible for conducting, handling, or supervising all matters arising under the internal revenue laws. The Tax Division has been given the authority to approve all tax-related indictments. Once prosecution is authorized, the trial itself may be handled by the local United States Attorney's office or, if requested, trial attorneys from the Tax Division can provide assistance or try the case. As with non-tax cases, the USAM requires that the evidence support a *prima facie* case and a reasonable probability of conviction. The USAM also instructs prosecutors to follow the policies of the Federal Tax Enforcement Program:

> The Federal Tax Enforcement Program is designed to protect the public interest in preserving the integrity of this nation's self-assessment tax system through vigorous, uniform enforcement of the internal revenue laws. The government's primary objective in criminal tax prosecutions is to get the maximum deterrent value from the cases prosecuted. To achieve

---

[7] USAM 9-27.001 *et seq.; see also* USAM 9-28.100 *et seq.* (Principles of Federal Prosecution of Business Organizations). In addition to the USAM, the CTM contains numerous important policy provisions, which will be discussed below and in other chapters of this book. Finally, the Internal Revenue Manual contains directives for IRS CID agents, some of which are publicly available. However, some of the most important parts of the Internal Revenue Manual, including prosecution thresholds, are secret.

[8] USAM 9-27.200. The USAM refers to this as the probable cause requirement.

[9] USAM 9-27.220.

[10] USAM 9-27.230.

[11] USAM 9-27.260.

> this objective, the government's tax enforcement activities must reflect uniform enforcement of the tax laws. Uniformity is particularly necessary because prosecution standards in the tax area potentially affect more individuals than in any other area of the law. Accordingly, the Federal Tax Enforcement Program is designed to have the broadest possible impact on compliance attitudes by emphasizing balanced enforcement, with respect to not only the types of violations prosecuted but also the geographic location and economic and vocational status of the violators. In view of the importance of the uniform prosecution program, the Tax Division has been delegated the responsibility of authorizing or declining investigation and prosecution in criminal tax matters.[12]

In attempting to convince federal prosecutors not to bring tax charges against your clients, what might you argue? What if your client is sick, aged, or mentally incompetent: can you convince the Government to drop the charges for these reasons? It's possible, but unlikely.[13]

Under the Justice Department's Health Policy established in 1953, whether an individual could physically survive the stress and strain of a trial is not a controlling consideration in deciding to bring a tax prosecution. Rather, the Tax Division's position is that whether a taxpayer should not be tried because of health reasons is a matter which can best be decided by the trial court, rather than on an administrative basis. "Only when it is clear beyond all doubt that a proposed defendant will never be able to stand trial because of a terminal physical condition is a case disposed of for reasons of health at the administrative level."[14] At the trial level, the Tax Division takes the position that:

> If a criminal defendant seeks a continuance or other delay of the trial on the ground that the defendant is not able to assist his counsel in presenting a defense and/or that a trial will pose a serious threat to the defendant's health, the prosecutor should ensure that the relevant facts and the court's decision are made a matter of record.
>
> The prosecutor should consider (1) asking the IRS special agent to conduct a discrete investigation to determine the extent of the defendant's daily activities and to eliminate the possibility of malingering; (2) asking the court to appoint a physician to conduct an examination, including hospitalization if necessary; and (3) requesting a hearing in open court to discuss the facts. [15]

The Tax Division is equally skeptical of claims of mental incompetency. "In criminal tax cases, where the taxpayer is in a money-producing activity during the prosecution years, lack of mental responsibility defenses are highly questionable." As we saw in Chapter 2A, the Government must prove willfulness beyond a

---

[12] USAM 6-4.010.

[13] Indeed, the Government recently prosecuted, albeit unsuccessfully, an 87-year-old man for conspiracy and filing false tax returns. *See* Shamik Trivedi, *Court Finds No Willfulness in Tax Conspiracy Acquittal*, 2013 TNT 56-2 (Mar. 22, 2013).

[14] CTM 4.04[1].

[15] CTM 4.04[2].

reasonable doubt, and willfulness is defined as "an intentional violation of a known legal duty." Thus, it would be rare for a case to be referred for prosecution by the IRS when there is clear and convincing evidence of a mental defense. As a result, except for cases in which very serious mental disorders are obvious, the Tax Division takes the position that it is up to the trial court to determine whether a taxpayer is competent to stand trial.[16]

C. Prosecution of Entities

Entities provide different prosecutorial challenges. While entities such as corporations can be charged with crimes, they cannot be incarcerated.[17] That said, entities can be fined and punished severely with fines. In some cases, most notably the demise of accounting giant Arthur Andersen after its indictment and conviction, a criminal charge can be a virtual death penalty.[18] As described in Chapter 12, indictment and conviction can severely affect other entities (e.g., those doing major business with the federal government), even when it is not fatal to them. Accordingly, when and how to prosecute corporations is an important policy issue. As a result, the Justice Department has adopted "Principles of Federal Prosecution of Business Organizations" to guide its prosecutors. This policy was updated in January 2003 by then-Deputy Attorney General Larry Thompson, in what is known as the Thompson Memorandum.[19] Several aspects of the Thompson Memorandum have come under attack in the high-profile prosecution of several former partners of the accounting firm of KPMG. Most notably, the Government used the threat of indictment and prosecution, which in Arthur Andersen's case was in essence a death sentence, to pressure KPMG into waiving its attorney-client privilege and cutting off payment of legal fees for individual partners of KPMG that had been indicted.[20] In response to the criticism, the Thompson Memorandum was revised in 2006 by Deputy Attorney General Paul McNulty, which has softened some of the more draconian aspects of the Thompson Memorandum.[21] The current

---

16 CTM 4.04[3].

17 *See, e.g.*, N.Y. Cent. & Hudson River R.R. Co. v. United States, 212 U.S. 481, 494 (1909) (corporations criminally liable for acts of agents). However, corporations cannot be tried for some crimes. For example, perjury under 18 U.S.C. section 1621 requires a false statement under oath. Since corporations cannot make statements under oath, they cannot be tried for perjury. On the other hand, as we saw in the *Ingredient Technology* case discussed in Chapter 2B, a corporation can be charged with section 7206(1) tax perjury, since the statute defines the crime as a false statement made under oath by a "person," which is defined to include corporations.

18 For a full discussion of the issues that arise in the prosecution of entities, *see* Lisa Kern Griffin, *Compelled Cooperation and the New Corporate Criminal Procedure*, 82 N.Y.U. L. Rev. 311, 321–322 (2007).

19 Memorandum from Larry D. Thompson, Deputy Attorney Gen., to U.S. Attorneys, regarding Principles of Federal Prosecutions of Business Organizations (Jan. 20, 2003), available at http://www.americanbar.org/content/dam/aba/migrated/poladv/priorities/privilegewaiver/2003jan20_privwaiv_dojthomp.authcheckdam.pdf.

20 United States v. Stein, 541 F.3d 130 (2d Cir. 2008) (sustaining the district court's dismissal of the indictments). The district court had earlier spotted the issue (United States v. Stein, 435 F. Supp. 2d 330, 367–73 (S.D.N.Y. 2006)), but only later dismissed the case when no other remedy was present. United States v. Stein, 495 F. Supp. 2d 390 (S.D.N.Y. 2007).

21 Memorandum from Paul J. McNulty, Deputy Attorney General to Head of Department Compo-

version of these policies is set forth in what is called the Filip Memorandum, named for then Deputy Attorney General Mark Filip.[22] The current version is substantially similar to the McNulty version discussed in the next paragraph.

As amended, the memo provides that corporations "should not be treated leniently because of their artificial nature nor should they be subject to harsher treatment. Vigorous enforcement of the criminal laws against corporate wrongdoers, where appropriate results in great benefits for law enforcement and the public, particularly in the area of white collar crime." The policy notes, however, that the Tax Division has a strong preference for prosecuting responsible individuals, rather than entities, for corporate tax offenses. In deciding whether to bring charges, prosecutors are instructed to consider the following factors in reaching a decision as to the proper treatment of a corporate target:

1. the nature and seriousness of the offense, including the risk of harm to the public, and applicable policies and priorities, if any, governing the prosecution of corporations for particular categories of crime;
2. the pervasiveness of wrongdoing within the corporation, including the complicity in, or condonation of, the wrongdoing by corporate management;
3. the corporation's history of similar conduct, including prior criminal, civil, and regulatory enforcement actions against it;
4. the corporation's timely and voluntary disclosure of wrongdoing and its willingness to cooperate in the investigation of its agents, including, if necessary, the waiver of corporate attorney-client and work product protection;
5. the existence and adequacy of the corporation's compliance program;
6. the corporation's remedial actions, including any efforts to implement an effective corporate compliance program or to improve an existing one, to replace responsible management, to discipline or terminate wrongdoers, to pay restitution, and to cooperate with the relevant government agencies;
7. collateral consequences, including disproportionate harm to shareholders, pension holders, and employees not proven personally culpable and impact on the public arising from the prosecution;
8. the adequacy of the prosecution of individuals responsible for the corporation's malfeasance; and
9. the adequacy of remedies such as civil or regulatory enforcement actions.[23]

---

nents and United States Attorneys available at http://www.usdoj.gov/dag/speeches/2006/mcnulty_memo.pdf.

[22] Memorandum from U.S. Deputy Attorney General Mark R. Filip, Principles of Federal Prosecution of Business Organizations (Aug. 28, 2008).

[23] Filip Memorandum at 3–4.

D. Deciding Which Crime to Charge

Once the Government has decided that the person's conduct merits indictment and prosecution, the next issue that must be resolved is which of the many crimes in the prosecutor's arsenal should actually be charged. As we saw in Chapters 2A, 2B, and 3, criminal conduct meant to lessen or eliminate a person's tax liability can be charged under a number of different statutes. For example, if the taxpayer fails to file a return and keeps a double set of books, should the crime be charged as failure to file or as tax evasion? Can the Government charge both crimes? What if the taxpayer and a few colleagues decide to file false returns claiming refunds they and others are not entitled to? Should the Government charge the conduct under section 7206(1) and (2), the general conspiracy statute of 18 U.S.C. section 371, or conspiracy to file false claims and filing false claims under 18 U.S.C. section 286 and 287? Can the Government charge every crime and let the jury pick its favorite?

In *United States v. Batchelder*,[24] the Supreme Court reviewed a defendant's conviction for being a felon in possession of a firearm. The defendant's conduct violated both 18 U.S.C. section 922(h), which had a maximum sentence of five years' imprisonment, and section 1202(a), which allowed no more than a two-year maximum sentence. The prosecutors indicted the defendant under the provision that allowed for a more severe sentence, and the trial court sentenced the defendant to the maximum five-year sentence. In rejecting the defendant's claim that these overlapping criminal statutes unconstitutionally enabled the prosecutors to select the punishment a defendant will receive, the Court stated: "This Court has long recognized that when an act violates more than one criminal statute, the Government may prosecute under either so long as it does not discriminate against any class of defendants. Whether to prosecute and what charge to file or bring before a grand jury are decisions that generally rest in the prosecutor's discretion."[25] Thus, if more than one statute clearly criminalizes certain conduct, prosecutors may freely choose which statute to charge.

The USAM requires that prosecutors charge "the most serious offense that is consistent with the nature of the defendant's conduct, and that is likely to result in a sustainable conviction."[26] The "most serious" offense is generally that which yields the highest range under the Sentencing Guidelines.

In addition to charging the most serious offense, may the Government also throw in extra goodies to sweeten the indictment? According to the USAM, the bringing of "unnecessary charges not only complicates and prolongs trials, it constitutes an excessive — and potentially unfair — exercise of power."[27] Of course, the key word in this quote is "unnecessary." As we have seen throughout this book, the Government is not shy about adding charges when doing so is to its advantage. In order to ensure appropriately limited exercises of the charging power, the USAM outlines three general situations in which additional charges may be

---

[24] 442 U.S. 114 (1979).

[25] *Id.* at 123–124 (citations omitted).

[26] USAM 9-27.300.

[27] USAM 9-27.320. In addition, the Sentencing Guidelines, discussed in Chapter 10, take much of the benefit out of bringing unnecessary charges.

brought: (1) when necessary to reflect the full nature and extent of the criminal conduct involved; (2) when necessary to provide the basis for an appropriate sentence under all the circumstances of the case; and (3) when an additional charge or charges would significantly strengthen the case against the defendant or a codefendant.[28]

E. Lesser Included Offense

A related issue that frequently arises because of the extensive overlap of criminal tax statutes deals with what are known as "lesser included offenses." The question of whether a crime is a lesser included offense looks at whether a separate criminal statute may, in some circumstance, be part of or included in another more serious criminal charge. For example, as noted above, failure to file (a misdemeanor) may in some circumstances be part of a tax evasion case, so-called *Spies* evasion. Is failure to file a lesser included offense of tax evasion under these circumstances? While the Sentencing Guidelines, discussed in Chapter 10, lessen the impact of this question, it is still an important, albeit confused, area of the law.

Why does this question matter? First, some courts have held that if a statute is a lesser included offense of another criminal statute, charging and sentencing for both violates the double jeopardy clause. For example, in *United States v. Kaiser*,[29] the defendant was convicted of both filing a false return and tax evasion for two tax years. The only affirmative acts of evasion alleged in the indictment supporting the evasion charge were the false returns used to support the section 7206(1) charge. The court held that the defendant could not properly be convicted and sentenced for both the greater offense of tax evasion and the lesser included offense of filing a false tax return, and it vacated the false return counts, holding:

> [W]e are confronted with a case in which the government must necessarily rely on all of the elements of the offense of false filing in order to establish an element of the greater offense of tax evasion. In a case such as this one, where tax evasion is charged solely by means of filing a false tax return under oath (i.e., a Form 1040), tax evasion includes as a legal necessity all the elements of false filing: filing a return under oath that is false as to a material matter, which the maker did not believe to be true, and which was willfully, as opposed to negligently done. Therefore, under the *Blockburger* test, the offense of filing a false return is a lesser included offense of tax evasion by means of filing the same false return.[30]

Second, if a charge is not considered a lesser included offense, the prosecutor might decide only to charge the more serious offense of tax evasion and not give the jury the option of convicting only on a misdemeanor failure to file count. If a jury has a choice only between conviction of a single offense and acquittal, the jury may believe that the conduct the defendant is charged with is still sufficiently serious that the jury is not willing to let the defendant simply walk. Juries in that situation would like a middle ground, but without a lesser-included offense charge, there is no

---

[28] *Id.*

[29] 893 F.2d 1300 (11th Cir. 1990).

[30] *Id.* at 1306; *see* Blockburger v. United States, 284 U.S. 299, 304 (1932).

middle ground. Jurors then must make the difficult choice of acquitting, when they think the defendant's conduct does not justify the greater charge the Government chose to pursue, or convicting the defendant of the greater charge in order to give some punishment. Accordingly, asking for a lesser included offense instruction may be essential to protecting your client from conviction of a more serious charge than he or she has committed.

The problem, however, is that the law on lesser included offenses in tax cases is far from clear. The rule, such as it is, is found in Fed. R. Crim. P. 31(c):

> (c) Lesser Offense or Attempt. A defendant may be found guilty of any of the following:
>
> (1) an offense necessarily included in the offense charged;
>
> (2) an attempt to commit the offense charged; or
>
> (3) an attempt to commit an offense necessarily included in the offense charged, if the attempt is an offense in its own right.

The courts have struggled with the phrase "necessarily included in the offense charged." In *Sansone v. United States,*[31] the Supreme Court addressed the issue of whether sections 7203 and 7207 were lesser included offenses of tax evasion.

SANSONE v. UNITED STATES

Unites States Supreme Court
380 U.S. 343 (1965)

The offense here charged was a violation of § 7201, which proscribes willfully attempting in any manner to evade or defeat any tax imposed by the Internal Revenue Code. As this Court has recognized, this felony provision is "the capstone of a system of sanctions which singly or in combination were calculated to induce prompt and forthright fulfillment of every duty under the income tax law and to provide a penalty suitable to every degree of delinquency." *Spies v. United States, supra*, 317 U.S. at 497. As such a capstone, § 7201 necessarily includes among its elements actions which, if isolated from the others, constitute lesser offenses in this hierarchical system of sanctions. Therefore, if on the facts of a given case there are disputed issues of fact which would enable the jury rationally to find that, although all the elements of § 7201 have not been proved, all the elements of one or more lesser offenses have been, it is clear that the defendant is entitled to a lesser-included offense charge as to such lesser offenses.

As has been held by this Court, the elements of § 7201 are willfulness; the existence of a tax deficiency, and an affirmative act constituting an evasion or attempted evasion of the tax. In comparison, § 7203 makes it a misdemeanor willfully to fail to perform a number of specified acts at the time required by law — the one here relevant being the failure to pay a tax when due. This misdemeanor requires only willfulness and the omission of the required act — here the payment of the tax when due. As recognized by this Court in *Spies*, the difference between a mere willful failure to pay a tax (or perform other enumerated actions) when due

[31] 380 U.S. 343 (1965).

under § 7203 and a willful attempt to evade or defeat taxes under § 7201 is that the latter felony involves "some willful commission in addition to the willful omissions that make up the list of misdemeanors." Where there is, in a § 7201 prosecution, a disputed issue of fact as to the existence of the requisite affirmative commission in addition to the § 7203 omission, a defendant would, of course, be entitled to a lesser-included offense charge based on § 7203. In this case, however, it is undisputed that petitioner filed a tax return and that the petitioner's filing of a false tax return constituted a sufficient affirmative commission to satisfy that requirement of § 7201. The only issue at trial was whether petitioner's act was willful. Given this affirmative commission and the conceded tax deficiency, if petitioner's act was willful, that is, if the jury believed, as it obviously did, that he knew that the capital gain on the sale of the property was reportable in 1957, he was guilty of violating both §§ 7201 and 7203. If his act was not willful, he was not guilty of violating either § 7201 or § 7203. Thus on the facts of this case, § 7201 and § 7203 "covered precisely the same ground." This being so, on the authorities cited, it is clear that petitioner was not entitled to a lesser-included offense charge based on § 7203.

Section 7207 requires the willful filing of a document known to be false or fraudulent in any material manner. The elements here involved are willfulness and the commission of the prohibited act. Section 7207 does not, however, require that the act be done as an attempt to evade or defeat taxes. Conduct could therefore violate § 7207 without violating § 7201 where the false statement, though material, does not constitute an attempt to evade or defeat taxation because it does not have the requisite effect of reducing the stated tax liability. This may be the case, for example, where a taxpayer understates his gross receipts and he offsets this by also understating his deductible expenses. In this example, if the Government in a § 7201 case charged tax evasion on the grounds that the defendant had understated his tax by understating his gross receipts, and the defendant contended that this was not so, as the misstatement of gross receipts had been offset by an understatement of deductible expenses, the defendant would be entitled to a lesser-included offense charge based on § 7207, there being this relevant disputed issue of fact. This would be so, for in such a case, if the jury believed that an understatement of deductible expenses had offset the understatement of gross receipts, while the defendant would have violated § 7207 by willfully making a material false and fraudulent statement on his return, he would not have violated § 7201 as there would not have been the requisite § 7201 element of a tax deficiency. Here, however, there is no dispute that petitioner's material misstatement resulted in a tax deficiency. Thus there is no disputed issue of fact concerning the existence of an element required for conviction of § 7201 but not required for conviction of § 7207. Given petitioner's material misstatement which resulted in a tax deficiency, if, as the jury obviously found, petitioner's act was willful in the sense that he knew that he should have reported more income than he did for the year 1957, he was guilty of violating both §§ 7201 and 7207. If his action was not willful, he was guilty of violating neither. As was true with § 7203, on the facts of this case §§ 7201 and 7207 'covered precisely the same ground,' *Berra v. United States*, *supra*, at 134, and thus petitioner was not entitled to a lesser-included offense charge based on § 7207.

Thus, depending upon the facts of an individual case, less serious charges like sections 7203, 7206(1), and 7207 might not be lesser included offenses. In *Schmuck v. United States*,[32] the Supreme Court adopted what it called the "elements test." Under that test, one offense is not "necessarily included" in another unless the elements of the lesser offense are a subset of the elements of the charged offense. Where the lesser offense requires an element not required for the greater offense, a lesser included offense instruction is not to be given under Rule 31(c).[33] In 1993, the Acting Assistant Attorney General in charge of the Tax Division issued a policy memorandum to Tax Division prosecutors, instructing them to adhere to the elements test. The Tax Division applies the elements test to tax cases as follows:[34]

> 1. In cases charged as *Spies*-evasion (*i.e.*, failure to file, failure to pay, and an affirmative act of evasion) under Section 7201, it is the government's position that neither party is entitled to an instruction that willful failure to file (Section 7203) is a lesser included offense of which the defendant may be convicted.
>
> 2. Similarly, in tax evasion cases, where the filing of a false return (Section 7206) is charged as one of the affirmative acts of evasion (or the only affirmative act), it is the Tax Division's policy that a lesser included offense instruction is not permissible, since evasion may be established without proof of the filing of a false return.
>
> 3. Although the elements of Section 7207 do not readily appear to be a subset of the elements of Section 7201, the Supreme Court has held that a violation of Section 7207 is a lesser included offense of a violation of Section 7201. *See Sansone v. United States*, 380 U.S. at 352; *Schmuck v. United States*, 489 U.S. at 720, n.11. Accordingly, in an appropriate case, either party may request the giving of a lesser included offense instruction based on Section 7207 where the defendant has been charged with attempted income tax evasion by the filing of a false tax return or other document.
>
> 4. Adhering to a strict "elements" test, the elements of Section 7207 are not a subset of the elements of Section 7206(1). Consequently, it is the government's position that in a case in which the defendant is charged with violating Section 7206(1) by making and subscribing a false tax return or other document, neither party is entitled to an instruction that willfully delivering or disclosing a false return or other document to the Secretary of the Treasury (Section 7207) is a lesser included offense of which the defendant may be convicted.
>
> 5. Prosecutors should be aware that the law in their circuit may be inconsistent with the policy stated in this memorandum. Nevertheless, since the government has now embraced the strict "elements" test and taken a position on this issue in the Supreme Court, it is imperative that the policy set out in this memorandum be followed.

---

[32] 489 U.S. 705 (1989).

[33] *Id.* at 716.

[34] CTM 8.11.

6. In tax cases, questions concerning whether one offense is a lesser included offense of another may not be limited to Title 26 violations, but may also include violations under Title 18 (i.e., assertions that a Title 26 charge is a lesser included violation of a Title 18 charge or vice-versa). The policy set out in this memorandum will also govern any such situations — that is, the strict elements test of *Schmuck v. United States*, 489 U.S. 705, should be applied.[35]

F. Dual and Successive Prosecution Policy ("Petite Policy")

An issue that arises frequently in federal charging decisions is whether a defendant who has been charged with a crime may be charged again for substantially the same conduct. This issue arises in tax cases when, for example, a defendant has been charged with evading state taxes, and the federal government wants to charge him again for evasion of federal taxes. It can also apply when a defendant has been charged with embezzlement or bank fraud, and the Government would like to bring a subsequent case against the defendant for tax fraud on the funds obtained from the prior crime. The policy, which is contained both in the CTM and the USAM,[36] gets its name from the case of *Petite v. United States*.[37] The policy provides:

> The federal government can prosecute a state criminal defendant on federal charges for similar conduct (*i.e.*, filing false federal tax returns that fail to report the same income that was not reported on state tax returns), and it can prosecute a federal criminal defendant for failing to pay taxes on ill-gotten gains from non-tax criminal conduct. The Justice Department's "Dual and Successive Prosecution Policy" calls upon prosecutors to evaluate whether it is a wise investment of federal resources and whether it is unfair to the defendant in a particular case, before the government brings federal charges that are based on "substantially the same act(s) or transaction(s)" as previous charges. *Id.*, § 9-2.031(A). The Tax Division adheres to the spirit of the policy when considering tax prosecutions, even if the two prosecutions in issue are not based on exactly the same acts or transactions. Thus, even though a tax prosecution based on unreported criminal proceeds is not based on the same acts or transactions as the underlying crime itself — *i.e.*, the tax prosecution is based on the filing or non-filing of a federal tax return, while the underlying crime may have nothing to do with federal taxes (*e.g.*, embezzlement from an employer or a Ponzi or other fraud scheme) — the Tax Division makes the kind of evaluation required under the policy. Likewise, the Tax Division makes such an evaluation where there has been a prior prosecution for state tax fraud, even though such a prosecution would be based on the filing or non-filing of state tax returns rather than federal tax returns.

---

35 *Id.*

36 CTM 4.02; USAM 9-2.031.

37 361 U.S. 529 (1960).

> The Department's policy precludes the initiation of a federal prosecution following a prior federal or state prosecution based on substantially the same act or transaction unless the Assistant Attorney General concludes that four conditions are satisfied:
>
> 1. the matter must involve a substantial federal interest;
>
> 2. the prior prosecution must have left that interest demonstrably unvindicated;
>
> 3. the defendant's conduct must constitute a federal offense for which the admissible evidence probably will be sufficient to obtain and sustain a conviction by an unbiased trier of fact; and
>
> 4. prosecution is otherwise justified under the Principles of Federal Prosecution. USAM, § 9-27.00.[38]

The Petite Policy applies whenever there has been a prior state or federal prosecution resulting in an acquittal, a conviction, including one resulting from a plea agreement, or a dismissal, or other termination of the case on the merits after jeopardy has attached. These policies are based upon prosecutorial discretion, rather than a legal requirement such as double jeopardy.[39] If the policy applies, approval of the Assistant Attorney General in charge of the Tax Division is required to pursue prosecution in dual or successive tax cases.

Even if the Petite Policy does not apply, if the putative defendant is currently incarcerated, the USAM instructs prosecutors to look at the criminal conduct for which he is serving time, and if "the offender is already subject to a substantial sentence, or is already incarcerated, as a result of a conviction for another offense, the prosecutor should weigh the likelihood that another conviction will result in a meaningful addition to his/her sentence, might otherwise have a deterrent effect, or is necessary to ensure that the record accurately reflects the extent of his/her criminal conduct."[40] The CTM provides, however, that "the most important issues in the exercise of prosecutorial discretion are the nature and seriousness of the proposed tax offense, the deterrent effect of a tax prosecution, and the probable sentence or other consequences if the person is convicted on the tax charges. If the target is already subject to a substantial sentence or is already incarcerated, the prosecutor should weigh the likelihood that a subsequent conviction on tax charges will result in a meaningful addition to his or her sentence."[41]

---

[38] CTM 4.02[1], *citing* USAM 9-2.031.

[39] Congress has, however, stated that in certain instances a state judgment of conviction or acquittal on the merits is a bar to any subsequent federal prosecution for the same act or acts. *See. e.g.*, 18 U.S.C. 659, 660, 2101, 2117.

[40] USAM 9-27.230(B)(8).

[41] CTM 4.03[2].

G. Plea and Sentencing Policies

The vast majority of federal prosecutions, including tax prosecutions, are resolved by a guilty plea. The review processes within the IRS and the Tax Division ensure that if a taxpayer is indicted for a tax crime, he or she is likely to be convicted. In addition, the cost of defending a criminal tax charge is often too prohibitive for many defendants to bear. As a result, criminal tax attorneys spend a good deal of their time negotiating plea agreements. That said, the charge to which the defendant will plead is often secondary to the amount of jail time the defendant will get. Clients are generally more interested in how long they will be guests of the federal government than they are in whether they plead to a section 7201 or a section 7206(1) charge. As we will see in Chapter 10, the sentence is driven primarily by the amount of "tax loss," which can be the subject of intense negotiation between prosecutor and defense counsel.

The USAM requires that in plea bargaining, "both charge bargaining and sentence bargaining, must honestly reflect the totality and seriousness of the defendant's conduct and any departure to which the prosecutor is agreeing, and must be accomplished through appropriate guideline provisions. The basic policy is that charges are not to be bargained away or dropped, unless the prosecutor has a good faith doubt as to the Government's ability readily to prove a charge for legal or evidentiary reasons."[42] In tax cases, the USAM imposes the "major count policy."

> The overwhelming percentage of all criminal tax cases are disposed of by entry of a plea of guilty. In most cases, the transmittal letter forwarding the case from the Tax Division to the United States Attorney will identify the major count(s) that have been authorized for prosecution. The United States Attorney's Office, without prior approval of the Tax Division, is authorized to accept a plea of guilty to the major count(s) of the indictment or information. The United States Attorney also is authorized to seek a plea to more than the major count(s) if it is considered warranted.[43]

In determining what is "the major count," prosecutors are instructed to consider the following factors:

- Felony counts take priority over misdemeanor counts.
- Tax evasion counts (7201) take priority over all other substantive tax counts.
- The count charged in the indictment or information which carries the longest prison sentence will be considered a major count.
- As between counts under the same statute, the count involving the greatest financial detriment to the United States (i.e., the greatest additional tax due and owing) will be considered the major count.
- Where there is little difference in financial detriment between counts, the determining factor will be the relevant flagrancy of the offense.

---

[42] USAM 9-27.400.

[43] USAM 6-4.310.

- Where the determination of the major count(s) is complicated by considerations not covered by the above rule, the United States Attorney is encouraged to consult the Tax Division.[44]

The Tax Division will not generally consent to reduce a charge from a felony to a misdemeanor merely to secure a plea. Beyond the major count policy, section 5.12 of the CTM provides the following guidance:

> **5.12[2] Plea Agreements and Major Count Policy for Offenses Committed After November 1, 1987**
>
> The advent of the Sentencing Guidelines in 1987 and the Department's adoption of policies pursuant thereto necessitated certain minor conforming changes to the Tax Division's Major Count Policy (U.S.A.M. 6-4.310).
>
> *A. Tax Offenses Which Are All Part of the Same Course of Conduct or Common Scheme or Plan*
>
> Normally, no change in the application of the Major Count Policy will be required by virtue of the Guidelines and the Department's plea policy for Guideline cases. In most cases, all of the tax charges in an indictment are related. Consequently, even if the defendant pleads to a single count and the remaining counts are dismissed, the tax loss from all of the years should be taken into account in determining the tax loss for the offense to which a defendant pleads. Thus, in the usual case, the Tax Division will continue to designate a single count as the major count according to the principles previously utilized in designating the major count. *See* U.S.A.M. 6-4.310.
>
> *B. Tax Offenses Which Are Not All Part of the Same Course of Conduct or Common Scheme or Plan*
>
> Where all of the tax charges are not part of the same course of conduct or common scheme or plan, however, the Department's plea policy for Guideline cases may require the Tax Division either to designate as major counts one count from each group of unrelated counts or to designate one count from one of the groups of unrelated counts as the major count and have the prosecutor obtain a stipulation from the defendant establishing the commission of the offenses in the other group (*See* USSG Sec. 1B1.2(c)). This will be the case where the offense level of the group with the highest offense level must be increased under USSG § 3D1.4.
>
> *C. Designating More Than One Count as a Major Count.*
>
> Designating more than a single year as a major count may also be required where the computed guideline sentencing range exceeds the maximum sentence which can be imposed under a single count.

---

44 *Id.*

D. Tax Charges and Non-Tax Charges.

In cases in which there are both tax counts and non-tax charges, the selection of which tax count to designate as the major count may not have any effect on the applicable guideline range because the offense level of the group or groups of non-tax offenses is 9 or more levels higher than the offense level of the group containing the tax charges (See USSG §§ 3D1.2, 3D1.4). In such cases, the Tax Division will normally continue to designate the major count by application of the usual rules for selecting the major count. However, the Tax Division may designate a less serious tax offense in the group as the major count if it is supplied with sufficient information establishing that such a selection will not affect the applicable guideline range and with adequate justification for a deviation from the Major Count Policy.

5.12[3] Nolo Contendere Pleas.

Department of Justice policy requires all government attorneys to oppose the acceptance of *nolo contendere* pleas. When pleading "*nolo*" the defendant may create the impression that the government has only a technically adequate case which the defendant elects not to contest. A guilty plea is preferred because it strengthens the government position when the defendant contests a civil fraud penalty in an ancillary proceeding, as a *nolo* plea does not entitle the government to use the doctrine of collateral estoppel. Federal prosecutors may not consent to a plea of *nolo contendere* except in the most unusual circumstances and only after a recommendation for doing so has been approved by the Assistant Attorney General, Tax Division. *See* U.S.A.M. 9-16.010 *and* 9-27.500. The government attorney also will oppose dismissal of any charges to which the defendant does not plead nolo contendere. *See* U.S.A.M. 9-27.530.

5.12[4] Alford Pleas

In *North Carolina v. Alford*, 400 U.S. 25 (1970), the Supreme Court upheld the validity of accepting a plea of guilty over the defendant's claims of innocence. United States Attorneys are instructed not to consent to a so-called "Alford plea" except in the most unusual circumstances and then only after a recommendation for so doing has been approved by the Assistant Attorney General, Tax Division, or a higher departmental official. *See* U.S.A.M. 9-16.015 *and* 9-27.440. Apart from refusing to enter into *Alford* plea agreements, however, the degree to which government attorneys can express their opposition to such pleas is limited. Prosecutors should discourage *Alford* pleas by refusing to agree to terminate prosecutions where such a plea is proffered to fewer than all of the charges pending. If an *Alford* plea to fewer than all charges is tendered and accepted over the government's objection, the government attorney will proceed to trial on all of the remaining counts not barred on double jeopardy grounds unless the Assistant Attorney General, Tax Division, approves dismissal of the charges.

5.12[5] Statements by Government Counsel at Sentencing; Agreeing to Probation

A. Rule 32(a), Federal Rules of Criminal Procedure, permits government counsel to make a statement to the court at the time of sentencing. Counsel for the government should make a full statement of facts, including if applicable, the amount of tax evaded in all of the years for which a defendant was indicted; the means utilized to perpetrate and conceal any fraud; the past criminal record of the taxpayer; and all other information that the court may consider important in imposing an appropriate sentence.

B. When recommendations are made to the court on sentencing, the Tax Division prefers that government counsel request the imposition of a jail sentence in addition to the fine, together with costs of prosecution. In the usual situation, the payment of the civil tax liability, plus a fine, costs, and probation, does not constitute a satisfactory disposition of a criminal tax case.

C. Notwithstanding the foregoing, government counsel may agree to a sentence of probation (preferably with alternative conditions of confinement) when (i) the defendant pleads guilty, (ii) the sentencing guidelines range is 0–6 months (and within Criminal History Category I), and (iii) the United States Attorney personally, by signature, must approve a written memorandum to the case file setting forth the unusual and exceptional circumstances, warranting such agreement (for example, the need to secure cooperation against a more culpable party, or serious post-indictment degradation in the evidence available for trial such as the death of a witness or the loss or suppression of evidence). A copy of the United States Attorney's written determination must be supplied to the Tax Division at the same time the United States Attorney's office is required to notify the Division that the case has been closed.

5.12[6] Compromise of Criminal Liability/Civil Settlement.

While statutory authority under 26 U.S.C. Sec. 7122(a) does exist for the Attorney General, after referral of a case to the Department, to enter into agreements to compromise criminal tax cases without prosecution, as a matter of longstanding policy, such authority is very rarely exercised. If it is concluded that there is a reasonable probability of conviction and that prosecution would advance the administration of the internal revenue laws, any decision to forego prosecution on the ground that the taxpayer is willing to pay a fixed sum to the United States, would be susceptible to the attack that the taxpayer was given preferential treatment because of his ability to pay whatever amount of money the government demanded.

Consequently, proposed criminal tax cases are reviewed without any consideration being given to the matter of civil liability or the collection of taxes, penalties, and interests. In short, proposed criminal tax cases are examined with the view to determining whether a violation has occurred to the exclusion of any consideration of civil liability.

Absent extraordinary circumstances, such as permanent loss of tax revenues unless immediate protective action is taken, settlement of the civil liability is postponed until after sentence has been imposed in the criminal case, except when the court chooses to defer sentencing pending the outcome of such settlement. In this event, the IRS should be notified so that it can begin civil negotiations with the defendant.

However, the Tax Division strongly encourages, but does not require, that a plea agreement include certain civil admissions by the defendant, including: (1) admission of either receipt of enumerated amounts of unreported income or claimed enumerated amounts of illegal deductions or improper credits for years set forth in the plea agreement; (2) a stipulation that defendant is liable for the fraud penalty imposed by the Internal Revenue Code (26 U.S.C. Sec. 6663) on the understatements of liability for the years involved; and (3) an agreement by the defendant to file, prior to sentencing, complete and correct initial or amended personal returns for the years subject to the above admissions and, if requested, to provide the IRS with information regarding the years covered by the returns and to pay, at sentencing, all additional taxes, penalties and interest which are due and owing and (4) an agreement by the defendant not to file thereafter any claims for refund of taxes, penalties, or interest for amounts attributable to the returns filed incident to the plea. See Memorandum, United States Department of Justice, Tax Division, "Civil Settlements in Plea Agreement," June 3, 1993, in the Tax Resource Manual.

Within the constraints of the Tax Division's policy, there is room to negotiate. As indicated, the "tax loss" attributable to a given crime will be a major part of the sentence. Prosecutors are often willing to agree on a certain tax loss, perhaps one that is lower than the one they could prove if the case were to go to trial, in exchange for a plea deal. Prosecutors prefer to avoid the expense of trial if they know they can obtain a guilty plea to the major count. Negotiating the amount of tax loss is often where defense counsel will have the most luck in obtaining the best deal for their client.

III. AFFIRMATIVE DEFENSES

A. In General

Affirmative defenses are fairly rare in criminal tax cases. The Government has the burden to prove each and every element of the offense beyond a reasonable doubt. As a result, the burden is generally on the Government to prove all the relevant facts to the jury, and the defendant may simply put on evidence that will counter the Government's proof.[45] Thus, while a defendant can put on facts that he or she did not have the requisite mental state to have committed tax evasion, putting on this evidence does not shift the burden from the prosecution to the defendant to prove that he or she lacked the required mental state. The burden remains firmly on the prosecution.[46] If the defense does wish to raise a defense to rebut an element of the offense, it must only present a prima facie case. The Second Circuit in *United States v. Moon*,[47] explained this important distinction:

> [T]he government must prove every element of the offense charged beyond a reasonable doubt. One of those elements is that Moon had income from the Chase accounts and the Tong Il stock distribution that he failed to report. Defendant may then present an "affirmative defense," one which does not rebut an element of the crime, or some other defense which rebuts an element of crime. If defendant asserts an affirmative defense he bears the burden of proof on it. Here, since the defense theory that Moon was acting only as a trustee rebuts the "ownership" element of the crime charged, it was not an affirmative defense. Hence, the only burden on Moon was to present a prima facie case that he held the assets in trust. If the defense had successfully introduced into evidence this prima facie rebuttal of the element of ownership, the trial court would have been obliged to instruct the jury on the law of trusts and the government would still have had to prove beyond a reasonable doubt that Moon "owned" the assets.

Despite this distinction, the courts and the Government nevertheless sometimes refer to claims by a defendant as "affirmative defenses." Keeping in mind the distinction articulated in *Moon*, we will discuss some of the most common defenses (affirmative and otherwise) in tax cases.

B. Forgotten-Deduction Defense

As we saw in Chapter 2A, the Government has the burden to prove in a tax evasion case that the defendant had a substantial tax deficiency. Defendants often try to show that there was no deficiency, their return was substantially accurate, or at least raise questions about the government's calculations, by arguing they had unclaimed deductions. Perhaps the most famous example of this is *United States v. Helmsley*,[48] discussed in Chapter 2A. In *Helmsley*, the defendant had used one method of depreciation on her return. When the government charged her with evasion and put on evidence of a deficiency, the defendant asserted the defense that there was no deficiency if she used an alternative method of depreciation. The court rejected that defense.

---

[45] In re Winship, 397 U.S. 358, 364 (1970) ("Lest there remain any doubt about the constitutional stature of the reasonable-doubt standard, we explicitly hold that the Due Process Clause protects the accused against conviction except upon proof beyond a reasonable doubt *of every fact* necessary to constitute the crime with which he is charged.").

[46] *See* Sandstrom v. Montana, 442 U.S. 510, 524 (1979).

[47] 718 F.2d 1210, 1224 (2d Cir. 1983), *cert. denied*, 466 U.S. 971 (1984).

[48] 941 F.2d 71 (2d Cir. 1991), *cert denied*, 502 U.S. 1091 (1992).

> Absent the Commissioner's consent, a taxpayer who has used a particular depreciation method may not defend an evasion charge on the ground that, under an alternative method, additional depreciation could have been claimed. *See Fowler v. United States*, 352 F.2d 100 (8th Cir. 1965), *cert. denied*, 383 U.S. 907 (1966). In *Fowler*, appellants were convicted of tax evasion and argued that the district court erred in excluding expert testimony that appellants could have taken greater depreciation on certain assets had the useful life of the assets been calculated under a different method. The Eighth Circuit disagreed, explaining that the exclusion of expert testimony was proper because appellants had "elected one method of determining depreciation and that election binds them for purposes of this action." *Id.* at 106.
>
> The law could hardly be otherwise. If it were, evaders with complicated returns would be allowed to evade taxes on one portion of their return while using a depreciation period that would be the most profitable in the long run if the evasion went undetected. If the evasion were uncovered, then they would need only to recalculate under a shorter depreciation period that would increase deductions for the years in which evasion is charged.[49]

This quote from *Helmsley* should not be read too literally to reject unclaimed deductions to eliminate tax due and owing, which, after all, is an element of the crime of tax evasion. The court was focusing only upon changing a method of depreciation which would generate the additional deductions. Under the method the defendant elected in filing her returns, the additional depreciation was not available and could only become available upon request to, and with the consent of, the Commissioner. As the Supreme Court said in *Sansone*, defendants in evasion cases can prove unclaimed deductions in order to eliminate the tax due and owing element of the crime.[50]

In *Siravo v. United States*,[51] the Government introduced evidence that the defendant had understated the gross income from his manufacturing business. The defendant argued that the Government failed to carry its burden of showing that he did not have labor costs offsetting the proved gross receipts. The court disagreed that the Government has any such burden.

> The applicable rule here is that uniformly applied in tax evasion cases — that evidence of unexplained receipts shifts to the taxpayer the burden of coming forward with evidence as to the amount of offsetting expenses, if any. Indeed, this case is necessarily included in that rule. For in a tax evasion case the government's ultimate burden is to show that the taxpayer received not only gross income but also taxable income, after deduction of

---

[49] *Id.* at 86–87. It should be noted, however, that the Supreme Court appeared to approve of the offsetting deduction defense. Sansone, *supra*, 380 U.S. at 352–53 ("if the jury believed that an understatement of deductible expenses had offset the understatement of gross receipts, while the defendant would have violated § 7207 by willfully making a material false and fraudulent statement on his return, he would not have violated § 7201 as there would not have been the requisite § 7201 element of a tax deficiency.").

[50] *Id.*

[51] 377 F.2d 469 473–474 (1st Cir. 1967).

> capital and non-capital expenses. If that is satisfied by proof of sales receipts, absent explanation, so must be the lesser burden here.[52]

The court held, however that if a defendant does offer evidence of offsetting costs, the burden is on the Government to persuade the jury that the costs are not allowable.[53] Thus, as we discuss in more detail in Chapter 2A, the critical issues in a trial will be whether the issue is in play and what level of proof is required for the defendant to have the issue of unclaimed deductions presented to the jury.

C. Good-Faith-Belief Defense

One of the elements of most tax crimes is willfulness — the Government must show that the defendant willfully evaded taxes or willfully filed a false return. Thus, the Government must prove that the defendant knew what the law provided and intentionally violated the law. This definition raises several avenues of opportunity for the defense. For example, the defendant may introduce evidence that he was mistaken as to the state of the law or that he had a good-faith misunderstanding as to what the law provided. Such a defense would negate willfulness and would enable the jury to acquit. On the other hand, a good-faith belief that the law is unconstitutional is *not* a defense to willfulness.[54]

Can a defendant assert reliance on the advice of counsel or other tax professional in showing a lack of willfulness? It depends upon the circumstances. If the defendant is arguing that he did not know what the law provides or that he believed a transaction to be legitimate, the defendant may properly assert a reliance defense. One court has held: "It is a valid defense to a charge of filing a false return if a defendant provides full information regarding his taxable income and expenses to an accountant qualified to prepare federal tax returns, and that the defendant adopts and files the return as prepared without having reason to believe that it is incorrect."[55] However, if the charge is failure to file a tax return, the law is clear that a taxpayer may not rely on or delegate to a professional the duty to file a timely tax return.[56]

The reliance-on-the-professional defense is a variation of the *Cheek* argument (i.e., the defendant did not know the law) and technically is an argument that the Government failed to meet its burden to prove willfulness, rather than a defense per se. The Government thus has to show that the defendant did not rely upon the tax professional in order to show willfulness. But, as in *Cheek*, the defendant has to put the "defense" in play by introducing some evidence of reliance on the tax

---

52 *Id.* at 473–74.

53 It is important to distinguish between the tax due and owing as an element of the tax evasion offense (which is a key element of the offense in the criminal trial case in chief) and the tax loss (which is the principal factor in computing the sentencing guideline range). Some courts do not permit unclaimed deductions in the calculation of the tax loss for sentencing, whereas courts seem to consistently permit unclaimed deductions to be in issue in the case in chief. We shall discuss this again in Chapter 10.

54 *See, e.g.*, Cheek v. United States, 498 U.S. 192, 201–06 (1991).

55 United States v. Whyte, 699 F.2d 375, 379–80 (7th Cir. 1983).

56 United States v. Boyle, 469 U.S. 241, 249–50 (1985).

professional. Once the defendant does that, it is then the Government's burden to show that the defendant did not rely.[57]

One way the Government can meet its burden is through the tax professional.[58] The tax professional may, however, have a bias to remember the events in a way that favors the professional rather than the defendant. By asserting reliance on the tax professional, the defendant waives any privilege (other than his own Fifth Amendment privilege, unless he has to waive it to assert the defense) that might otherwise apply. The tax professional may be called by the Government. Often the tax professional can testify as to certain representations made by the defendant or advice given to the defendant and that alone may be sufficient to rebut the defense or even affirmatively hang the defendant. Indeed, if there is no affirmative evidence of proper advice by the tax professional, the defendant may be convicted on the tax professional's testimony that it was his usual practice to give such proper advice. And, perhaps even more dangerously, any hope to successfully mount the defense will require the defendant to take the stand, thereby waiving his Fifth Amendment privilege. Doing so will open up the defendant to cross examination on the reliance issue and any other issue.

D. Cash-Hoard Defense

In Chapter 4, we discussed the various methods of proof, including the specific items, net worth, and bank deposit methods. In the indirect methods of proof, the Government must prove an increase in net worth or that deposits into the defendant's bank accounts proved unreported income. The most common defense to these indirect methods of proof is that the defendant had substantial quantities of cash at the beginning of the period under investigation. This defense is known as the cash hoard defense.[59] A typical cash hoard defense asserts that the defendant in earlier years received money from sources such as gifts or an inheritance, which he then spent during the prosecution period. The Supreme Court described the cash hoard defense as follows:

> Among the defenses often asserted is the taxpayer's claim that the net worth increase shown by the Government's statement is in reality not an increase at all because of the existence of substantial cash on hand at the starting point. This favorite defense asserts that the cache is made up of many years' savings which for various reasons were . . . not expended until the prosecution period. Obviously, the Government has great difficulty in refuting such a contention.[60]

While proving the negative that the defendant did not have cash is difficult, the Government must nevertheless establish with "reasonable certainty" the amount of

---

[57] United States v. Stadtmauer, 620 F.3d 238, 257 n.22 (3d Cir. 2010) ("to prove willfulness beyond a reasonable doubt, the Government would have to negate the [defendant's] claim that he relied in good faith on the advice of his accountant.").

[58] Note how the Government used the fact that Wesley Snipes consulted with one of his tax advisors to demonstrate he knew that his "861 argument" was meritless. *See* Appendix D, para. 26.

[59] United States v. Schafer, 580 F.2d 774, 779 (5th Cir.), *cert. denied*, 439 U.S. 970, (1978).

[60] Holland v. United States, 348 U.S. 121, 127 (1954).

cash that the defendant had in his possession at the beginning of the tax period.[61] The CTM instructs that one way to defeat such a claim is to show that the family member or friend alleged to be the source of the cash did not have sufficient resources to give the defendant the amount claimed.[62] The allegation of cash on-hand at the beginning of the prosecution period presents a factual issue for determination by the jury. Once the Government has established that a thorough investigation failed to uncover evidence of cash on hand, the burden shifts to the defendant to come forward with evidence of cash, and he remains silent at his peril.[63] As long as there is evidence from which a jury can conclude that the Government has established the amount of cash on hand with reasonable certainty, the defendant is not entitled to a judgment of acquittal on this issue.[64]

E. Fifth Amendment Defense

Criminal tax cases are littered with constitutional claims made by defendants. The tax protest movement in particular has spawned many constitutional defenses, all of which are spurious and some are down-right hilarious.[65] One example of a novel, but seriously-argued claim involves the gold-fringed flag defense.

> Various litigants, including tax defiers, argue that the placement in a court room of a gold-fringed American flag denotes: (1) admiralty jurisdiction; (2) suspension of constitutional governmental functions; and/or (3) martial law. Litigants call the gold-fringed American flag the "maritime flag of war," and claim its display signifies "[d]eprivation of rights under color of law." They maintain that a court that flies a gold-fringed flag: (1) lacks jurisdiction over those coming before it; and (2) deprives the litigant of due process rights.[66]

A sometimes valid constitutional defense is the Fifth Amendment right against self-incrimination. In *United States v. Sullivan*,[67] the Supreme Court held that the privilege against self-incrimination is not a defense to prosecution for failure to file, that is, a defendant may not rely on the Fifth Amendment in not filing at all. The Court stated in *dicta*, however, that the privilege could be claimed, in appropriate circumstances, as to specific information sought on a return. "If the form of return provided called for answers that the defendant was privileged from making he could have raised the objection in the return, but could not on that account refuse to make any return at all."[68] *Sullivan* is frequently cited for the proposition that a taxpayer may refuse to answer specific questions or disclose specific information if that disclosure would be incriminating. The courts have uniformly held, however, that disclosure of routine financial information on a tax return ordinarily does not, in itself, incriminate an individual, and does not violate the Fifth Amendment right

---

61 United States v. Wilson, 647 F.2d 534, 536 n.1 (5th Cir. 1981).

62 CTM 31.06[1].

63 United States v. Mackey, 345 F.2d 499, 506 (7th Cir.), *cert. denied*, 382 U.S. 824 (1965).

64 *See, e.g.*, United States v. Blandina, 895 F.2d 293, 302 (7th Cir. 1989).

65 For a discussion of various constitutional claims made by tax protestors, see CTM 40.05.

66 CTM 40.05[4][b] (citation omitted).

67 274 U.S. 259 (1927).

68 *Id.* at 263.

against self-incrimination.[69] However, a determination that the defendant's claim of the Fifth Amendment privilege is invalid does not prevent the defendant from arguing that he believed in good faith that he could properly assert the privilege. A good-faith Fifth Amendment claim, even if erroneous, is a valid defense to the element of willfulness.[70]

F. Statute of Limitations Defense

Perhaps the most important affirmative defense in tax cases is the statute of limitations. Section 6531 controls the statute of limitations periods for most criminal tax offenses. Under section 6531, the general rule is that the statute of limitations for criminal tax offenses is three years. However, the exceptions to the three-year rule essentially swallows up the general rule. The CTM includes a helpful table that sets forth the limitations periods for common tax offenses:[71]

Offense	Code Section	Statute of Limitations	Code Section
Tax Evasion	§ 7201	6 years	§ 6531(2)
Failure to Collect or Pay Over	§ 7202	6 years	§ 6531(4)
Failure to Pay	§ 7203	6 years	§ 6531(4)
Failure to File	§ 7203	6 years	§ 6531(4)
Failure to Keep Records	§ 7203	3 years	§ 6531
Failure to Supply Information	§ 7203	3 years	§ 6531
Supply False Withholding Certificate	§ 7205	3 years	§ 6531
False Tax Return	§ 7206(1)	6 years	§ 6531(5)
Aid or Assist in False Tax Return	§ 7206(2)	6 years	§ 6531(3)
Deliver or Disclose False Document	§ 7207	6 years	§ 6531(5)
Attempt to Interfere with Administration of Internal Revenue Laws	§ 7212(a)	6 years	§ 6531(6)
Conspiracy to Commit Tax Evasion	18 U.S.C. § 371	6 years	§ 6531(8)
Conspiracy to Defraud	18 U.S.C. § 371	6 years	§ 6531(1)
False Claim for Refund	18 U.S.C. § 286/ 287	5 years	18 U.S.C. § 3282
False Statement	18 U.S.C. § 1001	5 years	18 U.S.C. § 3282

[69] *See, e.g.*, California v. Byers, 402 U.S. 424, 428, 430 (1971) ("the mere possibility of incrimination is insufficient to defeat the strong policies in favor of a disclosure").

[70] *See, e.g.*, United States v. Goetz, 746 F.2d 705, 710 (11th Cir. 1984).

[71] CTM 7.01[2].

The statute of limitations defense is generally raised in a pretrial motion under Fed. R. Crim. P. 12 or at the latest, at trial. Significantly, a defendant may waive the defense either by a knowing voluntary waiver or, since it is an affirmative defense, by failure to assert the defense timely.[72]

1. When the Statute of Limitations Begins to Run

The statute of limitations begins to run when an offense is completed, that is, when all of the elements have occurred to complete the offense.[73] However, even if all of the elements have occurred by a certain date, the defendant may later take some action that will extend the statute. For example, in a tax evasion case the statute of limitations usually begins to run when a false return is filed. But if one of the affirmative acts of evasion charged is a subsequent false statement to IRS agents, the crime is completed at the time the false statement is made, not when the false return is filed.[74] Thus, the statute begins to run from the date of the last affirmative act. This is the case even when the return filed that is the subject of the evasion charge was filed outside the statute of limitations period.

For example, in *United States v. King*,[75] the defendant was a tax protestor who filed false Forms W-4 claiming excessive exemptions. An employer receiving suspicious W-4s is required to notify the IRS, and if the IRS has reason to believe that the W-4 forms are incorrect, the IRS can direct the employer not to honor the forms. In *King*, the defendant filed two such Forms W-4, the employer dutifully notified the IRS, and the IRS directed the employer not to honor the forms. However, for subsequent years the IRS did not direct the employer to refuse to honor the W-4s, and the employer honored them. The taxpayer did not file a tax return for any year after his first W-4 filing. The Government charged King with tax evasion for the years 1989 through 1991. The indictments were returned more than six years after the year King submitted his false W-4 to his employer, but within six years of the 1989 return being filed. The taxpayer argued that his tax evasion charge was outside the statute of limitations because it was based on the false W-4 that had been filed outside the statute. The taxpayer referred to the Regulations which said that a Form W-4 expires on February 15 after the year in which it is filed, even though some employers continue to honor a W-4 until a superseding form is filed. The Court rejected the argument that the false W-4 could not form a basis for indictment because it had technically expired, reasoning:

> If a defendant files a Form W-4 in which he falsely claims to be exempt from withholding, and he keeps the fraudulent form on file indefinitely, all the while believing that his employer will honor it until he files a new one, it is

---

[72] *See* United States v. Ramirez, 324 F.3d 1225 (11th Cir. 2003) (holding that, when the facts related to the statute of limitations defense are undisputed, the defense can be raised at trial to resolve the disputed facts but that, whne the facts related to the defense are undisputed from the face of the indictment, the defense is waived if not raised in a pretrial motion under Rule 12), *cert. denied*, 540 U.S. 881 (2003).

[73] Toussie v. United States, 397 U.S. 112, 115 (1970).

[74] United States v. Beacon Brass Co., 344 U.S. 43 (1952); United States v. Goodyear, 649 F.2d 226 (4th Cir. 1981).

[75] 126 F.3d 987 (7th Cir. 1997).

> only logical that the fraudulent W-4 may supply the affirmative act for § 7201 charges in later years, regardless of the fact that it technically expired pursuant to Treasury regulations. Maintaining a Form W-4 on file with one's employer effectively represents that one is still entitled to the number of allowances or exempt status claimed. If the form is false, the form certainly has the capacity to deceive for as long as it is kept on file. In this case, the fact that [the employer] failed to compel King to file a new W-4 each year, as requested by the IRS, in no way mitigates King's § 7201 liability. To find otherwise would be to allow the negligence of an employer to accrue to the benefit of an employee who has contravened the law in the first place by filing a false and fraudulent Form W-4. It would be inappropriate for us to judicially sanction a tax loophole like that.[76]

The defendant also argued that the required affirmative act (here the filing of the false W-4) must have occurred within the six-year statute of limitations in order to support timely criminal prosecution. The court rejected that argument as well, holding:

> This argument is unavailing. The indictment properly alleged that King's offenses occurred on the due dates of his returns for the prosecution years. A § 7201 offense is not complete until a tax deficiency exists, and a deficiency will not arise until the due date of a tax return. And, as we will discuss below, the act of filing and maintaining on file a false Form W-4 carries over to future years if the defendant files with the requisite intent to evade taxes.[77]

If the act that starts the running of the statute of limitations is the filing of a false return, when is the return considered to have been filed, the date the taxpayer mails the return, the date the return is received by the IRS, or some other date? The answer is, as always, it depends. The general rule is that the statute of limitations for the filing of a false tax return starts on the date the return is actually filed, that is the date received by the IRS.[78] However, if the return is filed prior to the due date for filing (*e.g.*, before April 15), section 6513(c)(1) provides that the statute of limitations does not start to run until the due date of the return. For example, if the taxpayer filed the return on March 15, the statute of limitations would begin to run on April 15. On the other hand, if the return is filed after the original due date, the statute of limitations begins running the day the return was actually filed, regardless of whether an extension was filed. For example, where a taxpayer was granted an extension to October 15 to file a return, but the return was actually filed on October 1, the statute of limitations begins to run on October 1. In addition, a return that is mailed on or before the due date of the return is deemed filed on the date of the postmark, regardless of whether it is received and processed by the IRS after the due date.[79] If the crime charged is failure to file a return, the statute of limitations begins to run when the return is due. If a defendant obtained an

---

[76] *Id.* at 991.

[77] *Id.* at 992.

[78] United States v. Habig, 390 U.S. 222, 223 (1968).

[79] IRC § 7502.

extension of time to file a tax return, the statute begins to run on the extension date.[80]

2. Statute of Limitations and Conspiracy Under 18 U.S.C. Section 371

The general statute of limitations for Title 18 offenses is five years.[81] However, if the offense charged is a conspiracy to commit an offense under the Internal Revenue Code or a conspiracy to defraud the IRS, section 6531 provides for a six-year statute of limitations. Defendants charged with tax conspiracy under section 371 have argued that the general five-year statute of limitations under 18 U.S.C. section 3282 should apply. The courts have routinely rejected this position and affirmed the application of the six-year limitations period to tax conspiracies.[82]

Similar to the tax evasion discussion above, the statute of limitations in a conspiracy begins to run from the date of the last overt act proved. In order for the overt act to count in the statute of limitations determination, the overt act must be in furtherance of the conspiracy. In *Grunewald v. United States*, the Supreme Court held that "the crucial question in determining whether the statute of limitations has run is the scope of the conspiratorial agreement, for it is that which determines both the duration of the conspiracy, and whether the act relied on as an overt act may properly be regarded as in furtherance of the conspiracy."[83] Thus, an act that is not in furtherance of a conspiracy but seeks to cover up a completed conspiracy does not necessarily start the statute of limitations running again. Of course, if the object of the conspiracy itself was to conceal the conduct in question, as is the case with many *Klein* conspiracies, the initial conspiracy carries through the acts in furtherance of that object.[84]

The Government is not required to prove that each member of a conspiracy committed an overt act within the statute of limitations period. Once the Government shows a member joined the conspiracy, his continued participation in the conspiracy is presumed until the object of the conspiracy has been achieved.[85] As discussed in Chapter 3, a member of a conspiracy may withdraw from the conspiracy. If the evidence shows that the defendant withdrew from the conspiracy before the expiration of the applicable limitations period (*i.e.*, more than six years prior to the indictment), withdrawal is a complete defense to a conspiracy charge. But if members wish to withdraw, they must do more than just stop taking an active role: "Mere cessation of activity is not enough to start the running of the statute; there must also be affirmative action, either the making of a clean breast to the authorities, . . . or communication of the abandonment in a manner reasonably

---

80 Phillips v. United States, 843 F.2d 438, 442–43 (11th Cir. 1988).

81 18 U.S.C. § 3282.

82 *See, e.g.*, United States v. Aracri, 968 F.2d 1512, 1517 (2d Cir. 1992).

83 Grunewald v. United States, 353 U.S. 391, 397 (1957).

84 *See, e.g.*, United States v. Vogt, 910 F.2d 1184, 1201–02 (4th Cir. 1990), *cert. denied*, 498 U.S. 1083 (1991); United States v. Pinto, 838 F.2d 426, 435 (10th Cir. 1988).

85 Grunewald, *supra*, at 397; Hyde v. United States, 225 U.S. 347, 369–70 (1912).

calculated to reach co-conspirators."[86] The defendant has the burden to prove withdrawal.[87]

3. Suspension and Tolling of the Statute of Limitations

While the statute of limitations generally expires within six years of the time the offense is completed, certain events can suspend or toll the running of the statute of limitations for tax crimes. First, the flush language of section 6531 contains its own tolling provision: "The time during which the person committing any of the various offenses arising under the internal revenue laws is outside the United States or is a fugitive from justice within the meaning of section 3290 of Title 18 of the United States Code, shall not be taken as any part of the time limited by law for commencement of such proceedings." Thus, the statute of limitations can be tolled if the defendant is outside the United States *or* is a "fugitive from justice." The terms "outside the United States" and "fugitive from justice" have been interpreted in the disjunctive. Mere absence from the United States without any intent to become a fugitive is sufficient to toll the statute of limitations.[88] As to the term "fugitive from justice," the circuits are split as to the intent required under this statute, with some circuits holding that mere absence from the jurisdiction, regardless of intent, is sufficient to toll the statute of limitations,[89] while other have held that intent to avoid arrest or prosecution must be proved before the person becomes a fugitive.[90]

Section 6531 also provides for extension of the statute of limitations period, "where a complaint is instituted before a commissioner of the United States within the period above limited, the time shall be extended until the date which is nine months after the date of the making of the complaint before the commissioner of the United States." The Government may file a complaint within the limitations period and effectively extend the statute period nine months. This is not a general grant to the Government for more time to bring an indictment. Rather, it was intended to be used in situations where the Government has made its case within the limitations period but cannot obtain an indictment within the limitations period because of the grand jury schedule.[91]

Outside of section 6531, section 7609(e) provides for the tolling of the statute of limitations in certain cases where there is not timely compliance with an IRS administrative summons. If the taxpayer files a motion to quash or intervenes in a

---

[86] United States v. Borelli, 336 F.2d 376, 388 (2d Cir. 1964) (internal quotation marks and citation omitted).

[87] Smith v. United States, 133 S. Ct. 714, 719 (2013) ("While the Government must prove beyond a reasonable doubt every fact necessary to constitute the crime with which the defendant is charged, . . . proof of the nonexistence of all affirmative defenses has never been constitutionally required. . . . Withdrawal does not negate an element of the conspiracy crimes charged here.").

[88] United States v. Marchant, 774 F.2d 888, 892 (8th Cir. 1985) (defendant's 11-day health and pleasure trip to Switzerland tolled the statute of limitations), *cert. denied*, 475 U.S. 1012 (1986).

[89] *See, e.g.*, In re Assarsson, 687 F.2d 1157, 1162 (8th Cir. 1982).

[90] *See, e.g.*, United States v. Marshall, 856 F.2d 896, 897–900 (7th Cir. 1988); United States v. Wazney, 529 F.2d 1287, 1289 (9th Cir. 1976).

[91] Jaben v. United States, 381 U.S. 214, 219–220 (1965).

summons enforcement proceeding, the statute is tolled during the period of the proceeding and any appeals. Tolling also occurs in the case of the issuance of any IRS administrative summons with no resolution as to the summonsed party's compliance. In that case, the statute is tolled from six months after the date of the summons until the party's compliance with the summons is resolved.

Section 3292 of Title 18 provides for the suspension of the statute of limitations to permit the United States to obtain foreign evidence. As the U.S. economy becomes more global, so do the tax schemes. Criminal tax prosecutions increasingly involve the use of evidence obtained from foreign sources. Chapter 7 discusses the methods by which the Government endeavors to obtain foreign evidence. We won't repeat that discussion here. For this discussion, section 3292 tolls the statute upon a Government application to a district court within the normal statute of limitations period if it has made an official request to a foreign government for evidence. The limitations period is tolled until the foreign government takes final action on the request, up to a maximum period of three years. The official request must be incident to a grand jury investigation and must be "a letter rogatory, a request under a treaty or convention, or any other request for evidence made by a court of the United States or an authority of the United States having criminal law enforcement responsibility, to a court or other authority of a foreign country."[92]

Finally, the statute of limitations is tolled during the course of a Collection Due Process appeal. Under sections 6320 and 6330, a taxpayer may appeal the IRS' issuance of a notice of intent to levy or a notice of federal tax lien to IRS Appeals and ultimately to the United States Tax Court. Section 6330(e) provides that the statutes of limitations, both the civil statute for collection as well as the criminal statute under section 6531, are suspended for the period during which the appeal is being considered and for an additional 90 days after the determination with regard to the appeal is made. This is yet another instance in which civil tax procedure has a direct impact on your criminal practice.

PROBLEM

You are preparing for the April 16, 2015 conference with the Tax Division CES attorney who is tasked with reviewing IRS CID's recommendation that your client be prosecuted. Your job is to convince the attorney to drop the charges. Your review of the file shows the following facts: Your client is a 72 year-old man named Paul. Paul has been the CEO and sole shareholder of a lumber company, St. Claire Lumber, located in Wisconsin. St. Claire Lumber is a C corporation, and it has annual gross sales of $30 million. Paul has been the driving force behind the company since its inception in 1958, and until recently there has not been even a whiff of problems with him or the company. However, in the last few years, Paul's behavior has become erratic. His temper is at times volatile and abusive, and he has been struggling with a fairly serious prescription drug problem. His doctor diagnosed him last year as having beginning stages of Alzheimer's disease. His wife, who used to be the company's bookkeeper, has left him because of his behavior. The IRS has been investigating St. Claire Lumber's corporate returns for

92 18 U.S.C. § 3292(c).

2007 through 2011. The CES attorney informed you that the CID agent has recommended indictment for tax evasion for both the corporate and Paul's personal returns, in violation of section 7201, and for conspiracy to commit tax evasion, in violation of 18 U.S.C. section 371. From interviews with Paul and from a detailed analysis by a forensic accountant you retained, you learn the following additional facts:

- There have been approximately $500,000 in withdrawals in each of the years 2007–2011 from the corporation's bank account into a bank account in Rochester, MN. The name on the Account is the Paul St. Claire Family Trust. The trust is a grantor trust, with Paul and his ex-wife as beneficiaries.
- The withdrawals were never reflected as compensation to Paul, nor were those amounts ever included in the corporation's income. Paul blames his ex-wife for what he refers to as a bookkeeping blunder. He says the amounts should have been treated as deferred compensation, which is why he did not report them on his personal return. He says that he did not extensively review the corporate return, but relied on his ex-wife and others to get the numbers right.
- St. Claire Lumber is a calendar year taxpayer. All of the corporation's returns for the years at issue were filed timely on March 15, and all of Paul and his ex-wife's joint returns were filed timely on April 15. The trust filed tax returns for all of the years as well, but the $500,000 deposits were never reflected on those returns.
- When the case was first being investigated by a civil Revenue Agent in 2011, Paul told the agent that he knew nothing about a trust bank account in Rochester, MN. Paul now claims he was merely mistaken, since he thought the bank account was in Duluth, MN, where he has a vacation home.
- In addition to his tax problems, Paul is also under criminal investigation by the local district attorney's office stemming from his prescription drug abuse.

1. With what crimes and for what years could the Government charge Paul and the corporation?

2. What defenses might you raise in the conference with the attorney?

3. Before you make your presentation at the conference, whom else might you want to interview and what other facts would you like to learn?

Chapter 6

INVESTIGATION AND DEVELOPMENT OF CRIMINAL TAX CASES

IRC: §§ 7602(b) & (c), 7608(a) & (b)

Regs: IRS Procedural Reg. § 601.107

I. INTRODUCTION

Chapter 1 described in skeletal fashion the key actors in the criminal tax process and the nature of criminal tax investigations. This Chapter 6 puts meat on those bones. The chapter considers the players in the criminal tax system and the administrative, grand jury, and hybrid channels through which criminal tax cases are developed. Thereafter, it considers the principal types of criminal tax cases and prosecution standards. Finally, this chapter discusses two strategic matters arising early: voluntary disclosure and egg shell audits.

II. THE PLAYERS

Both IRS and DOJ personnel are involved in the criminal tax system. Below, we describe the roles of IRS civil agents, Special Agents, and CI Counsel and of attorneys from DOJ Tax and the U.S. Attorneys Offices. We do so roughly in the order in which they enter the process.

A. IRS Civil Agents

IRS civil audits are performed by Examination personnel with various titles. In terms of their interface with the criminal tax system, Revenue Agents (typically the IRS's best trained and most experienced auditors) are the most important. Similarly, IRS collection work is performed by other civil personnel with various titles, most prominently Revenue Officers.[1]

As relevant here, Revenue Agents enter the process at three points. First, as discussed more fully in Part III below, referrals from Revenue Agents is a common path by which cases reach CI.[2] When a Revenue Agent or other examining agent conducting an audit has a firm indication of fraud, the agent will suspend further

---

[1] For further description of IRS functions and personnel, see David M. Richardson, Jerome Borison & Steve Johnson, Civil Tax Procedure ch. 1 (2d ed. 2007).

[2] To a lesser extent, cases involving evasion of payment after assessment may be referred to CI by Revenue Officers.

activity. Nothing further will happen on the civil side until the criminal referral is resolved either by prosecution or declination.

Second, after referral to CI, Special Agents may be assisted by one or more civil agents. The civil agents often are more adept at discovering and resolving any technical tax issues and in making the required tax computations.

Third, after resolution of the criminal aspects (whether by prosecution or declination), control of the case will be returned to the Examination function for completion of the audit and implementation of civil assessment procedures.[3] Thus, at least historically, the criminal facet of the case takes priority over the civil facet. This historic tendency may be mitigated somewhat by recent policy permitting parallel civil and criminal proceeding in some cases.

B. Special Agents

When CI gets the case from a civil agent (or other source), there will be new players. One or more CI agents, referred to as "Special Agents," will have primary authority for the case.

CI's staffing fluctuates. In recent years, CI has had about 2800 to 3000 Special Agents. Like other parts of the IRS, CI undergoes reorganization from time to time. Broadly speaking, CI has both national office and field functions. The national office sets policy and coordinates activities among areas. Special Agents in the field are divided among about three dozen local offices — often directed by Special Agents in Charge (SACs) — among fraud detection centers at IRS service centers, and among a number of liaison offices in foreign countries.

A Special Agent typically works on a variety of cases simultaneously and usually will have four or more major investigations ongoing at any given time. Special Agents are assisted by several types of nonagent CI personnel, including Investigative Analysts, Tax Fraud Investigation Assistants, Compliance Support Assistants, and computer specialists. During the pendency of the criminal investigation, CI will monitor and control the accounts of target taxpayers so that examination or collection activity does not occur that could compromise the criminal investigation.

C. CI Counsel

CI Special Agents may also be assisted by IRS Counsel who are in-house lawyers for CI. Such lawyers serve as advisors to CI during the investigation and help determine whether the case is appropriate to refer to DOJ. In their role as advisors, CI Counsel are available to assist with respect to legal issues and strategies. How involved Counsel may be during any given investigation varies. In the past, when Counsel was physically and institutionally separate from CI, Counsel's role was often more passive during CI's investigation. Now, with Counsel assigned to CI, Counsel is more proactive in counseling during the investigation and influencing the shape of the investigation. From the IRS's perspective, this

[3] Or, if post-assessment, control of the case will be returned to the Revenue Officer for initiation or resumption of collection procedures.

may mean higher quality investigations with fewer legal problems.

Often, the practitioner will not be aware of Counsel's role because it is played out behind the scenes. The astute practitioner will be able to see indications of Counsel's involvement in, for example, the document description in the summons (the "duces tecum" part of the summons). But there is usually nothing the practitioner can do other than observe and extrapolate as to what is happening with Counsel and what Counsel's involvement may mean for the client.

Counsel will become more active in those rare instances in which the investigation requires pre-referral interface with DOJ or the courts. The classic instance of this is when the agents desire a search warrant in support of the investigation. In that case, DOJ must be convinced to seek the search warrant and the court must review the request under the constitutional probable cause standard. Counsel is required to review and approve all Title 26 search warrants.

D. DOJ Tax

The IRS typically initiates criminal investigations, but DOJ controls whether the target will be prosecuted and, if so, for what charges. The two components of DOJ that are of principal significance are DOJ Tax (also called "Main Justice" in criminal tax circles) and the United States Attorney's Offices (USAOs).

Main Justice has a Tax Division, presided over by an Assistant Attorney General. The Tax Division has civil trial and appellate sections and, as relevant here, a Criminal Enforcement Section (CES). CES reviews potential criminal tax cases for suitability, and its attorneys sometimes try or assist in the trial of cases that proceed to prosecution.

There is a USAO in each of the country's judicial districts. Line attorneys in these offices are known as Assistant United States Attorneys (AUSAs). AUSAs try most of the criminal tax cases that go to trial. AUSAs also typically conduct grand jury proceedings as to both investigating and charging grand juries.

DOJ (either through DOJ Tax or the USAO) generally has no role in administrative investigations. Section 6103 prohibits the IRS from sharing any return information (virtually everything the IRS knows about the taxpayer) with DOJ personnel, unless and until either the IRS has referred the case to DOJ for criminal prosecution or a high ranking DOJ official has made written request for information. These strictures mean that DOJ has no legal role in an IRS administrative investigation. Where CI agents need legal advice during the IRS phase of the criminal investigation, they seek it from IRS Counsel.

There is one exception to this noninvolvement of DOJ during an administrative investigation. This occurs if the Special Agents desire to obtain a search warrant. In that event, the Special Agents will generally seek the assistance of the USAO.

DOJ Tax retains control over prosecution of tax crimes. Centralization and coordination are imperatives based upon the goal of the criminal tax system to support general tax compliance. This control is inherent in the processing of criminal tax investigations from CI through DOJ Tax. Thus, although the IRS usually investigates tax crimes, DOJ determines which among those investigated will be prosecuted.

The following is excerpted from an article written by Mark Matthews, former Deputy Assistant Attorney General in charge of CES.[4] The purpose of the article is to explain the Tax Division's function to AUSAs who approach tax cases differently than does the Tax Division. The article addresses concerns that usually arise when an AUSA is conducting a separate criminal investigation and has the opportunity to add a tax count or even feels that a tax count is the only way to nail a bad guy. The AUSA is not free to add tax counts just to further other goals. The article also addresses the situation in which the Tax Division has authorized one or more tax counts, has designated which counts are appropriate for a plea, and the AUSA believes that some other plea may be appropriate based on his or her view of the case.

> The Tax Division's criminal sections provide two basic criminal litigation roles: one is very popular; the other often decidedly unpopular. The popular role [is] direct and indirect litigation assistance to USAOs. The Tax Division provides very welcome and "user friendly" litigation assistance and expertise in evaluating and litigating tax cases. In fact, AUSAs are often thankful for the Tax Division attorney who is willing to wade into the mounds of paper in a complex tax case or the piles of frivolous motions filed by an illegal tax protester and for his or her contributions to the indictments, convictions, and sentences generated by complex tax litigation.
>
> The more difficult aspects of our relationship arise in the review process. This second, occasionally contentious, role is critical to the Tax Division, but is often dreaded by the AUSA and IRS case agent. The congenial relationship between the Tax Division and the local United States Attorney begins to deteriorate when we find it necessary to decline a case or a particular count or defendant. It becomes particularly more contentious when we decline to authorize a plea to a tax charge, which you believe would greatly simplify some difficult case in your district. This article attempts to explain what you might perceive as a schizophrenic Tax Division. How did the Division that produced an aggressive litigator who tried that difficult case for your district last year become such a meticulous, cautious reviewer, pointing out the problems in your case this year?
>
> In the review process, the Tax Division spends a lot of time listening to the concerns of AUSAs regarding the "how to's" of handling tax cases and dedicates a lot of energy to figuring out ways to make cases fit within Tax Division guidelines and meet the AUSA's goals as well. Frankly, as a former AUSA, I think I can safely attest that, in relation to handling the complexities of a tax investigation and weighty case load, AUSAs don't spend much time worrying about the Tax Division's mission and concomitant problems. I hope that this article will provide a useful perspective for

---

[4] Mark Matthews, *Through the Looking Glass: Reconciling the Mission of the Tax Division with the Goals of the United States Attorneys' Offices in Tax Prosecutions*, 46/3 USA BULLETIN 7 (Apr. 1998).

you or, at a minimum, help you to better evaluate your tax case's chances in the Tax Division.

The Tax Division review process can only be understood in terms of our mission. In all of law enforcement, we represent the extreme of general deterrence. We are trying to deter more taxpayers (over 200 million) with fewer prosecutions (approximately 1,500) than any other area of law enforcement. And, unlike other areas of law enforcement where the goal is usually to stop clearly unlawful conduct, we in the tax administration business have the goal of influencing hundreds of millions of Americans to take the affirmative steps of completing and filing often complex tax returns and making substantial payments to Uncle Sam.

This is a difficult mission by any measure, and we work hard to enforce compliance while ensuring uniform, fair enforcement in order to generate confidence in the system. One measure of our success is the "tax gap," which is the difference between what should be reported as owing and paid to the Government each year versus what is actually reported and paid. That figure is currently-estimated to be approximately $100 billion per year.[5] The Internal Revenue Service (IRS) estimates that the compliance rate is approximately 83 percent.

This tax gap is what causes us to place such a premium on every criminal tax case. Each tax case must be used to deter people who cheat or are willing to cheat on their taxes, but against whom we do not have the resources to investigate or prosecute. In these circumstances, it is easy to understand why we consider a tax case that is not publicized in any way a waste of resources. Even worse is a tax case that, if publicized, would undermine the voluntary compliance system. That can occur when the public perceives that the tax code has been used unfairly in some case, or more frequently, when the case and result is such that the public will perceive that perpetrators of tax crimes receive only a slap on the wrist, implying that tax crimes are somehow less serious than other Federal cases.

It is this phenomenon that sometimes challenges the relationship between a USAO and the Tax Division. The USAO tends to view a case through a more narrow lens than the Tax Division. The AUSA is concerned with effectuating substantial justice vis-à-vis a particular defendant in a particular factual circumstance. While those concerns are important to the Tax Division as well, we are much more focused on the impact the case will have on the public at large and tax compliance more generally. The AUSA may have a more acute understanding of the judge selected to handle the tax case or the likely reactions of local jurors to particular facts and witnesses. Therefore, the USAO frequently comes to the Tax Division with particular plea or charging proposals based on their view of the case, the

---

[5] [Authors' note: According to this 1998 article, the compliance rate was about 83% and the tax gap about $100 billion. By 2006, the compliance rate was about 80% and the tax gap was over $350 billion. *See* Richardson, Borison & Johnson, *supra*, at 94–95.]

judge, and the defendant and his or her attorney. We are often presented with a view that a particular course is the most appropriate or best the Government can achieve under the circumstances. We give great deference to those views, and in the vast majority of cases, come to agreement without much difficulty. The problem comes when we conclude that, despite the great weight given local views, the proposal is unacceptable because of its potential to undermine tax compliance and uniformity.

The most dramatic example of this tension arises when a Title 18 investigation has become more complex than anticipated, and the Government is looking for an efficient and just way to dispose of the case. In this often-repeated theme, a Title 18 investigation has begun and perhaps even been indicted with great prospects. The IRS is probably not involved in the case or is the tail on the dog of a much bigger case. In many instances, the Title 18 investigation or prosecution has received media attention, perhaps based, in an indicted case, on a press release announcing the Government's great efforts to address a particularly grave circumstance. Unfortunately, something has happened on the way to the jury. It could be the death of a witness; the unavailability of foreign evidence; the appearance of a dubious, but perhaps convincing alibi; the departure of the lead AUSA in a complex case; etc. The reason doesn't really matter; we often will agree that a serious problem has occurred.

The difficulty for the Tax Division occurs when the prosecutor and the defense attorney come to an agreement that a tax plea is a graceful way out for both parties. Often, the defense attorney is content with this result because the proposed sentencing guidelines will allow for an "acceptable" sentence, frequently probation or home confinement. We often understand that the proposal, viewed narrowly within the confines of the particular case, represents the most attractive alternative from your perspective. But when we evaluate this proposal in terms of our tax compliance mission, it presents us with great difficulty. We face the prospects of having the public perceive that a more "serious" Title 18 crime has been disposed of with a tax "slap on the wrist." We can actually write the defense attorney's statement to the media about how the Government, having utterly failed to prove the false and malicious charges against his or her client, has brought this "technical" tax case to which the client has reluctantly agreed to plead, particularly because no jail time is likely. We are concerned that taxpayers (who aren't committing other Title 18 crimes) will receive an erroneous message from this result. They will perceive that if these bad folks committing other crimes are pursued for tax crimes and receive small sentences, that they will not be pursued and will certainly avoid any jail sentence. Such a result is particularly damaging to tax enforcement.

A corollary problem for the Tax Division is this — to endorse the proposed course means that scarce resources available to prosecute tax crimes will be spent on a case that actually undermines compliance. A Criminal Investigation Division (CID) agent will still have to generate a special agent's report, and IRS counsel and Tax Division resources will be spent evaluating the plea. We have spent the last three years attempting to redress a sharp decline in CID resources directed to tax enforcement as opposed to narcotics and money laundering crimes. Plea agreements that do not take into consideration the tax enforcement mission of the Tax Division undermine these efforts.

As we begin to discuss these concerns with USAOs, we are sometimes confronted with an incredulous response along the following lines: "Would you rather have us let a criminal go completely free (or run a greater risk of an acquittal than normal)?" From the standpoint of the central mission of the Tax Division, the answer is "yes," we sometimes see a greater harm to tax administration from accepting that plea than from failing to charge the defendant or from dismissing the case.

Now, the good news is that we only infrequently face these more dramatic examples of conflict. Tax Division attorneys work with AUSAs to find a way out of the dilemma whenever possible. Because we are willing to give substantial weight to the views and concerns of USAOs, we struggle for alternative solutions or modifications to cases that will conform to Tax Division guidelines.

Less dramatic cases arise every day, however. We are asked to approve a failure to file misdemeanor when the facts more clearly show felony conduct. Or we are asked to approve a tax plea before the factual basis has been developed. Or we are asked to authorize a Spies evasion when other taxpayers have been charged with a failure to file on similar facts. These kinds of cases raise not only the issues above with respect to tax compliance, but also raise another important issue for the Tax Division — the uniform treatment of taxpayers. Given the applicability of our tax laws to all Americans, it is exceedingly important that they perceive the system as fundamentally fair. This means that the Government must act uniformly and fairly, and that, all factors being equal, the taxpayer referred for criminal prosecution in District A gets the same treatment as the taxpayer referred for prosecution in District B.

A breakdown in uniform treatment through disparate prosecution decisions, declinations, or pleas can harm voluntary compliance in other ways. The tax defense bar is a close knit group that meets often and exchanges information at the national level. Actions in one seemingly remote case can quickly wind up being used affirmatively against the Government in another setting.

This uniform treatment is a hallmark of why the Tax Division was created. The lack of a nationwide clearinghouse could (and did) generate diverse results that could undermine tax compliance. You may present what looks like an acceptable tax charge, but the Tax Division may oppose it on uniformity grounds. It may be that you propose a case with dollar thresholds substantially below those normally used by the IRS and the Tax Division. Or you may propose a case where the evidence of willfulness, while not negligible, differs substantially from the degree of proof we have required against other taxpayers. Or you may propose a criminal prosecution in an area of the tax code that has not been criminalized before and where there has been no antecedent aggressive civil enforcement by the IRS. In all of these instances, depending on the facts and other circumstances, the Tax Division may be much less enthusiastic about your case as a matter of fundamental fairness to other similarly situated taxpayers.

A more dramatic example illustrates the tension. We occasionally see proposed tax investigations or charges that involve political or other public figures. The structure of the entire tax review system, including career professionals at the IRS Chief Counsel's office and in the Tax Division, ensures both the reality and the public perception that individuals charged with criminal tax violations are selected for the crimes they commit, not because of who they are. No one involved in these cases wants a case to be, or to be perceived to be, investigated or brought for improper reasons. The availability of Tax Division review helps prevent either occurrence.

We occasionally receive comments during a review process that note the expertise and freedom of USAOs in many other areas of complicated white collar crimes. We, in the Tax Division recognize that expertise and struggle mightily not to convey the impression that we disagree because we are just wiser. It is simply that, unlike some USAOs, which at best see a couple dozen tax prosecutions a year, we see them all. We know precisely how we've handled similar matters in other districts. It is that experience that we bring to bear in the review process. I am quick to note, however, that the Tax Division and its prosecution policies have benefited greatly from the contribution of AUSAs, particularly a core of very experienced and committed Federal prosecutors who are very enthusiastic about tax enforcement. Further, I encourage you to contact the Tax Division in the early stages of a case so that we can work together to resolve any issues concerning the appropriate disposition of the case.[6]

III. ADMINISTRATIVE CASES

The traditional means of developing a criminal tax case is the so-called administrative route. This part describes administrative cases from six perspectives: (1) origin of the case; (2) investigation by CI; (3) moving the case from CI to DOJ; (4) case processing by DOJ; (5) conferences between the target and the Government; and (6) bringing criminal charges.

A. Origin of the Case

Traditionally, the largest stimulus for criminal tax investigations was IRS civil audits of tax returns. The IRM contains detailed instructions to Revenue Agents and other Examination personnel as to when to suspect that tax fraud has been committed.[7] The IRM identifies various badges of fraud, organized categorically as

---

[6] Matthews, *supra*, at 7–10.

[7] In this regard, the IRM does not distinguish qualitatively between civil and criminal fraud, but describes them as differing only in the requisite degree of proof: "beyond a reasonable doubt" for criminal purposes and "clear and convincing" for civil purposes. IRM 5.12.1.

to income, expenses or deductions, books and records, taxpayer conduct, and methods of concealment. Substantive clues include large unexplained increases in net worth and excessive deductions. Behavioral clues include procrastination, uncooperative attitude, quick agreement to adjustments, undue concern about closing the case quickly, concealing or destroying records, and transferring assets.[8] Obviously, care and discrimination is needed in applying such guidance since, read expansively, one or another badge of fraud arguably would exist in most, if not all, civil audits.

When the Revenue Agent observes affirmative acts or indications of fraud, the agent typically discusses the matter with his or her superior: the Group Manager or equivalent. They will then seek the aid of an IRS Fraud Referral Specialist, who is in the same division of the IRS and so is easily accessible to the agents. These officials will formulate a plan, if needed, to resolve "holes" in the development. Once they conclude that there are "firm indications necessary for a successful fraud case,"[9] the case will be referred to CI. Typically, the acceptance rate for such referrals is around 50%.

The volume of referrals from Examination to CI has fluctuated. After traditionally being the main source of criminal cases, such referrals declined for several decades at the end of the twentieth century. In the last few years, however, they appear to have been rebounding somewhat, as was discussed in Chapter 1 in connection with the Webster Report. In addition to referrals from other parts of the IRS, CI sometimes receives referrals from other federal or state agencies[10] whose work has uncovered indications of tax crimes.

Another source of case initiations is informants. CI assorts them into three classes: (1) anonymous informants; (2) confidential sources of information; and (3) confidential informants.[11] The second and third classes are eligible for rewards[12] although reaching agreement with the IRS about eligibility for and the amount of a reward is not always a smooth operation.[13] Who become informants for the IRS? If you're thinking former or disgruntled spouses[14] and former or disgruntled employees,[15] you've identified two of the leading categories.

---

[8] IRM 104.2.2.1 & 2.

[9] IRM 104.2.2.1(1).

[10] The IRS has announced nationwide expansion by 2009 of the State Reverse Filing Match Initiative, one of several programs in which the IRS and state tax departments share information to enhance income tax collection. *See* Karen Setze, *IRS-State Information Sharing Initiative to Go Nationwide in 2009, Brown Says*, TAX NOTES, June 18, 2007, at 1103.

[11] IRM 9.3.2.5.2. The difference between the second and third classes is that the confidential sources provide information they already know while confidential informants gather additional information at the direction of the IRS.

[12] IRC § 7623.

[13] The Tax Relief and Health Care Act of 2006, Pub. L. No. 109-432, attempted to ease such problems in order to enhance incentives for, especially, high-end whistle-blowing. *See* Jeremiah Coder, *IRS CI Division to Stay "Aggressive" Under New Chief*, TAX NOTES, May 21, 2007, at 705, 706.

[14] *E.g.*, United States v. Jackson, 578 F.2d 1162 (5th Cir. 1978).

[15] *E.g.*, United States v. Feffer, 831 F.2d 734 (7th Cir. 1987).

In addition to the foregoing, CI initiates some criminal investigations on its own. Special Agents read the newspapers and follow other media, alert for situations fraught with criminal tax potential. In addition, CI reviews forms filed under the Internal Revenue Code and the Bank Secrecy Act. Such forms include Forms 4789 and 8300 filed with the IRS or the Financial Crimes Enforcement Network ("FinCEN"). Similarly, CI has been receiving an increasing number of Suspicious Activity Reports ("SARs") filed by banks, brokerage houses, and other financial institutions.[16]

B. Investigation by CI

The Special Agents assigned to the case investigate through interviews with the target taxpayer, his or her representatives, and third parties involved in the relevant transactions. The Special Agents also attempt to gather pertinent documents. The techniques of CI information gathering and the major issues they raise are explored in Chapter 7.

C. Moving the Case from CI to DOJ

1. Recommending Criminal Prosecution

When CI concludes the investigation, it has two choices. First, and better for the taxpayer, CI could decline criminal prosecution and refer the case back to Examination. Second, CI could forward the case to DOJ with a recommendation for criminal prosecution. We shall focus on this second alternative.

CI recommends criminal prosecution when the case is otherwise within its priorities and "the evidence is sufficient to indicate guilt beyond a reasonable doubt; and a reasonable probability of conviction."[17] Typically, of course, CI will not have devoted investigative resources to a matter not within the priorities. But, if it has done so and has a substantial investment in the matter, CI may be inclined to recommend prosecution of a case only marginally within its priorities. It then becomes the lawyer's job to convince CI that it should not prosecute despite this investment of time. Failing convincing CI of that, the advocate may have a better opportunity of focusing this type of argument at the later decision points (DOJ Tax and, conceivably, the United States Attorney), who will have neither a time nor an emotional commitment to the case and can take a broader view of the Government's priorities.

2. The Special Agent's Report

CI prepares a Special Agent's Report (referred to as an SAR). The SAR pulls together the investigative work and tells the story of why the case is worthy of criminal prosecution. The SAR also develops the sentencing factors based on the

---

16 *See, e.g.*, Jon Almeras, *Fraud Referrals up, CI Official Says*, TAX NOTES, May 21, 2007, at 709 (quoting CI Deputy Chief John Imhoff to the effect that SARs provide great leads and are a "great tool for law enforcement").

17 IRM 31.31.1(1).

Sentencing Guidelines. The SAR will form the basis for further consideration in the steps between CI and actual criminal prosecution. The SAR will also be considered in the sentencing phase if the taxpayer is convicted.

Consistent with the general rule in our criminal tax system that the taxpayer is not entitled to discover the Government's criminal case (except, as discussed in Chapter 8, in the context of criminal discovery at the trial stage), the SAR is not provided to the target(s) of the investigation until much later in the process, if at all. By careful attention to the Special Agent's activities during the investigation, however, astute taxpayer's counsel will frequently have a very good idea of the contents of the SAR.

3. DOJ Referral

The IRS will refer a case for prosecution only "where the evidence is sufficient to indicate guilt beyond a reasonable doubt and where there appears to be a reasonable probability of conviction."[18] If the IRS decides to refer the case to DOJ with a recommendation for prosecution, the Special Agent will put the final touches on the SAR and Counsel will prepare a Criminal Reference Letter (CRL), which is a comprehensive summary of the recommendation and its basis.[19] In many respects, the CRL parallels the SAR, which is far more detailed and contains extensive exhibits in support. The contents of the CRL generally include discussion of the following topics:

- (a) Referral. The general nature of the referral and the statute of limitations;
- (b) Venue;
- (c) Case Origin and Initial Contact;
- (d) Taxpayer's Background;
- (e) Tax Liabilities and Computations;
- (f) Theory of Case;
- (g) Criminal Offense;
- (h) Principal Evidence;
- (i) Willfulness;
- (j) Indirect Methods of Circumstantial Proof;
- (k) Conferences and Defenses;
- (l) Sentencing Guidelines Calculations and Issues;
- (m) Whether any civil action has occurred or will or should occur;
- (n) Enclosed Transmittals. This will include, for example, the detailed SAR and its exhibits;
- (o) Return of Case Materials;
- (p) Pretrial Diversion;

---

[18] IRM 31.4.14.1(1).

[19] *See* IRM 31.4.7.

(q) Conclusion. The conclusion will include a statement "that Counsel is convinced of guilt beyond a reasonable doubt and believes there is a reasonable probability of conviction."[20]

In addition, the CRL may include a discussion of potential impeachment information about the Special Agents who may testify at trial.[21] Obviously, the CRL would be an invaluable document to obtain, but it is confidential.

D. Processing by DOJ

All recommendations except money laundering recommendations have elaborate processing and review requirements in CES. The requirements are designed to insure the case's suitability under the priorities for the criminal enforcement system. Money laundering recommendations are forwarded directly to the USAO since they do not implicate the criminal tax enforcement system. When, however, the money laundering charges are closely related to the tax recommendations, they will be processed the same as the tax recommendations. The following describes the processing of the CRL in the garden variety tax case.

1. Main Justice

CES attorneys review the CRL and make a recommendation as to whether to authorize criminal tax prosecution. The Assistant Attorney General or her delegate then makes the decision whether to prosecute.

The role of CES would be hard to overstate. All criminal tax prosecutions must be approved by CES (including the Assistant Attorney General who oversees CES) or must fall under one of the advance approval systems for certain limited types of cases. CES must insure that all tax prosecutions are consistent with national enforcement priorities. The practitioner must have some sense of national criminal tax enforcement priorities and the limited resources that require CES to only authorize prosecutions consistent with those priorities. Some taxpayers who have had the misfortune to slip through the IRS to CES may still not be within those enforcement priorities, and a case can still be made to the CES that they should not be prosecuted.

2. AUSA

Upon receipt of authorization from CES, the AUSA will seek an indictment from the grand jury or conduct such further grand jury investigation as may be necessary. On rare occasions, CES's decision to prosecute may not sit well with the United States Attorney or the AUSA. The USAO may not have the staff to handle the matter or its priorities may be elsewhere. The AUSA who would have to present the case to the grand jury and try the case may not think much of the case. The case can be sent back to CES for reconsideration, but if CES is intent upon prosecuting and cannot get the USAO to handle it, CES will field the attorneys required to present to the grand jury and try the case. Usually, however, there is a good

---

[20] IRM 31.4.7.2.

[21] ILM 199902018, *reproduced at* 1999 TNT 11-48 (Jan. 19, 1999).

working relationship between the USAO and CES and the processing of criminal tax cases in the USAO is quite professional.

As soon as the taxpayer's attorney has been advised that the case has been referred to the USAO, the taxpayer's attorney should contact that office, determine the AUSA to whom the case is assigned, and contact that AUSA. Although stopping the train is unlikely at that stage, defense counsel won't stop it unless he or she tries.

E. Conferences

1. CI Conferences

If the practitioner becomes convinced that there is a substantial possibility that CI will refer the case to DOJ, the practitioner should request a conference prior to the referral. The conference is the last shot at stopping the referral. Because CI has by that time determined to make the referral, stopping the referral is a long shot indeed. The practitioner should, however, attend and participate, at least at some level.

CI will usually grant the requested conference if it has tentatively decided to refer the case to DOJ Tax.[22] The conference will generally include the SAC or a person designated by the SAC, the Special Agent conducting the investigation, his or her manager, and perhaps CI Counsel. Generally, the conference must be formally requested by the taxpayer or his counsel although Special Agents occasionally suggest that one should be requested. A CI conference is not available if a grand jury is investigating the putative crime and the Special Agent involved is an assistant to the grand jury under Rule 6(e).

Whether the taxpayer himself should attend any such conference is a judgment call. Experienced counsel will usually discourage the taxpayer from attending. A taxpayer will communicate something to the IRS's attendees, even if only by body language. There is great risk that the communication will not be good. Without the taxpayer present, the taxpayer's attorney can focus on the presentation he or she wishes to make and on properly interpreting the IRS personnel's communications without being distracted by concern that the taxpayer may do something counter-productive.

The purpose of the conference is to permit the taxpayer's counsel to make any arguments and present any facts she may have to convince the IRS that the case should not be referred to DOJ Tax with a recommendation for prosecution. At the conference, CI will generally provide an oral statement of certain basic information for which a prosecution recommendation is being considered.[23] Practically, this means that CI will advise of the charges, the years, and the tax loss numbers involved. Despite the fact that the conference is not offered to allow discovery of the Government's case, the astute practitioner may learn a good deal from the

---

[22] *See generally* IRM 9.5.12. The provisions therein have not been updated based upon the new structure of CI after the reorganization based upon the Webster Report.

[23] IRS Proc. Reg. § 601.107(b)(2); IRM 9.5.12.2.2.

disclosures the IRS does make and from the nature of the questions they ask.

Many practitioners view the conference as a mere formality in terms of really trying to convince CI to change its mind. By that time, CI will have done a lot of work and is not likely to change its recommendation barring some blockbuster countervailing evidence. Even if counsel for the target has such evidence, he may be loath to play his hand at that stage. And, except in the rare case, such blockbuster evidence and arguments are not usually available. Instead, the target's counsel usually has various threads of evidence and arguments that might ultimately be persuasive at trial (particularly if the Government has not fully anticipated them) and is reluctant to play his hand at that stage for fear that CI will not be persuaded and CI and DOJ Tax will then be prepared to anticipate and deal with the defenses.

Many practitioners will nevertheless pursue a CI conference even while keeping their cards close to the vest in order to "discover" as much as possible about CI's case. Of course, the careful practitioner will have tracked the CI investigation from the beginning and will likely know more than CI knows and, equally important, will know the information that CI knows and therefore will have a good idea of the basis for the criminal recommendation. But the practitioner might still want to get a better feel for what is motivating CI. A carefully orchestrated CI conference sometimes permits the practitioner this type of additional discovery. The practitioner may thus make a presentation that really offers CI nothing more than it already knew and gives no insight into the taxpayer's defenses, but by playing back what the IRS already knew and making the obvious arguments (*i.e.*, the ones that would not have escaped CI anyway), the practitioner may flush out comments and questions from the CI agents that give significant insights into their thinking and the shape of the recommendation that will be made. This can be invaluable in marshalling the taxpayer's defenses in the later stages of consideration and in the trial.

2. DOJ Tax Conferences

DOJ Tax will also generally grant the taxpayer's representative a conference prior to authorizing prosecution.[24] As with the CI conference, the taxpayer's representative will be provided only limited information — basically the same information that CI provides with any adjustments that DOJ Tax may think is appropriate. However, as with the CI conference, in the give-and-take of the DOJ Tax conference, the astute practitioner may be able to learn other features of the case.

Moreover, in some cases, the DOJ conference can result in DOJ declining to pursue the case. That does not happen often, but, in the right case, this is an opportunity for defense counsel to pursue. If the DOJ Tax attorney tries the case, there will be opportunities in the pre-trial phase and even pre-indictment phase for the practitioner to have discussions with that prosecutor to further develop information in the client's best interests.

Taxpayers are usually afforded a conference in Washington and should make the request for the conference when advised that the case has been referred to CES.

---

[24] CTM 2.00 incorporating USAM 6-4.214; *see also* CTM DIR. 86-58 (May 30, 1986).

Some experienced practitioners make the request to CES for a conference when they first begin to believe that a referral to DOJ Tax is likely. The thinking is that, although CI may notify the taxpayer's attorney when the case is referred to CES, something may prevent a timely request after receipt of the formal notice. Advance notice will avoid the risk that the request would not otherwise be made for whatever reason. CES will receive the advance request and, when the case is referred, then treat the advance request as a timely request for conference.

The DOJ CES conferences (like the IRS conferences) are offered as a matter of Government general practice, but they are not matters of right. Thus, the Government may indict without offering the conferences.[25]

3. Conferences with AUSA

The taxpayer will usually have an opportunity to meet with the AUSA to try to thwart the prosecution although such a meeting is within the discretion of the AUSA. If such a meeting is held, it might offer the best opportunity to discover at least some of the Government's case. Similarly, there will be opportunities in the pre-trial phase and even pre-indictment phase for the practitioner to have discussions with the AUSA to further develop information and initiatives in the client's best interests.

F. Criminal Charges

1. Indictment, Information, or Complaint

The bringing of criminal charges marks the transition from the investigation phase to the prosecution phase. The charge is brought by an indictment issued by a grand jury, unless the defendant agrees to be charged by information.[26] Both the indictment and the information should be a plain, concise statement of the essential elements of the crimes charged. Sample indictments are in Appendices C, D, and E of this book.

The indictment or information begins a criminal case, as a complaint begins a civil case. It sets in motion the various procedures for processing the case to judicial resolution. It is not uncommon for the Government to file one or more superseding indictments. This is done to clean up problems in the first indictment and sometimes to add additional charges.

Sometimes the Government needs to start a criminal proceeding before an indictment can be obtained. The Government may file a complaint, which is "a written statement of the essential facts constituting the offense charged."[27] When a complaint is filed, upon a showing of probable cause to believe that a crime has been committed and that the individual named in the complaint committed it, the magistrate judge will issue an arrest warrant or, upon request of the Government,

---

[25] United States v. Ohle, 678 F. Supp. 2d 215, 233 (S.D.N.Y. 2010).

[26] Fed. R. Crim. P. 7(a) & (b).

[27] Fed. R. Crim. P. 3.

a summons.[28] As in grand jury proceedings, the determinations may be based upon hearsay evidence.[29] These are interim procedures to permit the Government to take action in exigent circumstances before the constitutionally required indictment can be obtained. For example, if a person who the Government believes should be considered for indictment is about to leave the country, the Government may file a complaint in order to obtain an arrest warrant.

When the Government thereafter presents the matter to the grand jury, it is possible that the grand jury will not indict. Federal grand juries consist of between 16 and 23 jurors.[30] Fed. R. Crim. P. 6(f) provides: "If a complaint or information is pending against the defendant and 12 jurors do not concur in finding an indictment, the foreperson shall so report to a federal magistrate judge in writing forthwith." This will result in a dismissal of the complaint or information. An indictment must be signed by the attorney for the Government.[31]

Given the standards that CES imposes for referring the matter to the grand jury in the first case, an indictment will probably come forth in the shortest time that the USAO's priorities permit. This is subject to one caveat as to timing. CES often prefers that tax indictments come in time that publicity could influence taxpayers during the filing season. Late March or early April indictments occur frequently. This timing may also be influenced by statute of limitations considerations. Frequently, the statute of limitations will fall on April 15, so that an indictment on or before April 15 is necessary to preserve the statute of limitations for the earliest prosecution year.

The indictment will usually be preceded by the lead Special Agent giving grand jury testimony as to his version of the taxpayer's skullduggery and offenses to the tax system. The testimony will be laced with hearsay, speculations, and even some hard evidence, but the grand jury will usually not bestir itself to ask critical questions or really understand the details of what happened. In short order, an indictment will come forth.

CES may require, or the AUSA may conduct, further investigation prior to seeking an indictment. If that occurs, the time to indictment will be longer. But even so, an indictment is usually forthcoming because CES will not usually refer the case for further investigation unless it believes the further investigation is likely to result in indictment. If there are simply too many holes of uncertain scope in the investigation, CES will usually kick the case back to the IRS, with either an admonition to close the case or to get it right before sending the case back.

Counsel should attempt to debrief any witnesses that appeared before the grand jury. Normally matters occurring before the grand jury are secret.[32] Grand jury witnesses, however, may disclose the contents of their testimony.[33] Also, witnesses

---

28 Fed. R. Crim. P. 4(a).

29 Fed. R. Crim. P. 4(b).

30 Fed. R. Crim. P. 6(a).

31 Fed. R. Crim. P. 7(c)(1).

32 Fed. R. Crim. P. 6(e).

33 Fed. R. Crim. P. 6(e)(2).

do not have to actually appear before the grand jury for their testimony to be considered by the grand jury. Hearsay testimony before the grand jury is acceptable, so frequently the IRS agents (or other Government agents) assigned to assist the grand jury in the investigation will interview witnesses who have been subpoenaed or threatened with a subpoena, and then those agents will summarize the information provided by the witness.

How will counsel know which witnesses have been subpoenaed or threatened with a subpoena? Counsel usually won't know unless the person subpoenaed or threatened tells since that information also is grand jury information that can be disclosed only by the witness. Thus, as a cautionary matter, counsel should contact persons who might be potential witnesses. If they will talk (there is no requirement that they do), counsel can debrief them to find out what they may have told the agents and/or the grand jury, what documents they provided the agents and/or the grand jury, and perhaps other useful information. (If counsel had been involved in the IRS administrative investigation phase, he or she might well have already interviewed the witness, but counsel should do so again to find out the focus of the grand jury investigation phase.) A financial institution may be prohibited from disclosing its receipt of a grand jury subpoena and delivery of documents to the grand jury for a period of 90 days.[34]

During this period, the taxpayer's counsel can consider what might be available through plea bargaining. Counsel can start that process upon the referral to DOJ Tax and, if no agreement is reached, continue it with the AUSA. Counsel also may want immunity for the client. Immunity requires that the client have something to offer the Government. In the typical criminal tax case, the client has nothing to offer but himself. Hence, plea negotiations offer the more fruitful possibilities.

2. Arrest or Summons for Initial Appearance

Historically, in tax cases, the attorney will have had substantial discussions with the AUSA shortly prior to the indictment. In those negotiations, the attorney will want to attempt to negotiate the process whereby the taxpayer or defendant makes his or her initial appearance. USAOs are beginning to insist that the taxpayer be formally arrested pursuant to an arrest warrant issued when the indictment is returned. Previously, at least in tax cases, the AUSA would usually agree, upon request, not to proceed by arrest warrant, but instead to issue a summons for the initial appearance before the federal magistrate judge. (Requiring arrest of a defendant who clearly will appear pursuant to a summons seems to make no sense and is one of the counterproductive fallouts of Enron and related excesses where the U.S. Attorney wanted to make a point with formal arrests, handcuffing, and transport to the courthouse. Hopefully, as we put these financial excesses behind us, clearer perspective will show that formal arrests should not be required when they really are not necessary.) Counsel will, of course, double check at this opening stage to see whether the statute of limitations bars prosecution for any or all of the charged offenses.[35]

---

[34] 12 U.S.C. § 3413(I).

[35] Statutes of limitations are discussed in Chapter 5.

3. Pre-Arraignment Issues

If the indictment does not fairly advise the taxpayer of the charge, counsel will want to consider filing a bill of particulars under Fed. R. Crim. P. 12. A bill of particulars serves the limited role of advising the defendant of the nature of the charge; it is not a discovery device.[36] A request for a bill of particulars is addressed to the sound discretion of the trial judge.

In addition to the arrest, counsel will want to negotiate issues such as conditions of release, bail if the Government desires bail, and the position the AUSA may take as to travel outside the district, including notice of travel and possession of a passport. Counsel will, of course, want to consider continuing the plea negotiations or starting them if they have not been had before.

4. Arraignment

At the arraignment, of course, the client will plead not guilty.[37] It is possible that a plea agreement could be reached and entered at the arraignment, but that is not usual in tax cases. At the arraignment, the Government may ask for bail or the court may raise the issue sua sponte. Counsel will seek release on the client's own recognizance unless, in the expectation of the court imposing bail, counsel has agreed in advance to the Government's bail request as a way to mitigate the damage.

In addition, the defendant will usually be asked to consider signing a waiver of the Speedy Trial Act,[38] which otherwise requires that a criminal defendant be brought to trial within seventy days from the latest of the arrest, the filing of an indictment, or the first appearance before the court. If there is no waiver and the time limit is exceeded, an indictment "shall be dismissed on motion of the defendant," with or without prejudice.[39] Certain delays are excludable from the 70-day period.[40] For example, court-ordered delays are excludable if the court makes a finding that the ends of justice served by the continuance "outweigh the best interest of the public and the defendant in a speedy trial."[41] Also, delays caused by pretrial motions are excluded as long as the delays are reasonable.[42]

Following the arraignment come the pre-trial, trial, sentencing, post-trial, and appellate phases. These are discussed in Chapters 8, 9, and 10 of this book.

---

[36] *E.g.*, United States v. Smith, 776 F.2d 1104, 1111 (3d Cir. 1985); United States v. Addonizio, 451 F.2d 49, 63 (3d Cir. 1971). In *United States v. Whatley*, 480 F. Supp. 307, 309 (W.D. Okla. 1978), the court noted the importance of a bill of particulars in a tax case in order "to enable the accused to prepare his defense and avoid surprise at trial, and a motion for a bill of particulars in a tax case should be liberally construed."

[37] Arraignments are addressed in Fed. R. Crim. P. 10.

[38] 18 U.S.C. §§ 3161-74.

[39] 18 U.S.C. § 3162(a)(2).

[40] *See* 18 U.S.C. § 3161(h).

[41] 18 U.S.C. § 3161(h)(8)(a).

[42] 18 U.S.C. § 3161(h)(1)(f); *see* Henderson v. United States, 476 U.S. 321, 323 (1986).

IV. GRAND JURY CASES

For our purposes, there are two kinds of grand juries, depending on their use: charging and investigative grand juries. Part III above described charging grand juries, *i.e.*, those used to obtain indictments. This Part IV describes investigative grand juries. As the name implies, investigative grand juries are used to investigate possible tax or related offenses, either as supplements to or replacements of the administrative investigative process described in Part III.

In most cases, the IRS prefers administrative investigations because they are more susceptible to the Service's institutional controls. However, in particularly important or visible cases, the Government often prefers to use a grand jury because it is a more effective investigative tool. Grand Jury investigation cases of this nature have recently included (i) the sprawling tax shelter criminal cases where many participants and several major professional firms (such as KPMG, Deutsche Bank and Jenkins & Gilchrist, a now defunct law firm) were involved and (ii) the juggernaut against UBS AG, a major Swiss bank, which marketed secret offshore accounts to U.S. persons and thereafter the investigation and prosecution of UBS account owners. Moreover, a grand jury is usually preferred in cases in which possible tax charges are mixed in with non-tax offenses which already are, or soon will be, subject to grand jury proceedings.

Despite the historical primacy of the administrative route, investigative grand juries have been involved in about half of all CI investigations in recent decades. Either CI or a USAO may initiate a request for use of an investigative grand jury.[43] In either event, such use usually must be approved by DOJ Tax.[44] However, USAOs are authorized — without needing prior approval from DOJ Tax — to expand non-tax grand jury investigations to include possible tax violations if there is reason to believe that such violations have occurred and the IRS has been asked, and has agreed, to provide assistance.

Subject to any applicable privileges, grand juries can compel testimony by witnesses via subpoena and can compel production of documents via subpoena duces tecum. A further aid to developing information is the ability to grant immunity. Immunity is not required in routine, legal source tax cases but may be useful in penetrating complicated, multi-actor schemes.

Witnesses are not entitled to have counsel with them during their testimony to the grand jury.[45] However, witnesses are permitted to step outside the grand jury room to consult with their attorneys.[46] The courts are divided as to whether and when a grand jury witness can obtain access to the transcript of his or her own testimony.[47] Grand jury testimony may be used against the witnesses,[48] but they

---

[43] IRM 9.5.2.2.

[44] CTM 2.00, incorporating USAM 6-4.121 & .122. CT Counsel often will review grand jury requests in tax cases. IRM 9.5.2.3.1.4.

[45] *E.g.*, Kirby v. Illinois, 406 U.S. 682 (1972).

[46] *E.g.*, United States v. Levinson, 405 F.2d 971 (6th Cir. 1968), *cert. denied*, 395 U.S. 906 (1969).

[47] A recent circuit court case noted the division, ruled that the appropriate test involves balancing of interests, and held that the witnesses were entitled under Rule 6(e)(3)(E)(i) to review transcripts of their

are entitled to assert the Fifth Amendment privilege against self incrimination.

An AUSA typically controls the grand jury proceeding. One or more Special Agents may assist the AUSA, but the agent's use of credentials is limited to identifying the agent as an "assistant to the attorney for the government in conjunction with a grand jury investigation."[49] Special Agents are authorized to conduct witness interviews and to receive subpoenaed documents outside the presence of the grand jury and the prosecutor. Civil actions against the subject of the grand jury investigation are suspended while the investigation is in progress absent specific approval to the contrary.

In a grand jury investigation, information may be solicited only for criminal purposes.[50] Grand jury proceedings and matters revealed before the grand jury are to be kept confidential by the jurors and Government personnel. However, the IRS may obtain such information for civil use in a number of ways. For example, (i) witnesses are free to discuss their testimony with anyone,[51] (ii) material may be disclosed to the IRS for civil purposes if the IRS makes a strong showing of "particularized need,"[52] (iii) grand jury materials that are "of public record" may be used,[53] (iv) material gathered in anticipation of grand jury consideration but which does not reveal the contents of grand jury proceedings, may be used civilly,[54] and (v) material predating the grand jury and independently generated, may be used civilly.[55]

After conclusion of the grand jury investigation, the IRS decides what, if any, tax charges to recommend for prosecution. Recommendations for prosecution of tax charges must be submitted to DOJ Tax for authorization. Taxpayer's counsel may request a conference with DOJ Tax.

V. HYBRID CASES

The normal rules as to administrative cases and grand jury cases can be varied to respond to exigencies. Impending expiration of the statute of limitation, flight of the target, concealment of assets, destruction of evidence, and the like may lead to streamlining or omitting some customary procedural steps.

---

own grand jury testimony in private at the USAO or a place agreed upon by the parties or designated by the court. It left to the sound discretion of the trial court whether to permit the witnesses' attorneys to accompany the witnesses as they reviewed the transcripts and whether to allow the witnesses or their lawyers to take notes. In re Grand Jury, 490 F.3d 978 (D.C. Cir. 2007) (per curiam).

[48] U.S.A.M. 9-11.260.

[49] IRM 9.5.2.5.3.

[50] United States v. Baggott, 463 U.S. 476 (1983). Grand jury materials may be disclosed to Special Agents in order "to enforce criminal law." Fed. R. Crim. P. 6(e)(3)(A)(ii).

[51] Fed. R. Crim. P. 6(e).

[52] United States v. Sells Engineering, 463 U.S. 418 (1983).

[53] *E.g.*, Bell v. Commissioner, 90 T.C. 878 (1988) ("[W]hen once-secret grand jury material becomes sufficiently widely known, it may lose its character as Rule 6(e) material"); In re Grand Jury, 490 F.3d 978 (D.C. Cir. 2007) (per curiam) (quoting In re North, 16 F.3d 1234, 1245 (D.C. Cir. 1994)).

[54] *E.g.*, Lombardo v. Commissioner, 99 T.C. 342 (1992).

[55] *E.g.*, United States v. Dynavac, Inc., 6 F.3d 1407 (9th Cir. 1993).

In addition to administrative and grand jury processes, tax crimes may come into the Government's cross-hairs in other ways in which the IRS and DOJ Tax may not be in the direct chain of processing. For example, a drug task force may desire to charge tax crimes incidental to the drug crimes it charges against a target of the investigation, perhaps based on the Capone factor (*i.e.*, that's the only way we can get the crook). For this purpose, even if a conviction on the drug charges could be obtained, the tax crime will not be grouped with the drug crimes, and thus, could have an enhancing effect on sentencing under the guidelines. The prosecutor(s) on a drug task force must seek DOJ Tax approval to charge tax crimes.[56] Further, in order to preserve its authority over tax crimes, DOJ Tax also has authority over Title 18 crimes related to tax crimes — such as mail fraud when the criminal act is the mailing of a return or form to the IRS.[57]

VI. TYPES OF CASES

CI has publicly announced compliance strategies to assist in identifying, developing, and investigating cases to foster confidence in the tax system and compliance with the tax law.[58] Here are some of the important enforcement and compliance categories.

A. Legal Source Cases

As discussed in Chapter 1, consistent with the Webster Report, the IRS is refocusing its efforts on legal source cases. Legal source cases are those in which the principal focus of the investigation is traditional tax crimes, not Title 18 or Title 31 crimes. Basically, this means a focus on people with income from legal sources who are not paying their taxes. CI will still be substantially involved in illegal source income and money laundering investigations, but will expend more of its resources on legal source cases. Within this area, the following items are among those that have hit CI's radar screen.

1. Nonfiler Enforcement Program

There are a large number of nonfilers who operate outside the tax system. An IRS-wide strategy is designed to bring them back into the system. CI's role in this strategy is to identify persons who have not responded to the IRS's efforts to bring them back into the system and to criminally prosecute them in order to encourage others to comply.

2. Employment Tax Enforcement Program

The IRS has identified significant noncompliance with respect to employment taxes. Even before a recent wave of protestor cases in which some small business owners simply refused to comply based on a host of frivolous arguments, the IRS had identified significant schemes in various iterations in which taxes were withheld

---

[56] USAM 6-4.218.

[57] CTM 2.00, incorporating USAM 6-4.210.

[58] CI's website, http://www.treas.gov/irs/ci/, sets forth some of its priorities and initiatives.

but not turned over to the IRS. In addition, there is traditional noncompliance exemplified by cases such as *Evangelista* (excerpted in Chapter 2B) involving section 7202 prosecution.

3. Abusive Trust Schemes

The IRS has identified a number of abusive trust schemes. Although there are various iterations, one such scheme might involve the use of several trusts that at some point move income offshore without paying tax on it. Such trusts are used essentially to hide the ball. There are both domestic trust schemes and foreign trust schemes, all of which are designed to conceal otherwise taxable income and create deductions for personal living expenses.

B. Illegal Source Cases

The IRS pursues illegal source income through a number of operational strategies, including a fraud program and a narcotics program. The fraud program covers "a broad range of illegal activity, primarily within legal industries."[59] The fraud program has a number of subprograms dealing with, among others, bankruptcy, excise tax violations, financial institution fraud, gaming, health care fraud, insurance fraud, public corruption, questionable refunds (including questionable earned income credit refunds), return preparer fraud, and telemarketing fraud.[60] Persons involved in these types of activities often do not report the income derived. Hence, the IRS has to maintain and renew enforcement efforts in such areas.

The IRS also has a narcotics related strategy. Income earned by persons involved in the illegal drug trade is taxable, but usually is not reported. Consistent with the Webster Report, the IRS will deploy less of its resources in this area, but it is by no means abandoning the area.

Formerly, CI had what it called general enforcement and special enforcement programs. Roughly speaking, the general enforcement program dealt with tax crimes involving legal source income. The special enforcement program involved illegal source income. CI no longer uses these terms, but practitioners sometimes still refer to general and special cases.

VII. STANDARDS FOR PROSECUTING TAX CRIMES

The Government is not required to prosecute persons whom it believes has violated the law. Certainly, in the tax context, only very small percentages of persons who are known or reasonably suspected by the Government to have committed some type of tax crime are investigated and prosecuted. Judgment calls are made from the first discovery of information through prosecution as to whether the case presents a fact pattern that is consistent with criminal enforcement.

---

59 IRM 9.1.1.4.1 & 9.5.3.2.

60 *See, e.g.*, IRM 9.1.3.2.

Given the limited resources that can be applied to tax prosecutions, the Government must be highly selective. Moreover, the Government can obtain a very high conviction rate because it is so selective. The message to taxpayers is: "sure, we don't try all tax cheats and don't even try all that we know about, but if we get you in our prosecution cross-hairs, you are dead."

DOJ states: "before authorizing prosecution, the Tax Division must conclude that the Government has: 1) sufficient evidence to support a prima facie case; and 2) a reasonable probability of conviction. . . . The Tax Division also considers factors such as uniformity, balanced and broad enforcement goals, and Department and IRS priorities and policies in criminal enforcement matters."[61] Actually, reasonable probability of conviction probably understates the quality of case the Government requires. The conviction rate is very high indeed. IRS's statistics reproduced in Chapter 1 indicate a conviction rate of around 90%.

In terms of supporting tax compliance, is it better to bring 2,000 prosecutions where the conviction rate is 90% or to bring 10,000 prosecutions where the conviction rate is 50%? Certainly, with the higher number of prosecutions and lower conviction rate, the Government puts more tax cheats in jail. But the message to the public would then be that, if the Government even decides to prosecute, there is a 50% chance to beat the rap. With the lower number of prosecutions and higher conviction rate, the message is that, if the Government gets you in its criminal tax cross-hairs, you are dead (or 90% dead, anyway). From the Government's perspective, not only is that a better message to the taxpaying (or non-taxpaying) public, it also consumes less of the country's limited investigation, prosecution, and judicial resources. For the Government as a whole, fewer cases and greater selectivity is "win-win."

Thus, if defense counsel can convince the Government that it has only a 50% chance of convicting the client, the Government probably should not even prosecute. Where's the break point? The Government probably will not bring a criminal prosecution in a garden variety tax case unless it assesses its chances of getting a conviction at 75 to 80% or better. Of course, cases are hard to assess in this percentage fashion, but all lawyers assess cases in broad strokes in that way. That's how settlements are achieved in civil cases, and plea bargains struck in criminal eases. Before reaching that stage, however, defense counsel will want to advocate that the Government's chances of prevailing are sufficiently lower than the critical 90% benchmark that the Government should not be even pursuing an indictment.

VIII. VOLUNTARY DISCLOSURE

A. Introduction

The question of whether to file an amended return to correct an original return that has criminal prosecution potential is an issue that a criminal tax lawyer will encounter frequently. The filing of an amended return correcting an original return in which the taxpayer had evaded reporting his correct tax liability will establish

[61] CTM 2.00, incorporating USAM 6-4.211A.

one of the key elements of tax evasion: tax due and owing. It will not by itself establish willfulness.[62] Most practitioners and well-counseled taxpayers will resist making any admission of any element of tax evasion unless there is something in it for them. The same question arises in the context of a taxpayer who has failed to file a return timely, thus being subject to potential prosecution for failure to file. He or she may want to file a delinquent return, but doing so will admit elements of the crime — *i.e.*, that a tax return was due and was not filed timely. They too will not want to file, unless there is something in it for them. What is in it for them is the opportunity to avoid prosecution under the so-called voluntary disclosure policy.

The IRS and DOJ have from time to time had voluntary disclosure policies.[63] The essence of the policies, in their various iterations, is that a taxpayer will not be prosecuted if he or she voluntarily discloses his or her misconduct before the IRS or DOJ is hot on his or her trail. There are various nuances of these policies, some of which are addressed here. It is a staple in the tax practitioner's bag of tricks to deliver quality service and results for taxpayers whose tax conduct might otherwise attract criminal tax attention.

The policy of not prosecuting tax cheats who come forward voluntarily is reflected in two types of government programs that overlap. The first — the one under discussion here — is the voluntary disclosure policy. The second is tax amnesty, a program implemented by a number of states and foreign countries but not by the federal government. Tax amnesty, where applicable, may purge criminal conduct and even some civil aspects of the taxpayer's conduct — penalties and sometimes even interest. Tax amnesty is discussed in Chapter 1. The two programs are basically the same in their principal bottom-line effect — relief from criminal prosecution. However, since the federal government does not yet have an amnesty program so labeled, we deal here with the voluntary disclosure policy.

As with all policies, voluntary disclosure involves a balancing of interests. On the one hand, everybody knows that there is a huge tax gap. Those taxpayers contributing to the gap — whether non-filers or evaders — need to be encouraged to come back into the system or become more honest with the system. This militates strongly in favor of the policy. In one sense, the policy gives the Government the best of both worlds — the Government continues to try as many criminal cases as it would anyway and it encourages many taxpayers to get right with the Government. Getting right with the Government includes ongoing compliance. If the Government had no policy or if the policy were extremely narrow so that few taxpayers benefited, the Government would lose revenue because taxpayers would have no incentive to get right with the system. Thus, a carefully structured and implemented voluntary disclosure policy is a win-win for

---

62 United States v. Dyer, 922 F.2d 105, 108 (2d Cir. 1990) (amended return supports inference of mistake, but not of willfulness).

63 The IRS policy is set forth in IRM 9.5.3.3.1.2.1, and will be discussed later in this part. A good discussion of the policy may be found in Allen D. Madison, *An Analysis of the IRS's Voluntary Disclosure Policy*, 54 TAX LAW. 729 (2001). Older but still valuable discussions of the policy maybe found in Cono R. Namorato & Scott D. Michel, *International Criminal Tax Cases*, 50 U. MIAMI L. REV. 617 (1996); John J. Tigue &; Linda A. Lacewell, *IRS Changes in the Rules on Voluntary Disclosure*, N.Y.L.J., Jan. 18, 1986, at 3. Some states have from time to time adopted voluntary disclosure policies. Here, of course, we deal only with federal voluntary disclosure policies.

the taxpayers who take advantage of it and for the Government.

In addition to the revenue effect, a taxpayer who voluntarily discloses puts pressure on the essential element for the Government to prosecute — the virtual certainty of conviction. To be sure, a delinquent return is proof of the original failure to file and an amended return reporting the taxes evaded is proof at least of the "substantial tax due" element for tax evasion. But the Government still has to prove willfulness. When the taxpayer has gotten right with the Government by voluntarily coming forward, that fact might give the jury sufficient incentive to find the willfulness element to be absent. It may not be relevant in a legal sense (since the criminal conduct is the failure to file or the filing of the false return), but it may avoid conviction by sympathetic jurors. Hence, the policy is also based upon the practical reality that, with so many other fish to fry to meet its enforcement goals, why should the Government expend and risk limited criminal enforcement resources after a voluntary disclosure?

At any given time, there may be two voluntary disclosure policies, with subtle differences between them. The IRS can have a policy, and DOJ Tax can have a policy. This works to the taxpayer's advantage. To the extent that the two policies differ (and they have differed at least in nuance from time to time), a taxpayer qualifying under the IRS's policy but not the DOJ policy wins because the matter never gets referred to DOJ Tax (at least if the IRS follows its policies). If, however, the taxpayer fails the IRS's policy but qualifies under the DOJ policy, the taxpayer still wins because DOJ Tax will not prosecute even if the IRS had the poor grace to refer the case to DOJ Tax.

B. IRS Voluntary Disclosure Policy

1. The Policy

The IRS policy is set out in the IRM. The IRM provision[64] is as follows:

> (1) It is currently the practice of the IRS that a voluntary disclosure will be considered along with all other factors in the investigation in determining whether criminal prosecution will be recommended. This voluntary disclosure practice creates no substantive or procedural rights for taxpayers, but rather is a matter of internal IRS practice, provided solely for guidance to IRS personnel. Taxpayers cannot rely on the fact that other similarly situated taxpayers may not have been recommended for criminal prosecution;
>
> (2) A voluntary disclosure will not automatically guarantee immunity from prosecution; however, a voluntary disclosure may result in prosecution not being recommended. This practice does not apply to taxpayers with illegal source income;
>
> (3) A voluntary disclosure occurs when the communication is truthful, timely, complete, and when:

---

[64] IRM 9.5.3.3.1.2.1. The latest iteration of the voluntary disclosure policy, called a "practice," is at IRM 9.5.11.9 (June 26, 2009). It does not materially differ from the practice quoted in the text.

a. the taxpayer shows a willingness to cooperate (and does in fact cooperate) with the IRS in determining his or her correct tax liability; and

b. the taxpayer makes good faith arrangements with the IRS to pay in full, the tax, interest, and any penalties determined by the IRS to be applicable.

(4) A disclosure is timely if it is received before:

a. the IRS has initiated a civil examination or criminal investigation of the taxpayer, or has notified the taxpayer that it intends to commence such an examination or investigation;

b. the IRS has received information from a third party (*e.g.*, informant, other governmental agency, or the media) alerting the IRS to the specific taxpayer's noncompliance;

c. the IRS has initiated a civil examination or criminal investigation which is directly related to the specific liability of the taxpayer; or

d. the IRS has acquired information directly related to the specific liability of the taxpayer from a criminal enforcement action (*e.g.*, search warrant, grand jury subpoena).

(5) Any taxpayer who contacts the IRS in person or through a representative regarding voluntary disclosure will be directed to Criminal Investigation for evaluation of the disclosure. Special agents are encouraged to consult Area Counsel, Criminal Tax on voluntary disclosure issues;

(6) Examples of voluntary disclosures include:

a. a letter from an attorney which encloses amended returns from a client which are complete and accurate (reporting legal source income omitted from the original returns), which offers to pay the tax, interest, and any penalties determined by the IRS to be applicable in full and which meets the timeliness standard set forth above. This is a voluntary disclosure because all elements of (3), above are met;

b. a disclosure made by a taxpayer of omitted income facilitated through a barter exchange after the IRS has announced that it has begun a civil compliance project targeting barter exchanges; however the IRS has not yet commenced an examination or investigation of the taxpayer or notified the taxpayer of its intention to do so. In addition, the taxpayer files complete and accurate amended returns and makes arrangements with the IRS to pay in full, the tax, interest, and any penalties determined by the IRS to be applicable. This is a voluntary disclosure because the civil compliance project involving barter exchanges does not yet directly relate to the specific liability of the taxpayer and because all other elements of (3), above are met;

c. a disclosure made by a taxpayer of omitted income facilitated through a widely promoted scheme regarding which the IRS has begun a civil compliance project and already obtained information which might lead to an examination of the taxpayer; however, the IRS has not yet commenced an examination or investigation of the taxpayer or notified the taxpayer of its intent to do so. In addition, the taxpayer files complete and accurate returns and makes arrangements with the IRS to pay in full, the tax, interest, and any penalties determined by the IRS to be applicable. This is a voluntary disclosure because the civil compliance project involving the scheme does not yet directly relate to the specific liability of the taxpayer and because all other elements of (3), above are met;

d. a disclosure made by an individual who has not filed tax returns after the individual has received a notice stating that the IRS has no record of receiving a return for a particular year and inquiring into whether the taxpayer filed a return for that year. The individual files complete and accurate returns and makes arrangements with the IRS to pay the tax, interest, and any penalties determined by the IRS to be applicable in full. This is a voluntary disclosure because the IRS has not yet commenced an examination or investigation of the taxpayer or notified the taxpayer of its intent to do so and because all other elements of (3), above, are met.

(7) Examples of what are not voluntary disclosures include:

a. a letter from an attorney stating his or her client, who wishes to remain anonymous, wants to resolve his or her tax liability. This is not a voluntary disclosure until the identity of the taxpayer is disclosed and all other elements of (3) above have been met;

b. a disclosure made by a taxpayer who is under grand jury investigation. This is not a voluntary disclosure because the taxpayer is already under criminal investigation. The conclusion would be the same whether or not the taxpayer knew of the grand jury investigation;

c. a disclosure made by a taxpayer, who is not currently under examination or investigation, of omitted gross receipts from a partnership, but whose partner is already under investigation for omitted income skimmed from the partnership. This is not a voluntary disclosure because the IRS has already initiated an investigation which is directly related to the specific liability of this taxpayer. The conclusion would be the same whether or not the taxpayer knew of the ongoing investigation;

d. a disclosure made by a taxpayer, who is not currently under examination or investigation, of omitted constructive dividends received from a corporation which is currently under examination. This is not a voluntary disclosure because the IRS has already initiated an examination which is directly related to the specific liability of this taxpayer. The conclusion would be the same whether or not the taxpayer knew of the ongoing examination;

e. a disclosure made by a taxpayer after an employee has contacted the IRS regarding the taxpayer's double set of books. This is not a voluntary disclosure even if no examination or investigation has yet commenced because the IRS has already been informed by the third party of the specific taxpayer's noncompliance. The conclusion would be the same whether or not the taxpayer knew of the informant's contact with the IRS.

2. How Is Disclosure Made?

Direct Disclosure (Often Called Noisy Disclosure[65]). The policy specifically discusses direct disclosure by contact with the IRS and requires that such disclosure be referred to and discussed with CI. Direct disclosure to CI usually proceeds as follows. The taxpayer's counsel contacts the SAC for the IRS area involved and arranges a conference. At the conference, the taxpayer's counsel provides a balanced summary of the criminal conduct, but without identifying the taxpayer. This type of submission is often referred to as a "proffer." The proffer will include facts otherwise bringing the taxpayer within the policy. The taxpayer's counsel will then seek CI's assurance not to prosecute if the taxpayer's identity is disclosed. In some cases, the oral proffer can be made in the initial telephone call rather than a separate meeting. This is often feasible when the practitioner and the taxpayer's counsel have had past dealings which have given the SAC confidence that he or she can rely upon taxpayer's counsel. CI may want the proffer of the facts to be put in writing to set in concrete the conditions of the assurance. CI can then give the assurance that, provided the facts prove to be as stated in the proffer, CI will not forward the matter to DOJ Tax with a recommendation for prosecution. Taxpayer's counsel then identifies the taxpayer. CI then conducts such investigation as it deems appropriate to assure itself that the proffer was a fair representation of the pertinent facts.

In this procedure for direct disclosure, IRS policy is that proper disclosure has not been made until and unless the taxpayer is identified to the IRS. Hence, there is conceivably a window in time between the practitioner's initial contact with CI and the actual disclosure of the taxpayer's identity during which the IRS could zero in on the taxpayer from independent sources and, strictly speaking, the policy would not apply. However, provided the policy would otherwise apply and there are no unreasonable delays from the taxpayer's side in making the required presentation to CI and then identifying the taxpayer, the IRS is not likely to cry foul simply because in that short interim period it starts an investigation.

Filing Disclosure (Often Called Quiet Disclosure). Another method to make the disclosure is to file with the service center (as opposed to filing with CI) an amended return correcting the deficiencies on the original return or a delinquent original return in case of failure to file. This is filing disclosure.

---

65 Use of the word "noisy" became popular in the criminal tax lexicon by analogy to disclosures directly to the SEC that might be required under Sarbanes Oxley. Practitioners adopted the noisy disclosure term for direct disclosures to IRS CI and added its tax counterpart — the "quiet" disclosure — to describe the very different process of simply filing amended returns without specific breast-beating before a live IRS CI agent.

Historically, most practitioners recommend filing disclosure. Filing disclosure may not result in direct IRS substantive consideration of the disclosure, while direct disclosure will. Although current IRS policy does not expressly approve or disapprove of filing disclosure, it is likely that, until and unless the IRS disapproves of filing disclosure (a practice well-known to the IRS and the bar), filing disclosure will remain a viable method for qualifying under the policy.[66]

As with the direct disclosure method, there will be a window between the time the taxpayer makes the decision to disclose and the time the taxpayer implements the disclosure by filing the amended return or delinquent original return. For example, an amended return may require that the taxpayer, his counsel, and his tax return preparer undertake due diligence to pull together adequate information to file a reasonably correct — *i.e.*, nonfraudulent — amended return. Sometimes this may take considerable time. In such a case, caution may dictate the direct disclosure method with implementation thereafter perhaps by the filing disclosure method if acceptable to CI. But when the return(s) can be prepared in a reasonable time frame, the filing disclosure method is usually preferable. As with the direct disclosure method, there will still be a window which could be troublesome. In order to address that issue, upon the taxpayer making the decision to file, prudent attorneys document the decision in writing then work with the taxpayer to insure that the return(s) is (are) prepared as expeditiously as possible. Should the IRS start an investigation in that interim, a persuasive argument can be made to the IRS that the policy should apply because the decision to make voluntary disclosure had been made and objective efforts — the taxpayer's, the lawyer's, and the preparer's — toward that end can be shown.

C. DOJ Tax Disclosure Policy

The 2008 version of section 4.01 of the CTM provides as follows:

> **4.01[1] Policy Respecting Voluntary Disclosure**
>
> Whenever a person voluntarily discloses that he or she committed a crime before any investigation of the person's conduct begins, that factor is considered by the Tax Division along with all other factors in the case in determining whether to pursue criminal prosecution. *See generally* USAM, § 9-27.220, et seq.

---

66 Indeed, there is a process for CI agent review of amended returns or substantially delinquent original returns received in the service center. The review is probably cursory in most cases and perhaps limited to certain material amounts of tax being reported. Amended returns and delinquent original returns seem to be rarely, if ever, referred to CI for criminal investigation. The win-win features of the voluntary disclosure policy means that it would be incredibly stupid for the IRS to discourage amended returns or delinquent original returns by investigating and prosecuting those who file them. Of course, it would be much nicer to have something in writing to offer a client other than that the IRS can't be that stupid. Notwithstanding the foregoing, in establishing the special voluntary disclosure initiative related to offshore credit cards, the IRS indicated that it has developed certain new criteria to screen amended returns filed directly with service centers in order to insure that the OVCI initiative was not circumvented.

> If a putative criminal defendant has complied in all respects with all of the requirements of the Internal Revenue Service's voluntary disclosure practice, the Tax Division may consider that factor in its exercise of prosecutorial discretion. It will consider, inter alia, the timeliness of the voluntary disclosure, what prompted the person to make the disclosure, and whether the person fully and truthfully cooperated with the government by paying past tax liabilities, complying with subsequent tax obligations, and assisting in the prosecution of other persons involved in the crime.
>
> A person who makes a "voluntary disclosure" does not have a legal right to avoid criminal prosecution. Whether there is or is not a voluntary disclosure is only one factor in the evaluation of a case. Even if there has been a voluntary disclosure, the Tax Division still may authorize prosecution. *See United States v. Hebel*, 668 F.2d 995 (8th Cir.), *cert. denied*, 456 U.S. 946 (1982).

Practitioners view this change to the CTM as bringing the DOJ Tax voluntary disclosure practice more in line with the IRS voluntary disclosure practice. But, the wording does suggest that DOJ Tax might prosecute even if the taxpayer has made a voluntary disclosure that the IRS would view as consistent with its practice. This raises the issue of whether DOJ Tax would or could prosecute when the IRS says that prosecution is not consistent with its administration of the tax laws. That is a big and potentially distractive issue, so we forgo it now.

D. Does Either Policy Confer Rights?

Both the IRM and the CTM specifically state that the practice or policy confers no rights on taxpayers. This is to reinforce the applicability of the *Caceres* doctrine.[67] Consider the case below.

UNITED STATES v. TENZER

United States Court of Appeals, Second Circuit
213 F.3d 34 (2000)

James L. Tenzer appeals from a judgment of conviction entered in February 1999 in the United States District Court for the Southern District of New York (Charles L. Brieant, J.) on an information charging him with four misdemeanor counts of failure to file timely tax returns for the years 1987–1990 in violation of 26 U.S.C. § 7203. The case comes before this court for the second time. In the first appeal, the government sought reversal of the district court's order dismissing the information because Tenzer's offer in compromise, submitted pursuant to the voluntary disclosure policy of the internal Revenue Service (IRS), had been improperly turned down. We reversed, holding that Tenzer's offer did not meet the requirements of that policy. *United States v. Tenzer*, 127 F.3d 222 (2d Cir. 1997) ("*Tenzer I*"). On remand, Tenzer again sought dismissal, based on allegedly new evidence produced by the government, but the district court held that the "mandate

[67] United States v. Caceres, 440 U.S. 741 (1979) (holding that the taxpayer could not challenge IRS action on the ground that the IRS violated its own internal rules).

rule" precluded it. Following a conditional guilty plea, Judge Brieant sentenced Tenzer to a year and a day incarceration, but declined to depart downward. Tenzer now appeals from his conviction and sentence. Tenzer argues that (1) the new evidence produced by the government on remand merits the reconsideration of our decision in *Tenzer I*; and (2) Judge Brieant did not fully understand his authority to downwardly depart. For the reasons set forth below, we affirm the conviction and remand for reconsideration of the sentence.

I. Background

A. The Civil Proceedings

Tenzer is an experienced tax attorney and one of the principals of a large accounting firm in Long Island, New York. It is uncontested that during the four years covered by the information, Tenzer earned substantial income but did not pay any tax. In October 1991, the IRS notified Tenzer that his account had been referred to the enforcement section and that he could still avoid enforcement action if he filed all his delinquent returns and paid all outstanding taxes within 10 days, or if he immediately contacted the IRS. Tenzer's attorney, Myron Weinberg, contacted the IRS and requested an extension of time for filing the returns, which the IRS granted. In February 1992, Tenzer filed complete and accurate returns for three of the years involved (1987–1989), but did not enclose any payments.

In October 1992, Tenzer began negotiating a payment plan with IRS revenue officer Elizabeth Kishlansky. At that time, Weinberg advised Kishlansky that Tenzer wanted to enter into an installment agreement with the IRS. Kishlansky notified Weinberg that the IRS would not consider any installment plan unless Tenzer immediately filed his delinquent 1990 and 1991 returns. Tenzer filed those returns in November 1992.

In January 1993, Kishlansky again met with Tenzer's lawyers, including Ernest Honecker, formerly a high-ranking attorney for the IRS, to discuss Tenzer's payment plan. At that meeting, Tenzer's lawyers sought assurances from Kishlansky that Tenzer's case was being handled as a civil matter. Tenzer's attorneys also informed Kishlansky that rather than enter into an installment plan with the IRS, whereby all delinquent payments would be made, Tenzer intended to make an "offer in compromise," that is, a partial payment in settlement of his tax liabilities. Kishlansky responded that such an offer would only be considered if Tenzer became current on his taxes due for 1992, and if the offer reasonably reflected his assets and potential earnings. Tenzer's lawyers then proposed $250,000 in compromise of his tax liability. Kishlansky indicated that she thought this amount would be unsatisfactory and that a more reasonable offer would be around $600,000. Nevertheless, when Tenzer submitted his $250,000 offer in a letter dated February 5, 1993, along with a $5000 payment, Kishlansky did not reject it but forwarded it to the IRS service center in Maine for review.

In early April 1993, the IRS returned Tenzer's offer in compromise letter, as well as the $5000 payment, as "unprocessable." The letter returning the offer explained that "for offers based on inability to pay, you must generally offer an amount equal to or in excess of the amount shown as 'equity in assets' on your financial statement(s)." The letter also invited Tenzer to amend his offer. On April 14, 1993, Honecker wrote a letter to the IRS disclosing his intention to resubmit the same offer in compromise, and explaining that $250,000 was a reasonable amount in light of the "forced sale" value of Tenzer's non-liquid assets. Later that month, Kishlansky notified Honecker that Tenzer's file was being transferred to the IRS office in Brooklyn, which covered the region where most of Tenzer's assets were located. Kishlansky also advised Honecker not to resubmit the offer until he was contacted by that office. At this point, all communication between Tenzer and the IRS regarding civil collection of his taxes ceased.

B. The Criminal Proceedings

In late June 1993, a "freeze" was placed on Tenzer's file halting any further collection efforts. The freeze was ordered by the IRS criminal investigation division, as a result of a separate investigation into criminal tax evasion by JRD, a corporate client of Tenzer's accounting firm. It was not until several weeks later that Tenzer's attorneys learned of the freeze and that Tenzer was now a subject of an IRS criminal investigation. The collection freeze on Tenzer's file was not lifted until February 25, 1999, shortly after Tenzer was sentenced by the district court.

In November 1994, consultation between agents of the IRS and the tax division of the Department of Justice led to a recommendation that Tenzer be prosecuted for his failure to timely file his tax returns. The recommendation reflected the IRS's conclusion that Tenzer did not meet the criteria of the voluntary disclosure policy. That policy provides that where a delinquent taxpayer comes forward and either pays or makes a bona fide arrangement to pay the applicable taxes, the IRS will not recommend prosecution. As a result of this policy, non-filers are seldom prosecuted. Nevertheless, in November 1995, the Justice Department charged Tenzer in the four-count information that led to this appeal.

Subsequently, Tenzer moved to dismiss the information. Tenzer argued that he had satisfied the requirements of the voluntary disclosure policy, and that by initiating criminal proceedings against him, the IRS failed to follow its own policy, thereby violating his due process rights. Following a four-day evidentiary hearing, the district court agreed and dismissed the information. The court reasoned that although Tenzer's initial offer in compromise was "laughable," he had intended in good faith to reach an acceptable compromise agreement with the IRS and thus complied with the voluntary disclosure program. The district court further concluded that the policy, which was widely publicized, afforded Tenzer due process rights, and that those rights were violated when the government decided, without affording Tenzer any advance notice, to freeze the civil collection effort and to prosecute him. The district court also noted that Tenzer's prosecution was "unique in the regular day to day administration of the [voluntary disclosure] Policy."

C. *Tenzer I*

In September 1997, we reversed the dismissal of the information, holding that prosecution was not barred because Tenzer did not comply with the voluntary disclosure policy. Because we held that Tenzer did not comply with the policy, we found it unnecessary to decide whether the policy afforded Tenzer any due process rights and whether those rights were violated by the IRS. The panel held that an "arrangement to pay" under the voluntary disclosure policy "may be a great variety of things, *e.g.*, an installation payment agreement, a promise to pay on a specific date, or an offer of a lump-sum payment in compromise." We also concluded that "under the express language of the policy, the 'bona fide arrangement' must have been 'made' for the policy to apply." Because Tenzer's offer had not been accepted by the IRS at the time he became the subject of a criminal investigation, his prosecution was not barred. Although we remarked that the government must negotiate in good faith toward the goal of achieving a settlement with the taxpayer, we found that in this case the government had provided Tenzer with sufficient opportunity to make an acceptable offer, and that he had not made such an offer. We concluded that "having thoroughly failed to bring himself within the letter of the voluntary disclosure policy, Tenzer cannot now claim the benefits of any protection it affords." Thus, we reversed the district court's dismissal of the information and remanded to the district court.

D. Proceedings on Remand

In the district court on remand, the government produced a new piece of evidence that prompted Tenzer to renew his motion to dismiss the information. The new evidence, a one-page computer-printout from the IRS processing center in Maine, shows that defendant's offer in compromise was "pending," as opposed to "rejected." The printout included a notation by one IRS official to another demonstrating, Tenzer argues, that the IRS expected resubmission of his offer. On this basis, Tenzer argued to the district court that the IRS's return of Tenzer's first offer as "unprocessable" is different from a return of the offer as "rejected." Since this distinction was not made clear on the previous appeal, Tenzer's argument went, this court's decision in *Tenzer I* was based on the erroneous assumption that Tenzer's offer was "firmly (and predictably) rejected." Additionally, Tenzer urged the district court to rule that the IRS denied him due process by failing to continue the settlement negotiations with him an issue, as already noted, that the panel in *Tenzer I* did not decide.

In a written opinion, Judge Brieant refused to grant Tenzer's renewed motion to dismiss the information. The opinion stated that "it seems to this Court that the IRS' unilateral decision to terminate negotiations with Mr. Tenzer without warning was unfair and was in violation of Mr. Tenzer's right to due process." But citing the "mandate rule," Judge Brieant held that "while this argument is attractive, this Court concludes that our Court of Appeals has already ruled on this issue, even if in an indirect way. The commission of a district judge does not extend to correcting the decisions of the Court of Appeals, or to placing a gloss on such decisions which would alter the practical outcome."

Thereafter, Tenzer entered a conditional guilty plea to all four counts of the information pursuant to Fed. R. Crim. P. 11(a)(2), reserving his right to appeal the district court's denial of his motion to dismiss and to appeal his sentence. The plea agreement set forth Tenzer's net offense level at 13 and his criminal history category as I.

At sentencing, Tenzer moved for a downward departure on various grounds that he claimed took this case out of the heartland of the sentencing guidelines. The most contentious of these concerned Tenzer's claim that his prosecution was unfair and in violation of his due process rights. Consistent with his two prior published opinions in this case, Judge Brieant stated at the sentencing proceeding, "I believe that the entire prosecution here is essentially unfair and in violation of public policies adopted by the Internal Revenue Service." In ultimately refusing to depart on this ground, however, Judge Brieant explained, "I do not believe that these issues alone or taken together provide a reasonable basis for the Court to depart downwardly in Mr. Tenzer's case. While courts have considerable power in connection with the fashioning of a sentence, a court must honor the mandates and decisions of the Court of Appeals, even when they're totally wrong." Judge Brieant also considered and rejected other grounds for departure. Tenzer was sentenced to concurrent terms of 12 months on counts one and two, and to concurrent terms of one day on counts three and four, making the total sentence a year and a day, at the bottom of the applicable guidelines range of 12 to 18 months. This appeal followed.

II. Discussion

A. Reconsideration of *Tenzer I*

We turn first to Tenzer's claim that new evidence supports reconsideration of our decision in *Tenzer I* under an exception to the law of the case doctrine. That doctrine has two principal prongs. Under one, a court of appeals must usually adhere "to its own decision at an earlier stage of the litigation." We have stated that "we will not depart from this sound policy absent 'cogent' or 'compelling' reasons. The major grounds justifying reconsideration are an intervening change of controlling law, the availability of new evidence, or the need to correct a clear error or prevent manifest injustice." Nonetheless, "this branch of the doctrine, while it informs the court's discretion, does not limit the tribunal's power."

The other prong of the "law of the case" doctrine, commonly referred to as the "mandate rule," describes the duty of the district court on remand. "When an appellate court has once decided an issue, the trial court, at a later stage of the litigation, is under a duty to follow the appellate court's ruling on that issue." We believe that, in refusing to dismiss the information, Judge Brieant correctly adhered to our prior decision, even though he evidently felt that the new evidence supported his disagreement with that decision.

However, the law of the case doctrine does not bind us with the same rigidity as it binds the district court. Thus, we are free to reconsider our holding in *Tenzer I*, if, as Tenzer claims, the new evidence sheds substantial doubt on that decision. As described above, the new evidence consists of a computer printout listing Tenzer's offer in compromise as "pending," rather than as "rejected." Tenzer argues that this evidence contravenes our finding in *Tenzer I* that "[Tenzer's offer of $250,000] was firmly (and predictably) rejected," and "arrangement to pay" would be reached.

Tenzer further argues that this error was fueled by the government's representation at oral argument in the prior appeal that the IRS rejected Tenzer's offer "out of hand." By contrast, Tenzer argues, the computer printout demonstrates that the IRS did not consider its negotiations with Tenzer to have ended and that Tenzer's offer was not "rejected." The government responds that there is nothing new in the evidence relied on by Tenzer. First, it is not surprising that Tenzer's case-file was designated as "pending," since the collection efforts on it had been frozen pending resolution of the criminal proceedings, as required by IRS regulations. Further, whether Tenzer's offer was "rejected," or "returned as unprocessable," was not material to our prior holding that an arrangement to pay had not been made, and therefore Tenzer could not enjoy the protection of the voluntary disclosure policy.

After carefully considering Tenzer's arguments and the district court's second opinion, we conclude that the new evidence does not warrant reconsideration of this court's previous decision in this case. The holding in *Tenzer I* was premised on Tenzer's failure, from the time he was notified of his tax delinquency to the time he submitted his first offer, to arrive at an arrangement to pay that was satisfactory to the IRS. The *Tenzer I* panel had before it the letter from the IRS returning Tenzer's first offer in compromise and the payment attached thereto. The court stated "the IRS subsequently returned the check and rejected the offer as being 'unprocessable' because it was below the minimum amount." Although the court did not distinguish between "return as unprocessable," and "rejection," it clearly understood, as Tenzer had at the time he received the letter, that Tenzer could attempt to restart the negotiations by submitting another offer. In other words, the court was aware that the return of Tenzer's first offer did not necessarily mark the end of the negotiations between Tenzer and the IRS. The point was not how we chose to characterize the IRS's response to Tenzer's initial offer, but rather our conclusion that it was not a bona fide offer, that Honecker's proposed resubmission was unlikely to change the situation, and that, at this point, the IRS was entitled to refer the matter to the DOJ for prosecution. The court stated that "it is clear that Tenzer was given ample opportunity, including a reasonable length of time, to comply with the voluntary disclosure policy, yet repeatedly failed to do so."

While Tenzer, and Judge Brieant, evidently disagree with the panel's conclusion in *Tenzer I*, the new evidence does not undermine it. The new evidence does not refer to the time period relevant to our prior decision, namely the period leading up to and including the return of Tenzer's first offer in compromise. Thus, it does not change the fact that no arrangement to pay had been made. Rather, it simply raises the speculative prospect that had the negotiations continued, they might (or might not) have resulted in an agreement between Tenzer and the IRS at some point down the line. Such speculation is not an appropriate basis for reconsideration. Since we do not disturb our holding in *Tenzer I* that Tenzer did not comply with the voluntary disclosure policy, we again find it unnecessary to decide whether the policy afforded Tenzer any due process rights and whether those rights were violated by the IRS.

If the decision whether to prosecute after a voluntary disclosure is a prosecutorial judgment call rather than a legal requirement, one can see why the prosecutorial judgment call was made against Mr. Tenzer, who showed recalcitrance at every stage that he could have. Any iteration of the voluntary disclosure policy requires that the taxpayer cooperate. Most practitioners advise their clients that the key to voluntary disclosure is to get right with the Government, which means real cooperation and not the type of resistance Mr. Tenzer showed.

E. Timeliness, Truthfulness, and Completeness

Voluntary disclosure under either policy requires timeliness, truthfulness, and completeness. When using filing disclosure, the return will usually not include a complete exposition of the underlying facts — either as to the nature of the erroneously reported item or the reason it was not included on the original return. Nevertheless, what the amended or delinquent original return should report is all of the information called for by the return instructions although it need not include a detailed mea culpa. Of course, if the IRS wants then to ask the taxpayer questions about the amended return or the delinquent original return, the taxpayer's responses will have to be complete and the taxpayer will have to be cooperative. Practitioners concerned about whether the filing disclosure is adequate without a complete discussion of the facts can simply include that discussion.

For many reasons, the taxpayer will often be unable to file a completely accurate amended return or delinquent original return. The taxpayer may not have kept good records, the taxpayer in furtherance of the original fraud may have destroyed records, the time elapsed may have made some third-party sources of relevant information unavailable, etc. Yet, something needs to be done and be done as accurately as possible, so that the taxpayer does not file a false amended return or false delinquent return, thereby compounding his or her problem.[68] Good return preparers will know how to undertake the type of due diligence to make the best return reasonably possible, and that should be acceptable. But, obviously a good faith, even if expensive, effort must be made to reconstruct the taxpayer's income, deductions, and credits, and proper disclosures should be made on the return when estimates and indirect methods of reconstruction are used. In many cases, this will require the return preparer to make judgment calls against the taxpayer in order to insure that the tax liability is not underreported. That is just a cost of the original fraud and insuring that the IRS will bless the voluntary disclosure, a less likely result if the taxpayer's disclosure by amended return is found wanting. Good faith is the key, and good faith will work to insure the application of the policy so long as the other requirements are met.

F. Taxpayer Cooperation

The taxpayer is required to be forthcoming and cooperative. Certainly, as to IRS inquiries regarding the taxes or potential penalties, the taxpayer must cooperate. Does cooperation require more?[69]

---

[68] *See* Blauner v. United States, 293 F.2d 723, 729–35 (8th Cir.), *cert. denied*, 368 U.S. 931 (1961).

[69] Cooperation appears in the Code in a number of civil contexts. For example, that the taxpayer "has cooperated with reasonable requests by the [IRS] for witnesses, information, documents, meetings, and interviews" is a prerequisite for shifting the burden of proof under section 7491(a)(2)(B). Thus far, there

For example, does cooperation mean in the case of filing disclosure that a taxpayer who knows he or she committed a criminal act is required to "self-impose" the appropriate civil penalties that would otherwise apply to the criminal conduct? Thus, if the original return were fraudulent, is the taxpayer required to advise the IRS on or with the amended return that he or she is subject to the civil fraud penalty and pay that penalty if possible? Most practitioners say that such self-imposed penalty assessments are not required to qualify for voluntary disclosure. The assessment of the penalty is not the prerogative of the taxpayer, but is instead the prerogative of the IRS. The IRS will often, even usually, assert some penalty upon receiving an amended return reporting substantial additional tax liability or for a delinquent original return, but the taxpayer should await the IRS's call on that one without great concern that he has not been cooperative.

The tougher question will be whether and how hard the taxpayer might want to fight the imposition of any penalty that the IRS asserts upon receipt of the return. Smart taxpayers, particularly in a fraud situation, might not want to fight for a host of strategic reasons. Often, the IRS will assert the 20% negligence or substantial understatement penalty upon rather cursory review of the return at the service center and without any independent investigation.[70] The IRS will not assert the fraud penalty (75%) without a somewhat detailed investigation which rarely occurs in a filing disclosure. Would acquiescing in the IRS's assertion of a 20% penalty when the taxpayer knows that the fraud penalty (75%) should apply be an indication of noncooperation? Most practitioners do not think so, and the IRM suggests that such taxpayer acquiescence is not noncooperation.[71]

Frequently, persons desiring to qualify under this policy will not have the funds to pay the taxes, penalties, and interest that are then due. *Tenzer II* indicates that, while full payment is not required, cooperation is required. The IRM provision quoted above appears to go farther — *i.e.*, the taxpayer must make "good faith arrangements with the IRS to pay in full, the tax, interest, and any penalties determined by the IRS to be applicable." Does this exclude from the policy taxpayers who cannot pay in full? Based on experience and a logical implementation of the policy, the answer probably is "no."[72] Of course, the taxpayer will want to avoid the delay and foot-dragging Tenzer employed, in order to meet the cooperation requirement. Accordingly, if the filing disclosure method is used, when the taxpayer can't fully pay, the taxpayer should include as much payment as possible with the return and a cover letter or a statement attached to the return saying that he or she cannot pay the amount required but desires to cooperate and

---

has been no attempt to define cooperation for voluntary disclosure purposes by reference to cooperation for section 7491 purposes.

[70] The 20% penalty can become a 40% penalty under the circumstances described in section 6662(h), but the service center is fairly unlikely to assert the 40% penalty rate.

[71] Paragraph (3)a merely requires the taxpayer to cooperate in determining his or her correct "tax liability" and does not mention penalties. Paragraph (4)b, by contrast, in requiring the taxpayer to make arrangements for payments does mention payment of "penalties determined by the IRS." The suggestion is that, if the IRS chooses to assert only the lesser penalties, the taxpayer need only cooperate in arranging payment of the penalties asserted.

[72] Indeed, under narrow circumstances, inability to pay may be a defense to failure-to-pay penalties under section 6651. *See* Reg. § 301.6651-1(c); Richardson, Borison & Johnson, *supra*, at 302–03.

work with the IRS under existing procedures to resolve the liability. The taxpayer should thereafter cooperate with the IRS collection personnel. Existing collection procedures include installment agreements and offers in compromise.[73] The key, of course, is for the taxpayer to show the good faith that eluded Tenzer.

If the IRS decides to investigate the circumstances of the original fraud or even the decision to disclose voluntarily, can the IRS require the taxpayer to waive his privileges in order to meet the cooperation requirement of the policy? The taxpayer has disclosed the underlying fraud itself and has thus waived his Fifth Amendment privilege as to that conduct.[74] But what if the taxpayer had other criminal conduct, not necessarily tax criminal conduct, but still related to the tax fraud? Could the taxpayer assert the Fifth Amendment privilege and still qualify? The IRS voluntary disclosure policy applies only to legal source income, so this might be a disqualification *ab initio* if the untaxed income is illegal source income.[75] Similarly, could the taxpayer assert the attorney-client privilege for advice he or she received in the course of considering and making voluntary disclosure? And, could the taxpayer claim the practitioner privilege under section 7525 to prevent the IRS from learning confidences incident to the original return preparation and still qualify for the privilege?[76] These issues are yet to be decided.

G. Events That Prevent Voluntariness

If the IRS gets on the taxpayer's trail or events are in place that will likely put the IRS on the taxpayer's trail, the voluntary disclosure policy does not apply. As set forth in the IRM, these events are a civil or criminal investigation, third-party information about that taxpayer's noncompliance, another civil or criminal investigation that would likely lead to the taxpayer or information from another criminal enforcement investigation.[77] This limitation on the policy is necessary. If all a taxpayer had to do to solve a criminal problem was to "fess up" when he was caught or was on the verge of being caught and maybe pay a few civil penalties, the cost-benefit ratio of playing the audit lottery with fraudulent activity would be heavily tilted in the taxpayer's favor.

There is one counterintuitive limitation in the examples in the policy. If an informant has pointed the IRS to the taxpayer before the taxpayer makes his or her disclosure, the disclosure will not qualify for the policy (at least the current IRS version of the policy). If the taxpayer does not know of the informant and is truly, from the taxpayer's perspective, making a voluntary disclosure not prompted

---

[73] *See* IRC §§ 6159 & 7122. These mechanisms are described in Richardson, Borison & Johnson, *supra*, at 367–70.

[74] Privileges are discussed in Chapter 7.

[75] Although the policies apply only to legal source income, a taxpayer with illegal source income might try the direct disclosure route to see if he or she can get the needed assurance from the Chief of CI. If the Chief gives the assurance, it will certainly be honored. That type of advance assurance cannot be achieved via the filing disclosure route.

[76] For discussion of section 7525, see Steve R. Johnson, *The Proposed Tax Advisor-Client Privilege: An Idea Whose Time Should Never Come*, 78 Tax Notes 1041 (1998). This privilege does not apply in criminal tax investigations. IRC § 7525(a)(2).

[77] *See* IRM 9.5.3.3.1.2.1(4).

by impending fear of IRS discovery by known events, the taxpayer still fails to qualify because of the unknown timing of the informant's action.[78] Of course, if the informant had threatened the taxpayer with turning him or her in to the IRS, the taxpayer's disclosure prompted by the threat would hardly be voluntary and would not be the type of disclosure that the policy seeks to reward. But when the taxpayer could not reasonably have known of the informant, a good case can be made that the policy should apply. The IRM says otherwise, perhaps because the IRS does not want to be committed in an area when what the taxpayer may have known might be uncertain.[79]

H. Practical Considerations

Your client filed a fraudulent return substantially underreporting his tax liability. He now has misgivings. He comes to you and expresses great concern and even a glimmer of remorse. What can you do for him?

Technically, he has filed a fraudulent return. The crime of tax evasion is complete upon filing the return. There is one exception to this. If the taxpayer filed his return before the normal due date (typically April 15 for an individual taxpayer and March 15 for a calendar-year corporation), he can purge the fraud by filing a nonfraudulent amended return on or before the normal due date.[80] This opportunity does not apply when the original return was filed late. If, as is usually the case, the taxpayer cannot qualify for this exception, the question becomes one of damage control. As described above, one possibility is making a voluntary disclosure. Assuming that your client otherwise qualifies, and you do it right, you can give him some comfort that a voluntary disclosure will avoid criminal problems for him.

You should advise your client, however, that there are no guarantees. As noted above, the voluntary disclosure policy is just that — a policy of the administrators of the law. It is not law itself. So, the taxpayer's ability to force the IRS to apply the voluntary disclosure to him may be limited under the noted previously *Caceres* rule. Nevertheless, most practitioners feel that the IRS will honor the policy, provided the taxpayer qualifies.

Assume first that you believe that your client can qualify for the voluntary disclosure policy. There are two ways to make the disclosure. First, you can discuss the matter on a "no-names" basis with CI. If you state a good case, CI will give reasonable assurance that there will be no prosecution. This can be a dicey procedure because you have to make sure that the facts are as you represent them to CI. Second, you can simply send in an amended return to the service center.

The next question you must answer is "who prepares the amended return?" It is usually not advisable to have the original tax return preparer prepare the amended

---

78 *See* IRM 9.5.3.3.1.2.1(e) (last sentence).

79 This may be a situation in which you will have to use your skills as an advocate to convince the IRS or DOJ Tax to make the prosecutorial judgment call in your client's favor because, although technically excluded from the policy, the facts show that your client was making a true voluntary disclosure without any immediate fear at which this limitation is obviously directed.

80 *See, e.g.*, Goldstone v. Commissioner, 65 T.C. 113, 116 (1975).

return. The reason has to do with controlling the flow of information and, specifically, putting up legal barriers to the IRS's access to information that might damage the client. In preparing the original return, the preparer had access to information and documents that are usually not privileged.[81] In a criminal investigation, the IRS can get to that information. Also, in preparing the amended return, the preparer should have access to other information that indicates that there were serious problems in the initial return filing and may even offer a roadmap to the fraud. If the original preparer is used for the amended return, the taxpayer will then be at risk that the return preparer cannot clearly establish what he learned prior to the time the privilege became applicable. The risk is usually not acceptable, even though there will be some additional costs to engaging a new preparer. In contrast, the preparer of the amended return will be brought under the cloak of privilege via the *Kovel* technique.[82] Assuming your client follows the advice or does not engage in utter stupidity as in *Tenzer*, that should really be the end of the matter.[83]

I. Voluntary Disclosure and Advocacy

Previously, the IRM suggested that the voluntary disclosure practice was not available if some series of events had transpired which made the IRS's discovery of the taxpayer's malfeasance inevitable. The limitation is not present in the current version of the practice. We urge the reader to go back and read the policy and consider why we say that this limitation is not in the current version. The reader will note that the practice is not available to a taxpayer if the IRS has started an investigation of another taxpayer as to a matter that is "directly related" to the taxpayer's liability. This limitation should be read carefully, and obviously the practitioner should be prepared to mount effective advocacy as to why his client's tax liability in the voluntary disclosure is not directly related to another previously discovered taxpayer's tax liability. Advocacy, even in a close case, might be effective here because the IRS could lose more than it could gain by applying the voluntary disclosure practice too narrowly. That is to say, IRS and DOJ Tax can get plenty of fodder for their criminal tax enforcement priorities without being stingy about voluntary disclosure. Your job may be to help the IRS and/or DOJ Tax CES realize that priority in your client's specific case.

---

[81] *See generally* Martin J. McMahon, Jr. & Ira B. Shepherd, *Privilege and the Work Product Doctrine in Tax Cases*, 58 TAX LAW. 405 (2005).

[82] United States v. Kovel, 296 F.2d 918 (2d Cir. 1961). The technique is discussed by Michael I. Saltzman, IRS Practice and Procedure ¶ 13.11[1][c] (rev. 2d ed. stud. ed. 2002); *see also* John A. Townsend, *The Accountant's Role — and Risks — in Koveling*, TAX PRAC. & PROC., Aug.–Sept. 2000, at 20.

[83] For further discussion, see Larry A. Campagna, *See No Evil, Hear No Evil, and Speak No Evil: Handling Voluntary Disclosures Without Creating a Witness Against Your Client*, ABA CENTER FOR CONT. LEG. EDUC. NAT'L INST. CRIMINAL TAX FRAUD (1997).

J. Special Voluntary Disclosure Initiatives

In major areas of noncompliance where the IRS's ability to detect noncompliance is limited or other special factors exist, the IRS may offer special "voluntary disclosure" initiatives in order to encourage compliance. Here are three prominent recent examples.

1. Offshore Voluntary Compliance Initiatives (and Related Audit Initiatives)

In the late 1990s, the IRS initiated a major initiative to identify taxpayers using offshore credit cards, and more broadly offshore financial institutions, as a means of implementing tax crimes with minimal (they thought) risk of detection. The IRS began tracing the credit card charges through the U.S. system of credit card transaction processors into tax haven foreign banks. With Sherlock Holmes techniques and some luck, the IRS could often identify the U.S. taxpayers and start U.S. audits and, where appropriate, criminal investigation processes. As an early part of this initiative, the IRS encouraged taxpayers with this problem to voluntarily disclose, and offered reasonable assurance that qualifying taxpayers would not be prosecuted. This initiative was called the Offshore Voluntary Compliance Initiative ("OVCI"). The IRS did not expect all taxpayers to accept this voluntary disclosure offer, and thus will still have plenty of taxpayers that it can identify and prosecute. But, for those taxpayers within the scope of the offer, the IRS did offer reasonable assurance that they would not be prosecuted. Still, during audits in which an offshore account was identified or suspected, the IRS usually offered the taxpayers a similar program with stiffened penalties (that were still much better than worst case) called the Last Chance Compliance Initiative ("LCCI").

2. Tax Shelter Initiatives

In the early 2000s, after a wave of abusive tax shelters, the IRS announced initiatives as to particular highly marketed shelters, permitting taxpayers to limit their risk by voluntary disclosure. These initiatives usually facially offer relief only with respect to the taxpayer's civil exposure, principally because the complexity of the shelters and the presence of "opinions" from major tax firms made criminal prosecution unlikely. But, in situations where the opinions were mere window dressing which the taxpayer really did not believe (often with the assistance of his own independent counsel), careful practitioners would at least be concerned that there might be criminal investigation or prosecution. The general thinking is that, in the unlikely event the taxpayer's conduct might otherwise be potentially subject to criminal prosecution, participation in the program with full disclosure will avoid the criminal problem.

3. 2009 Offshore Account Initiative

We discussed above the special 2009 Offshore Voluntary Disclosure Initiative, the most aggressive initiative for offshore financial accounts, and refer readers back to that discussion for context.

IX. EGG SHELL AUDITS

The IRS often audits taxpayers who, unbeknownst to the IRS at the start of the audit, have major criminal problems. The practitioner assisting such a taxpayer will have done his homework and ascertained that there is a problem and the parameters of the problem. The strategy then becomes damage control. This is often called an "egg shell audit." A traditional source of CI referrals is the civil audit in which the Revenue Agent discovers information that leads the Revenue Agent to believe that a tax crime has been committed.

As noted above, once the IRS commences the audit it may be too late to invoke the voluntary disclosure policy. Also, the practitioner needs to be very careful not to make the client's problems his problems, *i.e.*, by doing something in the course of the audit that is itself criminal or otherwise subject to penalty. As noted in Chapters 2B and 3, there are a panoply of provisions potentially applicable to the practitioner who does too much for his client by lying or otherwise frustrating the audit process. Examples include section 7212, 18 U.S.C. section 371 (*Klein* conspiracy), and 18 U.S.C. section 1001. You are, of course, a careful practitioner and would not do anything illegal. You might do something stupid, but not illegal. However, sometimes the line between stupid and illegal blurs.

One of the key danger points is encountered early on during the process of determining the parameters of the potential criminal problem. The careful practitioner will want to interview all potential witnesses as soon as possible. The reason is to learn the lay of the land. But, more subtly, there can be an important benefit to nailing down each witness's testimony before the civil agent has had an opportunity to affect the witness memories by leading questions and other mind-shaping techniques. The witness may be much more amenable to a taxpayer-favorable recollection before being put upon, even intimidated, by an IRS agent, particularly a Special Agent. Obtaining witness interviews in a potential criminal case, however, presents a danger point for the practitioner.

The practitioner will want first to acquire a balanced understanding of the witness's potential testimony, but beyond that will want a taxpayer-favorable version of the witness's memory. The latter imperative can lead the practitioner to suggest testimony and shading testimony to the witness, thus edging towards the risk of charges of witness tampering or obstructing justice. Accordingly, it is better form in these cases for the practitioner to be accompanied by another lawyer or paralegal from his firm who could be a potential witness in favor of the practitioner if that charge were ever made. In addition, if possible and helpful, it is important to get a statement from the witness, perhaps in affidavit form, to commit the witness to a version of the facts that is helpful to the client or, at a minimum, mitigates the potential for damage.

Even more fraught with danger than practitioner interviews of witnesses are attempts by the taxpayer himself to get or shape the witness's version. The taxpayer has a vested interest in what the witness would say and is much more likely to try to influence the witness improperly. The circumstances are ripe for the IRS to charge that the taxpayer acted improperly to influence the witness, which could ultimately result in an obstruction of justice charge. The better course is to prohibit the taxpayer from talking to the witness at all or, if there must be commerce between the taxpayer and the witness (*e.g.*, in a business setting), to prohibit the taxpayer from discussing the criminal matter with the witness.[84] After getting the lay of the land from all of the potential key witnesses and from careful review of all documentation, the practitioner is in a position to best serve the taxpayer in the egg shell audit.

During the audit, the practitioner should limit the contact between the agent and the taxpayer. This is good practice even if there is no criminal potential in the case. Ask that the agent make all requests for information through the practitioner. Even better, ask that the agent make all requests in writing so that there is no confusion about what the request was and whether the response was untruthful or misleading. Ultimately, if the agent persists in wanting a taxpayer interview,[85] make sure that the taxpayer is prepared to answer honestly or have you assert the Fifth Amendment or other applicable privileges when appropriate.

Taxpayer's counsel must also "audit" the auditor — track his investigation to know what he knows at all times. This task has been made easier under 1998 legislation. The IRS is now required to notify the taxpayer before contacting third parties and to keep a record of the third parties contacted, at least during the civil phase of an investigation.[86] Moreover, section 7609, as amended in 1998, now requires that the IRS notify the taxpayer of the summonses issued to third parties.[87] That notice requirement does not apply in criminal investigations,[88] but the investigation is not yet criminal, so counsel can track all third-party summonses issued. If, for any reason, counsel hears that third-party summonses have been issued and the taxpayer did not receive notice, counsel should inquire — either they were issued incident a criminal investigation or they were issued in violation of the notice requirement.

The civil agent's sources of information are: (1) the taxpayer himself; (2) third parties; and (3) other sources.[89] The practitioner will be able to monitor information from the taxpayer and will be aware of the IRS's obtaining information from third parties by compulsory process. The problem, of course, is that the IRS can obtain information from third parties without the need for compulsory process. So, this potential will make it doubly important for the practitioner to have interviewed and established a good relationship with the witnesses in advance. Remember to ask the witness to call the practitioner if he or she is contacted by the IRS. By careful

---

84 "Prohibit" is a strong word here and not technically applicable since an attorney cannot prohibit the client from doing something. The attorney can, however, use the strongest cautions possible in advising the client and thereby hopefully convince the client that the prohibition is in his interest.

85 In general, the taxpayer may be represented by an attorney (or some other authorized representative) during an audit. Usually, absent issuance of an administrative summons, the IRS cannot compel the taxpayer to accompany the attorney or other representative. IRC § 7521(c). This provision does not apply to criminal investigations. IRC § 7521(d).

86 IRC § 7602(c). This provision was one of the numerous taxpayer safeguards added by the Internal Revenue Service Restructuring and Reform Act of 1998, Pub. L. No. 105-206, 112 Stat. 685.

87 IRC § 7609(a)(1).

88 IRC § 7609(c)(2)(E).

89 For discussion of IRS investigation and information gathering in civil cases, see Richardson, Borison & Johnson, *supra*, ch. 4.

tracking of the agent's activities, the practitioner will know, within reasonable parameters, what the agent knows. It is important in this process to keep in touch with the agent. The practitioner can learn a lot, even if the agent does not specifically say that he suspects fraud or is in the process of transferring the matter to CI. Counsel should remember, of course, that cases such as *Kontny* suggest that the Revenue Agent can affirmatively mislead the taxpayer and his or her representative as to the nature of the investigation,[90] but generally agents are discouraged from doing that. The careful and experienced practitioner should be able to sense when the audit has turned criminal. In this regard, one of the classic indicia of a referral to CI is that the civil audit has turned quiet. Civil audits are conducted on a time line, which may vary from case to case, but, if the audit is not progressing, the practitioner needs to know why. Often, it is because an agent is swamped with other work or has been transferred, but it may also be that the civil agent has referred the case to CI. When the civil audit turns quiet, the practitioner should touch base with the agent or his or her supervisor to find out what is going on, without, of course, tipping the agent that he is overly concerned about it.

After the civil agent has worked on the case, it can take two directions. First, the agent may not perceive the case as having criminal potential and will proceed to close the audit with such civil recommendations as he thinks appropriate. Second, the agent may determine that the case has sufficient criminal potential that it should be referred to CI. This can happen anytime during the audit process, but it often happens toward the end when the agent analyzes what he or she has and consults with the group supervisor and/or an IRS fraud coordinator.

If an egg shell audit does turn criminal, the taxpayer will often want to just pay up whatever the Government says and move on — in the fantasy that the payment of the tax will cause the criminal problem to go away. It won't. The criminal investigators and prosecutors really don't care whether the taxpayer ever pays the tax. They want their criminal pound of flesh. Payment of the tax won't technically deflect a criminal investigation or prosecution. In appropriate cases, payment may permit the taxpayer to urge that he really wanted all along to pay the taxes that he owed and, when first advised that he may have underpaid, moved promptly to pay. However, the Government cannot generally accept that as a resolution of the criminal case because every target would simply pay the tax. The criminal enforcement program would be gutted, with every taxpayer cheating to his or her heart's content with the idea that, if caught, he or she would simply pay any taxes, penalties, and interest. This would dramatically tilt the risk or reward ratio in tax evasion.[91]

---

[90] United States v. Kontny, 238 F.3d 815 (7th Cir. 2001). *But see* United States v. Tweel, 550 F.2d 297 (5th Cir. 1977) (suppressing on Fourth Amendment grounds business records a Revenue Agent obtained deceptively at the behest of DOJ prosecutors). For discussion of these cases, see John A. Townsend, *Taxpayer Rights in Criminal Investigations*, 90 TAX NOTES 1842 (2001).

[91] For further discussion, see Larry A. Campagna, Caroline D. Ciraolo & Eric L. Green, *The Eggshell Audit Part I: A Primer*, J. TAX PRAC. & PROC., June–July 2012, at 21, & *The Eggshell Audit Part II: Indicators of Fraud and IRS Fraud Development Procedures*, J. TAX PRAC. & PROC., Feb.–Mar. 2013, at 29.

PROBLEM

Carlton Samber and his wife, Trudy, filed joint federal income tax returns for all years relevant to this Problem. Carlton had founded and was the sole owner of a corporation, CSC Ltd. In January 2000, Carlton sold all of his CSC stock to an unrelated person, realizing long-term capital gain of slightly over $50 million.

Realizing that he and Trudy were facing substantial federal income tax liability, Carlton let his friends and associates know that he would be receptive to tax planning to reduce his potential tax liability for 2000. For example, Carlton told Hamish Haverstock, Carlton's certified public accountant: "I don't want to get into trouble with the IRS, of course, but something creative, maybe even a bit aggressive could be in order. And what the IRS doesn't know won't hurt it — or me."

Carlton's "feelers" were rewarded. In October 2000, he was contacted by Agnes Armitage, a partner in ABCD, one of the largest accounting and business consulting firms in the country. Haverstock knew Armitage, and he contacted her on Carlton's behalf. On October 10, 2000, a meeting took place involving Carlton, Haverstock, and Armitage. At the meeting, Armitage explained that she was part of ABCD's High Net Worth or Tax Advantaged Investments Group, and she stated that her Group had a "tax product" that she believed would meet Carlton's needs.

Carlton asked Armitage how much tax help he could expect from her product. She replied: "I understand that you're looking at $50 million of taxable gains. We can set it up to generate $50 million of losses for you, which you can use to offset your $50 million of gains." Carlton said he wasn't interested in losing $50 million, to which Armitage replied: "No, these are paper losses, tax losses. Beyond paying our fees, you would be out of pocket almost nothing."

Carlton asked how it was possible to accomplish these results. Armitage replied: "I'll be glad to lay it out for you, but this tax product is proprietary. Before I describe the details, I'll need you both to sign this agreement." Carlton and Haverstock read the agreement Armitage proffered. It had three main provisions: (1) the taxpayer and his representative(s) agreed that they would not reveal the nature of the arrangement to anyone at any time, beyond claiming tax losses from it on the taxpayer's returns; (2) ABCD would provide instructions as to how to report the losses on the taxpayer's returns; and (3) the taxpayer and his representative(s) represented that they were not employees of the IRS or any state revenue authority and were not working with, cooperating with, or assisting the IRS or any state revenue authority.

After reading the agreement, Haverstock said: "I'm sorry. I have to be blunt. I don't know of anything legal that could produce the results you promise, and I get all the wrong vibes from what I just read. Carlton, if I were you, I'd walk away from this thing right now." Carlton said: "No, I want to hear more, but you leave if you feel you need to." Haverstock left immediately. He had no further involvement except that he prepared the bulk of the Sambers' 2000 Form 1040. He did not prepare the part of that return having to do with the ABCD tax product. Armitage prepared that part of the return.

During the remainder of the October 10 meeting and in succeeding meetings, Carlton learned that the tax product involved dealings in options in foreign currencies effected through partnerships, in a variation of the Son of BOSS tax shelter. For purposes of this Problem, you do not need to sift through all the details of the shelter.[92] The core facts that you need for this Problem are set out below.

After further discussions, Carlton decided to participate in the shelter. He paid $3 million in fees to ABCD. In return, ABCD (i) provided Carlton with a tax opinion as to the deal, (ii) through related entities, handled all the currency and related transactions, and (iii) prepared the portions of the Sambers' 2000 Form 1040 which dealt with losses through the shelter. As a result, the Sambers' 2000 Form 1040 (which was filed in August 2001 under an extension) reported the $50 million gain from sale of the business but offset that gain with over $50 million of losses from the shelter.[93] This resulted in zero reported taxable income and zero reported tax due.

The tax opinion that Carlton received from ABCD was written by Bernice Baccus, an experienced tax attorney and another ABCD partner. Carlton never met or spoke with Baccus. The opinion recounted a number of representations supposedly by Carlton even though Carlton had not actually made the stated representations. One of these representations was that Carlton was participating in the transactions with the objective of realizing an economic profit and not solely to produce tax savings. Based on the supposed representations and on an extensive (though not necessarily fully accurate) discussion of legal authorities, the opinion concluded that the claimed tax losses were "more likely than not" to be upheld were they challenged by the IRS and litigated.

---

[92] If, outside the confines of this Problem, you wish to satisfy your curiosity about the details of Son of BOSS shelters, you may wish to review the following cases: *Cemco Investors, LLC v. United States*, 515 F.3d 749 (7th Cir. 2008); *Klamath Strategic Investment Fund, LLC v. United States*, 440 F. Supp. 2d 608 (E.D. Tex. 2006), *further opinion*, 472 F. Supp. 2d 885 (E.D. Tex. 2007), *further opinion*, 2007-1 USTC ¶ 50,410 (E.D. Tex. 2007).

[93] Specifically, the $50 million loss was claimed on the Schedule D attached to the 2000 return. The shelter entailed offsetting short and long positions in foreign currencies. The long positions were contributed to a partnership, allegedly producing a high basis in the partnership interest under section 722. The partnership interest was then sold for a pittance, creating a capital loss under sections 1001 and 1222. This event was listed on the 2000 Schedule D as "sale of partnership interest," with the $50 million loss amount, the date of acquisition of the partnership interest, the date of sale of that interest, but no additional information.

Again, you do not need to delve deeply into the details of the shelter to grapple with this Problem. However, for the curious, some additional notes. First, the Sambers didn't actually lose money on the deal in a real economic sense. That's because their short positions covered their long positions. Second, the key to the shelter for tax purposes was the definition of "liabilities" under section 752. As the law appeared to stand before 2003, the short positions were not liabilities, so did not decrease the Sambers' basis in their partnership interest. On June 24, 2003, Treasury and the IRS closed that loophole with new regulations under section 752. The regulations were made retroactive to October 18, 1999. In the *Klamath Strategic* case noted above, the court held against the retroactivity. In the *Cemco* case noted above, the taxpayer did not challenge the retroactivity.

In August 2000 — about a year before the Sambers' filed their 2000 Form 1040 — the IRS issued Notice 2000-44 "Tax Avoidance Using Artificially High Basis."[94] The Notice described generically transactions like the one Carlton engaged in. It stated the IRS's position that losses claimed through such transactions are not allowable for federal income tax purposes, and it stated that the IRS could assert penalties on taxpayers claiming such losses (although it did not specify which penalties the IRS would impose). Carlton was aware of Notice 2000-44, and he read it in late 2000.

In November 2003, the Sambers' filed an amended return for 2000. That amended return withdrew the $50 million of losses claimed on the original return. The amended return was accompanied by full payment of the resulting substantial tax liability and interest on it. The IRS had not contacted the Sambers about their original return before they filed their amended return.

In February 2004, the Sambers reversed their field again. They filed a refund claim with the IRS, seeking refund of all of the taxes and interest paid in November 2003 as to the 2000 tax year. The IRS denied the refund claim,[95] and the Sambers filed a refund suit in federal District Court in July 2004.

In the meantime, in early 2003, the Government asserted criminal charges against ABCD and some of its partners, with respect to their roles in promoting abusive tax shelters. The Government obtained indictments against ABCD, Armitage, Baccus, and 10 other ABCD partners. The indictments did not specify Carlton's transaction, but it did identify many similar transactions. ABCD pleaded guilty to some of the charges. Armitage, Baccus, and the other partners pleaded "not guilty." At the times relevant to this Problem, they had not yet come to trial.

1. On the above facts, what might have been the criminal charges that the Government brought against ABCD and the ABCD partners? What would probably have been the best way for the Government to investigate and develop those charges?

2. Additional facts: In November 2004, Carlton was contacted by an IRS Special Agent investigating the Sambers with respect to 2000. You are the Sambers' attorney.

a. What charges might CI be considering as to the Sambers? Why?

b. What arguments would you advance on the Sambers' behalf? How do you assess the strength or weakness of those arguments?

c. When and how will you get to present your arguments? What is your best strategy for your clients?

---

[94] 2000-2 C.B. 255 (Aug. 13, 2000).

[95] The IRS concluded that the shelter losses were not allowable for two reasons: (1) the taxpayers' position on the meaning of liabilities under section 752 was wrong, both under the new, retroactive regulations and under prior law; and (2) the taxpayers did not enter into the transactions to make an economic profit, thus the transactions were a sham for tax purposes and were devoid of economic substance.

Chapter 7

GOVERNMENT INFORMATION GATHERING

IRC §§ 7525, 7602, 7603(b), 7609

18 U.S.C. § 6002

I. INTRODUCTION

Successful investigation and prosecution of a criminal case depends upon effective information gathering by the Government, both to establish the elements of its *prima facie* case and to negate possible defenses. This chapter will discuss the mechanisms available to the Government to develop information and evidence, as well as the means by which defense counsel may properly oppose the Government's efforts, including the assertion of privileges. Parts I through V will discuss information gathering from sources within the United States, including IRS administrative summonses, grand jury subpoenas, search warrants, and sting operations. Part VI will discuss the various privileges and defenses that may be asserted in response to a summons or subpoena. Finally, Part VII will analyze the means for gathering evidence abroad and securing other types of international assistance in criminal tax cases, including the use of mutual legal assistance treaties, tax treaties, tax information exchange agreements, court-sponsored procedures for taking depositions abroad, and letters rogatory.

II. IRS SUMMONS POWER

A. General IRS Authority

The IRS has numerous means to gather information, including the power to summons. The general statutory grant of authority to the IRS to obtain information is found in section 7602(a), which empowers the IRS to examine books and records, take testimony under oath, and summons the taxpayer or any other person the IRS may deem proper. While the IRS summons power has given rise to the most litigation, in most civil audits and criminal investigations, agents usually resort to a summons only when informal requests have proven inadequate.[1] It is often much easier to just pick up the phone and ask for documents or stop by a witness's residence or place of business, rather than issue a summons. Also, as we will see, issuing a summons can require notice to the taxpayer, and the

---

[1] IRM 25.5.1.4(1) instructs agents to attempt to obtain information voluntarily from taxpayers and witnesses prior to issuing a summons.

investigating agent might well prefer to fly below the radar with informal requests for documents and information. Nevertheless, summonses are utilized regularly, and you must become familiar with the rules and processes surrounding them.

B. Rules on the Issuing of Summons

A summons is essentially an administrative subpoena, in that it is a request (demand) for information, testimony, or documents. Unlike a subpoena, the IRS can issue a summons administratively without any judicial action. A summons is drafted by an IRS agent,[2] who signs it and serves it in one of the following three methods: delivery "in hand" to the witness, delivery by leaving a copy at the "last and usual place of abode," or if it is a so-called "third-party recordkeeper summons," delivery by certified or registered mail.[3] A summons requires the witness to appear at the time and place designated in the summons to give testimony and/or to produce documents. Appearance in response to a summons may take the form of a formal question-and-answer session under oath, an informal interview, or merely submission of the records summoned. The most common summons is a summons on a bank for records of a taxpayer. In criminal cases, a summons on the taxpayer for testimony is rare, since the taxpayer (or at least a well-advised taxpayer) will refuse to answer any questions, citing the Fifth Amendment privilege.

Is the taxpayer entitled to notice of a summons? If the taxpayer is entitled to notice, the he or she has the right to intervene in the summons enforcement case or bring a proceeding to quash the summons. If no notice is required, the taxpayer generally has no right to intervene or move to quash.[4] Taxpayers will obviously receive notice regarding a summons issued to them, and the IRS is generally required to notify taxpayers being investigated of the issuance of third-party summonses. However, the IRS is not required to give taxpayers notice (except in the case of a so-called "third-party recordkeeper summons") when the summons is "issued by a criminal investigator of the Internal Revenue Service in connection with the investigation of an offense connected with the administration or enforcement of the internal revenue laws."[5] Moreover, a taxpayer is not entitled to notice of a summons on a third-party if a court determines that there is "reasonable cause to believe the giving of notice may lead to attempts to conceal, destroy, or alter records relevant to the examination, to prevent the communication of information from other persons through intimidation, bribery, or collusion, or to flee to avoid prosecution, testifying, or production of records."[6] Section 7602(c) requires the IRS to give advance notice to taxpayers "that contacts with persons other than the taxpayer may be made" and thereafter requires the IRS to give periodic notice to the taxpayer of the persons who have been contacted. However, the statute does not require the IRS to say *who* will be contacted, just that persons

---

[2] Special Agents, Revenue Agents, and Revenue Officers can issue summonses.

[3] IRC § 7603.

[4] IRC § 7609(b); Prop. Reg. 153037-01, 71 Fed. Reg. 41377 (July 1, 2006), 2007-15 IRB 942.

[5] IRC § 7609(c)(2)(E).

[6] IRC § 7609(g).

other than the taxpayer may be contacted. More importantly, the notice provisions are suspended in the case of "criminal investigations." Thus, once the investigation is criminal, the IRS need not give the notice. Finally, after the criminal investigation has been referred to the Tax Division for criminal prosecution or for grand jury investigation, the IRS cannot continue to issue administrative summonses, but must rely instead on grand jury subpoenas.[7]

C. Summons Enforcement Proceedings

A summons is not self-enforcing; rather, it must be enforced by an action in U.S. District Court. A summons enforcement action begins with the Government filing a petition seeking an order to show cause, accompanied by an affidavit of the issuing IRS agent which provides the *prima facie* case to demonstrate compliance with the requirements for enforcement. The court's role in an enforcement proceeding is not to second guess the judgment of the IRS, but to determine whether the particular summons is a legitimate exercise of the IRS's investigative authority. In *United States v. Powell*,[8] the Supreme Court set out a fairly low standard for the enforcement of a summons.

> [T]he Commissioner need not meet any standard of probable cause to obtain enforcement of his summons, either before or after the three-year statute of limitations on ordinary tax liabilities has expired. He must show that the investigation will be conducted pursuant to a legitimate purpose, that the inquiry may be relevant to the purpose, that the information sought is not already within the Commissioner's possession, and that the administrative steps required by the Code have been followed — in particular, that the "Secretary or his delegate," after investigation, has determined the further examination to be necessary and has notified the taxpayer in writing to that effect. This does not make meaningless the adversary hearing to which the taxpayer is entitled before enforcement is ordered. At the hearing he "may challenge the summons on any appropriate ground," nor does our reading of the statutes mean that under no circumstances may the court inquire into the underlying reasons for the examination. It is the court's process which is invoked to enforce the administrative summons and a court may not permit its process to be abused. Such an abuse would take place if the summons had been issued for an improper purpose, such as to harass the taxpayer or to put pressure on him to settle a collateral dispute, or for any other purpose reflecting on the good faith of the particular investigation. The burden of showing an abuse of the court's process is on the taxpayer, and it is not met by a mere showing, as was made in this case, that the statute of limitations for ordinary deficiencies has run or that the records in question have already been once examined.

Thus, under *Powell*, the Government must make a *prima facie* showing that (1) the summons was issued for a legitimate purpose; (2) the material sought is relevant

[7] IRC § 7609(d).

[8] 379 U.S. 48, 57–58 (1964) (citations and footnotes omitted).

to that purpose; (3) the information sought is not already within the possession of the Commissioner; and (4) the administrative steps required by the Internal Revenue Code have been followed. The courts have given the term *relevance* an expansive definition:

> As the language of § 7602 clearly indicates, an IRS summons is not to be judged by the relevance standards used in deciding whether to admit evidence in federal court. . . . The language "may be" reflects Congress' express intention to allow the IRS to obtain items of even *potential* relevance to an ongoing investigation, without reference to its admissibility. The purpose of Congress is obvious: the Service can hardly be expected to know whether such data will in fact be relevant until [it is] procured and scrutinized. As a tool of discovery, the § 7602 summons is critical to the investigative and enforcement functions of the IRS . . . ; the Service therefore should not be required to establish that the documents it seeks are actually relevant in any technical, evidentiary sense.[9]

In practice, so long as the IRS can articulate almost any legitimate purpose for using the summons, a court will not interfere by quashing the summons or refusing to enforce it. Of course, the IRS must articulate some relevancy and materiality to a legitimate IRS function. In *United States v. Gertner*, which we will revisit later, the court provided a nice summary of the procedures a summons enforcement must take and the respective burdens on the parties:

> In determining whether to enforce IRS summonses under [the *Powell*] standards, we do not write on a pristine page. This court has constructed a three-tiered framework for expediting such determinations. To mount the first tier, the IRS must make a prima facie showing that it is acting in good faith and for a lawful purpose. This burden is not taxing, so to speak. Courts repeatedly have confirmed that an affidavit of the investigating agent attesting to satisfaction of the four Powell elements is itself adequate to make the requisite prima facie showing.
>
> Once this minimal showing surfaces, the burden shifts to the taxpayer to rebut the good-faith presumption that arises in consequence of the government's prima facie case. The taxpayer is not at this stage required to disprove the government's profession of good faith. She must, however, shoulder a significant burden of production: in order to advance past the first tier, the taxpayer must articulate specific allegations of bad faith and, if necessary, produce reasonably particularized evidence in support of those allegations. This showing does not demand that the taxpayer conclusively give the lie to the prima facie case, but only that she create a "substantial question in the court's mind regarding the validity of the government's purpose." To reach this goal, it is not absolutely essential that the taxpayer adduce additional or independent evidence; she may hoist her burden either by citing new facts or by bringing to light mortal weaknesses in the government's proffer.

---

[9] United States v. Arthur Young & Co., 465 U.S. 805, 814 (1984) (emphasis in original).

> If the taxpayer satisfies this burden of production, the third tier beckons. At this stage, the district court weighs the facts, draws inferences, and decides the issue. To do so, the court frequently will proceed to an evidentiary hearing, taking testimony and exhibits from both sides. But there is no hard-and-fast rule compelling an evidentiary hearing. A district court may, in appropriate circumstances, forgo such a hearing and decide the issues on the existing record.[10]

D. Third-Party Recordkeeper Summons

As noted above, normally, a taxpayer is not entitled to notice if a summons is served on a third party during a criminal investigation. In addition, even if the taxpayer somehow learned of the summons, there is no general right to intervene and move to quash a summons issued on a third party in a criminal case. The rules are different, however, if the summons is served on a so-called "third-party recordkeeper." A third-party recordkeeper is defined in section 7603(b) include banks, consumer reporting agencies, credit card companies, brokers, attorneys, accountants, barter exchanges, regulated investment companies, enrolled agents, and owners or developers of a computer software source code.

If a summons is issued to a third-party recordkeeper, the taxpayer has the right, under section 7609, to bring a proceeding to quash the summons or to intervene in a proceeding brought by the IRS to enforce the summons.[11] There are defenses to a third-party recordkeeper summons, especially those served on an attorney, and we will discuss those defenses below. However, these endeavors should not be undertaken lightly. Beyond the fact that these challenges rarely succeed given the low bar of the *Powell* test, the problem with this procedure is that it suspends the running of the civil and criminal statute of limitations during the pendency of the proceeding or any appeal.[12]

E. John Doe Summons

A *John Doe summons* is a summons issued to a third party, like a bank, seeking information regarding taxpayers whose identities are currently unknown to the IRS.[13] Thus, the purpose of a Joe Doe summons is not just to further an investigation of a given taxpayer. Rather, it is to find out who the taxpayers are so that an investigation may be undertaken in earnest. A typical example of a target of a John Doe summons is the promoter of an allegedly abusive tax shelter that has been widely sold, where the IRS desires to discover the names of all the investors. The John Doe summons procedures require the IRS to convince a court that (1) the investigation relates to a particular person or ascertainable group of persons; (2) there is reasonable cause to believe that the person or persons identified may not have complied with the tax laws; and (3) the information sought is not readily

---

[10] 65 F.3d 963, 966–67 (1st Cir. 1995) (citations and footnotes omitted).

[11] IRC § 7609(c)(2)(E).

[12] *See* Reg. § 301.7609-5. Statutes of limitation are discussed more fully in Chapter 5.

[13] In re Tax Liabilities of John Does, 671 F.2d 977, 978 (6th Cir. 1982).

available from other sources.[14] Since these proceedings are done *ex parte*, they are ripe for abuse.

In the case of a garden-variety third-party summons, the taxpayer receives notice and may contest the summons in a proceeding to quash. However, in the case of a John Doe Summons, the taxpayer is by definition not known and will not receive notice. Moreover, a taxpayer whose records or information are sought by the John Doe summons cannot intervene in the Government's initial *ex parte* application for service of the summons. That does not mean that the IRS routinely resorts to these procedures. Since a John Doe summons requires prior District Court approval, the IRS must obtain the assistance of Tax Division lawyers. The IRS must first convince DOJ Tax that it is worth presenting the matter to a frequently skeptical and almost always overworked District Court. Obviously, the IRS would much prefer just to use its administrative summons, which does not have these cumbersome steps.

A summons also may be issued for a dual purpose, that is, it may be issued in order to obtain both information relating to an identified taxpayer, as well as an unidentified taxpayer. In *United States v. Tiffany Fine Arts, Inc.*, the Supreme Court held that the IRS did not need to follow the cumbersome John Doe summons procedures to learn the identity of other taxpayers "as long as all the information sought is relevant to a legitimate investigation of the summonsed taxpayer."[15] The Court held that it is irrelevant whether the "primary" or "secondary" purpose of the summons relates to the tax liabilities of unidentified third parties, as long as the IRS is legitimately investigating the identified taxpayer.[16] *Tiffany Fine Arts* involved a tax shelter promoter who sold the shelters to unknown (at least to the IRS) third parties. By investigating the promoter's own tax liability as a basis of inquiry into whether it reported its income from those unknown third parties, the IRS could avoid the unwieldy *ex parte* procedures required for a John Doe summons, and summons the information under the general administrative summons rules. As a result, it could obtain the identity of unknown third parties and only have to meet the minimal requirements of *Powell*. The Supreme Court blessed that strategy and refused to require use of the John Doe summons procedure.

After *Tiffany Fine Arts*, the IRS seemed to have found liberation from the annoyances of the John Doe Summons procedures — simply find a reason to audit the third-party and find some pretext for obtaining the names of the third parties. The IRS tried that maneuver in *United States v. Gertner*, excerpted above. In *Gertner*, a client paid a law firm a large amount of cash, which required the firm to file a Form 8300 Currency Transaction Report (CTR) regarding the cash.[17] The client did not want his name divulged to the Government for fear that the Government might use the information against him. The law firm filed the CTR but asserted ethical obligations, attorney-client privilege, and constitutional

---

[14] IRC § 7609(f).

[15] 469 U.S. 310, 324 (1985).

[16] *Id.* at 317–18 n.5.

[17] We will discuss the ethical ramifications of receiving cash from clients in Chapter 11.

protections against naming the client. The John Doe summons would fit the situation like a glove, assuming of course that a court would have authorized the summons. Not to be slowed down, the IRS instead issued a regular summons for billing records and testimony that would identify the client. The law firm declined to comply, and the Government moved to enforce the summons. The district court refused to enforce the summons, finding that the IRS's use of the regular IRS summons was not in good faith. The court noted that *Tiffany Fine Arts* had approved the use of a regular summons that might have the collateral effect of identifying unknown taxpayers only if it related to an investigation of the person whose records were seized. The Government thus had to demonstrate that it had a legitimate interest in auditing the law firm. On appeal, the First Circuit agreed that the IRS failed to meet that burden:

> At the outset, we are constrained to note that the remarkably thin prima facie case established by Agent Ameno's declaration provides a shallow foundation for a presumption in favor of the government. While the declaration touches the requisite bases — it contains the bareboned allegations needed for the government's prima facie showing — it is utterly devoid of specifics. Though a conclusory affidavit is enough to satisfy the government's burden at the first tier of the framework, it can come back to haunt the proponent if it is not later supplemented by more hearty fare once the challenger succeeds in scaling the second tier.
>
> At any rate, the government effectuated its prima facie showing with little room to spare. The burden then shifted to the respondents to produce evidence and/or allegations of sufficient force and exactitude to warrant further inquiry. To meet this burden, the respondents argued that the summonses should be shelved because the government's professed purpose — linking the summonses to an investigation into the law firm's tax liability — was pretextual.
>
> Contrary to the government's dismissive suggestion, the respondents did not simply level the charge. In support of it, they submitted two affidavits. One affidavit incorporated the extensive correspondence between the firm and the IRS. The second affidavit chronicled the firm's meticulous attention to income reporting requirements, and asserted that the IRS already had the data it needed to determine whether the firm had fully complied with its tax-related obligations. In addition, the respondents documented several public statements which seem to imply that the IRS's purpose in issuing summonses to attorneys for the records of large cash-paying clients is designed less to monitor lawyers' compliance with the tax laws, and more to address money laundering, narcotics distribution, and kindred criminal activity on the part of lawyers' clients. Finally, the respondents pointed out that the Ameno declaration, which purported to describe the ongoing investigation of the law firm, was nothing but boilerplate.
>
> The lower court concluded on this chiaroscuro record that the government's supposed investigation of the law firm was a pretext for an anticipated investigation of John Doe. On appeal, the IRS rides two horses

> into the breach. First, it maintains that the district court erred in stabling the summonses without holding an evidentiary hearing. Second, it posits that, in all events, the court's ultimate finding of pretext, based on the record before it, is unsupportable. Both steeds are lame.
>
> In *Tiffany*, unlike here, the district court ascertained as a matter of fact that the IRS had a dual purpose, that is, an actual interest in the investigation of both the taxpayer and the John Doe. In this case, the district court ascertained, also as a matter of fact, that the IRS did not have an actual interest in the investigation of the taxpayer (the respondents' law firm), but only in learning more about John Doe. Thus, the two cases are not fair congeners except to the extent that, given Judge Brody's supportable factual finding that the summonses at issue here were not dual purpose summonses, the Supreme Court's opinion in *Tiffany* clearly indicates that we should respect that finding. And, once the judge determined as a matter of fact that the government's actual purpose in issuing the summonses was to further an investigation of the unnamed client, the follow-on conclusion that the government should have complied with the procedure for issuing John Doe summonses becomes irresistible.[18]

Recently, the most prominent instances of IRS use of the John Doe summons have been to identify U.S. taxpayers using offshore financial accounts to hide taxable income. For such clients playing the offshore account game, the expectation of secrecy is at the core of the game, so this activity is concentrated in countries that are referred to as "tax havens." The IRS is often unable to determine whether the U.S. taxpayer has a tax haven financial account or the amount in the account. The John Doe summons works well in such a case, at least when the party having information that can identify the U.S. taxpayers is within the IRS summons power (meaning that a U.S. court will impose meaningful sufficient pain via the contempt power to compel compliance).

Most tax haven financial institutions participating in this offshore evasion service for U.S. taxpayers try to avoid any U.S. presence that would subject them to the IRS summons and U.S. court contempt powers. They are not always successful. The IRS has used John Doe summonses in two prominent "waves." First, the IRS issued John Doe Summonses to U.S. credit and debit card processors who processed the credit and debit card transactions that U.S. taxpayers used to tap their offshore funds in a way that they and the tax haven banks thought would be invisible to the IRS. Once those debit and credit card transaction documents were obtained, the IRS might be able to match names or, in some cases, tie back to charges for U.S. taxpayer accounts at the U.S. vendor. The issuance and approval of the John Doe summonses to the credit and debit card transaction processors were covered with great fanfare in the press. Taking advantage of the press, the IRS created a special voluntary disclosure initiative whereby U.S. taxpayers having offshore accounts could solve their potential criminal exposure.[19]

---

[18] Gertner, *supra*, at 968–71.

[19] *See, e.g.*, Leandra Lederman, *The Use of Voluntary Disclosure Initiatives in the Battle Against Offshore Tax Evasion*, 57 VILL. L. REV. 499 (2012).

The second wave began in 2008, when the IRS issued a John Doe summons issued to the Swiss bank giant UBS. UBS, which had, and continues to have, a substantial U.S. presence, routinely assisted U.S. taxpayers hide their income from the IRS. Rather than sitting in Switzerland beyond the IRS summons power and U.S. court contempt power, UBS's Swiss bankers had regular contacts with clients in the U.S., in violation of U.S. law. The IRS learned of these activities and issued a John Doe summons to UBS for the names of the estimated 52,000 U.S. taxpayers maintaining accounts with UBS. UBS claimed that Swiss law prevented it from complying with the summons. The Swiss Government ultimately became involved in the dispute, which ended with a negotiated settlement between the U.S. and Swiss governments. While some names have been provided by UBS to the U.S. Government, the number is far fewer than the amount requested. However, more important than the number of names obtained, the Swiss Government agreed to reinterpret the exchange of information provision of the U.S. — Switzerland double tax treaty to permit UBS to make the disclosures of the names and account information for the taxpayers that the IRS had not identified. Thus, although the John Doe summons did not technically produce the information sought, the reinterpretation of the treaty is producing some of the information sought. Moreover, as discussed more fully below, the UBS case and the Government's new hardline against tax haven banks has fundamentally changed the way foreign financial evidence is obtained.

III. GRAND JURY SUBPOENA

Although the IRS usually conducts the initial phases of the investigation as an IRS administrative investigation, the grand jury and its processes may be used to fill any holes in the IRS investigation.[20] In addition, some tax investigations start out in the grand jury. The request for a grand jury investigation is a referral of the matter to the Department of Justice, and, while the referral is in effect, the IRS may not issue an administrative summons. If further investigative work is required or if assistance is needed to explain the case to the grand jury, an IRS Special Agent, usually the same agent conducting the administrative investigation, will be assigned to assist the grand jury. Instead of a summons, the Government uses the grand jury subpoena to investigate tax crimes. And, that process is powerful indeed — far more powerful than the IRS administrative summons.

How does the grand jury subpoena compare with the IRS administrative summons? First, a grand jury subpoena is self-enforcing — failure to comply with a grand jury constitutes contempt, whereas an IRS administrative summons is not self-enforcing and requires a subsequent summons enforcement action in the district court. Second, the witness must appear before the grand jury alone and cannot have his or her attorney present, whereas a witness appearing pursuant to an IRS summons has the right to have an attorney present. Although a grand jury witness can certainly leave the grand jury room to ask counsel for advice, there is tremendous pressure not to do so or to keep it to a minimum. Third, any IRS administrative summons to a third party requires notice to the taxpayer involved

[20] USAM 6-4.121.

under the rules discussed above. When a third-party summons requiring notice is involved, the taxpayer will know of both the existence of the investigation and the direction of the investigation by notice as to the types of information the IRS seeks. The grand jury subpoena, by contrast, has no notice requirements, and the taxpayer will not necessarily be advised of the existence or direction of the investigation. Indeed, as to some grand jury subpoenas, notifying the target of the subpoena is punishable as an obstruction of justice.

The grand jury subpoena is generally perceived as being more serious and requiring more prompt and serious attention than the IRS administrative summons. Moreover, the grand jury investigation is managed by seasoned DOJ prosecutors who know what information they need to shore up the case they will eventually be presenting to a jury for trial. By contrast, Special Agents must conduct their investigation not knowing what the prosecutor will want and without the guidance of those seasoned prosecutors.

"Targets" or "subjects" of grand jury proceedings usually are not subpoenaed to appear before the grand jury. USAM 9-11.151 defines the terms "target" and "subject" as follows:

> A "*target*" is a person as to whom the prosecutor or the grand jury has substantial evidence linking him or her to the commission of a crime and who, in the judgment of the prosecutor, is a putative defendant. An officer or employee of an organization which is a target is not automatically considered a target even if such officer's or employee's conduct contributed to the commission of the crime by the target organization. The same lack of automatic target status holds true for organizations which employ, or employed, an officer or employee who is a target.
>
> A "*subject*" of an investigation is a person whose conduct is within the scope of the grand jury's investigation.

That said, the line between target and subject has never been very clear, and a subject might well become a target without the person (or counsel) knowing of it. If the prosecutor or grand jury feels a need to hear from a target or subject, the prosecutor will normally "invite" the target or subject to appear rather than issuing a subpoena compelling the appearance. The USAM notes that while it is not improper for a grand jury to subpoena a subject or a target, "in the context of particular cases such a subpoena may carry the appearance of unfairness. Because the potential for misunderstanding is great, before a known 'target' is subpoenaed to testify before the grand jury about his or her involvement in the crime under investigation, an effort should be made to secure the target's voluntary appearance."[21] Of course, well-advised targets or subjects of the investigation invoke the Fifth Amendment privilege to the questions the prosecutor would want to ask. Thus, the target or subject will normally decline any invitation or opportunity to testify. And, if the target is subpoenaed to testify, he or she should usually be able to avoid having to appear by simply advising the prosecutor in writing that he or she will assert the Fifth Amendment.

---

[21] USAM 9-11.150.

The power of the grand jury subpoena does come with limitations that have significant applicability in tax contexts. Grand jury matters cannot be shared with the IRS to develop its civil tax position without a pending judicial proceeding and a court order.[22] This can put up a significant roadblock to the IRS pursuing a defendant's civil liability after the criminal proceedings have concluded. Thus, in order to obtain the more efficient criminal process by pursuing an investigation by grand jury, the IRS may limit its use of the fruits of the investigation in the ongoing civil tax investigation. As a result, most IRS investigations inhabit the administrative side of the house as long as possible, relying on the summons to furnish the necessary information.

IV. SEARCH WARRANTS

The IRS has increasingly used the search warrant as an investigative tool. Obtaining a search warrant requires the Government to establish that there is probable cause to believe that a crime has been committed. The object of the search may include "(1) property that constitutes evidence of the commission of a criminal offense; or (2) contraband, the fruits of crime, or things otherwise criminally possessed; or (3) property designed or intended for use or which is or has been used as the means of committing a criminal offense."[23] When Special Agents execute a search warrant, they generally take all books and records, papers, files, and computers (including, for some reason, the monitor and keyboard). Search warrants are normally not used against a person who is merely a witness and not the target or subject of the investigation. However, the Government will seek a search warrant if the circumstances suggest that the witness might have some reason not to respond properly to a summons or a subpoena.

If IRS Special Agents believe they can establish probable cause to seek a search warrant in an administrative investigation, they must consult with IRS Counsel, who review and approve all Title 26 search warrants and take an active role in preparing the proposed warrant and the supporting affidavit. With IRS Counsel approval, the Special Agent may ask the Department of Justice to seek the search warrant. Justice Department policies regarding the seeking of search warrants in tax cases are found in the CTM.[24] Generally, as to subjects or targets of a tax investigation, the request is made directly to the U.S. Attorney's office for the district in which the search warrant will be executed. Search warrants in tax cases on physicians, lawyers, accountants, public officials, clergy, news media representatives, labor union officials, and exempt organization officials require the approval of the Assistant Attorney General in charge of the Tax Division.[25] The documents that may support a tax crime are not within the traditional definition of contraband and may indeed be completely innocuous, and the Tax Division has urged some caution in using search warrants:

---

22 Fed. R. Crim. P. 6(e)(3)(C)(i).

23 Fed. R. Crim. P. 41(b).

24 *See* CTM 2.0, 3.0.

25 USAM 6-4.130.

> Aside from questions of strict legality, search warrants in tax investigations involve potential problems and issues intrinsic to tax cases. The concept of seizing personal or business books and records as the evidence or instrumentality of a crime is not as direct or simple a problem as is the seizure of a contraband. These documents usually contain much personal and confidential information and these very same documents, which, by their own nature, are not unusual, illegal or dangerous, will be the evidence of or the instrumentality of the crime to be charged. In addition to the controversial nature of such a seizure of documents, the requirement that the items to be seized must be named with specificity is more difficult to meet. In tax cases, the warrant must be specific, not only regarding the items to be seized and the place searched, but a specific time frame must also be stated.[26]

The most common issues regarding search warrants are the reasonableness of the search, the documents and other matters seized (like computers), and whether the search violated the Fourth Amendment right against unreasonable searches and seizures. The *Lefkowitz* case discusses those and other issues.

UNITED STATES v. LEFKOWITZ

United States Court of Appeals, Ninth Circuit
618 F.2d 1313 (1980)

Lefkowitz appeals from his convictions for various tax fraud offenses. He challenges the validity of the search warrants issued to search his home and his corporate offices, focusing on the failure of the supporting affidavit to disclose the identity of the IRS's secret informant: his estranged wife Helen. This failure, he says, prevented the magistrate from exercising an informed, independent judgment in issuing the warrants and renders the affidavit insufficient to support a finding of probable cause. He further argues that the privilege against adverse spousal testimony or the confidential marital communications privilege prohibits the use of his wife as an informant. We affirm.

Lefkowitz was convicted after a bench trial on stipulated facts of violating 18 U.S.C. §§ 371 and 1001 and 26 U.S.C. §§ 7201, 7203 and 7206(1). He was sentenced to four years imprisonment and placed on three years probation to begin after his prison term.

Lefkowitz was the president of several related small corporations, most of them in the car rental/leasing business. On June 12, 1975, IRS agents went to the Lefkowitz corporate offices, told Lefkowitz that he and his corporations were under investigation for possible violations of the tax laws and served him with a summons calling for the 1971–74 books and records of the Lefkowitz corporations to be produced at the IRS offices on June 23, 1975.

Sometime during the next week Lefkowitz, his lawyer Babic and his accountant Fisher met in Lefkowitz's private office to discuss the impending IRS document inspection. In response to Lefkowitz's concern over large cash shortages evidenced

[26] USAM 6-4.130; Tax Resource Manual 13.

by the 1973 books for N/U Rent-A-Car, one of the Lefkowitz entities, Fisher jokingly suggested burning the books. The less drastic solution of rewriting the books was chosen, and a secret, separate office was rented in which Fisher could perform his cosmetic accounting.

On June 23, the three conspirators met with agents at the IRS offices and Babic represented that the records called for in the summons did not exist or had been lost or destroyed. The date of July 14, 1975 was set for the production of whatever records could be found by then.

The next week Lefkowitz, with the help of his secretary Patricia Sullivan, Fisher, Mark Nestico (an employee) and Helen Lefkowitz, moved boxes of corporate records to Sullivan's apartment. On July 14, the IRS agents were given the then-completed spurious 1973 N/U Rent-A-Car records.

On November 7 and 10, 1975, IRS agents received information from a confidential source (later revealed to be Helen Lefkowitz). She told the agents about the falsified books and about the removal of the original records to Sullivan's apartment, and added that some of the original records had been moved back into the corporate offices after July 14, when the false N/U Rent-A-Car documents had been produced. She had seen these records in the corporate offices as late as mid-October.

On November 17, an IRS agent interviewed Nestico, who admitted that on Lefkowitz's instructions he had helped move some boxes of records from the Sullivan apartment to Lefkowitz's residence, where he had seen them as late as the end of October. Nestico also saw records in the corporate offices at the end of October.

On the basis of an affidavit by IRS agent Laffer reciting this and other information, search warrants were issued on November 17 for the Lefkowitz corporate offices and Lefkowitz's residence. The affidavit did not reveal that the secret informant was Helen Lefkowitz. Much of the evidence used to convict Lefkowitz was obtained through the execution of these warrants.

The threshold issue is whether the affidavit provided the magistrate enough essential facts to enable her to exercise her independent judgment and perform her function as a "neutral and detached magistrate." *See United States v. Beusch*, 596 F.2d 871, 874 (9th Cir. 1979); *Aguilar v. Texas*, 378 U.S. 108, 111 (1964), *quoting Johnson v. United States*, 333 U.S. 10, 14 (1948).

Aguilar announced a two-pronged test of the sufficiency of affidavits based on hearsay: first, the affidavit must provide information showing the reliability of the informant's information; second, the affidavit must provide information indicating the informant's credibility.

The affidavit here indicated that the informants had personally heard and observed that which they asserted. The first requirement, reliability, was therefore satisfied.

The affidavit here is replete with data indicating the informants' credibility: their information is firsthand, specific and highly detailed, thus it is "self-corroborating." Certain aspects of the information were independently corroborated by information already known to the IRS. The information was given to the IRS in circumstances subjecting the informants to possible personal or penal risk. In addition, Helen Lefkowitz's and Nestico's stories corroborated each other.

The affidavit is clearly sufficient on its face to support a finding of probable cause. The information from the two hearsay sources satisfied both prongs of the Aguilar test. Lefkowitz argues, however, that this court should look beyond the four corners of the affidavit and consider its sufficiency given Helen's identity and the accompanying credibility problems.

In *Franks v. Delaware*, 438 U.S. 154 (1978), the Supreme Court held that in order to challenge an affidavit valid on its face, a defendant must show (1) the affidavit contains intentionally or recklessly false statements, and (2) the affidavit purged of its falsities would not be sufficient to support a finding of probable cause.

Lefkowitz satisfies neither of these requirements. He asserts no intent or recklessness in the omission of Helen's identity (in fact, Laffer swore that he offered the identity to the magistrate, who declined it). Moreover, even if the affiant had revealed Helen's identity, the affidavit still would have sufficed to support a finding of probable cause to issue search warrants.

True, Helen Lefkowitz was the estranged wife of the appellant and as such may have had motivation to contact the IRS other than a sense of civic duty. After being married for 23 years, appellant and Helen Lefkowitz separated in August 1975. Appellant began living with Sullivan, his secretary, in September 1975. Helen Lefkowitz contacted the IRS in November 1975. The Lefkowitzes were eventually divorced in 1977. Inferences of spite, vengeance, and perhaps a desire to obtain advantageous property settlement information via an IRS investigation might spring from this scenario. However, the district court expressly found that the magistrate could have found Helen credible even considering her identity, and thus the affidavit would support a finding of probable cause even if the omission was cured. The district court's determination here was not clearly erroneous.

The nondisclosure of Helen Lefkowitz's identity does not require us to look beyond the four corners of the facially valid affidavit under the Franks v. Delaware test. Even considering her identity, she could still be found a credible informant.

[Authors' note: The court then turned to the defendant's allegation that the spousal testimony and confidential marital communications privileges prevented his wife from testifying against him.]

Although Lefkowitz confuses these privileges, they are distinct. The first can be invoked to prevent one spouse from testifying against the other. The second can be invoked to prevent the disclosure of confidential communications arising out of the marital relationship.

The privilege against adverse spousal testimony is of no use to Lefkowitz here because his wife did not "testify" against him, but provided information used to support the issuance of a search warrant. Moreover, this privilege does not preclude the use of a wife's statements against a defendant husband at trial when they are testified to by a third person. Here, Helen Lefkowitz did not personally appear before the magistrate; her information was recited in the affidavit of a third person. Therefore, the privilege did not bar this use of her statements.

The confidential marital communications privilege is also unavailable to Lefkowitz. It applies only to utterances or expressions intended to be communicative (i.e., to convey a message from one spouse to the other) and confidential.

The information Helen Lefkowitz provided to the IRS concerned the following facts: (1) the records turned over to the IRS were fraudulent; (2) the original records were removed from the corporate offices; (3) some of these records were moved to Sullivan's apartment; and (4) some of the original records were later moved back into the corporate offices (where they eventually were seized).

Her information that the records given to the IRS were false and that some of the original records were moved back into the corporate offices and remained there was based on her personal observations. There was no communicative utterance or expression by her husband and therefore her divulgence of this information did not violate the confidential marital communications privilege.

The original records were removed from the corporate offices in the presence, and with the assistance, of Sullivan, Fisher and Nestico. Even assuming such actions were communicative, the presence of others destroys confidentiality and renders the privilege inapplicable.

The only information based on a communication by Lefkowitz and arguably intended as confidential was that some records were moved to Sullivan's apartment. This piece of information can easily be disregarded without impairing the sufficiency of the affidavit. Nestico, the other informant relied on in the affidavit, provided essentially the same information, stating that he personally moved boxes of records, of a description strikingly similar to Mrs. Lefkowitz's description of the boxes of records she helped move, from Sullivan's apartment to the Lefkowitz residence. The fact that these records were ever in the Sullivan apartment, moreover, was not essential, because that apartment was never searched. The nature of these records was sufficiently demonstrated to the magistrate by the fact that Lefkowitz had warned Nestico not to tell anyone about them. The affidavit was therefore sufficient even disregarding Helen Lefkowitz's and Nestico's information about the Sullivan apartment.

Thus, neither the privilege against adverse spousal testimony nor the confidential marital communications privilege precluded the use of any facts obtained from Helen Lefkowitz which were essential to the sufficiency of the affidavit.

Mr. Lefkowitz committed one of the classic blunders. The most famous, of course, is never get involved in a land war in Asia,[27] but only slightly less well-known is, never use your wife to help you commit a crime and then dump her for your secretary. His assertion of the marital privilege was also not well-conceived. We will discuss below the various defenses and privileges that may be asserted in response to a summons, grand jury subpoena, and search warrant.

---

[27] THE PRINCESS BRIDE (Twentieth Century-Fox 1987).

V. STING OPERATIONS

In addition to summons, subpoenas, and search warrants, the IRS can use sting operations to gather evidence. Sting operations are often done in conjunction with other agencies, such as the FBI, and are usually conducted through a task force connected to a grand jury investigation. Most of the IRS sting operations are conducted as part of a money laundering investigation pursuant to 18 U.S.C. section 1956(a)(3). That subsection authorizes undercover operations when the Government or an informant can represent funds as being derived from a Specified Unlawful Activity (SUA).[28] Section 1956(a)(3) was added to the statute expressly to permit prosecution when the defendant believes the proceeds were derived from a SUA because of a representation made by a law enforcement officer or an informant.[29]

VI. DEFENSES AND PRIVILEGES

In this section, we will discuss the defenses and privileges that may be asserted in response to the Government's request for information. Obviously, these defenses also arise at trial and in other stages of criminal tax proceedings. Thus, some of these defenses, as well as the strategies that accompany them, are discussed in other chapters of this book. We will examine them here through the prism of the Government's information-gathering efforts.

Privileges are an evidentiary concept. The general rule in Anglo-American jurisprudence is that persons — both citizens and artificial entities — may be compelled to tell what they know to administrative agencies and courts in order to assist those agencies and courts administer the laws and dispense justice. In pithy language, the Supreme Court has admonished that "the public has the right to everyman's evidence."[30] Privileges, where applicable, permit persons to withhold what they know or, in a broader sense, evidence and hence to hamper the truth finding process in which courts and administrative agencies are involved. Privileges are thus justified only where there is some overriding public benefit — a public good transcending the normally predominant principle of utilizing all rational means for ascertaining truth. While other defenses and privileges can be raised, we will focus on the Fifth Amendment privilege, the attorney-client privilege, and the related work-product and accountant-client privileges.[31]

---

[28] We cover money laundering and SUAs in Chapter 3.

[29] IRM 9.5.5.2.1.3.

[30] Trammel v. United States, 445 U.S. 40, 50 (1980) (internal quotes and words omitted for clarity), *quoting* United States v. Bryan, 339 U.S. 323, 331 (1950).

[31] In addition to these traditional privileges a taxpayer can, as noted above, resist a summons if: (1) the four factors set out in *Powell* are not met, (2) the summons or subpoena is unreasonable as to place or time, (3) lack of proper service, (4) the summons was made after a case was referred to the Department of Justice, or (5) the summons was issued in bad faith (e.g., the Joe Doe summons in *Gertner*).

A. The Privilege Against Self-Incrimination

The Fifth Amendment to the Constitution provides that no person shall be compelled in any criminal case to be a witness against himself. Questions regarding this constitutional protection arise frequently throughout the life of a tax case, including: (1) in filing a tax return, the taxpayer may not want to respond to certain questions for fear it might expose nontax criminal activity (*e.g.*, drug dealing); (2) after filing, a taxpayer may face a similar dilemma in trying to decide whether to amend an original fraudulent or false return; (3) during an IRS civil or criminal investigation, the taxpayer may receive a summons to give testimony and/or produce documents that might be privileged; and (4) during the criminal trial, the taxpayer may consider testifying. We noted earlier that the Government does not usually summons the taxpayer or subpoena a target of a grand jury investigation to appear and testify before a grand jury, realizing it will result in the witness claiming the Fifth. During the Government's information gathering stage, Fifth Amendment concerns most often appear when a taxpayer or witness is asked to produce records or other documents.

It is well-settled that the Fifth Amendment privilege applies "in any proceeding, civil or criminal, administrative or judicial, investigatory or adjudicatory" where a person may tend to incriminate himself.[32] Federal jurisprudence on this issue attempts to balance the desire to protect individual citizens from excessive governmental intrusion that is the basis of the Fifth Amendment, against the Government's need to properly enforce the laws by using incriminating evidence "independently secured through skillful investigation."[33] The Fifth Amendment privilege protects only compelled testimonial disclosures. In order for the privilege to apply, the statements must be compelled at the time of they are made. Thus, a witness who voluntarily testifies or willingly produces documents in response to a summons subpoena cannot later claim the privilege. Likewise, documents that were seized pursuant to a search warrant were not obtained via testimony, and the privilege does not apply.

1. The Privilege and Testimony

The Fifth Amendment can be asserted in response to a summons, a subpoena, or informal interviews by the IRS. If a taxpayer or witness does assert the privilege, the witness bears the burden of establishing the right to the privilege. Thus, for the Fifth Amendment privilege to apply, the witness must show at least facially that a responsive answer to the question asked may tend to incriminate the witness. In the purely testimonial arena, issues surrounding the privilege occur most often when a taxpayer is interviewed by the IRS prior to representation. CID Agents like to surprise potential witnesses, and agents tend to show up at the taxpayer's home or place of business first thing in the morning or late at night. They usually travel in pairs, so that if the taxpayer makes damaging admissions, the IRS will have two witnesses to those admissions. Well-represented taxpayers are advised to claim the Fifth Amendment to *any* question, but CID Agents can appear to interview

---

32 Kastigar v. United States, 406 U.S. 441, 444 (1972).

33 Andresen v. Maryland, 427 U.S. 463 477 (1976), *citing* Watts v. Indiana, 388 U.S. 49, 54 (1949).

taxpayers before they know there is an investigation underway and that they even need representation. It is the damaging admissions given to the IRS prior to representation that can often be the undoing of a defendant.

Despite its shock tactics, the IRS does want to obtain admissible evidence. Thus, the IRM includes rules applicable to agents in their conduct of a noncustodial[34] interview:

1. The special agent will advise the individual of his/her constitutional rights during non-custodial interviews when the individual is a subject of an investigation, a corporate officer or employee who appears to be implicated in an alleged wrongdoing involving a corporation under investigation, or when a witness' statement would incriminate the witness.
2. The special agent will not use trickery, misrepresentation, or deception to obtain any evidence or information. Moreover, the special agent will not use language that could be interpreted as a promise of immunity or settlement of the subject's investigation, or that might be viewed as intimidation or a threat.
3. To defend against an attack on the admissibility of any statement or documentary evidence furnished by a subject under investigation, the special agent will always inform the subject of his/her constitutional rights at the beginning of a formal question and answer interview, even if the subject had previously been advised.
4. Failure to give subjects the constitutional warnings prescribed by Internal Revenue procedures has resulted in the exclusion of evidence obtained from the subjects.[35]

The IRM also instructs agents to identify themselves as Special Agents of the IRS, Criminal Investigation, display their badges and advise the witness, "[a]s a special agent, one of my functions is to investigate the possibility of criminal violations of the Internal Revenue laws and related offenses." Agents are then instructed to give the following *Miranda*-type warning:

> I advise you that under the Fifth Amendment to the Constitution of the United States, I cannot compel you to answer any questions or to submit any information if such answers or information might tend to incriminate you in any way. I also advise you that anything which you say and any documents which you submit may be used against you in any criminal proceeding which may be undertaken. I advise you further that you may, if you wish, seek the assistance of an attorney before responding. Do you understand these rights?

Agents are instructed to terminate the interview immediately if at any stage of an interview the witness indicates a desire to exercise the right to either withhold

[34] The Supreme Court held in Beckwith v. United States, 425 U.S. 341 (1976), that since the witness is not in custody, full Miranda warnings are not constitutionally required in a so-called noncustodial interview by Special Agents.

[35] IRM 9.4.5.11.3.1.

testimony or records, or to consult with an attorney.[36]

What happens, however, if the agents fail to follow these rules? In *United States v. Caceres*,[37] an IRS agent secretly recorded conversations with defendant. The agent had not obtained the approvals for the tapings as required by the IRM, and the issue was whether the fruits of the tapes could be suppressed. The Supreme Court held that they should not be:

> Regulations governing the conduct of criminal investigations are generally considered desirable, and may well provide more valuable protection to the public at large than the deterrence flowing from the occasional exclusion of items of evidence in criminal trials. Although we do not suggest that a suppression order in this case would cause the IRS to abandon or modify its electronic surveillance regulations, we cannot ignore the possibility that a rigid application of an exclusionary rule to every regulatory violation could have a serious deterrent impact on the formulation of additional standards to govern prosecutorial and police procedures. Here, the Executive itself has provided for internal sanctions in cases of knowing violations of the electronic-surveillance regulations. To go beyond that, and require exclusion in every case, would take away from the Executive Department the primary responsibility for fashioning the appropriate remedy for the violation of its regulations. But since the content, and indeed the existence, of the regulations would remain within the Executive's sole authority, the result might well be fewer and less protective regulations. In the long run, it is far better to have rules like those contained in the IRS Manual, and to tolerate occasional erroneous administration of the kind displayed by this record, than either to have no rules except those mandated by statute, or to have them framed in a mere precatory form.[38]

This case gave birth to the *Caceres* doctrine, which holds that internal agency rules that are not required by the Constitution or a statute do not generally confer rights upon citizens. Thus, if an agent violates an internal rule or procedure, the violation must rise to the level of a constitutional violation before the evidence obtained can be suppressed.

2. The Privilege and Document Production

Most of the litigation and confusion in the Fifth Amendment arena deal with the act of producing documents. Tax cases are heavily based on documents, and summonses and grand jury subpoenas routinely seek documents in addition to, or as part of, the witness's testimony. If the Government cannot get the requested documents, it often cannot make a case. The issue then becomes whether the taxpayer (or any witness) has a Fifth Amendment privilege with respect to documents that he or she possesses. As we shall see, in certain cases, the mere act

---

[36] IRM 9.4.5.11.3.1.1.

[37] 440 U.S. 741 (1979).

[38] *Id.* at 755–56.

of producing subpoenaed or summonsed documents implicates the Fifth Amendment.

The first question concerning the production of documents is whether the documents themselves are privileged. For example, business records that show that the taxpayer's actual net income is far in excess of the income reported on his return would obviously tend to incriminate the taxpayer. Can the taxpayer resist production of the records, citing the privilege against self-incrimination? In *Boyd v. United States*, the Supreme Court addressed the issue of whether the Fifth Amendment applies to subpoenaed business records. The Court held that "a compulsory production of the private books and papers of the owner of goods sought to be forfeited in such a suit is compelling him to be a witness against himself, within the meaning of the fifth amendment to the constitution"[39] From that high-water mark in 1886, however, the privilege attached to documents has dramatically receded.

In *Couch v. United States*, the Supreme Court held that business and tax records of a taxpayer, which were obtained through a summons on her accountant, were not subject to the privilege:

> In the case before us the ingredient of personal compulsion against an accused is lacking. The summons and the order of the District Court enforcing it are directed against the accountant. He, not the taxpayer, is the only one compelled to do anything. And the accountant makes no claim that he may tend to be incriminated by the production. Inquisitorial pressure or coercion against a potentially accused person, compelling her, against her will, to utter self-condemning words or produce incriminating documents is absent. In the present case, no "shadow of testimonial compulsion upon or enforced communication by the accused" is involved.[40]

Since the documents were in the hands of the taxpayer's accountant, the taxpayer herself could not have given any compulsory testimony. Therefore, the Court held that the privilege did not apply.

Several years later, in *Fisher v. United States*, the Supreme Court dealt with the next logical inquiry — whether documents of the taxpayer in his attorney's possession were subject to the Fifth Amendment privilege. *Fisher* also centered around an IRS summons for tax records, but this time the records were given to the taxpayer's attorney during the course of the attorney-client relationship. The parties agreed that if the Fifth Amendment would have excused the taxpayer from turning over the records had he still possessed them, the attorney would also be protected from releasing them. The Court held that the privilege did not apply. First, the Court reiterated its holding in *Couch*, that the Fifth Amendment privilege applies only to testimony and only to testimony that is compelled:

> The Amendment protects a person from being compelled to be a witness against himself. Here, the taxpayers retained any privilege they ever had not to be compelled to testify against themselves and not to be compelled themselves to produce private papers in their possession. This personal

[39] 116 U.S. 616, 634–35 (1886).

[40] 409 U.S. 322, 329 (1973).

> privilege was in no way decreased by the transfer. It is simply that by reason of the transfer of the documents to the attorneys, those papers may be subpoenaed without compulsion on the taxpayer. The protection of the Fifth Amendment is therefore not available.[41]

Since it was the attorney who received the IRS summons and was required to produce the documents, the taxpayer himself could not have engaged in any testimony, compelled or otherwise. Because of the attorney-client relationship and the extraordinary connection between attorney and client, the Court then addressed whether the privilege would have applied to these documents if a summons or subpoena was served on the taxpayer himself:

> A subpoena served on a taxpayer requiring him to produce an accountant's workpapers in his possession without doubt involves substantial compulsion. But it does not compel oral testimony; nor would it ordinarily compel the taxpayer to restate, repeat, or affirm the truth of the contents of the documents sought. Therefore, the Fifth Amendment would not be violated by the fact alone that the papers on their face might incriminate the taxpayer, for the privilege protects a person only against being incriminated by his own compelled testimonial communications. The accountant's workpapers are not the taxpayer's. They were not prepared by the taxpayer, and they contain no testimonial declarations by him. Furthermore, as far as this record demonstrates, the preparation of all of the papers sought in these cases was wholly voluntary, and they cannot be said to contain compelled testimonial evidence, either of the taxpayers or of anyone else. The taxpayer cannot avoid compliance with the subpoena merely by asserting that the item of evidence which he is required to produce contains incriminating writing, whether his own or that of someone else.
>
> The act of producing evidence in response to a subpoena nevertheless has communicative aspects of its own, wholly aside from the contents of the papers produced. Compliance with the subpoena tacitly concedes the existence of the papers demanded and their possession or control by the taxpayer. It also would indicate the taxpayer's belief that the papers are those described in the subpoena. The elements of compulsion are clearly present, but the more difficult issues are whether the tacit averments of the taxpayer are both "testimonial" and "incriminating" for purposes of applying the Fifth Amendment. These questions perhaps do not lend themselves to categorical answers; their resolution may instead depend on the facts and circumstances of particular cases or classes thereof. In light of the records now before us, we are confident that however incriminating the contents of the accountant's workpapers might be, the act of producing them the only thing which the taxpayer is compelled to do would not itself involve testimonial self-incrimination.[42]

Fisher stands today for the proposition that "the privilege against self-incrimination

---

[41] 425 U.S. 391, 398–99 (1976).

[42] *Id.* at 409–11.

protects only the act of producing subpoenaed evidence and not the evidence itself."[43]

Next, in *United States v. Doe*, the Court reaffirmed its holding in *Fisher* and answered the question it had left open in that case. The Court ruled that the Fifth Amendment does not protect the contents of an individual's business records in his own possession. Emphasizing that the Amendment protects the person asserting the privilege only from compelled self-incrimination, the Court held that because the documents at issue were voluntarily prepared, they did not contain compelled testimonial evidence in and of themselves. Although the documents at issue were business records, the Court held, "[i]f the party asserting the Fifth Amendment privilege has voluntarily compiled the document, no compulsion is present and the contents of the document are not privileged."[44]

In *Doe v. United States* (*Doe II*),[45] the Supreme Court addressed the issue of whether certain acts were "testimonial" for purposes of the Fifth Amendment. In *Doe II*, the Government sought a court order requiring the target of a grand jury investigation to sign forms consenting to disclosure of bank records from foreign bank accounts over which the Government knew or suspected that he had control. The Court first held that that the Fifth Amendment privilege applies only to acts that imply assertions of fact and that in order to be testimonial, an accused's communication must itself, explicitly or implicitly, relate a factual assertion or disclose information. "Only then is a person compelled to be a 'witness' against himself."[46] The Court then held that the consent directive itself was not "testimonial" because it did not acknowledge that an account at any of the banks existed or that it was controlled by the target:

> We read the directive as equivalent to a statement by Doe that, although he expresses no opinion about the existence of, or his control over, any such account, he is authorizing the bank to disclose information relating to accounts over which, in the bank's opinion, Doe can exercise the right of withdrawal. When forwarded to the bank along with a subpoena, the executed directive, if effective under local law, will simply make it possible for the recipient bank to comply with the Government's request to produce such records. As a result, if the Government obtains bank records after Doe signs the directive, the only factual statement made by anyone will be the *bank's* implicit declaration, by its act of production in response to the subpoena, that *it* believes the accounts to be petitioner's.[47]

---

[43] *See* William J. Stuntz, *The Substantive Origins of Criminal Procedure*, 105 YALE L.J. 393, 444 (1995). *See also* Thomas Kiefer Wedeles, *Fishing for Clarity in a Post-*Hubbell *World: The Need for a Bright-Line Rule in the Self-Incrimination Clause's Act of Production Doctrine*, 56 VAND. L. REV. 613 (2003).

[44] 465 U.S. 605, 612 (1984).

[45] 487 U.S. 201 (1988).

[46] *Id.* at 209–10.

[47] *Id.* at 217–18. *See also* United States v. Ghidoni, 732 F.2d 814 (11th Cir. 1984), where the court held that requiring a target to sign a consent directive that permitted the Government to obtain records from a Cayman Islands bank did not violate the target's Fifth Amendment rights. The court held the compelled act was neither testimonial nor incriminating, since the directive did not confirm the existence

The most recent treatment by the Supreme Court on the issue is *United States v. Hubbell.*[48] In *Hubbell*, the prosecutor had the grand jury issue broadly-worded grand jury subpoenas for a number of categories of financial records. Hubbell appeared before the grand jury and invoked his Fifth Amendment privilege. The prosecutor delivered to Hubbell an immunity order from the district court ordering him to comply and granting immunity "to the extent allowed by law." The immunity is referred to as derivative use immunity, meaning that, if the Government subsequently prosecutes the person, the Government must show that the prosecution is based on information other than the testimonial information it obtained only by the grant of immunity.[49] Hubbell then produced over 13,000 pages of documents. From the documents produced, the special prosecutor obtained an indictment of Hubbell for tax crimes and mail and wire fraud. The Government admitted that it could not prove that, without the compulsion, it knew of the documents with reasonable particularity. Based on that admission, the parties agreed that the charges would be dropped altogether if act-of-production immunity would bar prosecution. The Supreme Court held that the indictment should be dismissed:

> It is apparent from the text of the subpoena itself that the prosecutor needed respondent's assistance both to identify potential sources of information and to produce those sources. Given the breadth of the description of the 11 categories of documents called for by the subpoena, the collection and production of the materials demanded was tantamount to answering a series of interrogatories asking a witness to disclose the existence and location of particular documents fitting certain broad descriptions. The assembly of literally hundreds of pages of material in response to a request for "any and all documents reflecting, referring, or relating to any direct or indirect sources of money or other things of value received by or provided to" an individual or members of his family during a 3-year period, is the functional equivalent of the preparation of an answer to either a detailed written interrogatory or a series of oral questions at a discovery deposition. Entirely apart from the contents of the 13,120 pages of materials that respondent produced in this case, it is undeniable that providing a catalog of existing documents fitting within any of the 11 broadly worded subpoena categories could provide a prosecutor with a "lead to incriminating evidence," or "a link in the chain of evidence needed to prosecute."
>
> [W]e cannot accept the Government's submission that respondent's immunity did not preclude its derivative use of the produced documents because its "possession of the documents [was] the fruit only of a simple physical act — the act of producing the documents." It was unquestionably necessary for respondent to make extensive use of "the contents of his own mind" in identifying the hundreds of documents responsive to the requests in the subpoena. The assembly of those documents was like telling an inquisitor the combination to a wall safe, not like being forced to surrender

of any accounts or Ghidoni's control over them, nor did it authenticate any documents produced by the bank.

48 530 U.S. 27 (2000).

49 We will discuss derivative-use immunity below.

> the key to a strongbox. The Government's anemic view of respondent's act of production as a mere physical act that is principally non-testimonial in character and can be entirely divorced from its "implicit" testimonial aspect so as to constitute a "legitimate, wholly independent source" (as required by *Kastigar*) for the documents produced simply fails to account for these realities.
>
> In sum, we have no doubt that the constitutional privilege against self-incrimination protects the target of a grand jury investigation from being compelled to answer questions designed to elicit information about the existence of sources of potentially incriminating evidence. That constitutional privilege has the same application to the testimonial aspect of a response to a subpoena seeking discovery of those sources.

So where do these cases leave us? The answer is not entirely clear. As the court of appeals in the *Hubbell* case stated, determining the application of the act of production doctrine is an "admittedly abstract and under-determined area of the law."[50] But we can rely on these principles. First, voluntarily prepared documents are generally not privileged. In addition, documents that are business records, and not personal, are also not subject to a claim of privilege. The privilege applies only to compelled testimony. However, the act of producing the documents, *i.e.*, gathering, identifying, and authenticating them may be testimonial, is therefore subject to the act-of-production privilege.

Stated another way, the Government can compel production of documents in the face of a Fifth Amendment claim only where the summons or subpoena requests documents whose existence and possession are a "foregone conclusion." But what exactly does that mean? Reading it strictly in favor of the compelled party, the Government's hurdle is to know and be able to prove, if necessary, that the documents requested exist or likely exist. Still, that is a bit of an uncertain standard. In *United States v. Ponds*,[51] the D.C. Circuit attempted to bring more certainty to the inquiry by suggesting that the level of Government knowledge required to avoid an otherwise valid act of production privilege is the same as the "reasonable particularity" which echoes the standard used for search warrants. Courts deal routinely with the reasonable particularity standard and this might offer a good way to guide prosecutors and compelled parties as to the ground rules that apply. In *United States v. Bright*,[52] the Ninth Circuit that "the government must establish its independent knowledge of three elements: the documents' existence, the documents' authenticity and respondent's possession or control of the documents."[53] The question remains whether the court meant that the Government must establish those elements with reasonable particularity. Finally, in *In re Grand Jury Subpoena Duces Tecum Dated March 25, 2011*,[54] the Eleventh Circuit addressed the "foregone conclusion" issue in the context of encrypted computer files. The

---

[50] United States v. Hubbell, 167 F.3d 552, 570 (D.C. Cir. 1999), *aff'd*, 530 U.S. 27 (2000).

[51] 454 F.3d 313 (D.C. Cir. 2006).

[52] 596 F.3d 683, 692 (9th Cir. 2010).

[53] *Id. See also* United States v. Sideman & Bancroft, 704 F.3d 1197 (9th Cir. 2013).

[54] 670 F.3d 1335 (11th Cir. 2012).

prosecutors had obtained the target's computers in the course of a child pornography investigation. The computers contained vast quantities of encrypted files, and the prosecutors suspected that the files contained child pornography. However, the prosecutors had no evidence that the computers contained such illicit images or indeed, whether the files contained anything at all. The Eleventh Circuit refused to enforce the subpoena ordering the target to decrypt the files finding that "the Government has failed to show any basis, let alone shown a basis, with reasonable particularity, for its belief that encrypted files exist on the drives, that Doe has access to those files, or that he is capable of decrypting the files. The 'foregone conclusion' doctrine does not apply under these facts."[55]

What if the taxpayer is a corporation or other entity? Does the privilege apply when a corporate taxpayer receives a summons or subpoena for records? The short answer is no; the longer answer is: Corporations and other "collective entities" have no Fifth Amendment privilege. This is known as the "collective entity doctrine." Only the individual who responds on behalf of the corporation, known as the custodian of records, could potentially assert the privilege. However, in *Braswell v. United States*,[56] the Supreme Court held that the custodian of records and sole shareholder of a corporation that received a grand jury subpoena could not claim the privilege on behalf of the entity and refuse production. The Court then turned to the issue of whether the custodian of records can claim the privilege under the act of production doctrine for his own conduct. This question was particularly pointed for Braswell, since he was the sole shareholder of the corporations, and any production by the corporation would surely be viewed by the jury as having been done by the corporation's alter ego, Braswell:

> Although a corporate custodian is not entitled to resist a subpoena on the ground that his act of production will be personally incriminating, we do think certain consequences flow from the fact that the custodian's act of production is one in his representative rather than personal capacity. Because the custodian acts as a representative, the act is deemed one of the corporation and not the individual. Therefore, the Government concedes, as it must, that it may make no evidentiary use of the "individual act" against the individual. For example, in a criminal prosecution against the custodian, the Government may not introduce into evidence before the jury the fact that the subpoena was served upon and the corporation's documents were delivered by one particular individual, the custodian. The Government has the right, however, to use the corporation's act of production against the custodian. The Government may offer testimony — for example, from the process server who delivered the subpoena and from the individual who received the records — establishing that the corporation produced the records subpoenaed. The jury may draw from the corporation's act of production the conclusion that the records in question are authentic corporate records, which the corporation possessed, and which it produced in response to the subpoena. And if the defendant held a prominent position within the corporation that produced the records, the jury may, just as it

---

55 *Id.* at 1349.

56 487 U.S. 99 (1988).

would had someone else produced the documents, reasonably infer that he had possession of the documents or knowledge of their contents. Because the jury is not told that the defendant produced the records, any nexus between the defendant and the documents results solely from the corporation's act of production and other evidence in the case.[57]

After *Braswell*, there is very little left of the act-of-production doctrine for entities and their custodians of record. Counsel should nevertheless seek to obtain act-of-production immunity for their clients. Immunity, in all its various flavors, is covered in the following section.

3. The Required Records Doctrine

Prior to the Supreme Court's near-elimination of Fifth Amendment protection for business records in *Couch*, *Fisher*, and *Doe*, another exception to the Fifth Amendment had developed, known as the required records exception. Under this exception to the Fifth Amendment privilege against self-incrimination, a regulated business could not raise Fifth Amendment claims for documents that were required to be kept as a result of participating in the regulated industry.[58] The theory was that the documents sought by the summons or subpoena did not amount to compelled testimony because the records were required, compelled if you will, by virtue of the target's participation in the regulated industry. And, since the target voluntarily entered into the regulated industry, there was ultimately no compulsion at all. Until recently, the required records exception arose only sporadically in criminal tax cases. However, with the Government's increased attention on FBAR requirements and foreign bank accounts used to hide income, the exception has become more relevant to tax lawyers and their clients.

As we discussed in Chapter 3, the Bank Secrecy Act (BSA) imposes upon U.S. persons the obligation to file FBARs reporting their ownership or signatory authority over foreign bank accounts. The BSA also requires those persons to maintain records related to the foreign accounts and to produce them to the Government upon request. In the offshore bank initiative, grand juries across the country have issued grand jury subpoenas to taxpayers who the Government believes own or owned foreign bank accounts to produce the records required by the BSA. The taxpayers often moved to quash the subpoenas, urging that the Fifth Amendment privilege gave them the right to decline to produce the documents. All of the Courts to address this issue have held that the required records doctrine applies to these records and thus, there is no Fifth Amendment protection for these documents.[59] Such a broad construction of the term "required records" calls to

---

[57] *Id.* at 118–19.

[58] To constitute "required records," documents must satisfy a three-part test: (1) The requirement that they be kept must be essentially regulatory, (2) the records must be of a kind which the regulated party has customarily kept, and (3) the records themselves must have assumed "public aspects" which render them analogous to public documents. Grosso v. United States, 390 U.S. 62, 67–68 (1968).

[59] M.H. v. United States (In re Grand Jury Investigation M.H.), 648 F.3d 1067 (9th Cir. 2011), *cert. denied*, 133 S. Ct. 26 (2012); In re Special February 2011-1 Grand Jury Subpoena Dated September 12, 2011, 691 F.3d 903 (7th Cir. 2012), *cert. denied*, 133 S. Ct. 2338 (2013); In re Grand Jury Subpoena, 696 F.3d 428 (5th Cir. 2012).

mind Justice Jackson's dissent in an earlier required records doctrine case:

> The protection against compulsory self-incrimination, guaranteed by the Fifth Amendment, is nullified to whatever extent this Court holds that Congress may require a citizen to keep an account of his deeds and misdeeds and turn over or exhibit the record on demand of government inspectors, who then can use it to convict him. Today's decision introduces a principle of considerable moment. Of course, it strips of protection only business men and their records; but we cannot too often remind ourselves of the tendency of such a principle, once approved, to expand itself in practice "to the limits of its logic." That it has already expanded to cover a vast area is apparent from the Court's citation of twenty-six federal statutes that present parallels to the situation here under review. It would, no doubt, simplify enforcement of all criminal laws if each citizen were required to keep a diary that would show where he was at all times, with whom he was, and what he was up to. The decision of today, applying this rule not merely to records specially required under the Act but also to records "customarily kept," invites and facilitates that eventuality.[60]

B. Immunity

1. Immunity in General

The privilege against self-incrimination only applies, as we discussed above, when there is a reasonable possibility that the witness will be incriminated by the testimony. If the Government can remove any reasonable danger of self-incrimination, the witness may not assert the privilege in refusing to testify or produce documents. It is for this reason that the Government grants immunity to compel testimony that would otherwise have been privileged. Much like the law concerning the privilege itself, court decisions and federal statutes conferring immunity have evolved over the years.

Title 18 U.S.C. sections 6001 through 6005 contain the current statutory regime regarding compelled testimony and immunity. Section 6003 permits prosecutors to seek a court order to compel testimony of a witness appearing in court proceedings or before the grand jury. Prosecutors are authorized to request immunity when the testimony or other information that is expected to be obtained from the witness "may be necessary to the public interest." There are three types of immunity — transactional immunity, use immunity, and derivative use immunity. They are explained by the USAM's Criminal Resource Manual, 717–719:

> **717. Transactional Immunity Distinguished**
>
> Title 18 U.S.C. § 6002 provides use immunity instead of transactional immunity. The difference between transactional and use immunity is that transactional immunity protects the witness from prosecution for the offense or offenses involved, whereas use immunity only protects the

[60] Shapiro v. United States, 335 U.S. 1, 70–71 (1948) (Jackson, J. dissenting).

witness against the government's use of his or her immunized testimony in a prosecution of the witness — except in a subsequent prosecution for perjury or giving a false statement.

718. Derivative Use Immunity

The use immunity statute (18 U.S.C. § 6002) allows the government to prosecute the witness using evidence obtained independently of the witness's immunized testimony. Section 6002 provides:

> [N]o testimony or other information compelled under the order (or any information directly or indirectly derived from such testimony or other information) may be used against the witness in any criminal case, except a prosecution for perjury, giving a false statement, or otherwise failing to comply with the order.

The Supreme Court upheld the statute in *Kastigar v. United States*, 406 U.S. 441 (1972). In so doing, the Court underscored the prohibition against the government's derivative use of immunized testimony in a prosecution of the witness. The Court reaffirmed the burden of proof that, under *Murphy v. Waterfront Commission*, 378 U.S. 52 (1964), must be borne by the government to establish that its evidence is based on independent, legitimate sources:

> This burden of proof, which we affirm as appropriate, is not limited to a negation of taint; rather, it imposes on the prosecution the affirmative duty to prove that the evidence it proposes to use is derived from a legitimate source wholly independent of the compelled testimony.

719. Informal Immunity Distinguished From Formal Immunity

Statutory immunity, also known as formal immunity, should be distinguished from informal immunity. The latter term, often referred to as "pocket immunity" or "letter immunity," is immunity conferred by agreement with the witness. For example, the government and a cooperating defendant or witness might enter into a plea agreement or a nonprosecution agreement if the defendant or witness agrees to cooperate. Testimony given under informal immunity is not compelled testimony, but is testimony pursuant to an agreement and thus voluntary. The principles of contract law apply in determining the scope of informal immunity. Grants of informal immunity that do not expressly prohibit the government's derivative use of the witness's testimony will be construed to prohibit such derivative use. But a grant of informal immunity that expressly provides for derivative use of the testimony by the government will be upheld.

The most common type of immunity is derivative use immunity under 18 U.S.C. section 6002. Derivative use immunity has been held to be coextensive with the scope of the privilege against self-incrimination, and therefore is sufficient to compel testimony over a claim of the privilege. As noted above, the Fifth Amendment privilege may be asserted not only as to testimony that is itself incriminating, but also as to information that might lead to incriminating information. Derivative use immunity therefore prevents the prosecutor from using the testimony given pursuant to immunity order and the leads developed from that testimony. While this type of immunity may be obtained by statute, as we saw in *Hubbell,* it is usually obtained by agreement between the witness and the prosecutor prior to the witness actually having to formally assert the privilege.

Use immunity, a subset of derivative use immunity, provides only limited protection — the prosecutor will not use the statement made by the witness against him or her. This form of immunity permits the Government to use leads derived from the testimony to prosecute the witness. From the witness's perspective, therefore, this is the worst form of immunity. Since the immunity conferred by section 6002 is derivative use immunity, use immunity is available only by agreement with the prosecutor. Use immunity comes up most often in conferences with the Tax Division prior to indictment. As we saw in Chapter 6, DOJ Tax offers conferences to a taxpayer's attorney when it is considering whether to approve an indictment. The Tax Division has a policy conferring a type of use immunity for "vicarious admissions" made by an attorney for his or her client. In order to encourage effective conferences and free-flowing dialog in the conference, DOJ Tax commits to attorneys representing targets that it will not use admissions by the attorney against the client.[61]

Under transactional immunity, a witness is immunized from prosecution for the crime about which he or she is testifying. This is the broadest form of immunity. However, the federal immunity statute no longer provides absolute, or transactional, immunity. Thus, transactional immunity is rarely obtained in the federal system, and only through an agreement with prosecutors.

Finally, prosecutors may also give act-of-production immunity. As discussed above, the act of producing records concedes the existence and possession of the records called for by the summons or subpoena, as well as the witness's belief that the records are those described in the subpoena. Act-of-production immunity is generally obtained by agreement with the prosecutor.

Regardless of the type of immunity conferred, most immunity is conferred by agreement. An immunity agreement is essentially a contract between the witness and the prosecutor, and the negotiation for non-statutory immunity is simply a contract negotiation. Given the stakes, of course, the negotiation requires the most careful attention by practitioners. The negotiation becomes a prototypical free-market negotiation — what does the witness have (or what does the Government think the witness has) that the Government is willing to pay for? The Government's currency in this negotiation is its power to negotiate limitations upon ability to prosecute the witness. That negotiation, if successful, results in immunity.

The negotiations usually go like this: There will be some preliminary posturing between the parties in which the witness's lawyer insists that his client has information that the Government needs badly, and the prosecutor insists that the witness's information is important, but not critical. The opening offer is generally use immunity and then the negotiation is how limited that use immunity really is,

---

61 CTM 3.00, Tax Division Directive No. 86-58.

but derivative use immunity can be negotiated. The witness's lawyer may tantalize the prosecutor with certain portions of the information in an off-the-record way to lead the prosecutor into thinking the Government's need is greater. The negotiations then either fail, in which case the Government can either retreat to forced statutory immunity or forget information from that witness, or an agreement is reached. The terms of the contract are critical. The witness's lawyer will want the broadest scope possible (unequivocal transactional immunity) or, failing that, the best possible use immunity (preferably derivative use immunity). In any event, the writing, usually in the form of a letter from the prosecutor acknowledged by the witness and his or her lawyer, sets the terms of the contract.

2. *Kastigar* Hearings

Regardless of how the witness obtained immunity, the witness will want the benefit of the immunity. Obviously, if the witness has transactional immunity, a breach of the agreement can be easily spotted. However, it is less easy to spot breaches of derivative use immunity and use immunity. What does the witness do if the Government prosecutes the witness on the basis of evidence that the witness believes violates the immunity granted? The witness (now the defendant) may want to invoke a pretrial hearing process called a *Kastigar* hearing, named for the case upon which it is based, *Kastigar v. United States*.[62] In *Kastigar*, the Supreme Court considered whether the Government may compel testimony from an unwilling witness given use and derivative use immunity under the immunity statute or, on the other hand, may be compelled only by conferring transactional immunity. The Court reasoned:

> Petitioners argue that use and derivative-use immunity will not adequately protect a witness from various possible incriminating uses of the compelled testimony: for example, the prosecutor or other law enforcement officials may obtain leads, names of witnesses, or other information not otherwise available that might result in a prosecution. It will be difficult and perhaps impossible, the argument goes, to identify, by testimony or cross-examination, the subtle ways in which the compelled testimony may disadvantage a witness, especially in the jurisdiction granting the immunity.
>
> This argument presupposes that the statute's prohibition will prove impossible to enforce. The statute provides a sweeping proscription of any use, direct or indirect, of the compelled testimony and any information derived therefrom.
>
> This total prohibition on use provides a comprehensive safeguard, barring the use of compelled testimony as an "investigatory lead," and also barring the use of any evidence obtained by focusing investigation on a witness as a result of his compelled disclosures.
>
> A person accorded this immunity under 18 U.S.C. § 6002, and subsequently prosecuted, is not dependent for the preservation of his rights upon

[62] 406 U.S. 441 (1972).

the integrity and good faith of the prosecuting authorities. As stated in Murphy:

> "Once a defendant demonstrates that he has testified, under a state grant of immunity, to matters related to the federal prosecution, the federal authorities have the burden of showing that their evidence is not tainted by establishing that they had an independent, legitimate source for the disputed evidence." 378 U.S., at 79 n.18.

This burden of proof, which we reaffirm as appropriate, is not limited to a negation of taint; rather, it imposes on the prosecution the affirmative duty to prove that the evidence it proposes to use is derived from a legitimate source wholly independent of the compelled testimony.

This is very substantial protection, commensurate with that resulting from invoking the privilege itself. The privilege assures that a citizen is not compelled to incriminate himself by his own testimony. It usually operates to allow a citizen to remain silent when asked a question requiring an incriminatory answer. This statute, which operates after a witness has given incriminatory testimony, affords the same protection by assuring that the compelled testimony can in no way lead to the infliction of criminal penalties. The statute, like the Fifth Amendment, grants neither pardon nor amnesty. Both the statute and the Fifth Amendment allow the government to prosecute using evidence from legitimate independent sources.

The statutory proscription is analogous to the Fifth Amendment requirement in cases of coerced confessions. A coerced confession, as revealing of leads as testimony given in exchange for immunity, is inadmissible in a criminal trial, but it does not bar prosecution. Moreover, a defendant against whom incriminating evidence has been obtained through a grant of immunity may be in a stronger position at trial than a defendant who asserts a Fifth Amendment coerced-confession claim. One raising a claim under this statute need only show that he testified under a grant of immunity in order to shift to the government the heavy burden of proving that all of the evidence it proposes to use was derived from legitimate independent sources. On the other hand, a defendant raising a coerced-confession claim under the Fifth Amendment must first prevail in a voluntariness hearing before his confession and evidence derived from it become inadmissible.

There can be no justification in reason or policy for holding that the Constitution requires an amnesty grant where, acting pursuant to statute and accompanying safeguards, testimony is compelled in exchange for immunity from use and derivative use when no such amnesty is required where the government, acting without colorable right, coerces a defendant into incriminating himself. We conclude that the immunity provided by 18 U.S.C. § 6002 leaves the witness and the prosecutorial authorities in substantially the same position as if the witness had claimed the Fifth Amendment privilege. The immunity therefore is coextensive with the privilege and suffices to supplant it.[63]

Kastigar approved a process where, if the Government desires to prosecute a witness who has been compelled to testify under use or derivative use immunity, the Government must, upon the witness's request, demonstrate that it has made no direct or indirect use of the immunized testimony. As the Court noted, the ability to make the Government prove that it has lived up to the bargain is a substantial protection for a witness who was granted immunity, since the Government often cannot establish that it did not improperly rely upon the immunized testimony. The substantial burden will often discourage the Government from even seeking an indictment and, if it does obtain an indictment, the court may dismiss the indictment after a *Kastigar* hearing. The burdens imposed by the *Kastigar* hearing are the principal reason that federal prosecutors resist conferring derivative use immunity by agreement and are loath to seek statutory immunity. Nevertheless, if the witness's bargaining position is strong, obtaining derivative use immunity can effectively prevent the Government from attempting a prosecution where it anticipates that it will have significant *Kastigar* problems. A practitioner who stands his or her ground and obtains derivative use immunity may thus have insulated the witness from prosecution.

C. Attorney-Client and Work-Product Privileges

An important privilege that may be asserted in response to a summons or subpoena is the attorney-client privilege. Most of you will have a good deal of exposure to this privilege, and we will not give a lengthy dissertation here.[64] Instead, we will focus on the privilege in the context of criminal tax investigations. The classic statement of the privilege is from *Wigmore*:

> (1) Where legal advice of any kind is sought (2) from a professional legal adviser in his capacity as such, (3) the communications relating to that purpose, (4) made in confidence (5) by the client, (6) are at his instance permanently protected (7) from disclosure by himself or by the legal adviser, (8) except the protection be waived.[65]

Closely related to, and often confused with, the attorney-client privilege is the work-product privilege. The work-product doctrine is a judicially-created privilege for materials prepared or collected by an attorney in the course of preparation for possible litigation.[66] Materials within the scope of the work-product privilege include opinion work product (analysis or assessment of legal positions), as well as statements or summaries of the testimony of potential witnesses. With respect to both privileges, the issues that arise most often in tax investigations center around the identity of the client, whether the advice sought is "legal advice," and whether the privilege has been waived.

---

[63] 406 U.S. at 459–62.

[64] We also discuss the attorney-client privilege in Chapter 11.

[65] *See* 8 J. WIGMORE, EVIDENCE §§ 2292–2320 (McNaughton Rev. 1961).

[66] *See, e.g.*, Hickman v. Taylor, 329 U.S. 495 (1947).

1. Who Is the Client?

As we discuss in Chapter 11, the question regarding the identity of the client in the representation of a corporation or other entity is complex and confused. This is due in large part to the fact that corporations must act through living, breathing individuals. When the officer, director, or employee speaks with the corporation's attorney, is the communication privileged? Whose privilege is it, the individual officer/employee's or the corporation's? The seminal case on this issue is *Upjohn Co. v. United States*.[67] In *Upjohn*, IRS special agents issued a summons demanding production of files and records dealing with the corporation's own internal investigation of possible wrongdoing, including written questionnaires sent to managers of Upjohn and memorandums or notes of the interviews conducted by the attorney. The corporation, of course, declined to produce the documents on the grounds that they were protected from disclosure by the attorney-client privilege and constituted the work product of the attorneys. The Supreme Court agreed and held:

> The communications at issue were made by Upjohn employees to counsel for Upjohn acting as such, at the direction of corporate superiors in order to secure legal advice from counsel. As the Magistrate found, "Mr. Thomas consulted with the Chairman of the Board and outside counsel and thereafter conducted a factual investigation to determine the nature and extent of the questionable payments and to be in a position to give legal advice to the company with respect to the payments." Information, not available from upper-echelon management, was needed to supply a basis for legal advice concerning compliance with securities and tax laws, foreign laws, currency regulations, duties to shareholders, and potential litigation in each of these areas. The communications concerned matters within the scope of the employees' corporate duties, and the employees themselves were sufficiently aware that they were being questioned in order that the corporation could obtain legal advice. The questionnaire identified Thomas as "the company's General Counsel" and referred in its opening sentence to the possible illegality of payments such as the ones on which information was sought. A statement of policy accompanying the questionnaire clearly indicated the legal implications of the investigation. The policy statement was issued "in order that there be no uncertainty in the future as to the policy with respect to the practices which are the subject of this investigation." It began "Upjohn will comply with all laws and regulations," and stated that commissions or payments "will not be used as a subterfuge for bribes or illegal payments" and that all payments must be "proper and legal." Any future agreements with foreign distributors or agents were to be approved "by a company attorney" and any questions concerning the policy were to be referred "to the company's General Counsel." This statement was issued to Upjohn employees worldwide, so that even those interviewees not receiving a questionnaire were aware of the legal implications of the interviews. Pursuant to explicit instructions from the Chairman of the Board, the communications were considered "highly confidential" when made, and have been kept confidential by the company.

---

[67] 449 U.S. 383 (1981).

Consistent with the underlying purposes of the attorney-client privilege, these communications must be protected against compelled disclosure.

Application of the attorney-client privilege to communications such as those involved here, however, puts the adversary in no worse position than if the communications had never taken place. The privilege only protects disclosure of communications; it does not protect disclosure of the underlying facts by those who communicated with the attorney:

"[T]he protection of the privilege extends only to communications and not to facts. A fact is one thing and a communication concerning that fact is an entirely different thing. The client cannot be compelled to answer the question, 'What did you say or write to the attorney?' but may not refuse to disclose any relevant fact within his knowledge merely because he incorporated a statement of such fact into his communication to his attorney." Here the Government was free to question the employees who communicated with Thomas and outside counsel. Upjohn has provided the IRS with a list of such employees, and the IRS has already interviewed some 25 of them. While it would probably be more convenient for the Government to secure the results of petitioner's internal investigation by simply subpoenaing the questionnaires and notes taken by petitioner's attorneys, such considerations of convenience do not overcome the policies served by the attorney-client privilege.[68]

Despite the holding that the communications at issue were covered by the attorney-client privilege, the Court did not articulate any broad standards or tests that definitively resolve which officers or employees of a corporation are covered by the privilege. Rather, the Court's holding "resolves into a single question: Would application of the privilege under the circumstances of this particular case foster the flow of information to corporate counsel regarding issues about which corporations seek legal advice?"[69] Counsel representing a corporation must therefore be diligent in documenting the purpose and need for the communications between an officer or employee and the attorney.

A more controversial recent development in the law of attorney-client privilege and corporations involves the Government's efforts to pressure corporations to waive the privilege in exchange for more lenient treatment. The attorney-client privilege belongs to the client, not the attorney or anyone else. In the corporate context, the client is the corporation. Thus, corporations have the ability waive the privilege if they so wish. Recently, particularly in connection with the criminal investigation of large public accounting firms, the Government has pressured the firms to waive the privilege in exchange for a deferred prosecution agreement, so that the Government can then go after individual partners and members of the firm.[70] Similar pressure has been used in the sentencing arena, where the Government uses its power to recommend lighter or more severe penalties to

[68] *Id.* at 394–96.

[69] John E. Sexton, *A Post-*Upjohn *Consideration of the Corporate Attorney-Client Privilege*, 57 N.Y.U. L. REV. 443, 459 (1982).

[70] *See* the discussion in Chapter 5 regarding KPMG and the Thompson and McNulty memoranda.

persuade corporations to waive the privilege. These are controversial developments that have yet to be resolved.

2. Do You Want Legal or Tax Advice?

The next issue regarding the attorney-client privilege centers around whether the advice sought by the client is for legal advice and therefore subject to the privilege even under the best of circumstances. On one hand, it would seem to be a rather simple question — the client is seeking the advice of a lawyer, and lawyers give legal advice. However, where the advice entails tax advice, the scope of the privilege is quite limited. First, there is no privilege for communications relating to investment or business advice or services.[71] Hence, to the extent the advice sought regarding taxes can be construed as investment or business advice, the privilege does not apply.

In addition, the preparation of tax returns is generally not considered to be legal advice within the scope of the privilege. While preparation of tax returns may require some knowledge of the law, the courts have held that return preparation is primarily an accounting service.[72] Moreover, in *United States v. Arthur Young & Co.*,[73] the Supreme Court held that accountants' workpapers were not protected from IRS summons under the work-product doctrine. The Court also noted that there is no accountant-client privilege at common law. The problem with these cases is that the line between what constitutes return preparation and what amounts to legal advice with respect to a position on a return is hazy at best. For example, in *United States v. KPMG*,[74] the court held that a tax opinion regarding the tax consequences of certain investment portfolio transactions was not subject to the privilege because the opinion was "prepared in conjunction with preparation of a tax return. Indeed, the Court has not been presented a possible scenario in this case where the IRS would challenge a position that was *not* brought to the attention of the IRS by a means *other than a tax return*."[75] Read literally, this decision provides that any legal advice by a tax lawyer that ultimately ends up on the client's tax return is considered as given as part of return preparation and not covered by the privilege. It is difficult to conceive of much in the way of prospective tax advice that would not end up on a tax return. Fortunately, this does not appear to be the majority view. In *United States v. Frederick*,[76] Judge Posner took a more nuanced view of the privilege:

> Communications from a client that neither reflect the lawyer's thinking nor are made for the purpose of eliciting the lawyer's professional advice or other legal assistance are not privileged. The information that a person furnishes the preparer of his tax return is furnished for the purpose of

---

[71] *See, e.g.*, Matter of Walsh, 623 F.2d 489, 494 (7th Cir.), *cert. denied*, 449 U.S. 994 (1980).

[72] *See, e.g.*, United States v. El Paso Co., 682 F.2d 530, 539 (5th Cir. 1982), *cert. denied*, 466 U.S. 944 (1984).

[73] 465 U.S. 805, 817–18 (1984).

[74] 237 F. Supp. 2d 35 (D.D.C. 2002).

[75] *Id.* at 42 (emphasis in original).

[76] 182 F.3d 496, 500–501 (7th Cir. 1999), *cert. denied*, 528 U.S. 1154 (2000).

> enabling the preparation of the return, not the preparation of a brief or an opinion letter. Such information therefore is not privileged.
>
> We do not, however, accept the government's argument that there is no issue of privilege here because the information was transmitted to a tax preparer with the expectation of its being relayed to a third party, namely the IRS. It is true that "if the client transmitted the information so that it might be used on the tax return, such a transmission destroys any expectation of confidentiality." That is, the transmittal operates as a waiver of the privilege. But the tax preparer here was also the taxpayers' lawyer, and it cannot be assumed that everything transmitted to him by the taxpayer was intended to assist him in his tax-preparation function and thus might be conveyed to the IRS, rather than in his legal-representation function.

The law concerning the attorney-client privilege and tax advice continues to evolve. Counsel should therefore be aware that legal advice regarding the client's tax liability might not be subject to the privilege.

3. Waiver of the Privilege

The *Lefkowitz* case excerpted above showed how the marital privilege can be waived.[77] Likewise, the attorney-client privilege can be waived. As with *Lefkowitz*, the privilege can be waived if the communication is not made in confidence, *i.e.*, it was made in the presence of others. An important exception to the rule that disclosure to third parties waives the privilege is the so-called joint defense privilege. Under a joint-defense agreement, where co-defendants in a criminal case and their attorneys confer on matters of mutual interest, there is no waiver of the attorney-client privilege.[78] Joint defense agreements will be an important part of your practice.

4. The Privilege and Accountants

As we discussed above, there is no accountant-client privilege generally recognized in federal law. However, in 1998, Congress enacted a limited privilege for tax advice. Section 7525 provides that the same common law protections of confidentiality that apply to a communication between a taxpayer and an attorney will also apply to a communication between a taxpayer and any "federally authorized tax practitioner."[79] Thus, if the communication would be considered a privileged communication if it were between a taxpayer and an attorney, it will, subject to key limitations, be privileged if is between the taxpayer and any federally authorized tax practitioner. The term "federally authorized tax practitioners" include CPAs and enrolled agents and actuaries authorized to practice before the IRS.[80]

---

[77] *See also* United States v. Miller, 588 F.3d 897, 905 (5th Cir. 2009) (testimony by wife involved conversations about a joint criminal activity and thus is not protected by the confidential marital privilege).

[78] *See, e.g.*, United States v. Henke, 222 F.3d 633, 637 (9th Cir. 2000).

[79] IRC § 7525(a)(1).

[80] IRC § 7525(a)(3)(A).

While much ballyhooed at the time of enactment, the 7525 privilege does not provide much protection for communications between an accountant and his or her client. First, the privilege is only as broad as the attorney-client privilege. And, as we hope we have demonstrated, the applicability of the attorney-client privilege in tax matters is troublesome at best. Most importantly for this course, however, the privilege does not apply in any criminal investigation or prosecution.[81] Thus, if an investigation is or is about to be a criminal investigation or prosecution, anything said by the taxpayer to the taxpayer's accountant will not be privileged.

Discussions between a taxpayer and an accountant (or certain others) can be privileged, however, if the accountant is a so-called *Kovel* accountant. In delivering legal services, an attorney will often need the assistance of non-lawyers who will become privy to confidential information. For example, paralegals and other assistants in the lawyer's firm will become privy to the information. Disclosures of information to these personnel will not constitute a waiver of the privilege. In addition to in-house assistance, the attorney will often find it helpful to engage professionals outside the firm. In tax cases, attorneys routinely hire outside accountants to assist the attorney in delivering legal services to the client. The lawyer may want the accountant to meet with the client and obtain information directly from the client, and cloak that information in the attorney-client privilege just as if the lawyer obtained it directly rather than through the accountant. The traditional method by which that is done, at least in a tax practice, is through an arrangement whereby the lawyer engages the accountant to become part of the legal team. This arrangement was approved, and the attorney-client privilege was held to extend to the accountant, in the case *United States v. Kovel.*[82] Here, as in many areas of the law, it is imperative that if you are going to retain an accountant (and unless you are an accountant yourself, you should retain one), you do it correctly.

First, the attorney should engage the *Kovel* accountant, rather than having the client do so. This ensures that the accountant is working for the lawyer, and not for the client. It is also advisable to have the lawyer pay or at least approve the accountant's invoices for services provided. Equally as important, it is essential that a new accountant, rather than the client's existing accountant, be hired. The client will want his or her existing accountant to be used — the client is comfortable with the accountant, they presumably have a good relationship, and the accountant is up to speed with the client's issues. However, that is precisely the problem. It might be difficult to distinguish between what the accountant knows outside the *Kovel* engagement and what he or she knows only within the scope of the *Kovel* engagement (only the latter would be covered by the attorney-client privilege). Moreover, using the existing accountant requires that extra steps be taken to assure that the information related to the *Kovel* engagement is clearly separate from the information learned in the accountant's other engagements. It is best for the lawyer to start fresh and hire an independent accountant.

---

[81] IRC § 7525(a)(2).

[82] 296 F.2d 918 (2d Cir. 1961).

D. Work-Product Privilege

The work-product privilege (also referred to as the work-product doctrine) protects the work product and thought processes in preparing for litigation. The work-product privilege was blessed in the Supreme Court case of *Hickman v. Taylor*[83] and is now contained in Rule 26(b)(3) of the Federal Rules of Civil Procedure as follows:

> [A] party may obtain discovery of documents and tangible things otherwise discoverable . . . and prepared in anticipation of litigation or for trial by or for another party or by or for that other party's representative . . . only upon a showing that the party seeking discovery has substantial need of the materials in the preparation of the party's case and that the party is unable without undue hardship to obtain the substantial equivalent of the materials by other means. In ordering discovery of such materials when the required showing has been made, the court shall protect against disclosure of the mental impressions, conclusions, opinions, or legal theories of an attorney or other representative of a party concerning the litigation.

Work product subject to the privilege falls into two broad categories — (i) so-called "opinion work product," such as the mental impressions, conclusions, etc. of the attorney or other representative in the litigation; and (ii) other work product that relates to facts. Opinion work product is discoverable only by waiver through disclosure to the adverse party or if disclosed in a manner likely to become known to the adverse party. But even then the strict need requirements of the Rule must be met.[84] The work-product privilege is sometimes wrongly conceived as an attorney work-product privilege. The privilege is not limited to work done by or under the supervision of an attorney. Any work performed that is otherwise within the scope of the privilege may qualify. Thus, work performed by an accountant may qualify for the privilege.[85]

Unlike the attorney-client privilege, the work-product privilege is not absolute — with a strong showing of need an opposing party (here the Government) may be able to overcome the assertion of the privilege for non-opinion work product. Nevertheless, in most cases the Government likely will not be able to avoid the assertion of the privilege, if the privilege is otherwise well grounded. The work-product privilege is often asserted along with the attorney-client privilege. Since the attorney-client privilege is absolute, it will be better to avoid disclosure on that ground. Nevertheless where, for some reason, the attorney-client privilege is not available, *e.g.*, it is deemed to have been waived, the work-product privilege is a good fallback.

---

83 329 U.S. 495 (1947).

84 *See* FRCP 26(b)(3) ("[T]he court shall protect against disclosure of the mental impressions, conclusions, opinions, or legal theories of a party's attorney or other representative of a party concerning the litigation.").

85 *See, e.g.*, Adlman v. United States, 134 F.3d 1194 (2d Cir. 1998).

In *In re Grand Jury Subpoena Dated Oct. 22, 2001*,[86] two IRS Special Agents conducting an investigation interviewed the general counsel of the company being investigated. At some point, the investigation expanded to include the issue of whether the general counsel had lied in the interview. However, one of the Special Agents had died, and the Government's case was thus based solely on the testimony of the one live Special Agent. A grand jury investigating the company then issued a subpoena for the testimony of the lawyer who had appeared with the general counsel at the interview. The prosecutor represented to the subpoenaed attorney that her testimony was required only as to a factual report of what the client had said in the interview. The court of appeals held an attorney may properly assert the work-product privilege to avoid telling a grand jury what her client said to government agents during an interview in the lawyer's presence if the testimony may be used to indict the client for previous criminal conduct.

Finally, the work-product privilege may be waived, but the waiver of work product is not as broad as the attorney-client waiver. The attorney-client privilege is waived by intentional disclosure to anyone who is not an attorney (or deemed attorney via such doctrines as the *Kovel* concept or the joint defense group) or the client. The work-product privilege as often formulated requires a disclosure to someone having adverse interests.[87] An important and unresolved issue is whether a corporation's disclosure to its outside auditors of its tax accrual workpapers is a waiver of the work-product privilege.[88]

VII. INTERNATIONAL EVIDENCE GATHERING

A. Introduction

One of the highest enforcement priorities for the IRS and DOJ is international tax fraud. In its simplest form, international tax fraud will involve a taxpayer using an offshore bank account in a country whose secrecy laws place a premium on hiding the existence and ownership of the account and thus the taxable income that is in the account. An infinite number of more complex cross-border tax frauds exist, including concealing the existence of foreign investment accounts, reporting foreign sham transactions where the IRS's ability to discover the sham is more limited than if the transactions occurred in the U.S., and manipulating the complex foreign tax deferral regimes for foreign corporations controlled by U.S. persons. In these cases, it is not unusual to encounter a trust in the Channel Islands that owns shares in a Panamanian company that keeps funds in a Cyprus bank account. These cross-border schemes offer fertile ground for criminal investigations and prosecutions, assuming the Government can ever unwind the scheme within the statute of limitations period.

---

[86] 282 F.3d 156 (2d Cir. 2001).

[87] United States v. MIT, 129 F.3d 681, 687 (1st Cir. 1997).

[88] *Compare* United States v. Textron, Inc., 577 F.3d 21 (1st Cir. 2009), *cert. denied*, 560 U.S. 924 (2010); and United States v. Deloitte, 610 F.3d 129 (D.C. Cir. 2010); *see also* Steve R. Johnson, *The Work Product Doctrine and Tax Accrual Workpapers*, 124 Tax Notes 155 (2009).

The Government's job is to get as much information as possible from often unhelpful governments and businesses. Many countries' economies have been dependent on bank secrecy to attract funds, and they have been loath to turn over information simply to aid a U.S. tax investigation. The IRS and DOJ have faced significant roadblocks in obtaining evidence in foreign countries. However, after the high-profile cases against UBS and other international banks, governments around the world are focused as never before on bank secrecy, information exchange, and tax enforcement. This has led to new legislation, including the Foreign Account Tax Compliance Act (FATCA),[89] an amendment to the U.S.-Switzerland Tax Treaty that would broaden the information the Swiss will share in tax cases,[90] and the negotiation of numerous other tax information exchange treaties.[91]

While handling an international tax case conjures up images of Cayman Island beaches and snowcapped Swiss Alps, these cases are not all fun and games for defense counsel:

> When evidence sought is in a foreign country, it is necessary to observe not only applicable state or federal rules, but also the laws and regulations of the foreign country where the evidence is located. Procedures may vary in civil, criminal and administrative cases. Some countries view the taking of any form of evidence, even voluntary depositions, as an infringement on their judicial sovereignty. This applies to party and non-party witnesses. Telephone depositions are prohibited in many countries. Many countries do not permit the pre-trial discovery of documents. Attempting to obtain evidence without following the requirements of the foreign country may result in the arrest, detention, deportation or imprisonment of participants, including American counsel.[92]

The procedures available to the Government for obtaining foreign evidence are myriad and complex and include Mutual Legal Assistance Treaties (MLAT), tax information exchange agreements (TIEAs), tax treaties, and court-sponsored procedures for taking foreign depositions, including letters rogatory. Moreover, as noted above, the agreements in this area are frequently changing. We will only summarize the common tools to gather evidence.[93]

---

[89] Pub. L. No. 111-147, 124 Stat. 71, 97 (codified at IRC §§ 1471 *et seq.*).

[90] *See* Lauren Gardner & Daniel Pruzin, *Geithner Signs Protocol to U.S.-Swiss Treaty to Provide Greater Tax Information Exchange*, INT'L TAX MONITOR (BNA), Sept. 24, 2009.

[91] *See, e.g.*, Alison Bennett, *United States, Monaco Sign Agreement to Allow for Exchange of Tax Information*, DAILY TAX REP. (BNA), Sept. 10, 2009, at I-6; Rick Mitchell, *Island of Jersey, United Kingdom Sign Tax Information Exchange Agreement*, 46 DAILY TAX REP. (BNA), Mar. 13, 2009, at I-3; Daniel Pruzin, *Germany, Liechtenstein Approve TIEA Incorporating OECD Exchange Standards*, 169 DAILY TAX REP. (BNA). Sept. 3, 2009, at I-1; Daniel Pruzin, *Switzerland and Austria Conclude Accord on Tax Information Exchange*, 134 DAILY TAX REP. (BNA), July 16, 2009, at I-3; Rick Mitchell, *France, Switzerland Sign Tax Treaty Rider Aimed at Ending Banking Secrecy*, 165 DAILY TAX REP. (BNA), Aug. 28, 2009, at I-1.

[92] U.S. Department of State Circular: Obtaining Evidence Abroad, 739 PLI/LIT 1095, 1098 (2006).

[93] For a more detailed exposition on this subject, *see* Cono Namorato & Scott Michel, *International Criminal Tax Cases*, 50 U. MIAMI L. REV. 617 (1996); and James P. Springer, *Overview of International Evidence and Asset Gathering in Civil and Criminal Cases*, 22 GEO. WASH. J. OF INT'L L. & ECON. 278

B. Methods for Obtaining Foreign Evidence

The first methods for obtaining foreign evidence regarding tax violations are the traditional methods of summons and grand jury subpoena discussed above. The Government does not always have an effective mutual assistance means available for obtaining evidence abroad. If a foreign business engages in commerce in the United States, for example a foreign bank with a branch in the U.S., the Government may generally serve a summons or subpoena on the U.S. branch. However, the bank's compliance with the summons or subpoena may violate foreign law. Foreign businesses often contend that they might be prosecuted by their own government if they comply with the summons. In resolving these conflicts, courts have performed a balance of interests test, in which they look at the need for the evidence and international comity.[94] Since the Government is not involving a foreign government and is essentially forcing the foreign business to comply with its information request by threat of punishment on the local office, these methods are known as unilateral compulsory measures.

The next method by which foreign evidence can be obtained is through an MLAT. These treaties provide a defined and regularized method for obtaining a broad range of legal assistance for criminal matters, including taking testimony of witnesses, providing documents and other physical evidence in a form that would be admissible at trial, and executing searches and seizures. MLATs create a contractual obligation between the treaty partners to render each other assistance in criminal matters in accordance with the terms of the treaty. They are designed to facilitate the exchange of information and evidence for use in criminal investigations and prosecutions. Assistance is available under the MLAT at both the administrative and grand jury stages of an investigation, as well as at trial. Generally, MLATs have provisions restricting the use of evidence furnished under their provisions, including conditions of confidentiality. The Government must comply with these restrictions in using the information or evidence in the course of an investigation or prosecution.[95]

Similar to MLATs are Tax Information Exchange Agreements (TIEAs) and income tax treaties. The U.S. has numerous income tax treaties, most of which are designed to reduce double taxation. Most tax treaties do contain evidence sharing provisions. However, for the purposes of obtaining foreign evidence, TIEAs are more specialized and effective than tax treaties. TIEAs are agreements which specifically provide for mutual assistance in criminal and civil tax investigations and proceedings. This assistance includes obtaining foreign-based documents, including bank records, and testimony in admissible form. TIEAs are creatures of the Internal Revenue Code.[96] These provisions initially authorized the Secretary of the Treasury Department to conclude agreements with countries in the Caribbean Basin (thereby qualifying such countries for certain benefits under the Caribbean

(1988). Mr. Springer is also the principal author of the Criminal Tax Manual's provisions on foreign evidence gathering. *See* CTM 41.00 *et. seq.*, which are summarized below.

94 Namorato, *supra* at 623–24.

95 CTM 41.02.

96 *See* IRC § 274(h)(6)(C).

Basin Initiative), but later expanded this authority to conclude TIEAs with any country. All of the TIEAs and most of the tax treaties currently in effect contain language requiring that the information obtained under the agreements be used only for tax purposes. This creates problems for a prosecutor conducting a grand jury investigation directed at both tax and non-tax crimes.[97]

The final means by which prosecutors obtain foreign evidence are letters rogatory, also known as letters of request. This is the traditional method used by United States litigants to obtain the assistance of foreign authorities to obtain evidence abroad, in both civil and criminal cases. Essentially, a letter rogatory is a formal request from a court when a case is pending to a foreign court to perform some act. If the foreign court honors the request, it does so based on comity rather than any treaty obligation. A letter rogatory can usually only be used in a proceeding which has actually begun, such the post-indictment stages of a criminal case.

The route of a letter rogatory is quite circuitous and involves many diverse entities in an uncoordinated process. The Government initiates the process by applying to the court where the indictment is pending for the issuance of a letter rogatory. This application must be supported by a set of complicated and formalistic pleadings. If the court approves the request, the letter rogatory must be transmitted through diplomatic channels from the U.S. State Department to the foreign ministry of the country involved. The foreign ministry then delivers the request to the country's ministry of justice, which in turn delivers it to the foreign court. If the request is successfully executed, the evidence must retrace the path of the request back to the originating court.

While the letter rogatory procedure is the traditional method of obtaining assistance abroad, it has certain flaws: the process is convoluted and time-consuming; there is no obligation that the foreign country honor the request; the foreign country's bank secrecy laws may not permit the court to honor the request; there are no mutually agreed upon procedures to ensure that the evidence will be received in admissible form; and, the procedure is not available during the criminal investigation, when it is needed most. As a result, the Government usually relies on the more regularized and definite forms of obtaining foreign evidence like TIEAs and MLATs.[98]

PROBLEM

The IRS has been investigating Sharon Michael for more than a year. Sharon is the president and sole shareholder of *Michael's*, a high-end clothing manufacturing corporation. She travels extensively to Europe and Asia on business. On frequent trips through Zurich, she deposits large amounts of cash in an account at Grosser Schweizer Bank, which she refers to as her "retirement account."

The IRS investigation began as a civil audit, and Sharon was represented by her longtime accountant during that investigation. Sharon and her accountant resisted

---

[97] CTM 41.04.

[98] CTM 41.05.

the production of most of the documents requested by the revenue agent. A rather unnerving silence followed, and the accountant referred the case to you to see if anything could be done to pressure the agent to close the case. You advised Sharon and her accountant that the silence (plus the transfer of substantial sums by Sharon to a Swiss bank account) meant that there was a possibility that the case had been referred to IRS CID for criminal investigation. Your suspicions were confirmed when, within a week of your first meeting with the client, a flood of summons were issued by IRS Special Agent Moira McQuaid. A summons was issued to Sharon's U.S. bank for all records on all bank accountants for the past four years. Another summons was issued to Sharon's accountant, asking for all books and records on Sharon's business and personal taxes, all workpapers prepared by the accountant, and all written advice given by the accountant to Sharon. Finally, a summons was issued to Sharon herself to produce all records for her business, her records regarding her personal tax and financial information, and her personal calendar. The summons to Sharon asks her to provide "any and all documents relating to any direct or indirect sources of money or other things of value received from *Michael's*, and any records or information relating to transfers to any bank accountant outside the United States."

1. Sharon would like you to oppose, in court if necessary, all of the summonses. Which of the summonses do you recommend that she contest, and what privileges and defenses would you allege on her behalf?

2. Assume you are an attorney with IRS Chief Counsel's office. Special Agent McQuaid has come to you for advice. She suspects that Sharon has an account with the Zurich branch of Grosser Schweizer Bank and she wants to obtain the records of the account. The bank has offices in New York and San Francisco, as well as various other countries around the world. What are the various options the Government has to obtain the records on the Swiss bank account?

3. Once the summons issue is resolved, Sharon would like you to prepare a defense. She would like you to use her existing accountant should the need for forensic accounting arise. What do you advise?

Chapter 8

PRE-TRIAL ISSUES IN CRIMINAL TAX CASES

18 U.S.C. § 3500(a) & (e)

Fed. R. Crim. P. 12(b), 16(a), 47

I. INTRODUCTION

This chapter explores important issues that the parties face once a defendant has been charged with a criminal tax offense. We first discuss discovery. Criminal tax defendants are entitled only to limited discovery of the Government's case, so understanding the defendant's discovery rights is essential. Thereafter, we discuss dispositive motions and motions to suppress. Pre-trial motion practice can make or break the defense of a criminal case. This chapter concludes with consideration of questions of venue, bills of particulars, and shifting responsibility away from the taxpayer-defendant.

The field of pre-trial procedure is much broader than the scope of this chapter. Entire courses have been devoted to pre-trial procedural issues. Because the focus of this text is on criminal tax issues, this chapter does not address numerous pre-trial issues that are of great importance in all criminal cases — issues such as arrest, voluntary submission, the defendant's initial appearance, the detention hearing, bail and pre-trial release, supervision of the defendant by the United States Pretrial Services, arraignment, and speedy trial. These and many other pre-trial topics are not unique to tax cases, but are essential to practice in the criminal arena. Yet, they are beyond the scope of these materials, which focus on the tax aspects of certain pre-trial issues.

II. DISCOVERY OF THE GOVERNMENT'S CASE

A. The Problem of Limited Discovery

A person charged with a tax crime quickly learns a cruel paradox of our criminal justice system: discovery rights we take for granted in civil litigation are not available in criminal litigation. When a litigant's pocketbook is at risk in civil litigation, we allow wide-ranging discovery of anything that is relevant or is reasonably likely to lead to admissible evidence. But when a defendant's freedom hangs in the balance, the Federal Rules of Criminal Procedure generally provide only very limited discovery in advance of trial. The taxpayer's Fifth Amendment privilege blocks the Government from obtaining discovery of important information from the defendant, and the defendant's ability to compel discovery from the

Government is severely limited unless the presiding judge requires the Government to disclose additional information.

B. Practitioner Vigilance

Often, the best discovery is practitioner vigilance — moving quickly to learn material facts from available sources and keeping track of what the criminal investigators and prosecutors know. Defense counsel should aspire to stay one step ahead of the Government, and if that is impossible, no more than one step behind. Conducting an independent investigation of the facts, through the available witnesses and documents, is essential to the defense.

C. Administrative Disclosures

The practitioner should keep avenues of communication open with the investigators and prosecutors in order to learn as much as possible about the Government's case. As noted in Chapter 6, one of the key purposes of attending conferences with CI, DOJ Tax, and the AUSA is to learn more about the Government's evidence and theory of the case. Once charges have been filed, the Government communications should be made only through the prosecutor, unless express permission has been received to continue discussions directly with the investigating agents. Every contact with the investigators and prosecutors represents an opportunity for insight.

In many cases, the prosecution team willingly discloses information about the case that would not necessarily be discoverable under the federal rules. Sometimes these disclosures occur in the context of plea negotiations; sometimes the prosecutor simply is willing to discuss the case in greater detail than he or she might be required to disclose. As we discuss further below, some prosecutors essentially have an "open file" policy, which allows the defense to review practically the entire investigative file.

D. Freedom of Information Act and Privacy Act

The Freedom of Information Act (FOIA)[1] and the companion Privacy Act of 1974[2] offer additional avenues to discover at least portions of the Government's case. The basic concept of FOIA is that citizens should have the right to know how their Government operates. The basic concept of the Privacy Act is that a citizen should know what the Government's records say about him. These two acts are different in focus but share the underpinning that knowledge of Government in a free society is a good thing. In a democracy, citizens' knowledge is their power against an abusive government.

In a criminal case, the defendant and his lawyer ideally want to see everything in the Government's files. Just as in any other type of adversary proceeding (including civil trials), knowledge is power. Yet, historically, criminal investigations

---

[1] 5 U.S.C. § 552.

[2] 5 U.S.C. § 552a.

and trials offer the target limited ability to discover the information in the Government's files (and, correspondingly, the Government has limited ability to discover the defendant's files). This historical approach to criminal investigations and prosecutions severely limits the documentation that can be obtained via FOIA or the Privacy Act.

The federal statutory regime protects agency information from disclosure unless certain limited exceptions apply. The Privacy Act of 1974 sets out these protections, but it also permits parties to demand production of documents from the Government. The basic right to obtain production flows from 5 U.S.C. § 552a, which provides in pertinent part:

> (d) Access to Records. — Each agency that maintains a system of records shall—
>
> > (1) upon request by any individual to gain access to his record or to any information pertaining to him which is contained in the system, permit him and upon his request, a person of his own choosing to accompany him, to review the record and have a copy made of all or any portion thereof in a form comprehensible to him, except that the agency may require the individual to furnish a written statement authorizing discussion of that individual's record in the accompanying person's presence; . . .
> >
> > (5) nothing in this section shall allow an individual access to any information compiled in reasonable anticipation of a civil action or proceeding.
>
> (f) Agency Rules. — In order to carry out the provisions of this section, each agency that maintains a system of records shall promulgate rules, in accordance with the requirements (including general notice) of section 553 of this title, which shall—
>
> > (3) establish procedures for the disclosure to an individual upon his request of his record or information pertaining to him, including special procedure, if deemed necessary, for the disclosure to an individual of medical records, including psychological records, pertaining to him;
> >
> > (4) establish procedures for reviewing a request from an individual concerning the amendment of any record or information pertaining to the individual, for making a determination on the request, for an appeal within the agency of an initial adverse agency determination, and for whatever additional means may be necessary for each individual to be able to exercise fully his rights under this section; and
> >
> > (5) establish fees to be charged, if any, to any individual for making copies of his record, excluding the cost of any search for and review of the record.

Likewise, FOIA permits citizens to obtain copies of their personal information from Government files. Section 552(a) describes agency material subject to disclosure. Section 552(b) lists nine categories exempt from disclosure, and section 552(c) sets out additional exemptions. Since subsection (a) is a broad principle of disclosure, the controversy in FOIA cases typically involves the exemptions. Of particular relevance to our focus on criminal matters, FOIA expressly limits the availability of certain law enforcement records. Section 552(b)(7) provides that the Government may refuse production of records or information compiled for law enforcement purposes, but only to the extent that the production of such law enforcement records or information

> (A) could reasonably be expected to interfere with enforcement proceedings,
>
> (B) would deprive a person of a right to a fair trial or an impartial adjudication,
>
> (C) * * *,
>
> (D) could reasonably be expected to disclose the identity of a confidential source, including a State, local, or foreign agency or authority or any private institution which furnished information on a confidential basis, and, in the case of a record or information compiled by a criminal law enforcement authority in the course of a criminal investigation, or by an agency conducting a lawful national security intelligence investigation, information furnished by a confidential source,
>
> (E) would disclose techniques and procedures for law enforcement investigations or prosecutions, or would disclose guidelines for law enforcement investigations or prosecutions if such disclosure could reasonably be expected to risk circumvention of the law, or
>
> (F) could reasonably be expected to endanger the life or physical safety of any individual.

At least theoretically, virtually all of a criminal investigatory file (such as a file compiled by CI and by DOJ's CES) is likely compiled for law enforcement purposes. Nevertheless, given FOIA's purpose to narrowly construe the exemptions, most of the raw data in those files (*e.g.*, bank statements and cancelled checks) may be obtained in a FOIA request. For example, if a civil examination preceded the criminal investigation, much of the documentation in the civil examination file arguably was not compiled for law enforcement purposes. As a practical matter, while a criminal tax investigation is underway, a FOIA request will likely obtain for the taxpayer many of the underlying documents other than the documents generated by CI or DOJ in the criminal investigation itself.

Protecting the confidentiality of an informant is a high priority for criminal investigators. The Supreme Court has held, consistent with FOIA generally, that the informant exception in section 552(b)(7)(D) should be narrowly construed.[3] Specifically, in order to invoke the exemption, the investigating agency must show that the informant had supplied information under an express assurance of confidentiality or circumstances in which such an assurance was necessarily implied if not express. The Court noted in this regard that an assurance of confidentiality

[3] Department of Justice v. Landano, 508 U.S. 165 (1993).

does not mean an absolute assurance, for confidential informants often are required ultimately to testify at trial even if given some assurance of confidentiality. Should the matter be prosecuted, of course, the target (who is then a defendant) will have an opportunity for the limited discovery offered under the Federal Rules of Criminal Procedures and such doctrines as *Brady*. These rules and doctrines are discussed below.

E. Pre-Trial Discovery

1. Federal Rules of Criminal Procedure

Rule 16 of the Federal Rules of Criminal Procedure allows the defendant limited discovery of the Government's case. Since these general discovery rights are not unique to tax cases, they are not discussed here. Pre-trial discovery is prescribed by the rules of procedure, and most federal judges have their own individual or local district rules that also govern how much information is made available to a defendant prior to the commencement of trial.

2. Case Law Requiring Discovery

a. General

There are certain types of evidence that the Government must make available at some point. Most of this discovery results from a series of cases in which the Supreme Court has interpreted the Constitution and the Federal Rules of Criminal Procedure to require production of evidence pre-trial. The most important of these cases are *Brady*[4] and *Giglio*.[5] These decisions are so influential that criminal attorneys speak in a shorthand way by referring to "*Brady*" or "*Giglio*" when they are referring to certain types of information that must be made available before trial. For example, a defense attorney might ask, "When will we get the *Brady*?"

b. *Brady*

BRADY v. MARYLAND
United States Supreme Court
373 U.S. 83 (1963)

Opinion of the Court by Mr. Justice Douglas, announced by Mr. Justice Brennan.

Petitioner and a companion, Boblit, were found guilty of murder in the first degree and were sentenced to death, their convictions being affirmed by the Court of Appeals of Maryland. Their trials were separate, petitioner being tried first. At his trial Brady took the stand and admitted his participation in the crime, but he claimed that Boblit did the actual killing. And, in his summation to the jury, Brady's

---

[4] Brady v. Maryland, 373 U.S. 83 (1963).

[5] Giglio v. United States, 405 U.S. 150 (1972).

counsel conceded that Brady was guilty of murder in the first degree, asking only that the jury return that verdict "without capital punishment." Prior to the trial petitioner's counsel had requested the prosecution to allow him to examine Boblit's extrajudicial statements. Several of those statements were shown to him; but one dated July 9, 1958, in which Boblit admitted the actual homicide, was withheld by the prosecution and did not come to petitioner's notice until after he had been tried, convicted, and sentenced, and after his conviction had been affirmed.

Petitioner moved the trial court for a new trial based on the newly discovered evidence that had been suppressed by the prosecution. Petitioner's appeal from a denial of that motion was dismissed by the Court of Appeals without prejudice to relief under the Maryland Post Conviction Procedure Act. The petition for post-conviction relief was dismissed by the trial court; and on appeal the Court of Appeals held that suppression of the evidence by the prosecution denied petitioner due process of law and remanded the case for a retrial of the question of punishment, not the question of guilt.

We agree with the Court of Appeals that suppression of this confession was a violation of the Due Process Clause of the Fourteenth Amendment. The Court of Appeals relied in the main on two decisions from the Third Circuit Court of Appeals — *United States ex rel. Almeida v. Baldi*, 195 F.2d 815, 33 A.L.R.2d 1407, and *United States ex rel. Thompson v. Dye*, 221 F.2d 763 — which, we agree, state the correct constitutional rule.

This ruling is an extension of *Mooney v. Holohan*, 294 U.S. 103, where the Court ruled on what nondisclosure by a prosecutor violates due process:

> It is a requirement that cannot be deemed to be satisfied by mere notice and hearing if a state has contrived a conviction through the pretense of a trial which in truth is but used as a means of depriving a defendant of liberty through a deliberate deception of court and jury by the presentation of testimony known to be perjured. Such a contrivance by a state to procure the conviction and imprisonment of a defendant is as inconsistent with the rudimentary demands of justice as is the obtaining of a like result by intimidation.

In *Pyle v. Kansas*, 317 U.S. 213, 215–216 we phrased the rule in broader terms:

> Petitioner's papers are inexpertly drawn, but they do set forth allegations that his imprisonment resulted from perjured testimony, knowingly used by the State authorities to obtain his conviction, and from the deliberate suppression by those same authorities of evidence favorable to him. These allegations sufficiently charge a deprivation of rights guaranteed by the Federal Constitution, and, if proven, would entitle petitioner to release from his present custody.

The Third Circuit in the *Baldi* case construed that statement in *Pyle v. Kansas* to mean that the "suppression of evidence favorable" to the accused was itself sufficient to amount to a denial of due process. In *Napue v. Illinois*, 360 U.S. 264, 269, we extended the test formulated in *Mooney v. Holohan* when we said: "The same result obtains when the State, although not soliciting false evidence, allows it to go uncorrected when it appears." And *see Alcorta v. Texas*, 355 U.S. 28; *Wilde v.*

Wyoming, 362 U.S. 607. *Cf. Durley v. Mayo*, 351 U.S. 277, 285 (dissenting opinion).

We now hold that the suppression by the prosecution of evidence favorable to an accused upon request violates due process where the evidence is material either to guilt or to punishment, irrespective of the good faith or bad faith of the prosecution.

The principle of *Mooney v. Holohan* is not punishment of society for misdeeds of a prosecutor but avoidance of an unfair trial to the accused. Society wins not only when the guilty are convicted but when criminal trials are fair; our system of the administration of justice suffers when any accused is treated unfairly. An inscription on the walls of the Department of Justice states the proposition candidly for the federal domain: "The United States wins its point whenever justice is done its citizens in the courts."[6] A prosecution that withholds evidence on demand of an accused which, if made available, would tend to exculpate him or reduce the penalty helps shape a trial that bears heavily on the defendant. That casts the prosecutor in the role of an architect of a proceeding that does not comport with standards of justice, even though, as in the present case, his action is not "the result of guile," to use the words of the Court of Appeals.

Brady has been interpreted to require the Government to produce material known or reasonably knowable to the prosecutor that is (a) either exculpatory (favorable to the defendant) or potentially useful for impeachment of Government witnesses and (b) material (in an importance sense) and prejudicial to the defendant.[7] The Government thus bears this mandatory production burden, even if the defendant does not request the evidence.[8] Thus, the defendant theoretically need not file a motion for *Brady* material. Nonetheless, it is good form to make the request early, in writing, and in some cases, often. There is no specific time when *Brady* materials must be disclosed, and most judges have a particular pre-trial schedule that is followed in routine cases. But the defendant should not hesitate to demand early disclosure, particularly in complex cases, so that the *Brady* material can be used effectively by the defendant. Courts generally require the disclosures before trial, but it sometimes can be a challenge to obtain the material far enough in advance of trial to make timely use of the information.

---

[6] [2] Judge Simon E. Sobeloff when Solicitor General put the idea as follows in an address before the Judicial Conference of the Fourth Circuit on June 29, 1954:

> The Solicitor General is not a neutral, he is an advocate; but an advocate for a client whose business is not merely to prevail in the instant case. My client's chief business is not to achieve victory but to establish justice. We are constantly reminded of the now classic words penned by one of my illustrious predecessors, Frederick William Lehmann, that the Government wins its point when justice is done in its courts.

373 U.S. at 87, n.2.

[7] *E.g.*, United States v. Gil, 297 F.3d 93, 101–05 (2d Cir. 2002); *see* Strickler v. Greene, 527 U.S. 263 (1999).

[8] Kyles v. Whitley, 514 U.S. 419, 432–33 (1995).

c. *Giglio*

In *Giglio v. United States*,[9] the defendant was convicted of passing forged money orders. While his appeal was pending, his attorney discovered new evidence indicating that the Government had failed to disclose an alleged promise made to the key Government witness that the witness would not be prosecuted if he testified for the Government before the grand jury and at trial. The Supreme Court granted certiorari to determine whether the undisclosed evidence required a new trial under the due process criteria of *Napue v. Illinois*[10] and *Brady*. The Court relied on *Brady* for the principle that suppression of material evidence justifies a new trial "irrespective of the good faith or bad faith of the prosecution," and on *Napue* for the rule that when the reliability of a witness may be determinative of guilt or innocence, "nondisclosure of evidence affecting credibility" falls within the general rule established in *Brady*. Since the Government's case depended almost entirely on the testimony of the witness who allegedly had been promised that he would not be prosecuted, the Court concluded that in the absence of such testimony there would have been no indictment or evidence sufficient for the case to reach the jury. Thus, the witness' credibility was important to the case, and the jury was entitled to know of any agreements made with the witness regarding future prosecution.

As a result of *Giglio*, the Government is required to produce any material evidence that may be used for impeachment, including most prominently, agreements that have been reached with prosecution witnesses.[11] As with *Brady*, it is a good form for the defendant to file a motion demanding disclosure of any impeachment evidence, although the Government is required to produce material impeachment evidence without such a motion.

d. *Henthorn* Requests

If the Government intends to use an IRS employee as a witness at trial, the defense is entitled to evidence that would impeach the testimony of the IRS employee just as with any other witness. One prophylactic measure is to request that the IRS employee's personnel file be reviewed in camera for potential impeachment evidence. The IRM refers to this request as a *Henthorn* request.[12] Both the Attorney General and the Secretary of the Treasury have guidelines to ensure disclosure of all *Giglio* and *Brady* information, including appropriate personnel files. When the IRS employee's file is known to present a problem for the Government, the *Henthorn* material should be disclosed and discussed in the CRL (the referral letter from the IRS to DOJ Tax).[13] The Government views *Henthorn* as requiring only a review of the personnel file, so that the files are not furnished to

[9] 405 U.S. 150 (1972).

[10] 360 U.S. 264 (1959).

[11] *See also* Fed. R. Crim. P. 16. Even implicit plea agreements might be covered by *Giglio*. *See* Peter A. Joy & Kevin C. McMunigal, *Implicit Plea Agreements and Brady Disclosure*, 22 ABA CRIM. JUSTICE 50 (2007).

[12] United States v. Henthorn, 931 F.2d 29 (9th Cir. 1991); *see* IRM 9.6.3.7.1.1.

[13] ILM 199902018 (Nov. 20, 1998), *published at* 1999 TNT 11-48 (Jan. 19, 1999).

the defense unless something relevant and material is uncovered in that review. Defense counsel should consider a specific request for the personnel file as part of the discovery demands in the case.

3. The Jencks Act

The Jencks Act[14] requires, upon request, production of Government witness statements concerning the subject of their testimony on direct examination.[15] However, no statement or report made by a Government witness is discoverable until the witness has testified on direct examination.[16] Rule 26.2 of the Federal Rules of Criminal Procedure incorporates the Jencks Act and contains certain procedures for witness statements to be reviewed in camera to protect privileged information. Although the production of a witness statement is not required until after the witness has testified, some AUSA's voluntarily produce Jencks material early in order to make the trial more efficient, and some judges will require production of the required material earlier for the same reason.[17] One very common practice is for the witness statement to be produced to the defendant the night before the witness testifies.

Requests or motions for Jencks statements should be made sooner rather than later. Jencks materials should also be requested early, in writing, in some cases often, and in all cases no later than the conclusion of the testimony of each witness. Many defense counsel also file motions at the outset of the case to require the Government to preserve Jencks material.

Among the materials subject to the Jencks Act are the portions of: (i) the SAR that relate to the Special Agent's testimony if given at trial;[18] and (ii) grand jury testimony that relates to a witness' testimony at trial.[19]

The Government's disclosure obligations are not met by including the required materials in a larger document set without specifically identifying the material as *Brady, Giglio*, or Jencks Act materials, particularly if it would strain the defendant's resources under all the circumstances to identify the materials and use them in a meaningful way.[20] In other words, in a complex case with hundreds of thousands of documents, it is not sufficient for the Government to produce all the documents and then say, "If there is any *Brady, Giglio*, or Jencks, it's in there."

---

[14] 18 U.S.C. § 3500.

[15] The statute's name derives from the case that inspired the legislation, Jencks v. United States, 353 U.S. 657 (1957).

[16] 18 U.S.C. § 3500(a).

[17] *See* United States v. Campagnuolo, 592 F.2d 852, 858 (5th Cir. 1979); United States v. Murphy, 569 F.2d 771, 774 (3d Cir. 1977), *cert. denied*, 435 U.S. 955 (1978).

[18] United States v. Cleveland, 507 F.2d 731 (7th Cir. 1974).

[19] 18 U.S.C. § 3500(e)(3).

[20] *See, e.g.*, United States v. Gil, 297 F.3d at 106–07.

4. The Prosecutor's Duties

The combination of prosecutorial duties created by *Brady*, *Giglio*, and the Jencks Act provides the potential for significant discovery by the defendant before and during trial. The following case provides an example of how one court has interpreted the limits of the combination of duties imposed on the Government's to produce information to the defense.

UNITED STATES v. RODRIGUEZ

United States Court of Appeals, Second Circuit
496 F.3d 221 (2007)

LEVAL, J.

This appeal raises questions about the Government's obligations in a criminal case to make notes of, and to disclose, information that may impeach its witnesses or exculpate the defendant. Ramiro Rodriguez was convicted of drug dealing in a multi-defendant trial in which the Government's case rested primarily on the testimony of two cooperating witnesses. During the direct examination of one cooperating witness, the Government elicited that the witness had lied "about everything" during her initial interviews with investigators. Defense counsel demanded that the Government disclose investigators' notes from the interviews, and demanded to be informed of the substance of the witness's false statements. The Government advised that no notes had been made of the false statements and refused to disclose the substance of the lies. The district court at first indicated that the Government should make such a disclosure, but expressed doubt whether disclosure could properly be required where the false statements were not memorialized in a document or a recording, and ultimately declined to compel the disclosure.

Rodriguez contends he suffered a violation of his rights under the Jencks Act, under *Brady v. Maryland* and *Giglio v. United States* and under the Sixth Amendment's Confrontation Clause. He contends the Government's investigators were obligated to take notes during their interviews with the cooperating witness, so that the notes could be turned over to the defense, and that, in any event, the Government was obligated under *Brady* to disclose the substance of the witness's lies.

We reject Rodriguez's argument that the Government was obligated to take notes during its interviews with its witness. As for Rodriguez's further arguments — that the Government was obligated to disclose the substance of the witness's lies — we cannot resolve them at this stage of the case. If the district court's reason for declining to compel disclosure was that the statements were not recorded, we do not agree. When the Government is in possession of material information that impeaches its witness or exculpates the defendant, it does not avoid the obligation under *Brady or Giglio* to disclose the information by not writing it down.

It does not necessarily follow, however, that the failure to disclose in this case violated any right of Rodriguez. The disclosure obligations of *Brady* and *Giglio* apply only to impeaching or exculpatory information that is of sufficient importance to be deemed "material." The district court was never advised of the nature of the lies and never ruled on whether the witness's undisclosed prior statements were sufficiently material to give rise to a disclosure obligation. We remand to the district court for a determination of materiality and prejudice.

Discussion

a. The Government's Failure to Take Notes

Rodriguez argues that by failing to take notes during interviews with Lopez and by taking only minimal notes during interviews with Espada, the Government violated his rights under the Jencks Act, under *Brady* and *Giglio*, and under the Sixth Amendment's Confrontation Clause. He suggests that the Government deliberately refrained from memorializing the witnesses' statements in order to evade any obligation to turn over exculpatory and impeaching information to the defense. He equates the Government's behavior with the destruction of evidence — here, "the destruction . . . not of written notes, but rather of any record of the witness[es'] oral statements by failing to preserve them in written form." Moreover, according to Rodriguez, "[b]y snuffing out the record . . . the [G]overnment immunized its two chief witnesses from full and fair cross-examination."

The Jencks Act requires the Government to produce to the defendant any "statement" by the witness that "relates to the subject matter as to which the witness has testified." 18 U.S.C. § 3500(b); *see id.* § 3500(e) (defining "statement"). The term "statement," however, is defined to include only statements that have been memorialized in some concrete form, whether in a written document or electrical recording. *Id.* § 3500(e). The obligation has no application where, as here, no such memorialization has been created in the first place. *See United States v. Houlihan*, 92 F.3d 1271, 1288 (1st Cir. 1996) ("The Jencks Act does not impose an obligation on government agents to record witness interviews or to take notes during such interviews.").

We reject Rodriguez's contention that *Brady* or the Confrontation Clause requires the Government to take notes during witness interviews. While *Brady* and *Giglio*, as discussed below, obligate the prosecutor in certain circumstances to disclose to the defense material exculpatory and impeaching information, those cases have not been generally construed to require the Government to make written notes for the defendant's benefit.[21] This is in part because the Government's

[21] [3] We need not and do not consider whether, in some cases, the preservation of exculpatory or impeaching information in a concrete form — such as by note taking — may be necessary to ensure that the information can be relayed accurately to the defense. In this case, there is no reason to doubt the ability of the AUSA to inform the defense of any of the witnesses' prior statements that were materially exculpatory or impeaching. Further, although the Government has no obligation to make written notes for the defendant's benefit, we do not reach here the issue of whether the Government, for the purpose of avoiding the disclosure of the initial falsities and inconsistencies of persons who may become Government trial witnesses, may permissibly instruct an agent not to follow the customary practice of taking notes of witness interviews. That question is not before us in this case because, although defense counsel speculated at trial that the Government had specifically directed agents not to follow their alleged ordinary practice of taking notes of interviews with witnesses, the district court expressly gave

representative may have no way of knowing, upon hearing a witness's statement, that the statement is inconsistent with what the witness will say at a later time. Rodriguez contends that in order to protect the obligation of the Government to turn over inconsistent statements of witnesses once it becomes aware of the inconsistencies, the Government is obligated to take notes of all interviews of potential witnesses. *Brady, Giglio*, and the Confrontation Clause have not been construed to impose this obligation, and we decline to extend them in this manner.

b. The Government's Disclosure of Brady Information

Whether the Government was obligated to make notes of a potential witness's statements and whether it was required to disclose the witness's lies are very different questions. From the fact that the Government is not required to make notes of a witness's statements, it does not follow that the Government has no obligation to inform the accused of information that materially impeaches its witness. *Brady* and its progeny require the Government to disclose material information that is "favorable to the accused, either because it is exculpatory, or because it is impeaching." *Strickler v. Greene*, 527 U.S. 263, 281–82 (1999); *see also Brady*, 373 U.S. at 87 (due process obligation to disclose to the defendant "evidence favorable to an accused"). This obligation is designed to serve the objectives of both fairness and accuracy in criminal prosecutions. To begin with, it recognizes the possibility that the evidence on which the prosecution relies to prove the defendant's guilt is not necessarily truthful, accurate, or complete, especially when the prosecution's investigations have made it aware of evidence or information that might be favorable to the defense in controverting the Government's proofs.

Brady information must be disclosed, furthermore, in a manner that gives the defendant a reasonable opportunity either to use the evidence in the trial or to use the information to obtain evidence for use in the trial. Thus, the Government must make disclosures in sufficient time that the defendant will have a reasonable opportunity to act upon the information efficaciously. *See DiSimone v. Phillips*, 461 F.3d 181, 197 (2d Cir. 2006) ("The more a piece of evidence is valuable and rich with potential leads, the less likely it will be that late disclosure provides the defense an 'opportunity for use.' " (quoting *Leka v. Portuondo*, 257 F.3d 89, 103 (2d Cir. 2001)). Similarly, disclosures must be sufficiently specific and complete to be useful. *See Leka*, 257 F.3d at 103 (finding *Brady* not satisfied where Government did not disclose details of potential witness's knowledge, because defendant was left to gamble on what witness would say).

If the district court's reason for declining to compel the Government to make disclosure was that the lies were not set forth in any document or recording ("I have never seen anything that says the government has to turn over oral information."), we disagree. As noted above, we agree with the district court that the absence of such memorialization is determinative with respect to any obligation to disclose a witness's statements under the Jencks Act. The considerations under *Brady* and *Giglio*, however, are quite different. *Brady* and *Giglio* obligations, which apply only

---

defense counsel the opportunity to examine the key agent outside the presence of the jury on this point, and defense counsel declined to take advantage of that opportunity.

to material exculpatory and impeaching information, arise because it would be unfair to the defendant — and might cast doubt on the reliability of the verdict — for the trial to be conducted without informing the defendant of such information. The obligation to disclose information covered by the *Brady* and *Giglio* rules exists without regard to whether that information has been recorded in tangible form.[22]

Even if the district court relied on an inappropriate reason for declining to compel disclosure, that would not necessarily mean that a *Brady* violation occurred, which would require overturning Rodriguez's conviction. A *Brady* violation occurs only where there is a "reasonable probability" that a different verdict would have resulted from disclosure of the information that the defendant claims was suppressed. The Government declined to disclose the substance of Lopez's lies because it contended at trial that it had satisfied all of its obligations under *Brady*, and the district court, which ruled on a different basis, never considered whether the failure to disclose Lopez's lies would violate *Brady*. Because we do not know what Lopez's lies were, we cannot determine whether disclosure was mandated under *Brady or Giglio* or whether the Government's refusal to make disclosure more extensive than Lopez's testimony that she lied "about everything" caused the defendant prejudice. The district court is far better positioned to make this appraisal. Accordingly, we remand, in accordance with the procedures set forth in *United States v. Jacobson*, 15 F.3d 19, 22 (2d Cir. 1994), so that the district court can evaluate these questions in the first instance.

In the event the court determines that disclosure was mandated, the court will need to consider the Government's argument that any disclosure obligation was fully discharged when the AUSA elicited on the direct examination of Lopez that she had lied "about everything." The Government takes the position that this disclosure gave the defendant the full protection of the *Brady* rule because it armed defense counsel with sufficient information to learn the specifics of Lopez's lies by cross-examining her.

We express no definitive views on the Government's argument because the conclusion may vary depending on the nature of the undisclosed material. But at least in some circumstances, telling the defendant that a witness lied, but leaving it for defense counsel to find out what the lies were by questioning the witness before the jury, might as a practical matter foreclose effective use of the impeaching or exculpatory information. Defense counsel would be in the difficult position of having to question the witness blindly in the jury's presence, not knowing whether the answers elicited might seriously incriminate or prejudice the defendant. *See Leka*, 257 F.3d at 103 ("The opportunity for use under *Brady* is the opportunity for a responsible lawyer to use the information with some degree of calculation and

[22] [4] Although courts sometimes loosely describe the *Brady* rule as an obligation to turn over favorable "evidence," *see, e.g., Youngblood v. West Virginia*, 126 S. Ct. 2188, 2190 (2006) ("A *Brady* violation occurs when the government fails to disclose evidence materially favorable to the accused."), it is no answer that the specifics of the lies told by Lopez would not necessarily be admissible evidence. The Government's obligations under *Brady* to disclose such information does not depend on whether the information to be disclosed is admissible as evidence in its present form. The objectives of fairness to the defendant, as well as the legal system's objective of convicting the guilty rather than the innocent, require that the prosecution make the defense aware of material information potentially leading to admissible evidence favorable to the defense.

forethought. A responsible lawyer could not put [the potential witness] on the stand without essential groundwork.").

After hearing the parties, the district court will determine whether there was a *Brady* violation, including whether Lopez's undisclosed statements were sufficiently material that the Government was obligated under *Brady* or *Giglio* to make disclosure; if so, whether the Government discharged that obligation by its partial disclosure; and whether the defendant knew or should have known the information in question.

Prosecutors have a duty to aggressively pursue justice and the public interest, and virtually all federal prosecutors take that duty seriously. The Government is not prone to overzealousness in its pre-trial discovery tactics, but if it unfairly limits the defendant's access to material information about the case, justice is not served. Occasionally, the Government becomes overly aggressive, withholding discovery that the courts later find to have been constitutionally mandated. The best prosecutors respect their discovery duties and endeavor to fulfill them responsibly and fully. They take to heart the admonition of Justice Sutherland in *Berger v. United States*:[23]

> The United States Attorney is the representative not of an ordinary party to a controversy, but of a sovereignty whose obligation to govern impartially is as compelling as its obligation to govern at all, and whose interest, therefore, in a criminal prosecution is not that it shall win a case, but that justice shall be done. As such, he is in a peculiar and very definite sense the servant of the law, the twofold aim of which is that guilt shall not escape or innocence suffers. He may prosecute with earnestness and vigor — indeed, he should do so. But, while he may strike hard blows, he is not at liberty to strike foul ones. It is as much his duty to refrain from improper methods calculated to produce a wrongful conviction as it is to use every legitimate means to bring about a just one.

The *Rodriguez* opinion reaffirms that *Brady* materials must be provided to the defense in a "manner that gives the defense a reasonable opportunity either to use the evidence in the trial or to use the information to obtain evidence for use in the trial." If the only opportunity accorded to the defense is to use the information to cross-examine the witness at trial, *Brady* has not been satisfied. Thus, to avoid any question about whether the defendant had a reasonable opportunity to use the *Brady* material, the U.S. Attorney's Manual urges prosecutors to make exculpatory material available to the defense promptly after it is discovered and to make impeachment material available at a reasonable time in advance of trial.[24]

---

[23] Berger v. United States, 295 U.S. 78, 88 (1935).

[24] USAM 9-5.001(D)(1) and (2).

5. Other Discovery Motions in Tax Cases

The rules of criminal procedure provide for limited discovery, and these general rules apply to tax prosecutions just as they apply to other criminal prosecutions.[25] The particular facts and circumstances of each case determine what discovery the parties need. Many prosecutors will agree to certain discovery motions as long as the discovery is reciprocal. Does that mean that defense counsel's witness interview notes must be provided to the Government? In many cases, the prosecutor will make the entire Government file available, a policy that is discussed in more detail below.

In addition to such standard defense motions as motions for disclosure of impeachment information and preservation of Jencks material, a particular case may suggest that other motions will yield discoverable information or will help posture the defendant's case for trial. For example, in cases involving taxpayers who blame their return preparers for the errors, motions should be considered to compel disclosure of particular impeaching information with regard to the preparer. In rare tax cases, electronic or other surveillance may have been conducted, and the defendant should consider a motion for disclosure of the results of that surveillance.[26] In some cases, a motion for a bill of particulars will be necessary in order to understand the Government's theory of the case.

Some examples of discovery from the Government that may be particularly useful in tax cases include:

- documents and tangible objects available under Rule 16(a)(1)(E);
- the taxpayer's statements, available under Rule 16(a)(1)(A);
- reports of experiments and tests under Rule 16(a)(1)(F);
- a written summary of the Government's expert witness testimony under Fed. R. Evid. 703 to 705, but caveat the requirement of reciprocal discovery;
- electronic and mechanical surveillance under Rule 16(a)(1)(A);
- statements of alleged indicted or unindicted co-conspirators;[27]
- evidence the Government intends to offer under Fed. R. Evid. 404(b); and
- production of documents in advance of trial per Rule 17(c).

Some portions of the SAR or SOI may be available as discovery,[28] although many courts will not require the report to be produced unless the agent testifies as a witness. Sometimes the DOJ attorney or AUSA will provide the defense with the

---

[25] Fed. R. Crim. P. 16.

[26] Electronic surveillance is not authorized for investigations of Title 26 (tax) crimes. *See* 18 U.S.C. §§ 2510, 2516. However, law enforcement officers investigating other specific offenses listed in 18 U.S.C. § 2516 are permitted to obtain court approval for wiretapping and other electronic surveillance, and the evidence obtained is sometimes turned over to IRS special agents. IRS agents also may be detailed to work with other agencies in investigations that result in multiple charges including tax counts. *See* IRM 38.1.1.5.

[27] United States v. Jackson, 757 F.2d 1486 (4th Cir.), *cert. denied*, 474 U.S. 994 (1985).

[28] United States v. Cleveland, 507 F.2d 731 (7th Cir. 1974).

entire Special Agent Report. It does not hurt to ask.[29]

In the event either party is concerned about preserving testimony that may not be available at trial (*e.g.*, because a witness has a fatal illness), the party may move to take testimony by deposition.[30] The taxpayer may pursue discovery from third parties by use of the subpoena for testimony and/or documents under Rule 17(c).[31] And, of course, the defendant's counsel should pursue informal discovery by communications with the AUSA.

F. Prosecutors' Open File Policy

1. Concept and General Practice

A relatively recent trend is for the prosecutor in a tax case to adopt an "open file" policy, in which the defendant is given access to all of the files except certain privileged documents (such as the portions of the SAR that are privileged, informants' statements, and witness statements to the extent not required under *Brady* or *Giglio*). This policy avoids much of the need for the court to address discovery issues.

The policy also has much to commend it from the prosecutor's perspective. If the prosecutor insists on providing only the discovery required under the criminal rules, the prosecution team must expend resources to review documents and determine which must be disclosed. In most cases, it takes far less work to pull out select portions of the SAR and then let the defendant have the rest of the files.

More importantly, an open file policy helps insulate prosecutors from potential constitutional errors that can occur if *Brady, Giglio*, or other discoverable material is not produced to the defense. In one relatively simple process, the Government "opens the kimono" but helps ensure that if a conviction is obtained, there will be no reversible error related to discovery.

2. Massive Document Cases

In most tax cases the volume of documents is relatively manageable, and the open file policy is simple to execute. However, when the documentary evidence is voluminous, significant issues come into play.

The open file policy in a massive document case presents a troublesome process for a defendant with limited resources. An example of this problem occurred in one of the largest tax crime prosecutions in history, the prosecution of 19 defendants in the Southern District of New York relating to tax shelters promoted by the KPMG

[29] Remember the great scene in the movie *My Cousin Vinny* in which Vinny schmoozes the DA who responds by offering him the entire prosecution file. Vinny boasts to his hairdresser girlfriend (and auto mechanic expert) of his schmoozing ability, but she puts him in his place by telling Vinny that state law required the DA to give up the files. Two lessons can be learned here: (1) it helps to read the law books; and (2) much effort, schmoozing or otherwise, can be avoided by knowing the law.

[30] Fed. R. Crim. P. 15.

[31] *See* United States v. Nixon, 418 U.S. 683, 699–700 (1974).

accounting firm.[32] KPMG avoided indictment by agreeing to an onerous deferred prosecution agreement (DPA). That DPA inured only to the benefit of KPMG as an entity, while individual lawyers and accountants at the KPMG firm remained at risk, as did numerous clients, tax preparers, counsel and organizations with whom KPMG allegedly conspired. Nineteen of those individuals were indicted, and they faced a conspiracy trial involving literally millions of documents.

The prosecutors in the KPMG case adopted an open file policy, thus making over 25 million pages of documents theoretically available to the defendants, some in hardcopy format, some in digital format, and some in both formats. The digitized documents were sometimes produced in a litigation software format (Concordance), while others were in native formats (*e.g.*, .xls or .doc files). The Government sought to mitigate criticism of such a huge document production by arguing that because some of the documents were produced in searchable formats rather than by just dumping the entire load of documents on the defendants, the defense counsel would be able to "efficiently and effectively analyze what are admittedly voluminous materials." The Government also argued that it had made available many more paper documents than it was required to produce under Rule 16.

Defense counsel often refer to this method of meeting the Government's *Brady* and Jencks Act obligations as a "document dump." They complain that the Government has buried the potentially exculpatory and impeachment material within millions of documents that the defense has neither the time nor the financial resources to review adequately. The court's preliminary orders in the KPMG case observed that: "The government contends — and the defendants have given no reason to doubt — that the core of the material gathered in the investigation is contained in a word searchable electronic data base that is available to the defendants."[33] The issue eventually became somewhat moot. By the time the case finally went to trial, two of the defendants had pled guilty, charges against 13 of the remaining 17 defendants were dismissed, and the four remaining defendants apparently had sufficient financial means to permit them to wade through the massive document database. The problem was not as severe as it had seemed when the earlier dismissed defendants were in the case. The Government also may have made more specific disclosures before going to trial, but the reported opinions are not clear on that point.

The issues and sensitivities involved in such massive document productions also were addressed in a pre-trial order in *United States v. Anderson*.[34] Like the KPMG case, *Anderson* involved a large document set turned over by the prosecutors under an open file policy. Anderson cried foul in several respects, and he moved for relief

32 United States v. Stein, 435 F. Supp. 2d 330 (S.D.N.Y. 2006). Although it might be more proper to refer to this as the "Stein" case, most practitioners and publications have referred to it as the "KPMG" case.

33 Order, Dkt. # 89 (Nov. 1, 2005).

34 416 F. Supp. 2d 110 (D.D.C. 2006). Although the IRS has referred to *Anderson* as the largest criminal tax case involving an individual taxpayer in history, that characterization is questionable. *See* Statement of Commissioner Everson, *reported at* Allen Kenney, *Telecom Tycoon Charged with Evading $200 Million in Taxes*, 2005 TNT 39-1.

from the district court. The *Anderson* court held that:[35]

(1) The prosecutors must notify the defendant of the documents otherwise discoverable under Rule 16 (in this case the documents seized pursuant to search warrant) that the prosecutors intend to use in the case-in-chief as Rule 12(b)(4)(B) specifically requires. The court noted that the Government's notice need not include documents that may be used at trial "for such purposes as refreshing its witnesses' recollection, impeaching defendant's witnesses, or presenting its rebuttal case, so long as the use of [those documents] was not planned in advance of trial." However, if the prosecutors fail to give notice of one or more key documents and then try to shoehorn them into these exceptions, the court indicated that it was likely to take a dim view.

(2) The prosecutors must notify the defendant of the grand jury materials that would be used in the case-in-chief as covered by Rule 16(a)(1)(E)(ii). In view of the massive number of documents, the court rejected the prosecutors' argument that the turnover of the documents was all that Rule 16 required. The court reasoned:

> Given the enormous volume of material produced in this case and defendant's limited resources, it is apparent that requiring defendant's counsel to peruse each page of the materials at issue here — in effect, to duplicate the work of document review presumably already done by the government — would materially impede defendant's counsel's ability to prepare an adequate defense or, as repeatedly emphasized by defendant's counsel at oral argument, to evaluate meaningfully the government's plea offer and to engage in fruitful plea negotiations.
>
> The government's obligation to identify the material that it intends to use in its case-in-chief at trial parallels the defendant's obligation under Rule 16(b)(1)(A), which requires a defendant seeking discovery under Rule 16(a)(1)(E) to afford the government the opportunity to inspect and copy material that is "within the defendant's possession, custody, or control" and that "the defendant intends to use . . . in the defendant's case-in-chief at trial." As this Court previously has held, the government's possession of documents that a defendant intends to use in the defendant's case-in-chief does not eliminate the defendant's duty to disclose those documents and identify them as such under Rule 16(b)(1)(A). The defendant cannot satisfy that obligation simply "by providing the government with the thousands of pages of discovery [he] received from the government and stating that the documents upon which [he] intends to rely are found somewhere therein." United States v. Hsia, 87 F. Supp. 2d 10, 2000 WL 195067, at *1 (D.D.C. 2000). The reverse must also be true. A reciprocity of obligations between the defendant and the government clearly is consistent with the intent of the Rules Advisory Committee, which in 2002 specifically amended Rule 16(b)(1)(B) to "track the similar language in revised Rule 16(a)(1)." Fed. R. Crim. P. 16, Advisory Committee Note to 2002 Amendment. In short, for the intended reciprocity to be effectuated, the government must identify what it intends to rely on in its case-in-chief at trial before the defendant

---

[35] 416 F. Supp. 2d at 113.

> must identify what he intends to rely on in his.
>
> It is in both Mr. Anderson's and the government's interest that the defendant be able to mount an adequate defense and/or engage in meaningful plea discussions, and it is the Court's view that the identification and production of the requested information will help to ensure that he can. For these reasons, the Court will grant plaintiff's motion under Rule 16, insofar as it seeks the identification of which grand jury materials the government intends to use in its case-in-chief. Again, this Order will not prevent the government from using evidence not previously identified for limited purposes such as refreshing recollection, impeachment, and rebuttal, so long as the use of that evidence was not planned in advance of trial. Neither will the granting of plaintiff's motion under Rule 12 and Rule 16 preclude defendant from seeking further discovery if, on the basis of the material identified, defendant believes he is entitled to it.[36]

The *Anderson* order properly recognizes that a mass document dump gives the prosecutor an unfair advantage, the harm of which can be mitigated by the tools available to the court under the discovery and related rules. The fairness of a particular document production in response to a discovery request or in an attempt to comply with *Brady, Giglio*, or Jencks is decided based on the unique facts of the case, with the ultimate issue being one of fairness. On the facts, the judge in *Anderson* did not think the prosecutors' ploy was fair. Now, consider the following opinion, in which the District Court for the Southern District of New York considered an analogous, but even more massive document dump in the context of the prosecutors' *Brady* obligations:[37]

> Defendants contend that the Government cannot discharge its *Brady* obligations by turning over exculpatory documents as part of "a voluminous file that is unduly onerous to access." . . . *United States v. Skilling*. 554 F.3d 529, 577 (5th Cir. 2009), *aff'd in part and vacated on other grounds*, 130 S. Ct. 896, 177 L. Ed. 2d 619 (2010)). In this case, defendants note that the "database that the government produced comprises several gigabytes of data, including millions of separate files extending to several million pages in length. [Moreover], the 'database' consists of nine separate databases . . . [, and any] document search has to be conducted on a database-by-database basis." . . . Defendants cite *United States v. Salyer*, 2010 U.S. Dist. LEXIS 77617 . . . (E.D. Cal. Aug. 2, 2010), to the effect that "the government cannot meet its *Brady* obligations by providing [the defendant] with access to 600,000 documents and then claiming that she should have been able to find the exculpatory information in the haystack." . . . Thus, defendants maintain that even though all of the documents at issue were available for inspection upon request and all but a handful were included as part of the pretrial electronic discovery, the Government violated *Brady* because the materials were unduly onerous to access.

---

36 416 F. Supp. 2d at 114–15.

37 United States v. Ohle, 2011 U.S. Dist. LEXIS 12581 (S.D.N.Y. Feb. 7, 2011), *aff'd without published opinion*, 2011 U.S. App. LEXIS 21275 (2d Cir. Oct. 20, 2011).

However, the principal case defendants cite in support of this proposition, *United States v. Skilling*, 554 F.3d 529, 577 (5th Cir. 2009), is far more nuanced than defendants suggest. The Fifth Circuit first noted that there is "little case law on whether a voluminous open file can itself violate *Brady*, and the outcomes of these cases seem to turn on what the government does in addition to allowing access to a voluminous open file." 554 F.3d at 577. In *Skilling*, the Government "did much more than drop several hundred million pages on Skilling's doorstep." Id. Instead, the file was electronic, indexed, and searchable, and the Government highlighted particularly relevant documents. Id. Although Skilling argued that the Government should have scoured the open file in search of every piece of potentially exculpatory evidence, the Court determined that the Government "was in no better position to locate any potentially exculpatory evidence than was Skilling." Id. Thus, although the Court did not hold that the use of a voluminous open file could never violate *Brady*, especially if there were "evidence that the government 'padded' an open file with pointless or superfluous information to frustrate a defendant's review of the file," the Court determined that, in light of "the additional steps the government took beyond merely providing Skilling with the open file, the equal access that Skilling and the government had to the open file, the complexity of Skilling's case, and the absence of evidence that the government used the open file to hide potentially exculpatory evidence or otherwise acted in bad faith, we hold that the government's use of the open file did not violate *Brady*." Id.

The general principles articulated by the *Skilling* court are particularly relevant here. Undoubtedly there were many documents — not least because of the efforts that the defendants and their coconspirators took to obscure their egregious fraud — but the Government, to facilitate review of the documents, provided defense counsel with an electronically searchable Concordance database. Both the Government and defense counsel had equal access to this database. Thus, the defendants were just as likely to uncover the purportedly exculpatory evidence as was the Government. Moreover, as a general rule, the Government is under no duty to direct a defendant to exculpatory evidence within a larger mass of disclosed evidence. *See United States v. Mulderig*, 120 F.3d 534, 541 (5th Cir. 1997); *United States v. Alvarado*, No. 01 Cr. 156 (RPP), 2001 U.S. Dist. LEXIS 21100, at *13–*14 (S.D.N.Y. 2001) ("The Defendants have pointed to no authority for the proposition that where there is a large mass of material that has been made available to the Defendants, it is the Government's duty to root out *Brady* material for the Defendants. Indeed the only authority is to the contrary.").

The defendants further argue that, notwithstanding the equal access of both sides to the database in question, the Government may have a heightened obligation to uncover exculpatory evidence in light of its allegedly extensive resources and subpoena powers. The Court rejects this argument. "While the Supreme Court in *Brady* held that the Government may not properly conceal exculpatory evidence from a defendant, it does not place any burden upon the Government to conduct a defendant's investigation or assist in the presentation of the defense's case." *United States v. Marrero*, 904 F.2d 251, 261 (5th Cir. 1990). Placing a higher burden on the Government to uncover such evidence would place prosecutors in the untenable position of having to prepare both sides of the case at once. Indeed, the adversarial system presumes that the defense will be more highly motivated to uncover exculpatory evidence, so if anything the onus is on defense counsel to conduct a more diligent search for material potentially favorable to his client. This is especially true considering that, if exculpatory evidence exists, the defense is in the best position to know what such evidence might be and where it might be located.

As the Court noted in *United States v. Skilling*, 554 F.3d 529, 577 (5th Cir. 2009), exceptions to these general principles may exist if it is found that the Government deliberately hid documents within a larger mass of materials or somehow purposefully confounded the defendant's search for exculpatory material. As this Court previously found, however, there is no evidence of bad faith that has been proffered in this case. Accordingly, the Court holds that the Government did not violate *Brady* by failing to specifically highlight the particular documents defendants now claim are relevant to the defendants' case.

G. The Civil Case Gambit

Commencement of some type of civil case during the pendency of a criminal investigation or prosecution poses severe hazards for a taxpayer, because the Government may seek discovery from the taxpayer free of the restraints of the Fifth Amendment privilege and the limited discovery available under the criminal rules. Nevertheless, for the risk-taker, the taxpayer might consider instigating some civil litigation to attempt to take advantage of the more liberal discovery rules in civil cases. However, the courts frequently stay civil cases pending resolution of the criminal matter.[38]

III. DISPOSITIVE MOTIONS AND MOTIONS TO SUPPRESS EVIDENCE

Pre-trial Motions are governed by Fed. R. Crim. P. 12(b)(2), 12(b)(3), and 47. As in all criminal cases, serious thought should be given to whether a motion to suppress evidence or to dismiss the case is appropriate. If the defendant has a dispositive motion to present, it should be filed as soon as possible. If granted, such a motion may terminate the case.

[38] *E.g.*, Campbell v. Eastland, 307 F.2d 478, 487–89 (5th Cir. 1962) (stay of civil discovery or protective order may have been appropriate remedy while criminal proceeding pending).

A. Motions to Dismiss

A classic pre-trial dispositive motion is a motion based on the defense that the statute of limitations bars any prosecution of the defendant for the crimes charged in the indictment. Another example would be a motion to dismiss based on uncertainty in the law, relying on cases such as *James*, *Critzer*, and *Garber* to attempt to eliminate the willfulness element as a matter of law.[39] These sorts of arguments are particularly well suited for pre-trial resolution. Even if the motion to dismiss is denied, the Government's response to such a pre-trial motion may well divulge details of the prosecution's case in chief that would not otherwise have been discoverable. The motion also will educate the judge about the nature of the defense and some of the issues that will be addressed at trial and in the potential jury instructions.

B. Motions to Suppress

Motions to suppress also may essentially be dispositive motions, because the trial court's decision on whether evidence will be suppressed or admitted is very likely to determine the outcome of the case.[40] A successful motion to suppress often results in dismissal of the case, since the Government may not be willing to pursue the prosecution without the benefit of the suppressed evidence. In the event that any unconstitutional or otherwise illegal investigatory efforts were undertaken by the Government, a motion to suppress evidence may be the appropriate vehicle to obtain redress.

1. The *Tweel* Issue

Perhaps the most famous example of a motion to suppress in a tax case occurred in *United States v. Tweel*.[41] Tweel had been audited previously by the IRS and considered for a criminal investigation. In a subsequent civil examination, the examination from which Tweel's indictment arose, Tweel's representative was concerned that CID might be involved, so he inquired specifically of the revenue agent whether CID was involved. The Revenue Agent responded negatively, which was technically a correct answer. CID was not involved. The taxpayer's representative assumed from the answer that the investigation therefore was civil and did not have a criminal focus. The revenue agent, who certainly understood the purpose of the question, failed to advise that the nominally civil tax examination was being conducted at the behest of the Organized Crime and Racketeering Section of the Department of Justice, which had authority only to conduct criminal investigations. Tweel's representative then cooperated with the Revenue Agent. He delivered records to the Revenue Agent without the necessity of a summons.[42] Upon

---

[39] These cases are discussed in Chapter 2A.

[40] See, e.g., *United States v. Ramirez*, CR H-00-395 (S.D. Tex. 1995), where the taxpayers pled guilty after an attempt to suppress a confession obtained during the civil examination.

[41] 550 F.2d 297 (5th Cir. 1977).

[42] In a summons proceeding the taxpayer would have been able to assert rights to withhold some or all of the documents, because *Tweel* occurred before the Supreme Court cases substantially limiting the ability to assert the Fifth Amendment privilege as to documents.

indictment, the taxpayer moved to suppress the documents, urging that they had been obtained by the Revenue Agent in violation of the Fourth Amendment because the taxpayer's consent was obtained through deception — the failure to advise the taxpayer of the criminal nature of the investigation. The district court denied the motion to suppress.

The Fifth Circuit held that the evidence should be suppressed based on deception, although it remanded the case to the District Court to determine what evidence should be suppressed. The conviction was reversed because a consent obtained by a Government official's deceit, trickery, or misrepresentation violated the Fourth Amendment. The court agreed that the mere failure to advise the taxpayer that anything he or she says may be used against him or her is not alone fraud, deceit, or trickery. But, the court held, "Silence can only be equated with fraud where there is a legal or moral duty to speak or where an inquiry left unanswered would be intentionally misleading."[43] The court then held:

> From the facts we find that the agent's failure to apprise the appellant of the obvious criminal nature of this investigation was a sneaky deliberate deception by the agent under the above standard and a flagrant disregard for appellant's rights. The silent misrepresentation was both intentionally misleading and material. Any findings to the contrary under the facts of this case are clearly erroneous.
>
> Appellant showed Miller knew that the IRS was acting at the request of the Organized Crime and Racketeering Section of the Justice Department which is undeniably an instrument for criminal investigation. Miller obviously knew the accountant inquired whether a special agent was involved to determine whether he was conducting a criminal audit. Miller's response, although on the face of it true, misled appellant to such a degree that his consent to the "search" must be vitiated by the agent's silence concerning the origin of this investigation.
>
> In this case, the agent testified he intended, if appellant had consented to an interview, to advise him of his rights. Because the IRS requires only special agents to warn taxpayers of their rights, by assigning a revenue agent the IRS still succeeded in masking the undeniable criminal nature of this investigation and materially deceived this appellant.[44]

The IRS responded to the *Tweel* decision by adopting a rule "explicitly prohibiting a civil agent from developing a criminal case against a taxpayer in the guise of a civil investigation."[45] The IRS's spin on *Tweel* is that it requires termination of a civil examination and transfer to CI once the revenue agent finds a "firm indication of fraud."[46] This rule is designed to transfer the case to special

---

[43] 550 F.2d at 299, quoting United States v. Prudden, 424 F.2d 1021 (5th Cir.), *cert. denied*, 400 U.S. 831 (1970).

[44] United States v. Tweel, 550 F.2d 297 (5th Cir. 1977).

[45] *See* United States v. McKee, 192 F.3d at 541 (citing United States v. Powell, 835 F.2d 1095, 1100 n.12 (5th Cir. 1988)).

[46] The Internal Revenue Manual specifically cites *Tweel* in IRM 25.5.6.5.2. *See also* IRM Fraud Handbook 25.1.

agents, who presumably will be sensitive to implications of *Tweel* and *Miranda* and will make sure that no deception occurs and that appropriate warnings are given to taxpayers. However, in practice, revenue agents who suspect fraud are taught to work with a Fraud Technical Advisor to develop enough proof of the fraud to convince CI to accept the case.[47] Although the Internal Revenue Manual requires referral upon finding a "firm indication of fraud," the practical result is that the taxpayer is asked to provide documents and oral statements well after the civil agent has uncovered firm indications of fraud, even to the point of being asked to appear for a "confrontation" interview at the end of the examination to allow the agent to confront the taxpayer with the evidence of fraud and obtain the taxpayer's response.

The IRS believes that the use of civil agents to develop the evidence of fraud before referral to CI completely avoids the issue in *Tweel*, since there is no criminal agent using the civil agent as a stalking horse for a criminal investigation as there was in *Tweel*. The defense bar views the use of a fraud technical advisor rather than a criminal investigator as a distinction without a difference, since the IRS is gathering proof for a criminal case without warning the taxpayer that the case is not just a standard civil examination and is likely to become a criminal matter.

In any event, the viability of *Tweel* as authority to suppress information obtained during a civil examination has eroded over the years. Other circuit courts have limited the rule to prohibit only the use of evidence obtained via affirmative misrepresentations by IRS agents.[48] Moreover, some courts have taken the rule to a more restrictive result. For example, in *United States v. Rutherford*,[49] the Sixth Circuit held that the defense must demonstrate that the IRS misrepresentations must have altered the defendant's conduct, such as cases where the agent's conduct actually compelled the taxpayer to speak against his will. And the Seventh Circuit in *Kontny* has shown that some judges would be willing to allow government agents to lie to taxpayers if necessary to uncover crimes.[50]

2. Motions to Suppress Evidence from Illegal Searches and Seizures

One of the most common motions to suppress in criminal cases is the motion to suppress evidence illegally obtained by the Government. Although these motions are more common in non-tax prosecutions, occasionally defendants claim that the evidence supporting a criminal tax charge was obtained in violation of the Constitution.

Consider *United States v. Srivastava*,[51] in which the district court considered the suppression of evidence obtained pursuant to three search warrants that authorized

---

[47] See IRM 25.1.3 & 25.1.8.

[48] *See, e.g.*, United States v. McKee, 192 F.3d 535, 537–38 (6th Cir. 1999); United States v. Peters, 153 F.3d 445, 447 (7th Cir. 1998), *cert. denied*, 525 U.S. 1070 (1999).

[49] 555 F.3d 190 (6th Cir. 2009).

[50] 238 F.3d 815 (7th Cir. 2001).

[51] 445 F. Supp. 2d 385 (D. Md. 2006), *rev'd*, 540 F.3d 277 (4th Cir. 2008), *cert. denied*, 557 U.S. 919 (2009).

the search of Defendant Srivastavas home and two medical offices for "financial, business, patient, and other records related to" his "business . . . which may constitute evidence of violations of Title 18 U.S.C. § 1347," a statute prohibiting health care fraud. In the course of the searches, FBI agents and HHS agents uncovered documents in Srivastava's residence reflecting that the Srivastava had failed to report all his capital gains and losses and documents from his office reflecting transfers to an undisclosed foreign bank account. The records were delivered to IRS agents and ultimately led to Srivastava's indictment for tax evasion and filing a false tax return. The district court suppressed all the tax-related documents, holding that the files and documents were outside the scope of the warrant, since they did not relate to Srivastava's medical practice and were not evidence of health care fraud. Following on that conclusion, the trial court suppressed all the evidence seized under the warrants, based on the inappropriate conduct of the agents in seizing documents beyond the scope of the search warrants.

The Fourth Circuit reversed the suppression order in *Srivastava*, finding that the tax records related to Srivastava's medical practice and potentially could have provided fragments of evidence related to health care fraud. Thus, the documents were properly seized under the warrants, and the objective reasonableness of the agent's actions meant that the blanket suppression order also had to be reversed. Nevertheless, *Srivastava* serves as a reminder that although most tax cases do not involve potentially unconstitutional evidence gathering, both prosecutors and defense attorneys should not overlook the possibility that evidence may have been obtained in violation of the Fourth Amendment.

IV. VENUE ISSUES

A. General Venue Provisions

In general, a federal criminal offense may be prosecuted in any district in which the offense was begun, continued, or completed.[52] Fed. R. Crim. P. 18 provides that a prosecution shall be in "a district in which the offense was committed" unless otherwise permitted by a statute or the rules. Rule 18 further allows "the District Court to fix the place of trial with due regard to the convenience of the defendant and the witnesses and the prompt administration of justice."

Although the Tax Division reviews each referral for purposes of determining proper venue, it is incumbent upon prosecutors and defense counsel to verify the venue as proper. If charges are brought in a venue that is improper, a motion to transfer venue is the appropriate remedy.

[52] 18 U.S.C. § 3237(a). The Constitution requires that trials be held in the "State and district wherein the crime shall have been committed." U.S. Const., amend. VI. *See also* Art. III, § 2, par. 3 ("The trial of all Crimes . . . shall be held in the State where the said Crimes shall have been committed.").

B. Venue in Evasion Cases

Applying the general rule of 18 U.S.C. section 3237(a), tax evasion can be prosecuted in any district where the attempt to evade taxes was begun, continued, or completed. For example, evasion can be prosecuted in the district where the defendant's tax returns were prepared and signed.[53] If false records were made in furtherance of the attempt to evade, the charges could be brought in the district where a corporation maintaining those records has its principal place of business.[54] Since the fraudulent returns normally would be filed with an IRS Service Center, the charges also could be brought at the location of the Service Center, where the crime would have been "completed."

C. Venue in Failure to File Cases

The offense of failure to file a tax return occurs both at the defendant's place of residence and at the Service Center (or other location) where the return should have been filed.[55]

D. Venue in False Return Cases

Prosecutions under section 7206(1) may be brought where the return was made or subscribed, where the return was filed, or where the preparer received information from the defendant.[56] Thus, venue is proper where the return was prepared and signed, even if the return was filed and received elsewhere.[57]

E. Venue in Aiding or Assisting Cases

The language of section 7206(2) does not indicate the location in which the tax violation occurs. However, the statute proscribes conduct that "aids or assists in, or procures, counsels, or advises" the preparation of false tax returns. As a result, venue generally would be considered proper in any district in which actions were taken by the defendant to aid or assist the preparation of the false return.[58]

F. Motions to Transfer Venue

In most criminal tax prosecutions, the defendant may move the court to change venue and may elect to be tried in the district in which he or she was residing at the time the offense was committed.[59] Thus, a defendant normally has an absolute right to transfer the prosecution to his or her home district, and this ability to

---

[53] United States v. Slutsky, 487 F.2d 832 (2d Cir. 1973), *cert. denied*, 416 U.S. 937 (1974).

[54] United States v. DeFabritus, 605 F. Supp. 1538 (S.D.N.Y. 1985).

[55] United States v. Hicks, 947 F.2d 1356 (9th Cir. 1991); United States v. Garman, 748 F.2d 218 (4th Cir. 1984), *cert. denied*, 470 U.S. 1005 (1985); United States v. Clinton, 574 F.2d 464 (9th Cir.), *cert. denied*, 439 U.S. 830 (1978).

[56] *E.g.*, United States v. Lawhon, 499 F.2d 352 (5th Cir. 1974), *cert. denied*, 419 U.S. 1121 (1975).

[57] *E.g.*, United States v. Rooney, 866 F.2d 28 (2d Cir. 1989).

[58] *See, e.g.*, United States v. Hirschfeld, 964 F.2d 318 (4th Cir. 1992), *cert. denied*, 506 U.S. 1087 (1993).

[59] 18 U.S.C. § 3237(b).

transfer venue applies even when an indictment covers both Internal Revenue Code violations and other criminal conduct.[60]

Under Fed. R. Crim. P. 18, motions to transfer venue also can be based on the convenience of the defendant, the witnesses, or the interests of justice. In *United States v. Auffenberg*,[61] charges were brought in the Southern District of Illinois against a local car dealer and numerous other defendants who allegedly conspired to commit wire fraud and evade taxes by falsely taking advantage of an "Economic Development Program:" of the United States Virgin Islands (USVI). The Government alleged that the defendants falsely claimed residency in the USVI and claimed that their income was "effectively connected" with businesses conducted in the USVI, all allegedly for the purpose of reducing the individuals' federal income taxes by approximately 90%. The defendants moved to transfer the venue of the case to the USVI, claiming that the convenience of the witnesses and parties, as well as the interests of justice, would best be served by trial there.

The court granted the motion to transfer, based primarily on the approximately 215 witnesses in the USVI whom the defendants intended to call at trial. The defendants demonstrated that the testimony from these witnesses was essential to establishing the defendants' financial ties to the USVI, their business operations, and their residency. The witnesses included public officials, service providers, retail merchants, and real estate agents. The court found that these witnesses would suffer unwarranted personal and financial hardship to travel to the Southern District of Illinois. Moreover, the court gave credence to the defendants' suggestion that a jury in the Southern District of Illinois might have difficulty appreciating the unique practical living conditions and experiences of the USVI. Understanding those conditions would be important to a juror's understanding of the issues in the case because the administration of the Economic Development Corporation program by the USVI was "deeply enmeshed in island life." Finally, the court "found that the local car dealer might have significant difficulty obtaining a fair and impartial jury in Illinois on the issue of whether he was a bona fide resident of the USVI.[62]

The change of venue paid off for the defendants. The jury in the Virgin Islands returned a verdict of acquittal on all charges.[63]

V. MOTION FOR BILL OF PARTICULARS

Fed. R. Crim. P. 7(f) permits the court to direct the filing of a bill of particulars. The purpose of a bill of particulars is to provide the defendant with a supplement to the indictment that includes information necessary to prepare a defense, to avoid surprise at trial, or to eliminate the risk of double jeopardy.[64] The defendant may

---

[60] *E.g.*, United States v. Nathanson, 813 F. Supp. 1433 (E.D. Cal. 1993).

[61] United States v. Auffenberg, 07-30042-MJR (S.D. Ill. Mar. 26, 2007).

[62] United States v. Auffenberg, 07-30042-MJR (S.D. Ill. Mar. 26, 2007), Memorandum and Order filed July 5, 2007.

[63] United States v. Auffenberg, 1:07-cr-00047 (D. V.I. Mar. 6, 2009), Verdict announced March 4, 2009.

[64] United States v. Horton, 526 F.2d 884 (5th Cir.), *cert. denied*, 429 U.S. 820 (1976).

file a motion for a bill of particulars before arraignment or within ten days after arraignment, or at a later time if the court permits.

Many tax indictments include little more than the amount of tax reported and the amount the Government believes should have been reported. So, defendants often move for a bill of particulars to request information regarding the method of proof that the Government will offer at trial. In a false return case, a bill of particulars often can isolate the particular false statements that are alleged and can specify what documents the Government intends to rely upon to show the falsity. A bill of particulars does not permit the defendant to obtain the Government's evidence in the case or extensive information regarding the Government's legal theories.[65] In essence, a bill of particulars is not intended as a discovery device, and the court has broad discretion about whether or not to grant a motion for a bill of particulars.

The test for a defendant's motion for a bill of particulars is whether the indictment has adequately advised the defendant of the crime charged.[66] In essence, the defendant must show prejudice and lack of the essential facts necessary to understand the charges that are pending.

VI. SHIFTING THE RESPONSIBILITY

First man: I have a CPA do my income tax return.

Second man: Why do you do that?

First man: It saves me time.

Second man: How much time?

First man: Maybe 5 to 10 years.

— Old Joke[67]

In many criminal tax cases, the defense contends that the taxpayer relied on the advice of counsel, on the return preparer, or on some other tax practitioner. This defense assumes that the taxpayer sought such assistance in good faith and provided the relevant information to the attorney or tax practitioner. The defense could implicate the advisor in criminal conduct or could just create a never-never land in which neither party is subject to criminal exposure.

Taxpayer-defendants often consider the prospect of obtaining a "deal" by offering up their tax advisor for prosecution. Many a prosecutor would prefer to root out a cheating tax advisor who caused numerous taxpayers to defraud the Government rather than pursuing one individual taxpayer, even if that individual was complicit with the advisor. The individual taxpayer might obtain an agreement not to be prosecuted or a plea to a lesser crime. At minimum, the taxpayer can ask the prosecutor to agree to a downward sentencing adjustment for cooperation.

---

65 United States v. Pottorf, 769 F. Supp. 1176 (D. Kan. 1991).

66 *Id.* at 1182.

67 *Quoted in* Burgess J.W. Raby & William L. Raby, *Penalty Protection for the Taxpayer: Circular 230 and the Code*, 2005 TNT 105-65 (June 2, 2005).

Even if the taxpayer sought the advice or assistance of a qualified tax practitioner and gave the advisor all the relevant and material information, the practitioner could still have completed the return incorrectly. That does not necessarily absolve the taxpayer of responsibility if the taxpayer knew that the return understated his or her tax liability.[68] Nevertheless, the Government usually finds it difficult to convict the taxpayer if the tax practitioner was given all the pertinent information by the taxpayer.

In order to succeed with this defense, a taxpayer usually will have to take the stand and testify credibly. In *United States v. Stone*,[69] a doctor was charged with willful tax evasion and asserted reliance on his tax accountant as his defense. His accountants had determined the doctor's taxable income from his daily log books, monthly bank statements, canceled checks, check stubs, and from the interest income recorded in savings account passbooks. On cross-examination, the taxpayer admitted destroying these source documents before the Government could check them.

The Government therefore used the net worth method to determine taxable income. The taxpayer did not seriously question the results of that methodology. Instead, the taxpayer attempted to negate his willfulness by arguing that he relied in good faith on his accountant. The court said:

> Appellant argues further that he placed total, good faith reliance upon a competent CPA to compute his tax returns accurately, and the deficiencies were the result of the accountant's negligence. This contention goes both to the sufficiency of the evidence and to the attack on the Court's jury charge. The credibility of this contention was purely a question of fact for the jury, who decided it adversely to Dr. Stone. Based upon a thorough review of the record we are in accord with their finding.
>
> It just may be that this defense was the worst one the Doctor could have asserted. For it established that whatever the accountants had they obtained from the Defendant. And what he furnished turned out to be spectacularly wrong.
>
> Mr. Weiner, Appellant's accountant for over 15 years, testified that he had computed Dr. Stone's account during each of those years, including 1962–1964. He personally made an annual visit to Dr. Stone's office to obtain all of his sources of taxable income, and relied completely upon the Doctor or his wife to supply him with a comprehensive register of the taxable income. Mr. Weiner would then take this material to his office where either he or his employees would compute the Doctor's returns. Once this was finished he returned both the records and his worksheets to the Doctor. Mr. Weiner inadvertently retained possession of his worksheets for 1962. Those worksheets reveal that Dr. Stone had reported only $5,800.00 in taxable income for 1962. The reconstructed records show that in that same year the Doctor made life insurance payments of $5,900.00, increased

68 United States v. Olbres, 61 F.3d 967, 970–71 (1st Cir.), *cert. denied*, 516 U.S. 991 (1995).

69 431 F.2d 1286 (5th Cir. 1970), *cert. denied*, 401 U.S. 912 (1971).

his bank deposit nearly $25,000.00, and had personal expenditures alone of $11,000.00.

The accountant's employees similarly testified that any tax returns they computed were based upon all of the Doctor's taxable income, the source of such information being the Doctor himself. It rounds this out to state that the effort to put the blame on others — a tactic with built-in hazards — was not accepted by the jury.[70]

Courts encountering the "blame the preparer" defense often say that, in order to succeed, the taxpayer must have made full disclosure to the accountant.[71] Obviously, a taxpayer who knowingly withholds information that the accountant needs to prepare a true and accurate return has not relied upon his accountant. But what of the taxpayer who simply turns over his or her basic records with the expectation that the accountant will ask any necessary and appropriate questions?

The following example presents a common fact pattern. The taxpayer sells an asset for $1,000,000 at a formal closing where the closing agent pays the taxpayer by cutting checks for $900,000 to pay off certain of the taxpayer's debts and providing the taxpayer with a check for $100,000. That $100,000 is deposited into the checking account for the taxpayer's sole proprietorship, which reports on the cash method. On the check records, the taxpayer simply notes that $100,000 was deposited into the account and that the payor on the check was XYZ Title Company, which, of course, is correct. But the records then do not show that the taxpayer sold assets or received a much larger amount. The accountant then just compiles all of the deposits — including this $100,000 amount — into gross revenue without any understanding that the deposit was for assets sold or that the taxpayer received a much larger amount than was reflected in the cash records. The accountant asks no questions. In a situation like this, the taxpayer has relied upon the accountant and may not intentionally have hidden anything.[72] But some might argue that the taxpayer should have put more information in the cash records relating to such a large transaction, or should specifically have brought the transaction to the accountant's attention. The taxpayer bears the risk that an investigator might not perceive the omission of income as benign. Even if the return preparer arguably should have discovered problems based on the information provided by the taxpayer, the return preparer's negligence constitutes no defense if the Government can otherwise prove the taxpayer's intentional violation of a known legal duty. In a recent case, the defendant sought to introduce expert testimony that the return preparer knew or should have known of the omission of income, but the trial judge sustained the Government's objection to the evidence. The First Circuit held that, even if the return preparer's conduct were negligent, the mere failure to discover and properly treat the undisclosed income would not be a defense in a case where the evidence showed beyond a reasonable doubt that the taxpayer willfully omitted

---

[70] 431 F.2d at 1288–89.

[71] *E.g.*, United States v. Bishop, 291 F.3d 1100 (9th Cir. 2002), *cert. denied*, 537 U.S. 1176 (2003).

[72] Indeed, depending on the taxpayer's basis in the asset sold, the taxpayer may not have omitted any taxable income at all, or conceivably may have a deductible loss.

the income.[73] The First Circuit did acknowledge that, in cases where the preparer's neglect could be relevant (presumably where the evidence is not overwhelming as to the taxpayer's intent), such expert evidence might be admissible at trial. So, for a defendant asserting a reliance on professional defense, the taxpayer must convince the trial judge to admit the evidence as bearing on defendant's reliance.

Taxpayers have blamed the accountant or the preparer in a plethora of cases, many of which describe the potential pitfalls of such a defense.[74] Students would be well advised to revisit the *Pomponio* case in Chapter 2A to see how catastrophic the results of this defense can be.

Tax practitioners must remain ever vigilant to avoid the risks that come with the reliance on tax advisor defense. If the taxpayer blames the preparer, be certain to investigate the allegations fully, as taxpayers who are under investigation may falsely attempt to place blame on the preparer or other tax advisor in a desperate attempt to avoid prosecution. Unless the taxpayer's representative proceeds cautiously, communicating a false allegation against the taxpayer's preparer could expose the representative to civil suit by the preparer or even criminal problems if the Government believes that the representative knowingly misrepresented the facts. Never make the client's problems your problems.

PROBLEM

Mr. and Mrs. Cashcow have operated the Golden Cow family restaurant for several decades. They had a checking account with their local bank and a payroll account at the same bank. Receipts from the restaurant were deposited into the checking account, and transfers were made from the checking account to the payroll account to pay wages and employment taxes. The Cashcows had no other income outside of the restaurant business for most of their lives, but in later years, they opened a securities account with a discount brokerage firm, and they had some small amounts of interest and dividends that they reported from that account.

From time to time over the years, Mr. and Mr. Cashcow took small amounts of cash from the cash register to pay for personal items or to pay vendors. For many years, those cash amounts were fairly small, but as Mr. and Mrs. Cashcow approached their retirement, they began to keep more and more of the cash out of the restaurant cash register. These "skimmed" amounts from the Golden Cow were deposited directly into the brokerage account.

For over 20 years, the Cashcows have had their income tax returns prepared by Sloppy Sam. Many years ago, Sam learned how the Cashcow restaurant business operated, and he prepared the annual Cashcow individual income tax return each year by reviewing the restaurant bank account statements and the returned checks to determine the income and deductions for the Golden Cow, which he then included on a Schedule C on the Cashcows' individual income tax returns. In

---

[73] United States v. Pierre, 599 F.3d 19 (1st Cir. 2010).

[74] *E.g.*, United States v. Brimberry, 961 F.2d 1286, 1290 (7th Cir. 1992); United States v. Wilson, 887 F.2d 69, 73 (5th Cir. 1989); United States v. Meyer, 808 F.2d 1304, 1306 (8th Cir. 1987); United States v. Pomponio, 563 F.2d 659, 662 (4th Cir. 1977), *cert. denied*, 435 U.S. 942 (1978).

addition, Sam obtained the restaurant cash register tape in order to compare the total receipts of the restaurant to the deposits in the bank account each year. Mr. and Mrs. Cashcow gave Sam the dividends and interest from the brokerage account each year, but Sam never asked to see the brokerage account statements.

Mr. and Mrs. Cashcow's 2012 income tax return was selected for civil examination by the Internal Revenue Service. Revenue Agent Diligent Dan, an IRS civil examiner with more than 20 years of experience, conducted the examination. In addition to reviewing the cash register tapes, the bank accounts, and all of Sloppy Sam's files, Agent Dan met with Mr. and Mrs. Cashcow several times during the 14 months that he examined the Cashcow income tax returns. In the initial interview with Mr. and Mrs. Cashcow, Agent Dan confirmed from the taxpayers that "no income was deposited into other bank accounts." Within two months of that initial interview, Agent Dan conducted another interview with Mr. and Mrs. Cashcow. The agent's notes reflect that the second interview was requested "after it was discovered that they were depositing business money to an undisclosed bank account." In the second interview, Mr. and Mrs. Cashcow again told Agent Dan that the restaurant checking account was the only checking account they had and that no income had been deposited to other accounts. After that interview, Agent Dan met with his group manager and discussed the fact that he had found significant deposits into a securities account at a brokerage firm. The agent and manager decided to expand the examination to add the year 2013, to summon both the bank and the brokerage firm for copies of all relevant documents, and to track the case for fraud.

During the first 12 months of the civil examination by Agent Dan, Mr. and Mrs. Cashcow were represented in the examination by Sloppy Sam. Agent Dan also interviewed Sam and nailed down the fact that Mr. and Mrs. Cashcow had never advised Sam of the existence of any Golden Cow income beyond the deposits to the checking account and the dividends and interest from the brokerage firm.

After numerous meetings with the fraud coordinator to review the data obtained during the examination, Agent Dan scheduled one final interview with Mr. and Mrs. Cashcow. At that interview, Agent Dan confronted Mr. and Mrs. Cashcow with the documents he had obtained from the brokerage firm showing the skimmed cash deposits. Mr. and Mrs. Cashcow broke down and admitted that the amounts deposited into that bank account were cash skimmed from the restaurant.

Based on the documents and the confessions at the interview, the case was referred to Criminal Investigation. At that point, Mr. and Mrs. Cashcow hired an attorney. During the criminal investigation, Mr. and Mrs. Cashcow were summoned, but they claimed their Fifth Amendment privilege and gave no further statements to the special agents. After another year of review, the matter was referred to the Department of Justice Tax Division. Despite the best efforts of their lawyer to convince the IRS and the Tax Division that there was no proof of anything but a mix-up in the preparation of the returns, the Tax Division sent the case to the U.S. Atttorney's office, which obtained a grand jury indictment against Mr. and Mrs. Cashcow, charging them with income tax evasion for the years 2012 and 2013.

1. Assuming that within the first two months of the civil examination Agent Dan found numerous "firm indications of fraud" as defined in *Tweel*, what type of motion would you consider filing to argue that Agent Dan violated the constitutional rights of Mr. and Mrs. Cashcow?

2. Are Mr. and Mrs. Cashcow likely to succeed if they blame Sloppy Sam?

3. Assume that Sloppy Sam has a long list of clients who have been the subject of civil examinations and criminal investigations by the Internal Revenue Service. In virtually every one of those cases, the IRS found a separate bank account where the taxpayers had deposited income that was unreported on the returns prepared by Sloppy Sam. What special discovery will the Cashcows need in order to make use of this fact in their defense?

4. Mr. and Mrs. Cashcow learned during the IRS examination that Agent Dan was once investigated for an alleged bribe received from one of the taxpayers that he was examining. What particular type of motion would be used by the Cashcows to learn information regarding that potential bribe?

Chapter 9

TRIAL AND POST-TRIAL

Fed. R. Evid. 401–05

I. INTRODUCTION

In this chapter, we introduce some major themes that practitioners confront in criminal cases involving federal tax crimes. We will cover some general themes applicable in criminal trials and weave in some specific themes applicable to criminal tax trials. Because this is such a large subject, the presentation here is necessarily selective based on the authors' experiences and the selection is necessarily subjective.

The criminal trial is the culmination of the process that has occupied so much of our attention before this chapter. The largest component of the overall work is the pretrial work, including the pretrial processes upon and after indictment. By the time the trial starts, the lawyer should know his or her case and be prepared to try the case as expeditiously and as effectively as possible. We have noted that perhaps 95% of the cases plead without a trial, a phenomenon driven by (i) the care with which the Government selects its criminal cases and (ii) the sentencing incentives to plead via the acceptance of responsibility downward adjustment and, possibly, a 5K1 departure for substantial assistance to the prosecution.[1] This chapter is thus devoted to 5%, more or less, of cases that go to trial.

II. TRIALS DETERMINE JUSTICE, NOT TRUTH

We start with general comments on trials as a search for and discovery of truth. That is a myth, but a very useful myth because it gives us some feeling that our system of justice is good. The outcome of a trial is not truth, but truth as the fact finder determines based upon the evidence presented, the law presented to the fact finder (by instruction in the case of a jury trial), and how that evidence and the law as presented factors into the fact finder's life experience. Truth in any objective or perfect sense is not determined in a trial.

So the theory goes, if both parties pursue their self-interests at trial, a version of the truth will emerge sufficient for the trier of fact to dispense justice in the case at hand. There will be imperfections along the way, but material imperfections are sufficiently rare as to be acceptable.

[1] Sentencing is the topic for Chapter 10.

So the theory also goes in a criminal setting, the prosecutors' self interest is to serve the system by pursuing truth and justice wherever they lead. As famously noted by the Supreme Court, the interest of the government "in a criminal prosecution is not that it shall win a case, but that justice shall be done."[2] The aspiration is that the prosecutor will season zeal with judgment. Sometimes, however, a prosecutor suspends judgment, pursuing conviction with only a distorted view of whether the pursuit serves justice. This phenomenon is more than just academic in the general criminal prosecution universe.[3] However, with one notable exception,[4] the authors have not experienced this phenomenon in federal tax cases.

The defense counsel's duty is only to the client. In a criminal setting, this means the obvious — avoiding indictment if that is possible, avoiding conviction if that is possible, and, if those are not possible, mitigating the punishment. The defense attorney owes no duty to the system or the abstract concept of justice, other than to avoid illegal or unethical conduct. Indeed, in the adversarial setting, the notion is that the defense lawyer serves justice by representing his or her client zealously within the legal and ethical boundaries.

So, in sum, if it is not about truth, what is it about? Shakespeare told us in Hamlet — "The play's the thing."[5] Each counsel is a director of the play. In a dissenting opinion remarkable for other reasons, Judge Posner noted, in discussing the notion of trials as competitive events and judges as referees: "They [Judges] are not umpires when it comes to management of the trial; they are directors of the drama that we call trial by jury. (Trials are closer to theater than they are to ball games.)"[6] Judges are, of course, the ultimate director of the competing dramas, but each party's case and themes are the drama that party presents. As a director, you must play your "truth" to the intended audience — you must put on a credible show. It is about telling a credible version of the truth and that requires elements of performance — drama, pathos (as appropriate), humor, remorse (if appropriate), and even error and fallibility.

---

[2] Berger v. United States, 295 U.S. 78, 88 (1935).

[3] The phenomenon is, however, not uncommon in other areas. Recently, the press has often carried horror stories of injustice at the hands of overzealous prosecutors, particularly in death penalty cases. As just an example of this genre, we offer Raymond Bonner, *Anatomy of Injustice: A Murder Case Gone Wrong* (Knopf 2012). Prosecutors in tax cases avoid this phenomenon in most cases because of their professionalism and the multi-levels of review imposed upon tax prosecutions.

[4] The exception is the largest tax criminal case in history, United States v. Stein et al. (S.D.N.Y. Dkt # 05 Cr. 888 (LAK)). The judge presiding over the sprawling case found that the prosecutors let their "zeal get in the way of [their] judgment" in forcing KPMG to withhold attorneys fees to those current and former partners and employees under investigation who did not cooperate, in the prosecutors' view; the judge accordingly dismissed 13 of 18 defendants in the case. United States v. Stein et al., 495 F. Supp. 2d 390 (S.D.N.Y. 2007); see also United States v. Stein et al., 435 F. Supp. 2d 330 (S.D.N.Y. 2006) (where the judge made many of the critical findings and conclusions leading to the dismissal); *aff'd* 541 F.3d 130 (2d Cir. 2008).

[5] The complete, out of context quotation is: "The play's the thing wherein I'll catch the conscience of the king." Hamlet, Act II, Scene II.

[6] United States v. Warner, 506 F.3d 517, 521 (7th Cir. 2007).

III. PLANNING THE TRIAL

A. Anticipating and Planning

You must plan in advance of the trial. Trial will inevitably present unexpected events — things you could not have anticipated or, in any event, did not anticipate. But, even with that potential uncertainty, you must plan the case. And you must have the flexibility to deal with the unexpected.

B. The Theme of the Case[7]

The most important element of trying any case is a theme. Story tellers and screen writers call it a story or plot. We use the term theme here. Sometimes there may be more than one theme, but even then there must be a central theme that ties all subordinate themes together. Everything the lawyer does must be guided by the theme.

1. Rules concerning themes

- The theme must be simple. Sometimes, if there is little in the way of evidence that affirmatively establishes a defense, the theme must be that the Government's proof does not establish guilt beyond a reasonable doubt. That may be the only theme that finally can be exploited consistent with the other key rule for themes.
- The theme must be credible. Not only must it logically hang together, but the theme must be believable in the context of the evidence at trial.
- The theme must be repeated early and often.[8] Opening argument (usually), evidence presentation (always, even if the precise relationship to the theme may require tying up in closing argument), and in closing argument (always). And, it can be a persuasive touch to have elements of the theme supported by the Government's witnesses — usually in cross-examination — thus, interrupting the flow of the Government's show with reinforcement for the defense themes.
- The theme must be referred to in the instructions. The judge will give preliminary jury instructions and it will be helpful if your theme is in those instructions. Most importantly, you want to insure that you have laid a

---

[7] The presentation in this subparagraph is inspired by and sometimes drawn verbatim from Charles M. Meadows and Harvey M. Silets, *The Trial of a Criminal Case*, pp. H-12–H-14, published in an ABA publication titled *Criminal Tax Fraud 2004*. Mr. Meadows granted the authors permission to use these materials.

[8] "There's nothing so absurd that if you repeat it often enough, people will believe it." William James, the father of modern psychology. This concept appears in various forms. For samplings, see Wikipedia: http://en.wikipedia.org/wiki/Proof_by_assertion. Of course, there is a counter to this theme as well. Franklin D. Roosevelt said: "We Americans begin to know the difference between the truth on the one side and the falsehood on the other, no matter how often the falsehood is iterated and reiterated. Repetition does not transform a lie into a truth." Radio Address to the New York Herald Tribune Forum on October 26, 1939, reproduced at http://www.presidency.ucsb.edu/ws/index.php?pid=15828 (visited 10/20/12).

record predicate for having instructions consistent with the theme at the close of the evidence. In anticipating what instructions will be given so that you can develop your theme during trial, you must be reasonable in your expectations as to the instructions you can expect the judge to give. It would be bad to develop a theme as to which the judge gives no instructions or, worse, an adverse instruction.

2. Examples of Themes in Tax Cases

- The tax law is complex and, in this case, given the underlying milieu of the facts, the defendant's failure to report the tax liability was not an intentional violation of a known legal duty (the Cheek defense).
- The defendant accepts responsibility for any taxes which he owes and has paid these taxes.
- The defendant has already paid a heavy price (public embarrassment, strain and stress on family, costs incurred to deal with this).
- Expert testimony regarding traits in the defendant's personality/behavior that mitigate his culpability (if not wipe it out altogether as in a successful insanity defense).
- The defendant is a nice guy and a sympathetic figure.[9]
- The Government has not been fair in the conduct of the investigation or trial. In tax cases, this sub-theme may be developed, for example, by showing sloppiness and inferring vindictiveness in overreaching tax calculations. This is usually not per se a defense that will, alone, convince the jury to acquit the defendant, but it can be helpful in the context of other facts that, by themselves, would not have been sufficient to obtain acquittal.
- The Government cannot/has not proved its case beyond a reasonable doubt. This theme in a tax cases often revolves around the element of willfulness, the common element for tax crimes. This is the ultimate fall back. A danger with this defense is that the defendant is the ultimate best witness on what was in his or her mind; the jury will want to hear from the defendant. For a credible defense, the defendant may be forced to waive the Fifth Amendment and testify. Failing that, of course, the theme that the Government has not proved its case may be all that is left to exploit and you must get the jurors to imagine that they are in the dock and this could happen to them unless they require the Government to prove its case. This theme needs to be played carefully so that it is not viewed as an admission of guilt with an escape via a failure of the Government to meet some high level of proof, however important imposing that level of proof may be.

---

[9] A prominent criminal tax example in which making the defendant appear to be a sympathetic figure was an uphill and ultimately unsuccessful task is United States v. Helmsley, 941 F.2d 71 (2d Cir.), *cert. denied*, 502 U.S. 1091 (1991), involving, by media reputation, the "Queen of Mean" (*see* Wendt v. Wendt, 1998 Conn. Super. LEXIS 1023, 35 (Mar. 31, 1998)).

Counsel must abandon any theme that is not credible under the evidence after all attempts to dress up that pig. Indeed, counsel must know in advance whether counsel can gussy that pig up and forego trotting it out to the jury if that can't be done credibly. Defenses that are not credible hurt more than they help. "Never mind" is not a good response to a theme that the jury determines is not credible.

C. Plan and Shape the Trial Consistent with the Themes

A trial is a specific context for the triple-reinforcement process often touted as a powerful teaching, lecturing or writing technique — tell them what you are going to tell them, then tell them, then tell them what you told them.[10] In opening argument, each party tells the jury what he or she is going to tell the jury by evidence in the main show. During the main show (the trial), each party tells the jury the story by orchestrating the presentation of evidence. In closing argument, each party tells the jury what he or she previously told them in opening argument and during trial and points the jury to a conclusion favorable to the client. This process must be planned for effect.

The Government opens the criminal trial, both with argument and opening evidence.[11] By being first, even with the substantial criminal burden of proof, the Government has a powerful opportunity to shape the discussion, reinforcing its themes of the case and mitigating the force of anticipated defense themes of the case. That advantage may be blunted even before the Government closes its case-in-chief. Unless the defense defers its opening argument to the beginning of the defense case (not usual), the defense presents its themes in a unified summary argument format following the Government opening argument.[12] That argument must be shaped by the defense theme of the case, of course, and must meet all of the points noted above, particularly as to credibility. The defense also can reinforce its themes of the case by cross-examination of the Government witnesses. By the time the Government rests its case-in-chief, the jury will (i) know the themes of the defense from a credible opening argument and (ii) have heard evidence in support of those themes during the Government's show, usually by cross-examination. The defense will then use its case-in-chief to reinforce and establish persuasively the relationship of the evidence to the themes.

---

[10] The examples of the application of this technique are too numerous to mention. *See, e.g.*, Scott Longman, *The Architecture of Legal Writing*, 15 CBA RECORD 40 (2001). We have heard a pungent and helpful reminder as the fourth element — "sit down."

[11] This is consistent with the normal trial procedure where the party bearing the burden of persuasion opens and closes.

[12] Sometimes, for best effect, a theme can be presented cryptically. I am reminded of an opening argument that exploited other golden rules of presentations — pungency and brevity. Vincent ("Vinny") LaGuardia Gambini, played by Joe Pesci, in *My Cousin Vinny*, presented the following opening argument in response to the prosecution's opening argument: "Everything that guy just said is bullshit. Thank you." He was brief, the jury could easily remember what he said, and he was courteous. Powerful. The judge did sustain the prosecutor's objection as follows: "Sustained. Counselor's entire opening statement, with the exception of 'thank you,' will be stricken from the record." At least the courteous part survived the objection and, of course, the power — not the same as cogency — of the stricken part did also. Ultimately, of course, Vinny "pulled it altogether" and obtained dismissal before the case was submitted to the jury, but the evidence did show that Vinny had it right in his opening argument.

D. Be (or Appear to Be) Reasonable to the Judge and Jury

You, as the representative of your client, must appear reasonable (do not hack the judge or jury off). This is totally within your control (except as you might face an aberrational judge or juror).

IV. JURY SELECTION

The parties have no control over the jury pool from which the trial jury will be drawn. This is an overstatement, for the Government's venue choices may influence this pool of potential jurors.[13] For example, the Government may have a choice of where to indict participants in a large conspiracy. The Government will likely make that choice based, in part, on its theme of the case and its imagination of differences in the profile jury pools of available districts for indictment. For example, for more sophisticated financial crimes involving large investor losses, the Government might prefer a jury pool that is better educated, more urbane, and even more financially well-off so as to be better able to personalize the damage felt when the people work hard, save and lose everything. Setting aside venue choices (discussed elsewhere in the text), however, the parties have no control over the pool of potential jurors.

When jurors are called to be at the court for possible service in trials, jurors submit basic information which will be made available to the court and the parties. From the jurors that appear, a sufficient number will be selected randomly so that, based on experience with an expected number of challenges, the number is adequate to permit the final jury of 12 (plus alternates if appropriate) to be seated. For example, a jury pool of 25 might be drawn for a run of the mill one defendant federal criminal case expected to last less than a week. That pool will be subject to a process known as voir dire whereby the prospective jurors are examined under oath to determine their competence or suitability. Fed. R. Crim. P. 24 permits the court to make the examination and allows the court to permit counsel for the parties to make some or all of the examination.[14] If the court does not permit counsel for the parties to make the examination, it will consider requests from the parties as to questions to ask. You must know your case well and ask or propose questions that will flush out key information that might be material to your case. For example, standard questions in a tax case include some variation of the following: (i) whether the jurors work for the IRS or any government agency or a law enforcement agency and (ii) whether the jurors have been audited and were dissatisfied in any way about the results of or treatment during the audit. More case specific questions might be formulated to develop information that might suggest that a juror could have case-relevant information outside the evidence to be presented in the case or might have some bias related to the evidence the juror will hear.

The district court may dismiss any prospective juror for cause based on the voir dire. The parties may dismiss a certain number of jurors without cause, provided in

[13] Venue is discussed in Chapter 8.

[14] The defendant is not entitled to have his attorney conduct the examination. Hamer v. United States, 259 F.2d 274 (9th Cir. 1958), *cert. denied*, 359 U.S. 916 (1959), *reh'g denied*, 359 U.S. 962 (1959); Fox v. United States, 296 F.2d 217 (5th Cir. 1961), *cert. denied*, 369 U.S. 888 (1962).

the case of the prosecution a constitutionally prohibited factor such as race is not the basis for the dismissal. This dismissal by a party is called a peremptory challenge and colloquially is referred to as a "strike." In a noncapital felony criminal case, the prosecution has six peremptory challenges and the defendant(s) has 10; in a misdemeanor case, each side has three peremptory challenges.[15] In multi-defendant cases, the court may allow other peremptory challenges.[16] Jury selection is also an art form and making the choice of peremptory challenges requires careful attention to all of the communications, including body language, from the jury pool.

V. THE JUDGE AND THE JURY

A. General

Most criminal tax trials are to a jury. The parties may waive trial by jury, but that is the exception and not the norm. The jury will generally accept as true everything the judge says. Even if the judge is off base legally, the jury will likely not perceive it and will take what the judge has to say at face.

B. Jury Instructions

The judge will have many occasions to interact with the jury. Generally, the judge's instructions to the jury are the most critical. Except in cases of jury nullification, those jury instructions — particularly the final jury instructions — are the lens through which the jury sees the evidence and judges the case. The judge's words are critical; a key function of the lawyer is to influence the judge in the choice of words that he or she speaks from Mount Olympus.

There are two key points at which the judge will give a significant block of jury instructions. At the beginning of the case and at the end of the case. During the trial, the judge may give specific instructions to the jury based upon events at trial. For example, if the jury hears evidence that the judge believes the jury should not have heard, the judge will contemporaneously instruct the jury to disregard the evidence. Typically, those instructions are ad hoc and relatively routine and uncontroversial. To the extent, however, that the lawyers can anticipate such events that are controversial or not routine, the better part of wisdom would be either (1) to deal with the issue by motion in limine before the trial starts or (2) to have some

---

[15] Fed. R. Crim. P. 24(b)(2) & (3). Some tax crimes, most prominently failure to file, are misdemeanors. Fed. R. Crim. P. 24(b)(3) provides for 3 peremptory challenges for each side. As we noted elsewhere, the Sentencing Guidelines have obscured differences between misdemeanors and felonies. For example, in tax cases, section 7203 failure to file is a misdemeanor, but because the Government almost always charges more than one count and the Base Offense Level is determined by the tax loss, the potential sentence in a tax misdemeanor conviction will be determined much the same as a tax felony conviction. Accordingly, the ultimate outcome in terms of a sentence for a tax misdemeanor will be calculated the same as a related tax felony. If more than 3 peremptory challenges are important in a tax misdemeanor prosecution, either or both sides might be able to argue for more, even up to the felony level. We are aware of no authority for that, but we doubt that there would be authority since the number of peremptory challenges is unlikely to be contested further.

[16] Fed. R. Crim. P. 24(b).

wording and authority in writing to present to the judge in order to help the judge shape a favorable instruction to the jury.

The opening and closing instructions to the jury are not routine. The parties submit proposed instructions. The lawyers' submissions of proposed jury instructions thus must be supported by both the evidence and the law. The goal in drafting the proposed jury instructions is to have those instructions support the conclusions you desire from the evidence that establishes your themes of the case. The preliminary goal, however, is to draft the instructions in a manner that the judge will agree to give to the jury. To state the obvious, it does your client no good if you write a dynamite jury instruction that will hook the jury on the defense and the judge declines to give the instruction. You may have an appeal, and there are certainly cases where you must submit proposed jury instructions that the judge may not give in order to assure that you can appeal. But the first goal, if possible, is to submit an instruction that you believe the judge can give consistent with your goal to obtain the result your client desires.

In discussing some of the criminal offenses earlier in Chapters 2A and 2B, we have provided examples of jury instructions that explain elements of the offenses in language that juries understand. Most of these examples were drawn from a circuit court's approved forms for jury instructions, often referred to as pattern instructions.[17] Federal circuit courts often adopt pattern jury instructions. These pattern instructions are often drafted and approved initially by a blue ribbon panel of practitioners and judges from the circuit. They are designed to assist busy parties and district judges in drafting proper instructions on common themes and issues in cases. Such pattern instructions are not necessarily correct in the sense that any court has approved in advance their use in the case. However, the care with which they are drawn and the vetting they have had usually assure that they are good starting points for the parties in proposing instructions to the court. Busy district courts will tend to accept these instructions verbatim in appropriate cases except to the extent that the attorneys convince the judge that, in the particular case at hand, a fair trial requires some variance. In marshaling your arguments for variance from these instructions, you will use all of those lawyer skills available, including research of the cases where similar variances may have been made and your general arguments that the law and justice requires a variance in this case.

Where there are no such pattern jury instructions, you will have to prepare the jury instructions from other sources and convince the judge that they properly instruct the jury as to the law in the context of the case. There are several sources for form jury instructions. One source that is particularly important in criminal tax cases is the proposed jury instructions in the CTM.[18] The CTM's proposed instructions must be approached with care; they are one advocate's imagination of proper jury instructions. As with pattern jury instructions, they may or may not be correct statements of the law in general or correct statements as applied to the

---

[17] For example, the Fifth Circuit's pattern jury instructions are on the web at: http://www.lb5.uscourts.gov/juryinstructions/ which also contains links to other Circuits' pattern jury instructions.

[18] The following URL's may be used for the current edition (2008) of the CTM: http://www.justice.gov/tax/readingroom/2008ctm/CTM%20TOC.htm. DOJ's form jury instructions are: http://www.justice.gov/tax/readingroom/2008ctm/CTM%20JI%20-%20Title%2026.pdf.

case at hand. But, a circuit court's pattern jury instructions are drafted with a lot more real or perceived objectivity than the CTM's instructions. Hence, the CTM's instructions should be viewed skeptically. If the defense proposes an instruction substantially consistent with a CTM instruction, it is likely not to be controversial and is likely to be given. If, however, the prosecution proposes a CTM instruction that the defense has a legitimate concern about, the defense should be prepared to refute the instruction and to object if it is given.

Drafting your proposed jury instructions is an art form. On the one hand, you want to present the instructions in the light that you imagine achieves the best result for your client. On the other hand, you don't want to present such one-sided instructions that the judge will deny your requested instructions for good reasons, thus bullet-proofing the denial on appeal.

VI. THE TRIAL

A. General

Once the trial starts, it's all about what the jury hears or sees or intuits.[19] In theory at least, this is shaped principally by the evidence and the instructions.

B. Opening Instructions

The judge will usually give some form of opening instructions to advise the jury of the general nature of the case, their duties in the case, and certain generic types of trial matters that they are likely to experience (*e.g.*, evidentiary objections, side-bar conferences and the like). These opening instructions will be general as to the substantive law that they will ultimately apply in reaching their verdict. The purpose of these preliminary instructions is to give the jury some context for what the jury will be hearing. The purpose is not to give the jury a definitive statement of the law they should consider when they ultimately begin deliberation at the close of the case, but to give them sufficient overview so that, as the trial proceeds, the jury can have some context to make the evidence meaningful.

These are important instructions, even though preliminary and subject to fine-tuning at the close of the evidence. If possible, you will want the judge to give preliminary instructions consistent with the theme(s) of your case.

C. Opening Arguments

Opening argument is a major opportunity for each party to present and put some minimal bones around the themes of the case and anticipate the evidence in support of the theme(s). In anticipating the evidence in support of the theme(s), however, it is important that the attorney not overstate his or her case — either the evidence that will in fact be presented or the reasonable inferences that may be drawn from the evidence. We noted above that credibility is important and will

[19] The unknown and usually unknowable in any practical sense is a juror's knowledge and prejudices that influence the final outcome but were not flushed out in voir dire.

disappear if the attorney overstates his client's case.

One of the danger points in opening argument is to refer to evidence that then does not materialize at trial. Generally, this is poor form because the attorney will have failed to deliver something important he promised to deliver. However, it is particularly troublesome if the attorney refers to testimony he expects from his client, the defendant. In a criminal tax trial, a key factual issue — often the only one in material dispute — is whether the defendant had the requisite "willfulness" and the related issue of whether the defendant was not willful because of reliance on a tax professional. The defendant will usually be best positioned to testify on that subject. However, the defendant does not have to testify at trial. The Government is required to prove its case — including the defendant's wilfulness — without the defendant's testimony and, in an otherwise weak prosecution case, may be able to achieve its objective only through cross-examining the defendant. In any event, in many and perhaps most criminal tax cases, the final decision of whether the defendant will testify will not be made until the Government has rested its case-in-chief. The jury will view skeptically any statement in opening argument that the defendant will testify if the defendant thereafter does not testify. Be careful about making those types of commitments in opening argument because you may want to preserve the flexibility to have the defendant not testify. Of course, as noted, this same point is true for other forms of evidence you may discuss in opening argument — if you promise evidence that does not materialize in the trial, the jury may well draw negative inferences that may infect other aspects of the case. Promise only what you can and will deliver.

D. Government's Case

1. Introduction

The prosecution proceeds first with its evidence. The prosecution will continue until it rests its case.

2. Proving the Elements of the Crime

Chapter 4 discussed the principal proof issues arising in tax cases. We introduce here a related concept: "bad act" evidence which the Government often uses to put the defendant in a bad light in the eyes of the jury.

Tax crimes require that the defendant act "willfully," meaning that the defendant must have intentionally violated an objectively knowable and subjectively known legal duty. Focusing on the latter, the Government must prove specific intent. Intent is rarely directly provable, but is proved by circumstantial evidence.

It is not uncommon for the Government to seek to prove the defendant's willfulness (or intent) by reference to other crimes or conduct. Under Fed. R. Evid. 404(a), the Government may not prove character or a character trait of a defendant as proof of charged action in conformity with the character or trait (often referred to as "propensity" evidence), unless the defendant introduces such evidence in his or her defense. However, under Fed. R. Evid. 404(b), the Government may introduce evidence of "other crimes, wrongs, or acts" for purposes other than showing character or character trait; thus, it may be admitted to show "intent," "knowledge," "absence of mistake or accident," etc. This type of evidence is often called "uncharged crimes," "other crimes," or "bad acts" evidence. Because the evidence shows the defendant in a bad light, it will further prejudice the defendant in the jury's mind even apart from its persuasiveness as to the charged crimes in the case. Bad conduct evidence avoids 404(b)'s limitations altogether if the conduct is "inextricably intertwined" with the charged conduct, because the Government is permitted to tell the whole story of the charged conduct.[20]

The difference between impermissible 404(a) evidence of bad character from which to infer guilt and 404(b) permissible bad acts evidence has been conceptualized as follows:

> Although the distinction between acts offered to prove propensity and acts offered for another purpose is not easily drawn, it is helpful to consider whether the factfinder is asked to engage to infer from behavior on one occasion something about the nature of a person and then to infer from that how the person probably would have behaved on another occasion, when the only connection between the two occasions is that the factfinder believes that people of a certain type would act the same way both times. If so, then the evidence is character evidence. If the factfinder can reason from one act about another without going through the first step, the evidence is not character evidence.[21]

In layman's terms, the concept is captured in the following Fifth Circuit Pattern Jury Instruction:

> You have heard evidence of acts of the defendant which may be similar to those charged in the indictment, but which were committed on other occasions. You must not consider any of this evidence in deciding if the defendant committed the acts charged in the indictment. However, you may consider this evidence for other, very limited, purposes.
>
> If you find beyond a reasonable doubt from other evidence in this case that the defendant did commit the acts charged in the indictment, then you may consider evidence of the similar acts allegedly committed on other occasions to determine:
>
> Whether the defendant had the state of mind or intent necessary to commit the crime charged in the indictment;
>
> or
>
> whether the defendant had a motive or the opportunity to commit the acts charged in the indictment;

---

20 *E.g.*, United States v. Tarwater, 308 F.3d 494, 517 (6th Cir.), *reh'g and reh'g en banc denied*, 2002 U.S. App. LEXIS 26465 (6th Cir. Dec. 19, 2002) (citing United States v. Everett, 270 F.3d 986, 992 (6th Cir. 2001); United States v. Hilgeford, 7 F.3d 1340 (7th Cir. 1993)).

21 Stephen A. Saltzburg, Daniel J. Capra & Michael M. Martin, *Commentary on Rule 404, in* Lexis-Nexis Federal Criminal Laws and Rules Selected Federal Court Rules (CD-Rom edition) (Current as of January 31, 2012).

> or
>
> whether the defendant acted according to a plan or in preparation for commission of a crime;
>
> or
>
> whether the defendant committed the acts for which he is on trial by accident or mistake.
>
> These are the limited purposes for which any evidence of other similar acts may be considered.[22]

The Government can use the uncharged conduct with a level of proof that is significantly below the level required if the indictment had charged the conduct.[23] Thus, the jury does not have to find the defendant "guilty" of the bad act beyond a reasonable doubt. At least in theory, this means that, if the Government did not charge the "bad act" because it realized it could not meet that level of proof for that conduct, it might still use evidence of the conduct to convince the factfinder to find guilt on charged conduct. That is counter-intuitive and points out the dangers in 404(b) evidence.

Because of its risk of prejudice, courts require that the inference the prosecution seeks from the bad acts be an inference that is really in issue. For example, where this usually arises in tax cases is with respect to the willfulness or intent element of the crime. In this context, the Government will only be allowed to introduce the evidence if the defendant is contesting willfulness.[24] Since the Rule requires that, upon request, the prosecution must notify the defendant of such evidence, that request is routinely made in criminal cases and, sometimes even when not requested, simply required by the Court as part of a comprehensive pretrial scheduling plan that sets forth dates for such notice and dates for pretrial motions in limine as to the admissibility of the evidence. Conceivably, the defendant might pre-empt the issue by conceding willfulness, but in most cases the defendant may not be willing to do that because the prosecutors' inability to prove willfulness beyond a reasonable doubt is his or her only viable defense. So the defendant must look to mitigate the damage by challenging the logical nexus between the evidence and the allegation of intent which it is supposed to prove and by obtaining a favorable limiting instruction.

Consider the following example of bad acts evidence in a tax case:

---

[22] Fifth Circuit Pattern Jury Instruction 1.30 (2012 edition, which is the edition current as of April 17, 2013).

[23] Huddleston v. United States, 485 U.S. 681 (1988) (rejecting an argument that the judge make a preliminary finding of the bad act by a preponderance of the evidence and requiring only that the judge determine that the Government's evidence is sufficient to permit the jury to reasonably conclude by a preponderance of the evidence that the defendant committed the alleged bad act).

[24] *E.g.*, United States v. Bok, 156 F.3d 157 (2d Cir. 1998).

UNITED STATES v. JOHNSON

United States Court of Appeals, Fourth Circuit
634 F.2d 735 (1980)

Johnson is a medical doctor, who inherited her practice from her deceased brother. She filed tax returns for 1972, 1973, and 1974, which understated her income by approximately $120,000.00 and her tax liability by approximately $31,000.00. Her defense at trial was inadvertence: she has had nothing to do with preparing her tax returns because she cared nothing for money and chose, instead, to devote her time to the demanding personal needs of her patients. To support this defense, she produced seven local witnesses — three physicians, a school board member, a public school teacher, a mortician, and a minister — who testified to her truthfulness, honesty, and compassion, and to the busy nature of her practice.

In attempted rebuttal of this portrait of Johnson as an altruistic healer of the sick, whose concerns lay elsewhere than attending to her financial interests and resulting legal responsibilities, the government called Robert Pemberton, an auditor for the U.S. Department of Health, Education & Welfare. Pemberton testified at length about his investigation of Johnson's billings for Medicaid services for 1976–78. His study showed that Johnson reported four times as many services per patient as other Virginia doctors. Johnson did not object to the general course of Pemberton's testimony. In fact, the following day Johnson again took the stand in order to testify that she had not signed the Medicaid billings upon which Pemberton had based his investigation. During cross-examination, government counsel asked Johnson, "Who would have received the benefit of all the fraudulent forms for Medicaid that were filed?" Johnson's counsel objected and moved for a mistrial because use of the term, "fraudulent," unduly prejudiced the jury. The trial judge overruled the motion, directed government counsel to rephrase the question, and gave the jury a cautionary instruction.

We hold that Pemberton's testimony was admissible under Fed. R. Evid. 404(b), which provides:

> Evidence of other crimes, wrongs, or acts is not admissible to prove the character of a person in order to show that he acted in conformity therewith. It may, however, be admissible for other purposes, such as proof of motive, opportunity, intent, preparation, plan, knowledge, identity, or absence of mistake or accident.[25]

The first sentence of Rule 404(b) brings forward the traditional rule that extrinsic acts evidence is inadmissible solely to prove that defendant is a bad character and, therefore, likely to have committed the crime charged. Extrinsic acts evidence, however, may be admissible for other purposes including those listed in Rule 404(b). The Rule's list is merely illustrative, not exclusive. Rule 404(b) of course commits to trial judge discretion the determination whether extrinsic act evidence shall be admitted under its second sentence. In exercising that discretion the judge first must determine if the proffered evidence is relevant to an issue other than the

---

25 [Authors' note: The latter sentence now concludes with a procedural requirement that, upon request, the prosecution notify the defendant of the 404(b) evidence it intends to use.]

accused's character. If so, then the trial judge must balance the evidence's probative value against the dangers of undue prejudice aroused by this form of evidence. This may concededly pose particularly difficult problems. The Advisory Committee Notes to Rule 404(b) state:

> No mechanical solution is offered. The determination must be made whether the danger of undue prejudice outweighs the probative value of the availability of other means of proof and other factors appropriate for making decisions of this kind under Rule 403 (confusion of issues, misleading the jury, undue delay, waste of time, and needless presentation of cumulative evidence).

Within this general guideline for the exercise of trial court discretion, we think the evidence here challenged was properly admitted. The general prohibition contained in the first sentence of Rule 404(b) is designed to prevent prosecutorial overreaching by a means whose obvious effectiveness has made it an inescapable temptation for advocates over the years. The second sentence, however, reflects the perception that evidence of "other acts" may sometimes be critical to proof on a dispositive issue related to a defendant's state of mind. The ambivalence reflected in the Rule but serves to emphasize the particular delicacy of the discretionary rulings its administration may require. There is no gainsaying that the ruling here posed just such a problem for the trial judge, but we think he properly resolved it.

Particularly where, as here, a defendant in a criminal case by her own testimony and that of others has deliberately sought as the primary means of defense to depict herself as one whose essential philosophy and habitual conduct in life [are] completely at odds with the possession of a state of mind requisite to guilt of the offense charged, that defendant may be considered in effect to have forfeited any protection that the first sentence of the Rule might otherwise have provided against the type of "other act" evidence here challenged. See Walder v. United States, 347 U.S. 62 (1954). In such circumstances, testimony such as that of Pemberton may well be the only effective way to rebut evidence designed generally to plant in the jury's mind a reasonable doubt that such a person could have possessed the culpability of mind requisite to convict of the crime charged. Balancing the probative value of the challenged evidence against its potential for unfairly prejudicing the defendant, and on the latter point taking into account that the defendant deliberately chose to base her defense upon evidence not otherwise effectively rebuttable, we conclude that the district judge's admission of Pemberton's evidence lay well within the bounds of the discretion reposed in him.

We think that government counsel's unfortunate reference to "fraudulent" Medicaid forms was sufficiently corrected by the trial judge's cautionary actions so that the risk of prejudice was adequately removed.

As noted in Johnson, the Government's 404(b) evidence, if otherwise proper, is still subject to exclusion "if its probative value is substantially outweighed by the danger of unfair prejudice, confusion of the issues, or misleading the jury, or by considerations of undue delay, waste of time, or needless presentation of cumulative evidence."[26]

3. Government Witnesses

We discussed in Chapter 4 some types of Government witnesses encountered in tax crimes trials. In addition, if there are still legal uncertainty issues lurking in the case a la Garber and similar cases, you may try to flesh that out from the Government witnesses, particularly the Special Agent who testifies. The Special Agent is frequently not a real expert in the tax law, and may succumb to unexpected cross examination over the legal basis for the conclusions.

E. Prosecutorial Misconduct

1. Comment on Defendant's Exercise of Fifth Amendment

Prosecutors sometimes misbehave in trials. Judges have a range of remedies to correct the damage from such misbehavior, including declaring a mistrial or in particularly egregious cases dismissing the indictment. Alternatively or in addition, judges may punish the offending prosecutor.

In terms of what a judge may do, it is important to keep in mind that our system is designed to give a defendant a fair trial, not a perfect trial. (A perfect trial, like the search for objective truth, is elusive.) The following exemplifies a type of misbehavior that implicates the defendant's Fifth Amendment right to have the Government prove its case beyond a reasonable doubt without his testimony. In order to protect that right, the prosecution is not able to call the defendant to the stand to force the defendant to invoke the right or even in any other way try to gain advantage from the fact that the defendant does not testify. In this case, the prosecutor in a moment of zeal untempered by judgment sought to exploit the interface of that black letter law with a corollary rule that, once the defendant does testify, he or she is fair game for the prosecutor unfettered by Fifth Amendment claims.

UNITED STATES v. EVANGELISTA

United States Court of Appeals, Second Circuit
122 F.3d 112 (1997)

[Authors' note: Another portion of the Evangelista decision was excerpted in Chapter 2B. For the facts of the case, see that previous excerpt.]

During the government's cross-examination of Reffsin, Evangelista, Sr. [the Defendant] audibly answered "yes" in response to the prosecutor's pending question. The prosecutor reacted by saying: "I call Louis Evangelista to the stand." Judge Wexler immediately told the prosecutor to sit down, and admonished Evangelista, Sr. to "keep [his] mouth quiet." Then, at defense counsel's request, Judge Wexler convened a side-bar with all counsel, and promptly thereafter instructed the jury: "A statement was made by the defendant and a statement was made by the prosecution. Disregard them both. I think that it was in the heat of

---

[26] 25 Fed. R. Evid. 403.

excitement where it came out, it should not have come out. They were both wrong. So disregard it." The defense made no contemporaneous objection to the court's curative instruction.

The Evangelistas claim that this "egregious act of prosecutorial misconduct amounted to a deliberate effort to undermine [their] constitutional rights" not to testify, and was "in no way cured by the District Court's instruction" to the jury.

This Court has stated that "inappropriate prosecutorial comments, standing alone, would not justify a reviewing court to reverse a criminal conviction obtained in an otherwise fair proceeding; such remarks must be examined within the context of the trial to determine whether the prosecutor's behavior amounted to prejudicial error." "In making this assessment, this Court has focused primarily on three factors: the severity of the misconduct, the measures adopted to cure it, and the certainty of conviction in the absence of the misconduct." * * *

Under this standard, the prosecutor's comment — while plainly improper — does not warrant reversal. We agree with the government that the comment ultimately had no prejudicial effect on Evangelista, Sr., or on his son Claude, when considered in light of the district court's immediate curative instruction and the weight of evidence against both defendants.

The severity of the prosecutor's single improper statement was also "mitigated somewhat in this case because the remark appears to have been an aberration in an otherwise fair proceeding." *Id.* "Most of the cases in which we have reversed convictions as a result of prosecutorial misconduct have involved repeated improper statements whose aggregate effect was more likely to undermine the fairness of the trial." *Id.* The prosecutor's statement here had no bearing on the credibility of the defense witness on the stand at the time, or on the validity of the evidence against the Evangelistas. We emphasize that there is no one-free-bite rule for prosecutors, but the record reflects and supports Judge Wexler's view that the comment was a heated, momentary response to provocation rather than a tactical move. In short, the prosecutor's comment is an insufficient ground for reversal.

2. Prosecutor Comments on Prosecutor's Personal Beliefs

A criminal trial should be about the evidence and whether the evidence proves the criminal charges beyond a reasonable doubt. A prosecutor should avoid stating his or her personal belief about the weight of the evidence.

Consider the following in a tax prosecution:

UNITED STATES v. WOODS

United States Court of Appeals, Fourth Circuit

710 F.3d 195 (2013)

As discussed above, the government maintained that Woods profited from his fraudulent scheme by charging clients a $500 premium for the inclusion of false dependent information on those clients' tax returns. Woods, however, testified that the $500 sums represented repayments of loans he had made to clients before they received their tax refunds. The part of the government's closing argument at issue here occurred when the prosecutor stated:

> So, Mr. Woods was right in the middle of getting these $500 payments for the fake dependents and he lied about it under oath when he testified this morning (emphasis added).

According to Woods, this statement was improper and constituted reversible error. In response, the government argues that the statement was neither improper nor prejudicial.

First, we disagree with the government's contention that this statement was proper. We long have rebuked government counsel for making inflammatory statements of this nature. Twenty years ago, in *United States v. Moore*, 11 F.3d 475 (4th Cir. 1993), we strongly criticized a prosecutor's statement during closing argument that the crime was "compounded when the defendant . . . comes into a federal court, takes the oath on the Bible, and lies." 11 F.3d at 480. We explained unequivocally that "it is highly improper for the government to refer to a defense witness as a liar," and further noted that we had "continually admonished the government not to engage in such conduct." *Id.* at 481 (emphasis added). Applying plain error review in Moore, we held that the prosecutor's statement was error that was plain, and we "strongly admonished [the government] to 'clean up its act,'" issuing the warning "hopefully for the last time." *Id.* at 482 n.9; see also *United States v. Weatherless*, 734 F.2d 179, 181 (4th Cir. 1984) (noting that government counsel's multiple statements that the defendant was a liar and a "loser" fell "well beneath the standard which a prosecutor should observe"); *cf. United States v. Loayza*, 107 F.3d 257, 262 (4th Cir. 1997) ("It is improper for a prosecutor to directly express his opinion as to the veracity of a witness.") (quoting *Moore*, 11 F.3d at 481).

Our reasoning in Moore applies with equal force in the present case, because "any statement of personal belief jeopardizes the integrity of the trial process." *Loayza*, 107 F.3d at 262 (quoting *United States v. Harrison*, 716 F.2d 1050, 1052 (4th Cir. 1983)). When a prosecutor comments on the veracity of a witness, the prosecutor's statement presents two discrete risks: (1) of improperly suggesting to the jury that the prosecutor's personal opinion has evidentiary weight; and (2) of improperly inviting the jury to infer that the prosecutor "had access to extra-judicial information, not available to the jury." *United States v. Moore*, 710 F.2d 157, 159 (4th Cir. 1983).

The gravity of these risks is amplified in the case of a criminal defendant exercising his constitutional right to testify in his own defense. Here, by stating that Woods lied under oath, the prosecutor suggested to the jury that Woods abused this constitutional right and attempted to manipulate the outcome of the trial to avoid being held responsible for his true actions. Based on these grave concerns, we reiterate our holding in Moore that error that is plain results when a prosecutor states that a defendant has lied under oath during trial, and we conclude that such an error occurred here.[27]

---

[27] [4] We are not persuaded by the government's attempt on appeal to distinguish between a situation in which the prosecutor referred to the defendant as a "liar," and, as in this case, a situation in which the prosecutor stated that the defendant "lied."

[Omitted sections reviews the evidence as to Woods' guilt.]

In light of this volume of evidence of Woods' guilt, we conclude that, even in the absence of the prosecutor's improper statement, Woods' credibility would have been significantly weakened by the direct conflict between his testimony and that of the several government witnesses and the documentary evidence. Moreover, a considerable portion of the government's evidence directly contradicted Woods' theories of defense. Accordingly, although we strongly criticize the prosecutor's argument that Woods had lied under oath, we conclude that Woods' substantial rights were not violated and that this trial error does not warrant reversal of Woods' convictions.

Focus on the court's footnote 4 above. The footnote is cryptic as to precisely what the Government's argument was, but the argument was:

> In the instant case, government counsel did not call the defendant a liar. Nor did counsel express his personal opinion about the defendant's veracity. Rather, counsel commented on the veracity of the defendant's testimony which was clearly contradictory to the testimony of government witnesses and the documentary evidence that was admitted at trial. Since the defendant's credibility was in issue, it was permissible for government counsel to argue from the evidence that the defendant was untruthful.[28]

While it is permissible for the prosecutor to argue that the jury can determine credibility and that defendant or any witness lied, the fine line is suggesting to the jury that the defendant or the witness lied. This is a very fine line, because most jurors would know that the prosecutor would not have made the argument unless the prosecutor believes the defendant or witness lied. Still fine lines are important in the criminal arena.

3. Golden Rule Argument

Golden rule arguments are attempts to personalize for the jury some aspect of the case, so that the jury may be less objective in making its decisions.[29] Usually, the argument asks the jury to put themselves in the place of one of the parties. Prosecutors do it; defense attorneys do it. The following is an example of prosecutor use of the golden rule argument:

> Of the various remarks Mr. George challenges, we find that three in particular were improper. During its closing argument and final summation, the prosecution made the following remarks: (1) that the defendants "were stealing from you and they were stealing from me and everyone else that's paying into the system"; (2) that the defendants were "living large off of your tax dollars"; and (3) that without citizens filing accurate tax returns, "we would have no tax revenue, . . . no way to build schools . . . no way to fight wars." There is no doubt that these "golden rule" remarks were

---

[28] Gov't Brief pp. 60–61.

[29] The allusion is to the golden rule attributed to Jesus in Luke 6:31 to do to others what you would have them do to you.

> improper, as they directly suggested that the jurors had personal stakes in the outcome of the case and they placed the prosecution together with the jury in a joint effort to combat fraud. *See United States v. McGarity*, 669 F.3d 1218, 1246 (11th Cir. 2012) ("[B]y telling the jury that the victims of the child pornography are 'our daughters and granddaughters, neighbors, friends,' the prosecutor here crossed the line . . . 'demarcating permissible oratorical flourish from impermissible comment.' "). *See also United States v. Lopez*, 590 F.3d 1238, 1256 (11th Cir. 2009) ("Improper suggestions, insinuations and assertions calculated to mislead or inflame the jury's passions are forbidden in the presentation of closing arguments."). We expect prosecutors from the Tax Division of the Department of Justice to refrain from this kind of argument in the future.
>
> Nonetheless, as in *McGarity*, 669 F.3d at 1246–47, the improper remarks did not so prejudicially affect Mr. George's rights that a different outcome might have been achieved in their absence. First, the district court instructed the jury on at least three separate occasions that the arguments of counsel were not evidence. *See United States v. Rodriguez*, 765 F.2d 1546, 1560 (11th Cir. 1985) (holding issuance of three curative instructions was sufficient to cure damage arising from prejudicial comments made by prosecutor). Second, there was overwhelming evidence against Mr. George. The improper remarks did not affect Mr. George's substantial rights, even when considered cumulatively. *See Ladson*, 643 F.3d at 1342 ("There is no cumulative error where the defendant cannot establish that the combined errors affected his substantial rights.") (internal quotation marks omitted). As a result, the prosecution's improper statements do not require reversal.[30]

We noted that either side may attempt golden rule arguments for its own purpose to influence the jury. When prosecutors do it and obtain a conviction (whether based on the argument or not), the defense can appeal and complain.

Note that this golden rule strategy was presented in the prosecution's closing argument where it is probably most effective. But it can be a theme of the prosecution's case presented earlier in the trial, perhaps in more subtle ways. Practitioners should be careful to object and request curative instructions if this implication is presented to the jury at any stage.

F. Defense Motion for Judgment of Acquittal

The defendant may move for judgment of acquittal at the conclusion of the Government's case or at the conclusion of all the evidence.[31] The motion essentially argues that, taking the Government's case as the Government has presented it, no reasonable jury could conclude beyond a reasonable doubt that the defendant was guilty of a crime. These motions are rarely granted but do serve as a check on

---

[30] United States v. Hunte, 2014 U.S. App. LEXIS 4729 (11th Cir. Mar. 13, 2014).

[31] Fed. R. Crim. P. 29. Rule 29(b) permits the court to reserve decision on the motion even until after the jury verdict.

abuse of the Government's raw power to incite a grand jury to indict.[32]

G. Defendant's Case

If the Government's case is still viable after the Government presents its case, the defendant will then present the defendant's evidence.

1. Defense Witnesses

a. Defense Summary Witnesses

Just as the Government can use summary witnesses, so can the defense. For example, in a complex tax case where the Government uses a summary witness to establish the net worth method of reconstructing taxable income,[33] the taxpayer could have a summary witness making different calculations or even countering problems in the Government's proffered summary.

b. Defendant as Witness

Of course, probably the key witness question facing the defense is whether the defendant will testify. That decision is based on experience, a reading of the trial judge and jury, and careful preparation with the defendant to project how he would appear.

c. Character Witnesses

FRE 404(a) permits the defendant to present character witnesses in support of the defense case. In tax cases, a character witness's testimony goes to the willfulness element along the following lines (highly summarized): "I have known the defendant for X number of years in a context which permits me to draw fair and reliable inferences about his or her ability and predilection to willfully commit this type of crime; and I am here to tell you no way Jose." That type of evidence is rarely sufficient by itself, although one can certainly imagine a case where it would be. It is easier to imagine character evidence contributing to the outcome with other evidence that defendant did not act willfully or the Government's proof the defendant did act willfully has some flaws. Often, however, the jury will just consider the evidence as nice — everybody can find someone who speaks well of him or her, but it's nice to know that someone likes this defendant — but not determinative or even important to their resolution of the case in light of all the other evidence presented. In this setting, the prosecution will often not cross-examine or conduct cross-examination "light," perhaps just to suggest that the witness may not have had sufficient opportunity to draw conclusions as to the inner recesses of the mind or heart of this defendant.

The downside to opening up character evidence is that it can be outcome

---

32 For an example of a successful motion of this type, see United States v. Pappathanasi, 383 F. Supp. 2d 289 (D. Mass. 2005) (granting defendants' motion under Fed. R. Crim. P. 29 and entering judgments of acquittal in an 18 U.S.C. section 371 *Klein* conspiracy case).

33 See Chapter 4 for discussion of summary witnesses and the net worth method.

determinative in favor of the prosecution. Rule 404(a) permits the prosecution to present character evidence once the defendant has opened that door and to attack the defendant's character witnesses with a vengeance. The prosecutors will have to tread lightly so as not to appear to the jury to be abusive or unfair, but if it can clear that hurdle it might present to the jury much about the defendant's character that affirmatively supports or affirms its theme of the case.

2. Defense Themes

a. The Limits of Jury Appeal

(1) When You Just Can't Put Lipstick on the Pig

I said that you must make your client a sympathetic figure. Sometimes, that just can't be done. The classic tax case is the tax evasion trial of Leona Helmsley, wife of a prominent New York land baron. At least as the press reported the evidence (including the courtroom demeanor evidence) at her trial, it was clear that Ms. Helmsley was not a likeable person. She was sometimes referred as the "queen of mean." Those around her, including employees and other retainers, who felt abused by her were more than willing at trial to trot out the bad stuff. For example, she was quoted in the tax trial as saying "only little people pay taxes." That does not play well in front of a jury of people who pay taxes. And her general disdainful treatment of others also did not play well. So how did the lawyer — Jerry Feffer, one of the best — present the unlikeable client? Feffer starts his closing argument as follows: "I don't believe Ms. Helmsley is charged in the indictment with being a tough bitch." Unfortunately for the client, this tactic and her other defenses were not successful.[34] However, my sense is that Feffer's candor with the jury on the point that had been a strong presence as the trial developed did not hurt. Generally, it certainly does not hurt to state the obvious and, indeed, in this context could have been marginally favorable except for the other evidence of guilt that carried the day.

(2) The Golden Rule

In *United States v. Roman*,[35] the Defendant was precluded on motion in limine from presenting a golden rule defense.

> Before the trial kicked off, the government filed a motion in limine to preclude Roman from making a so-called "Golden Rule" appeal, i.e., that the jury should place itself in his shoes. In support of its motion, the government relied on United States v. Teslim, 869 F.2d 316, 328 (7th Cir. 1989), for the proposition that such arguments are improper. Judge Kennelly agreed and granted the government's motion.
>
> Teslim ironically involved an improper "Golden Rule" argument by the government: "[I]f it happened to you and you had nothing to hide —" Here,

---

[34] United States v. Helmsley, 941 F.2d 71 (2d Cir.), *cert. denied*, 502 U.S. 1091 (1991).

[35] 492 F.3d 803 (7th Cir. 2007).

Roman was rebuffed when he sought to argue that the jurors should put themselves in his shoes and consider "There but for the grace of God go I."

This proposed argument was correctly foreclosed by Judge Kennelly. As we explained in Teslim, a "Golden Rule" appeal in which the jury is asked to put itself in the defendant's position "is universally recognized as improper because it encourages the jury to depart from the neutrality and to decide the case on the basis of personal interest and bias rather than on the evidence." 869 F.2d at 328.

In his brief, Roman writes:

> In a tax evasion case such as this, it is a logical extension to ask the jury to think about evil versus stupid, to speculate what they would do, were they to be placed in the subjective shoes of the defendant. This is precisely what "there, but for the grace of God" requests. No more no less than the objective discernment of evil as viewed from the defendant's subjective eyes. "God" in this context being a surrogate for the all knowing introspective "See," the diviner of the secrets in men and women's heart.

Whatever can be said about this contention, one thing is certain: it's not persuasive. We see no reason why the rule against arguing about the Golden Rule should be reconsidered in this case.[36]

H. Government's Rebuttals

The Government may then present evidence in favor of a conviction. Usually, the new evidence addresses matters that arose in the defendant's defense in chief. If the Government could have anticipated the need for the evidence in advance, it likely would have admitted its evidence in its case-in-chief, but sometimes for strategic reasons the Government will want to get the defendant committed to a particular view of the facts which often happens only during the defendant's case-in-chief and then spring its contrary view of the facts.

The taxpayer may then renew its motion for acquittal, again on the ground that a reasonable jury could not find each element of the offense charged beyond a reasonable doubt.[37] Again, such motions are usually denied.

I. Closing Argument

The parties will then make their closing arguments. Before doing that, the judge will again instruct the jury as to the purpose of this phase of the trial. The judge will say the expected things — such that arguments are not evidence and that the arguments should be credited only to the extent (1) persuasive, (2) consistent with the facts they heard in the trial, and (3) consistent with the law as the judge will instruct the jury in making the submission of the case to the jury.

---

[36] 492 F.3d at 805–806.

[37] Fed. R. Crim. P. 29.

The prosecution then goes first, arguing the facts and the law that, in its view, support a finding of guilt for each element of each charged count. The defense goes next, arguing that the facts and the law do not support a finding of guilt beyond a reasonable doubt for each element of each charged count. The prosecution will then make a short rebuttal.

J. Closing Instructions

1. Introduction

Closing instructions are given at the conclusion of the case. They are the last words from Mount Olympus and, in some variation, the judge will instruct the jury that they are to accept those last words in their deliberations.

The judge will then instruct the jury. As a predicate for this, the judge will have required the parties to have submitted proposed jury instructions. Each party will present to the judge proposed jury instructions designed to be consistent with (1) the facts at trial, (2) the law, and (3) that party's view of the case. The judge will make the decision as to the actual jury instructions to give.

2. Charge Specific Instructions

The judge will then actually present the jury instructions. We have presented specific examples of jury charges in discussing the statutory crimes.

3. Specialized Charges

Either party may request special charges based upon the facts in dispute at trial and the law that relates to such facts. Often, the defense requests special charges related to a theory of its defense. Thus, it is not uncommon to seek special instructions going to a *Cheek* good faith defense. Consider the following example:

> Chavin and Litwin argued as part of their defense to the tax-fraud charges that they relied in good faith on the advice of Chavin's accountant Kessler and therefore did not "willfully" perpetrate the tax fraud. Defendants tendered a theory-of-defense jury instruction that covered this point. The district court, however, refused to give the instruction to the jury, stating that the theory of defense was sufficiently covered by other instructions; specifically, by the pattern instruction on good faith and a further instruction that made clear that defendants must have acted "willfully" within the precise definition of that term.
>
> We review a district court's refusal to give a theory-of-defense instruction de novo. *United States v. Meyer*, 157 F.3d 1067, 1074 (7th Cir. 1998). To be entitled to a theory-of-defense instruction, a defendant must satisfy a four-part test by showing (1) that the proposed instruction is a correct statement of law; (2) that the evidence in the case supports the theory of defense; (3) that the theory of defense is not already part of the charge; and (4) that failure to include the proposed instruction would deny the defendant a fair trial. *Id.*

> Here, defendants have, at the very least, failed to satisfy the third element. We have recognized in prior tax-evasion cases that a " 'good faith reliance' defense is essentially a claim that the [defendant] did not act 'willfully.' " *United States v. Brimberry*, 961 F.2d 1286, 1291 (7th Cir. 1992). Consequently, when, as here, instructions are given that require the jury to find that a defendant acted "willfully" and those instructions define "willfulness" and "good faith" as mutually exclusive, then a further "good faith reliance" theory-of-defense instruction would be unnecessarily redundant. *Id.*; *United States v. Kelley*, 864 F.2d 569, 573 (7th Cir. 1989). Therefore, we find that the instructions given by the district court adequately covered the defendants' theory of defense.[38]

In considering the foregoing, keep in mind that the Court was not saying that it would be error to give the requested charge. All the Court held was that it was not error not to give the charge. Accordingly, upon request, a trial court may well give this type of instruction even though it is redundant to some degree.

K. The Verdict

The jury will then retire for deliberation. If the jury can reach a verdict based on the judge's instructions, the jury will so advise the judge and the case will be convened in the court for the jury to present its verdict.

VII. POST-TRIAL

A. Post-Trial Motions

The defendant will have available the standard post-trial motions — new trial, etc.[39]

B. Pre-Sentence Investigation Report

If the defendant is convicted as to any count, the Probation Office will prepare a Pre-Sentence Investigation Report ("PSR"). We review the PSR in Chapter 10 in discussing sentencing, but summarize the key points here: The PSR will contain all relevant factors known to the probation officer that should affect sentencing, a summary of the statutory and Sentencing Guidelines sections applicable, and a calculation of the sentencing level. The most critical determinant for the PSR review and sentencing recommendation is the tax loss number we discussed earlier in the text. Another factor often present in tax cases will be acceptance of responsibility. Other relevant factors also will be discussed.

Both sides may heavily lobby for inclusions and exclusions from the PSR. How successful such lobbying is depends upon the facts, the persuasiveness of the attorneys and the particular probation officer involved.

---

[38] United States v. Chavin, 316 F.3d 666, 670 (7th Cir. 2002).

[39] *E.g.*, Fed. R. Crim. P. 33.

It is best if the parties can agree upon the content of the PSR. Busy judges will then have the assurance that the proposal in the PSR fairly balances the competing interests of the Government and the defendant and have been independently reviewed and approved by the Probation Office which has the duty to present any significant factors that have not been fairly treated by the parties. If complete agreement cannot be achieved, the parties should work hard with the Probation Office to narrow their differences with the PSR. The parties will then have an opportunity at the sentencing to present their views on any remaining differences and have the judge resolve them.

C. Sentencing

As we noted above, the Probation Office will submit a PSR to the court to assist the court in sentencing. The goal is to have an agreed PSR — or at least one as to which neither party objects. If either party does not agree with any portion of the PSR, that party may contest that portion and any disputes are resolved at the sentencing hearing. Factual disputes are resolved on a preponderance of the evidence standard (not the beyond a reasonable doubt in the criminal case in chief). Disputes in the application of the Sentencing Guidelines are resolved by the judge based on his or her legal determinations.

D. Appeal

The defendant will have the usual opportunities to appeal. Appeals from the conviction and sentence are called direct appeals. Key points (some of which are review) regarding appeals are:

First, the taxpayer may appeal from errors that substantially affected the trial phase proceedings below. These errors can range the gamut from insufficiency or variance of the indictment, evidentiary errors, procedural errors, erroneous instructions to the jury, etc. Second, the taxpayer may appeal from the sentencing. Third, timely appeal is a jurisdictional requirement. Rule 4(b), Federal Rules of Appellate Procedure ("FRAP"), requires filing the notice within 10 days of the judgment or order being appealed or the filing of the government's notice of appeal.[40] The Government may not appeal where the double jeopardy clause would prevent further prosecution.[41] Practically speaking, this means that appeal after trial is limited to a defendant's appeal after conviction.

During the pendency of the appeal (including petition for certiorari to the Supreme Court), the defendant is required to begin his or her sentence of incarceration unless the court finds (1) by clear and convincing evidence, that the defendant is not likely to flee or pose a danger to the safety of another person or the community, and (2) the appeal is not for delay and raises a substantial question of law or fact likely to result in reversal, an order for new trial, a sentence that does not include a term of imprisonment, or a sentence reduced to a term of

---

[40] Because appellate jurisdiction turns upon a timely filed appeal, careful attention to the filing of the notice of appeal is critical. In addition to FRAP 4(b), you should review FRAP 26(a) regarding how the 10 day period is computed.

[41] 18 U.S.C. § 3731.

imprisonment less than the total of the time already served plus the expected duration of the appeal process.[42] Fed. R. Crim. P. 9 allows prompt appellate review of a district court decision to deny release pending appeal of the conviction or sentence. The court of appeals may order release on that prompt request or order release later before decision on the substantive issues, after reviewing the briefs or hearing oral argument on the substantive issues if it determines that there is a substantial issue involved that might require reversal or further proceedings.

E. Post-Appeals Remedies (Collateral Attacks; Expungement)

The defendant's post-appeal remedies are limited. At some point litigation must cease and the result accepted (regardless of whether it is right or wrong in any purist sense). Nevertheless, certain "collateral attack" remedies are available.

The most commonly used collateral attack where the convicted defendant is in custody is via 28 U.S.C. § 2255 which is a statutory successor to the common law writ of habeas corpus procedure, although it is not the same.[43] Section 2255 permits relief for the sentence imposed on convicted defendants who are in custody in the following situations: (1) the sentence was imposed in violation of the Constitution or federal law; (2) the sentencing court did not have jurisdiction to impose the sentence; (3) the sentence exceeded the maximum allowed by law; and (4) the sentence is otherwise "subject to collateral attack." Despite the breadth of the language, not every alleged violation is cognizable under § 2255. Rather, they must involve a "fundamental defect which . . . results in a complete miscarriage of justice."[44]

On § 2255 review, a court will not redetermine matters presented on an earlier appeal and will address matters not previously appealed only if there is (1) an intervening change in the law or newly discovered evidence or (2) a claim of ineffective counsel that is typically not presented on direct appeal.[45]

Some types of collateral attacks may also be pursued under 28 U.S.C. § 2241, also a type of habeas corpus procedure.[46] This procedure applies where the § 2255 motion would be inadequate or ineffective.[47] Since § 2255 is generally deemed

---

[42] 18 U.S.C. § 3143(b).

[43] For good summaries, see Allan Ellis and James H. Feldman, Jr., *A 2255 and 2241 Primer*, 26 CHAMPION 26 (2002); and Brent E. Newton, *A Primer on Post-Conviction Habeas Corpus Review*, 29 CHAMPION 16 (2005).

[44] Davis v. United States, 417 U.S. 333, 346 (1974).

[45] Massaro v. United States, 538 U.S. 500, 504–505 (2003) (holding that generally, "a motion brought under § 2255 is preferable to direct appeal for deciding claims of ineffective-assistance" because the district court is "the forum best suited to developing the facts necessary to determining the adequacy of representation during an entire trial"). *See also, e.g.*, United States v. Galloway, 316 F.3d 624, 634 (6th Cir. 2003); and United States v. Jake, 281 F.3d 123, 132 n. 7 (3d Cir. 2002). Some courts, however, allow this issue to be presented on the direct appeal in rare cases when the record before the court has fully developed the issue. *E.g.*, United States v. Barnes, 324 F.3d 135 (3d Cir. 2003).

[46] For a good summary, see Allan Ellis and James H. Feldman, Jr., *A 2255 and 2241 Primer*, 26 CHAMPION 26 (2002).

[47] *Id.*

adequate to preserve legitimate attacks on convictions and sentences, this procedure is generally not available.

In rare and exceptional circumstances, the writ of coram nobis may provide relief for persons who are not in custody.[48] The error(s) complained of via this writ must not have been known or reasonably knowable at an earlier stage where a more appropriate remedy of the types discussed above would have worked and the error(s) must continue to cause fundamental injustice even after release from custody.[49]

Finally, there may be a narrow — microscopically narrow — window of opportunity to obtain an expungement of a criminal conviction. The authority to expunge is not granted by statute and thus runs squarely into the general rule that federal courts are courts of limited jurisdiction. Nevertheless, some courts have found authority to expunge based upon ancillary jurisdiction. One court suggested that expungement might be available when the other post-conviction remedies are not available and the convicted person is able to establish some basis going to the integrity of the process; equitable factors alone will not suffice.[50]

VIII. ATTORNEYS FEES — THE HYDE AMENDMENT

Legislation commonly referred to as the "Hyde Amendment,"[51] allows a prevailing party in a criminal case to recover attorneys fees and litigation expenses from the government in cases where the government's position was vexatious, frivolous, or in bad faith. The Hyde Amendment is the criminal counterpart to the Equal Access to Justice Act ("EAJA"), 28 U.S.C. § 2412, which authorizes courts to award attorneys fees and costs in most civil cases. In civil tax taxes, Section 7430 covers the recovery of attorneys fees.

The fees and expenses that may be recovered include those incurred in the criminal prosecution itself and also those incurred incident to the preceding criminal investigation, including the IRS phase of the investigation. The defendant must prove that he or she is the prevailing party and that the government's position was vexatious, frivolous, or in bad faith. Merely prevailing, i.e., being acquitted in a criminal prosecution or receiving a Government or court dismissal of the indictment, is not alone sufficient to make the required showing of vexatious, frivolous, or in bad faith. And then, even when the defendant makes those showings, a court may still nevertheless deny the request for attorneys fees if it finds that special circumstances make awarding such fees unjust.

---

[48] Brent E. Newton, *A Primer on Post-Conviction Habeas Corpus Review*, 29 Champion 16 (2005).

[49] *Id.*

[50] United States v. Meyer, 439 F.3d 855, 861–62 (8th Cir. 2006).

[51] P.L. 105-119, Title VI section 617, 111 Stat. 2440, 2519 (1997). This amendment is not formally codified, but is commonly referred to as 18 U.S.C. § 3006A (Note).

In *United States v. Lindquist*,[52] the indictment charged a conspiracy with respect to taxes[53] and conspiracy to structure currency transactions. The jury convicted. The defendant appealed. The Ninth Circuit reversed on the ground that the Government's proof failed to show the requisite intent required for the crimes. The Court remanded. On remand, the district court denied the defendant's request for attorneys fees under the Hyde Amendment. On appeal, the Ninth Circuit held that the grant or denial of attorneys fees under the Hyde Amendment is reviewed on an abuse of discretion standard. The Court then held that the district court had not abused its discretion in denying attorneys fees:

> As a preliminary matter, we note that a defendant bears the burden of proving that the government's position was vexatious, frivolous, or in bad faith. The Amendment states that awards "shall be granted pursuant to the procedures and limitations (but not the burden of proof) provided for an award under [the EAJA]." Under the EAJA, the government bears the burden of proof. Thus, by rejecting the EAJA's approach to burden of proof, the Hyde Amendment places the burden of proof on the movant.
>
> We also note that the standard for recovering fees under the Hyde Amendment is more demanding than under the EAJA. Lindberg argues that in order to prevail, he only has to show that the government's position was not "substantially justified," the standard for recovery under the EAJA. However, legislative history undermines his claim. When Representative Hyde first introduced the Amendment, it contained the same language as the EAJA. *See* 143 Cong. Rec. H7786-04, H7791 (daily ed. Sept. 24, 1997). But several legislators criticized the "substantially justified" standard as too relaxed, *see id.* at H7792; *Gilbert*, 198 F.3d at 1300–02, and when the final version was passed, it provided that a criminal defendant could only recover fees and expenses if the government's position was vexatious, frivolous, or in bad faith. This clearly illustrates that a defendant must show more than that the government's position was not substantially justified.
>
> Several courts have grappled with the issue of what exactly a defendant must show under the vexatious, frivolous, or in bad faith standard. The Eleventh and Fourth Circuits have relied on Black's Dictionary to illuminate these terms. At least one district court has followed suit. Although this approach seems sensible enough, we find it unnecessary to settle on a precise formula here because under any articulation of the standard, we would be hard-pressed to conclude that the district court abused its discretion.
>
> Lindberg argues that the government's prosecution of him was vexatious and frivolous because it lacked any evidence that he knew it was illegal to structure currency transactions or that he knew the object of the conspiracy was tax evasion. Because such knowledge is required before a

[52] 220 F.3d 1120 (9th Cir. 2000).

[53] The opinion is not clear, but it appears that the conspiracy count may have alleged both an offense conspiracy and a defraud, *Klein* conspiracy.

defendant can be found guilty, Lindberg argues that the government knew its case against him was baseless.

Although Lindberg is correct that he could not be convicted of conspiracy unless he had the requisite knowledge, the prosecution was not required to present direct evidence of Lindberg's knowledge. In *Ratzlaf*, the Supreme Court stated that "[a] jury may, of course, find the requisite knowledge on defendant's part by drawing reasonable inferences from the evidence of defendant's conduct." 510 U.S. at 149 n.19. Thus, the government's lack of direct evidence as to Lindberg's knowledge does not demonstrate that its case was baseless. A jury could have inferred that knowledge on the basis of Lindberg's conduct.

Indeed, that appears to be what the jury did. The jury convicted Lindberg on the evidence presented by the government, and the district court refused to grant Lindberg's motion for acquittal. It is true that this court subsequently reversed the conviction. But as several courts have stated, a defendant must prove more than that his conviction was reversed on appeal; otherwise, almost every reversal would result in an award of attorneys fees.

The district court, which also presided over the trial in this case, concluded during its consideration of Lindberg's Hyde Amendment claim that "there [was] no question in [its] view that there was evidence by which a jury could draw inferences." We find no reason to second-guess the court's firm conviction that the charges in this case were neither vexatious nor frivolous.

Lindberg also argues that the government's prosecution of him was in bad faith because it was motivated by a desire to gain plea-bargain leverage against his mother and to obtain his apartment through forfeiture. To support this claim, he cites various statements made by the prosecution during trial. But these statements simply reflect the government's spin on the evidence; they do not indicate bad faith. At one point, for instance, the prosecutor urged the jury not to compartmentalize the evidence, but to look at each defendant's association with the group. Contrary to Lindberg's claim, this statement does not demonstrate that the prosecutor knew the case against Lindberg was baseless. Under our case law, once the existence of a conspiracy is established, evidence showing that a defendant was even slightly connected with the conspiracy is sufficient for a conviction. Thus, it was only natural for the prosecutor to focus on each defendant's association with the conspiracy.[54]

IX. INCARCERATION

The overwhelming number of tax crimes that are charged result in a conviction. Accordingly, attention early on in the process must focus on the Sentencing Guidelines. As an adjunct to that, particularly as sentencing approaches, the

---

[54] 200 F.3d at pp. 1124–1126.

practitioner must spend some time preparing the convicted client for incarceration if required by the sentence. Persons convicted of tax crimes will often qualify for the prisons with less severe confinement environments — dare I say country club prisons. This subject is beyond any detailed exposition here, but just be aware that there are certain pro active things that can be done in the process to make convicted defendants better candidates for these prisons.[55]

X. WHEN ALL ELSE FAILS — THE PRESIDENTIAL PARDON

The Constitution provides: "The President . . . shall have Power to grant Reprieves and Pardons for Offenses against the United States, except in cases of Impeachment."[56] This power includes the power to pardon for a convicted crime and to pardon prospectively for a crime that has been or might be charged.[57] This power also includes the prospective commutation of a sentence not yet served,[58] although more frequently pardons as to convicted crimes come after the sentence has been served. This power is often not consciously considered in the process of representing a person alleged to have offended the tax system or convicted of having done so. I suspect that this is principally because most tax persons in the prosecutors' sights do not present the type of factors that would offer a reasonable prospect for a presidential pardon.

Since the President's power to pardon is plenary and not subject to review (except in the proverbial court of public opinion where there is no power to reverse), there is no roadmap to the factors that the President considers in determining whether to pardon. However, history has shown that there can be any number of factors — including mercy and politics — that move the process.[59]

---

[55] Alan Ellis is a leading practitioner in this niche area of the law of sentencing and post-conviction law and has written extensively on this subject. You can find useful resources, including key guidebooks, in this area at his website: http://www.alanellis.com/.

[56] Art. II, § 2, cl 1.

[57] The quintessential example of the prospective pardon for crimes not yet charged was the pardon granted to former President Nixon by then President Ford after President Nixon resigned, thus making Ford the President. In the tax universe, the quintessential example of a pardon for crimes charged but not tried was the pardon President Clinton granted to the elusive fugitive billionaire Marc Rich.

[58] Margaret Colgate Love, *Reviving the Benign Prerogative of Pardoning*, 32 ABA LITIGATION 25, 26 (Winter 2006); Samuel T. Morison, *The Politics of Grace: On the Moral Justification of Executive Clemency*, 9 BUFF. L. REV. 1, 32 n.63 (2005). The commutation of uncompleted sentences is akin to the parole process; indeed, "[p]arole grew out of pardon, though it never entirely replaced it." Love, *supra*, at 27. However, parole has been abolished in the federal system. Thus, this safety valve complement to the pardon power is no longer present. As a result of its absence, one would have thought that the number of pardons would increase, but it has not.

> Even the defenders of the pardon power appear willing to concede that it is often beyond the effective reach of rational moral justification, and attempt to fend off the critics by arguing that clemency decisions do not, after all, require any such justification. As one sympathetic commentator recently put it, the president has a duty to pardon, not just where moral desert has been established in a particular case, but also as a more general obligation of office. This latter aspect of the duty to pardon is neither grounded in nor limited by considerations of law and morality, but is essentially one of politics.

[59] Samuel T. Morison, *The Politics of Grace: On the Moral Justification of Executive Clemency*, 9

Recent Presidents have used their pardon powers sparingly, albeit with some dramatic instances of conferring the pardon where some suggestion of favoritism unrelated to traditional pardoning rationales were involved.[60] Presidents do not pardon all sinners against society's criminal norms, but they do pardon some. Ordinary tax sinners may have a great deal of difficulty getting the sponsorship or stroke required for a pardon. Still it may be a shot. So at least consider it.

PROBLEM

Alan is a partner with a large accounting firm. Alan was involved in his firm's tax shelter initiatives. Alan and several other partners from his firm were indicted for three of its tax shelters with the following acronyms (as was common in this era of tax shelters): MAGIC, CRAP, and WET. All of these shelters produced alleged tax benefits through a perceived loophole in the tax code deploying complex entity structures that were mostly paper and that affected no appreciable change in a taxpayer's wealth or risk, except to the extent of the fees paid to various lawyers, accountants, banks, and other intermediaries to effect the structures. The tax shelters were illegal, and after a grand jury investigation, the prosecutors believe that they can prove illegality beyond a reasonable doubt. The claimed tax underpaid from the charged conduct is $800 million, which is far above the highest possible Guideline Base Offense of 36, applying when the tax loss exceeds $400 million. In planning with respect to the scope of the indictment, the prosecution estimated that its case-in-chief would take three months.

In the grand jury investigation prior to indictment, the prosecution team identified another tax shelter that these defendants marketed. This one, WILD, is of equal complexity but exploited an unrelated perceived loophole of the Code. The prosecution believed that WILD was also illegal. The prosecution estimated that, if WILD were charged in the indictment, an additional month would be added to the Government's case-in-chief. Furthermore, the prosecution was less certain that criminal conduct could be proved beyond a reasonable doubt. Moreover, since the Sentencing Guidelines' maximum Base Offense Level is reached over $400 million, adding the shelter to the indictment would not achieve a greater Guidelines sentence even if conviction were obtained.

1. You are the DOJ attorney assigned to handle this case. What do you perceive to be the advantages and disadvantages of including WILD-related criminal tax charges in the indictment? Would you decide to include them in or exclude them from the indictment?

2. You are still the prosecutor. Assume that you decide to omit the WILD-

---

BUFF. L. REV. 1, 3 (2005) (quotation marks and footnotes omitted).

[60] An example is the commutation of I. Lewis Libby's sentence for perjury. Libby was the chief aide to Vice President Chaney who shaded the truth in a special prosecutor investigation of a leak that cast doubt on the White House's claimed basis for entering the Iraq War. Libby was prosecuted, convicted, and sentenced to 30 months for perjury. President Bush, a parsimonious user of the pardon power, commuted Libby's incarceration to zero months. President Clinton, a more frequent user of the pardon power, closed out his administration with some pardons, including a pardon for Marc Rich who was charged with a tax crime and fled the country rather than face the music. In both instances (Libby and Rich), many found disingenuous the Presidents' articulated bases for exercising the pardon power.

related charges from the indictment. Could you nonetheless attempt to use Alan's WILD activities in some other fashion in order to advance the goal of convicting Alan with respect to the other charged tax shelters?

3. Switch roles. You now are Alan's defense counsel. The prosecution has omitted the WILD activities from the indictment. However, thinking along the lines of Question 2 above, you plan a strategy to attempt to defeat any effort by the prosecution to use Alan's WILD activities to increase the chance of conviction as to the shelters that were charged. What could you do to attempt to exclude WILD-related evidence or to mitigate the harm of its admission?

4. If the indictment does not include the WILD shelter, what factor, if any, could the WILD shelter play in sentencing?

Chapter 10

SENTENCING IN TAX CASES

United States Sentencing Guidelines §§ 2T1.1, 2T4.1, 3E1.1, 5C1.1, 5E1.2

I. INTRODUCTION

Sentencing issues are arguably the most important part of a federal criminal tax case. When clients learn they are under criminal investigation, the first questions are often: "How long will I have to spend in jail?" "Can I avoid jail altogether?" In addition, since the vast majority of all indicted defendants plead guilty, sentencing issues are often the only issues in a criminal tax case. Thus, it is essential that you become proficient with the applicable sentencing rules and procedures. This will require you to have a detailed knowledge of the United States Sentencing Guidelines. The Guidelines, although only advisory after the Supreme Court's decision in *United States v. Booker*,[1] are nevertheless the mandatory staring point in every sentencing proceeding. Section II of this chapter will provide an overview of the United States Sentencing Guidelines and the general rules applicable in all federal criminal cases. Section III will discuss the procedural aspects of sentencing. Section IV contains the history of the Sentencing Guidelines from their adoption, to their semi-demise at the hands of the Court in *Booker*, and the Court's post-*Booker* case law. Finally, Section V will discuss the Sentencing Guideline provisions specifically applicable in tax cases.

II. OVERVIEW OF THE SENTENCING GUIDELINES

A. In General

The United States Sentencing Guidelines[2] were the result of a joint effort by Congress (in the Sentencing Reform Act of 1984)[3] and the United States Sentencing Commission to provide more certainty and less disparity in federal sentences. In developing the Guidelines, the Commission studied the sentences imposed in 10,000 actual cases and attempted to follow what was "typical past practice," and imposed sentencing ranges that were the average of these prior sentences.[4] Using a detailed set of rules, tables, and adjustments that look at the

---

[1] 543 U.S. 220 (2005).

[2] 18 U.S.C. sections 3551–3568 & 28 U.S.C. sections 991–998.

[3] Title II of the Comprehensive Crime Control Act of 1984, Pub. L. 98-473, section 217(a), 98 Stat. 1837, 2017-34.

[4] Stephen Breyer, *The Federal Sentencing Guidelines and the Key Compromises upon Which They*

entire conduct of a convicted defendant, the Guidelines produce a numerical score or "offense level," which then translates into a range of months of imprisonment. As the Sentencing Table from the Guidelines in Exhibit 10.1 illustrates, the higher the offense level, the longer the defendant's sentence will be. For example, an offense level of 10, would result in a sentence of between six and 12 months, while an offense level of 13 would result in a sentence of twice that length. Thus, the goal of a defendant in any plea negotiations or sentencing proceeding is to obtain the lowest offense level possible.[5]

The Sentencing Reform Act of 1984 established the parameters for the Guidelines and dramatically changed how sentences for federal crimes were determined. Prior to the Act, an enormous amount of discretion was given to sentencing judges for federal crimes, with the judges limited only by statutory maximums. The Act transferred the power that had been exercised by the sentencing judge and the Parole Commission to the United States Sentencing Commission, and it directed the Sentencing Commission to promulgate Guidelines to be used for sentencing. The Act also made all sentences basically determinate or fixed. Thus, unlike the prior sentencing regime in which a prisoner would be released under the Act only after serving only a portion of his or her sentence, a prisoner will be released at the completion of the full sentence, reduced only by any credit earned by good behavior while in custody.[6] Finally, the Act made the Sentencing Commission's Guidelines binding on the courts,[7] although it preserved for the judge the discretion to depart from the guideline in certain, limited circumstances.[8]

The Sentencing Commission issued its first set of Sentencing Guidelines in 1987. The Commission has the authority to submit guideline amendments each year to Congress, and the Commission has amended the Guidelines regularly since their initial promulgation. The new amendments take effect on November 1st of that year. In order to calculate the offense level and appropriate guideline range, the Guidelines require that the determinations regarding the base offense, specific offense characteristic, adjustments and enhancements be made.[9]

Rest, 17 Hofstra L. Rev. 1, 7–8 (1988). However, in certain cases, like white collar crime cases, the Commission increased the severity of sentences imposed over prior practice. Indeed, under pre-guidelines practice, roughly half of all tax defendants were sentenced to probation without imprisonment. The tax Guidelines drastically curtailed the number of pure probationary sentences.

[5] Conversely, the goal of the Government is often to obtain the highest offense level. However, the Government may trade a lower offense level than it might otherwise get in exchange for a guilty plea.

[6] 18 U.S.C. section 3624(a) and (b).

[7] The Supreme Court's decision in Booker held that the portion of the Act making the guidelines mandatory and binding was unconstitutional.

[8] 18 U.S.C. section 3553(a), (b), and (c).

[9] U.S.S.G. section 1B1.1.

Ex. 10.1

SENTENCING TABLE
(in months of imprisonment)

	Offense Level	Criminal History Category (Criminal History Points) I (0 or 1)	II (2 or 3)	III (4, 5, 6)	IV (7, 8, 9)	V (10, 11, 12)	VI (13 or more)
	1	0-6	0-6	0-6	0-6	0-6	0-6
	2	0-6	0-6	0-6	0-6	0-6	1-7
	3	0-6	0-6	0-6	0-6	2-8	3-9
	4	0-6	0-6	0-6	2-8	4-10	6-12
Zone A	5	0-6	0-6	1-7	4-10	6-12	9-15
	6	0-6	1-7	2-8	6-12	9-15	12-18
	7	0-6	2-8	4-10	8-14	12-18	15-21
	8	0-6	4-10	6-12	10-16	15-21	18-24
	9	4-10	6-12	8-14	12-18	18-24	21-27
Zone B	10	6-12	8-14	10-16	15-21	21-27	24-30
	11	8-14	10-16	12-18	18-24	24-30	27-33
Zone C	12	10-16	12-18	15-21	21-27	27-33	30-37
	13	12-18	15-21	18-24	24-30	30-37	33-41
	14	15-21	18-24	21-27	27-33	33-41	37-46
	15	18-24	21-27	24-30	30-37	37-46	41-51
	16	21-27	24-30	27-33	33-41	41-51	46-57
	17	24-30	27-33	30-37	37-46	46-57	51-63
	18	27-33	30-37	33-41	41-51	51-63	57-71
	19	30-37	33-41	37-46	46-57	57-71	63-78
	20	33-41	37-46	41-51	51-63	63-78	70-87
	21	37-46	41-51	46-57	57-71	70-87	77-96
	22	41-51	46-57	51-63	63-78	77-96	84-105
	23	46-57	51-63	57-71	70-87	84-105	92-115
	24	51-63	57-71	63-78	77-96	92-115	100-125
	25	57-71	63-78	70-87	84-105	100-125	110-137
	26	63-78	70-87	78-97	92-115	110-137	120-150
	27	70-87	78-97	87-108	100-125	120-150	130-162
Zone D	28	78-97	87-108	97-121	110-137	130-162	140-175
	29	87-108	97-121	108-135	121-151	140-175	151-188
	30	97-121	108-135	121-151	135-168	151-188	168-210
	31	108-135	121-151	135-168	151-188	168-210	188-235
	32	121-151	135-168	151-188	168-210	188-235	210-262
	33	135-168	151-188	168-210	188-235	210-262	235-293
	34	151-188	168-210	188-235	210-262	235-293	262-327
	35	168-210	188-235	210-262	235-293	262-327	292-365
	36	188-235	210-262	235-293	262-327	292-365	324-405
	37	210-262	235-293	262-327	292-365	324-405	360-life
	38	235-293	262-327	292-365	324-405	360-life	360-life
	39	262-327	292-365	324-405	360-life	360-life	360-life
	40	292-365	324-405	360-life	360-life	360-life	360-life
	41	324-405	360-life	360-life	360-life	360-life	360-life
	42	360-life	360-life	360-life	360-life	360-life	360-life
	43	life	life	life	life	life	life

-395- November 1, 2013

Each of the Guidelines sections are divided into the actual guideline provisions themselves and the commentary. The commentary includes notes, background statements, definitions, and policy statements. Often, the commentary section of the Guidelines is more illuminating than the Guidelines themselves. The officially-published versions of the Guidelines manual also contains all of the "legislative history" surrounding adoption of each of the amendments as well as the prior versions of each section of the Guidelines.

Since the Guidelines are amended each year, a common issue is, which version of the Guidelines should be used, the version of the Guidelines in effect when the crime was committed or the version in effect at the time of sentencing? Section 1B1.11(a) of the Guidelines requires that a court "[use] the Guidelines [Manual] in effect on the date [that the defendant is sentenced]."[10] However, if the court determines that using that version of the Guidelines would violate the *Ex Post Facto* Clause,[11] the court "shall use the Guidelines Manual in effect on the date that the offense was committed."[12] Thus, if the sentencing guideline in effect at the time the offense was committed is more favorable to the defendant than the guideline in effect at the time of sentencing, the court must apply the more favorable guideline. Generally, for *ex post facto* purposes, the completion date of the offense controls the version of the Sentencing Guidelines to be applied.[13] In *Peugh v. United States*,[14] the Supreme Court held that the *Ex Post Facto* Clause is violated when the Guidelines in effect at the time of sentencing call for a greater punishment than when the crimes were completed. Section 1B1.11 also establishes the "one book" rule, which provides that the "Guidelines Manual in effect on a particular date shall be applied in its entirety."[15] A court cannot pick and choose selected provisions of various versions of the Guidelines.

Another of the unique aspects of the Sentencing Guidelines is the concept of "relevant conduct." Under the Guidelines, a defendant is sentenced for the total harm caused by his or her actions, not just for the crimes for which the defendant was actually convicted. This is achieved by allowing the sentencing judge to consider all relevant conduct of the defendant. Under § 1B1.3, "relevant conduct" includes not only the conduct for which the defendant was convicted, but also uncharged conduct, actions that took place beyond the applicable statute of limitations, actions for which the defendant was actually acquitted, and even the conduct of other people, as long as that conduct was both in furtherance of, and reasonably foreseeable in connection with, the criminal activity jointly undertaken by the defendant.[16]

B. Base Offense Level and Specific Offense Characteristics

In calculating the guideline's sentence, one must first select the applicable offense guideline section from Chapter 2 of the Guidelines corresponding to the crime committed. Chapter 2 is organized by the types of crimes, with specific subchapters dedicated to broad classes of crimes. For example, drug offenses are in subchapter 2D, firearm offenses are in subchapter 2K, and espionage offenses are in subchapter 2M. The offense Guidelines generally applicable to tax crimes

---

[10] United States v. Fitzgerald, 232 F.3d 315, 318 (2d Cir. 2000).

[11] U.S. Const. art. I, section 9, cl. 3.

[12] U.S.S.G. section 1B1.11(b)(1).

[13] U.S.S.G. section 1B1.11, cmt. n.2.

[14] 133 S. Ct. 2072 (2013).

[15] *See* U.S.S.G. section 1B1.11(b)(2).

[16] U.S.S.G. section 1B1.3.

are in subchapter 2T. Once the applicable Guidelines provision is selected, the "base offense level" must be calculated. As discussed below, in tax cases, the offense level is generally determined by the amount of tax attempted to be evaded.

In addition, the any appropriate "specific offense characteristics" contained in the particular guideline section must be applied. Each Guidelines provision outlines certain conduct that the Sentencing Commission believed made the conduct worse than the usual crime. If the defendant's conduct falls within these offense characteristics, the base offense level is increased by the points corresponding to the particular characteristic. In tax cases, for example, the base offense level is increased by two points if the defendant failed to report income exceeding $10,000 from a criminal activity in any year.[17] We will discuss the specific offense characteristics applicable in tax cases later in this chapter.

C. Adjustments to the Offense Level

After the offense level corresponding to the specific crime has been calculated, other adjustments applicable to all offenses, which are set forth in Chapter 3 of the Guidelines, must be applied. First, the sentencing level may be enhanced 2 levels for obstruction of justice.[18] The obstruction must have occurred during the investigation, prosecution or sentencing. Examples of conduct that would warrant an adjustment for obstruction include: threatening, intimidating, or otherwise unlawfully influencing a co-defendant, witness, or juror; committing, suborning, or attempting to suborn perjury; producing or attempting to produce a false, altered, or counterfeit document or record; and destroying or concealing or directing or procuring another person to destroy or conceal evidence that is material to an official investigation.[19] While conduct such as this normally results in an obstruction enhancement, courts may refuse to apply the enhancement if they think that the conduct was essential to one of the counts of conviction, and increasing the sentence would be double-counting. For example, there are two obstruction offenses frequently employed in tax cases — 7212(a) and *Klein* conspiracy — which necessarily involve conduct that might be viewed as obstructive. It would generally be inappropriate to sentence the defendant for the crime of conviction and increase the offense level for obstruction of justice. However, the court might still impose an obstruction of justice enhancement if the court finds the defendant lied on the stand, including asserting a defense that was false.[20]

Another potential upward adjustment is found in section 3B1.1(a), which provides for a four level enhancement "if the defendant was an organizer or leader of a criminal activity that involved five or more participants or was otherwise

---

[17] U.S.S.G. section 2T1.1, cmt. n.3.

[18] U.S.S.G. section 3C1.1.

[19] U.S.S.G. 3C1.1, cmt. n. 4. Wesley Snipes received a two-level enhancement for obstruction because he instructed an employee not to respond to a grand jury subpoena. United States v. Snipes, 611 F.3d 855, 871 (11th Cir. 2010), *cert. denied*, 131 S. Ct. 2962 (2011).

[20] *See* United States v. Holmes, 406 F.3d 337, 365–66 (5th Cir.), *cert. denied*, 546 U.S. 871 (2005).

extensive."[21] Many tax crimes are "loner" crimes with only one or two persons at most involved. However, tax preparers who violate section 7206(2) or 18 U.S.C. sections 286 and 287 may receive this enhancement if they have at least one knowing participant and prepare many returns which are deemed equivalent to at least five knowing participants.

The most important downward adjustment involves "acceptance of responsibility." Overwhelmingly, tax indictments are resolved by plea rather than trial. One of the principal factors encouraging a defendant to plead guilty is the two- or three-level downward adjustment resulting from acceptance of responsibility.[22] The adjustment is two levels if the offense level prior to adjustment is below 16, and the adjustment is three levels if the level is 16 or greater and "upon motion of the government stating that the defendant has assisted authorities in the investigation or prosecution of his own misconduct by timely notifying authorities of his intention to enter a plea of guilty, thereby permitting the government to avoid preparing for trial and permitting the government and the court to allocate their resources efficiently."[23] In tax cases, this adjustment is generally achieved by a plea agreement and acceptance of responsibility sufficiently before the trial date that the Government avoids expending significant resources.

D. Calculating the Sentence

The calculation of the offense level is only one half of the equation. As you can see from Ex. 10.1, the length of a defendant's sentence depends on the offense level (the vertical axis) and the defendant's criminal history (the horizontal axis). Thus, the defendant's criminal history category must be determined under Chapter Four of the Guidelines. The more prior convictions defendants have, the higher their criminal history category. For most defendants in tax cases, the count of conviction is their first offense, and their criminal history category will therefore be 1.

Now that the final offense level and the criminal history categories have been calculated, the actual sentence from the Sentencing Table can finally be determined. The guideline calculation will result in a range of months of imprisonment. The Sentencing Table (Ex. 10.1) is divided into four zones, Zone A through Zone D. These zones limit the discretion of the sentencing judge in imposing a sentence other than a sentence of imprisonment. If the applicable guideline range is in Zone A, a sentence of imprisonment is not required, and any or all of the sentence could be served on supervised release or some form of alternative confinement.[24] Obviously, getting a defendant into Zone A via a plea agreement or otherwise is ideal for the defendant. If the applicable guideline range is in Zone B, the sentencing term may be satisfied by a sentence of imprisonment or alternative confinement, as long as one month of the sentence is satisfied by

---

[21] U.S.S.G. section 3B1.1(a).

[22] U.S.S.G. section 3E1.1.

[23] *Id.*

[24] The guidelines list intermittent confinement, community confinement, and home detention as alternatives to normal confinement in prison. *See* U.S.S.G. section 5C1.1.

imprisonment.[25] If the guideline range is in Zone C, at least one-half of the minimum term must be satisfied by imprisonment, and if the range is in Zone D, all of the sentence must be satisfied by imprisonment.[26]

The judge must also impose other parts of the defendant's sentence, including fines and restitution, as set forth in Chapter Five of the Guidelines. As discussed throughout this book, the various criminal statutes provide maximum fines in addition to maximum incarceration periods. 18 U.S.C. section 3571 overrides these mandatory sentences by providing higher potential fines, including a fine of $250,000 in the case of an individual convicted of a felony and $500,000 fine in the case of an organization.[27] Compare IRC section 7201, which has a maximum fine for individuals of $100,000. The Guidelines then set forth the rules for imposing the fines up to the maximum allowed. Section 5E1.2 of the Guidelines provides a table, similar in methodology to the sentencing table, to determine the range of appropriate fines.

The Guidelines also permit the judge, in certain cases, to order restitution. Restitution is designed to reimburse the victim of the crime. Restitution is generally only allowed where it is provided for by statute and, where restitution is authorized, it takes priority over fines.[28] Restitution to the victim of the offense of conviction may be imposed by the court pursuant to two overlapping provisions, the general restitution provision[29] and the Mandatory Victim Restitution Act.[30] These provisions allow restitution to the victim in convictions under Title 18 and certain specified offenses, all of which are nontax offenses. Restitution is thus not statutorily-authorized for a pure tax offense of conviction (i.e., a conviction only for a Title 26 offense).[31] This is not an anomaly — in tax cases the victim is the United States and the harm is the tax not paid. The Government possesses extensive procedures for determining and collecting taxes independent of the criminal justice system. As noted in Chapter 13, the IRS will normally employ these procedures after the criminal case is concluded.

Although the statute does not permit restitution in tax cases, the court may order restitution if the parties agree to it.[32] While the underlying tax liability is not normally addressed in the criminal phase of a case, the civil tax liability may on occasion be addressed in the plea agreement.[33] The plea agreement is a contract, and the sentencing court may include an agreement reached as to restitution in the

---

[25] The sentencing judge can, of course, impose a sentence of imprisonment for the entire guideline range.

[26] U.S.S.G. section 5C1.1.

[27] 18 U.S.C. section 3571.

[28] 18 U.S.C. section 3572(b); U.S.S.G. section 5E1.1.

[29] 18 U.S.C. section 3663.

[30] 18 U.S.C. section 3663A.

[31] *See* United States v. Stout, 32 F.3d 901, 904–5 (5th Cir. 1994).

[32] *See* 18 U.S.C. section 3663(a)(3). In cases where the taxpayer is the defendant, DOJ Tax practice is now, at least generally, to require a plea agreement contractual provision for restitution for the tax loss number agreed to for sentencing.

[33] Prudence may dictate that the civil tax liability be resolved and paid prior to sentencing, if possible,

sentence imposed.[34] In addition, the court may impose restitution as a condition of some benefit that it is giving the defendant, such as supervised release.[35] In this case, if the defendant wants the benefit (supervised release), he or she must accept the cost of the benefit (restitution).[36]

In addition, as discussed in Chapter 3, other crimes are often charged with tax crimes and may be inseparable from the tax crimes. Some of these non-Title 26 crimes, for example conspiracy under 18 U.S.C. section 371, do permit restitution. Given the Government's ability to collect taxes in any event, is the Government likely to tack on a Title 18 charge just to get restitution? For the taxpayer-defendant, the obligation of restitution for the tax evaded is arguably unnecessary, given the IRS's civil tax authority, and the sentence imposed often just ignores restitution or states generally that the taxpayer will pay the tax determined ultimately to be due. For defendants other than the "taxpayer," however, an order of restitution might be imposed. In the case of conspiracy, persons other than the taxpayer, for example, preparers or advisors, may be convicted of the conspiracy. In these cases, particularly where the Government is for some reason unable to collect from the taxpayer, the Government may seek an order of restitution.

E. Departures

The Guidelines, at least until the *Booker* decision,[37] were binding on the sentencing court, and the court had limited authority to impose a sentence outside the parameters of the applicable Guidelines range. The discretion recognized by the Commission to deviate from the Guidelines is known as a departure, and the departure rules are contained in subparagraph 5K. A sentencing judge may depart upward from the Guidelines' range if certain aggravating factors are present,[38] and the judge may depart downward if certain mitigating factors are present.[39] The sentencing court may also depart downward if the defendant has provided "substantial assistance" in the investigation or prosecution of another person who has committed an offense.[40] The substantial assistance departure is different from the adjustment for acceptance of responsibility discussed above, where the

---

in order to strengthen the argument that the defendant qualifies for the acceptance of responsibility downward adjustment.

[34] *See e.g.*, United States v. Miller, 406 F.3d 323, 330 (5th Cir.), *cert. denied*, 546 U.S. 929 (2005).

[35] *See* 18 U.S.C. § 3583(d). Supervised release is the Guidelines-era equivalent of parole. To get an idea of the conditions that may be imposed with respect to supervised release, see Appendix F (the judgment in the *Snipes* case).

[36] Congress amended the Internal Revenue Code in 2010, to make the amount ordered for restitution of tax immediately assessable and collectible without the usual predicate notice of deficiency. § 3(a) of the Firearms Excise Tax Improvement Act of 2010, Pub. L. 111-237, 124 Stat. 2497, effective for restitution orders entered after August 16, 2010. The IRS is required to assess the restitution amount once the criminal judgment becomes final. A notice of deficiency is not required as a predicate to assessment of the restitution amount. The defendant/taxpayer may not thereafter contest civilly the tax restitution amount so assessed.

[37] *See* Booker, *supra* note 1.

[38] *See, e.g.*, U.S.S.G. sections 5K2.0 to 5K2.8.

[39] *See, e.g.*, U.S.S.G. sections 5K2.11 to 5K2.16.

[40] U.S.S.G. section 5K1.1.

sentencing judge looks at whether the defendant accepted full responsibility for his or her own conduct. The substantial assistance departure is for helping the Government convict someone else. In addition, a defendant is not required to affirmatively assist the Government in order to qualify for the acceptance of responsibility adjustment. Thus, the substantial assistance departure is thus designed to give the defendant an incentive to cooperate. While tax crimes often involve only one defendant, some crimes — such as the massive crimes involved in the abusive trust schemes — offer the players some opportunity to provide substantial assistance in delivering up others. In these cases, a target may be in a real position to take advantage of this basis for departure.

The Guidelines not only list grounds for departure, they also list certain factors that cannot be the basis of a departure. Section 5K2.0 provides that the judge may not base a departure on matters such as race, sex, national origin, creed, religion, and socio-economic status; any circumstance that is specifically prohibited as a ground for departure, such as drug or alcohol dependence; or any ground that has already taken into account under another portion of the Guidelines, such as the defendant's acceptance of responsibility.

If defense counsel contemplates requesting the sentencing court to make a downward departure, it is important to first convince the prosecutor regarding the departure. Obviously, if the prosecutor objects to the downward departure, the sentencing court will be less likely to grant the departure. If, however, the prosecutor signals the sentencing court that the Government will not object to a downward departure, the court will have much more latitude for a downward departure because, with that signal, the court knows that the Government will not appeal a downward departure.

III. PROCEDURES FOR SENTENCING

A. Overview

Prior to sentencing, the defendant's probation officer must conduct an interview of the defendant and prepare a Presentence Report ("PSR").[41] In the PSR, the probation officer will calculate the defendant's offense level and criminal history category; state the resulting sentencing range and kinds of sentences available; identify any factors relevant to kind of sentence (*e.g.*, probation, imprisonment); recommend a sentence within the applicable sentencing range; and identify any basis for departing from the applicable sentencing range.[42] The PSR must also contain the defendant's prior criminal record (if any), the defendant's financial condition, and if the crime for which the defendant was convicted provides for restitution, information sufficient to calculate a restitution order.[43]

The defendant is entitled to be represented by counsel at the interview with probation officer, and it is imperative that counsel take advantage of that right and

---

[41] *See* U.S.S.G. section 6A1.1.

[42] Fed. R. Crim. P. 32(d).

[43] *Id.*

be present at the interview. The PSR will be the starting point at the sentencing hearing, and judges give deference to the recommendations of the probation officer. Not only is the PSR instrumental in the sentencing judge's determination, it will also follow the defendant throughout his or her time in prison and could well affect the defendant's life in prison and during any period of probation or supervised release. After the probation officer has completed the PSR, the report must be disclosed to the defendant, the defendant's attorney, and the prosecutor at least 35 days prior to the sentencing date. The parties then have an opportunity to make any objections to the PSR.

B. The Sentencing Hearing — Proof Issues

The actual sentence imposed by the judge is pronounced after a sentencing hearing. At the sentencing hearing, both the defense and the prosecution will have an opportunity to make any formal objections to the PSR, present additional evidence and witness testimony, and make arguments. The Federal Rules of Evidence do not apply to the admission of testimony or other evidence, as long as "the information has sufficient indicia of reliability to support its probable accuracy."[44]

The judge resolves factual issues relevant to sentencing under a "preponderance of the evidence" standard, not the "beyond a reasonable doubt" standard that applied in determining guilt at trial.[45] Notwithstanding this general rule as to a preponderance burden of proof, the 9th Circuit requires that the sentencing proof be "clear and convincing" as to sentencing factors that have a "disproportionate impact" on the length of the sentence.[46] This requirement is designed to ensure that that criminal defendants receive adequate due process and to ensure that legislatures "cannot evade [the constitutionally required standard of proof] by reclassifying an element of a crime as a sentencing factor."[47] The "totality of the circumstances" and, apparently a keen intuition, inform the sentencing court when this higher standard should apply, but the following are considered:

1. whether the enhanced sentence falls within the maximum sentence for the crime alleged in the indictment;
2. whether the enhanced sentence negates the presumption of innocence or the prosecution's burden of proof for the crime alleged in the indictment;
3. whether the facts offered in support of the enhancement create new offenses requiring separate punishment;
4. whether the increase in sentence is based on the extent of a conspiracy;
5. whether an increase in the number of offense levels is less than or equal to four; and
6. whether the length of the enhanced sentence more than doubles the length

---

[44] U.S.S.G. section 6A1.3(a); *see also* 18 U.S.C. section 3661; U.S.S.G. section 1B1.4.

[45] U.S.S.G. section 6A1.3, cmt.

[46] United States v. Treadwell, 593 F.3d 990, 1000 (9th Cir.), *cert. denied*, 131 S. Ct. 488 (2010).

[47] *Id.*

> of the sentence authorized by the initial sentencing guideline range in a case where the defendant would otherwise have received a relatively short sentence.

Further, the court may consider any evidence "without regard to its admissibility under the rules of evidence applicable at trial, provided that the information has sufficient indicia of reliability to support its probable accuracy."[48] Thus, for example, a sentencing court may consider "reliable hearsay evidence,"[49] as well as out-of-court declarations by an unidentified informant, "where there is good cause for the non-disclosure of the informant's identity and there is sufficient corroboration by other means."[50] The net result of these procedures is that a defendant's sentence can be based on evidence and things other than the crime of conviction.

IV. *UNITED STATES v. BOOKER*

The Sentencing Guidelines were first adopted in November 1987, and the constitutionality of the Guidelines was challenged almost immediately. That challenge quickly reached the United States Supreme Court, in *Mistretta v. United States*,[51] where the court examined whether the Guidelines and the Sentencing Commission that created them, violated separation of powers.

MISTRETTA v. UNITED STATES

Supreme Court of the United States
488 U.S. 361 (1989)

For almost a century, the Federal Government employed in criminal cases a system of indeterminate sentencing. Statutes specified the penalties for crimes but nearly always gave the sentencing judge wide discretion to decide whether the offender should be incarcerated and for how long, whether he should be fined and how much, and whether some lesser restraint, such as probation, should be imposed instead of imprisonment or fine. This indeterminate-sentencing system was supplemented by the utilization of parole, by which an offender was returned to society under the "guidance and control" of a parole officer.

Both indeterminate sentencing and parole were based on concepts of the offender's possible, indeed probable, rehabilitation, a view that it was realistic to attempt to rehabilitate the inmate and thereby to minimize the risk that he would resume criminal activity upon his return to society. It obviously required the judge and the parole officer to make their respective sentencing and release decisions upon their own assessments of the offender's amenability to rehabilitation. As a result, the court and the officer were in positions to exercise, and usually did exercise, very broad discretion. This led almost inevitably to the conclusion on the part of a reviewing court that the sentencing judge "sees more and senses more"

---

48 U.S.S.G. § 6A1.3(a).

49 U.S.S.G. § 6A1.3, cmt.

50 *Id.*

51 488 U.S. 361 (1989).

than the appellate court; thus, the judge enjoyed the "superiority of his nether position," for that court's determination as to what sentence was appropriate met with virtually unconditional deference on appeal.

Historically, federal sentencing — the function of determining the scope and extent of punishment — never has been thought to be assigned by the Constitution to the exclusive jurisdiction of any one of the three Branches of Government. Congress, of course, has the power to fix the sentence for a federal crime, and the scope of judicial discretion with respect to a sentence is subject to congressional control. Congress early abandoned fixed-sentence rigidity, however, and put in place a system of ranges within which the sentencer could choose the precise punishment. Congress delegated almost unfettered discretion to the sentencing judge to determine what the sentence should be within the customarily wide range so selected. This broad discretion was further enhanced by the power later granted the judge to suspend the sentence and by the resulting growth of an elaborate probation system. Also, with the advent of parole, Congress moved toward a "three-way sharing" of sentencing responsibility by granting corrections personnel in the Executive Branch the discretion to release a prisoner before the expiration of the sentence imposed by the judge. Thus, under the indeterminate-sentence system, Congress defined the maximum, the judge imposed a sentence within the statutory range (which he usually could replace with probation), and the Executive Branch's parole official eventually determined the actual duration of imprisonment.

Serious disparities in sentences, however, were common. Rehabilitation as a sound penological theory came to be questioned and, in any event, was regarded by some as an unattainable goal for most cases.

The Act, as adopted, revises the old sentencing process in several ways:

1. It rejects imprisonment as a means of promoting rehabilitation, 28 U.S.C. § 994(k), and it states that punishment should serve retributive, educational, deterrent, and incapacitative goals, 18 U.S.C. § 3553(a)(2).
2. It consolidates the power that had been exercised by the sentencing judge and the Parole Commission to decide what punishment an offender should suffer. This is done by creating the United States Sentencing Commission, directing that Commission to devise Guidelines to be used for sentencing, and prospectively abolishing the Parole Commission. 28 U.S.C. §§ 991, 994, and 995(a)(1).
3. It makes all sentences basically determinate. A prisoner is to be released at the completion of his sentence reduced only by any credit earned by good behavior while in custody. 18 U.S.C. §§ 3624(a) and (b).
4. It makes the Sentencing Commission's Guidelines binding on the courts, although it preserves for the judge the discretion to depart from the guideline applicable to a particular case if the judge finds an aggravating or mitigating factor present that the Commission did not adequately consider when formulating Guidelines. §§ 3553(a) and (b). The Act also requires the court to state its reasons for the sentence imposed and to give "the specific reason" for imposing a sentence different from that described in the guideline. § 3553(c).

5. It authorizes limited appellate review of the sentence. It permits a defendant to appeal a sentence that is above the defined range, and it permits the Government to appeal a sentence that is below that range. It also permits either side to appeal an incorrect application of the guideline. §§ 3742(a) and (b).

The Commission is established "as an independent commission in the judicial branch of the United States." § 991(a). It has seven voting members (one of whom is the Chairman) appointed by the President "by and with the advice and consent of the Senate." "At least three of the members shall be Federal judges selected after considering a list of six judges recommended to the President by the Judicial Conference of the United States." *Ibid.* No more than four members of the Commission shall be members of the same political party. The Attorney General, or his designee, is an ex officio non-voting member. The Chairman and other members of the Commission are subject to removal by the President "only for neglect of duty or malfeasance in office or for other good cause shown." *Ibid.* Except for initial staggering of terms, a voting member serves for six years and may not serve more than two full terms. §§ 992(a) and (b).

Petitioner argues that in delegating the power to promulgate sentencing Guidelines for every federal criminal offense to an independent Sentencing Commission, Congress has granted the Commission excessive legislative discretion in violation of the constitutionally based nondelegation doctrine. We do not agree.

The nondelegation doctrine is rooted in the principle of separation of powers that underlies our tripartite system of Government. We also have recognized, however, that the separation-of-powers principle, and the nondelegation doctrine in particular, do not prevent Congress from obtaining the assistance of its coordinate Branches. In a passage now enshrined in our jurisprudence, Chief Justice Taft, writing for the Court, explained our approach to such cooperative ventures: "In determining what [Congress] may do in seeking assistance from another branch, the extent and character of that assistance must be fixed according to common sense and the inherent necessities of the government co-ordination." *J.W. Hampton, Jr., & Co. v. United States*, 276 U.S. 394, 406 (1928). So long as Congress "shall lay down by legislative act an intelligible principle to which the person or body authorized to [exercise the delegated authority] is directed to conform, such legislative action is not a forbidden delegation of legislative power." *Id.*

Applying this "intelligible principle" test to congressional delegations, our jurisprudence has been driven by a practical understanding that in our increasingly complex society, replete with ever changing and more technical problems, Congress simply cannot do its job absent an ability to delegate power under broad general directives.

In light of our approval of these broad delegations, we harbor no doubt that Congress' delegation of authority to the Sentencing Commission is sufficiently specific and detailed to meet constitutional requirements. Congress charged the Commission with three goals: to "assure the meeting of the purposes of sentencing as set forth" in the Act; to "provide certainty and fairness in meeting the purposes of sentencing, avoiding unwarranted sentencing disparities among defendants with similar records . . . while maintaining sufficient flexibility to permit individualized sentences," where appropriate; and to "reflect, to the extent practicable, advancement in knowledge of human behavior as it relates to the criminal justice process." 28 U.S.C. § 991(b)(1). Congress further specified four "purposes" of sentencing that the Commission must pursue in carrying out its mandate: "to reflect the seriousness of the offense, to promote respect for the law, and to provide just punishment for the offense"; "to afford adequate deterrence to criminal conduct"; "to protect the public from further crimes of the defendant"; and "to provide the defendant with needed . . . correctional treatment." 18 U.S.C. § 3553(a)(2).

We cannot dispute petitioner's contention that the Commission enjoys significant discretion in formulating Guidelines. The Commission does have discretionary authority to determine the relative severity of federal crimes and to assess the relative weight of the offender characteristics that Congress listed for the Commission to consider. But our cases do not at all suggest that delegations of this type may not carry with them the need to exercise judgment on matters of policy. Developing proportionate penalties for hundreds of different crimes by a virtually limitless array of offenders is precisely the sort of intricate, labor-intensive task for which delegation to an expert body is especially appropriate.

With *Mistretta*, the constitutionality of the Guidelines, at least with regard to the nondelegation and separation of powers issues, was settled. However, more constitutional challenges were to come. These later, and more successful, challenges, examined the way in which offense levels were calculated by the sentencing judge. The constitutional challenge to the federal sentencing Guidelines was preceded by decisions involving state sentencing procedures. The two leading cases were *Apprendi v. New Jersey*[52] and *Blakely v. Washington*.[53] In these and other cases, defendants challenged the rules that allowed a sentencing judge to determine a sentence based on facts or evidence that was never presented to a jury. The Court held that these state regimes violated the Sixth Amendment right to trial by jury.

With these cases added to the defense bar's arsenal, a full frontal assault on the Guidelines was inevitable. The result was the Supreme Court's decision in *United States v. Booker*,[54] a multi-part decision with two majority opinions and four dissents, two of which were authored by the justices who decided one of the Court's majority opinions. The first part of the majority's decision dealt with the question of whether Guidelines provisions allowing the sentencing judge to base a sentence on conduct that was not found by the jury violates the Sixth Amendment right to a jury trial. The Court found that the Guidelines indeed were unconstitutional. The second part of the opinion, with a different majority of justices,[55] then dealt with the question of what the remedy should be, given the constitutional infirmity.

---

[52] 530 U.S. 466 (2000).

[53] *See* Blakely v. Washington, 542 U.S. 296 (2004).

[54] 543 U.S. 220 (2005).

[55] Only Justice Ginsburg joined both parts of the Court's opinion.

UNITED STATES v. BOOKER

Supreme Court of the United States
543 U.S. 220 (2005)

JUSTICE STEVENS delivered the opinion of the Court in part.

The question presented in each of these cases is whether an application of the Federal Sentencing Guidelines violated the Sixth Amendment. In each case, the courts below held that binding rules set forth in the Guidelines limited the severity of the sentence that the judge could lawfully impose on the defendant based on the facts found by the jury at his trial. In both cases the courts rejected, on the basis of our decision in *Blakely v. Washington* 542 U.S. 296 (2004), the Government's recommended application of the Sentencing Guidelines because the proposed sentences were based on additional facts that the sentencing judge found by a preponderance of the evidence. We hold that both courts correctly concluded that the Sixth Amendment as construed in *Blakely* does apply to the Sentencing Guidelines. In a separate opinion authored by Justice Breyer, the Court concludes that in light of this holding, two provisions of the Sentencing Reform Act of 1984 (SRA) that have the effect of making the Guidelines mandatory must be invalidated in order to allow the statute to operate in a manner consistent with congressional intent.

I

Respondent Booker was charged with possession with intent to distribute at least 50 grams of cocaine base (crack). Having heard evidence that he had 92.5 grams in his duffel bag, the jury found him guilty of violating 21 U.S.C. § 841(a)(1). That statute prescribes a minimum sentence of 10 years in prison and a maximum sentence of life for that offense. Based upon Booker's criminal history and the quantity of drugs found by the jury, the Sentencing Guidelines required the District Court Judge to select a "base" sentence of not less than 210 nor more than 262 months in prison. The judge, however, held a post-trial sentencing proceeding and concluded by a preponderance of the evidence that Booker had possessed an additional 566 grams of crack and that he was guilty of obstructing justice. Those findings mandated that the judge select a sentence between 360 months and life imprisonment; the judge imposed a sentence at the low end of the range. Thus, instead of the sentence of 21 years and 10 months that the judge could have imposed on the basis of the facts proved to the jury beyond a reasonable doubt, Booker received a 30-year sentence.

II

It has been settled throughout our history that the Constitution protects every criminal defendant "against conviction except upon proof beyond a reasonable doubt of every fact necessary to constitute the crime with which he is charged." *In re Winship*, 397 U.S. 358, 364 (1970). It is equally clear that the "Constitution gives a criminal defendant the right to demand that a jury find him guilty of all the elements of the crime with which he is charged." *United States v. Gaudin*, 515 U.S.

506, 511 (1995). These basic precepts, firmly rooted in the common law, have provided the basis for recent decisions interpreting modern criminal statutes and sentencing procedures.

In *Apprendi v. New Jersey*, 530 U.S. 466 (2000), the defendant pleaded guilty to second-degree possession of a firearm for an unlawful purpose, which carried a prison term of 5 to 10 years. Thereafter, the trial court found that his conduct had violated New Jersey's "hate crime" law because it was racially motivated, and imposed a 12-year sentence. This Court set aside the enhanced sentence. We held: "Other than the fact of a prior conviction, any fact that increases the penalty for a crime beyond the prescribed statutory maximum must be submitted to a jury, and proved beyond a reasonable doubt." *Id.*, at 490.

The fact that New Jersey labeled the hate crime a "sentence enhancement" rather than a separate criminal act was irrelevant for constitutional purposes. As a matter of simple justice, it seemed obvious that the procedural safeguards designed to protect Apprendi from punishment for the possession of a firearm should apply equally to his violation of the hate crime statute. Merely using the label "sentence enhancement" to describe the latter did not provide a principled basis for treating the two crimes differently.

In *Blakely v. Washington*, 542 U.S. 296 (2004), we dealt with a determinate sentencing scheme similar to the Federal Sentencing Guidelines. There the defendant pleaded guilty to kidnaping, a class B felony punishable by a term of not more than 10 years. Other provisions of Washington law, comparable to the Federal Sentencing Guidelines, mandated a "standard" sentence of 49-to-53 months, unless the judge found aggravating facts justifying an exceptional sentence. Although the prosecutor recommended a sentence in the standard range, the judge found that the defendant had acted with " 'deliberate cruelty' " and sentenced him to 90 months.

In *Ring v. Arizona*, 536 U.S. 584 (2002), we reaffirmed our conclusion that the characterization of critical facts is constitutionally irrelevant. There, we held that it was impermissible for "the trial judge, sitting alone" to determine the presence or absence of the aggravating factors required by Arizona law for imposition of the death penalty. "If a State makes an increase in a defendant's authorized punishment contingent on the finding of a fact, that fact — no matter how the State labels it — must be found by a jury beyond a reasonable doubt." *Id.*, at 602. Our opinion made it clear that ultimately, while the procedural error in Ring's case might have been harmless because the necessary finding was implicit in the jury's guilty verdict, "the characterization of a fact or circumstance as an 'element' or a 'sentencing factor' is not determinative of the question 'who decides,' judge or jury," *id.*, at 605.

As the dissenting opinions in *Blakely* recognized, there is no distinction of constitutional significance between the Federal Sentencing Guidelines and the Washington procedures at issue in that case. This conclusion rests on the premise, common to both systems, that the relevant sentencing rules are mandatory and impose binding requirements on all sentencing judges.

If the Guidelines as currently written could be read as merely advisory provisions that recommended, rather than required, the selection of particular sentences in response to differing sets of facts, their use would not implicate the Sixth Amendment. We have never doubted the authority of a judge to exercise broad discretion in imposing a sentence within a statutory range. Indeed, everyone agrees that the constitutional issues presented by these cases would have been avoided entirely if Congress had omitted from the SRA the provisions that make the Guidelines binding on district judges; it is that circumstance that makes the Court's answer to the second question presented possible. For when a trial judge exercises his discretion to select a specific sentence within a defined range, the defendant has no right to a jury determination of the facts that the judge deems relevant.

The Guidelines as written, however, are not advisory; they are mandatory and binding on all judges. While subsection (a) of § 3553 of the sentencing statute lists the Sentencing Guidelines as one factor to be considered in imposing a sentence, subsection (b) directs that the court "*shall* impose a sentence of the kind, and within the range" established by the Guidelines, subject to departures in specific, limited cases. Because they are binding on judges, we have consistently held that the Guidelines have the force and effect of laws.

All of the foregoing support our conclusion that our holding in *Blakely* applies to the Sentencing Guidelines. We recognize, as we did in *Jones*, *Apprendi*, and *Blakely*, that in some cases jury fact finding may impair the most expedient and efficient sentencing of defendants. But the interest in fairness and reliability protected by the right to a jury trial — a common-law right that defendants enjoyed for centuries and that is now enshrined in the Sixth Amendment — has always outweighed the interest in concluding trials swiftly. *Blakely*, 124 S. Ct., at 2542–43. As Blackstone put it:

> [H]owever *convenient* these [new methods of trial] may appear at first (as doubtless all arbitrary powers, well executed, are the most *convenient*) yet let it be again remembered, that delays, and little inconveniences in the forms of justice, are the price that all free nations must pay for their liberty in more substantial matters; that these inroads upon this sacred bulwark of the nation are fundamentally opposite to the spirit of our constitution; and that, though begun in trifles, the precedent may gradually increase and spread, to the utter disuse of juries in questions of the most momentous concerns.

4 Commentaries on the Laws of England 343–344 (1769).

Accordingly, we reaffirm our holding in *Apprendi:* Any fact (other than a prior conviction) which is necessary to support a sentence exceeding the maximum authorized by the facts established by a plea of guilty or a jury verdict must be admitted by the defendant or proved to a jury beyond a reasonable doubt.

[Authors' note: With this portion of the Court's decision, the Guidelines, as drafted, were found to be unconstitutional because the Guidelines permitted a sentencing judge to base a sentence on conduct that was not found by or even considered by the jury. What possible fix could remedy this constitutional defect? The Court could have invalidated the Guidelines altogether, it could have required that all facts affecting a sentence be decided by a jury, or it could have invalidated the relevant conduct provisions. However, the remedy ultimately crafted by a different majority of justices (referred to in the dissents as the "remedial majority") was to turn the mandatory Guidelines with the force and effect of law into merely *advisory* Guidelines.]

Justice Breyer delivered the opinion of the Court in the part.

We here turn to the second question presented, a question that concerns the remedy. We must decide whether or to what extent, "as a matter of severability analysis," the Guidelines "as a whole" are "inapplicable . . . such that the sentencing court must exercise its discretion to sentence the defendant within the maximum and minimum set by statute for the offense of conviction."

We answer the question of remedy by finding the provision of the federal sentencing statute that makes the Guidelines mandatory, 18 U.S.C.A. § 3553(b)(1), incompatible with today's constitutional holding. We conclude that this provision must be severed and excised, as must one other statutory section, § 3742(e), which depends upon the Guidelines' mandatory nature. So modified, the Federal Sentencing Act makes the Guidelines effectively advisory. It requires a sentencing court to consider Guidelines ranges, but it permits the court to tailor the sentence in light of other statutory concerns as well.

I

We answer the remedial question by looking to legislative intent. We seek to determine what "Congress would have intended" in light of the Court's constitutional holding. In this instance, we must determine which of the two following remedial approaches is the more compatible with the legislature's intent as embodied in the 1984 Sentencing Act.

One approach, that of Justice Stevens' dissent, would retain the Sentencing Act (and the Guidelines) as written, but would engraft onto the existing system today's Sixth Amendment "jury trial" requirement. The addition would change the Guidelines by preventing the sentencing court from increasing a sentence on the basis of a fact that the jury did not find (or that the offender did not admit).

The other approach, which we now adopt, would (through severance and excision of two provisions) make the Guidelines system advisory while maintaining a strong connection between the sentence imposed and the offender's real conduct — a connection important to the increased uniformity of sentencing that Congress intended its Guidelines system to achieve.

Both approaches would significantly alter the system that Congress designed. But today's constitutional holding means that it is no longer possible to maintain the judicial factfinding that Congress thought would underpin the mandatory Guidelines system that it sought to create and that Congress wrote into the Act in 18 U.S.C.A. §§ 3553(a) and 3661. Hence we must decide whether we would deviate less radically from Congress' intended system (1) by superimposing the constitutional requirement announced today or (2) through elimination of some provisions of the statute.

To say this is not to create a new kind of severability analysis. Rather, it is to recognize that sometimes severability questions (questions as to how, or whether, Congress would intend a statute to apply) can arise when a legislatively unforeseen constitutional problem requires modification of a statutory provision as applied in a significant number of instances.

In today's context — a highly complex statute, interrelated provisions, and a constitutional requirement that creates fundamental change — we cannot assume that Congress, if faced with the statute's invalidity in key applications, would have preferred to apply the statute in as many other instances as possible. Neither can we determine likely congressional intent mechanically. We cannot simply approach the problem grammatically, say, by looking to see whether the constitutional requirement and the words of the Act are linguistically compatible.

Nor do simple numbers provide an answer. It is, of course, true that the numbers show that the constitutional jury trial requirement would lead to additional decisionmaking by juries in only a minority of cases. Prosecutors and defense attorneys would still resolve the lion's share of criminal matters through plea bargaining, and plea bargaining takes place without a jury. Many of the rest involve only simple issues calling for no upward Guidelines adjustment. And in at least some of the remainder, a judge may find adequate room to adjust a sentence within the single Guidelines range to which the jury verdict points, or within the overlap between that range and the next highest.

But the constitutional jury trial requirement would nonetheless affect every case. It would affect decisions about whether to go to trial. It would affect the content of plea negotiations. It would alter the judge's role in sentencing. Thus we must determine likely intent not by counting proceedings, but by evaluating the consequences of the Court's constitutional requirement in light of the Act's language, its history, and its basic purposes.

While reasonable minds can, and do, differ about the outcome, we conclude that the constitutional jury trial requirement is not compatible with the Act as written and that some severance and excision are necessary.

Congress, had it been faced with the constitutional jury trial requirement, likely would not have passed the same Sentencing Act. It likely would have found the requirement incompatible with the Act as written. Hence the Act cannot remain valid in its entirety. Severance and excision are necessary.

We now turn to the question of *which* portions of the sentencing statute we must sever and excise as inconsistent with the Court's constitutional requirement. Although, as we have explained, we believe that Congress would have preferred the total invalidation of the statute to the dissenters' remedial approach, we nevertheless do not believe that the entire statute must be invalidated. Most of the statute is perfectly valid. And we must "refrain from invalidating more of the statute than is necessary." Indeed, we must retain those portions of the Act that are (1) constitutionally valid, *id.*, at 652–653, (2) capable of "functioning independently," and (3) consistent with Congress' basic objectives in enacting the statute.

Application of these criteria indicates that we must sever and excise two specific statutory provisions: the provision that requires sentencing courts to impose a sentence within the applicable Guidelines range (in the absence of circumstances that justify a departure), and the provision that sets forth standards of review on appeal, including *de novo* review of departures from the applicable Guidelines range. With these two sections excised (and statutory cross-references to the two sections consequently invalidated), the remainder of the Act satisfies the Court's constitutional requirements.

We do not doubt that Congress, when it wrote the Sentencing Act, intended to create a form of mandatory Guidelines system. But, we repeat, given today's constitutional holding, that is not a choice that remains open. Hence we have examined the statute in depth to determine Congress' likely intent *in light of today's holding*. And we have concluded that today's holding is fundamentally inconsistent with the judge-based sentencing system that Congress enacted into law. In our view, it is more consistent with Congress' likely intent in enacting the Sentencing Reform Act (1) to preserve important elements of that system while severing and excising two provisions (§§ 3553(b)(1) and 3742(e)) than (2) to maintain all provisions of the Act and engraft today's constitutional requirement onto that statutory scheme.

Ours, of course, is not the last word: The ball now lies in Congress' court. The National Legislature is equipped to devise and install, long-term, the sentencing system, compatible with the Constitution, that Congress judges best for the federal system of justice.

Do you agree with the remedial majority's resolution of the constitutional issue? Is it the proper role of the Supreme Court to attempt to discern the intent of Congress in 1984 in choosing which of the two options is the lesser of evils? Perhaps a relevant factor in at least Justice Breyer's decision is that he, then Judge Breyer of the First Circuit Court of Appeals, was a member of the Sentencing Commission that promulgated the original Guidelines in 1987.

The post-*Booker* sentencing world has been fraught with confusion and division. This is in part due to the incongruity of the two *Booker* majority opinions. The Stevens' majority opinion ends with the sentence: "Accordingly, we reaffirm our holding in *Apprendi:* Any fact (other than a prior conviction) which is necessary to support a sentence exceeding the maximum authorized by the facts established by a plea of guilty or a jury verdict must be admitted by the defendant or proved to a jury beyond a reasonable doubt."[56] This is simply not true in the post-*Booker*, non-binding Guidelines world. With the remedial majority's opinion making the Guidelines merely advisory, sentencing judges can and do find facts that impact a defendant's sentence which have not been found by the jury.[57] Given this, how should the Guidelines be implemented, what can a sentencing judge consider, and what is the role of courts of appeals in reviewing sentences? The Supreme Court has

---

[56] 543 U.S. at 243.

[57] Wesley Snipes made an argument based on this sentence from *Apprendi.* The appeals court rejected it, noting: "the use of extra-verdict enhancements in a non-mandatory guidelines system is not unconstitutional . . . . Since the district court correctly observed that the guidelines were purely advisory, *Apprendi* does not apply to this case." Snipes, *supra*, 611 F.3d at 871 n. 8.

had to return to the issues raised by *Booker* numerous times to flesh out the rules that govern sentencing.

First, in *Rita v. United States*,[58] the Court held that when a district court sentences within the range the Sentencing Commission deems appropriate, the court of appeals may presume that the sentence is reasonable. Thus, following *Rita*, the courts of appeals may apply a "presumption of reasonableness" to a sentence that reflects a proper application of the Sentencing Guidelines.

The Court then issued two decisions on the same day, *Gall v. United States*[59] and *Kimbrough v. United States*,[60] in which the Court attempted to resolve further the application of the Guidelines and the extent of appellate review of sentences imposed. In *Gall*, the defendant had been a member of a conspiracy to distribute the drug ecstasy while he was in college. Several months after joining the conspiracy, Gall advised the coconspirators that he was withdrawing from the conspiracy, and he did not sell illegal drugs of any kind thereafter. He then graduated from college, obtained gainful employment, and put his prior life of crime behind him. Several years later, he was indicted and pleaded guilty for his role in the drug conspiracy. Under the Guidelines, Gall's sentencing range was 30 to 37 months of imprisonment. However, the district court, noting Gall's brief participation in the conspiracy and his rehabilitation, sentenced him to probation for a term of 36 months.[61] The court of appeals reversed, holding that a sentence outside of the Guidelines range must be supported by a justification that is proportional to the extent of the difference between the advisory range and the sentence imposed. The court of appeals determined that the difference between a sentence of probation and the bottom of Gall's advisory Guidelines range of 30 months was "extraordinary" because it amounted to a 100% downward variance. It held that such a variance must be supported by "extraordinary circumstances."[62] The Supreme Court reversed the court of appeals and reinstated the original sentence, rejecting the notion that a sentence outside the Guidelines range must be justified by "extraordinary" circumstances.

The Supreme Court then set up the procedure by which sentencing courts should determine and impose sentences. First, the court should begin by calculating the applicable Guidelines range, noting that, in an effort to maintain nationwide consistency, the Guidelines should be the starting point.[63] Then, after giving both parties an opportunity to argue for whatever sentence they deem appropriate, the sentencing court should then consider all of the § 3553(a) factors to determine whether they support the sentence requested by the party. Those factors are as follows:

(1) the nature and circumstances of the offense and the history and characteristics of the defendant;

---

[58] 551 U.S. 338 (2007).

[59] 552 U.S. 38 (2007).

[60] 552 U.S. 85 (2007).

[61] *Gall*, 128 S. Ct. at 592–93.

[62] 128 S. Ct. at 594.

[63] *Id.* at 596.

(2) the need for the sentence imposed—

(A) to reflect the seriousness of the offense, to promote respect for the law, and to provide just punishment for the offense;

(B) to afford adequate deterrence to criminal conduct;

(C) to protect the public from further crimes of the defendant; and

(D) to provide the defendant with needed educational or vocational training, medical care, or other correctional treatment in the most effective manner;

(3) the kinds of sentences available;

(4) the kinds of sentence and the sentencing range established for—

(A) the applicable category of offense committed by the applicable category of defendant as set forth in the guidelines;

* * *

(5) any pertinent policy statement;

(6) the need to avoid unwarranted sentence disparities among defendants with similar records who have been found guilty of similar conduct; and

(7) the need to provide restitution to any victims of the offense.[64]

In applying these factors, the sentencing court must make an individualized assessment based on the facts presented. If the sentence is outside the Guidelines' range, the court must ensure that the justification is sufficiently compelling to support the degree of the variance. Finally, the judge must adequately explain the chosen sentence to allow for meaningful appellate review and to promote the perception of fair sentencing.[65]

The Court then turned to the nature of appellate review, and held that courts of appeals must review the sentence under an abuse-of-discretion standard. First, the reviewing court must ensure that the district court committed no significant procedural error, such as failing to calculate the Guidelines range or failing to consider the § 3553(a) factors. The appellate court must also consider the substantive reasonableness of the sentence imposed under an abuse-of-discretion standard. When conducting this review, the court must take into account the totality of the circumstances, including the extent of any variance from the Guidelines range. If the sentence is within the Guidelines range, the appellate court may, but is not required to, apply a presumption of reasonableness. But if the sentence is outside the Guidelines range, the court may not apply a presumption of unreasonableness. It may consider the extent of the deviation, but must give due deference to the district court's decision that the § 3553(a) factors, on a whole, justify the extent of the variance.[66]

In *Kimbrough*, the Supreme Court addressed the situation in which it was the Guidelines themselves, rather than the exceptional conduct of the defendant, that

---

[64] 18 U.S.C. § 3553(a).

[65] *Gall*, 128 S. Ct. at 596.

[66] *Id.* at 597–98.

were the basis of a sentence below the Guidelines range. Kimbrough had pleaded guilty to various drug-related charges, including possession with intent to distribute crack cocaine. Under the Guidelines, Kimbrough's sentencing range was 228 to 270 months, but the district court sentenced Kimbrough to 180 months in prison and stated that the case "exemplified the disproportionate and unjust effect that crack cocaine guidelines have in sentencing."[67] The Fourth Circuit reversed, holding that a sentence imposed "outside the guidelines range is per se unreasonable when it is based on a disagreement with the sentencing disparity for crack and powder cocaine offenses."[68] The Supreme Court disagreed and held that as long as the sentencing judge follows the requirements of *Gall* (*i.e.*, there was no procedural error and the sentence was substantively reasonable) a sentence outside the Guidelines range, even if based on a disagreement with the Guidelines themselves, is not reversible error.[69]

Finally, in *Spears v. United States*,[70] the sentencing judge disagreed with powder-to-crack cocaine ratio of 100:1 set forth in the Guidelines, and he imposed the sentence using his own 20:1 ratio. The court of appeals reversed, holding that while sentencing judges may disagree with the Guidelines as applied, they cannot adopt their own categorical crack-powder ratios in place of the Guidelines ratio. The Supreme Court summarily reversed the decision of the Eighth Circuit and held that sentencing courts are entitled to reject and vary categorically from the crack cocaine Guidelines based on a policy disagreement with those Guidelines.[71]

After these slew of cases, we are left with the following principles: First, a sentencing court must begin by calculating the Guidelines sentence. It is reversible error not to calculate the Guidelines range or to calculate it incorrectly. However, having calculated the Guidelines, the judge range may disregard that range, even if the judge simply disagrees with the Guidelines range on policy grounds. The sentencing judge must explicitly consider all of the § 3553(a) factors, as well as the Guidelines' policy statements. In imposing a sentence, the judge must ensure that a sentence outside the Guidelines has a justification that is "sufficiently compelling" to support the degree of the variance, and the judge must adequately explain the chosen sentence to allow for "meaningful appellate review." Finally, the court of appeals may only review a sentence for an abuse of discretion. Even with these cases providing guidance, the lower courts continue to struggle with the scope and application of appellate review.

Tomko,[72] a 2009 circuit court decision, illustrates the unpredictable sentencing occurring in the post-*Booker* era. The defendant, the head of a construction company, pleaded guilty to one count of evading taxes, using the "tax savings" in part to finance construction of his multimillion dollar mansion. The Guidelines

---

[67] 128 S. Ct. at 565. Kimbrough would have received a Guidelines range of 97 to 106 months had he been sentenced for an equivalent amount of powder cocaine.

[68] *Id.*

[69] 128 S. Ct. at 575–76.

[70] 555 U.S. 261 (2009).

[71] *Id.* at 266–67.

[72] United States v. Tomko, 562 F.3d 558 (3d Cir. 2009).

recommended a range of 12 to 18 months of incarceration. The defendant argued for probation and home detention, maintaining that his incarceration could cause his business to fail (threatening over 300 jobs) and that his construction expertise could be used by requiring him to do work for Habitat for Humanity. The Government countered that it would be unseemly to confine the defendant to the mansion built by the illegally diverted taxes and that incarceration would send the message that rich defendants can't buy their way out of jail. The sentencing judge agreed with the defendant, imposing probation and home detention. A sharply divided *en banc* circuit court affirmed. *Tomko* was highly controversial and has been distinguished by several subsequent decisions.[73]

V. THE SENTENCING GUIDELINES IN TAX CASES

A. In General

For most tax crimes, the applicable Guidelines section will be in Part T of Chapter Two, generally section 2T1.1. However, if a tax crime is charged as a non-Title 26 crime, the sentence may be calculated under another Guidelines section. For example, if a defendant was convicted of filing a false claim for refund under 18 U.S.C. section 287, the applicable Guidelines section would be section 2B1.1, which is applicable to offenses involving theft and fraud. FBAR convictions for conduct having tax evasion (or related tax crimes) as their focus are being sentenced under the Tax Guidelines, the first step of which is § 2T11. As with all of the guideline provisions in Chapter 2, the offense level under section 2T1.1 is calculated by determining the base offense level and then making any adjustments for specific offense characteristics.

B. Calculating the Base Offense Level

The base offense level under section 2T1.1, as well as other sections under subchapter 2T, is calculated using the tax loss — the greater the tax loss to the government, the higher the offense level (and consequently, the longer the sentence). The Guidelines employ the Tax Table of section 2T4.1 for this calculation.

---

[73] *See, e.g.*, United States v. Engle, 592 F.3d 495 (4th Cir. 2010). For a more extensive discussion of the *Tomko* case, *see* Scott A. Schumacher, Tomko *and Sentencing Guidelines After* Booker, 125 Tax Notes 149 (2009).

4. TAX TABLE

§2T4.1. Tax Table

	Tax Loss (Apply the Greatest)	Offense Level
(A)	$2,000 or less	6
(B)	More than $2,000	8
(C)	More than $5,000	10
(D)	More than $12,500	12
(E)	More than $30,000	14
(F)	More than $80,000	16
(G)	More than $200,000	18
(H)	More than $400,000	20
(I)	More than $1,000,000	22
(J)	More than $2,500,000	24
(K)	More than $7,000,000	26
(L)	More than $20,000,000	28
(M)	More than $50,000,000	30
(N)	More than $100,000,000	32
(O)	More than $200,000,000	34
(P)	More than $400,000,000	36.

Historical Note: Effective November 1, 1987. Amended effective November 1, 1989 (see Appendix C, amendment 237); November 1, 1993 (see Appendix C, amendment 491); November 1, 2001 (see Appendix C, amendment 617); January 25, 2003 (see Appendix C, amendment 647); November 1, 2003 (see Appendix C, 653).

Under section 2T1.1, how the tax loss is calculated depends upon the crime for which the defendant was convicted. For example, if the defendant was convicted of tax evasion and the offense involved the filing of a return that underreported income, the amount of the tax loss is generally equal to 28% of the unreported income (34% if the taxpayer is a corporation).[74] However, if the defendant was convicted of willful failure to file, the tax loss is equal to 20% of the gross income (25% if the taxpayer is a corporation).

Prior to amendments adopted in 1993, the tax loss calculation was fixed at these percentages, regardless of whether the amount of tax actually evaded was different, and courts held that the tax loss could not be reduced by unclaimed deductions.[75] In 1993, the definition of tax loss was amended to provide that the percentage calculations of 20% or 28% for individuals and 25% and 34% for corporations should be treated as the tax loss, "unless a more accurate determination of the tax loss can be made."[76] This amendment raised the question as to whether the defendant could now get the benefit of unclaimed deductions. The circuits were split on this issue, with the majority holding that a sentencing court may not consider unclaimed deductions to reduce the tax loss.[77] The Sentencing Commission resolved that

---

[74] These percentage rates were chosen because they reflected prevailing individual and corporate income tax rates at the time. The rates have changed since then for general tax purposes, but they remain unchanged for U.S. Sentencing Guidelines purposes.

[75] *See, e.g.*, United States v. Valentino, 19 F.3d 463 (9th Cir. 1994).

[76] U.S.S.G. section 2T1.1(c)(1)(A).

[77] *See* United States v. Clarke, 562 F.3d 1158, 1164–65 (11th Cir. 2009) (citing cases in adopting this majority view), *cert. denied*, 558 U.S. 1077 (2009); United States v. Delfino, 510 F.3d 468, 473 (4th Cir. 2007) ("The law simply does not require the district court to engage in [speculation as to what deductions

circuit split with amendments to section 2T1.1 in 2013:

> Unclaimed Credits, Deductions, and Exemptions. — In determining the tax loss, the court should account for the standard deduction and personal and dependent exemptions to which the defendant was entitled. In addition, the court should account for any unclaimed credit, deduction, or exemption that is needed to ensure a reasonable estimate of the tax loss, but only to the extent that (A) the credit, deduction, or exemption was related to the tax offense and could have been claimed at the time the tax offense was committed; (B) the credit, deduction, or exemption is reasonably and practicably ascertainable; and (C) the defendant presents information to support the credit, deduction, or exemption sufficiently in advance of sentencing to provide an adequate opportunity to evaluate whether it has sufficient indicia of reliability to support its probable accuracy.[78]

As with other areas of the Guidelines, when calculating the tax loss, the court may consider all relevant conduct. For taxes, that means that the court may include the tax loss from years barred by the statute of limitations,[79] uncharged conduct,[80] the tax loss attributable to counts the defendant was acquitted of,[81] and even state taxes that were evaded if those taxes would be part of the common scheme or plan of the federal counts of conviction.[82] However, the tax loss calculation cannot include penalties or interest.[83]

How should the tax loss be calculated if the crime involved skimming profits from a closely held corporation? This type of crime involves the evasion of two different taxes — the corporate level taxes and the shareholder-employee's taxes. Should the corporation get the benefit of a compensation deduction prior to the 34% tax loss calculation? The Seventh Circuit addressed this issue first.

UNITED STATES v. HARVEY

United States Court of Appeals, Seventh Circuit
996 F.2d 919 (1993)

The Sentencing Guidelines use "tax loss" as the foundation for determining the appropriate sentence for tax evasion and other violations of the revenue laws. The Guidelines define "tax loss" as "28 percent of the amount by which the greater of gross income and taxable income was understated, plus 100 percent of the total amount of any false credits claimed against tax. If the taxpayer is a corporation, use

would have been allowed], nor does it entitle the Delfinos to the benefit of deductions they might have claimed now that they stand convicted of tax evasion."); United States v. Phelps, 478 F.3d 680, 682 (5th Cir. 2007); United States v. Chavin, 316 F.3d 666 (7th Cir. 2002); *but see* United States v. Hoskins, 654 F.3d 1086 (10th Cir. 2011); United States v. Martinez-Rios, 143 F.3d 662, 671 (2d Cir. 1998).

[78] U.S.S.G. section 2T1.1, cmt. n.3. The burden is on the defendant to establish any such credit, deduction, or exemption by a preponderance of the evidence. *Id.*

[79] United States v. Valenti, 121 F.3d 327, 334 (7th Cir. 1997).

[80] United States v. Meek, 998 F.2d 776, 781 (10th Cir. 1993).

[81] United States v. Kelly, 147 F.3d 172, 178 (2d Cir. 1998).

[82] U.S.S.G. section 1B1.3; United States v. Fitzgerald, 232 F.3d 315, 320–21 (2d Cir. 2000).

[83] U.S.S.G. section 2T1.1, cmt. n.1.

34 percent in lieu of 28 percent." U.S.S.G. § 2T1.3(a). This rough-and-ready calculation applies the highest marginal rate to the amount of concealed income, disregarding deductions that would have been available had the taxpayer filed an honest return.

Our case presents the question: What happens when a single crime causes both corporate and personal income to be understated? One common tax crime occurs when the manager and dominant investor in a closely held corporation distributes the firm's income to himself, not reporting it at either the corporate or personal level. Here is a simple example: the manager and principal shareholder of a corporation sells some of the corporation's inventory, producing a $100,000 profit that he diverts to his own use. This is a disguised dividend from the corporation, with income taxable at two levels: the corporation is supposed to pay an income tax on its profits, and the manager owes tax on the dividend income. Suppose the manager, responsible for both the corporation's and his own failure to pay, is convicted of tax evasion. There are at least three ways to compute the "tax loss": (a) apply the 28% rate to the manager's income of $100,000, for a tax loss of $28,000; (b) apply the corporate rate of 34% to the unreported profit of $100,000 and the personal rate of 28% to the unreported income of the same $100,000, for a tax loss of $62,000; (c) apply the corporate rate of 34% to the unreported profit of $100,000 and reduce the imputed dividend by the amount of imputed taxes, then apply the personal rate of 28% to the reduced dividend of $66,000, for a tax loss of $52,480. Method (c) assumes that the corporation, having paid $34,000 to the United States, distributes as a "dividend" only $66,000, the after-tax profit.

James Harvey pleaded guilty to tax evasion patterned after our example, except that the corporation distributed scrap aluminum rather than cash. Harvey sold the aluminum and kept the proceeds (some $81,000), reporting neither corporate nor personal income. The district court applied Method (b) to this amount. Insisting that Method (b) is "double taxation", Harvey argues for Method (a). We conclude that Method (c) is more accurate than either.

One may debate the wisdom of the corporate income tax, but our current system calls for sequential taxation of the same income. Corporate profits are taxed to the corporation, then taxed as personal income after distribution to the investors. Dividends, unlike repayments of debt, are not deductible at the corporate level even though both reflect the firm's cost of capital. When a single transaction bypasses both corporate and personal taxes, any effort to determine the "tax loss" must include both. (Harvey's corporations did not qualify under Subchapter S of the Internal Revenue Code, which ascribes corporate income directly to the investors and avoids sequential taxation.) Harvey refers to the last sentence of § 2T1.3(a): "If the taxpayer is a corporation, use 34 percent rather than 28 percent." This means, he insists, that the judge cannot apply *both* 28% and 34% to the same income. True enough: the personal rate is 28%, and the corporate rate 34%; no one has a rate of 62%. Still, the sentence speaks of "the taxpayer", not "the defendant" and does not speak directly to the person whose crime causes two taxpayers to understate their income and pay less to the Internal Revenue Service.

Application Note 3 to § 2T1.3 implies an answer to the multiple-taxpayer case in remarking: "In determining the total tax loss attributable to the offense . . . , all conduct violating the tax laws should be considered as part of the same course of conduct or common scheme or plan unless the evidence demonstrates that the conduct is clearly unrelated." In other words, the Sentencing Commission wants the judge to consider the entire tax loss produced by the defendant's criminal conduct. If one person causes two taxpayers to understate their incomes, both underpayments count.

Reaching this point, the district court applied Method (b), which the prosecutor proposed and the presentence report endorsed. The difficulty is that Method (b) overstates the revenues lost to the Treasury. If the corporation has a profit of $100,000, it must pay $34,000 to the United States. (Here we disregard, as the tax loss table does, all deductions and credits.) Only $66,000 remains for distribution, and only the amount distributed as a dividend is subject to personal income taxation. If the investor-manager obeys the tax laws, the tax revenues will be $52,480: a 34% tax on $100,000 at the corporate level, and a 28% tax on the $66,000 the stockholder receives as a dividend. If this corporation nonetheless distributes $100,000 to an investor-manager, the $34,000 difference must be a return of capital, which is not taxable income (although it reduces the investor's basis in his stock). If we understand the extra $34,000 as an implicit wage or bonus to the recipient in his role as manager rather than an implicit dividend to the recipient in his role as investor, then this sum is deductible to the corporation, which may deduct compensation to its employees, and again sequential taxation does not occur. Method (c) will not be precise; characterizing the $34,000 increment in this example as a bonus rather than a return of capital would reduce the marginal rate from 34% to 28%; but the tax loss is not supposed to be a perfect reflection of actual tax revenues foregone. All in all, Method (c) approximates the loss better than Method (b). The district judge therefore should have deducted the (imputed) corporate income tax before determining the personal taxable income that Harvey was required to report.

As it happens, the difference between Method (b) and Method (c) does not affect Harvey's sentence. Explaining why requires a short tour through the numbers. The scrap aluminum that should have been reported as corporate income fetched Harvey $80,613, which also represented unreported personal income to Harvey. Applying Method (b) to the $80,613 yields a tax loss of almost $50,000. Under Method (a) the tax loss is $22,571. Method (c) implies a tax loss of $42,306. Harvey also concealed approximately $344,000 in additional personal income, representing a tax loss of roughly $96,000. Adding that $96,000 to the tax losses under each method comes to roughly $118,600 for Method (a), $146,200 for Method (b), and $138,500 for Method (c). The table in U.S.S.G. § 2T4.1 specifies that a tax loss between $70,000 and $120,000 translates to 12 offense levels, while a tax loss between $120,000 and $200,000 calls for 13 offense levels. Harvey thus gets the extra level under either Method (b) or Method (c). Nothing in the district judge's thorough sentencing memorandum suggests that the choice of a sentence within the guideline range turned on the precise calculation of the tax loss. Indeed, Harvey received the lowest penalty within the sentencing range. A remand is accordingly unnecessary — unless there is some other problem in the calculation.

Harvey insists that there is. The district court included about $58,000 of unreported personal income from 1985, although Harvey was not charged with any crime in connection with that tax year. Deleting all of the 1985 income would not depress the tax loss below $120,000, so this contention, too, turns out not to matter. The $58,000 accounts for less than $16,300 of the tax loss; subtract that from the $138,500 we have calculated, and $122,200 remains. We add for completeness that there was no error. Tax offenses, like embezzlements and drug crimes, fall within the rule that relevant conduct includes the whole scheme. Application Note 3 to § 2T1.3 refers to § 1B1.3(a)(2), the cornerstone of the relevant-conduct rules that have led to the inclusion of quantities of drugs in addition to those charged in the offenses of conviction. *United States v. White*, 888 F.2d 490, 497 (7th Cir. 1989), explains how the Guidelines produce this result for drug offenses. Tax offenses work the same way.

The Sixth Circuit calculated the tax loss differently, in its decision in *United States v. Cseplo*.[84] The *Cseplo* court rejected the reasoning of *Harvey* and determined that the tax loss should be computed by adding 34% of the understated corporate income and 28% of the underreported individual income (what the *Harvey* court called Method (b)), and that the defendant should not get the benefit of any deduction at the corporate level:

> The decision in *Harvey* assumes that the defendant has committed "a single crime, [that] causes both corporate and personal income to be understated." [996 F.2d] at 920. It further assumes that the funds diverted to the defendant's personal use constitute a "disguised dividend" the size of which would have been reduced by the amount of the corporate tax if the "dividend" had been paid openly. *Id.* at 920.
>
> We are not prepared to indulge any of these assumptions in the case at bar. Mr. Cseplo pleaded guilty not to having committed a single crime, but to having committed two separate crimes. One offense, involving a corporate tax return, was committed in May of 1990, and the other, involving an individual tax return, was committed five months later. The guidelines are very specific about the necessity of aggregating the tax losses, and we see no justification for proceeding as if only one crime had been committed.[85]

The Sentencing Commission resolved this dispute by adopting the aggregate method articulated in *Cseplo*:

> If the offense involved both individual and corporate tax returns, the tax loss is the aggregate tax loss from the individual tax offense and the corporate tax offense added together. Accordingly, in a case in which a defendant fails to report income derived from a corporation on both the defendant's individual tax return and the defendant's corporate tax return, the tax loss is the sum of (A) the unreported or diverted amount multiplied by (i) 28%; or (ii) the tax rate for the individual tax offense, if sufficient information is available to make a more accurate assessment of that tax rate; and (B) the unreported or diverted amount multiplied by (i) 34%; or

---

[84] 42 F.3d 360 (6th Cir. 1994).

[85] *Id.* at 364.

(ii) the tax rate for the corporate tax offense, if sufficient information is available to make a more accurate assessment of that tax rate. For example, the defendant, the sole owner of a Subchapter C corporation, fraudulently understates the corporation's income in the amount of $100,000 on the corporation's tax return, diverts the funds to the defendant's own use, and does not report these funds on the defendant's individual tax return. For purposes of this example, assume the use of 34% with respect to the corporate tax loss and the use of 28% with respect to the individual tax loss. The tax loss attributable to the defendant's corporate tax return is $34,000 ($100,000 multiplied by 34%). The tax loss attributable to the defendant's individual tax return is $28,000 ($100,000 multiplied by 28%). The tax loss for the offenses are added together to equal $62,000 ($34,000 + $28,000).[86]

C. Specific Offense Characteristics

Calculating the tax loss is just the first step. As discussed in section II above, the Guidelines require that the base offense level be increased if the defendant engaged in conduct that the Sentencing Commission has determined makes the crime more egregious, the so-called "Specific Offense Characteristics." Under section 2T1.1, the Guidelines set forth two types of conduct that warrant an offense level increase — a failure to report income from a "criminal activity" and "sophisticated means."

Section 2T1.1(b)(1) provides that if the defendant "failed to report or to correctly identify the source of income exceeding $10,000 in any year from criminal activity, increase by 2 levels. If the resulting offense level is less than level 12, increase to level 12." The phrase *criminal activity* is defined as "any conduct constituting a criminal offense under federal, state, local, or foreign law."[87] The policy behind this adjustment is as follows: "Failure to report criminally derived income is included as a factor for deterrence purposes. Criminally derived income is generally difficult to establish, so that the tax loss in such cases will tend to be substantially understated."[88]

The other Specific Offense Characteristic under section 2T1.1 is for "sophisticated means."[89] This two-level enhancement is reserved for "especially complex or especially intricate offense conduct pertaining to the execution or concealment of an offense. Conduct such as hiding assets or transactions, or both, through the use of fictitious entities, corporate shells, or offshore financial accounts

---

86 U.S.S.G. section 2T1.1 cmt. n.7.

87 U.S.S.G. section 2T1.1, cmt. n.4. This commentary was amended in 1993, by adding foreign law to the range of laws a violation of which would result in the specific offense increase. This amendment was in response to the Ninth Circuit's decision in United States v. Ford, 989 F.2d 347, 350–51 (9th Cir. 1993), which held that a sentencing court could not increase the offense level of a defendant for a failure to report more than $10,000 of income derived from criminal activity that only violated Canadian law.

88 U.S.S.G. section 2T1.1 cmt.

89 This Specific Offense characteristic has also been denominated, "sophisticated concealment," in prior versions of the Guidelines. The two terms, sophisticated concealment and sophisticated means, appear to have the same meaning.

ordinarily indicates sophisticated means."[90] The Seventh Circuit held that the conduct does not have to be terribly sophisticated in order for the enhancement to be applied:

> In light of its purpose and context, we think "sophistication" must refer not to the elegance, the "class," the "style" of the defrauder — the degree to which he approximates Cary Grant — but to the presence of efforts at concealment that go beyond (not necessarily far beyond, for it is only a two-level enhancement that is at issue, which in this case added roughly six months to the defendants' sentences) the concealment inherent in tax fraud.[91]

Courts have imposed the sophisticated means enhancement in a variety of cases,[92] including: using shell corporations,[93] fictitious names or entities,[94] using false documents,[95] using offshore bank accounts,[96] and depositing funds in a bank account either not directly linked to the defendant or in a non-interest bearing business bank accounts to avoid detection.[97] Conversely, merely making misrepresentations on a tax return likely does not justify an enhancement for sophisticated means.

D. Other Guidelines Applicable in Tax Cases

While the vast majority of tax crimes are sentenced under section 2T1.1, there are other guideline provisions in subchapter 2T about which you should be aware.[98] For example, if the defendant was charged with aiding and assisting the filing of a false tax return under section 7206(2), the offense level would be calculated under section 2T1.4. The offense level calculation is nearly identical to that of section 2T1.1, with only a change in the specific offense characteristics. If the defendant was convicted of a *Klein* conspiracy[99] or a conspiracy to commit a tax offense, the offense level would be calculated under section 2T1.9.

Other significant Guidelines sections are section 2T1.6, which applies to offense where the defendant failed to collect or pay-over taxes, section 2T1.7, where the defendant failed to deposit taxes into a trust account as required, and section 2T1.8, which applies to offenses relating to withholding statements.

---

[90] U.S.S.G. section 2T1.1, cmt. n.5.

[91] United States v. Kontny, 238 F.3d 815, 821 (7th Cir.), *cert. denied*, 532 U.S. 1022 (2001).

[92] *See* CTM 5.03[2][b].

[93] United States v. Paradies, 98 F.3d 1266, 1292 (11th Cir. 1996), *cert. denied*, 522 U.S. 1014 (1997).

[94] United States v. Veksler, 62 F.3d 544, 550–51 (3d Cir. 1995), *cert. denied*, 516 U.S. 1075 (1996).

[95] United States v. Madoch, 108 F.3d 761, 766 (7th Cir. 1997).

[96] United States v. Whitson, 125 F.3d 1071, 1075 (7th Cir. 1997).

[97] United States v. Lewis, 93 F.3d 1075, 1081–83 (2d Cir. 1996); United States v. Middleton, 246 F.3d 825, 848 (6th Cir. 2001).

[98] As already noted, some tax crimes are completely outside subchapter 2T. For example, if a defendant was convicted of filing a false claim for refund under 18 U.S.C. section 287, the applicable guidelines section would be section 2B1.1, which is applicable to offenses involving theft and fraud.

[99] United States v. Klein, 247 F.2d 908, 915 (2d Cir. 1957). For a discussion of *Klein* conspiracies, see chapter 3.

PROBLEM

Laura is an accomplished jewel thief who is under criminal investigation by the Government. Given her expertise and cunning, the prosecutors cannot pin any of the thefts on her. However, the IRS was able to obtain bank records of Laura's Cayman Island bank account. Laura made deposits of $125,000 into the account while on her annual scuba diving trip in each of the years under investigation, and the Government suspects that these deposits are proceeds from robberies. Nevertheless, the Government can prove that these amounts were not reported on her tax return, and she is indicted for tax evasion for the years 2010, 2011, and 2012.

1. Assuming Laura goes to trial and loses, what is the potential sentence (i.e., range of months of imprisonment) she could receive under the United States Sentencing Guidelines?

2. In determining her potential sentence, what specific offense characteristics might be applicable? What arguments would you make for the application of the specific offense characteristics, and what arguments would you make against their application?

3. Assume that, in response to the summons on the local branch of the Cayman Island bank, Laura filed a proceeding to quash the summons, and asserted spurious Fifth Amendment and other constitutional claims. What arguments would you, as prosecutor, assert in asking for an increase in the offense level for obstruction of justice?

4. Assume instead of being a jewel thief, Laura is the president of a printing company, and the $375,000 in omitted income was profits skimmed from her C corporation, which was placed in a bank account in her mother's name in a different city. Assume also that Laura decides to plead guilty as soon as the omitted income is discovered by the IRS. What is the potential sentence she could receive under these facts?

Chapter 11

ETHICAL ISSUES IN CRIMINAL TAX PRACTICE

Treasury Circular 230, §§ 10.20, 10.23, 10.33, 10.34, 10.37, 10.50 & 10.51

ABA Model Rules 1.6, 1.7, 1.13 & 3.3

I. INTRODUCTION

This chapter will focus on the ethical issues applicable to tax lawyers who represent clients in criminal tax cases. We will discuss the sets of ethical rules applicable to tax lawyers, the sometimes conflicting duties owed to clients, the courts, and the government, and some of the common ethical dilemmas that tax lawyers routinely face. Our goal is to alert you to ethical fishhooks you will face, as well as to give you the gear and tackle with which to deal with these issues. That said, many of the ethical issues you will face in practice have no clear answer, and the rules and strategies discussed in this chapter will be, at least for those issues, no more than a guide.

A subject as broad as this warrants an entire book to itself, and in fact, depending upon the focus of one's inquiry, several books have been written that would be useful to resolving these issues.[1] Some of the subjects discussed in other chapters of this book necessarily implicate ethical issues. For example, Chapter 6 discusses the issues surrounding the filing of original or amended returns during a criminal tax investigation, a specially sticky situation. Likewise, Chapter 7, which deals with the government's efforts to gather evidence and information, contains a scintillating discussion on the reach and contours of the attorney-client privilege. We will not rehash those issues here.

Part of the challenge of ethically representing clients in a criminal tax case is that the lawyer is often more than just a criminal defense lawyer — as with nearly every subject covered in this book, a lawyer must be both an expert criminal defense lawyer and fully knowledgeable in federal tax law. Civil tax matters almost always accompany a criminal tax case, either as part of the criminal case or after the conclusion of the investigation or prosecution. The ethical issues are no different. In this context, it is important to highlight the unique role of tax lawyers in the system of tax administration. Tax lawyers are called upon to represent their clients but also may at times have a duty to protect the government fisc. In representing clients in

---

[1] *See, e.g.*, John Wesley Hall, Jr., Professional Responsibility in Criminal Defense Practice (3d ed. 2005); Bernard Wolfman, et al., Ethical Problems in Federal Tax Practice (4th ed. 2008); Deborah L. Rhode, Professional Responsibility, Ethics by the Pervasive Method (2d ed. 1998); and Jonathan G. Blattmachr, et al., The Circular 230 Deskbook (2006).

tax planning matters, tax lawyers can impact, either positively or negatively, how close to the line, or how far over the line, their clients go. The government's indictment and prosecution of members of prominent accounting firms for allegedly assisting their clients in committing tax evasion demonstrates just how dangerous this can be. In addition, tax lawyers, with their ability to bless tax structures and thereby protect clients from penalties, hold the key to a client's ability to take aggressive positions on tax returns.[2] Many commentators assert that tax professionals, when giving tax planning advice to clients, have an affirmative duty to the IRS and "the system."[3] Thus, while any criminal practice will have its share of ethical dilemmas, the convergence of civil and criminal tax issues makes criminal tax practice particularly challenging.

II. SOURCES OF LAW

In order to properly analyze ethical issues in criminal tax cases, a tax lawyer must first gain a facility with the various sources of law applicable to ethical issues. Not only must a lawyer be well-versed in tax, constitutional, and criminal law, he or she must also master the ethical rules and opinions promulgated by state bar associations and supreme courts, the American Bar Association, the Treasury Department and IRS, and the Securities and Exchange Commission.[4] Each of these bodies of law contains detailed rules and duties applicable to lawyers, and many of the rules overlap and sometimes conflict.

A. State Ethics Rules and Opinions

The first set of ethical rules are the ones that are probably the most well-known to all lawyers — state ethics rules. Each state has its own rules of professional conduct applicable to lawyers admitted to practice in that state, and each state's bar association renders regular opinions on common ethical dilemmas facing lawyers in their state. Most states' rules of professional conduct are patterned after the American Bar Association's Model Rules of Professional Conduct, but there are some notable exceptions, including California and New York. Moreover, even those state ethics rules that are patterned after the ABA's Model Rules contain some key differences. Given the myriad variations in the rules governing lawyer's practice among the states, we will not attempt to outline state rules and opinions. Nevertheless, you should be mindful that while the remainder of this chapter will examine the ABA's Model Rules and Ethics Opinions, as well as the ethical rules applicable to practice before several federal agencies, your state will likely have detailed rules on these very same issues, and the state's rules (which govern your ability to be a lawyer at all) may be contrary to the more general national rule.

---

[2] *See* Treas. Reg. section 1.6664-4(b) & (c) (reasonable reliance on a tax expert can be a defense to most of the penalties under section 6662 and 6663).

[3] *See, e.g.*, Camilla E. Watson, *Tax Lawyers, Ethical Obligations, and the Duty to the System*, 47 U. Kan. L. Rev. 847 (1999).

[4] Other sources, while not constituting binding authority, can be extremely helpful. *See, e.g.*, Restatement of the Law Third, The Law Governing Lawyers; ABA Standards for Criminal Justice: Prosecution and Defense Function (3d ed. 1993).

B. ABA Rules and Opinions

The next important set of rules are the American Bar Association's Model Rules of Professional Conduct and Formal Ethics Opinions. The ABA's Model Rules and opinions are only advisory, and state rules are binding. Nonetheless, it could be argued that the ABA's rules and opinions are more significant, given that the Model Rules have been the model for most states' rules and the ABA's ethics opinions have generally been regarded as the most authoritative voice on common ethical issues facing lawyers.

C. Treasury Circular 230 and the Internal Revenue Code

Treasury Circular 230 comprises the rules promulgated by the Department of Treasury that govern practice before the Internal Revenue Service, and is codified in 31 C.F.R. Part 10. These rules cover everything from a lawyer's conduct in dealings with the IRS to standards for giving tax advice and other dealings with clients.[5] We will discuss some of the Circular 230 provisions relevant to criminal tax practice below.

The provisions of Circular 230 are amplified by the Internal Revenue Code, which also contains standards of tax practice, as well as penalties applicable to practitioners who fail to live up to those standards. These penalties are assessed against practitioners who render erroneous tax advice, and the penalties can be draconian.[6] Penalties applicable to tax shelters can be even more severe.[7] Finally, lawyers and other tax advisors who become a bit too enthusiastic in helping their clients meet their tax saving goals can and do find themselves under indictment and criminal prosecution for conspiracy, aiding and abetting, and other substantive crimes.[8]

D. SEC Standards of Professional Conduct

In 2003, the Securities and Exchange Commission, pursuant to the Sarbanes-Oxley Act of 2002,[9] promulgated Standards of Professional Conduct for Attorneys Appearing and Practicing Before the Commission in the Representation of an Issuer. The Sarbanes-Oxley Act was enacted in response to corporate scandals like Enron, and the Act sets forth rules relating to corporate governance, financial disclosure, and public accounting, all designed to restore public confidence in corporate disclosures. The regulations promulgated pursuant to Sarbanes-Oxley concern lawyers' practice before the SEC, and are codified at 17 C.F.R. Part 205. While at first blush these regulations would appear to have perhaps limited application to most criminal tax lawyers, the definition of "practice before the

[5] In the context of a criminal tax case, Circular 230 applies only during the administrative stages of the case.

[6] The penalty imposed under IRC section 6694 is *the greater of* $1,000 per return or 50% of the fees earned or to be earned. IRC section 6694(a)(1).

[7] *See, e.g.*, IRC sections 6700, 6707, 6707A.

[8] *See, e.g.*, 18 U.S.C. sections 2 & 371; IRC sections 7206(2) & 7212.

[9] P.L. 107-204, 116 Stat 745 (2002).

Commission" is sufficiently broad to cover advice by attorneys to corporate clients. In this regard, 17 C.F.R. section 205.2(a)(1)(iii) defines *appearing and practicing before the Commission* to include

> [p]roviding advice in respect of the United States securities laws or the Commission's rules or regulations thereunder regarding any document that the attorney has notice will be filed with or submitted to, or incorporated into any document that will be filed with or submitted to, the Commission, including the provision of such advice in the context of preparing, or participating in the preparation of, any such document.

The breadth of the language, "or incorporated into any document that will be filed with or submitted to, the Commission" should give any lawyer pause. No lawyer can predict where his or her work product will end up in the future. It is therefore essential that an attorney representing a corporate client be familiar with the SEC's Standards of Professional Conduct.

III. GENERAL ETHICAL DUTIES

The rules of professional conduct, both at common law and under state-codified rules, impose three general sets of duties on lawyers. The first is the duty of loyalty to the client. This duty prohibits conflicts of interest between the lawyer and two or more clients and between lawyer's interests and clients' interests.[10] It also requires the lawyer to act as a zealous advocate in furthering the client's case.[11] It is the duty of loyalty that is at the heart of what it means to be a lawyer. This ethic originated, perhaps, from Lord Broughman's defense of Queen Caroline, in which he argued:

> An advocate, in the discharge of his duty, knows but one person in all the world, and that person is his client. To save that client by all means and expedients, and at all hazards and costs to other persons, and amongst them, to himself, is his first and only duty; and in performing this duty he must not regard the alarm, the torments, the destruction which he may bring upon others.[12]

As we will discuss more fully below, this duty is not absolute, and a lawyer must balance this duty of loyalty against duties of candor and fairness. The duty of loyalty also requires that the lawyer strike the delicate balance between on the one hand, allowing the client to make all important decisions regarding the disposition of the case, and on the other hand, ensuring that the lawyer, as the expert in these matters, makes all other decisions and controls the case.[13]

The second general duty is the duty of competence. This duty requires the lawyer to be knowledgeable, diligent, and to keep clients informed of the progress in their cases.[14] If a lawyer is not competent to handle a matter, he or she must refer

---

[10] *See, e.g.*, ABA Model Rules ("Model Rules") 1.7 & 1.8.

[11] *See, e.g.*, Model Rule 3.1, cmt. 1.

[12] Hall, *supra* note 1, at 342.

[13] Hall *supra* note 1, at 369–370.

[14] *See, e.g.*, Model Rule 1.1, 1.2, 1.3 & 1.4.

the case to someone who is. Given the stakes inherent in criminal cases, the duty of competence, as well as the duty to refer the case if the lawyer is not competent, is arguably higher than in a civil case.[15]

The final general duty is the lawyer's duty to the system of justice. This duty requires the lawyer to exercise candor toward a tribunal, to bring only meritorious claims, and to act with decorum and fairness to opposing party.[16] Some of the most vexing ethical problems arise when the duty to the client and the duty to the system intersect.

For tax lawyers, the varied roles of the IRS make the ethical duty owed to the Service a moving target. The IRS fills pretty much every governmental role in tax law: the IRS is lawmaker (it promulgates Regulations and Revenue Rulings); administrator (it collects and processes returns); investigator (civil auditors and CID agents); settlement officer (IRS Appeals); litigator (IRS counsel attorneys represent IRS in some courts); judge/decision-maker (when it rules on Private Letter Rulings requests); ethics board (the IRS creates ethical rules for practice before the IRS); and ethics enforcement officers (when it enforces its own ethical rules through its Office of Professional Responsibility). Depending upon the role the IRS is performing, or more accurately, depending upon the role the practitioner is playing when he or she deals with the IRS in its various roles, the practitioner may have different ethical duties.

Tax lawyers who handle criminal cases have their own ethical challenges. The point at which a tax investigation goes criminal is not always clear. During these so-called egg-shell audits, the client and attorney may know of the client's fraudulent activity, but the IRS has yet to learn of it. As we will discuss, Circular 230 requires candor and cooperation with the IRS, that may be appropriate in a civil case, but would be singularly inappropriate once the case becomes criminal. At the other end of the spectrum, the end of a criminal tax case is rarely the end of the client's tax problems. There are nearly always civil tax consequences that the attorney should plan for and resolve. Thus, criminal tax practice often is an exciting mix of civil and criminal tax law.

IV. DUTIES OWED TO THE IRS

A. General Duties and Standards of Conduct

While lawyers are always bound by their state's rules of professional conduct, when they practice before the IRS, they are also bound by another set of rules — Circular 230. Practice before the IRS includes all matters connected with the presentation to the IRS relating to a taxpayer's rights, privileges, or liabilities under the tax laws.[17] This includes preparing and filing returns and other documents and presenting cases and arguments to the IRS. Any attorney admitted

---

[15] Hall *supra* note 1, at 348–349. In complicated criminal matters, one should heed the advice of H. Callahan, who opined, "A man has got to know his limitations." Magnum Force (Warner Bros. 1973).

[16] *See, e.g.*, Model Rule 3.3, 3.4 & 4.1.

[17] 31 C.F.R. section 10.2(d).

to the bar of a state is automatically admitted to practice before the IRS.[18]

The rules of practice set out in Circular 230 are in some ways quite similar to state bar rules, which are applicable in all roles a lawyer serves. Circular 230 prohibits conflicts of interest,[19] restricts the kinds of advertising a practitioner may engage in,[20] and prohibits practitioners from endorsing or negotiating any refund check which has been issued to a taxpayer.[21] However, since the rules were drafted by the IRS, Circular 230 also contains explicit rules dealing with how practitioners are supposed to act when dealing with the IRS. For example, a practitioner is required to provide records or information in any matter before the IRS, if the request is "proper and lawful." The rules also prohibit a practitioner from interfering with any proper and lawful effort by the IRS, unless "the practitioner believes in good faith and on reasonable grounds that the records or information are privileged."[22] Another section provides: "No practitioner shall unreasonably delay the prompt disposition of any matter before the Internal Revenue Service."[23] How do these requirements mesh with a lawyer's duty to zealously represent his client? Is it not the lawyer's duty to delay a criminal investigation if that will benefit the client?

While many of these rules were not drafted with criminal investigations in mind, you must nevertheless be cognizant of their existence and their potential reach. This is especially so, given that section 10.50 of Circular 230 allows the Director of the Office of Professional Responsibility to suspend or disbar any practitioner from practice before the Internal Revenue Service, if the practitioner is "shown to be incompetent or disreputable, who refuses to comply with any regulation in this part, or who, with intent to defraud, willfully and knowingly misleads or threatens a client or prospective client." The term *disreputable conduct* is defined in Section 10.51 as follows:

> (a) Incompetence and disreputable conduct. Incompetence and disreputable conduct for which a practitioner may be sanctioned under § 10.50 includes, but is not limited to—
>
> (1) Conviction of any criminal offense under the Federal tax laws.
>
> (2) Conviction of any criminal offense involving dishonesty or breach of trust.
>
> (3) Conviction of any felony under Federal or State law for which the conduct involved renders the practitioner unfit to practice before the Internal Revenue Service.
>
> (4) Giving false or misleading information, or participating in any way in the giving of false or misleading information to the Department of the Treasury or any officer or employee thereof, or to any

---

[18] 31 C.F.R. section 10.3.

[19] 31 C.F.R. section 10.29.

[20] 31 C.F.R. section 10.30.

[21] 31 C.F.R. section 10.31.

[22] 31 C.F.R. section 10.20.

[23] 31 C.F.R. section 10.23.

tribunal authorized to pass upon Federal tax matters, in connection with any matter pending or likely to be pending before them, knowing the information to be false or misleading. Facts or other matters contained in testimony, Federal tax returns, financial statements, applications for enrollment, affidavits, declarations, and any other document or statement, written or oral, are included in the term "information."

(5) Solicitation of employment as prohibited under § 10.30, the use of false or misleading representations with intent to deceive a client or prospective client in order to procure employment, or intimating that the practitioner is able improperly to obtain special consideration or action from the Internal Revenue Service or any officer or employee thereof.

(6) Willfully failing to make a Federal tax return in violation of the Federal tax laws, or willfully evading, attempting to evade, or participating in any way in evading or attempting to evade any assessment or payment of any Federal tax.

(7) Willfully assisting, counseling, encouraging a client or prospective client in violating, or suggesting to a client or prospective client to violate, any Federal tax law, or knowingly counseling or suggesting to a client or prospective client an illegal plan to evade Federal taxes or payment thereof.

(8) Misappropriation of, or failure properly or promptly to remit, funds received from a client for the purpose of payment of taxes or other obligations due the United States.

(9) Directly or indirectly attempting to influence, or offering or agreeing to attempt to influence, the official action of any officer or employee of the Internal Revenue Service by the use of threats, false accusations, duress or coercion, by the offer of any special inducement or promise of an advantage or by the bestowing of any gift, favor or thing of value.

(10) Disbarment or suspension from practice as an attorney, certified public accountant, public accountant, or actuary by any duly constituted authority of any State, territory, or possession of the United States, including a Commonwealth, or the District of Columbia, any Federal court of record or any Federal agency, body or board.

(11) Knowingly aiding and abetting another person to practice before the Internal Revenue Service during a period of suspension, disbarment or ineligibility of such other person.

(12) Contemptuous conduct in connection with practice before the Internal Revenue Service, including the use of abusive language, making false accusations or statements, knowing them to be false, or circulating or publishing malicious or libelous matter.

(13) Giving a false opinion, knowingly, recklessly, or through gross incompetence, including an opinion which is intentionally or recklessly misleading, or engaging in a pattern of providing incompetent opinions on questions arising under the Federal tax laws. False opinions described in this paragraph (a)(13) include those which reflect or result from a knowing misstatement of fact or law, from an assertion of a position known to be unwarranted under existing law, from counseling or assisting in conduct known to be illegal or fraudulent, from concealing matters required by law to be revealed, or from consciously disregarding information indicating that material facts expressed in the opinion or offering material are false or misleading. For purposes of this paragraph (a)(13), reckless conduct is a highly unreasonable omission or misrepresentation involving an extreme departure from the standards of ordinary care that a practitioner should observe under the circumstances. A pattern of conduct is a factor that will be taken into account in determining whether a practitioner acted knowingly, recklessly, or through gross incompetence. Gross incompetence includes conduct that reflects gross indifference, preparation which is grossly inadequate under the circumstances, and a consistent failure to perform obligations to the client.

(14) Willfully failing to sign a tax return prepared by the practitioner when the practitioner's signature is required by Federal tax laws unless the failure is due to reasonable cause and not due to willful neglect.

(15) Willfully disclosing or otherwise using a tax return or tax return information in a manner not authorized by the Internal Revenue Code, contrary to the order of a court of competent jurisdiction, or contrary to the order of an administrative law judge in a proceeding instituted under § 10.60.

(16) Willfully failing to file on magnetic or other electronic media a tax return prepared by the practitioner when the practitioner is required to do so by the Federal tax laws unless the failure is due to reasonable cause and not due to willful neglect.

(17) Willfully preparing all or substantially all of, or signing, a tax return or claim for refund when the practitioner does not possess a current or otherwise valid preparer tax identification number or other prescribed identifying number.

(18) Willfully representing a taxpayer before an officer or employee of the Internal Revenue Service unless the practitioner is authorized to do so pursuant to this part.

B. Standards for Giving Tax Advice

A criminal tax attorney must also be familiar with the standards applicable to giving tax advice to clients. Criminal defense attorneys are often called upon to give civil tax advice either during or after the criminal case. The standards for giving a favorable tax opinion to a client are found in Code section 6694 and sections 10.34 and 10.37 of Circular 230.

Clients seek tax advice for several reasons. First, they wish to know what the law is and whether they may take a particular position on a tax return. Second, they want to know how far they can go in aggressively planning and minimizing their tax liabilities. Even before Judge Learned Hand uttered his famous dictum regarding taxes — "Any one may so arrange his affairs that his taxes shall be as low as possible; he is not bound to choose that pattern which will best pay the Treasury; there is not even a patriotic duty to increase one's taxes"[24] — taxpayers have sought to pay as little taxes as they may legally get away with. Finally, clients seek advice from attorneys and other tax professionals because reliance on the advice of a tax expert would generally protect taxpayers from penalties the IRS may impose, should the position of the taxpayer be successfully challenged.[25] It is therefore important for attorneys to know not only the substantive law, but also the standards for giving advice on aggressive (or conservative) position to their clients.

What are the standards for giving tax opinions, and under what circumstances may an attorney give a favorable opinion to a client? For the first 50 years of the income tax's existence, there were no published standards regarding when a lawyer could advise a client to take a given position on a tax return. Then in 1965, the ABA Tax Section issued Formal Opinion 314. The ABA opined that an attorney may give an opinion on a reporting position if the position had a "reasonable basis." This standard created some controversy. Many commentators realized that something could be entirely reasonable and have very little chance of success. As a result, in 1985, the ABA issued Formal Opinion 85-352. That opinion provides that a lawyer may advise taking a position on a tax return if the lawyer believes the position "is warranted in existing law or can be supported by a good faith argument for an extension, modification or reversal of existing law." The opinion further defines "good faith" as requiring that there be "some realistic possibility of success if the matter is litigated." Opinion 85-352 did not attempt to quantify what a "realistic possibility of success" meant. However, an ABA Tax Section Task Force the next year quantified the standard as a 1-in-3 chance of success. The "realistic possibility of success" standard was later adopted by Congress in the preparer penalties of section 6694, and then by Treasury in Circular 230. Thus, from the 1980s and for the next 20 years, "realistic possibility of success" was the opinion standard that governed the majority of tax advice.[26]

However, in 2008 Congress amended section 6694 and significantly revised the opinion standard regime.[27] As amended, section 6694 applies to all "return preparers," which includes anyone who either signs a tax return or gives advice with respect to a position on the tax return after the transaction at issue has been completed. A return preparer must either have "substantial authority" for the tax

---

[24] Helvering v. Gregory, 69 F.2d 809, 810 (2d Cir. 1934).

[25] *See* Treas. Reg. section 1.6664-4(b) & (c).

[26] If the transaction entered into by the taxpayer was deemed a "tax shelter," the standard the tax professional was required to use was "more likely than not," which is defined as a little more than 50 percent.

[27] Pub. L. 110-343, div. C, title V, § 506(a), Oct. 3, 2008, 122 Stat. 3880.

position, or the position must be disclosed.[28] The substantial authority standard is "defined" as follows:

(i) There is substantial authority for the tax treatment of an item only if the weight of the authorities supporting the treatment is substantial in relation to the weight of authorities supporting contrary treatment. All authorities relevant to the tax treatment of an item, including the authorities contrary to the treatment, are taken into account in determining whether substantial authority exists.

(ii) Nature of analysis. The weight accorded an authority depends on its relevance and persuasiveness, and the type of document providing the authority.[29]

Thus, before rendering advice, a tax advisor must weigh all of the authorities in favor of the taxpayer's position and all authorities against that position. If the authorities in favor of that position are "substantial" (whatever that means), the professional may advise the taxpayer to take the position on the return without disclosure. However, what happens if, as is often the case statutes, there are no authorities either for or against the position? Tax lawyers are routinely employed to render advice on a new or relatively new amendment to the Code where the IRS has provided no guidance and the courts have not addressed the issue. In this regard, the Treasury Regulations provide: "There may be substantial authority for the tax treatment of an item despite the absence of certain types of authority. Thus, a taxpayer may have substantial authority for a position that is supported only by a well-reasoned construction of the applicable statutory provision."[30] Remarkably then, the "substantial authority" for a newly-minted Code provision is merely the tax professional's interpretation of that Code provision. The standards of section 6694 have since been incorporated in revised section 10.34 of Circular 230 and as a result, "substantial authority" is *the* standard for all non-tax-shelter advice.

V. CLIENT CONFIDENTIALITY AND DEALINGS WITH GOVERNMENT AGENCIES

Another set of ethical issues that frequently arises is when a lawyer learns that his or her client has made false or misleading representations, or has engaged in "misleading silence" when dealing with a government agency like the IRS. The lawyer's duties in these circumstances are both unclear and contradictory, heightening the ethical dilemma for the professional. Model Rule 3.3 (Candor to the Tribunal) provides one set of rules:

(a) A lawyer shall not knowingly:

(1) make a false statement of fact or law to a tribunal or fail to correct a false statement of material fact or law previously made to

[28] IRC section 6694(a). A disclosed position must also have a "reasonable basis."

[29] Treas. Reg. section 1.6662-4(d).

[30] Treas. Reg. section 1.6662-4(d)(3)(ii).

the tribunal by the lawyer;

(2) fail to disclose to the tribunal legal authority in the controlling jurisdiction known to the lawyer to be directly adverse to the position of the client and not disclosed by opposing counsel; or

(3) offer evidence that the lawyer knows to be false. If a lawyer, the lawyer's client, or a witness called by the lawyer, has offered material evidence and the lawyer comes to know of its falsity, the lawyer shall take reasonable remedial measures, including, if necessary, disclosure to the tribunal. A lawyer may refuse to offer evidence, other than the testimony of a defendant in a criminal matter, that the lawyer reasonably believes is false.

(b) A lawyer who represents a client in an adjudicative proceeding and who knows that a person intends to engage, is engaging or has engaged in criminal or fraudulent conduct related to the proceeding shall take reasonable remedial measures, including, if necessary, disclosure to the tribunal.[31]

Is the IRS a "tribunal" within the meaning of Rule 3.3, and is it entitled to the candor accorded a tribunal? ABA Formal Opinion 314 opined that the IRS is not a tribunal:

> The Internal Revenue Service is neither a true tribunal, nor even a quasi-judicial institution. It has no machinery or procedure for adversary proceedings before impartial judges or arbiters, involving the weighing of conflicting testimony of witnesses examined and cross-examined by opposing counsel and the consideration of arguments of counsel for both sides of a dispute. While its procedures provide for "fresh looks" through departmental reviews and informal and formal conferences procedures, few will contend that the service provides any truly dispassionate and unbiased consideration to the taxpayer. Although willing to listen to taxpayers and their representatives and obviously intending to be fair, the service is not designed and does not purport to be unprejudiced and unbiased in the judicial sense.[32]

Formal Opinion 314 also provides that a lawyer appearing as an advocate before the IRS is under no duty to disclose weaknesses in the client's case if the case is "fairly arguable." And, to emphasize its position, the ABA stated that there is no duty to disclose weak facts. "Negotiation and settlement procedures of the tax

---

[31] ABA Model Rules of Professional Conduct, 2014 Edition. Copyright © 2014 by the American Bar Association. Reprinted with permission. Copies of ABA Model Rules of Professional Conduct, 2014 Edition are available from Service Center, American Bar Association, 321 North Clark Street, Chicago, IL 60654, 1-800-285-2221. This information or any or portion thereof may not be copied or disseminated in any form or by any means or stored in an electronic database or retrieval system without the express written consent of the American Bar Association.

[32] Formal Opinion 314 © 1965 by the American Bar Association. Reprinted with permission. All rights reserved. This information or any or portion thereof may not be copied or disseminated in any form or by any means or stored in an electronic database or retrieval system without the express written consent of the American Bar Association.

system do not carry with them the guarantee that a correct tax result necessarily occurs, just as it might happen with regard to other civil disputes."[33]

Despite these rather broad statements, the ABA hastened to emphasize: "It by no means follows that a lawyer is relieved of all ethical responsibility when he practices before this agency. There are certain things which he clearly cannot do, and they are set forth explicitly in the canons of ethics."[34] The ABA reinforced this notion in Formal Opinion 85-352, which states: "In all cases, however, with regard both to preparing returns and negotiating administrative settlements, the lawyer is under a duty not to mislead the IRS deliberately, either by misstatements or by silence or by permitting the client to mislead." However, Rule 1.6, the rule dealing with keeping client confidences, prevents the disclosure of client confidences except to prevent the commission of a crime or fraud. But if the statements do not rise to the level of criminal or fraudulent behavior, may an attorney disclose client confidences? Arguably not without violating the affirmative prohibition against disclosure of Rule 1.6. At the same time, section 10.51(d) defines *incompetence and disreputable conduct* to include giving false or misleading information, or participating in any way in the giving of false or misleading information to the Department of the Treasury. Thus, a lawyer may be caught between the duties imposed by the Model Rules, state bar rules (many of which do not follow the relatively liberal disclosure rules of Model Rule 1.6), and the duty not to mislead the IRS imposed by Circular 230.

This already difficult situation is made even worse if the misleading statements can be seen to be continuing. For example, a client may have submitted a financial document to the IRS through the attorney, and the attorney later learns that it contains misleading or incorrect factual information. Assume also that the IRS may rely on that false or misleading information in determining or resolving the client's tax liability. What do the rules require under these circumstances? Not surprisingly, the rules are not consistent.

First, the attorney must recognize that he or she has been used to perpetrate what may be fraud or a crime. The attorney therefore may have exposure to both civil and criminal liability. Nevertheless, many states' ethics rules do not permit the attorney to reveal the client's confidences. The lawyer may and indeed might be required to withdraw under Formal Opinion 314. ABA Formal Opinion 92-366 states that a lawyer should not only withdraw, but may disavow his or her prior work product and submissions, using what is known as a "noisy withdrawal."[35]

These various requirements (disclosure, nondisclosure, withdrawal, noisy withdrawal) put an attorney in a difficult ethical bind. In addition, regardless of what the attorney does under the ethical rules, he or she runs the risk of being sued by the client, charged with conspiracy, or disbarred or suspended from practice. As with other similar ethical quandaries, the best course of action is to solicit an opinion from the state bar association of which the attorney is a member and/or an ethics attorney.

---

[33] *Id.*

[34] *Id.*

[35] ABA Formal Opinion 92-366.

VI. THE CHALLENGES OF REPRESENTING AN ENTITY CLIENT

A. Who Do You Represent?

A threshold ethical question that must always be resolved is, who is my client? For many lawyers, the answer to this question is obvious — it is the person sitting across the conference room table, the person who retained the lawyer. However, for the lawyer representing an entity client or representing an entity and the principal owner of the entity, the question — who is my client? — is often the most difficult ethical question the lawyer will face.[36]

The general rule for identifying the client is set forth in ABA Model Rule 1.13, which provides simply that a "lawyer employed or retained by an organization represents the organization acting through its duly authorized constituents." But even this simple declarative sentence raises numerous questions. What does it mean that lawyer represents the entity acting through the duly authorized constituents? Who are "the duly authorized constituents?" Is it the interests of the constituents or the interests of the organization that the lawyer must protect? How can the lawyer tell the difference? What if those constituents disagree as to what is in the best interest of the organization?

This general rule is confused by the substantive law surrounding how entities are characterized. With corporations, there is not much confusion. It is well settled that a corporation is a separate legal entity, a separate legal "person." However, the law is much less settled with regard to general partnerships, limited partnerships, limited liability partnerships, limited liability companies, and all of the other related hybrid entities. Are partnerships and LLCs separate entities, or are they merely an aggregate of their individual members?

The predominant theory in cases that have examined this issue is that partnerships, LLCs, and similar entities are entities, rather than aggregates of their owners, and that the lawyer represents the entity and not the owners.[37] However, other courts have found that the lawyer did in fact represent the owners as well as the entity.[38] Nearly every court to have addressed this issue has based its determination on the facts of the individual case.

Given the rather uncertain state of the law regarding the identity of the client when representing partnerships and LLCs, the ABA has attempted to set forth a bright-line (or at least a brighter-line) rule on this issue. In ABA Formal Opinion 91-361 (1991), the ABA held that a partnership is an "organization" within the

---

[36] Difficult ethical questions also arise when a lawyer seeks to represent both a husband and wife in a case.

[37] *See, e.g.*, Hopper v. Frank, 16 F.3d 92 (5th Cir. 1994); Quintel Corp., N.V. v. Citibank, N.A., 589 F. Supp. 1235 (S.D.N.Y. 1984) (lawyer representing the limited partnership and its general partners did not necessarily have a client-lawyer relationship with limited partners).

[38] *See, e.g.*, Margulies v. Upchurch, 696 P.2d 1195 (Utah 1985) (holding that law firm's representation of a limited partnership in commercial litigation gave rise to and implied attorney-client relationship with respect to the individual partners, who according to the court reasonably believed that the law firm was acting for their individual interests as well as those of the partnership).

meaning of Rule 1.13, and that, generally, a lawyer who represents a partnership represents the entity rather than the individual partners. However, the ABA also stated that the facts of any given case may well show that the attorney also represents one or more of the partners.

Thus, the answer as to whether a lawyer representing a partnership or LLC represents the entity itself or an aggregate of its members cannot be definitely answered. Moreover, depending upon the circumstances, a lawyer may wish to represent only the partnership or LLC, while in other cases, the lawyer may want to represent the partners or members as well.

The Code is of little help in conceptualizing the relationships between partnerships and LLCs on the one hand and their owners on the other. Subchapter K of the Code is the main source of the substantive rules governing income taxation in the partnership and LLC contexts.[39] Unfortunately, Subchapter K makes no clean and consistent choice. Partnerships and LLCs are sometimes treated as aggregates, sometimes as entities, sometimes as aggregate/entity blends, and sometimes as aggregates or entities depending upon what the organization elects.[40] Similarly, partnerships and LLCs can be subject to multiple procedural rules. Sometimes, dispute resolution procedures operate purely at the entity level;[41] sometimes they operate purely at the owner level;[42] and sometimes they operate in a hybrid entity/owner dual-level fashion.[43]

An example of the problems that may stem from this uncertain treatment relates to a lawyer's liability for penalties under the Code. Section 6694 imposes penalties against income tax return preparers, if the preparer negligently or willfully fostered a tax underpayment. The question then becomes can a lawyer who prepares a return for a partnership or LLC be held liable as a return preparer with respect to the individual partners or members? Treasury has taken the following position:

> [T]he sole preparer of a partnership return of income or a small business corporation income tax return is considered a preparer of a partner's or a shareholder's return if the entry or entries on the partnership or small

---

[39] The great majority of LLCs are treated as partnerships for income tax purposes, either because they affirmatively so elect or because of the check-the-box default rules. *See* Treas. Reg. sections 301.7701-1 to -3.

[40] *See, e.g.*, William S. McKee, William F. Nelson & Robert L. Whitmire, Federal Taxation of Partnerships and Partners (2004) ¶ 1.02[3] ("The drafters of Subchapter K combined the entity and aggregate concepts in developing a comprehensive scheme for the taxation of partnerships. * * * As this book repeatedly demonstrates, this blending of aggregate and entity concepts is one of the primary sources of uncertainty in the interpretation and application of Subchapter K.").

[41] For example, so-called master or publicly traded limited partnerships are treated as corporations, and therefore entities, for all purposes. IRC section 7704.

[42] An example is partnerships not subject to the so-called TEFRA audit and litigation rules, where audit and subsequent procedural states deal with the partners individually. *See* David M. Richardson, Jerome Borison, and Steve Johnson, Civil Tax Procedure, ch. 6 (2d ed. 2007).

[43] The TEFRA partnership rules centralize audit and litigation at the partnership level but also provide for notice and participation by the partners themselves. IRC sections 6221–6234.

> business corporation return reportable on the partner's or shareholder's return constitutes a substantial portion of the partner's or shareholder's return.[44]

In *Goulding v. United States*,[45] the Seventh Circuit held that a lawyer who prepared partnership returns and schedules for a limited partnership was also liable for the preparer penalty of section 6694 for each of the limited partners' returns as well. The assessed liability against Mr. Goulding was more than $44,000. In so holding, the court examined the structure of the Code and the nature of partnerships in general:

> Here the government's position reflects both the congressional intent and the realities of the limited partnership relationship. Partnerships are hybrids — for some purposes they are entities separate from the partners, for other purposes they are aggregates of the individual partners. Under the Internal Revenue Code, partnerships are not taxpayers or taxable entities. When a partnership receives income, the partners record their share of that income on their individual returns and are taxed on it, whether or not that income is actually distributed to them. Partners also deduct partnership losses on their individual returns. Partnerships are "entities for purposes of calculating and filing informational returns;" otherwise they "are conduits through which the taxpaying obligation passes to the individual partners in accord with their distributive shares." *United States v. Basye*, 410 U.S. 441, 448 (1973).
>
> As the partnership is both entity and aggregate, the tax preparer's relationship to the partnership is necessarily dual — he is dealing with the partnership both as entity and as aggregate of partners. Appellant was retained to analyze the partnership operation; however, the analysis of the partnership operation was a making of decisions and calculations for all the individual partners, to whom the tax liability or deductions would flow through the partnership. These decisions and calculations were directly reflected on the returns of the partners; all the individual partners depended upon Mr. Goulding's analysis. Thus while appellant was retained by the partnership and compensated by the partnership, in reality his work was for all the partners.[46]

According to the *Goulding* court, which analyzed and applied what it believed were the rules set out by Congress in the Code and by Treasury in its Regulations, a lawyer advising and representing a partnership "in reality" works for all of the partners, if under the facts of the case the partners depended upon the advice of the lawyer.

While this inconsistent treatment of entities and owners is bad enough, what is especially troubling is that the determination of who the client is may be based in some cases not on objective factors but on the subjective beliefs *of the clients*. ABA

---

[44] Treas. Reg. section 1.301.7701-15.

[45] 957 F.2d 1420 (7th Cir. 1992).

[46] *Id.* at 1427–28 (footnotes omitted).

Formal Op. 91-361 provides that whether a relationship between a lawyer and one or more of the partners has been created almost always will depend on an analysis of the specific facts involved, including "whether there was evidence of reliance by the individual partner on the lawyer as his or her separate counsel, or of the partner's expectation of personal representation." Likewise in *Goulding*, the court held that while Goulding represented the partnership and made decisions on the tax treatment of certain partnership-level items, "these decisions and calculations were directly reflected on the returns of the partners; all the individual partners depended upon Mr. Goulding's analysis."[47]

It is therefore imperative that a practitioner (1) determine as many facts as possible about case and the parties; (2) decide which of the parties he or she will represent; (3) clearly communicate to all parties involved (whether being represented or not) who the practitioner will be representing; and (4) to the extent possible, obtain consents or acknowledgements from all of the parties as to the extent and limitations of that representation.

B. The Attorney-Client Privilege in the Context of Misconduct by an Owner or Employee

A significant ethical issue in representing entities concerns the situation in which the lawyer learns that one or more of the owners, employees, or other constituents has done something that is either illegal or contrary to the best interests of the entity. As has been established, a lawyer represents the entity as a separate entity. Yet, entities can only act through individual owners and employees. Who speaks for the entity when there is a dispute and to whom should the lawyer listen? Model Rule 1.13(a) provides that an organization acts through its "duly authorized constituents." However, particularly in the case of closely-held businesses, it is not always clear who the duly authorized constituents are.

Model Rule 1.13(b) sets out the basic rules on how the professional should act in these circumstances:

> If a lawyer for an organization knows that an officer, employee or other person associated with the organization is engaged in action, intends to act or refuses to act in a matter related to the representation that is a violation of a legal obligation to the organization, or a violation of law that reasonably might be imputed to the organization, and that is likely to result in substantial injury to the organization, then the lawyer shall proceed as is reasonably necessary in the best interest of the organization. Unless the lawyer reasonably believes that it is not necessary in the best interest of the organization to do so, the lawyer shall refer the matter to higher authority in the organization, including, if warranted by the circumstances to the highest authority that can act on behalf of the organization as determined by applicable law.[48]

---

[47] *Id.* at 1428.

[48] ABA Model Rules of Professional Conduct, 2014 Edition. Copyright © 2014 by the American Bar Association. Reprinted with permission. Copies of ABA Model Rules of Professional Conduct, 2014 Edition are available from Service Center, American Bar Association, 321 North Clark Street, Chicago,

Thus, Rule 1.13(b) reemphasizes that the lawyer's primary duty is to act in the best interest of the organization. In addition, the lawyer must, if the circumstances warrant, report the misconduct to the "highest authority" within the organization. However, this does not answer the situation in which the malevolent actor *is* the highest authority within the organization.

Rule 1.13 was substantially revised in August 2003. Under the prior version of the Rule, once the highest authority that can act on behalf of the organization was informed of the misconduct within the organization, it was proper for the lawyer to conclude that the organization as client has been notified and that the lawyer's professional obligation had been fulfilled.[49] If the highest authority within the organization refused to take action against the misconduct, Rule 1.13(c) permits the lawyer to resign in accordance with Rule 1.16.[50] Significantly, however, no disclosure was permitted by the lawyer.

The revised version of Rule 1.13(c) changes that. Under the revised Rule, a lawyer may reveal information about the organization's (or constituent's) misconduct, even though revealing that information would not normally be permitted by Rule 1.6:

> If (1) despite the lawyer's efforts in accordance with paragraph (b) the highest authority that can act on behalf of the organization insists upon or fails to address in a timely and appropriate manner an action, or a refusal to act, that is clearly a violation of law, and (2) the lawyer reasonably believes that the violation is reasonably certain to result in substantial injury to the organization, then the lawyer may reveal information relating to the representation whether or not Rule 1.6 permits such disclosure, but only if and to the extent the lawyer reasonably believes necessary to prevent substantial injury to the organization.[51]

Thus, if the lawyer knows that an owner or employee is engaged in action in a matter related to the representation that is a violation of a legal obligation to the entity, or that the action is a violation of law that reasonably may be imputed to the entity and that will likely result in substantial harm to the entity, then the lawyer should proceed as is reasonably necessary in the best interest of the entity. The

---

IL 60654, 1-800-285-2221. This information or any or portion thereof may not be copied or disseminated in any form or by any means or stored in an electronic database or retrieval system without the express written consent of the American Bar Association.

49 *See* ABA Comm. on Professional Ethics, Formal Op. 93-375 (1993) (lawyer may not reveal client's lie to bank examiner but must "climb corporate ladder" or withdraw if client persists in fraudulent conduct).

50 *See also* Ass'n of the Bar of the City of N.Y., Comm. on Professional Ethics, Op. 1994-10 (1994) (when general partner of limited partnership engages in activities that may harm entity, lawyer may be required to withdraw from representation of partnership, individual general partner, and individual limited partner if independent professional judgment likely to be affected by differing interests).

51 Model Rule 1.13(c). ABA Model Rules of Professional Conduct, 2014 Edition. Copyright © 2014 by the American Bar Association. Reprinted with permission. Copies of ABA Model Rules of Professional Conduct, 2014 Edition are available from Service Center, American Bar Association, 321 North Clark Street, Chicago, IL 60654, 1-800-285-2221. This information or any or portion thereof may not be copied or disseminated in any form or by any means or stored in an electronic database or retrieval system without the express written consent of the American Bar Association.

lawyer's action will be determined by the circumstances, but ordinarily this means referral to a higher decision-making person or group within the organization. The lawyer may, but is not required to, reveal facts relating to the representation, even if not expressly permitted by Rule 1.6, but only if and to the extent the lawyer reasonably believes necessary to prevent substantial injury to the organization.

C. Conflicts of Interest: Representing Entities and Owners

Even though the general rule is that a lawyer represents the entity and not the individual owners, the situation routinely arises in which the lawyer may be asked to represent one or more of the owners in addition to the entity itself. In addition, lawyers representing an entity will inevitably develop a relationship with one or more of the owners and, if the lawyer has been effective on behalf of the entity, an owner may wish to retain the services of the lawyer. Is it acceptable under the rules to represent an owner while also representing the entity?[52] Under Model Rule 1.7, a lawyer may represent parties with potential conflicts of interest, but only if the lawyer believes his or her representation will not be affected, and each client consents in writing. Comment 6 to Model Rule 1.7 sets forth the policy basis of the rule:

> Loyalty to a current client prohibits undertaking representation directly adverse to that client without that client's informed consent. Thus, absent consent, a lawyer may not act as an advocate in one matter against a person the lawyer represents in some other matter, even when the matters are wholly unrelated. The client as to whom the representation is directly adverse is likely to feel betrayed, and the resulting damage to the client-lawyer relationship is likely to impair the lawyer's ability to represent the client effectively. In addition, the client on whose behalf the adverse representation is undertaken reasonably may fear that the lawyer will pursue that client's case less effectively out of deference to the other client, i.e., that the representation may be materially limited by the lawyer's interest in retaining the current client.[53]

Model Rule 1.13(g) confirms that the conflict provisions of Rule 1.7 apply to the representation of an organization and one or more of its constituents. Rule 1.13(g) imposes the additional requirement that the consent required by Rule 1.7 be given by an owner other than the owner who will be represented by the lawyer for the entity. Accordingly, if a lawyer will be representing both the corporate client and one of the shareholders or the partnership client and one of the partners, the lawyer should obtain written consents from both the entity and the other individual to be represented, with the consent on behalf of the entity from an owner other than the one to be represented.

---

[52] *See* Hall, *supra* note 1, at 577 *et seq.*

[53] ABA Model Rules of Professional Conduct, 2014 Edition. Copyright © 2014 by the American Bar Association. Reprinted with permission. Copies of ABA Model Rules of Professional Conduct, 2014 Edition are available from Service Center, American Bar Association, 321 North Clark Street, Chicago, IL 60654, 1-800-285-2221. This information or any or portion thereof may not be copied or disseminated in any form or by any means or stored in an electronic database or retrieval system without the express written consent of the American Bar Association.

Can the entity pay the legal fees of the officer or shareholder? The ABA Standards provide:[54]

> In accepting payment of fees by one person for the defense of another, defense counsel should be careful to determine that he or she will not be confronted with a conflict of loyalty since defense counsel's entire loyalty is due the accused. Defense counsel should not accept such compensation unless:
>
> (i) the accused consents after disclosure;
>
> (ii) there is no interference with defense counsel's independence of professional judgment or with the client-lawyer relationship; and
>
> (iii) information relating to the representation of the accused is protected from disclosure as required by defense counsel's ethical obligation of confidentiality. Defense counsel should not permit a person who recommends, employs, or pays defense counsel to render legal services for another to direct or regulate counsel's professional judgment in rendering such legal services.[55]

A colorful example of these principles was front and center in the appeal of mob-boss John Gotti from his conviction on multiple counts, including tax fraud.

UNITED STATES v. LOCASCIO

United States Court of Appeals, Second Circuit
6 F.3d 924 (1993)

On July 18, 1991, a grand jury in the Eastern District of New York returned a thirteen count superseding indictment against Gotti and Locascio. The indictment also named two other defendants, Salvatore Gravano and Thomas Gambino, who are not parties to this appeal. All four defendants were charged with violating the Racketeer Influenced and Corrupt Organizations Act ("RICO"), 18 U.S.C. § 1962(c)–(d) (1988), for unlawfully conducting and participating in the affairs of a criminal enterprise through a pattern of racketeering activity. The charged enterprise was the Gambino Organized Crime Family of La Cosa Nostra ("the Gambinos," "The Gambino Family," or "the Gambino Crime Family"). Gotti was charged as the head of the organization, and Locascio was accused of being the "underboss," or second-in-command.

Trial began in February 1992. The government's proof to support the allegations that Gotti and Locascio had been in command of an extensive criminal enterprise was comprised mostly of lawfully intercepted tape-recorded conversations of the defendants-appellants and other alleged members of the Gambino Family. The government introduced tape recordings from four different locations over an eight-year period.

---

[54] ABA Standards, *supra* note 4, § 4-3.5(e).

[55] Reprinted with permission from the ABA Standards for Criminal Justice: Prosecution and Defense art 1993 © by the American Bar Association. All rights reserved. This information or any or portion thereof may not be copied or disseminated in any form or by any means or stored in an electronic database or retrieval system without the express written consent of the American Bar Association.

The most significant evidence consisted of conversations intercepted at 247 Mulberry Street in New York during the period from late 1989 until early 1990. The government had installed three listening devices in that building: in the Ravenite Social Club on the first floor, in a hallway behind the club's rear door, and in an apartment two stories above the club ("the Ravenite Apartment"). It was this last location that proved the most fruitful for the government, and the most damaging for the defendants-appellants. In the discussions in the Ravenite Apartment, Gotti, Locascio, and other Gambino Family members discussed various illegal acts. These discussions formed the core of the proof against the defendants-appellants at trial. Another major source of evidence was the testimony of Salvatore Gravano, who cooperated with the government following the indictment. As a high-level insider in the Gambino Family, Gravano's testimony was especially damaging.

Following a six-week trial, the jury found Gotti guilty of all charges in the indictment. Locascio was found guilty of all charges except the count relating to a gambling operation in Queens, New York. Each defendant-appellant was sentenced by the district court to life in prison on the RICO and murder counts, and the statutory maximum prison terms on all remaining counts, with all sentences to run concurrently.

I. *Disqualification of Counsel*

Prior to trial, the district court disqualified attorneys for both Gotti and Locascio. Gotti and Locascio now contend that these disqualifications were unwarranted and violated their Sixth Amendment rights.

The Sixth Amendment to the Constitution provides that "[i]n all criminal prosecutions, the accused shall enjoy the right . . . to have the Assistance of Counsel for his defence." U.S. Const. amend. VI. The accused, however, does not have the absolute right to counsel of her own choosing. *See Wheat v. United States*, 486 U.S. 153, 159 (1988). As the Court stated in *Wheat*,

> while the right to select and be represented by one's preferred attorney is comprehended by the Sixth Amendment, the essential aim of the Amendment is to guarantee an effective advocate for each criminal defendant rather than to ensure that a defendant will inexorably be represented by the lawyer whom he prefers.

Id. Similarly, although a criminal defendant can waive her Sixth Amendment rights in some circumstances, that right to waiver is not absolute, since "[f]ederal courts have an independent interest in ensuring that criminal trials are conducted within the ethical standards of the profession and that legal proceedings appear fair to all who observe them." *Id.* at 160. The question of disqualification therefore implicates not only the Sixth Amendment right of the accused, but also the interests of the courts in preserving the integrity of the process and the government's interests in ensuring a just verdict and a fair trial.

In deciding a motion for disqualification, the district court recognizes a presumption in favor of the accused's chosen counsel, although this presumption can be overcome by a showing of an actual conflict or potentially serious conflict. We accord the district court's decision to disqualify an attorney "substantial latitude," and review the decision only for an abuse of discretion.

There are many situations in which a district court can determine that disqualification of counsel is necessary. The most typical is where the district court finds a potential or actual conflict in the chosen attorney's representation of the accused, either in a multiple representation situation or because of the counsel's prior representation of a witness or co-defendant. Courts have also considered disqualification where the chosen counsel is implicated in the allegations against the accused and could become an unsworn witness for the accused or where the chosen counsel is somehow unable to serve without unreasonable delay or inconvenience in completing the trial.

In this case, the government moved to disqualify attorneys for both Gotti and Locascio on multiple theories. We consider each of the defendants-appellants in turn.

B. *Gotti*

Bruce Cutler served as Gotti's attorney in previous criminal trials in federal court. Prior to trial, the government moved to disqualify Cutler from acting as Gotti's attorney. Although the motion also dealt with the disqualification of other Gotti attorneys, only the disqualification of Cutler has been challenged on appeal.

Gotti now appeals the district court's ruling, arguing that the disqualification was an abuse of discretion. We disagree, and affirm the disqualification on two grounds: (1) Cutler's role as house counsel to the Gambino Crime Family; and (2) Cutler's anticipated role as an "unsworn witness" for Gotti had he been allowed to serve. We note that, importantly, Gotti does not challenge the effectiveness of his replacement trial counsel. Although the government cannot justify an otherwise unwarranted disqualification by arguing that the disqualification did not result in the accused receiving ineffective assistance of counsel, the fact that Gotti received more than competent representation is an additional consideration strongly supporting the district court's otherwise entirely correct ruling.

2. *Cutler's Role as House Counsel*

Gotti argues that the facts before the district court did not merit the conclusion that Cutler had acted as "house counsel" to the Gambino Crime Family. Rather, Gotti argues that Cutler was merely his personal attorney.

Ethical considerations warn against an attorney accepting fees from someone other than her client. As we stated in a different context, the acceptance of such "benefactor payments" "may subject an attorney to undesirable outside influence" and raises an ethical question "as to whether the attorney's loyalties are with the client or the payor." *In re Grand Jury Subpoena Served Upon John Doe*, 781 F.2d 238, 248 n.6 (2d Cir. 1985) (in *banc*), *cert. denied*, 475 U.S. 1108 (1986). In this context, proof of house counsel can be used by the government to help establish the existence of the criminal enterprise under RICO, by showing the connections among the participants.

Contrary to Gotti's assertions, there was sufficient evidence for the district court to determine that Cutler had acted as house counsel to the Gambino Crime Family. For example, the court cited one conversation in which Gotti, in the time-honored tradition of legal clients, complained about his legal fees:

> I gave youse [sic] 300,000 in one year. Youse [sic] didn't defend me. I wasn't even mentioned in none of these [expletive deleted] things. I had nothing to do with none of these [expletive deleted] people. What the [expletive deleted] is your "beef?" . . . Before youse [sic] made a court appearance, youse [sic] got 40,000, 30,000 and 25,000. That's without counting [attorney] John Pollok. . . . You standing there in the hallway with me last night, and you're plucking me. . . . "Tony Lee's" lawyer, but you're plucking me. I'm paying for it. . . . Where does it end? Gambino Crime Family? This is the Shargel, Cutler and who do you call it Crime Family.

Gotti thus demonstrated that he was incurring the legal fees for representation of others. As support for disqualification, the government indicated that it would introduce the testimony of Michael Coiro, who would testify that he had paid nothing to Cutler and another attorney for their services to him, presumably because Gotti paid for his defense.

Cutler's role as house counsel to the Gambinos raised a credible issue of the ethical propriety of his representation of Gotti in this case. An attorney cannot properly serve two masters, and the evidence before the district court indicated that Cutler had represented the Gambino Family as a whole. Moreover, Cutler's status as house counsel was potentially part of the proof of the Gambino criminal enterprise. We cannot say that the district court abused its discretion in disqualifying Cutler on this basis, considering the volume of proof of Cutler's proximity to the affairs of the Gambino Crime Family offered by the government in this case.

3. *Cutler's Role as an Unsworn Witness*

An even stronger basis for disqualification, however, was the possibility that Cutler would function in his representational capacity as an unsworn witness for Gotti. An attorney acts as an unsworn witness when his relationship to his client results in his having first-hand knowledge of the events presented at trial. If the attorney is in a position to be a witness, ethical codes may require him to withdraw his representation.

Even if the attorney is not called, however, he can still be disqualified, since his performance as an advocate can be impaired by his relationship to the events in question. For example, the attorney may be constrained from making certain arguments on behalf of his client because of his own involvement, or may be tempted to minimize his own conduct at the expense of his client. Moreover, his role as advocate may give his client an unfair advantage, because the attorney can subtly impart to the jury his first-hand knowledge of the events without having to swear an oath or be subject to cross examination.

This is different from the situation in *Wheat,* since the conflict in *Wheat* — multiple representation — was a conflict inuring to the detriment of the accused. In such a case, waiver by the accused of the conflict can conceivably alleviate the constitutional defect, so long as the representation by counsel does not seriously compromise the integrity of the judicial process. When an attorney is an unsworn witness, however, the detriment is to the government, since the defendant gains an unfair advantage, and to the court, since the factfinding process is impaired. Waiver by the defendant is ineffective in curing the impropriety in such situations, since he is not the party prejudiced.

The district court disqualified Cutler partially on the ground that his representation of Gotti would place him in the role of such an unsworn witness. The clearest support for this finding was Cutler's presence during the Ravenite Apartment discussions taped by the government. The government was legitimately concerned that, when Cutler argued before the jury for a particular interpretation of the tapes, his interpretation would be given added credibility due to his presence in the room when the statements were made. This would have given Gotti an unfair advantage, since Cutler would not have had to take an oath in presenting his interpretation, but could merely frame it in the form of legal argument.

Gotti argues, however, that the district court erred in disqualifying Cutler where the government had no intention of calling Cutler. He also maintains that Cutler's presence and participation on the government's tapes could have been redacted to eliminate references to and statements by Cutler, thereby eliminating the unsworn witness problem. The first contention is meritless, since the district court explicitly and correctly noted that "whether the government will or will not call . . . Cutler . . . has no significance for this motion." 771 F. Supp. at 562. The second contention is equally unavailing, since the district court explicitly found that redaction of the tapes would have eviscerated the government's case. We are not in a position to second-guess the district court's clearly supported factual findings on review. Moreover, we agree with the district court that the government's case should not be unfairly impaired so that an accused can continue with conflicted counsel.

The unsworn witness problem arises not only in relation to the Ravenite tapes, but to other grounds cited by the district court in support of disqualification. For example, the court found that Gotti's references to Cutler's acceptance of fees "under the table" were relevant to the government's case on the tax fraud count. Had Cutler argued Gotti's defense to that count, he would not only have had a conflict of interest but he would have been arguing as to events in which he was allegedly involved.

We are aware that disqualification is a drastic remedy to the unsworn witness problem. We are also, however, cognizant that this is an unusual case, in that Cutler had allegedly entangled himself to an extraordinary degree in the activities of the Gambino Crime Family: he is recorded on government tapes when discussions of allegedly illegal activity took place; he is allegedly involved in the tax fraud count against Gotti; his role as house counsel could be used to prove the criminal enterprise; and his representation of government witnesses caused a conflict with his representation of Gotti. Although we are cognizant of the right of the accused to secure representation, we are also conscious of the institutional interest in protecting the integrity of the judicial process. If an attorney will not perform his ethical duty, it is up to the courts to perform it for him. Bruce Cutler had no place representing John Gotti in this case, and the district court properly determined that he should be disqualified.

While it is unlikely that you will be asked to represent members of an organized crime family, you may nevertheless face the issue of whether you may represent both an entity and one or more of its principals. Is this permissible under the reasoning of *Gotti*? What steps could you take to ensure that you are not disqualified? Potential conflicts can be waived, even in criminal defense cases, as long as the waiver is made knowingly.[56] As we saw in *Gotti*, it is not entirely up to the defendant to determine whether a conflict can be waived. Another potential conflict of interest that can arise in tax litigation involves the situation in which the tax lawyer who advised on a deal or planned the deal, seeks to represent his client when the deal is challenged by the IRS. *Para Technologies* set forth below outlines some of the pitfalls in this arrangement.

PARA TECHNOLOGIES TRUST v. COMMISSIONER

United States Tax Court
64 TCM 922, T.C. Memo. 1992-575 (1992)

Each of these cases is before the Court for ruling on respondent's Motion to Compel Withdrawal of Petitioners' Counsel of Record for Conflict of Interest. The issue for decision is whether a conflict of interest exists that requires the disqualification of petitioners' counsel of record.

Nassau Life Insurance Company, Ltd. (Nassau Life), promoted the use of domestic and foreign entities to shelter United States business and investment income from United States Federal income taxation. Nassau Life engaged in this activity through representatives known as "information officers" and through the dissemination of printed materials. From 1982 through 1988, Joe Alfred Izen, Jr. (Izen), was counsel to Nassau Life. In the course of that representation, among other services, he prepared and issued two opinion letters that related to the multiple-entity tax shelter promoted by Nassau Life. In a legal opinion letter dated September 26, 1983, Izen discussed the legal status of "contractual trust companies" that were being promoted by Nassau Life (the 1983 opinion letter).

Ferber is a songwriter with a high school education. Anderson completed the eighth grade. At the time of hearing on the pending motions, Ferber was 36 years old and Anderson was 30 years old.

Ferber and Anderson met in India in 1977 and became friends. In late 1984, Anderson began to engage in an electronics business, VideoLab, as a sole proprietor. Because of his limited education, Anderson wanted to adopt a structure for VideoLab that would minimize the amount of paperwork that was necessary to carry on the business. He discussed his plans with Ferber, who was then employed as an information officer for Nassau Life. Ferber, relying at least partially on the 1983 opinion letter, advised Anderson, who also had access to the 1983 opinion letter, to structure his business as a trust such as those promoted by Nassau Life.

In January 1985, Anderson formed Para Tech as a common-law business trust. From its creation and thereafter, Para Tech conducted the business in which

---

[56] *See, e.g.*, Glasser v. United States, 315 U.S. 60 (1942).

VideoLab had previously been engaged. Ferber was the trustee of Para Tech. The beneficial owner of Para Tech was another trust, Atram Investment Group (Atram), formed under the laws of the Turks and Caicos Islands, British West Indies. Anderson was one of the beneficiaries of Atram.

In a legal opinion letter prepared for Nassau Life dated June 20, 1985, Izen discussed the tax aspects of contractual trust companies (the 1985 opinion letter). Among other things, the letter concluded that the grantor trust provisions of the Internal Revenue Code did not apply to "contractual trust companies". Izen's letter failed to discuss decided cases contrary to the positions he was espousing. Anderson and Ferber gained access to the 1985 opinion letter.

Respondent determined deficiencies in petitioners' Federal income taxes for 1987 and 1988. Respondent determined that Para Tech was an association taxable as a corporation for Federal income tax purposes and disallowed its claimed distribution deductions. Respondent determined that Anderson and Ferber were each taxable on an amount equal to the taxable income of Para Tech. Respondent asserted three alternative theories in support of this determination. First, because Para Tech should be taxed as a corporation and because of their control over Para Tech and Atram, Anderson and Ferber were in constructive receipt of dividend income equal to the amounts transferred from Para Tech to Atram. Second, if Para Tech was a trust, it was a grantor trust owned by Anderson and Ferber, who were therefore taxable on Para Tech's income. Third, because both Para Tech and Atram were sham entities that should be disregarded for Federal income tax purposes, Anderson and Ferber are taxable on the income from Para Tech's business. Respondent also determined that all three petitioners are liable for additions to tax for fraud.

Para Tech, Anderson, and Ferber filed petitions for redetermination with this Court. Izen is counsel of record for petitioners in these cases. Nassau Life is bankrupt. All legal fees are being paid by Para Tech. No discovery and no settlement negotiations have taken place, and none of the cases has been set for trial.

Respondent's counsel in these cases wrote letters to Izen dated September 19, 1991, and November 15, 1991, questioning Izen regarding possible conflicts of interest in his representation of petitioners. Izen did not respond to these letters. Respondent, therefore, moved the Court to compel withdrawal of Izen as petitioners' counsel.

Discussion

Petitioners contend, based on *Appeal of Infotechnology, Inc.*, 582 A.2d 215 (Del. Super. 1990), that respondent lacks standing to make this motion because a nonclient litigant does not have the power to enforce a technical violation of the Model Rules of Professional Conduct (Model Rules). These cases, however, are distinguishable from *Appeal of Infotechnology, Inc., supra*, in which the court held that it had "become apparent that [the opposing party] was seeking to use disqualification as a litigation tactic." *Id.* at 221. The Court is generally reluctant to disqualify counsel of a taxpayer's choice on motion of the adversary. *See Alexander v. Superior Court*, 685 P.2d 1309, 1317 (Ariz. 1984). In these cases, however, respondent promptly moved for disqualification prior to conducting discovery or engaging in settlement negotiations and before these cases were set for trial. *See Duffey v. Commissioner*, 91 T.C. 81, 84 (1988).

Rule 201(a) provides that "Practitioners before the Court shall carry on their practice in accordance with the letter and spirit of the Model Rules". This Court, therefore, has the power to compel withdrawal of petitioners' counsel if such representation would violate the Model Rules. Specifically, Rule 24(f) provides:

> If any counsel of record (1) was involved in planning or promoting a transaction or operating an entity that is connected to any issue in a case, [or] (2) represents more than one person with differing interests with respect to any issue in a case, then such counsel must either secure the informed consent of the client ; withdraw from the case; or take whatever other steps are necessary to obviate a conflict of interest or other violation of the ABA Model Rules of Professional Conduct, and particularly [Rule] 1.7.

Rule 24(f), which became effective July 1, 1990, emphasizes the provisions of the Model Rules to which practitioners before this Court were already subject. Rule 24(f) was added "to insure that the bar of this Court disclose or rectify any conflict of interest." Rules of Practice and Procedure of the United States Tax Court, 93 T.C. 821, 858 Note.

Model Rule 1.7(b) provides:

> A lawyer shall not represent a client if the representation of that client may be materially limited by the lawyer's responsibilities to another client or to a third person, or by the lawyer's own interests, unless:
>
> (1) the lawyer reasonably believes the representation will not be adversely affected; and
>
> (2) the client consents after consultation. When representation of multiple clients in a single matter is undertaken, the consultation shall include explanation of the implications of the common representation and the advantages and risks involved.

Petitioners contend that Izen's representation of them does not violate Model Rule 1.7(b) because no potential conflict of interest exists among petitioners. Petitioners contend that each petitioner is contesting the deficiency and will argue that Para Tech should be recognized as a trust and that Para Tech's Federal income tax returns for 1987 and 1988 were correct.

Respondent contends that Izen's representation of each petitioner may be materially limited by his responsibilities to the other petitioners and by his own interests. Respondent states:

> There are positions which can be advanced on behalf of each Petitioner which, if established, would enable that Petitioner to avoid liability for all or part of the deficiencies and additions to tax determined against that Petitioner, but which cannot be established without irreparably damaging some other Petitioner's case.

As set forth above, respondent determined that Anderson and Ferber were each taxable on an amount equal to the taxable income of Para Tech. One of respondent's alternative theories is that Para Tech is a grantor trust. Generally, the grantor trust rules apply to a person, such as Anderson, who created the trust. See secs. 671 through 678. Anderson formed the trust and transferred his business to it and is a beneficiary of the trust. Ferber, although serving as a trustee, is less likely to be a grantor. Ferber, and, hypothetically, Para Tech, would avoid taxation if respondent successfully established that the income was taxable to Anderson as the grantor.

Further, respondent has determined that each petitioner is liable for the additions to tax for fraud. In support of that determination, respondent's answer alleges that books and records made available to respondent during the examination of petitioners' returns were false and fraudulent, that petitioners "individually and in concert, refused to cooperate with Respondent's agents and attempted to obstruct Respondent's examination by various means", and that each petitioner understated or failed to report taxable income and tax due from them. In this regard, Anderson and Ferber can each argue that the other was responsible for maintaining the books and records of Para Tech and for preparing its tax returns and that each relied on the other. Each may also claim that he relied on Izen's opinion letters. In addition, Ferber, as trustee of Para Tech, is putatively making decisions for Para Tech, including using its funds to pay for litigation of these cases, while Anderson, not Ferber, has a beneficial interest in Para Tech.

Although it is too early in this litigation to anticipate all of the arguments that will be made, and the foregoing possibilities may not be the positions that petitioners should or will adopt at trial, there is a serious possibility that petitioners' positions may become adverse to each other.

Izen's personal interests in this case may also conflict with the interests of petitioners. Anderson and Ferber relied, at least partially, on opinion letters that Izen had written. Therefore, Izen has an interest in vindicating the positions he took in the opinion letters in order to maintain his professional reputation and to protect himself from any potential future liability to petitioners. He would therefore be less likely to advise petitioners disinterestedly with regard to such matters as accepting a settlement offer. Izen's failure to advise petitioners of the potential adverse defenses or affirmative claims available to them would constitute a breach of his duty of loyalty to them. Finally, Izen is potentially a witness with respect to matters set forth in his tax opinion, and testimony on that subject could appropriately be obtained without violation of the attorney-client privilege.

Izen and petitioners contend that petitioners have been informed of and waive Izen's conflict of interest. We are not persuaded, however, that the apparent consent of petitioners is informed and voluntary.

We are not persuaded that Izen made a full and fair disclosure or that petitioners understood the inherent potential conflicts between them. The backgrounds of the individuals suggest a lack of sophistication in assessing matters such as these, and they relied solely on the advice of Izen in deciding to waive the conflicts of interest. It appears to us that the waiver is not based on informed consent but on the cost of employing independent and separate counsel and having such counsel become familiar with the underlying facts of the cases.

Izen admitted during the hearing on respondent's motion that he had not secured written consents or waivers from petitioners and that he had not contacted Nassau Life or other beneficiaries of the Para Tech trust. Under these circumstances, we conclude that it is "more important that unethical conduct be prevented than [that petitioners] have an unfettered right to counsel of [their] choice." *Kevlik v. Goldstein*, 724 F.2d 844, 849 (1st Cir. 1984). The potential for unfairness to petitioners and damage to the integrity of the judicial process is too serious to permit Izen's representation of petitioners to continue, even in the face of an apparent waiver.

Therefore, Izen must be disqualified from representing petitioners in these cases.

There is nothing per se improper about receiving fees from an entity to represent an officer or employee of the entity. Indeed, the ABA Standards noted above approve of the practice if handled properly, and it is quite common for fees to be paid by the entity/employer. Moreover, in the high-profile criminal case against former partner KPMG partners, the District Court dismissed the indictments against 13 of the 16 defendants, finding that the Government had pressured KPMG to cut off the payment of legal fees to their former employees.

> The government threatened to indict, and thus to destroy, the giant accounting firm, KPMG LLP. It coerced KPMG to limit and then cut off its payment of the legal fees of KPMG employees. KPMG avoided indictment by yielding to government pressure. Many of its personnel did not. They now await trial, four of them deprived of counsel of their choice and most of the others unable to afford the defenses that they would have presented absent the government's interference.
>
> This Court previously held that the government's interference with KPMG's payment of the legal fees of its employees and former employees violated the employees' constitutional rights. The government now concedes that thirteen of the sixteen individuals formerly employed by KPMG are entitled to dismissal, assuming that this Court's previous ruling was correct. But the government does not concede the correctness of that ruling. Accordingly, the Court has reconsidered *Stein I* carefully in light of the government's arguments. It remains convinced that the ruling was correct. Indeed, additional evidence not previously considered strongly supports the Court's decision. The government, however, now has focused for the first time on the specific circumstances of certain of these defendants. The Court concludes that three of the defendants have not established that KPMG would have paid their defense costs even if the government had left KPMG to its own devices. The indictment therefore will be dismissed as to thirteen of the sixteen KPMG Defendants.[57]

---

[57] United States v. Stein, 435 F. Supp. 2d 330 (S.D.N.Y. 2007), *aff'd*, 541 F.3d 130 (2d Cir. 2008).

VII. CASH FOR SERVICES

Under section 6050I, any business that receives more than $10,000 in cash in a single transaction or related series of transactions must file an IRS Form 8300. Lawyers and law firms are included within the definition of "any business" for these purposes. Failure to file the Form 8300 and supply all required information called for by the form, including the identity of the payor, may subject the business to civil or criminal penalties.[58] And yet, the client may wish that his identity not be disclosed to the IRS on a Form 8300. Can the lawyer refuse to disclose that information? The Second Circuit dealt with this precise issue in the context of a high-profile criminal defense attorney.

LEFCOURT v. UNITED STATES

United States Court of Appeals for the Second Circuit
125 F.3d 79 (1997)

Title 26, section 6050I, of the United States Code requires "[a]ny person . . . engaged in a trade or business" who "in the course of such trade or business, receives more than $10,000 in cash . . ." to report to the IRS the person from whom the cash was received, the amount of cash received, the date and nature of the transaction, and "such other information as the Secretary may prescribe." Form 8300 is the form used to report such a transaction.

During the summer of 1993, Lefcourt, a law firm specializing in criminal defense work, undertook the representation of a client facing federal drug and money laundering charges. The client paid Lefcourt over $10,000 in cash for legal services. On July 9, 1993, the law firm submitted a Form 8300 to the IRS, stating that it had received in excess of $10,000, and particularizing the date of the payment. The firm, however, deliberately omitted the payor's name. In doing so, Gerald Lefcourt, the law firm's name partner, attached to the Form 8300 an affidavit asserting that revealing the client-identifying information called for by § 6050I would prejudice the interests of a client whom the law firm was actively representing and that the confidentiality of the information was protected by the Fifth and Sixth Amendments of the Constitution and by the Lawyers' Code of Professional Responsibility.

On December 14, 1993, the IRS served the law firm with a Notice of Proposed Penalties under 26 U.S.C. § 6721(e), which allows for the imposition of a penalty where "intentional disregard" of § 6050I's reporting requirements is established. Over the following four months, Lefcourt initiated numerous correspondences with the IRS to request a conference with the IRS's Office of Appeals concerning the proposed penalty, and to explain the basis for its failure to provide the name of its client on the Form 8300. The overtures resulted in an apparently unsuccessful pre-settlement conference between Lefcourt and the IRS on April 12, 1994: on August 8, 1994 the IRS assessed the law firm a $25,000 penalty pursuant to § 6721.

---

[58] *See* sections 6721(e) & 7203.

DISCUSSION

I. *Intentional Disregard*

We first turn to the question of whether, by declining to provide its client's name as called for by Form 8300, the law firm acted with "intentional disregard" of § 6050I's filing requirements.

As noted earlier, 26 U.S.C. § 6050I requires "[a]ny person . . . engaged in a trade or business" who "in the course of such trade or business, receives more than $10,000 in cash . . ." to file a report with the IRS that specifies the person from whom the cash was received, the amount of cash received, the date and nature of the transaction, and "such other information as the Secretary may prescribe." 26 U.S.C. § 6050I(a), (b). When a party is deemed to have failed to file the information required by § 6050I because of "intentional disregard of the filing requirement," the Internal Revenue Code provides that the party shall be fined the greater of $25,000 or the amount of cash received in the transaction. *See* 26 U.S.C. § 6721(e)(2)(C). Title 26, section 301.6721-1(f)(2)(ii), of the Code of Federal Regulations indicates that "a failure is due to intentional disregard if it is a knowing or willful . . . [f]ailure to include correct information."

The district court found that the $25,000 penalty was properly assessed against Lefcourt because the government satisfied its burden of demonstrating that the law firm acted with intentional disregard of its legal obligations — that is, that "[p]laintiff knew what § 6050I required and voluntarily, consciously, and intentionally failed to comply."

On appeal, Lefcourt argues that the district court applied the incorrect *mens rea* standard to § 6721's enhanced penalty provision. Lefcourt takes the position that under § 6721, a good faith belief in the legality of one's conduct — even where that belief later proves to be mistaken or unreasonable — precludes a finding of intentional disregard. Put another way, Lefcourt argues that one must be aware of the law's requirements in order to disregard them, and thus, a subjective good faith belief that one's conduct is lawful precludes the imposition of the penalty. Lefcourt suggests that Congress chose to adopt this heightened "bad faith" requirement because the penalties provided for by the statute are severe.

The principal case Lefcourt points to is *Cheek v. United States*, 498 U.S. 192 (1991), which involved the criminal prosecution of a defendant who failed to pay federal income taxes for several years on the basis of his (erroneous) view that, under the tax laws, wages did not constitute taxable income. The Supreme Court held that in order to convict a defendant of criminal tax evasion in violation of 26 U.S.C. § 7201, it is not sufficient for the government to show only that the defendant acted voluntarily, as opposed to by accident or mistake. The Court held that the government also must prove willfulness, which, "as construed by . . . prior tax cases, requires the Government to prove that the law imposed a duty on the defendant, that the defendant knew of this duty, and that he voluntarily and intentionally violated this duty." *Id.* at 201. A defendant's genuinely held — albeit erroneous or even unreasonable — belief in the legality of his conduct is thus a defense to a prosecution for willful tax evasion.

Lefcourt's reliance on *Cheek*'s willfulness standard is unavailing. *Cheek* was a criminal case, and we are persuaded that its rationale does not apply in the context of the civil tax penalties at issue here.

Section 6721 does not use the term "willful"; it uses the term "intentional disregard." But 26 C.F.R. § 301.6721-1(f)(2)(ii) defines "intentional disregard" as synonymous with "willfulness." Thus, in our view, the "intentional disregard" set forth in § 6721's penalty provision means conduct that is willful, a term which in this context requires only that a party act voluntarily in withholding requested information, rather than accidentally or unconsciously. Once it is determined, as it was here, that the failure to disclose client-identifying information was done purposefully, rather than inadvertently, it is irrelevant that the filer may have believed he was legally justified in withholding such information. The only question that remains is whether the law required its disclosure.

As it is uncontested that Lefcourt was aware that Form 8300 asked for its client's identity and nonetheless chose to refuse to provide the name, there is no dispute that Lefcourt acted voluntarily. We thus agree with the district court that, as a matter of law, Lefcourt's failure to disclose the client-identifying information was willful and in "intentional disregard" of the law firm's obligation.

II. *Mandatory Waiver*

Lefcourt argues that even if the law firm acted with intentional disregard of § 6050I's reporting requirements, it was entitled to the automatic penalty waiver under 26 U.S.C. § 6724. That section sets forth the waiver rules that apply to the penalties for failure to comply with certain IRS reporting requirements. It provides that "[n]o penalty shall be imposed under this part with respect to any failure if it is shown that such failure is due to reasonable cause and not to willful neglect." 26 U.S.C. § 6724(a). The burden of showing reasonable cause is on the party seeking the waiver. We hold that Lefcourt was not entitled to the waiver because the law firm failed to establish that it had an objectively reasonable argument for failing to disclose its client's identity.

Although we have found no cases discussing the phrase "due to reasonable cause and not to . . . willful neglect" within the meaning of § 6724, the Supreme Court in *United States v. Boyle*, 469 U.S. 241, 243 (1985), considered the meaning of a virtually identical phrase used in 26 U.S.C. § 6651(a)(1), which states the penalty for the late filing of a tax return. In that context, the Court stated that " 'willful neglect' may be read as meaning a conscious, intentional failure or reckless indifference." *Boyle*, 469 U.S. at 245. However, we do not believe that *Boyle*'s definition applies to § 6724's waiver provision. In *Boyle*, the Supreme Court explicitly limited its definition to the term "willful neglect" as used in § 6651. *See Boyle*, 469 U.S. at 245. More to the point, if *Boyle*'s definition were applied in this context, the circumstances that would trigger a penalty would be such as to negate the waiver provision in the first place because once a willful violation under § 6721 were found, a filer would never be entitled to a waiver under § 6724. Put another way, a filer found to have acted in a "voluntary, conscious, and intentional" manner so as to be subject to the penalty would also necessarily be found to have acted with "willful neglect" as defined in *Boyle* — that is, consciously and intentionally, *see id.* — and would thus be ineligible for the waiver. We do not believe that Congress would create such a phantom waiver clause. Rather, we believe that "reasonable cause and not willful neglect" must refer not simply to whether the taxpayer acted voluntarily in the sense of acting consciously, but also to whether the filer's reason for so acting was objectively reasonable under the circumstances.

This interpretation of the meaning of the phrase "reasonable cause and not willful neglect" is supported by the definition of the term "reasonable cause" in 26 C.F.R. § 301.6724-1. To be entitled to the reasonable cause waiver, the filer must satisfy several criteria. Relevant here is the objective standard found in the regulation's requirement that the filer must have acted in a responsible manner by exercising reasonable care, "which is that standard of care that a reasonably prudent person would use under the circumstances in the course of its business in determining its filing obligations." 26 C.F.R. § 303.6724-1(d)(i).

Further, we believe that the regulation's reference to reasonableness "under the circumstances in the course of its business" permits a court to consider specific relevant features of the filer's particular business in assessing whether the filer acted with reasonable care in intentionally disregarding his or her § 6050I obligations. Thus the appropriate inquiry in this case is whether the law firm's decision to withhold client-identifying information was consistent with the standard of care that a reasonably prudent attorney would use under the circumstances in the course of his or her business.

Preliminarily, we acknowledge that a reasonable attorney carefully attends to the attorney-client privilege. Not only is the attorney bound to do so under the various codes of professional responsibility that govern the practice of law, but also, to many attorneys, the privilege between attorney and client "is essential to enhancing frank and complete communication between attorney and client, which, in turn, promotes compliance with the law and facilitates the administration of justice." Brief of the Amici Curiae at 4.

Yet the attorney-client privilege, however important to our system of justice, is not a license for an attorney to act "unreasonably" in willfully failing to comply with clear federal law. Thus, in the context presented here, if a reasonable attorney would have no basis for concluding that nondisclosure of client-identifying information was justified under existing law, the attorney- client privilege cannot serve to excuse the imposition of a penalty under § 6721. Accordingly, we turn to Lefcourt's rationale for nondisclosure to determine whether it was objectively reasonable.

Lefcourt argued to the IRS and to the district court that under Second Circuit law the attorney-client privilege protects an attorney from disclosing the client-identifying information required under § 6050I in certain "special circumstances." The law firm contended that it did not submit the required information principally because it believed that a special circumstance might be found to exist where the completed Form 8300 would provide the government with evidence of its client's unexplained wealth — evidence that could incriminate the client in the same proceedings for which the client had retained the law firm. Lefcourt also referred to the fact that disclosure of the client's identity might lead eventually to Lefcourt's being called as a witness against the client, which would in turn result in the law firm's disqualification.

Our assessment of the reasonableness of the law firm's claimed "special circumstances" begins with *United States v. Goldberger & Dubin, P.C.*, 935 F.2d 501 (2d Cir. 1991). In *Goldberger*, upon a law firm's refusal to file a completed Form 8300, the IRS issued a summons, subsequently enforced by the district court, directing the firm to produce its clients' names. On appeal, the attorneys argued that § 6050I's reporting requirements were unconstitutional and violative of the attorney-client privilege. We rejected both claims and affirmed the district court's order directing disclosure of the client-identifying information.

With respect to the attorney-client privilege, we held that "absent special circumstances . . . the identification in Form 8300 of respondents' clients who make substantial cash payments is not a disclosure of privileged information." *Goldberger*, 935 F.2d at 505. Thus, we suggested that although a client's identity is generally not privileged, there might be "special circumstances" where such information would be protected from disclosure.

Lefcourt relies on *Goldberger*'s reference to "special circumstances" to support the proposition that in this circuit, there are occasions when an attorney's noncompliance with § 6050I will be excused. The law firm argues further that *Goldberger* left open the possibility that one such special circumstance could be where the disclosure of the client-identifying information would "prejudice [the client's] interest and undermine [the law firm's] ability to provide effective representation." We do not accept that reading of *Goldberger* and the cases on which *Goldberger* relied.

As a general rule, a client's identity and fee information are not privileged. Although the court in *Goldberger* did not elaborate on the meaning of the special circumstances exception to the rule, it offered some guidance as to what might and what might not constitute such a circumstance. Significant to this case, the court expressly rejected the essence of Lefcourt's claim when it stated that the "asserted possibility" that a client may be incriminated by disclosure does not constitute a special circumstance. *See* 935 F.2d at 505.

In so doing, the court cited *In re Grand Jury Subpoena Duces Tecum Served Upon Gerald L. Shargel*, 742 F.2d 61 (2d Cir. 1984), which involved a defense attorney's appeal of a district court order denying a motion to quash a subpoena issued by a grand jury that sought to compel the attorney to produce records of money he had received from several clients who had been indicted for RICO violations. The government in *Shargel* admitted that the grand jury wanted the information as possible evidence that the defendants possessed unexplained wealth. Shargel argued that disclosure of the information would violate the attorney-client privilege by incriminating his clients in the RICO case. The court unequivocally rejected this "incrimination rationale" that Lefcourt now claims provided a reasonable basis for its own noncompliance:

> We have consistently held that client identity and fee information are, absent special circumstances, not privileged. This result follows from defining the privilege to encompass only those confidential communications

> necessary to obtain informed legal advice. This definition, which focuses upon facilitating the role of the lawyer as a professional advisor and advocate, is to be distinguished from the so-called "incrimination rationale," which focuses upon whether the materials sought may be used as evidence against the client. While the attorney-client privilege historically arose at the same time as the privilege against self-incrimination, it was early established that the privileges had distinct policies and that the "point of honor" — the attorney's reluctance to incriminate his client — was not a valid reason to invoke the attorney-client privilege.

Shargel, 742 F.2d at 62–63 (citations and footnote omitted). The court thus held that "information is not protected by the privilege even though the client may strongly fear the effects of disclosure, including incrimination." *Id.* 742 F.2d at 63.

Thus the law is clear, and was so when Lefcourt refused to file its completed Form 8300: to the extent that the legal advice exception exists in any jurisdiction, it plainly is not recognized as a special circumstance in this circuit. Lefcourt's argument that nondisclosure in this case was warranted under the attorney-client privilege because the client-identifying "information could be used against the client in the very case in which the Firm was engaged to provide criminal defense representation," Brief of Appeal of Gerald B. Lefcourt, P.C. at 3 — a phrase that parrots the classic definition of the legal advice exception set forth in *Anderson*, 906 F.2d at 1488 — was not objectively reasonable.

Most of the courts that have considered this issue agree with the Second Circuit in *Lefcourt.*[59] However, despite this consensus in the federal courts on this issue, state bar associations have imposed a contradictory duty on their members. For example, the Washington and Wisconsin state bar associations have issued ethics opinions holding that an attorney may not ethically disclose a client's identity on a Form 8300 unless the client consents.[60] Under these opinions, the attorney must not only refuse to disclose the client's identity (and presumably face the civil penalties imposed in *Lefcourt*), the attorney must also contest any IRS effort to obtain that information through summons or subpoena. While some of these ethics opinions strike a rather nonchalant pose regarding the imposition of penalties, the Indiana bar seems to recognize the untenable position attorneys face:

> It is the opinion of this Committee that the reporting requirements of 26 U.S.C. § 6050I of the Internal Revenue Code create an ethical dilemma for attorneys confronting the problem that, absent client consent to disclose the information, may prove insoluble. On the one hand, the attorney is bound to hold sacred the confidences of his client; on the other, as an officer of the court and as a citizen of the United States, the attorney is bound to obey the law, including § 6050I of the Internal Revenue Code. The problem

---

[59] *See, e.g.*, United States v. Blackman, 72 F.3d 1418 (9th Cir. 1995), *cert. denied*, 519 U.S. 911 (1996); United States v. Ritchie, 15 F.3d 592 (6th Cir.), *cert. denied*, 513 U.S. 868 (1994); United States v. Leventhal, 961 F.2d 936 (11th Cir. 1992).

[60] Washington Formal Op. 194 (1997); Wisconsin Ethics Op. E-90-3; *see also* Hall, *supra* note 1, at 322 n.4.

> is that in some cases, by reporting a client's cash transaction activity on Form 8300, a lawyer may attract the attention of the IRS as well as law enforcement authorities to a client who was not previously being investigated.
>
> The answer to the question posed at the beginning of this opinion, as to whether an attorney is forbidden by the Indiana Rules of Professional Conduct from disclosing client information on IRS Form 8300, is, in the opinion of this committee, that Rule 1.6, and possibly Rules 1.8 and 1.9 as well, do forbid such disclosures. At the same time, Rule 4.1(b) appears to compel such disclosures. The committee believes that this absurd result can only be definitively addressed by legislative action. Until this situation is remedied in Congress, the options open to the lawyer are few. The only way in which the lawyer can avoid the ethical dilemma is to disclose in advance to the client the existence of 26 U.S.C. § 6050I and the reporting requirements of Form 8300. The ethical lawyer will advise the client that if the client wishes to avoid placing a lawyer in an impossible bind, he will not confront the lawyer with cash or bearer transactions that appear reportable. If the client does not consent to representation on those terms, the net effect will be that the client will likely seek a less ethical lawyer, who will agree not to make any report on Form 8300.[61]

Not only do attorneys face civil penalties for failing to file or fully complete a Form 8300, there are potentially *criminal* sanctions that can be applied. As discussed in Chapter 2B, section 7203 makes it a crime to willfully fail to file a return. Normally, a failure to file is a misdemeanor. However, if the failure to file involves a Form 8300 (a violation of section 6050I), the offense becomes a felony. Thus, the stakes in this game are extremely high, and an attorney should only accept cash for services after having thoroughly analyzed the situation.

A related problem deals with representing defendants who are not garden-variety tax cheats who have evaded taxes on legitimately-derived income, but rather whose booty is more of the ill-gotten variety. It is not unusual for lawyers to represent clients in a criminal tax case in which the income allegedly underreported came from illegal activities like drug dealing.

If the client uses proceeds from certain crimes to pay his lawyer, the fees may be subject to forfeiture by the government. For example, 21 U.S.C. section 853 empowers the government to seize from a defendant who has been convicted of certain narcotics offenses "any property constituting, or derived from, any proceeds the person obtained, directly or indirectly, as the result of such violation."[62] The phrase "any property" in section 853 has been interpreted to include fees paid to an attorney. In *Caplin & Drysdale v. United States*,[63] the Supreme Court held that forfeiting fees paid to attorneys does not violate a defendant's Sixth Amendment right to counsel. Attorneys should therefore be extremely careful in ensuring that any funds used to pay their fees came from a legitimate source of the client.

---

[61] Indiana State Bar Association Legal Ethics Committee Opinion No. 1 (1995).

[62] 21 U.S.C. section 853(a)(1).

[63] 491 U.S. 617 (1989).

PROBLEM

Your firm has been contacted by Acme Construction Company, Inc., a C corporation. The company is currently under audit by an IRS revenue agent (a civil auditor). At the first meeting with the client, you learn that majority shareholder and CEO of the company, Mark, has been using company funds, assets, and materials to remodel his palatial waterfront home. He has been charging the work to other jobs and deducting the costs of material and labor. Mark did not report the value of the improvements as income. The revenue agent has served requests for documents to which the company has not yet responded. Among the documents requested are records that will show that both the company and Mark committed tax fraud.

(1) Mark would like to retain you and your firm to represent him. In order to save money, he would like you to represent the company as well (he argues that the cases involve the same transactions, and therefore the defenses will be identical). He proposes to have the company pay the retainer and all subsequent fees for both him and the company, since it is the company that is under audit. May you ethically represent both the company and the CEO? What steps should you take to ensure that your representation of either or both of the parties is handled ethically?

(2) The client asks that you not respond to the request for records. Can you decline to provide the requested documents and not be disciplined for failing follow the requirements of Circular 230? Would your answer be different if the IRS agent were a CID agent?

(3) Assume that instead of the CEO using company assets for his use, your fact investigation reveals that the company's Chief Financial Officer, Keli, was embezzling funds to remodel her downtown condo. Since she was the CFO, she was able to doctor the books to charge the expenses to other jobs, and the tax returns filed for the years under investigation show these expenses were deducted as costs of goods sold, rather than salary. What are your obligations to the company and what ethical standards are applicable?

(4) During the course of your representation, October 15th rolls around and the company would like to file its tax returns. The offending remodeling was completed before the beginning of the taxable year, so there is no risk of damaging the client's position in the current investigation by filing a return. Nevertheless, the company would like to take a rather aggressive position on certain repair expense deductions for construction done on the company's headquarters facilities, and the company would like to pay you to draft an opinion letter stating that the position is acceptable for tax purposes. Can you ethically draft an opinion for the client? Should you? Assuming you do draft the opinion letter, what ethical standards are applicable to you as a tax professional in issuing such an opinion?

Chapter 12

MAJOR COLLATERAL ISSUES

IRC: Read §§ 6103(a) & (b), 7213(a)(1), 7213A, 7216, 7301, 7302, 7303, 7431; Skim §§ 6103 (remainder), 7304 & 7321–7342

I. INTRODUCTION

Understandably, the first concerns of taxpayer's counsel in a criminal tax case are to prevent the taxpayer's incarceration or at least to minimize its duration. However, as important as those goals are, they cannot fix the limit of counsel's horizon. Counsel's vision also must encompass a number of important secondary considerations.

This chapter and the following one describe those considerations. This Chapter 12 addresses: (1) forfeiture of assets; (2) civil disabilities arising as a result of conviction; (3) effect on immigration status of alien defendants; (4) professional sanctions as to tax advisers who commit tax offenses; (5) adverse publicity; and (6) potential disruption of business privileges and relationships. Chapter 13 addresses civil tax liabilities and penalties.

II. FORFEITURE

A. Introduction

Congress has provided forfeiture for some of the crimes considered here, principally money laundering and currency transaction reporting. Forfeiture law is a separate subject in itself, and this subchapter does little more than introduce the subject.[1] We start with background on forfeiture law generally, to provide perspective for the tax-specific rules.

Forfeiture has been defined as "divestiture without compensation of property used in a manner contrary to the laws of the sovereign."[2] There are two types of

---

[1] For further discussion of forfeiture, see Levy, *License to Steal: The Forfeiture of Property* (1996), the title of which should give you an idea of the author's view of the subject. Another good discussion of tax and money laundering is 2 Ian M. Comisky, Lawrence S. Feld & Steven M. Harris, *Tax Fraud and Evasion* chs. 12 & 13 (2006); *see also* Dee R. Edgeworth, Asset Forfeiture: Practice and Procedure in State and Federal Courts (2d ed. 2008); Stefan D. Cassella, Asset Forfeiture Law in the United States (2d ed. 2013).

[2] J.W. Goldsmith, Jr.-Grant Co. v. United States, 254 U.S. 505, 511 (1921) (*quoting* Blackstone's Commentaries).

forfeiture — one criminal, also referred to as in personam, and the other civil, referred to as in rem.

In rem forfeiture is a civil action against a thing.[3] Society finds the thing offensive and therefore allows a civil action by the sovereign to forfeit the thing. Forfeiture of the thing is not punishment and not subject to the Excessive Fines Clause.[4] Illegal drugs are a good example. The owner of such drugs (if he or she will admit to being the owner) has no claim for the seizure and forfeiture of illegal drugs.

In personam forfeiture is an adjunct of criminal action against a person. Forfeiture is imposed in addition to the criminal penalties otherwise provided statute. At common law, the felon forfeited all personal property to the crown and all real property to his temporal lord. This type of full forfeiture against the felon is forbidden by the Bill of Attainder prohibition of the Constitution.[5] Bills of Attainder have been described as follows:

> In English law, the extinction of civil and political rights resulting from a sentence of death or outlawry after a conviction of treason or a felony. The most important consequences of attainder were forfeiture and corruption of blood. For treason, the offender's lands were forfeited to the king. For felony, they were forfeited to the king for a year and a day and then escheated (forfeited) to the lord from whom the offender held his tenure, a result of the concept that felony was a breach of the feudal bond.[6]

Although the Government may not forfeit property solely by virtue of a person's felon status, the Government may fine a felon for his or her criminal conduct. Fines are subject to the Excessive Fines prohibition in the Eighth Amendment because they are punishments. Fines may take the form of forfeiture of the means or fruits of a crime (as opposed to all property whether or not related to the crime being punished).

The Tax Division of the Department of Justice intends soon to establish a formal policy to govern forfeitures in civil and criminal tax cases. Currently no general policy exists; each U.S. Attorney's Office follows its own approach. Prosecutors do not use forfeiture in most tax cases.[7]

B. General Federal Forfeiture Rules

Forfeiture has been a governmental prerogative since the inception of the United States. In 1970, in Congress' first forays in the war on crimes, Congress enacted criminal forfeiture first for RICO (Racketeer Influenced and Corrupt Organizations) and then in the continuing criminal enterprises. Thereafter, in 1986, Congress enacted forfeiture for the money laundering crimes. Although there are

---

[3] *See* IRM 9.7.2.1.

[4] U.S. Const. amend. 8.

[5] U.S. Const. art. I, § 9, cl. 3.

[6] "Attainder," Encyclopaedia Brittanica (2007).

[7] *ABA Meeting: DOJ Working on Formal Forfeiture Policy*, 2012 TNT 181-6 (Sept. 18, 2012) (quoting DOJ officials).

forfeiture rules scattered through the federal statutes,[8] the general forfeiture rules are set forth in 18 U.S.C., Part I, Ch. 46.[9]

Two types of forfeiture are allowed — civil forfeiture under 18 U.S.C. section 981 and criminal forfeiture under 18 U.S.C. section 982. Civil forfeiture is the in rem type of forfeiture noted above. It is separate from, and not dependent upon, any criminal prosecution. Criminal forfeiture is the in personam type of forfeiture noted above and is an adjunct to a criminal proceeding, in which the forfeiture is imposed at the time of sentencing.

1. Civil Forfeiture

Contraband, being property illegal to own per se, is forfeitable even without the statute. The statutes deal principally with property used in the commission of crime or proceeds from the commission of crime and are in rem forfeitures.[10] As pertinent to this course, civil forfeiture is available for property involved in a money laundering transaction under 18 U.S.C. sections 1956, 1957, or 1960.[11] And, in pertinent part, proceeds from the commission of certain crimes, including specifically crimes involving "specified unlawful activity (as defined in section 1956(c)(7))" are forfeitable.[12] Civil forfeiture is not prescribed in these general provisions for tax offenses. (However, the Internal Revenue Code provides certain forfeitures, which we shall cover below.) The statute confers title in the United States from the time of commission of the underlying offense.[13]

Seizures generally require a court seizure warrant obtained in a manner similar to a search warrant, but there are some key exceptions.[14] Upon satisfaction of this initial requirement, the Attorney General generally makes the seizure, but the Secretary of the Treasury makes the seizure for crimes investigated by Treasury, including the IRS.[15]

As usual in such a large bureaucracy, the Secretary of the Treasury has delegated the authority and, through redelegations, the authority resides in local IRS management.[16] The property, once seized, is not repleviable.[17] The Government may bring a judicial proceeding for forfeiture but in most cases may also forfeit administratively, subject to the property owner's right to invoke judicial remedies by following certain requirements.[18] Under the administrative forfeiture

---

[8] *See* Comiskey, Feld & Harris, *supra*, at 12-8 (noting over 140 federal forfeiture statutes).

[9] 18 U.S.C. § 981 *et seq.*

[10] IRM 9.7.2.3.

[11] 18 U.S.C. § 981(a)(1)(A).

[12] 18 U.S.C. § 981(a)(1)(C).

[13] 18 U.S.C. § 981(f).

[14] 18 U.S.C. § 981(b)(2).

[15] 18 U.S.C. § 981(b)(1).

[16] *See generally* IRM 9.7, "Asset Seizure and Forfeiture." See IRM 9.7.2.2 for delegations to the IRS with respect to Bank Secrecy Act and Money Laundering seizures and forfeitures.

[17] 18 U.S.C. § 981(c).

[18] 18 U.S.C. § 981(d) (incorporating customs procedures under 19 U.S.C. § 1602 *et seq.*); *see* IRM

procedures, the IRS will notify all known claimants to the property that the IRS intends to forfeit the property and will advise those persons that they have either a judicial remedy or an administrative remedy. The judicial remedy is obtained by filing a claim of ownership. The Government's right to make the seizure and forfeit the property is contestable under the procedures in section 983 discussed below. The civil forfeiture proceeding may be stayed if discovery in the proceeding might prejudice the Government's investigation or the taxpayer's rights.[19]

The civil forfeiture provisions were substantially revised by the Civil Asset Forfeiture Reform Act of 2000 (CAFRA).[20] As relevant to this course, the following are key features of civil forfeiture under the CAFRA revision of section 983:

1. General rules for forfeiture proceedings are provided to permit timely, independent judicial review of the Government's assertion of its right to forfeit.[21] One of the most prominent reforms is that the putative property owner does not have to post a bond to obtain judicial review of the Government's right to forfeit.
2. Indigent property owners may obtain representation if they have indigent representation in a related federal criminal case. Further, indigent property owners may obtain representation if the Government seeks to forfeit a primary residence.[22]
3. The Government must prove by a preponderance of the evidence that it is entitled to make the forfeiture.[23] If the Government's ground for forfeiture is that the property facilitated the commission of the offense, the Government must prove that there is a substantial connection between the property and the offense.[24] This allocation of the burden of proof is a substantial departure from the prior rules which permitted seizure for forfeiture merely upon a showing of probable cause and, after seizure, the claimant for property had the burden of showing by a preponderance of the evidence that forfeiture was either unjustified or inappropriate.
4. Innocent owners of property, including bona fide purchasers, who did not participate in the criminal offense or know of the conduct may avoid

---

9.7.3.6.1 (stating that administrative forfeiture is preferred, unless the nature of the property requires civil judicial forfeiture or prosecutorial considerations favor criminal judicial forfeiture).

[19] 18 U.S.C. § 981(g).

[20] P.L. 106-185, 114 Stat. 202.

[21] 18 U.S.C. § 983(a). Prompt judicial review is a due process requirement, United States v. Melrose E. Subdivision, 357 F.3d 493, 499 (5th Cir. 2004), similar to the due process requirements for jeopardy and termination assessments in tax cases. *See* Commissioner v. Shapiro, 424 U.S. 614 (1976) (giving rise to the elaborate procedures under section 7429 for judicial and administrative review of jeopardy and termination assessments). In *Melrose East*, the Fifth Circuit addressed the level of proof required to continue preliminary restraint on the assets when such restraint allegedly hindered the person's ability to engage counsel. This is related to the Supreme Court's holdings in *Caplin & Drysdale v. United States*, 491 U.S. 617 (1989), discussed later in this chapter and its companion case, *United States v. Monsanto*, 491 U.S. 600 (1989).

[22] 18 U.S.C. § 983(b).

[23] 18 U.S.C. § 983(c)(1).

[24] 18 U.S.C. § 983(c)(3).

forfeiture.[25]

5. Administrative forfeitures that have not been properly noticed may be set aside.[26]
6. Expedited release from forfeitures may be granted in cases of hardship.[27]
7. These forfeiture protections apply generally to forfeitures under any applicable federal law except in specifically enumerated circumstances, one of which is forfeitures under the Internal Revenue Code discussed below.[28] Since forfeitures under the Internal Revenue Code are not material for general crimes that we consider in this course, this exception is also not material for this course. Judicial proceedings related to civil forfeiture are handled under the Federal Rules of Civil Procedure.

An additional constitutional question is whether civil in rem forfeiture after conviction of the crime constitutes punishment for purposes of the double jeopardy guarantee.[29] The Supreme Court has held that it does not.[30]

2. Criminal Forfeiture

Criminal forfeiture is provided under 18 U.S.C. section 982. Criminal forfeitures are in personam forfeitures limited to the property of the defendant.[31] The court in imposing sentence after conviction may provide for forfeiture of property used in certain offenses, including the money laundering offenses, and traceable proceeds of certain crimes. The indictment or information must allege, and there must be a special verdict (or provision of the guilty plea) as to the extent of, the defendant's interest in the property.[32] If the property cannot be located after the exercise of due diligence, substitute property owned by the defendant may be forfeited instead.[33] Although an adjunct to a criminal proceeding, the Government need prove its right to forfeit only by a preponderance of the evidence.[34]

In *United States v. Bajakajian*,[35] the Supreme Court held that criminal forfeiture is subject to the Constitution's prohibition against Excessive Fines and further held that the forfeiture under consideration violated that constitutional guarantee. In that case, a citizen with a Middle Eastern background attempted to

---

[25] 18 U.S.C. § 983(d).

[26] 18 U.S.C. § 983(e).

[27] 18 U.S.C. § 983(f).

[28] 18 U.S.C. § 983(i)(2)(B).

[29] U.S. Const. amend. V.

[30] United States v. Ursery, 518 U.S. 267 (1996).

[31] *See* IRM 9.7.3.

[32] Fed. R. Crim. Proc. 7(c)(2) & 32.2.

[33] 18 U.S.C. § 982(b) & 21 U.S.C. § 853(p). Criminal forfeiture overrides other rules that otherwise could limit alienability, such as the Code's nonforfeiture provision IRC § 408(a)(4) and ERISA's Anti-Alienation provisions. *See* United States v. Vondette, 352 F.3d 772 (2d Cir. 2003), *judgment vacated on other grounds*, 543 U.S. 1108 (2005).

[34] *E.g.*, United States v. Voigt, 89 F.3d 1050 (3d Cir.), *cert. denied*, 519 U.S. 1047 (1996).

[35] 524 U.S. 321 (1998).

leave the United States with a large sum of cash ($356,144). The cash was not derived from a criminal enterprise, or at least so the Court assumed, and was being transported to repay a legitimate debt. The citizen failed to disclose on the CMIR (Cash and Monetary Instrument Report) that must be filled out upon exiting the United States, that he was transporting the cash. Using "cash-sniffing" dogs, Customs officials discovered the cash and inquired of the citizen, whereupon he told a falsehood about the cash. The citizen was arrested and indicted for failing to report the cash as required pursuant to 31 U.S.C. section 5316(a)(1) and making false statements to Customs under 18 U.S.C. section 1001. The Government also sought forfeiture of the $357,144 pursuant to 18 U.S.C. section 982(a)(1), the criminal forfeiture provision. The Government could not have asserted civil forfeiture because the money was not criminally derived. The Court held that criminal forfeiture under the circumstances violated the Excessive Fines guarantee.

The Court started its analysis as follows:

> The touchstone of the constitutional inquiry under the Excessive Fines Clause is the principle of proportionality: The amount of the forfeiture must bear some relationship to the gravity of the offense that it is designed to punish. Until today, however, we have not articulated a standard for determining whether a punitive forfeiture is constitutionally excessive. We now hold that a punitive forfeiture violates the Excessive Fines Clause if it is grossly disproportional to the gravity of a defendant's offense.[36]

The Court discussed the critical distinction between civil in rem forfeiture and criminal forfeiture. The Court determined that the section 982 forfeiture at issue was criminal in personam forfeiture. The offense for which the forfeiture was sought was solely the failure to fill out the CMIR properly. The offense of lying to Government agents under 18 U.S.C. section 1001 was not a basis of the forfeiture. Relative to the crime of failing to fill out the CMIR properly, a 100 percent forfeiture was disproportional. In this regard, the Court noted that the cash was not the instrumentality of a crime, such as a pistol or drugs.

As the dissent noted, the Court's holding only applies to criminal forfeitures.[37] Civil forfeitures are not subject to the Excessive Fines prohibition; civil forfeiture statutes frequently provide for full forfeiture.[38] Hence, as the dissent cautioned, the wave of the future could be to provide for civil forfeitures as a substitute for criminal forfeitures. Subsequently, CAFRA was amended to provide in the case of civil forfeiture that proportionality will apply, thus resolving for the present this potential overreaching in the civil forfeiture provisions.[39]

---

[36] *Id.* at 334.

[37] *Id.* at 347 (Kennedy, J., dissenting).

[38] *See, e.g.*, 18 U.S.C. § 981(a)(1)(A) (imposing civil forfeiture for property involved in a transaction or attempted transaction in violation of §§ 1956, 1957, or 1960 money laundering provisions).

[39] 18 U.S.C. § 983(g).

C. Internal Revenue Code Forfeitures

1. Generally

Sections 7301 and 7302 set out the general Code forfeiture provisions. As noted earlier, the Secretary of the Treasury — thus, by delegation, the IRS — has authority over forfeitures related to crimes other than the crimes set out in the Code.

Forfeiture plays virtually no role in criminal tax prosecutions for substantive tax crimes. Forfeiture plays a big role in money laundering crimes and the crimes that underlie money laundering, including drug trafficking. Because this case book is principally devoted to tax crimes, we shall here focus only on the forfeitures related to tax crimes and specifically on the Internal Revenue Code provisions noted above. However, we also discuss general forfeitures as they relate to attorneys fees because of their importance to practitioners.

2. Proceeds and Tracing

Section 7302 does not permit proceeds forfeiture or tracing. The IRS takes the position that section 7302 forfeiture is permitted for violations of the currency reporting rules in section 6050I, but only the actual funds could be seized in any event and fungibility issues may make that effort impractical.[40]

3. Types of Assets

These provisions do not apply to real property. They may apply to books, records, ledgers, and papers. However, these are generally of limited value.

In one case, a tax shelter promoter peddled his product with backdated documents. The forfeiture was based on use of an automobile in the scheme, and the court approved the forfeiture of the automobile.[41] The IRS similarly takes the position that computers and equipment used in false refund schemes are subject to section 7302 forfeiture. Section 7302 is used in motor fuel excise tax cases to permit the IRS to seize trucks, vessels, and goods involved in the scheme to evade.

For most tax crimes (setting aside the non-tax crimes arising from the War on Crimes in which forfeiture is a principal punishment), forfeiture is not an issue. The IRS does participate in forfeiture of currency or monetary instruments with respect to which a report is required under 31 C.F.R. section 103.23, *i.e.*, the Customs CMIR for transportation of currency or monetary instruments into or out of the United States.[42]

---

[40] *See* CCDM (31)810(1).

[41] United States v. One 1954 Rolls Royce Silver Dawn, 777 F.2d 1358 (9th Cir. 1985).

[42] *See also* 31 C.F.R. pt. 103.

4. Procedures

As noted above, forfeitures generally are subject to the procedural safeguards in CAFRA, but CAFRA expressly exempts IRC forfeitures from its safeguards. Most seizures in which the IRS is involved, however, are not IRC forfeitures. For example, the IRS is authorized to conduct investigations under the money laundering provisions and incident thereto to make forfeitures as authorized for money laundering instruments or proceeds. These non-IRC forfeitures are generally subject to CAFRA's safeguards.

D. Attorneys Fees Forfeitures

We now consider a subject near and dear to all of us — attorneys fees. Are they subject to forfeiture? What additional considerations are applicable in this type of case?

In *Caplin & Drysdale v. United States*,[43] a prominent Washington law firm (with a major tax practice) undertook representation of a person the grand jury was investigating for drug-related crimes. An indictment was brought alleging the client to be in the drug business which was a continuing criminal enterprise in violation of 21 U.S.C. section 848. Relying on forfeiture provisions in the statute, the indictment sought forfeiture of the client's property. Shortly after the indictment, the district court entered a restraining order forbidding the client from transferring the listed assets that were potentially forfeitable. Notwithstanding the restraining order, the defendant paid the firm $25,000 for pre-indictment legal services a few days after the indictment was handed down. This sum was placed by the law firm in an escrow account. The firm continued to represent the defendant following the indictment.

The law firm, on behalf of the client, moved the district court to modify the restraining order to permit the use of the restrained assets to pay the law firm and also sought to exempt from any post-conviction forfeiture order the assets that he intended to use to pay petitioner. Before the court acted, the client pled guilty and, pursuant to the plea agreement, agreed to forfeit all of the specified assets listed in the indictment. The district court then denied his earlier motion to modify the restraining order, concluding that the plea and forfeiture agreement rendered moot any further consideration of the propriety of the court's pretrial restraints. Shortly thereafter the district court entered an order of forfeiture.

The client then brought a proceeding under the forfeiture law for adjudication of the rights of claimants to the forfeited assets. The law firm claimed an interest in $170,000 of the assets for services it had provided in conducting the defendant's defense. It also claimed an interest in the $25,000 being held in the escrow account. The client argued alternatively that assets used to pay an attorney were exempt from forfeiture under the statute and, if not, that the failure of the statute to provide such an exemption rendered it unconstitutional. The district court granted the motion.

---

[43] 491 U.S. 617 (1989).

On appeal, a panel of the circuit court found that the forfeiture statute, by not allowing payment of attorney's fees, violated the defendant's Sixth Amendment right to the counsel of his choice. On *en banc* rehearing, the court of appeals reversed.

The Supreme Court held that the forfeiture was valid and did not impermissibly infringe on the taxpayer's constitutional right to counsel. The Court first rejected an interpretation of the statute that would have given the district courts equitable discretion to release forfeited property to defray attorney's fees. Then, the Supreme Court held that the Sixth Amendment right to counsel did not give a defendant the right to use assets subject to forfeiture to employ counsel of his choice. The Court held that the system has guarantees that will assure a defendant the right to adequate counsel and even counsel of his choice, if he can afford such counsel from his nonforfeitable resources. It does not assure him, however, that he can use assets subject to forfeiture to underwrite his counsel of choice.

This holding has two related aspects. First, and ostensibly most immediately at issue in *Caplin & Drysdale*, the defendant may find criminal practitioners wary about undertaking representation when there is a risk that they will not be paid. Second, it cautions practitioners who are entitled to be paid for our services that we need to be wary about the type of engagements we accept. Consider the following:

> The attorney in a white-collar case — just as in other matters — should know the statutes and prosecutorial policies that govern money laundering, currency reporting requirements, and forfeiture of legal fees that may affect the attorney's ability to retain fees paid. Arguably, in federal cases, under the so-called "relation-back" doctrine, title to the proceeds of a crime vests in the government at the time of its commission. Thus, even though a client may pay his or her attorney pre-accusation, before the attorney has any knowledge or belief that the government will seek forfeiture, an argument can still be made that the funds are forfeitable. The "relation-back" doctrine does not, however, prevent the attorney from asserting that he or she is an "innocent owner." While the federal government has generally not sought to forfeit legal fees paid in instances where the attorney does not have notice of the possibility of forfeiture, the practice has been upheld. If the forfeiture prevents the defendant from having funds to have counsel of choice, however, a probable cause hearing may be required to determine if there is a sufficient basis to believe the funds are forfeitable. To avoid such a hearing, some prosecutors will consent to the payment of reasonable trial fees out of restrained funds.
>
> There is a statutory exemption under the money laundering laws for financial transactions "necessary to preserve a person's right to representation as guaranteed by the Sixth Amendment to the Constitution," which, presumably, was drawn to exempt criminal attorneys paid with the proceeds of criminal conduct from prosecution for money laundering. Many cases hold, however, that the Sixth Amendment right to counsel does not attach until indictment. Therefore, an argument can be made that money laundering laws are applicable to attorneys who receive tainted funds from

clients for pre-indictment legal services.[44]

III. CIVIL DISABILITIES ARISING FROM CONVICTION

A felony conviction may result in civil disabilities.[45] These are largely the result of state law, but they can have federal consequences. For example, some states disqualify felons from voting,[46] which thereby disqualifies them from voting in federal elections since the right to vote in federal elections is determined by the right to vote in state elections.[47] Other examples of disqualification under state law may include the right to hold public office, the right to serve on juries, and the right to engage in certain professions and regulated industries. Federal law also authorizes federal agencies to refuse to do business with contractors who have been convicted of crimes which bear upon their business integrity (*e.g.*, making false statements related to business).[48]

IV. IMMIGRATION MATTERS ARISING FROM CONVICTION

Immigration status may be affected by conviction of an "aggravated felony."[49] An aggravated felony is defined to include an offense that:

> (i) involves fraud or deceit in which the loss to the victim or victims exceeds $10,000; or
>
> (ii) is described in section 7201 of [the Internal Revenue Code] (relating to tax evasion) in which the revenue loss to the Government exceeds $10,000.[50]

The second subpart makes clear that a conviction under section 7201 is an aggravated felony. The question arises, however, whether other tax crimes that, in general parlance, might be viewed to include fraud or deceit are covered in the first subpart. For example, as we have noted, the Government often charges section 7206(1) (tax perjury) in a case in which it could have charged tax evasion, and then the sentencing phase will require proof of a tax loss number that is the number the taxpayer fraudulently sought to avoid reporting or paying. U.S. Immigration and Customs Enforcement (a successor to the former Immigration and Naturalization Service) is charged with administering the immigration laws. The agency takes the

---

[44] Lawrence S. Goldman & Jill R. Shellow-Lavine, *Pre-Indictment Representation in White Collar Cases*, 24 CHAMPION 18 (2000). Reprinted by permission.

[45] *See, e.g.*, 1 ROBERT FINK, TAX CONTROVERSIES: AUDITS, INVESTIGATIONS, TRIALS § 22.03 (2007) (summarizing these disabilities).

[46] *See* Richardson v. Ramirez, 418 U.S. 24 (1974) (holding constitutional a California statute denying convicted felons right to vote).

[47] U.S. Const. art. I, § 2 & amend. XVII.

[48] 48 CFR § 9.406-2(a)(3), (5).

[49] 8 U.S.C. § 1227(a)(2)(A)(iii). *See generally* Scott A. Schumacher, *Criminal Tax and Immigration: A Search for Clarity*, TAX NOTES, Oct. 11, 2010, at 235.

[50] 8 U.S.C. § 1101(a)(43)(M).

position that section 7206(1) may constitute an aggravated felony as defined in the first subpart. Resolving a split in the lower courts, the Supreme Court has held that convictions under sections 7206(1) and (2) in which the Government's revenue loss exceeds $10,000 qualify as aggravated felonies for this purpose.[51]

The Court also has held that failure to advise of immigration consequences can be ineffective assistance of counsel in violation of the Sixth Amendment.[52] An attorney actually misadvising the client as to immigration consequences also would raise Sixth Amendment issues.[53] In your practice, be sure to cover this point with clients and cover it effectively.

V. PROFESSIONAL SANCTIONS

Adverse professional repercussions, including possible loss of license to practice, need to be considered with respect to both the defendant and the defendant's advisers.[54]

A. Defendant

If the defendant is a professional, conviction can imperil his or her livelihood. As examples:

- If the defendant is a financial planner, certification as such and membership in organizations of financial planners can be key business assets. Certification and membership have been denied in a number of cases in which the planner was convicted of criminal tax violations or even had civil tax penalties imposed upon her.
- Those who practice before the IRS — including attorneys, accountants, appraisers, and enrolled agents — are subject to the professional responsibility rules set out in Treasury Circular 230.[55] Violation of those rules can lead to a variety of sanctions, depending on the seriousness of the conduct involved. Disbarment, suspension, reprimand, and monetary penalties all are possible.[56] One possible cause of sanctions is derelictions as to the practitioner's own returns, such as conviction of a tax crime.[57]

---

[51] Kawashima v. Holder, 132 S. Ct. 1166 (2012) (rejecting defendants' contentions based on the Code, the sentencing guidelines, and the rule of lenity); *see also* John Doe v. Attorney General, 659 F.3d 266 (3d Cir. 2011) (wire fraud is removable offense).

[52] Padilla v. Kentucky, 559 U.S. 356 (2010); *see also* Lilia S. Stantcheva, Padilla v. Kentucky*: How Much Advice Is Enough?*, 89 N.Y.U. L. Rev. 1836 (2014) (reviewing post-*Padilla* cases and commentary).

[53] *See, e.g.*, United States v. Kwan, 407 F.3d 1005, 1015–16 (9th Cir. 2005) (collecting and discussing cases, including United States v. Couto, 311 F.3d 179, 187–88 (2d Cir. 2002)).

[54] For comprehensive discussion and critique of professional and other sanctions — with particular emphasis on tax offenses — see Joshua D. Blank, *Collateral Compliance*, 162 U. Pa. L. Rev. 719 (2014).

[55] 31 C.F.R. pt. 10.

[56] *See* 31 C.F.R. § 10.50; IRS Notice 2007-39, 2007-20 I.R.B. 1.

[57] *E.g.*, Director, Office of Prof'l Responsibility v. Navatsyk, No. 2010-03 (Nov. 5, 2010), available at 2011 TNT 148-11 (Aug. 2, 2011) (attorney disbarred from practicing before the IRS for disreputable conduct including willful failures to file returns and pay tax); *see also* Senyszyn v. Department of

- Attorneys, accountants, and some other types of professionals also are subject to regulation by their states, and they may face state professional sanctions as a result of tax peccadilloes. Consider these examples from two states, Texas and New York:

  > On Nov. 21, the Board of Disciplinary Appeals suspended Peter S. Gross [#08537000], 71, of San Antonio. Gross was convicted in the U.S. District Court, Western District of Texas, San Antonio Division, of conspiracy to defraud the United States and to impair and impede the lawful function of the Internal Revenue Service (18 U.S.C. § 371), an intentional crime as defined in the Texas Rules of Disciplinary Procedure. Gross was placed on probation for 15 months beginning Jan. 24, 1999. This probation was terminated early by the court on Jan. 13, 2000. The board suspended Gross from the practice of law for the term of his criminal probation, from Jan. 24, 1999 and its early termination on Jan. 13, 2000.
  >
  > On Nov. 23, the Board of Disciplinary Appeals suspended Steven J. Zauft [#22251300], 52, of San Antonio, Zauft was convicted in the U.S. District Court, Western District of Texas, San Antonio Division, of conspiracy to defraud the United States and to impair and impede the lawful function of the Internal Revenue Service (18 U.S.C. § 371), an intentional crime as defined in the Texas Rules of Disciplinary Procedure. Zauft was placed on probation for 15 months beginning Jan. 24, 1999. Zauft's probation was terminated early by the court on Jan. 13, 2000. The board suspended Zauft from the practice of law for the term of his criminal probation, from Jan. 24, 1999 and its early termination on Jan. 13, 2000.[58]

  Roger Roisman, a New York Big Law attorney (and holder of an LL.M. degree in tax law) who failed to file tax returns, had his license to practice law suspended for one year.[59]

B. Defendant's Advisers

When a tax adviser crosses the line and becomes an aider-and-abettor, the adviser may become personally subject to prosecution under the tax crimes set out in the Code or more general federal criminal statutes.[60] Even if the adviser avoids criminal prosecution, breach of ethical duties in representation can lead to imposition on the adviser of the federal and state professional sanctions described

---

Treasury, 2012 U.S. App. LEXIS 2596 (Fed. Cir. Feb. 10, 2012) (upholding firing of IRS revenue agent found guilty of filing false tax returns, tax evasion, structuring financial transactions, and bank fraud).

[58] Texas Lawyer, Jan. 2001, at 81–82.

[59] In re Roisman, 89 A.D.3d 164 (N.Y. App. Div. 2011). For other examples of New York attorneys suspended or publicly censured for tax violations, see In re Goldman, 71 A.D.3d 9 (N.Y. App. Div. 2009) (per curiam) (citing additional cases); In re Howley, 70 A.D.3d 218 (N.Y. App. Div. 2009) (citing cases); In re Eppner, 62 A.D.3d 151 (N.Y. App. Div. 2009).

[60] For example, see the discussion of section 7206(2) in Chapter 2B and the discussion of 18 U.S.C. section 371 in Chapter 3.

above.[61]

Section 6694 is one of the principal provisions imposing civil penalties on tax advisers who negligently, willfully, or recklessly lead their clients astray. The section 6694 penalty is imposed on advisors who prepare returns or refund claims containing understatements. There are reasonable cause, disclosure, and substantial authority defenses, especially as to non-tax-shelter transactions. The penalty amount is the greater of $1,000 (raised to $5,000 in cases of willfulness or recklessness) or 50% of the income derived by the preparer. Other sections — including sections 6695A, 6700, 6701, and 7408 — impose penalties and other sanctions on advisors who are not return preparers.

VI. PRESS RELEASES

The IRS and the Department of Justice have policies allowing them to issue press releases regarding enforcement activity, including criminal tax prosecutions and convictions. IRS Policy P-1-183 states in part as to criminal prosecutions and convictions:

> (1) News coverage to advance deterrent value of enforcement activities encouraged: The Service will endeavor to obtain news coverage of its enforcement activities in order to: (a) help deter violations of the internal revenue laws; and (b) increase the confidence of conscientious taxpayers that the Service prosecutes violators. In achieving these goals, the Service will act with due regard for an individual's right to a fair trial as set forth in the Attorney General's guidelines, 28 CFR § 50.2, as well as the public's right to know. Accordingly, the Service will promote news coverage of its enforcement activities in the following manner:
>
> > 1. General information concerning the work of a particular division or divisions involved may be furnished;
> >
> > 2. Information which is a matter of public record (such as pleadings filed with the United States Tax Court or an indictment which has been made public) may be supplied upon request;
> >
> > 3. In cases pending with a U.S. Attorney, the Service will cooperate with him/her to obtain news coverage;
> >
> > 4. In strike force cases, the Service will cooperate with the on-site strike force attorney to obtain news coverage;
> >
> > 5. All news releases concerning criminal actions will be submitted to the U.S. Attorney for approval before distribution to the news media. News releases may be prepared for attribution either to the U.S. Attorney, or for joint attribution to both the Service and the U.S. Attorney. Jointly attributable news releases may be issued on IRS masthead after clearance through the Disclosure Officer and the U.S. Attorney, and may be distributed by Service officials. News releases

---

61 See Chapter 11 for discussion of ethical issues in criminal tax practice.

which are attributed only to the U.S. Attorney may be distributed by Service officials upon request of the U.S. Attorney. Because of statutory prohibition on the disclosure of tax information, it is imperative that material contained in news releases be limited to facts that are a matter of public record;

6. Designated Service officials may participate in press conferences relating to enforcement actions at the invitation of U.S. Attorneys.[62]

The purpose of these news releases should be clear. The IRS has limited resources, particularly in the criminal enforcement area. So, it must choose its targets well, get a high conviction rate, and make sure that the criminal enforcement actions are publicized.

Thus, the practitioner needs to caution her client that the IRS may publicize an indictment or conviction. Most clients would prefer to keep their indictments and convictions confidential, so your client must understand that publication may be a nonstatutory further punishment that may be imposed in the IRS's zeal to encourage others to do right.

One of the major controversies that has arisen is whether the IRS has breached other obligations in its press releases in criminal matters. Section 6103 generally prohibits the IRS from releasing taxpayer return information.[63] Information the IRS gathers in its audit or criminal investigation of a taxpayer is taxpayer return information generally prohibited from disclosure. Of course, in order for DOJ to consider the taxpayer for criminal prosecution and thereafter to prosecute the taxpayer, the taxpayer's return information has to be disclosed to DOJ. Thus, there are exceptions from the general prohibition on disclosure. The exceptions allow disclosure to various persons and governmental bodies under particular circumstances, including disclosures to DOJ and the courts.[64] If the taxpayer is prosecuted, of course, the return information may be disclosed in the prosecution — in the indictment, in the plea agreement if one is reached, in the record at trial if the case is tried, and other documents filed of record in the criminal proceeding.[65] But what if the IRS in making a press release upon conviction discloses information from its files that was not part of the public record? The courts generally hold that such disclosures violate section 6103. Does it make a difference if the IRS pulls the information from the public record in the criminal trial? Most courts hold that that is acceptable. Then, does it make a difference if the IRS pulls the information from its files and the same information just happens to also be in the public court record? Some courts approve that disclosure; others do not.[66]

---

[62] IRM 1.2.1.2.41.

[63] *See generally* Baskin v. United States, 135 F.3d 338, 340–42 (5th Cir. 1998) (discussing the history of disclosure prohibitions).

[64] IRC § 6103(h)(2) & (h)(4). In 2007, the IRS made about 4.5 billion legal disclosures to various recipients. Jt. Comm. Tax'n, *Disclosure for Public Inspection Pursuant to Internal Revenue Code Section 6103(p)(3)(C) for Calendar Year 2007* (JCX-47-08) (June 3, 2008).

[65] IRC § 6103(h)(4).

[66] 1 Joint Committee on Taxation, Study of General Disclosure Provisions (Jan. 28, 2000) (summarizing the cases).

Because the various circuits apply the nuances of section 6103, the IRS has to be cautious in the press releases that are so important to its criminal enforcement strategy. The IRS thus instructs its employees that the following procedures are to apply:

> (1) No person involved in the investigation, preparation, or litigation of the case at issue [should] be involved of the drafting of the press release;[67]
>
> (2) All information to be included in the press release must be obtained from an independent source, such as court files, newspapers, previous press releases, published court opinions, and never from internal Service files. Great care should be exercised in determining whether tax information has actually become a matter of public record, as information which is supplemental to that which has become public is subject to the confidentiality provisions of section 6103;
>
> (3) Retrieve (and maintain) copies of documents (pleadings, indictments, arrest or search warrant affidavits, recorded notices of federal tax lien) independently from the public source, or use transcripts or copies of documents containing a court stamp;
>
> (4) Attribute any statements made directly to the public record document. Press releases should only contain information set forth in the public record and should indicate that the source of the information is the public record;
>
> (5) Press releases should be reviewed by the local disclosure office, and if necessary, by the National Office, before being published;
>
> (6) Information made public by a taxpayer or third party, which is identical to returns or return information in the possession of the Service, remains confidential pursuant to section 6103. Thus, the Service cannot use return information to confirm information made public by any other party unless specifically authorized to do so by I.R.C. section 6103;
>
> (7) Only information that has become a matter of public record in connection with tax administration may be publicized by the Service. The Service draws a distinction between general public record information, such as divorce decrees and mortgage deeds of trust, and return information that has become a matter of public record through tax administration. In this way, the Service avoids linking otherwise innocuous public information with a person's tax liability.[68]

Some of these "fixes" to the potential problem may seem more cosmetic than substantive.

Congress has enacted a variety of civil and criminal penalties to put teeth into disclosure prohibition. Section 7431 allows taxpayers to seek damages from the IRS

---

[67] IRM 9.3.2 (Publicity and Internal Communications) directs the Special Agent in Charge (SAC) to either draft or assist in the preparation of the press release. *See also* IRM 9.3.2.4.1, 9.3.2.10.1.1, 9.3.2.10.1.1.1(11).

[68] ILM 200316011, *reproduced at* 2003 TNT 76-22 (Apr. 21, 2003).

for negligent (or worse) disclosure of tax returns or tax return information.[69] Section 7213 makes it a crime for federal employees and designated other persons to willfully and wrongfully disclose returns or return information. Section 7213A criminalizes willful improper inspection of returns or return information by federal employees and certain other persons. Section 7216 makes illegal knowing or reckless improper disclosure of return-related information by tax return preparers.

VII. CONTRACT VIOLATIONS

The taxpayer may have contractual obligations to third parties to comply with — or at least not violate — laws, including tax laws. In one case,[70] franchisors sought to revoke the franchise of a franchisee based on violation of the tax laws. The franchisee had not even been prosecuted for tax evasion. Instead, an anonymous informant advised the franchisors of the violation of tax and employment laws. The tax violation was the charging of significant personal expenses to the business, thereby underreporting the net business income and underpaying tax. The court found the owner had committed tax evasion, and also analyzed the case under section 7206(1) (tax perjury), finding that the misstatements (overstated expenses) were material. In sustaining the termination of the franchise agreement, the court also relied upon employment law violations. The court made the following finding:

> The Defendants have not been convicted, indicted, fined, or otherwise cited by any governmental agency as a result of the Defendants' noncompliance with federal income tax on employment laws. Moreover, the Plaintiffs have not shown that any person, other than the parties and their representatives, are aware of the Defendants' noncompliance with the federal laws or that Plaintiffs have lost any customers or attracted any adverse public attention as a result of Defendants' noncompliance with the federal laws.

Nonetheless, the court allowed the franchisers to terminate. Moreover, the public record — fully available to the IRS — now alerts the IRS as to potential taxes and civil and criminal penalties from the conduct.

PROBLEM

Eddie Jones was an executive with Allcities Insurance Company (AIC) and was employed at its headquarters in Tacoma, Washington. Jones began in 1979 with AIC as an agent. By 2008, he had become executive vice-president and a member of the board of directors. He and Rex Coburn, AIC's president, reported directly to the board.

In 2012, the IRS began auditing AIC and its key executives, including Jones and his wife. Upon discovering discrepancies, the examining agent referred the matter

[69] *See, e.g.*, Snider v. United States, 468 F.3d 500 (8th Cir. 2006) (defining "return information" and exploring calculation of damages under section 7431).

[70] Dunkin' Donuts Inc. v. Martinez, U.S. Tax Cas. (CCH) ¶ 50291 (S.D. Fla. 2003).

to the IRS Criminal Investigation Division (CID), which assigned the case to Robert G. Stern, a Special Agent.

Following an investigation, CID referred the case to the Department of Justice to prosecute Jones and his wife for tax evasion for the years 2009 and 2010. The case was assigned to Assistant United States Attorney James L. Parker. In February 2014, Parker advised Jones's attorney, Robert I. Williams, that he planned to seek an indictment of both Jones and his wife, but, if Jones pled guilty to a one-count criminal information that he underpaid his 2010 taxes (by approximately $9,500), the Government would not prosecute his wife for either 2009 or 2010, would not prosecute Jones for 2009, and would recommend a probated sentence.

Jones kept AIC's executive committee, president, and counsel fully apprised of the situation. Williams and Jones were reassured that, even if Jones pled guilty to a crime, as long as there was no publicity that would embarrass AIC, Jones could continue with AIC as executive vice-president. Williams therefore determined to ensure that Jones's identity would never be disclosed — that, if someone looked at the district court file, he could not associate Jones with AIC.

Williams notified Parker that publicity of a conviction would be extremely damaging, and Parker evidently agreed, as he had with Williams on other occasions for other defendants, to preserve Jones's relative anonymity. Parker agreed to let Williams seek the district court's authorization to have the pre-sentence investigation performed before charges were filed. The completed pre-sentence investigation report was delivered the court on April 2, 2014. Jones's case was to be heard on Friday, April 21, at 4:00 p.m. in the Tacoma courthouse. Williams requested that the criminal information be filed at the time of the hearing, along with Jones's waiver of indictment and the plea bargain agreement; and that the "Defendant's Information" sheet give Williams's office address for Jones's address. Parker agreed to these precautions and agreed that no press release would be issued concerning Jones. But Parker did not advise the IRS of this "no publicity" agreement.

At approximately 4:00 p.m. on April 21, proceedings on the record commenced. Williams had confirmed that the district judge had no other business that Friday afternoon, and Parker had agreed to that time to minimize the risk of publicity. Williams and Jones searched the Tacoma courthouse for members of the press and found none, so the only people present for the hearing were Jones, Williams, Parker, the district judge, and court personnel. Jones signed and filed a waiver of indictment.

The "Defendant Information" sheet, identifying Jones as "Edward Jones" was also filed. In fact, although Jones's full name is Edward E. Jones, he was known as "Eddie" Jones by friends, AIC executives and employees, and business acquaintances. He signed all correspondence as "Eddie." The sheet gave as Jones' address the address of his lawyer's office, not Jones' actual home ("25 Alder Circle") or business address.

A criminal information, charging Jones with tax evasion for 2010 in the amount of $9,474.97, was filed, and he signed and swore to a written "Plea of Guilty." After a Fed. R. Crim. P. 11 hearing, the court sentenced Jones to six months confinement, suspended, and one-year of supervised probation. None of the documents filed on April 21 mentioned Jones's employment. At the plea hearing, the district judge did make reference to Jones being "an executive with Allcities Insurance Company." The following Monday, April 24, a judgment of conviction and sentence was filed.

According to Jones, when returning from court on April 21, he notified AIC's president about what transpired, and Coburn responded favorably that the IRS matter was over and that he (Jones) should move forward because he was important to AIC. By the end of business on Tuesday, April 25, Jones informed other members of AIC's executive committee that he had pled guilty to a tax crime and put the matter behind him. Jones testified that he was not asked to resign. Instead, he was told the "best interest of the company is served by keeping you exactly where you are."

The day before, however, Monday, April 24, Sylvia Shram, an IRS Public Affairs Officer, had prepared the following press release about Jones's conviction, entitled "Insurance Executive Pleads Guilty in Tax Case": "TACOMA, WASHINGTON — In U.S. District Court here, Apr. 21, Edward E. Jones, 59, pled guilty to a charge of federal tax evasion. Judge Hugh Gibson sentenced Jones, of 25 Alder Circle, to a six-month suspended prison term and one year supervised probation. Jones, an executive vice-president for the American Insurance Corporation, was charged in a criminal information with claiming false business deductions and altering documents involving his 2009 and 2010 income tax returns. In addition to the sentence, Jones will be required to pay back taxes, plus penalties and interest."

Shram had prepared the release with the help of Special Agent Stern, relying, with one exception (the paragraph regarding back taxes, penalties, and interest), solely on information she received from him. She did not ask Stern about the source of that information although she knew Stern had not been in the courtroom for Jones's hearing on April 24. The last paragraph of the release (penalty portion) was not based on information received from Stern. It was boilerplate language in the form Shram used.

According to Stern, he learned of the conviction from Parker on either Friday, April 21, or Monday, April 24. Stern testified that, based on that conversation, he prepared on Monday, April 24, the following internal "Report of Legal Action": "On April 21, 2014, AUSA JIM PARKER filed a criminal information charging JONES with tax evasion under 26 U.S.C. § 7201 for the years 2009 and 2010. JONES pled guilty on the same day to one count of section 7201 for 2010, and the 2009 count was dismissed. Judge GIBSON sentenced JONES to six months to serve with this six months being suspended and placed him on one year supervised probation. No fine was assessed, and no appeal is expected. This legal action occurred in Tacoma."

In addition to not attending Jones's hearing, neither Shram nor Stern had any of the court documents. Stern, who was in Seattle, was not advised by Parker about either the plea agreement or hearing in Tacoma until approximately two hours before the hearing, when Parker was leaving his Seattle office to travel to Tacoma for the hearing. Because of such short notice, another matter prevented Stern from attending the hearing. Stern, however, did not check the public record before giving the information to Shram.

After preparing a draft of the release, Shram telephoned Stern and read it to him. Stern testified that he copied it verbatim. Stern then contacted Shram and told her that Parker had approved the release.

Shram also called Michael Ordway, a CID supervisory employee, and read the release to him. After Ordway approved the release, Shram mailed it on April 24 to nearly two dozen media outlets in the Seattle or Tacoma area.

On April 26, a Tacoma journalist telephoned AIC to inquire about Jones's conviction. Jones learned of the press release and contacted Williams, who immediately contacted Parker. Parker denied any knowledge of the release and assumed the IRS was responsible.

Williams also telephoned and wrote to the IRS about the release. It was then that the IRS realized that the release contained erroneous information: that Jones had been charged only for 2010; and that the criminal information did not charge him with claiming false business deductions or altering documents.

Jones informed AIC president Coburn and two executive committee board members of the release on April 26 and provided Coburn with a copy of the release that same day. On learning from Williams that the IRS would not withdraw the release, Jones told Coburn that all AIC board members should be informed. Coburn advised Jones that he (Coburn) would contact the entire board. On Saturday, April 29, and Monday, May 1, Coburn asked Jones to resign from his positions as executive vice president and board member, which Jones did. Jones was reassigned to another office and given a less important position. He continues to serve there at considerably diminished compensation.

At this point, Jones hires you as his new lawyer. Identify and evaluate legal recourse available to Jones.

Chapter 13

CIVIL TAX CONSIDERATIONS

IRC: §§ 66(c), 6015(a)–(d) & (f) (skim), 6501(a)–(c), 6651(f), 6662(a)–(c), 6663, 6664(b) & (c), 7122(a), 7454(a), 7525

11 U.S.C. §§ 507(a)(8), 523(a)(1)(c), 727

I. INTRODUCTION

We have said that the civil tax attorney, ignorant of criminal tax, is dangerous to the attorney's clients. So is the criminal tax attorney who is ignorant of civil tax rules. Your client's gratitude that you kept him out of jail will be considerably dampened if he is saddled with ruinous civil tax liabilities. Comprehensive discussion of civil tax considerations is beyond the scope of this chapter.[1]

This chapter considers six contexts in which the criminal and civil rules interact: (1) timing and other coordination between civil and criminal tax investigations; (2) civil penalties; (3) collateral estoppel; (4) the statute of limitations on assessment of tax liabilities; (5) measures by which to mitigate liabilities for tax years involving tax offenses; and (6) return filing with respect to subsequent tax years.

II. CIVIL-CRIMINAL COORDINATION

A. Timing

Historically, the Government has proceeded with criminal tax investigation and prosecution first, suspending audit and collection until culmination of the criminal proceedings. This policy reflected several considerations, including fears that: (1) civil discovery could reveal too soon, too much of the Government's criminal case; (2) an inconsistent position taken in the civil case could compromise the criminal case; (3) witnesses might be strained or inconvenienced by having to testify in two sets of roughly simultaneous proceedings; (4) other evidence might be scattered or lost between two sets of simultaneously active proceedings; and (5) the criminal prosecution could be painted as spite occasioned by the IRS's frustrations, failures, and delays as to civil collection. In addition, especially in failure-to-file and fraud cases, the Government reasoned that the civil statute of limitations on assessment will still be open even if the criminal case takes years to resolve.

[1] For fuller discussion, see David M. Richarson, Jerome Borison & Steve Johnson, *Civil Tax Procedure* (2d ed. 2007); Michael I. Saltzman & Leslie Book, *IRS Practice and Procedure* (rev. 2d ed., 2009 as updated).

This historical view is expressed in IRS Policy Statement P-4-84:

> 1. *Criminal and Civil Aspects in Enforcement.* The purpose of criminal tax investigations is to enforce the tax laws and to encourage voluntary compliance. Experience has demonstrated that attempts to pursue both the criminal and civil aspects of a case concurrently may jeopardize the successful completion of the criminal case. It is, therefore, necessary in the overall interests of enforcement of the law to identify those instances when criminal actions generally will take precedence over the civil aspects.
>
> 2. *Civil enforcement actions on taxable periods of the same and other types of tax not involved in the criminal investigation:* Civil enforcement actions, including enforced collection activity, with respect to taxable periods of the same and other types of tax not included in the criminal investigation, generally, do not imperil successful criminal investigation or subsequent prosecution. Therefore, civil enforcement actions for tax liabilities, for such other taxable periods or different types of tax for the same periods will proceed concurrently, unless there is agreement between Division Chiefs of the responsible field functions to withhold civil action in whole or in part during pendency of the criminal investigation or, if agreement cannot be reached, the District Director determines that such action should be withheld. District Directors make the determination in districts which do not have Division Chiefs. On matters involving a grand jury investigation, this determination will be made by a management official, not lower than a Division Chief, appointed by the District Director who will not have access to any grand jury information.[2]
>
> 3. *Civil Enforcement Actions on Matters Involved in Criminal Investigation.* Civil enforcement actions with respect to the same taxable periods and same types of taxes for those periods included in the criminal investigation may imperil subsequent prosecution. Therefore, the consequences of civil enforcement actions on the criminal investigation and prosecution case should be carefully weighed, and in general, only such actions will be taken, as Division Chiefs of the responsible field functions agree, should be taken or, if agreement cannot be reached, the District Director makes the determination. However, there generally should be no suspension of collection action on assessed amounts of tax liabilities reported on filed returns.
>
> 6. *Civil enforcement actions after referral to Counsel by District Directors:* Civil actions concerning a case referred to Counsel for criminal prosecution should generally be deferred until the criminal aspects are closed. However, if the District Director or his or her designee, not lower than Division Chief, determines that such deferral would imperil ultimate collection of the civil liability, and that the contemplated civil action would not adversely affect the criminal case, Counsel should be advised of the specific proposed action. Chief Counsel Policy requires Counsel to notify

[2] As a result of reorganizations of the IRS, these positions have been eliminated and their authority has been redelegated to other IRS officials.

> the District Director, expeditiously and without undue delay, of Counsel's concurrence or nonconcurrence with the proposed action. If Counsel and the District Director do not reach an agreement, the matter should be referred to the National Office for resolution.[3]

Even if the Government doesn't suspend the civil proceedings, a court might. The concern is that the Government might use civil proceedings to force the taxpayer to either waive his Fifth Amendment privilege or face some penalty in the civil proceeding. Courts sometimes mitigate these concerns by staying the civil case pending resolution of the criminal investigation and/or prosecution.[4]

The historic policy of deferring to the criminal investigation or prosecution may be changing. The Chief of CI is reported to have said: "Gone are the old rules about ceasing a civil audit once a matter has been referred for criminal activity."[5] It is too early in the game, however, to perceive how this change in policy may play out. The Government has proceeded simultaneously, civilly and criminally, in some prominent tax shelter cases, but this has not become a pattern in more "routine" cases.

B. Civil Liability and Pleas

Chapter 10 discusses sentencing. One sentencing consideration is that a judge might be more inclined to allow a downward adjustment for "acceptance of responsibility" if the taxpayer-defendant has paid or agreed to pay the tax liability. Payment is not an admission of liability or an admission that the limitations period remains open. The taxpayer will still be able to argue about the liability later.

In some cases, a restitution provision is incorporated into the plea agreement. The IRS's ability to proceed civilly backstops the Government's revenue interest when the plea agreement does not contain an adequate restitution provision. For example, in 2006, Walter C. Anderson, a telecommunications entrepreneur, pleaded guilty to two counts of tax evasion, for which he received nine years in concurrent prison terms.[6] After the original sentencing order, DOJ moved to correct the sentence to require restitution, arguing that restitution was "implied" in the plea agreement. The court denied the motion. Nonetheless, the Government has various means by which it can get some or all of its money eventually. The IRS issued a notice of deficiency to Anderson, ultimately seeking around $250 million in back taxes and penalties (not counting interest).[7]

---

3 IRM 1.2.1.4.25; *see also* IRM 9.5.13.2.1.

4 *See generally* Milton Pollack, *Parallel Civil and Criminal Proceedings*, 129 F.R.D. 201 (1990) (discussing risks of parallel proceedings). For a leading case involving the taxpayer's institution of a civil refund suit in order to discover the fruits of the criminal investigation, *see Campbell v. Eastland*, 307 F.2d 478, 487–89 (5th Cir. 1962), *cert. denied*, 371 U.S. 955 (1963) (stay of civil discovery or protective order may have been appropriate remedy while criminal proceeding pending).

5 Sheryl Stratton, *IRS, Justice Officials Discuss Booming Criminal Tax Business*, 2004 TNT 214–13.

6 In addition to eight years (later reduced to four years) for one count of defrauding the District of Columbia.

7 Anderson v. Comm'r, T.C. Memo. 2009-44 (granting IRS's motion for partial summary judgment as to civil fraud penalties), *aff'd*, 698 F.3d 160 (3d Cir. 2012), *cert. denied*, 133 S. Ct. 2797 (2013).

C. Grand Jury Material and Civil Liability

As described in greater detail in Chapter 6, Federal Rule of Criminal Procedure 6(e) prohibits the IRS from using grand jury matters in developing its civil tax position as to the taxpayer's liability without a pending judicial proceeding and a Rule 6(e)(3) order. However, if the taxpayer resolves his civil tax liability incident to the plea negotiation, grand jury matters apparently can be used. One may question whether this result is consistent with the integrity of Rule 6(e).

III. CIVIL PENALTIES

Whether the IRS wins or loses in the criminal tax proceeding, it nearly always also attempts to establish civil liabilities against the taxpayer. This usually happens after conclusion of the criminal process although, as explained in Chapter 1, the IRS sometimes proceeds concurrently on the civil and criminal fronts. The Internal Revenue Manual instructs Special Agents to be alert to possible civil penalties.[8] The civil liabilities the IRS will pursue include deficiencies for the years involved, plus interest on the deficiencies,[9] plus civil penalties,[10] plus interest on the civil penalties.[11]

A. Civil Fraud Penalties

The penalty the IRS most often asserts in such cases is the civil fraud penalty. There are many reasons for this, as we mention here then describe more fully below. First, the fraud penalty is the largest civil tax penalty in dollar magnitude: 75% of the understatement attributable to fraud. Second, when fraud is established, there is no statute-of-limitations impediment to the assessment of the civil liabilities. Third, a determination of fraud undercuts the possibility of the taxpayer discharging the liabilities in a later bankruptcy proceeding. Fourth, although the burden of proof as to civil fraud is higher than that as to other civil penalties, it is lower than the burden as to criminal fraud.

A taxpayer seeking fraudulently to prevent or minimize assessment of taxes may file a false return or may refrain from filing a return at all. The former situation is covered by section 6663. Section 6663(a) imposes a penalty equal to 75% of the portion of the underpayment which is attributable to fraud.[12] In the case of married-filing-jointly returns, fraud by one spouse is not attributed to the other. Under section 6663(c), the penalty applies only to the spouse(s) whom the IRS proves to have committed fraud.

Civil tax fraud consists of:

---

[8] IRM 9.5.13.2.2.

[9] IRC §§ 6601 & 6621; *see* Richardson, Borison & Johnson, *supra*, ch. 12.

[10] *See* Richardson, Borison & Johnson, *supra*, ch. 11.

[11] IRC § 6601(e)(2).

[12] "Underpayment" is defined in section 6664(a). Under section 6663(b), if the IRS proves that any part of the underpayment is due to fraud, a rebuttable presumption arises that all of the underpayment is due to fraud.

> the intentional commission of an act or acts for the specific purpose of evading a tax believed to be owing. Fraud implies bad faith, intentional wrongdoing, and a sinister motive. It is never imputed or presumed. Whether fraud has been committed is a question of fact to be determined from the entire record.[13]

Since direct proof of fraudulent intent is usually not available, the scienter element typically is inferred from objective facts, *i.e.*, the existence of one or more of the so-called "badges of fraud."[14] These badges are familiar from the section 7201 context. They include, among others: a multi-year pattern of understating income, failing to maintain adequate books and records, failing to file returns, concealing assets, lying to or failing to cooperate with IRS agents, receiving illegal source income, giving implausible or inconsistent explanations, dealing in cash, consistently and substantially overstating deductions, keeping multiple sets of books, creating false documents or entries, destroying information, and deceptively structuring transactions or business.[15]

Under section 6664(b), the section 6663 penalty applies only to filed returns.[16] Failure to file and late filing are penalized under section 6651. The normal delinquency penalty under section 6651(a)(1) is five percent per month (or part of a month) capped at 25%. When the failure to file is due to fraud, however, section 6651(f) raises the delinquency penalty to 15% per month (or part of a month) capped at 75%.

The IRS bears the burden of proving civil fraud by clear and convincing evidence,[17] which is a lower standard than the "beyond a reasonable doubt" quantum required for criminal conviction.[18] "Reasonable cause" is a defense against both the section 6651[19] and the section 6663 penalties.[20]

Taxpayers sometimes have argued that imposition of a civil fraud penalty on top of a criminal tax penalty violates the Double Jeopardy Clause of the Fifth Amendment and/or the Excessive Fines Clause of the Eighth Amendment. By now,

---

13 Estate of Spruill v. Commissioner, 88 T.C. 1197, 1241–42 (1987).

14 *E.g.*, Spies v. United States, 317 U.S. 492, 499 (1943); Rowlee v. Commissioner, 80 T.C. 1111, 1123 (1983).

15 *E.g.*, Laurins v. Commissioner, 889 F.2d 910, 913 (9th Cir. 1989); Petzoldt v. Commissioner, 92 T.C. 661, 699 (1989); IRM 20.1.5.12.1.

16 It does not apply to substitutes for returns under section 6020(b). For discussion of substitutes for returns, *see* Steve R. Johnson, *Swallows Holding as It Is: The Distortion of National Muffler*, 112 Tax Notes 351, 355 n.44 (2006).

17 IRC § 7454; Tax Ct. R. 142(b).

18 Curiously, some studies suggest that jurors sometimes perceive "clear and convincing" to be a higher standard than "beyond a reasonable doubt." Lawrence Solan, *Refocusing the Burden of Proof in Criminal Cases: Some Doubt About Reasonable Doubt*, 78 Tex. L. Rev. 105, 128–29 (1999). Bench trials presumably would not present this logical inconsistency but may suffer from judges' relaxed assessments of the quantum of proof needed to get "beyond a reasonable doubt."

19 IRC § 6651(a)(1); Reg. § 301.6651-1(c); IRM 20.1.1.3.1.

20 IRC § 6664(c); Reg. § 1.664-4; IRM 20.1.5.6. This defense applies as well with respect to the 6662 accuracy-related penalty.

however, the courts appear to have decisively rejected such contentions.[21]

B. Accuracy-Related Penalty

The section 6662 accuracy-related penalty is an alternative to the fraud penalty. Under section 6662(a), the penalty amount is 20% of the underpayment, raised to 40% in some situations. The penalty applies when any of seven bases are present. They include negligence or disregard of tax rules,[22] substantial understatements of tax, substantial valuation misstatements, adjustments based on lack of economic substance, and undisclosed foreign financial asset understatements. A reasonable cause defense is available under section 6664(c) as to all of the bases except the base related to lack of economic substance.[23] After the IRS meets an initial burden of production as to the accuracy penalty, the taxpayer typically bears the burden of proof (at a "preponderance of the evidence" standard) as to the section 6662 penalty.[24]

Despite this burden-of-proof difference, the accuracy-related penalty typically is inferior to the fraud penalty from the IRS's standpoint in cases also subject to criminal investigation and prosecution. The penalty amount is smaller, and section 6662 does not help the IRS as to the statute of limitations on assessment or with respect to bankruptcy. Accordingly, the section 6662 penalty usually is asserted in previously criminal cases only in the rare situation when the IRS has a weak fraud case but the statute of limitations on assessment somehow remains open.

C. Delinquency Penalties

The civil penalty applicable to failure to timely file returns is section 6651(a)(1). The elements of this penalty are the same as the elements of the section 7203 failure-to-file offense. The taxpayer must have a duty to file and must have failed timely to file.

In general, the section 6651(a)(1) penalty is five percent per month, with a maximum penalty of 25%. However, under section 6651(f), if the failure to file is fraudulent, the penalty rate becomes 15% per month, with a maximum of 75%. A fraudulent failure to file is not the same as section 7201 tax evasion since the latter requires an affirmative act in addition to the failure to file. There is limited case law

---

[21] *E.g.*, Louis v. Commissioner, 170 F.3d 1232 (9th Cir. 1999) (also rejecting the taxpayer's Fifth and Sixth Amendment arguments), *cert. denied*, 528 U.S. 1115 (2000). As to the Double Jeopardy Clause, see also *Helvering v. Mitchell*, 303 U.S. 391 (1938), and *Roberts v. Commissioner*, 73 T.C. Memo. (CCH) 2745 (1997).

[22] IRC § 6662(b)(1) & (2). Negligence "includes any failure to make a reasonable attempt to comply with the [Code]," and disregard "includes any careless, reckless, or intentional disregard." IRC § 6662(c).

[23] As to when reliance on advice from a tax advisor constitutes reasonable cause, see Larry A. Campagna, Caroline D. Ciraolo & Ellis L. Reemer, *But I Relied on My Accountant! The Scope of the Reasonable Cause Defense to Penalties*, J. TAX PRAC. & PROC., Aug.–Sept. 2012, at 41; Steve R. Johnson, *Does Reliance on the Advice of an Insider Provide Penalty Protection?*, J. TAX PRAC. & PROC., Aug.–Sept. 2008, at 35.

[24] IRC § 7491(a) & (c); *see* Steve R. Johnson, *The Dangers of Symbolic Legislation: Perceptions and Realities of the New Tax Burden-of-Proof Rules*, 84 IOWA L. REV. 413 (1999).

as to whether section 7203 conviction estops a taxpayer from denying the applicable of the section 6651(f) penalty.

In general, the failure-to-file civil penalty base is the tax required to be shown on the return.[25] However, that base is reduced by the tax that has been paid — for example, by withholding or estimated taxes — by the due date of the return.[26]

In addition to section 6651(a)(1), the Code provides a number of other penalties for failure to timely file returns or to timely pay tax liabilities. They include sections 6651(a)(2) (failure to pay tax shown on return), 6651(a)(3) (failure to pay deficiencies after notice and demand), 6652 (failure to file certain information returns), 6653 (failure to pay stamp tax), 6654 and 6655 (failure to pay estimated taxes by individuals and corporations, respectively), 6656 (failure to make deposit of taxes), 6657 (payment via bad check), and 6721 (failure to file information returns).

D. Other Civil Penalties

There are a host of other civil penalties that parallel criminal penalties or could apply in circumstances in which criminal tax prosecution is a potential. Identifying them all would be beyond the scope of this chapter. A number of civil penalties relate to tax advisers. Section 6694(a) penalizes income tax return preparers who, in effect, negligently advise taxpayers leading to tax understatements. Section 6694(b) raises the penalty when the preparer's conduct was willful or reckless.[27] Section 6700 penalizes those who organize, sell interests in, or otherwise participate in the promotion of abusive tax shelters and similar arrangements. Section 6701 imposes a penalty for aiding and assisting (including advising) with respect to a document in connection with a material matter involving the tax laws when the person knows or has reason to know that the document will result in a tax understatement.

Section 6662A imposes an accuracy-related penalty on understatements with respect to tax shelters. Section 6676 establishes a penalty with respect to excessive claims for refund or credit. Sections 6698 and 6699 are penalties for failure to file partnership returns and S corporation returns, respectively. Section 6707A penalizes failure to provide information as to reportable transactions. Section 6708 penalizes failure to maintain lists of advisees as to reportable transactions.

IV. COLLATERAL ESTOPPEL

The party who prevails in the criminal phase of the controversy would prefer to win in the civil phase as well — as quickly and as inexpensively as possible. Sometimes the doctrine of collateral estoppel allows the prevailing party to prevail on the principal issue in the civil case or one or more subissues without having to

---

[25] IRC § 6651(a)(1).

[26] IRC § 6651(b).

[27] *See, e.g.*, Scott A. Schumacher, *Section 6694 Preparer Penalties and Tax Advice: The Latest on the Constantly Moving Target*, PRAC. TAX LAW., Winter 2009, at 19.

retry the merits.[28] Below, we consider five patterns: (1) the taxpayer prevailed in the criminal tax trial; (2) the Government prevailed on a section 7201 charge; (3) the Government prevailed but on a charge other than section 7201; (4) the taxpayer lost a case other than a tax case; and (5) sentencing determinations are asserted as the basis for estoppel.

A. Taxpayer Prevailed

As noted above, the Government must satisfy a higher standard of proof (beyond a reasonable doubt) in a criminal case than it must satisfy as to civil fraud (clear and convincing), as to other civil penalties (initial burden of production), or as to deficiencies (preventing the taxpayer from establishing a preponderance of the evidence). Accordingly, the taxpayer gains no collateral estoppel traction in the civil case when the Government failed to obtain a conviction in the previous criminal tax case.[29]

B. Government Prevailed on Section 7201 Charge

When a court of competent jurisdiction enters a final judgment on the merits of a case, the doctrine of *res judicata* bars the parties to the case and parties in privity with them from relitigating "not only as to every matter which was offered and received to sustain or defeat the claim [but also] as to any other admissible matter which might have been offered for that purpose."[30] Both convictions after trial and guilty pleas have preclusive effect.[31] Many (though not all) courts hold that all independently sufficient alternative findings receive preclusive effect.[32] Absent fraud or some other factor which invalidates the judgment, these matters may not be relitigated in any later case.

However, "where the second action between the same parties is upon a different cause, . . . the principle . . . is applied much more narrowly." Specifically, the judgment "operates as an estoppel, not as to matters which might have been litigated and determined, but 'only as to those matters in issue or points controverted, upon the determination of which the . . . verdict was rendered.' "[33] Thus, the analytical framework for determining whether collateral estoppel may be applied includes the following steps:

> (1) An identification of the issues in the two actions for the purposes of determining whether the issues are sufficiently similar and sufficiently material in both actions to justify invoking the doctrine; (2) an examination

---

28 *See, e.g.*, John A. Townsend, *Collateral Estoppel in Civil Cases Following Criminal Convictions*, 2005 TNT 4-28 (Jan. 6, 2005).

29 *E.g.*, McHan v. Comm'r, 558 F.3d 326 (4th Cir. 2009) (forfeiture judgment); Neaderland v. Commissioner, 52 T.C. 532 (1969), *aff'd*, 424 F.2d 639 (2d Cir.), *cert. denied*, 400 U.S. 827 (1970).

30 Cromwell v. County of Sac, 94 U.S. 351, 354 (1877).

31 When conviction results from a guilty plea, the preclusive effect extends to all issues necessarily admitted in the plea. *E.g.*, DeCavalcante v. Comm'r, 620 F.2d 23, 27 n.9 (3d Cir. 1980).

32 *E.g.*, Anderson v. Comm'r, 698 F.3d 160, 165 (3d Cir. 2012), *cert. denied*, 133 S. Ct. 2797 (2013).

33 Commissioner v. Sunnen, 333 U.S. 591, 598 (1948) (quoting *Cromwell, supra*, 94 U.S. at 353).

of the record of the prior case to decide whether the issue was "litigated" in the first case; and (3) an examination of the record of the prior proceeding to ascertain whether the issue was necessarily decided in the first case.[34]

The courts have held that the term "willfully" as used in section 7201 encompasses all of the elements of fraud as used in the civil fraud penalties. Accordingly, when a taxpayer is convicted of section 7201 tax evasion, the taxpayer will be collaterally estopped from disputing the IRS's fraud determination in a later civil tax proceeding.[35]

Collateral estoppel applies equally to convictions based on guilty pleas as to convictions based on trial on the merits.[36] Courts will rarely look behind the circumstances of a guilty plea in applying collateral estoppel. The burden is on the opponent of estoppel to prove that the plea was entered involuntarily, that counsel was incompetent, that there was prosecutorial misconduct, or that any other reason exists to look behind the plea.[37] An *Alford* plea (a guilty plea entered by a defendant who nevertheless claims to be innocent) is treated as a guilty plea for this purpose, so gives rise to collateral estoppel in the civil case.[38] Despite a few contrary decisions, a plea of *nolo contendere* does not support collateral estoppel.[39] However, under principles discussed below, a *nolo* plea may be offered in evidence as part of the IRS's civil fraud case.[40]

Whether persons are sufficiently closely related to be in privity for collateral estoppel purposes is a question of fact. In some cases, a shareholder may be bound by a prior adjudication in a suit to which the corporation is a party.[41] However, the gate appears not to swing the other way. In a frequently cited case, the corporation's president and principal shareholder was criminally convicted for filing or causing the corporation (a C corporation) to file false and fraudulent corporate returns. The president and shareholder was held to be estopped from denying fraud for what is now section 6663 purposes. However, the corporation — which had not

---

[34] United States v. McLaurin, 57 F.3d 823, 826 (9th Cir. 1995) (emphasis omitted). Other courts express the same substance in slightly different formulations. *E.g.*, McGowan v. Commissioner, 187 F. App'x 915, 917 (11th Cir. 2006) (describing a four-part test).

[35] *E.g.*, Stratton v. Commissioner, 54 T.C. 255, 282–84, *supp. op.*, 54 T.C. 1351 (1970), *acq. in part*, 1970-2 C.B. XVIII; Amos v. Commissioner, 43 T.C. 50, 55 (1964), *aff'd*, 360 F.2d 358 (4th Cir. 1965).

[36] *E.g.*, United States v. Killough, 848 F.2d 1523, 1528 (11th Cir. 1988).

[37] *E.g.*, Yarbrough Oldsmobile Cadillac, Inc. v. Commissioner, 65 T.C.M. 1766, 1768, T.C. Memo. 1993-20 (1993).

[38] *E.g.*, Blohm v. Commissioner, 994 F.2d 1542 (11th Cir. 1993); *see* North Carolina v. Alford, 400 U.S. 25 (1970). *Alford* pleas are discussed in Chapter 9.

[39] *E.g.*, Bell v. Commissioner, 320 F.2d 953 (8th Cir. 1963).

[40] In one case, the court forbade the Government from using the *nolo* plea even for the limited purpose of impleading the taxpayer. Mickler v. Fahs, 243 F.2d 515 (5th Cir. 1957). However, this case preceded adoption of Federal Rule of Evidence 609, the legislative history of which permits such impeachment. Accordingly, *Mickler* no longer is good law. United States v. Sonny Mitchell Ctr., 934 F.2d 77, 79 (5th Cir. 1991).

[41] *See, e.g.*, Jaffe v. Grant, 793 F.2d 1182, 1188 (11th Cir. 1986); Dudley v. Smith, 504 F.2d 979, 982–83 (5th Cir. 1974).

been a party to the criminal case — was held not to be so estopped.[42]

A final aspect of collateral estoppel after section 7201 conviction involves the amount of the underpayment. In one case, the taxpayer attempted to turn criminal defeat into partial civil victory. In the criminal case, the Government had stipulated the exact amount of the underpayment. Later, in its notice of deficiency, the IRS asserted a higher underpayment amount. The taxpayer argued that the IRS was collaterally estopped from doing so. The court rejected this argument because determination of the exact underpayment is not essential to a section 7201 judgment.[43] For the same reason, criminal conviction under section 7201 does not estop the taxpayer from challenging, in the later civil case, the precise amount of the deficiency.[44]

C. Government Prevailed on a Charge Other than Section 7201

At one time, the Tax Court took the position that conviction under section 7206(1) for filing a false return collaterally estopped the taxpayer from challenging imposition of a civil fraud penalty.[45] However, other decisions have established that intent to evade — a necessary element for civil fraud — is not an element of section 7206(1). On this basis, other courts criticized, and the Tax Court abrogated, the Tax Court's earlier view.[46] Similarly, neither a "failure to file" conviction under section 7203[47] nor conviction of mail or wire fraud under 18 U.S.C. sections 1341 or 1343[48] precludes the taxpayer from later challenging a civil fraud penalty.

These holdings give the criminal tax defendant and the defendant's attorney additional motivation to attempt to bargain down a section 7201 charge to a lesser charge. Sometimes, the Justice Department attorney handling the case cares mainly about disposing of the criminal case and pays limited attention to civil tax consequences, so may be amenable to such a plea arrangement. A Justice Department attorney with a broader perspective on the Government's interests may resist bargaining down the criminal charge unless the defendant agrees not to contest a to-be-determined-later civil fraud penalty (except perhaps contesting the dollar magnitude of that penalty).

Although not dispositive, the taxpayer's conviction on charges other than section 7201 is quite helpful to the IRS in the civil case. Such a conviction is at least

---

42 C.B.C. Super Markets, Inc. v. Commissioner, 54 T.C. 882, 894–96 (1970); *see also* American Lithofold Corp. v. Commissioner, 55 T.C. 904, 924 (1971).

43 Moore v. United States, 360 F.2d 353 (4th Cir. 1965).

44 *E.g.*, Uscinski v. Commissioner, T.C. Memo 2006-200, 92 T.C.M. (CCH) 285, 287 (2006).

45 *E.g.*, Goodwin v. Commissioner, 73 T.C. 215, 224 (1979); Considine v. Commissioner, 68 T.C. 52, 61, 68 (1977).

46 *E.g.*, Considine v. United States, 683 F.2d 1285, 1287 (9th Cir. 1982); Wright v. Commissioner, 84 T.C. 636 (1985), *acq. in part*, 1988-2 C.B. 1 (I.R.S. 1988).

47 *E.g.*, Kotmair v. Commissioner, 86 T.C. 1253 (1986).

48 Carmel v. United States (*In re* Carmel), 134 B.R. 890 (Bankr. N.D. Ill. 1991).

evidentiary — "while not dispositive, [it] will be one of the facts to be considered in a trial on the merits."[49]

In this context, it is helpful to distinguish between claim preclusion and issue preclusion. Conviction of an offense other than section 7201 does not preclude the taxpayer from challenging the IRS's claim that the taxpayer is liable for the civil fraud penalty. However, such conviction may preclude the taxpayer from contesting certain issues or facts that are part of the IRS's case in support of its civil fraud penalty claim.

For example, assume that the taxpayer did not file an income tax return for a particular year and was convicted under section 7203. If the IRS later asserts the section 6651(f) delinquency fraud penalty, the taxpayer will be able to argue that the scienter needed to support the penalty (an intent to evade tax known to be owing) was not present. However, the taxpayer will not be allowed to deny: (i) that he or she failed to file the return; or (ii) that this failure was willful — since these are elements of the section 7203 offense and so were necessarily determined in the criminal proceeding. Clearly the criminal conviction does not get the IRS all the way to its section 6651(f) goal, but it advances the IRS far in that direction.[50]

D. Taxpayer Lost a Non-Tax Case

The IRS may gain some fact or issue preclusion benefit from a non-tax loss by the taxpayer. For example, in one case, an employee was successfully sued by his employer in an accounting action for wrongfully diverting the employer's funds to himself. In a subsequent civil tax case, the IRS argued that the judgment in the accounting action collaterally estopped the employee, as taxpayer, from denying his diversion of the funds (which he had not reported on his income tax return). The Tax Court, noting the erosion of the doctrine of mutuality in estoppel, agreed with the IRS.[51]

E. Sentencing Determinations as the Basis for Estoppel

There has been relatively little exploration of whether judicial determinations made as part of sentencing in a criminal case can give rise collateral estoppel for civil tax purposes. One can imagine several permutations of criminal charges and civil tax issues. Here, we will confine ourselves to two matters as to civil fraud.

The first arises out of *Maciel*, a circuit court decision.[52] After initially charging Maciel with two section 7201 counts, the Government filed a superseding information charging him with two section 7206(1) counts. Maciel admitted guilt as to both counts in a plea agreement. The plea agreement calculated Maciel's

---

49 *Wright, supra*, 84 T.C. at 643–44.

50 *See, e.g.*, *Considine, supra*, 683 F.2d at 1288 (a finding of an intent to evade is a "natural inference" when willful underpayment by a sophisticated, knowledgeable taxpayer has been established).

51 Meier v. Commissioner, 91 T.C. 273 (1988) (citing Montana v. United States, 440 U.S. 147 (1979); Parklane Hosiery Co. v. Shore, 439 U.S. 322 (1979)).

52 Maciel v. Commissioner, 489 F.3d 1018 (9th Cir. 2007), *aff'g in relevant part*, 87 TCM 881, T.C. Memo 2004-28 (2004).

adjusted offense level as eight. The Pre-sentence Report (PSR) concluded that Maciel had intended to evade tax, which would have raised the adjusted offense level. At the sentencing hearing, Maciel urged the court to reject that conclusion in the PSR. The prosecutor responded only tepidly, and the court agreed with Maciel.

Later, the IRS issued to Maciel a statutory notice of deficiency for the years in question. The notice asserted deficiencies and the section 6663 fraud penalty. The years in question were open to adjustment only if the IRS could establish that the returns were fraudulent.[53] In challenging the IRS's civil fraud determinations, Maciel argued that the district court's "no fraud" conclusion in the sentencing hearing precluded the IRS from asserting civil fraud. Following a line of Second Circuit non-tax cases,[54] the Ninth Circuit rejected Maciel's argument and upheld the IRS's fraud determinations. The court concluded that "findings made in a criminal sentencing proceeding ordinarily should not have preclusive effect in a subsequent civil case." This holding reflected the parties' realization throughout the process that the criminal and civil aspects of the case were proceeding on different tracks and reflected as well the fact that, given the plea agreement, the criminal prosecutor had limited incentive to defend the fraud recommendation in the PSR.

The second matter we will consider here is the reverse of the *Maciel* facts. What if the sentencing court had agreed with the PSR and held that Maciel had fraudulent intent? Could the IRS have used that determination to argue that Maciel was precluded from denying the fraud determinations in the notice of deficiency? The answer should be "no." As noted in Chapters 9 and 10, sentencing determinations are made on a "preponderance of the evidence" standard, which is below the "clear and convincing" standard that the IRS must meet to carry civil fraud.

F. Examples

Example 1: For tax year 1, Taxpayer fraudulently claimed large deductions, thus wiping out his year 1 income tax liability and creating a net operating loss on the tax year 1 tax return filed on April 15 of year 2. Under section 172(b)(3), Taxpayer elected not to carry back his losses and therefore carried them forward. He claimed some portion of the NOL carry forward in each of the years 2 through 4 on April 15 of each succeeding year (*i.e.*, the year 2 tax return is filed on April 15 of year 3, etc.). On May 1 of year 5 (shortly after filing the year 4 tax return), Taxpayer was indicted for tax evasion for years 1 through 3, each year being a separate count.[55] He was subsequently convicted on all counts. Based on the foregoing, the conviction of tax evasion for years 1 through 3 effects collateral estoppel as to civil fraud in years 1 through 3. But, does the year 1 conviction collateral estoppel on the civil fraud issue as to the year 4 return? One court has so

---

[53] *See* IRC § 6501(c)(1). This provision is discussed in Part IV below.

[54] *See* United States v. United States Currency in the Amount of $119,984, 304 F.3d 165 (2d Cir. 2002) (civil forfeiture by Customs Service); SEC v. Monarch Funding Corp., 192 F.3d 295 (2d Cir. 1999) (securities fraud).

[55] Set aside the question of why Taxpayer would have been so stupid as to file the return claiming the fraudulent NOL carry forward to the year 4 return when he knew (as he certainly would have) that he was under investigation and likely indictment for tax evasion for years 1 through 3.

held, reasoning that the claiming of a fraudulent NOL carry forward perforce renders the return fraudulent and, since the fraudulent claiming of the NOL loss itself has already been litigated between the parties in the NOL year (year 1 in this example and, by extrapolation, years 2 and 3 for which he was convicted for carrying the fraudulent loss to those years), it gives rise to collateral estoppel in the subsequent nonconviction year (year 4 in the example).[56] What would you argue in response?

You might argue that the convictions in the prior years are not preclusive on the issue of whether the taxpayer had the requisite intent in the fourth year. It is at least conceivable that he did not. For example, what if the carry forward to year 4 was relatively small in amount, and Taxpayer perhaps just did not think about the issue in year 4 (his return preparer just carried it forward from last year's return without discussing it with Taxpayer)? By analogy, in the criminal proceeding involving tax evasion charges for years 1 through 3, could the judge have instructed the jury that, if it found Taxpayer guilty for year 1, it must find him guilty for years 2 and 3? Probably not, because even though the fraudulent tax benefit traced to year 1, the issue is Taxpayer's guilt at the time he filed his year 2 or 3 return. If that finding of guilt is not preclusive in the criminal proceeding, why should a finding of guilt be preclusive in a noncharged year?

Example 2: Start with the same facts as in Example 1. In the sentencing phase, the Government established by a preponderance of the evidence that the tax loss number for each year is $100,000. Focus first on years 1-3 for which the taxpayer was convicted. In the ensuing civil fraud case, the parties agree that the total underpayment in each year was $200,000. Assume that the Government establishes by collateral estoppel its initial burden to show fraud by clear and convincing evidence. Then, assume that the evidence in the civil trial would show that $50,000 is not due to fraud. Under section 6663, the civil fraud penalty base would appear to be $150,000. Assume that the quality of proof for the $150,000 remaining is that the evidence shows by a preponderance of the evidence that $100,000 is attributable to fraud and $50,000 is in equal balance as to fraud. (Trial lawyers would say that the finder is in a state of equipoise as to that $50,000 and thus is unable to conclude that the taxpayer has established the right to have it excluded from the civil penalty base.) In the sentencing proceedings where the Government must establish the tax loss number by a preponderance of the evidence, the amount in the state of equipoise would not be included in the tax loss number. However, at least conceptually, in the civil penalty proceeding, the amount in equipoise is included in the civil penalty base. At least conceptually, therefore, the civil penalty base would be $150,000 in this example for years 1–3. Focus next on year 4 for which there is no conviction. Year 4 is considered in the criminal case only in calculating the sentence under the relevant conduct concept. Here, since the Government cannot rely upon collateral estoppel to establish its initial burden for the civil fraud penalty, it would have to make a fresh showing of fraud by clear and convincing evidence and thereafter the same process would apply (*i.e.*, taxpayer could exclude only the portion of the underpayment that he shows by a preponderance is not attributable to fraud).

---

[56] Gandy Nursery, Inc. v. United States, 318 F.3d 631 (5th Cir. 2003).

This example illustrates that the only difference between the sentencing finding as to the tax loss number and the civil fraud base is with respect to a possible inclusion in the amount as to which the proof in the civil case is in equipoise. Equipoise is a useful tool for analyzing burden of proof but is not helpful in real world cases where it is only the rare case that has key findings turn upon a state of equipoise.[57] For this reason, for judicial estoppel and prudential reasons, the sentencing findings as to the tax loss number should determine the civil penalty base.[58]

Example 3: Assume that, in the sentencing phase, the sentencing court is unable to determine a tax loss number and thus determines the guidelines without a tax loss number. The Base Offense Level would then apply in that case.[59] Is the sentencing court's inability to determine a tax loss number by a preponderance of the evidence collateral estoppel against the IRS on that issue in the subsequent civil case? It could be argued that it should be. If the Government has been unable to prove any fraudulent underpayment in the sentencing phase by a preponderance of the evidence, why should it be allowed to have a second bite at the judicial resource apple when it is required to make an affirmative showing by clear and convincing evidence?

If collateral estoppel were to apply to the tax loss number sentencing findings (still an open issue), the preclusive effect would be a two-way street. It would preclude the IRS from getting a larger civil penalty base but would also preclude the taxpayer from getting a lower one — provided, of course, that the IRS meets its initial burden of showing fraud by clear and convincing evidence (a showing it can make by collateral estoppel from a criminal finding to that level of proof, *i.e.*, guilt of tax evasion) or by actual evidence in the civil case.

Returning from this esoterica of collateral estoppel, the main point is that the civil fraud penalty is a big penalty that attends tax misconduct. The taxpayer can count on the fraud penalty being asserted if he or she is convicted. Even if the taxpayer is acquitted, the IRS can and usually will assert the fraud penalty when it has recommended the taxpayer for prosecution even if ultimately there is no prosecution and conviction. Moreover, fraud not only controls application of the section 6663 penalty, but also usually governs whether the statute of limitations on assessment of the tax liabilities remains open.

---

[57] *See* Cigaran v. Heston, 159 F.3d 355, 357 (8th Cir. 1998) ("The shifting of an evidentiary burden of preponderance is of practical consequence only in the rare event of an evidentiary tie."); *see also* Polack v. Commissioner, 366 F.3d 608, 613 (8th Cir. 2004) (citing *Cigaran*); Steve R. Johnson, *The Dangers of Symbolic Legislation: Perceptions and Realities of the New Burden-of-Proof Rules*, 84 Iowa L. Rev. 413, 444–46 (1999).

[58] This is the view of at least one of the authors of this book. *See* John A. Townsend, *Collateral Estoppel in Civil Cases Following Criminal Convictions*, 106 Tax Notes 243 (2005). As discussed in the article, the IRS and the courts had declined to apply collateral estoppel to set the civil fraud base at the tax loss number. For the reasons noted, those positions are based upon incomplete understanding of the role of the tax loss number in the scheme of the Sentencing Guidelines.

[59] A variation on this theme happened in *United States v. Roselli*, 366 F.3d 58 (1st Cir. 2004).

V. STATUTE OF LIMITATIONS

Our focus here is on the statute of limitations as to assessment of taxes for the year(s) involved in the criminal investigation. In general, the IRS must assess any tax, or issue a notice of deficiency, with respect to a tax year within three years of when the return for the year was filed or was due to be filed, whichever is later.[60] However, as set out principally in sections 6501 and 6503, many conditions can extend or suspend the running of this limitations period.

Four aspects of these rules are of principal significance in the criminal tax context. First, if the criminal investigation was occasioned by the taxpayer's failure to file a return, an important tactical question is whether to file the return(s), however belatedly. The statute of limitations on assessment is one consideration bearing on this question. Under section 6501(c)(3), the limitations period does not begin to run until the return for the year is filed.

Second, under section 6501(c)(4), the taxpayer can consent to extend the limitations period. Before the matter "went criminal," an IRS revenue agent may have asked the taxpayer to enter into such a consent. Subject to certain coordination rules, such a solicitation may even be made after referral of the case to the Department of Justice.[61] Again, many considerations bear on the decision as to how to respond to such a request.[62] Some experienced counsel recommend against granting consents when there is an appreciable chance of criminal investigation. If, nonetheless, the decision is made to grant the consent, counsel should distinguish between the two IRS forms principally used for this purpose. Form 872 extends the limitations period for a specified duration while Form 872-A extends the period until the agreement is revoked by either party (plus 90 days thereafter). Since greater control is retained, Form 872-A may be the form of choice when there is criminal potential.

Third, when the allegedly criminal conduct consisted of omitting income from the return, another of the exceptions may come into play. Section 6501(e) provides for a six-year limitations period in the case of substantial omissions from gross income on income tax returns. An omission or set of omissions is substantial for this purpose if the total omitted exceeds 25% of the gross income shown on the return. In such cases, counsel should calculate the extended six-year date and monitor movement towards it.

Fourth, there is no limitations period — *i.e.*, the tax may be assessed at any time — if the return is "false or fraudulent . . . with the intent to evade tax" (section 6501(c)(1)) or if, in the case of taxes other than income, estate, gift, or generation-skipping transfer taxes, there is "a willful attempt in any manner to defeat or evade tax" (section 6501(c)(2)). Given these provisions, the IRS will often let the normal three-year period elapse if it feels confident that it can establish fraud. The effect of these provisions on the statute of limitations on assessment should be one factor

---

60 IRC §§ 6501(a) & 6503(a).

61 *See* CCDM 31.4.2.0:2.

62 *See* Richardson, Borison & Johnson, *supra*, at 93–95.

in the taxpayer's decision-making as to possible terms on which to settle the criminal case.

As noted in Subpart II.A above, the section 6663 fraud penalty cannot be asserted against a spouse simply by virtue of his or her having made a joint return for the year with the other spouse who did commit fraud. There must be proof of fraud on both spouses' parts before the IRS can assert the fraud penalty against both spouses. However, for statute of limitations purposes, the question is whether the return is fraudulent, not whether one or both of the spouses participated in the fraud. Thus, for example, assume that the return is fraudulent because it contains fraudulent items of the husband's. Assume further that the wife did not know the items were wrong. Section 6501(c) would still give the IRS an unlimited period to assess any deficiencies and interest against the wife (as well the husband). The IRS could not assess the section 6663 penalty against her (because of section 6663(c)), and the wife might qualify for spousal relief under section 6015, but she would not have a statute of limitations defense under section 6501.[63]

The IRS need not show that the entire return is fraudulent. The unlimited assessment period applies as long as any part of the return is fraudulent.[64] However, criminal conviction for one or some years does not create a presumption that inaccuracies on returns for other years was attributable to fraud.[65]

If the taxpayer files a fraudulent original return, the statute of limitations generally is unlimited even if the taxpayer later files a nonfraudulent amended return for the same tax year.[66] The exception is when: (i) the fraudulent original is filed before the due date or extended due date of the return; and (ii) the nonfraudulent amended return also is filed on or before the due date or extended due date. Under those conditions — which are rare in the real world — the amended return (called a superseding return) will be treated as the original return for all purposes. If the taxpayer initially fraudulently fails to file but later files a nonfraudulent (although late) return, the normal three-year limitations period begins to run from the date the return was filed.[67]

VI. MITIGATING TAX LIABILITIES

The goal of the criminal prosecution is to fortify the better instincts of the mass of taxpayers by showing them what may happen if they yield to temptation. However, once the defendant has served this "object lesson" function criminally, the IRS will want to assess and collect whatever additional liabilities the taxpayer owes. In general, criminal conviction does not displace the civil processes of assessing and

---

[63] *E.g.*, Ballard v. Commissioner, 740 F.2d 659, 663 (8th Cir. 1984); CCA 200205027 (Feb. 1, 2002).

[64] *E.g.*, Corson v. Commissioner, 369 F.2d 367, 368 (3d Cir. 1966) (per curiam), *cert. denied*, 387 U.S. 919 (1967). Moreover, fraud by the return preparer suffices even if the taxpayer him or herself did not have the requisite fraudulent intent. Allen v. Commissioner, 128 T.C. 37 (2007).

[65] *E.g.*, United States v. Diehl, 460 F. Supp. 1282, 1287 (S.D. Tex.), *aff'd per curiam*, 586 F.2d 1080 (5th Cir. 1978).

[66] Badaracco v. Commissioner, 464 U.S. 386 (1984).

[67] *See, e.g.*, Bennett v. Commissioner, 30 T.C. 114 (1958); Rev. Rul. 79-178, 1979-1 C.B. 435.

collecting such liabilities.[68] Typically, the IRS will still have to issue a notice of deficiency, triggering the opportunity for Tax Court review. After the deficiency process has run its course, the IRS must assess the determined liabilities. If the taxpayer does not "voluntarily" pay the liabilities after assessment, the IRS will have to use the enforced collection options the Code provides, subject to remedies and defenses available to the taxpayer and any affected third parties.[69]

Once tax liabilities have been assessed, the IRS has at its disposal an imposing array of enforced collection tools. The collection powers of the IRS exceed those of ordinary creditors.[70] These powers include jeopardy and termination assessments, general and special tax liens, administrative levy and sale, and judicial sale.[71] They also include techniques of secondary liability, such as transferee liability, fiduciary liability, and the section 6672 trust fund recovery penalty (also known as the 100% penalty and the "responsible person" penalty).[72]

Nonetheless, taxpayers and affected third parties have access to a variety of administrative and judicial remedies by which to oppose improper IRS collection efforts or to mitigate effects of proper collection efforts.[73] In general, these remedies remain available even to taxpayers who have gone through criminal investigation and prosecution. However, there are exceptions. Below, we consider three important collection areas: offers in compromise, spousal relief, and bankruptcy.

A. Offers in Compromise

Section 7122 gives the Government authority to compromise tax liabilities by accepting something less than the full amounts that have been or could be assessed. Currently, compromise may be effected on any of three grounds: (1) doubt as to liability (the substantive tax law, correctly applied, would make the taxpayer liable for less than the IRS has assessed or intends to assess); (2) doubt as to collectibility (the taxpayer's assets plus foreseeable future income in excess of reasonable living expenses would permit only partial payment of the tax liabilities); and (3) promotion of effective tax administration (a less-than-precisely-defined and rarely granted category of relief that balances effects of collection on the taxpayer and the IRS).[74]

The first and third grounds are unlikely to be available in matters that have gone through both criminal and civil investigation. The second ground may be

---

[68] Sometimes a plea agreement in the criminal case includes agreement as to the civil liabilities. Other times the plea agreement or sentencing order includes a requirement that the taxpayer-defendant cooperate with the IRS in determining the correct amount of the civil liabilities. *E.g.*, McGowan v. Commissioner, 187 F. App'x 915, 916 (11th Cir. 2006). *See generally* U.S. Att. Man. 6-4.200; DOJ Tax Div. Man. 4-25; CCDM 31.4.7.0.2.

[69] These rules of assessment and collection are described in Richardson, Borison & Johnson, *supra*.

[70] *See* Steve R. Johnson, *The IRS as Super Creditor*, 92 Tax Notes 655 (2001).

[71] *See* Richardson, Borison & Johnson, *supra*, chs. 7 & 13.

[72] *See* Richardson, Borison & Johnson, chs. 14 & 15.

[73] These remedies are described in Richardson, Borison & Johnson, *supra*, at 339–50.

[74] Reg. § 301.7122-1(b).

available. IRS policy expressly allows consideration of an offer in compromise in criminal tax situations although special rules exist requiring coordination of the evaluation of the offer with the Criminal Investigation function.[75] In practice, results have been mixed as to offers to compromise fraud-related deficiencies, interest, and penalties. Some such offers have been accepted. Others, in light of the history and circumstances, have received chilly reception.

The stage which the matter has reached will determine which department has authority to enter into a compromise. Section 7122(a) provides that the IRS "may compromise any civil or criminal [tax] case" before referral to the Department of Justice for prosecution or defense but that Justice has compromise authority after such referral. After referral, the Department of Justice has broad authority to settle the civil aspects of a case which are germane to the criminal referral.[76]

The outer limits of section 7122(a) have not yet been mapped. In one case, a taxpayer who had been convicted of multiple tax offenses submitted an offer in compromise to the IRS. The court held that section 7122(a) did not preclude the IRS from considering the offer but did preclude the IRS from accepting it without approval by the Department of Justice.[77] Just when the IRS regains unilateral authority to accept or reject offers has not been definitively resolved.

B. Spousal Relief

Assume that fraudulent items attributed to Spouse A appear on a return filed jointly with Spouse B. Spouse B could have trouble even if he or she did not participate in the fraud. As explained in preceding sections, although neither civil nor criminal fraud sanctions could be imposed on Spouse B, the fraud on the return would keep the statute of limitations open to assessment of the deficiency and interest. Moreover, under section 6013(d)(3), both of the spouses would be jointly and severally liable for the deficiency and interest.

To avoid or minimize such liability, Spouse B will hope to qualify for relief under section 6015. Since 1998, section 6015 has provided for three categories of relief. Section 6015(b) allows relief from joint liabilities regardless of current marital status as long as a number of requirements are met, including that the spouse seeking relief did not know or have reason to know of the understatement and did not materially benefit from it. Section 6015(c) allows widowed, divorced, or separated spouses to elect proportionate liability, each spouse being liable for the taxes as to his or her items only. Section 6015(f) allows relief from liability for underpayment when, based on all of the facts and circumstances, it would be inequitable to impose liability on one of the spouses.[78]

---

[75] *See* IRM 9.5.14.6.

[76] *E.g.*, Aviation Corp. v. United States, 46 F. Supp. 491, 494 (Ct. Cl. 1942), *cert. denied*, 318 U.S. 771 (1943). *But see* United States v. McCue, 178 F. Supp. 426 (D. Conn. 1959) (purported compromise agreement entered into by U.S. Attorney's Office held invalid).

[77] Isley v. Comm'r, 141 T.C. 349, at 363–66 (2013). To similar effect, see United States v. Jackson, 511 Fed. Appx. 200, 203 (3d Cir. 2013); Faust v. United States, 28 F.3d 105 (9th Cir. 1994); Chief Counsel Notice CC-2011-020 (Sept. 13, 2011).

[78] These relief avenues are described in detail in Richardson, Borison & Johnson, *supra*, ch. 3.

Criminally punishable tax behavior plays out in several ways against this statutory framework. For one thing, practically if not doctrinally, spousal relief cases often take on a comparative aspect. The worse that Spouse A behaved, the more likely it will be that Spouse B will be held to qualify for relief.

More important, though, are the nature and extent of Spouse B's activities. If Spouse B knew or should have known of Spouse A's tax peccadilloes or if Spouse B materially benefited from them, section 6015(b) relief would be unavailable. If the IRS proves that Spouse B had actual knowledge of the deficiency or that assets were transferred by Spouse A to Spouse B, section 6015(c) relief would be imperiled.[79] Likewise, of course, similar facts would alter the balance of equities as to section 6015(f) relief.

C. Bankruptcy

Bankruptcy can be an important option for taxpayers with substantial liabilities.[80] Part of the attractiveness is the possibility of receiving discharge of unpaid debts. Whether tax debts are dischargeable depends on the interaction of three portions of the Bankruptcy Code (Title 11 of the United States Code): sections 507, 523, and 727.[81]

In the criminal tax context, a significant exception to discharge is set out in 11 U.S.C. section 523(a)(1)(C), prohibiting discharge when the taxpayer-debtor willfully attempted to evade or defeat tax. This exception has been the subject of an increasing volume of judicial decisions, and some of the decisions have been less than fully consistent.[82] The Government bears the burden of proof as to the exception, with a "preponderance of the evidence" standard of proof.[83] The exception has two elements: intent (willfulness) and conduct (attempt). The conduct element can be satisfied both by acts of commission and acts of omission.[84]

VII. SUBSEQUENT YEARS' RETURNS

Taxpayers under criminal investigation often face important and difficult decisions with respect to filing returns for tax periods subsequent to the periods under investigation. Although section 6103(a) typically makes tax returns and tax return information confidential, the Code permits their disclosure to IRS special agents for

---

79 *See* IRC § 6015(c)(3)(C), (4).

80 For detailed discussion of bankruptcy in federal tax collection, *see* William D. Elliott, Federal Tax Collections, Liens, and Levies, ch. 20 (2d ed. 2005).

81 A federal tax lien comes into existence upon assessment followed by notice and demand for payment. IRC §§ 6321 & 6322. Even if the underlying taxes themselves are dischargeable, the tax lien, if it exists, remains in place. *E.g.*, Wrenn v. American Cast Iron Pipe Co. (*In re* Wrenn), 40 F.3d 1162 (11th Cir. 1994). Section 6672 "responsible person" liabilities are not dischargeable in bankruptcy. *E.g.*, United States v. Sotelo, 436 U.S. 268 (1978).

82 Instructive cases interpreting the exception include: United States v. Jacons (In re Jacobs), 490 F.3d 913 (11th Cir. 2007); United States v. Fretz (In re Fretz), 244 F.3d 1323 (11th Cir. 2001); Roper v. Barclay (In re Roper), 294 B.R. 301 (B.A.P. 8th Cir. 2003).

83 *E.g.*, Grogan v. Garner, 498 U.S. 279, 291 (1991).

84 *E.g.*, Mathis v. United States (In re Mathis), 310 B.R. 468, 472 (Bankr. S.D. Fla. 2004).

use in criminal investigations and to the Department of Justice for use in criminal prosecutions (and for other tax administration purposes).[85] Statements made on tax returns may constitute admissions that help the special agents to develop their case.[86]

If the taxpayer files a timely and accurate return for the later year, admissions contained therein may help the Government obtain conviction in the criminal case. For instance, the issue in the earlier year(s) criminal case may involve unreported income from a business. If a later-year return accurately reports far higher income from the business than was reported in the criminal year(s), absent some major change in the business or other explanation the later return could complicate the taxpayer's ability to deny the earlier omission of income.

The taxpayer could seek to avoid damaging admissions by reporting on later-year returns which is consistent with the reporting on the return(s) for the earlier, criminal year(s). However, if consistency is purchased at the price of knowing inaccuracy, the taxpayer could be inviting further criminal (section 7601 or 7602) and civil (section 6663 or 6662) liability, particularly because each tax year stands on its own and can give rise to independent liability. If the taxpayer seeks to avoid Scylla and Charybdis of the above approaches by not filing at all and not paying with respect to the later year(s), the taxpayer risks criminal and/or civil liability under other sections (section 7201 or 7203 and section 6651, respectively).

The above problems are real, but they are somewhat mitigated by four possibilities. First, in some circuits, the taxpayer may offer the filing of accurate returns or amended returns and the payment of associated taxes as evidence to negate willfulness.[87] Second, the taxpayer may be able to assert the Fifth Amendment privilege against self incrimination as the basis for not filing the later return(s) during the pendency of criminal proceedings or at least for omitting some information from the later return(s).[88] Third, if the taxpayer chooses not to file on time for the later year(s), the taxpayer should at least consider making a deposit in the nature of a cash bond with respect to the later year(s).[89] Civilly, making such a deposit will minimize interest accruals. Criminally, it may help to show that the taxpayer is attempting to comply with his or her tax obligations. Fourth, as a matter of administrative policy, the IRS sometimes chooses to forgo use of later year returns in prosecutions involving earlier years.

In general, when a criminal case is pending in the Department of Justice, the IRS will not examine subsequent tax years of the taxpayer's without first soliciting

---

85 *See* IRC § 6103(h)(1), (2), (4) & (i)(1)–(4).

86 *E.g.*, United States v. Hornstein, 176 F.2d 217, 220 (7th Cir. 1949).

87 *E.g.*, Hill v. United States, 363 F.2d 176, 180 (5th Cir. 1966).

88 For treatment of the many issues that can arise in this regard, see Siffert & Michael Saltzman, *The Fifth Amendment and Tax Returns: The Viability of the Deferred Filing/Current Payment of Tax Approach Pending a Criminal Investigation*, 4 White-Collar Crime Rep. 1 (Jan. 1990). See Chapter 7 for additional discussion of the privilege against self incrimination. *But see* United States v. Radtke, 415 F.3d 826, 840–41 (8th Cir. 2005) (holding that an amended return filed post-indictment was of little or no probative value, thus evidence of the filing was properly excluded).

89 *See, e.g.*, Baral v. United States, 528 U.S. 431 (2000); Rev. Proc. 84-58, 1984-2 C.B. 506.

Justice's approval.[90] However, the IRS may issue a notice of deficiency for subsequent years without such advance coordination when tax adjustments are obvious from the face of the later-years' returns.

PROBLEM

Aaron Ascher has an eighth-grade education. In 1996, he began operating Ascher Construction Corporation (ACC), an S corporation. The corporation has been profitable. Aaron has at all times been the president and sole shareholder of ACC. In 2010, Aaron married Brenda Barnes, who owns and operates a clothing manufacturing business.

Later in 2010, Aaron hired Charles Cranch, Brenda's accountant, to revise ACC's accounting and payroll records and to prepare tax returns. In 2011, Aaron bought a computer for ACC, and Charles installed, on the computer, an accounting software program to record general ledger, payroll, invoice, and accounts receivable information. ACC's clerical staff did not have any previous bookkeeping experience, but Charles trained the staff to perform bookkeeping functions.

Each year, Aaron and ACC's clerical staff kept a handwritten ledger to record all work performed, invoices prepared, and customer checks received. Aaron or his staffers opened ACC's mail and collected customer checks. They would match each check with its corresponding invoice and record, in the handwritten ledger, that the invoice had been paid. In addition, the staffers recorded, in the general ledger, the customer checks they deposited in ACC's bank account and used this information to prepare monthly financial statements.

From 2011 through 2013, Aaron and the staffers recorded the receipt of all of the customer checks in Aaron's handwritten ledger. During these years, Aaron cashed, or deposited into his personal bank account, customer checks and used the proceeds for his personal benefit. ACC's balance sheets for each year reflected significant balances in the shareholder equity accounts, which included shareholder loans, capital stock, retained earnings, and current earnings.

Beginning in 2011, Brenda became concerned because some of the customer checks were not being deposited into ACC's account. She informed Charles that she did not want to file a joint federal income tax return with Aaron for 2011. Charles asked Aaron whether all customer checks were being properly accounted for. Aaron told Charles that all of the income was being recorded in ACC's books. Based on this assurance, and on Charles' belief that Brenda would qualify as an innocent spouse under section 6015 even if Aaron were underreporting his income, Charles convinced Brenda to sign a joint return for 2011.

Before signing a return for 2012, Brenda sought legal advice to determine whether she would qualify as an innocent spouse if Aaron failed to report all of his income on their joint return. Brenda subsequently refused to sign a 2012 joint return with Aaron. This decision led to Brenda and Aaron's separation in 2012 and divorce in early 2013. Thereupon, Brenda contacted the IRS and alleged that Aaron

---

[90] *See* CCDM 31.4.7.0.

had taken funds from ACC and had not reported them on his tax returns.

Charles had access to, but did not review, the handwritten ledger, accounts receivable, and invoices. He relied exclusively on ACC's bank records and financial statements (which were prepared from the information in the general ledger) to prepare ACC's Forms 1120S.

The IRS launched a criminal investigation. In 2015, Aaron was convicted under section 7201 with respect to his and Brenda's individual return (Form 1040) for 2011, convicted under section 7206(1) for his Form 1040 for 2012, convicted under section 7206(2) for ACC's Form 1120S for 2012, and acquitted of all criminal charges with respect to his Form 1040 and ACC's Form 1120S for 2013.

On April 30, 2016, the IRS issued a notice of deficiency to Aaron. It determined deficiencies and section 6663 fraud penalties against Aaron, based on unreported income from ACC, for tax years 2011, 2012, and 2013.

1. Aaron retains you to represent him with respect to the notice of deficiency. He tells you that, if he is called in any civil trial, he will testify that he believed at the time that the checks he converted to his personal use had been included in the shareholder accounts as a loan to him. He now understands that they weren't, however, and he acknowledges that the unreported income amounts stated in the notice of deficiency are correct. He also will testify that he cooperated with all IRS requests for information and that he made all relevant information available to his clerical staffers, who prepared records for Charles to use in preparing the individual and corporate tax returns.

Evaluate the issues and Aaron's prospects for success in contesting the determinations in the notice of deficiency. Identify any factual ambiguities and describe their potential significance.

2. In the course of your discussions, Aaron mentions that ACC has continued to operate profitably. However, because of the then ongoing criminal investigation and prosecution, neither Aaron individually nor ACC has filed any federal income tax returns for 2014 or 2015. What should Aaron do?

3. Change the facts. You do not represent Aaron. Instead, Brenda retains you. She tells you that she has heard that Aaron received a notice of deficiency from the IRS for 2011 through 2013. She is worried that the IRS might "come after" her too. Although it hasn't happened yet, Brenda also wonders what she should do if the IRS asks her to extend the section 6501 limitations period as to any return. What do you say to Brenda?

4. Change the facts again. To pay his legal fees, Aaron sells ACC. The new owner of ACC retains you. She is worried that the IRS may "come after" ACC for inaccurate Forms 1120S filed while Aaron was the owner. What advice do you give? Consider both civil and criminal tax sanctions.

Chapter 14

PUTTING IT ALL TOGETHER

Regs. § 301.7602-1

Review the materials in previous chapters regarding the procedures followed by the IRS, U.S. Attorney's Office, and Department of Justice Tax Division in investigating and prosecuting criminal tax cases. Pay particular attention to the individuals involved and their responsibilities and duties.

I. INTRODUCTION

In the prior chapters, we addressed by topic specific issues related to federal tax crimes. In this chapter, we review the process of a criminal tax case from investigation through sentencing, with two goals in mind. First, we hope to present some of the materials from earlier chapters in practical scenarios that will aid students in their understanding of the materials. Second, we discuss some of the strategic issues that must be addressed in typical criminal tax cases. We will not regurgitate the materials previously covered. Instead, we hope to examine some of the same ground in a different way, with a view toward applying some of the concepts previously addressed.[1]

II. UNDERSTANDING THE PLAYERS WITHOUT A SCORECARD

Perhaps only a few of those who read this case book intend to devote their careers to the prosecution and defense of criminal tax cases. Nevertheless, anyone who has studied these materials has probably spent more time thinking about criminal tax issues than most of the accountants, tax planners, financial planners, estate planners, revenue agents, revenue officers, and even IRS counsel who do not work with CI. Thus, the reader hopefully has absorbed the fundamentals regarding the personnel involved in tax investigations, the procedures that will be followed in criminal tax cases, and the strategies that might apply to a particular set of circumstances. There truly is no substitute for mastery of the procedures and personnel. No amount of strategic discussion makes much sense if the student has not thoroughly understood what opportunities exist for negotiation and discussion with the opposing parties. And those opportunities will be squandered if the student misunderstands the duties or motivations of the parties with whom the negotiations will take place.

[1] Although many of the examples in this chapter are presented from the defense point of view, hopefully future prosecutors will also benefit from the scenarios.

Neither laypersons (such as most taxpayers) nor most of the accountants and lawyers who deal regularly with the civil tax arena are prepared for the intricacies of criminal tax cases. For example, accountants and even sophisticated tax planners often refer to most IRS field personnel as "revenue agents," without regard to whether the IRS employee might be a collection officer or special agent as opposed to an actual revenue agent. The consequences of assuming that a client-taxpayer (or the accountant or lawyer who referred that client) has properly understood the role of the IRS personnel can be calamitous. One of the authors of this case book once listened in on a phone call in which an accountant with 30 years of experience called a revenue officer who had made contact with the taxpayer. After introducing himself, the accountant revealed that the taxpayer had hired the accountant to bring the taxpayer's books and records up to date and to have some delinquent income tax returns prepared. The accountant then stated that he could have the returns ready for filing within two weeks, and he asked the revenue officer if that time frame was acceptable. Only then did the revenue officer reveal that he had actually contacted the taxpayer regarding some apparent overpayments on the taxpayer's payroll tax accounts! Thus, the accountant had brought the non-filing problem to the attention of the IRS unnecessarily. Imagine if a similar mistake was made in a discussion with a special agent, whose job is to recommend cases for prosecution.

Similarly, even experienced criminal defense lawyers frequently misunderstand the tools of IRS criminal investigation. For example, a common error is to refer to a document as a "subpoena," when in fact it may be an IRS special agent summons. Even when the distinction is pointed out, most lawyers and civil tax practitioners do not fully comprehend the important distinctions between an IRS administrative investigation and a grand jury investigation. We hope the readers of this book now know those differences in their bones. Without such an intuitive understanding, neither prosecutors nor defense counsel can make sophisticated decisions with regard to the handling of criminal tax cases.

In many fields of endeavor, it is common to hear something described as being "more art than science." The "science" of criminal tax practice involves developing the particular facts of each case and knowing the precedent that applies. The "art" involves determining your client's best possible arguments and deciding which personnel in the process will be most receptive to your best presentation of the facts and the law. Learning the "art" comes in part from experience and the judgment that experience permits a practitioner to bring to the table. Some of that experience can be vicarious (*e.g.*, attending seminars or reading advance sheets and articles), but the experience must become so ingrained that it permits the practitioner to extrapolate in new contexts, because the facts are never exactly the same from case to case. In the criminal tax field, many situations arise in which the prosecutor or defense counsel must decide whether to press an argument at a particular time or save it for later. Likewise, it can be difficult to decide whether to reveal a fact or use it at a different point in the process. Those daily choices, compounded by the months and months that go by in a typical criminal tax investigation, make it difficult to provide bright line tests or formulas that apply to criminal tax practice.

The balance of this chapter suggests some areas that deserve your particular attention and review, as well as some of the sophisticated strategic decisions that often come into play in handling criminal tax cases.

III. SOME EXAMPLES OF STRATEGIC DECISION-MAKING IN CRIMINAL TAX CASES

In Chapter 1 we introduced the players and procedures involved in the criminal tax process. In Chapter 6, we presented more thorough discussions of both administrative and grand jury criminal tax investigations. There is no substitute for thorough familiarity with the procedures described in those two chapters. Let's look at the various stages of an IRS administrative criminal tax case and some of the decisions that might be considered during those phases.

A. After Return Filing But Before Audit

Your client filed a fraudulent return substantially underreporting his tax liability. He now has misgivings. He comes to you and expresses great concern and even a glimmer of remorse. What can you do for him?

The crime of tax evasion is complete upon filing the return. There are two possible exceptions. If the taxpayer filed the return before the normal due date (April 15 for an individual taxpayer and March 15 for a calendar year corporation), the taxpayer can purge the fraud by filing a non-fraudulent amended return on or before the normal due date. This opportunity also applies if a superseding return purges the fraud during an applicable extension period. If, as is usually the case, the taxpayer cannot qualify for these exceptions, the question becomes one of damage control.

Since you are familiar with the voluntary disclosure policy, you can consider with your client the idea of making a voluntary disclosure to avoid prosecution. You must explore carefully whether the client qualifies for voluntary disclosure treatment. Will the disclosure be timely and complete? Will the taxpayer be in a position to cooperate with any examination of the tax returns? What about the ability to pay or make arrangements to pay? If the facts fit the IRS policy, you can give the client some comfort that a voluntary disclosure will avoid a criminal investigation or prosecution. You should advise your client, however, there are no guarantees. Why?

As noted above, the voluntary disclosure policy is just that — a policy of the administrators of the law. It is not law. So, the taxpayer's ability to force the IRS to apply the voluntary disclosure policy is limited under the *Caceres* doctrine.[2]

Nevertheless, most practitioners feel that the IRS will honor the policy, provided the taxpayer qualifies. But you must always ask: is there some other fact that might impel the IRS to prosecute despite an honest effort by your client to voluntarily disclose? For example, is your client a politician or other well-known figure for whom the publicity from a criminal tax conviction will be too juicy for the IRS to forgo? If so, perhaps the voluntary disclosure should begin with an anonymous contact to the SAC to receive assurances that the IRS will not pursue a criminal case if the disclosure is made.

---

[2] United States v. Caceres, 440 U.S. 741 (1979), discussed in Chapter 7.

Let's assume that you believe your client can qualify for the voluntary disclosure policy. If you decide to discuss the matter on a "no-names" basis with CI, you must make sure that the facts are fully and accurately presented. Otherwise, any assurance received from CI will not be considered binding. If you decide to simply send in an amended return to the service center, the client takes more risk, although the risk may be minimal under your facts. But the decision to take that risk should be the client's decision after discussing the pros and cons.

The next question: who should prepare the amended return(s)? It is usually not advisable to use the original tax return preparer, who is already exposed as a potential witness against the client and possesses information that cannot be erased from memory. The original preparer had access to information and documents that typically are not privileged. In preparing an amended return, additional information will be learned that may offer a roadmap to the fraud. If the original preparer works on the amended return, the taxpayer will then be at risk that the return preparer cannot clearly establish what information was learned only after the privilege became applicable. This risk usually is not acceptable, even though the taxpayer faces additional costs by engaging a new preparer.

The preparer of the amended return should be brought under the cloak of the attorney-client privilege via a *Kovel* agreement.[3] However, the IRS still could assert that the amended return preparer is nothing more than a preparer (not needed to perform legal services) or perhaps that the information received by the *Kovel* accountant is not privileged because it was intended to be disclosed. When the budget permits, the *Kovel* accountant should assist the lawyer by gathering and analyzing all potentially relevant information, and then the lawyer should determine what portion of the information to disclose to an independent return preparer who is not covered by a *Kovel* arrangement. In that way, the preparer's knowledge is discoverable by the IRS, but the information disclosed to the *Kovel* accountant should remain privileged. Keeping the roles distinct best preserves the attorney-client privilege.

Assuming your client makes a full disclosure and does not engage in utter stupidity (remember the lessons of *Tenzer*), the voluntary disclosure should succeed, and the risk of prosecution should be eliminated.

B. The Eggshell Civil Tax Audit

In an "eggshell audit," you must walk on eggshells to represent your client effectively in the civil examination without exposing the fraud, all the while honoring your duties to the tax system not to mislead the revenue agent.[4] Although a voluntary disclosure is theoretically untimely once the civil examination has begun, by careful attention and advocacy, the practitioner may be able to obtain a reasonable level of assurance that the civil agent will not refer the matter to CI, so

[3] United States v. Kovel, 296 F.2d 918 (2d Cir. 1961), discussed in Chapter 7.

[4] There is a healthy dose of self-interest here because of the panoply of potential crimes that might be charged if the IRS believes the practitioner has intentionally misled the examination agent. In addition, sanctions can be imposed by the Office of Professional Responsibility if the practitioner does not comply with accepted standards of conduct.

that disclosure of the fraud to the agent will not result in a referral for criminal investigation. There are many circumstances in which disclosure to the agent may be the best option. For example, if the taxpayer has failed to report income that almost certainly will be discovered in the examination, the revenue agent may be willing to allow the taxpayer to disclose the problem, pay a reduced penalty, and move on without a criminal referral. Agents often are happy to close a case with an adjustment that results in additional tax collected. In other cases, the best strategy may be to disclose an error in the hope that by correcting the item, the disclosure will undercut the willfulness issue to the point that CI may not be interested in the case if a referral is made. Special agents generally have more cases to work than they can handle, so the supervisory special agents often choose to drop cases in which the taxpayer has disclosed the item and paid the appropriate tax plus a penalty. This strategy often requires the taxpayer to "open the kimono" in order to convince the agent that the taxpayer is acting in good faith and deserving of such grace as the agent and the group manager can confer.

Assuming that the civil examination will proceed without a full disclosure by the client, the practitioner usually should limit the contact between the agent and the taxpayer. This is good practice even if there is no criminal potential in the case. Ask that the agent make all requests for information through the practitioner. Even better, ask that the agent make all requests in writing so that there is no confusion about what the request was and whether the response was untruthful or misleading. Ultimately, if the agent persists in demands for a taxpayer interview, make sure that the taxpayer is prepared to answer honestly or to assert the Fifth Amendment and other applicable privileges when appropriate. The practitioner should remain vigilant at the interview to prevent the client from accidentally answering questions for which the privilege should be asserted.

The defense must also "audit" the agent, *i.e.*, track the investigation to keep abreast of what the agent knows. IRS civil agents are required to notify the taxpayer before contacting third parties and to keep a record of the third parties contacted, at least during the civil phase of an investigation. And section 7609 requires that the IRS notify the taxpayer of summonses issued to third parties. That notice requirement does not apply in criminal investigations,[5] but here we are discussing the civil examination phase, and the notice requirement applies. If third-party summonses have been issued and the taxpayer did not receive notice, those summonses probably were: (1) issued incident a criminal investigation, (2) issued with notice sent to the wrong address, or (3) issued in violation of the notice requirement. If a witness voluntarily provided information when requested by the civil agent, without the need for a third-party summons, the record of the third-party contact will sit in the file, generally until the defense requests the information. Thus, establishing a good relationship with potential witnesses is an important part of the job during the civil examination, and witnesses should be asked to call the taxpayer's counsel if the IRS makes contact with the witness.

---

[5] There is an exception for summonses issued to third party recordkeepers as defined in section 7603(b). The notice procedures must be followed for recordkeeper summonses even in criminal cases. IRC § 7609(c)(2)(E)(ii).

The taxpayer's counsel should strongly consider the use of a forensic accountant in eggshell audits (as well as in criminal investigations). The *Kovel* accountant should be engaged as early in the process as possible to garner the maximum benefit from the accountant's work. Since many defense lawyers are not equipped to handle the tax issues that arise in eggshell audits and criminal investigations, it is common for some practitioners to engage former IRS CI agents in addition to the forensic accountant, in order to "audit" the examination agent's activity and help prepare a cogent defense.

Often, important information can be gleaned simply by keeping in touch with the agent. The taxpayer's counsel can learn a lot, even if the agent does not specifically say that fraud is suspected or that the matter is in the process of being referred to CI. Cases such as *Kontny* suggest that the IRS revenue agent (civil agent) can affirmatively mislead the taxpayer and the taxpayer's representative, but generally agents are discouraged from doing that. The careful and experienced practitioner often will sense that a Fraud Technical Advisor has been consulted and that the examination has turned into a de facto fraud investigation.

One of the paradoxes of civil tax examinations is that two diametrically opposite patterns of activity by the civil agent each suggest that a fraud referral may result. The first common pattern involves an agent who starts copying voluminous documents, reconciling every sales invoice to the general ledger, or otherwise spending far more time on the case than would ordinarily be expected. Often this additional activity involves the agent following the direction of a fraud technical advisor to button up details before a referral to CI. But the opposite pattern also may suggest a potential referral, because a case that turns quiet sometimes indicates that the agent and the managers may have made a referral to CI and are waiting for a response. Civil examinations are conducted on a time line, which may vary from case to case, but if the audit does not progress for an extended period of time, the practitioner needs to know why. Often, it is because an agent is swamped with other work, has been out for extended training, or has been transferred. But inactivity may also mean that the civil agent has referred the case to CI. When the civil audit turns quiet, the practitioner should touch base with the agent or the supervisor to find out what is going on. Of course, the practitioner should not act overly concerned about the delay. A FOIA request should be considered if it becomes clear that the case will be referred.

After the civil agent has finished work on the case, it can take two directions. First, the agent may not perceive the criminal potential and may close the civil examination with proposed adjustments or a no-change letter. Second, the agent may determine that the case has sufficient criminal potential to be referred to CI. Although the IRM requires that the agent refer the case to CI when he or she has a "firm indication of fraud," agents currently are taught to consult with their group managers and the fraud technical advisors to review the fraud potential in an examination. Thus, although a referral can occur anytime during the civil examination process, it usually happens near the end.

C. The CI Phase

When CI receives the referral from the civil agent, a special agent will be assigned primary responsibility for the case. While with CI, the criminal aspects of the case ordinarily take priority over the civil. The civil examination usually will not progress to the point of a notice of deficiency or assessment until after the criminal investigation is resolved, but the CI special agents may be assisted by a civil agent who is often more adept at technical tax issues and tax computations. The key issue for defense counsel may be to determine what sorts of information to share, if any, with the special agents.

In order to stop the case short of a criminal referral to DOJ Tax, the defense counsel must also convince the IRS criminal tax counsel, who serve as the in-house lawyers for CI. These attorneys advise the special agents during the investigation in determining whether the case is appropriate to refer to the DOJ. The involvement of counsel in any given investigation varies, but special agents and their supervisors often rely on counsel during the investigation, particularly with respect to legal issues and strategies for the investigation. Any information provided to the investigators in an attempt to eliminate the criminal case likely must pass muster with the criminal tax counsel as well as the special agents.

Often, counsel's role is played out behind the scenes. The astute practitioner will see hints of counsel's involvement in, for example, the document description in the summons (the "duces tecum" part of the summons). Under the applicable regulations, counsel is authorized to conduct the Q&A at summons appearances.[6] Barring that type of overt counsel involvement, there is usually nothing the practitioner can do other than observe and extrapolate as to what is happening with counsel and its implications to the client. But in the appropriate case, the taxpayer's counsel should not hesitate to make contact with the local IRS criminal tax counsel.

What sorts of facts or legal issues are most likely to convince special agents to terminate their criminal investigation? Although we will address a few examples of matters that were successfully brought to a conclusion by meeting with special agents or with the IRS criminal tax counsel, perhaps the question is best answered by considering its opposite. What sorts of facts or defenses are best saved for discussions with the DOJ Tax Division or with the U.S. Attorney's Office rather than presenting them to the special agents? In the era before criminal tax counsel were embedded within the criminal investigation function, many taxpayer defense counsel adopted the view that attempting to convince the special agents was usually a waste of breath, that most issues were best explained to lawyers for the IRS or potentially at the Tax Division or the U.S. Attorney's Office. For example, if the taxpayer had a classic *James* or *Garber* or *Dahlstrom* defense (that the law was sufficiently unclear so that willfulness could not be inferred from the facts), most practitioners would make that pitch in Washington to the Tax Division or once the case was referred to the U.S. Attorney's Office. Many practitioners perceived that the special agent would be unlikely to be moved by such an argument. So, what arguments will work with a special agent and the criminal tax counsel?

---

6 Reg. § 301.7602-1(b).

A recent example of a criminal investigation that was terminated after a presentation to IRS criminal tax counsel and the SAC involved an investigation of a return preparer who was accused of having "manufactured" phony Schedule C deductions in order to save his clients or taxpayers significant amounts of tax. During the course of the criminal investigation, the taxpayer's counsel interviewed every Schedule C taxpayer who could be found. The results of the interviews showed that with the exception of four individual taxpayers, every taxpayer was adamant that he or she really did conduct a proprietorship-type business, and most of the taxpayers were able to produce records of the business to the preparer's defense counsel. More importantly, the four taxpayers who were the exceptions all had worked together at the same company, and each one had referred the next one to become a client of the preparer who was under investigation. As a result, defense counsel was able to convince the IRS criminal tax counsel that there was a substantial likelihood that each of those four individuals had conspired with the others to create bogus Schedule C businesses and had been referred seriatim to the same preparer. By combining those facts with other pieces of information, such as the many hours of continuing education that had been taken by the preparer, the preparer's efforts to train others in his offices regarding the proper methods for preparing tax returns, and other personal items, the preparer's counsel was able to convince IRS criminal tax counsel and the SAC that the criminal investigation should not continue and that no referral should be made to the DOJ Tax.

Another classic example of a case killed at the criminal investigation stage involved a taxpayer who was under investigation for possible money laundering and tax evasion. The taxpayer had become addicted to the state lottery. The taxpayer was cashing checks several times a day to purchase lottery tickets and "Pick 3" tickets, to the tune of hundreds of dollars per day. The IRS had uncovered the numerous cashed checks and occasional large deposits from winnings, which caused the special agents to wonder if the taxpayer was laundering money. Defense counsel was able to obtain affidavits from the individuals at various convenience stores who regularly sold lottery tickets to the taxpayer, in order to demonstrate that the funds were being used for a legal (albeit stupid) purpose. Moreover, the taxpayer was interviewed by a psychologist who presented an extensive statement about the psychological impairment that caused the taxpayer to become addicted to the lottery. Once the special agent saw the legitimate source of the deposits to the taxpayer's account and the legitimate use of the funds to purchase Pick 3 and lottery tickets, the criminal investigation was terminated.

Another scenario that occurs frequently in criminal investigations involves families of recent immigrants. It is common practice in many immigrant cultures for a long- settled and respected member of the community to act as a "private bank." When families or neighbors pool their bank deposits in this way, the IRS frequently finds from analysis of the bank deposits or from other indirect methods of proof what the IRS believes to be unreported income. With the help of a savvy forensic accountant (and additional facts from witnesses), the lawyer may prove that the funds did not belong to taxpayer. Affidavits from depositors and a well-crafted report from the forensic accountant often can convince the IRS that the deposits are not income to the account owner.

Defense counsel frequently fear that by revealing the essential facts or theories of the defense, special agents will simply "dig deeper" in an attempt to rebut whatever information has been received from the taxpayer's representatives. For that reason, it is quite common for the taxpayer to remain silent during the criminal investigation and for the taxpayer's counsel to have few exchanges of information with the special agents conducting the investigation. Frequently, facts and theories are revealed only when the case is ready for the conference with the SAC. By that point, the special agent essentially has completed work on the case, and the defense counsel has little hope to prevent a referral to the DOJ Tax Division. However, some preliminary discussion of the defense theory often seems appropriate to pave the way for a more extensive presentation at the DOJ or the US Attorney's Office.

1. The Initial Surprise Interview

In cases where a civil tax examination has turned criminal, the practitioner will have filed a power of attorney, Form 2848, with the IRS. If the CI agents desire to interview the taxpayer, they should make the request through the attorney.[7] However, where there has been no civil tax examination, and even sometimes when there is a power of attorney on file, it is not unusual for the CI special agent and a sidekick (usually another CI special agent) to show up without advance notice to "chat" with the taxpayer. The special agents will identify themselves as special agents and usually provide business cards identifying themselves. The lead special agent will read the taxpayer the IRS's special modified version of the *Miranda* warnings. The taxpayer is not in custody, and the full blown *Miranda* warnings are not required. If for any reason the special agents do not give that warning, the taxpayer may be able to suppress any damaging statements he or she makes during the interview, although *Kontny* may suggest otherwise.

This surprise interview without an attorney is dangerous for the taxpayer, even an innocent taxpayer. The best thing the taxpayer can do is to decline politely the special agents' invitation to talk and advise that the taxpayer's counsel will contact the special agents. The worst thing the taxpayer can do is to engage in a discussion with the special agents. The chances of the taxpayer convincing the special agents to fold their tents and go away are not great. It is far more likely the taxpayer will say something quite damaging. Thus, practitioners should warn their clients that the IRS might attempt an "ambush" interview, and the clients should be taught how to respectfully decline to answer and refer the agents to the taxpayers' counsel.

For example, the taxpayer may be sorely tempted to tell a little lie, either going to the heart of the matter or peripheral issues. As in *Beacon Brass* and any number of other cases, the taxpayer may then have violated 18 U.S.C. § 1001, may have violated the omnibus clause of § 7212, or may have refreshed a statute of limitations that had either expired or would have expired before the IRS and DOJ could have completed the work necessary to prosecute.

Even if the taxpayer has a good story to tell, it can be best told through a lawyer. If the taxpayer has the good sense to call a lawyer before proceeding with the

---

[7] IRM 9.5.1.3.3.

interview, the attorney generally should not let the special agents interview the taxpayer.

2. Other Taxpayer Interviews

It is a rare case in which the attorney should allow CI to interview the taxpayer anytime during the investigation (even after the possible surprise visit). There are always exceptions to this rule. Many practitioners have had occasional cases in which they allowed the special agents to interview a target taxpayer, but only after the attorney fully understood the lay of the land and had fully prepared the taxpayer. That preparation invariably includes testing, *e.g.*, cross-examining, to find out what problems might arise. If there is no positive reason for the interview, it simply should not occur, or the taxpayer should invoke the Fifth Amendment.

3. Witnesses

Just as the Special Agent will seek to interview third-party witnesses, the taxpayer's counsel should interview all of the witnesses who can be identified. If you begin your representation only after the criminal investigation has started, you will have a lot of work to do. Interview the key potential witnesses as quickly as you can, and consider whether it makes sense to record the witnesses' recollections in a signed affidavit or other written statement.

It is also good practice to touch base periodically with the witnesses to determine whether they have been contacted by CI. If they have, it is important to debrief them again to determine: (1) what lines of questioning CI pursued and (2) what information and/or documents the witness provided to CI.

4. The Taxpayer's Documents

The taxpayer's ability to assert the Fifth Amendment privilege to withhold documents is problematic. The "act of production doctrine" that saved Web Hubbell's bacon may sometimes be available to protect against the testimonial aspect of producing documents. But the target of the investigation will not willingly deliver up incriminatory documents even if they are not subject to a privilege. What do you do when the IRS issues a summons for the documents you would rather the IRS not have?

The target may be tempted to destroy the documents, but that is illegal, and the lawyer should have cautioned the taxpayer to retain relevant documents. The taxpayer could simply refuse to comply with the IRS's administrative summons, hopefully asserting some colorable defense to compelled disclosure. The IRS may then seek judicial enforcement of the summons. Taxpayers rarely win summons enforcement cases under the *Powell* criteria. Likewise, in grand jury cases, the required records doctrine has been used to enforce subpoenas where the taxpayer's Fifth Amendment privilege does not apply. But *Hubbell* teaches that a narrow window of opportunity exists to avoid enforcement if the IRS has too broadly defined the scope of a summons or has otherwise implicated the act of production doctrine.

5. Vicarious Admissions

Under agency principles, the attorney is generally deemed to have authority to make representations for the client, and the admissions can generally be used against the client.[8] The IRM provides that the IRS may use vicarious admissions.[9] We discussed this policy in an earlier chapter in the context of the SAC conference, but it is important to keep this policy in mind throughout the investigation, for statements of the attorney may be used against the client in the subsequent criminal case.

6. Concluding the Investigation

CI concludes its investigation in one of two ways. First, and the best for the taxpayer, CI can decline criminal prosecution and refer the case back for civil examination. Second, CI can forward the case to DOJ Tax with a recommendation for criminal prosecution.

CI recommends criminal prosecution when the case is otherwise within its priorities and the evidence "is sufficient to indicate guilt beyond a reasonable doubt and a reasonable probability of conviction."[10] Typically, CI will not have devoted investigative resources to a matter outside its current priorities. But, if a substantial investment in the matter has already been made, CI may be inclined to recommend prosecution of a case only marginally within its priorities. The taxpayer's attorney must then convince CI that it should not prosecute despite the investment of time and resources. This type of argument may be better received by a later decision-maker (DOJ Tax or the United States Attorney) who will have neither the time nor the emotional commitment to the case and can take a broader view of the Government's priorities.

7. The Special Agent's Report

The Special Agent's Report (SAR)[11] summarizes the results of the investigation and describes why the case is worthy of criminal prosecution. The SAR also develops the sentencing factors from the Sentencing Guidelines. The SAR is not provided to the target(s) of the investigation until much later in the process, if at all. By careful attention to the Special Agent's activities during the investigation, however, the astute lawyer will frequently have a very good idea of the contents of the SAR. As noted below, the defense should request a copy of the SAR if the taxpayer reaches the unfortunate point of preparing for a sentencing hearing.

---

[8] Fed. R. Evid. 801(d)(2)(C) & (D).

[9] IRM 38.2.1.4.14.

[10] IRM 38.2.1.6.1.12.

[11] The SAR is usually used in administrative investigations. In grand jury investigations, the Summary of Investigation (SOI) format may be used. IRM 9.5.8.2.

8. The SAC Conference

Almost invariably, CI invites the taxpayer to attend a conference with the SAC (or often with the Assistant SAC and CI's counsel) prior to any referral for prosecution. This SAC conference is the last shot at stopping the referral. CI by that time has determined to make the referral, so stopping the referral is a long shot. In fact, the authors of this casebook have never seen a case declined at a SAC conference. Nevertheless, the taxpayer's attorney ordinarily should attend and participate.

Even if the taxpayer's attorney has no reasonable prospect of stopping the referral, the conference may still be in the taxpayer's best interest. The taxpayer's attorney may be able to learn important information and nuances of the IRS's view of the case. The IRS does not offer the conference as an opportunity for taxpayer discovery, but conferences reveal important information from the questions asked and the information disclosed. The SAC conferences usually are attended by CI's criminal tax counsel and a delegate for the SAC. Sometimes, the special agent(s) or the SAC may attend. The taxpayer's attorney will attend, but the taxpayer typically does not attend. Even a taxpayer who has been carefully prepared to remain silent may communicate something to the IRS at the SAC conference, if only by body language. There is great risk that the communication will be damaging or will be misinterpreted. Without the taxpayer present, the taxpayer's attorney can focus more clearly on the presentation and on properly interpreting the IRS personnel's communications, without being distracted by a concern that the taxpayer may be doing something that would be counterproductive.

9. DOJ Referral

The IRS will refer a case for prosecution only "where the evidence is sufficient to indicate guilt beyond a reasonable doubt and where there appears to be a reasonable probability of conviction."[12] If the IRS decides to refer the case to the DOJ with a recommendation for prosecution, the special agent will put the final touches on the SAR and counsel will prepare a Criminal Reference Letter (the CRL), which is a comprehensive summary of the recommendation and its basis.[13] In many respects, the CRL parallels the SAR, which is far more detailed and contains extensive exhibits in support.

The CRL invariably includes a representation that "Counsel is convinced of guilt beyond a reasonable doubt and believes there is a reasonable probability of conviction."[14] In addition, the CRL may include a discussion of potential impeachment information about the IRS special agents who may testify at trial.[15] This is in anticipation of *Giglio/Henthorn* issues that may arise at trial. Obviously, the CRL would be an invaluable document for the defense. Do you think that you can obtain

---

[12] IRM 38.2.1.6.1.12.

[13] USAM 6-4.110.

[14] USAM 6-4.211.

[15] ILM 199902018, *reproduced at* 1999 TNT 11-48.

it? Why not? (Is the latter a leading question in anticipation that your answer to the first question is no?)

D. Review by the Department of Justice Tax Division

DOJ Tax Criminal Enforcement Section (CES) attorneys review the CRL and make a recommendation as to whether to authorize criminal tax prosecution. The AAG or her delegate then makes the decision whether to prosecute. Taxpayers are usually afforded a conference in Washington and should request a conference as early as possible.

Some experienced practitioners make the conference request to the CES during the criminal investigation, when they first begin to believe that a referral to the CES is likely or when they learn of a grand jury investigation. Their thinking is that CI may not notify the taxpayer's attorney of the referral or may not timely notify of the referral. Hence, an early request to the CES should avoid the risk that the conference request would be untimely and the opportunity for a DOJ conference would be missed. The CES will receive the premature request and notify the taxpayer's attorney that, except for unusual cases, it is the policy to grant such a conference. Then, when the case is referred to DOJ Tax, an invitation to hold a conference will be sent to the taxpayer's representative.

All criminal tax prosecutions must be approved by CES (including the AAG who oversees the CES) or must fall under one of the advance approval systems for certain limited types of cases. The CES must insure that all tax prosecutions are consistent with overall national enforcement priorities. The practitioner must have some sense of the national criminal tax enforcement priorities and the limited resources that require the CES to authorize only prosecutions consistent with those priorities. Some taxpayers who have had the misfortune to be referred to the CES may still not be within those enforcement priorities, and a case can still be made to the CES that they should not be prosecuted.

What arguments or evidence are likely to convince DOJ Tax to decline to prosecute? As discussed above, many defense attorneys believe that arguments based on legal defenses, such as a *James* or *Garber* or *Dahlstrom* theory that unsettled law obviates willfulness, are best presented at DOJ Tax. But the law need not be completely unsettled for such an argument to succeed. Often, by combining various facts of the case with a substantive legal argument to show that the tax treatment adopted by the taxpayer was either correct or arguably correct, the taxpayer's counsel can undercut the willfulness element to the point that the reviewing attorney will agree there is no reasonable probability of conviction. Well prepared defense counsel often present a memorandum to the Tax Division before the review conference, outlining the relevant fact and authorities. It is also common to make verbal presentations independent of any memorandum. No matter what method of presentation is chosen, the typical conference focuses on the sufficiency of the evidence of guilt and any defenses that undercut the probability of conviction.

Although DOJ Tax primarily reviews the case to determine the sufficiency of the evidence and a reasonable probability of conviction, it is possible to obtain a declination that does not focus on those two particular elements. For example, if the taxpayer can demonstrate that the tax loss was immaterial in comparison to the dollars involved in the matter, the case might be declined. Of course, materiality depends on the circumstances of the taxpayer and the returns at issue. Also, some taxpayers face such terrible health that they might not be prosecuted for that reason alone — for example, persons dying of AIDS or cancer typically are not prosecuted. And, although age itself is not a reason to drop a prosecution, only very notorious 80 or 90-year olds seem to face indictment.

Defense attorneys commonly try to "personalize" the taxpayer by providing some biographical information at the DOJ conference. Sometimes those personal details can make all the difference, but often they are presented as the framework for the presentation of other defenses. If the taxpayer has a record of military or other public service; if the taxpayer's children suffer from a debilitating disease that is expensive to treat; if the taxpayer has an exemplary record of charitable service; if the taxpayer has overpaid taxes in other years not investigated by the IRS; any of these or a myriad of other personal items have the potential to resonate with the reviewing attorney at the Tax Division. Although none of these issues are likely to change the reviewer's analysis of the quantum of proof or the probability of conviction, it is always possible that in a close case the sympathetic client may escape a decision to prosecute, while the client whose personal life remains a mystery to the reviewer stands a greater risk of prosecution.

Of course, any information that is provided to DOJ Tax concerning the insufficiency of the evidence can result in the case being returned to the IRS for further investigation or approved for prosecution with instructions to the US Attorney's Office to conduct further investigation through the grand jury in order to plug the potential evidentiary holes. For that reason alone, some practitioners are loath to discuss too many facts with DOJ Tax or to reveal the Government's potential evidentiary weaknesses, preferring to save those potential arguments for a trial on the merits. Likewise, defense counsel should carefully weigh whether the arguments that undercut a reasonable probability of conviction truly have the potential to result in a declination rather than simply educating the Government on what defenses it will face in court.

E. Review by the United States Attorney's Office

The United States Attorney usually acts through an AUSA assigned to handle the tax cases in that district. Upon receipt of authorization from the CES, the AUSA will seek an indictment from the grand jury or conduct such further grand jury investigation as may be necessary. As soon as the taxpayer's attorney has been advised that the case has been referred to the United States Attorney's Office, the taxpayer's attorney should contact that office, determine the AUSA to whom the case is assigned, and contact the AUSA. Conferences with the AUSA often present the best opportunity to kill the case, and at worst, the plea bargaining process can begin.

On rare occasions, CES's decision to prosecute may not sit well with the United States Attorney or the AUSA. The United States Attorney's Office may not have the staff to handle the matter, or the priorities in that particular district may be focused on other types of cases. The AUSA may not think the case will play as well before a local jury as the folks in Washington thought. The case might be rejected by the USAO and sent back to the CES for reconsideration. If the CES is intent upon prosecuting and cannot convince the United States Attorney to prosecute, the CES has the option to field the attorneys required to present the case to the grand jury and try the case. Usually, there is a very good working relationship between the USAO and the CES. The CES will respectfully consider any deficiencies in the case or priorities that the United States Attorney or the designated AUSA raises, and DOJ Tax may well decline to pursue the matter further. The case will then be returned to the IRS for further civil processing as may be appropriate. Rejection of the case by the local AUSA is the exception and not the norm. Usually once the case has been approved by DOJ Tax, it will be presented to the grand jury, indicted, and a trial or plea will ensue.

In some districts, the AUSAs who handle tax cases have an abundance of cases to try, and they are thus more likely than most to be convinced to decline to prosecute a case that has been approved by DOJ Tax. For many years, certain prominent and experienced criminal tax defense attorneys touted the notion that they were much more likely to succeed in killing a case by presenting information to the AUSA than they were by presenting the identical information to the CES reviewing attorney in Washington. While that sentiment may ring true for defense attorneys in some districts, statistically the percentages of cases declined by the CES are similar to those declined by the USAO. Moreover, skipping the CES conference to focus all efforts on discussions with the AUSA risks the possibility that if the US Attorney declines the case after DOJ Tax has approved the prosecution DOJ Tax may devote its own manpower to prosecute the case.

Sometimes the same argument that fails to convince the reviewing attorney in Washington will mean much more to the AUSA who must actually prosecute the case. Though the reviewing attorney at DOJ Tax may find the evidence sufficient and a reasonable probability of conviction, a savvy AUSA will think through every argument presented by defense counsel, compare it to the evidence that has been mustered in the CI investigation, and think long and hard about whether a local jury will convict. The prosecutor who actually must present the case to the jury might be more attuned to the weaknesses of the case than the CES attorney who simply has to review and sign off on whether the case rises to the necessary standard for prosecution.

For example, an immigrant from Taiwan who had built a successful grocery supply business was targeted for prosecution after a civil IRS agent uncovered material cash receipts that had been deposited to a personal account at a brokerage house rather than to the corporate operating account. Although the taxpayer's representatives told the revenue agent that the failure to pay corporate or personal income tax on those cash collections was an inadvertent mistake resulting from the return preparer's neglect to ask for copies of the brokerage statements, the revenue agent pressed on. The agent tied down every cash invoice, receipt, and deposit, and then referred the case to CI. CI likewise turned a deaf ear to the argument that the taxpayer disclosed all of the capital gains from the numerous transactions in the brokerage account, so it was clear that the return preparer had been made aware of the brokerage account and simply failed to ask where the equity had come from to conduct the trading in that account. The reviewing attorney in the CES listened patiently to the same explanation but promptly approved the case for prosecution. However, the local AUSA who received the case quickly concluded that the defense had legs, and he declined to prosecute the case. He then wrote a 15-page memorandum detailing why the defense had merit and undercut a reasonable probability of conviction. Although the DOJ Tax reviewing attorney was livid when the case was returned from the US Attorney's Office, after reading the AUSA's memo, the reviewing attorney had to concede that the defense was potentially meritorious, and DOJ Tax declined to prosecute the case. The case was returned to the IRS for civil tax adjustments.

F. Forum Shopping

The venue rules often present several choices of district in which the Government has the right to prosecute a tax case. In most tax evasion cases, the Government can indict in the district in which the false return was prepared, mailed, or filed, and the Government also has the option of prosecuting in the taxpayer's district of residence. The Government virtually always chooses to indict in the taxpayer's district of residence. While most defendants prefer to stand trial where they reside, sometimes the attendant publicity or the circumstances of the case make the district of residence a poor choice. The *Auffenberg* case discussed in Chapter 8 is an example of a case in which the location of the taxpayer's witnesses, the nature of the case, and the peculiar law of the U.S. Virgin Islands combined to convince the district court in Illinois that justice would be better served by transferring venue to the Virgin Islands. There are numerous tales of defense counsel who have urged DOJ Tax or the local AUSA to consider bringing the charges in another district, usually for transparent reasons that the Government promptly rejects. The publicity attendant to a prosecution in the taxpayer's home district supports the Government's policy goals by increasing the deterrent effect of its prosecution. However, occasionally both the Government and the defense agree that a case belongs in a venue other than the taxpayer's place of residence.

If appropriate, it is best to raise the venue issue during the DOJ Tax review process, or as soon as the case reaches the USAO. Then, the case can be filed in the forum of choice rather than dealing with a change of venue. A motion to transfer venue is a tool too often neglected by the defense in tax cases.

G. Plea Bargaining

There are probably as many different ways to plea bargain as there are AUSAs and defense attorneys. Because the DOJ Tax "major count" policy makes it difficult to dispose of tax cases by bargaining felonies down to misdemeanors, other issues normally become the central focus of negotiations for plea agreements in tax cases. Although there are many ways to approach the issues, here are some of the essential elements to consider:

1. Horse Trading

Can your client obtain a better plea bargain by assisting the Government with information about other potential defendants? Compared to most criminal cases, criminal tax defendants infrequently have information of value to the Government relating to other parties. More commonly, a defendant is charged with evading his or her own income taxes or the income taxes of an entity that the defendant controlled. However, when the defendant has information of value with regard to third parties who may be prosecuted, the defense has bargaining power. The defendant might begin by requesting immunity from prosecution in exchange for proffered information, particularly in a grand jury investigation. More commonly, the defendant provides the information in exchange for an agreement by the prosecutor to file a motion under Sentencing Guidelines § 5.K.1 advising the court of the extensive cooperation received from the defendant.

Even if immunity or a 5.K.1 agreement is impossible to achieve, there may still be much to gain from a plea agreement. An agreed plea normally results in the Government proceeding via a complaint as the charging instrument rather than seeking an indictment from a grand jury. The defendant usually obtains the benefit of voluntary surrender rather than facing the prospect of an arrest. Avoiding the potential that the defendant will be arrested in front of family, friends, or co-workers may be worth quite a bit to particular defendants. Even if the plea agreement provides no other benefits, this may be a sufficient inducement to plead in some towns where an arrest is likely to result in excessive publicity.

2. Criminal Tax Loss

Since the amount of criminal tax loss constitutes the primary determinant of a sentence in a criminal tax case under the Sentencing Guidelines, plea negotiations often focus on trimming the amount of the tax loss. Defense counsel use a myriad of techniques to try to reduce the loss, and often the AUSA is willing to bargain on the amount of the criminal tax loss as long as the resulting Guidelines range is acceptable. Some items to consider include: eliminating some of the purported criminal conduct by questioning the willfulness of the taxpayer on a specific item or items; pointing out overlooked expenses or excessive inclusions of income in the SAR's calculation of tax loss; and eliminating certain years from relevant conduct by distinguishing the cause of tax losses computed for those years.

The importance of calculating and agreeing on a criminal tax loss amount cannot be overstated. In fact, some defense counsel claim that if the criminal tax loss amount is not agreed, then the defendant might as well just stand up and plead guilty without a plea agreement, because the plea agreement is not likely to contain sufficient benefits to justify the other provisions that virtually every U.S. Attorney's Office demands, such as waiver of the right to appeal.

The prosecutor and the defense counsel have not finished their jobs simply because they have calculated and agreed to a criminal tax loss. Unless the special agent agrees to defend the criminal tax loss calculation vigorously, the parties are at serious risk that the U.S. Probation Office will rely on the SAR and other information from the special agent to present its own criminal tax loss position to the sentencing judge, and the agreed criminal tax loss number in the plea agreement might be for naught. In fact, the Probation Officer can be expected to request a copy of the SAR, so it behooves the parties to prepare an explanation of why the IRS and the USAO have changed the amount of the criminal tax loss from the computation that was originally proposed in the SAR. Typically, this explanation includes line item adjustments with explanations, and savvy defense counsel will have obtained the special agent's agreement to those adjustments. Although the Probation Officer may never request such an explanation and may be perfectly willing to go along with the criminal tax loss amount stated in the plea agreement, one should never expect such cooperation. In fact, once a plea agreement is reached, the defense should ask for a copy of the SAR so that both parties can be fully prepared to defend the criminal tax loss number presented in the plea agreement.

By defining the criminal tax loss number in the plea agreement, the prosecution and defense both gain a measure of certainty regarding the Sentencing Guideline range that will be argued to the sentencing judge. Although probation officers and judges are free to question the criminal tax loss amount, most do not second guess an agreed number in a plea agreement. Moreover, by entering the plea agreement, the parties bind themselves to defend that number even if questions are raised by the Probation Office or the judge. If the special agent has been properly prepared and is on board, then it is rare for a different tax loss amount to be determined at sentencing.

3. Civil Tax Issues

Until recent years, restitution was not commonly ordered in tax cases.[16] But now the DOJ Tax has instructed its attorneys and AUSAs to demand restitution in tax cases. Sentencing judges frequently require the defendant to cooperate with the IRS in payment of his or her taxes. Both the prosecution and the defense benefit from a provision in the plea agreement clarifying that the criminal tax loss number is a calculation determined under the Sentencing Guidelines and is not the precise amount of civil tax liability due from the defendant for the years in issue.

The defendant has two essential choices for handling the civil tax liability. The most common alternative is for the defendant to expressly reserve the right to challenge (in Tax Court or elsewhere) the amount of the civil tax liability and/or penalties. The prosecution thus gains the collateral estoppel effects of a conviction, with restitution assessed by statute as a civil liability and the IRS free to assert additional tax liabilities beyond the criminal tax loss that the court ordered as restitution. The defendant gains the right to contest certain issues that may not have been decided in the criminal case.

The alternative approach is to attempt to resolve the civil liability simultaneously with the criminal case. This approach has become common and expected in many parts of the country but remains rare in other districts. One item worthy of particular attention by the defense is a plea agreement clause that requires the

[16] 18 U.S.C. § 3663 does not authorize restitution in tax cases unless the defendant agrees or the judge makes it a condition of supervised release under 18 U.S.C. § 3583. United States v. Nolen, 472 F.3d 362 (5th Cir. 2006).

defendant to file amended tax returns for the years in issue. This provision carries the attendant risk that the taxpayer has other errors or omissions on the returns that may need to be corrected even if the Government never uncovered those issues during the criminal case. The taxpayer must be counseled carefully if there are other issues unknown to the prosecution.

4. Guidelines Issues

Most plea agreements include an extensive recitation of facts regarding the offense, facts which the defendant sometimes has difficulty accepting when they are originally proposed by the AUSA. By negotiating the plea agreement carefully, most AUSAs will work with defense counsel to craft the wording of the factual statement to make it acceptable to both parties. The statement should demonstrate to the court the essential facts necessary for a conviction as well as the defendant's acceptance of responsibility.

In addition to the factual recitation, many plea agreements include express provisions addressing Sentencing Guidelines issues that the parties anticipate. This portion of the plea agreement can be particularly problematic. For example, is it smart for the prosecutor and defense counsel to include a sentence in the plea agreement expressly agreeing that the defendant did not use "sophisticated means," or is it best to orally agree to defend that position at sentencing rather than suggesting to the Probation Office that the sophisticated means issue is in play? Similar difficult decisions often occur with regard to: the defendant's role in the offense; whether the defendant's source of income was from "criminal activity"; whether the defendant committed the offense as part of a pattern or scheme of aiding, assisting, or advising tax fraud; and whether certain years or activities should be added to the criminal tax loss as relevant conduct.

In fact, the elimination of various years of "relevant conduct" often has a significant impact on the defendant's ultimate sentence. By carefully crafting the factual statement and the description of the means used by the defendant to commit the crime(s), both the prosecution and defense can determine whether certain conduct in other years may be added as relevant conduct in determining the sentence. If the defendant has cheated the Government for decades, finding a way to eliminate many years of potential relevant conduct may be the most important task the defense counsel faces in trying to bargain for the least onerous punishment.

The bottom line in plea negotiation is to decide whether the plea agreement constitutes an attempt to define an agreed specific sentence, will fix the guideline range by agreeing on sentencing factors, or will leave quite a few issues open for the sentencing judge. Although Fed. R. Crim. P. 11(c)(1)(C) permits the parties to reach a plea agreement that binds the sentencing judge and permits the defendant to withdraw the guilty plea if the judge will not follow the agreed sentence, many AUSAs are prohibited by local policy from entering such agreements. Moreover, many federal district court judges will not accept binding pleas. If the defendant faces trial in a district where the judge is willing to accept a binding plea agreement and sentence, by all means the parties should consider it in order to eliminate uncertainty. If not, the parties may be able to achieve a high measure of certainty by drafting a plea agreement that binds both the Government and the defendant on as many of the open issues as possible.

H. Pre-Indictment Issues

If all attempts to reach an agreed plea have failed, and the AUSA is set on obtaining an indictment against the taxpayer, there is still much good that a defense counsel can accomplish. For example, in most white collar cases, defense counsel should be able to arrange for the defendant to appear voluntarily and be processed by the U.S. Marshal's Service rather than being arrested. Most districts do not require "perp walks" and have now returned to the more common practice that formal arrests should not be required when the defendant is willing to submit voluntarily.

In addition to avoiding arrest, most AUSAs are willing to discuss important issues that will be faced at the detention hearing, such as conditions of release, bail if the Government desires bail, and issues regarding business travel outside the district. Ideally, these issues will be agreed upon before the AUSA seeks an indictment from the grand jury.

I. Post-Indictment/Pretrial Issues

1. Local Counsel

Although judges are assigned randomly and neither the Government nor the taxpayer has the ability to select which judge will try the case, the defendant may have one advantage in this regard: the defense can always try to choose a local counsel who is viewed favorably by the judge while the Government typically has only one or two AUSAs who handle tax cases in each district. Considering the addition of a prominent local counsel to the defense team, hopefully one who has an excellent relationship with the trial judge, can often accomplish more benefit for the defense team than most lawyers may realize. Good local counsel may know the personnel in the clerk's office, the judge's courtroom deputy, the judge's briefing attorney, and other court personnel. The local counsel should be familiar with the local rules as well as the actual practice in the particular judge's courtroom. All of this adds up to a very significant impact on cases in some particular districts, while all the familiarity in the world has virtually no influence on other judges.

Knowledge of the particular judge's preferences can be invaluable in making the numerous tactical decisions that will be faced during the course of pretrial procedures and the trial. Each of these decisions may be subtly or even overtly influenced by the information available concerning the judge. Even in a jury trial, the judge has considerable discretion that can substantially influence the outcome of the case, and every attorney who appears in the courtroom should constantly remain aware of the impression that is being made on the judge and jury by each action taken.

2. Judge vs. Jury

Federal criminal cases are tried to a jury unless the defendant waives the right to a jury trial, the Government consents, and the court agrees.[17] Because criminal tax cases often focus on taxpayers of extreme wealth (or taxpayers whose wealth increased extremely as a result of their alleged actions), many taxpayer-defendants can expect significant prejudice from a jury of average local citizens. In several recent cases, taxpayer-defendants have attempted to waive jury trials, only to have the Government insist on a jury. But a trial to the court is often much more efficient and much more promptly completed than a jury trial, so the parties should at least consider whether waiver of a jury trial would be advantageous in each particular case.

J. Voir Dire

Although most federal district court judges conduct the voir dire of prospective jurors themselves, Fed. R. Crim. P. 24 allows for counsel to handle all or a part of the examination of the jury pool. Many judges permit this, although they cannot be compelled to allow voir dire by the parties.[18] Counsel who have not practiced in states where voir dire by the parties is commonplace should not underestimate the power of voir dire to influence the outcome of a case.

When the judge allows the parties to conduct voir dire rather than just submit questions for the judge to ask the jury, the opportunity exists for counsel to explain a bit about the case, root out hidden prejudices, and begin to establish the themes of the defense. Effort should be made to learn each potential juror's level of tax and business acumen, attitudes toward the IRS and the Government in general, and receptiveness to the burden of proof beyond a reasonable doubt. Skillful civil lawyers have long known that the voir dire is where many cases are won or lost. While that may be a bit of an exaggeration in a criminal tax case, the tone of the entire trial can be set by counsel in voir dire, and the opportunity should not be missed.

K. Sentencing

In addition to the extensive materials presented in earlier chapters regarding sentencing, readers should be aware that a cadre of lawyers around the country have become known as sentencing experts and are often associated to assist in the sentencing phase of major cases. In addition to assisting defense counsel with the typical issues under the Sentencing Guidelines and under 18 U.S.C. § 3553, these sentencing specialists often provide tips on influencing the Bureau of Prisons to assign the defendant to a favored location, easing the defendant's transition from freedom to incarceration, helping the defendant with medical and other personal issues that can create problems during the surrender process, and many other

---

[17] Fed. R. Crim. P. 23(a).

[18] *E.g.*, Hamer v. United States, 259 F.2d 274 (9th Cir. 1958), *cert. denied*, 359 U.S. 916 (1959), *reh'g denied*, 359 U.S. 962 (1959); Fox v. United States, 296 F.2d 217 (5th Cir. 1961), *cert. denied*, 369 U.S. 888 (1962).

issues. Since most tax attorneys rarely handle criminal cases, and since most criminal tax attorneys have little experience with the process of sentencing and incarceration (remember, most tax defendants received probation before the Guidelines started becoming more onerous in the late 1990s), considering the use of a consultant who specializes in sentencing issues sometimes makes good sense.

IV. A FINAL CAUTION

The practitioner must be vigilant to avoid making the client's problems the practitioner's problems, *i.e.*, doing something in the course of the audit, criminal investigation or prosecution that subjects the attorney to criminal or civil penalties. As we noted above, a panoply of provisions potentially apply to the practitioner who does too much for his client by lying or otherwise frustrating the tax process.[19] Most defense counsel would never intentionally do anything illegal — maybe something stupid, but not illegal. Unfortunately, the line between stupid and illegal sometimes is blurred.

One of the key danger points involves the handling of witnesses. The careful defense practitioner will want to interview all potential witnesses as soon as possible, in order to learn the lay of the land. Also, there can be great benefit from nailing down each witness's testimony before the civil or criminal agent potentially starts to alter the witness's memory by asking leading questions, threatening the witness, and otherwise eliciting "facts" that the witness does not realize are inaccurate. The witness may be much more amenable to a taxpayer-favorable recollection before facing the uncomfortable prospect of being interviewed by an IRS agent, particularly a special agent. Obtaining witness interviews in a potential criminal case, however, presents risk for the attorney.

The careful practitioner, whether prosecutor or defense counsel, wants a balanced understanding of the witness's potential testimony. But it is unrealistic to put this goal on a pedestal and divorce the process from the subconscious tendency to hear what we expect or want to hear in order to benefit our client (or the Government). The desire to help the client can lead defense counsel to suggest testimony and shadings of testimony to the witness, thus subtly risking potential charges of witness tampering or obstruction of justice. Accordingly, most defense attorneys make it a habit to conduct witness interviews with another lawyer or a paralegal present. Special agents routinely conduct interviews with two agents present for the same reason: the second interviewer is available as a potential witness in case there is any question about what was said by the interviewer or the interviewee. Likewise, the careful prosecutor will interview witnesses with the case agent or another attorney present to negate claims of intimidation or implicit promises. If possible, a written statement should be obtained from the witness, perhaps in affidavit form, to commit the witness to a particular version of the facts.

Defense counsel also must take steps to prevent the possibility that the taxpayer under investigation may try to shape the witness' memory before anyone interviews the witness. The taxpayer has a vested interest in what the witness will say and is

[19] *See, e.g.*, IRC § 7212; 18 U.S.C. § 371 (*Klein* conspiracy); 18 U.S.C. § 1001.

much more likely to try to improperly influence the witness, primarily because the taxpayer generally is a layperson who has never been educated about the rules governing witness tampering. The circumstances are ripe for the IRS to charge that the taxpayer acted improperly to influence the witness to say something that was not true. The best strategy is to prohibit the taxpayer from talking to the witnesses at all. If there must be commerce between the taxpayer and the witness (*e.g.*, in a business setting), defense counsel should instruct the taxpayer not to discuss the relevant tax matters with the witness. The attorney must warn the client about possible allegations of witness tampering and obstruction of justice, using the strongest possible cautions to convince the client that the prohibition on communications is in the client's best interests.

Both prosecutors and defense counsel serve as officers of the court, with commensurate duties of candor tempering the admonition to zealously advocate their positions. Moreover, the tax controversy world is a narrow one — the same Government attorneys and taxpayer counsel interact repeatedly on case after case, sometimes for decades. There is room for common courtesies to be maintained even when stark disagreements occur. By careful attention to the rules of engagement, the combatant parties' counsel should be able to protect themselves from personal risk, vigorously advocate their positions, yet remain cordial and businesslike in the process. Who knows, some friendships may even develop! We wish you that success, among many others.

PROBLEM

The taxpayer is the subject of a criminal investigation for failing to timely file corporate income tax returns and then filing delinquent returns that bore little resemblance to the actual income and expenses of his family business. The defense counsel learns from family members that the taxpayer has lifelong history of symptoms of bipolar disorder. The taxpayer's father, brother, and daughter all have also been diagnosed and treated for the disease, prior to the taxpayer's criminal investigation. The family provides counsel with numerous examples of the taxpayer's difficulties in school, despite an extremely high IQ and ultimate graduation in engineering from a prestigious university. The family also describes the taxpayer's difficulties in accurately completing tasks much simpler than filing a tax return and an extensive history of argumentative and inconsiderate behavior that has caused difficulties with employees and family members.

After consultation with psychologists and psychiatrists, the taxpayer is diagnosed with bipolar disorder and begins treatment for the disorder. Extensive reports are prepared by the consulting doctors. Defense counsel believes that these reports will constitute powerful proof that willfulness would be a difficult hurdle for the Government to cross. Assume that the taxpayer's counsel can present a combination of affidavits from family members, college professors, a psychiatrist, and a psychologist, all demonstrating that despite the taxpayer's extreme intelligence, his ability to complete common tasks was so obscured by his disorder that he often believed that he had completed necessary duties that he had not even begun. Also, during the taxpayer's manic phases, he would undertake a whirlwind of work and accomplish an impressive number of tasks, although employees and family members could not rely on the accuracy of the work the taxpayer has completed.

At what stage of the proceedings should such a defense be offered? Should the defense be presented to the investigating agents, used at the SAC conference, documented for the Tax Division CES reviewing attorney, presented to the Assistant U.S. Attorney, or saved for trial? If the complete defense will not be offered immediately, should some portion of the defense be presented at an early stage in the process in order to plant the seeds for the defense? If so, how should those seeds be watered so that they may sprout and bloom at trial?

Appendix A

GLOSSARY OF ACRONYMS AND INITIALISMS

AAG — Assistant Attorney General, in this context, the AAG for the Tax Division, Department of Justice.

AFMLS — DOJ's Asset Forfeiture and Money Laundering Section.

ATF — Treasury's Bureau of Alcohol, Tobacco and Firearms.

AUSA — Assistant United States Attorney, in the context of the materials here usually means the local prosecutor as to a federal tax crime.

ATF — Bureau of Alcohol, Tobacco and Firearms, Department of Treasury.

BSA — Bank Secrecy Act, the Bank Records and Foreign Transaction Act, Titles I and II of Pub. L. 91-508, as amended, codified at 12 U.S.C. § 1829b, 12 U.S.C. §§ 1951–1959, and 31 U.S.C. §§ 5311–5330.

CAFRA — Civil Asset Forfeiture Reform Act of 2000, Pub. L. 106-185, 114 Stat. 202.

CATEPS — Criminal Appeals & Tax Enforcement Policy Section of DOJ Tax.

CBI — Caribbean Basin Initiative, the popular name for the Caribbean Basin Economic Recovery Act of 1983.

CCE — a continuing criminal enterprise subject to 21 U.S.C. § 848.

CES — Criminal Enforcement Section of DOJ Tax. This section has the primary responsibility for authorizing criminal tax prosecutions and setting and coordinating the Government's criminal tax enforcement priorities. It is broken down into geographical units, including Northern, Southern, and Western. The geographical divisions may be viewed at http://www.usdoj.gov/tax/cessoump1.htm

CFEA — 18 U.S.C. § 3571 (sometimes referred to as the Criminal Fine Enforcement Act of 1984 (Pub. L. No. 98-596)).

CFR — Code of Federal Regulations.

CFTC — Commodity Futures Trading Commission.

CI — Criminal Investigation, the branch of the IRS principally responsible for investigating tax crimes. This is often referred to as CID, an acronym for a prior name for this branch.

CMIR — Report of International Transportation of Currency or Monetary Instruments, Form 4790, for use by any person to report the transportation into or out of the United States of currency and certain other monetary instruments on any one occasion in excess of $10,000.

CRL — Criminal Reference Letter, a letter from IRS CI to DOJ Tax's CES referring a case with a recommendation of indictment or further investigation by a grand jury.

CTM — Department of Justice Tax Division Criminal Tax Manual.

CTR — Currency Transaction Report, Form 4789, for use by financial institutions to report currency transactions exceeding $10,000. An analogous report (Currency Transaction Report by Casinos (CTRC), Form 8362) is required for casinos.

DCC — Treasury's Detroit Computing Center where FBARs are filed.

DEA — Drug Enforcement Administration, Department of Justice.

DOJ — Department of Justice.

DOJ Tax — DOJ's Tax Division.

DPA — Deferred Prosecution Agreement, an agreement between a defendant and DOJ under which the defendant agrees that he, she, or it has committed a specified crime but DOJ agrees to defer prosecution pending the defendant's satisfaction of specified conditions.

EOAF — Executive Office of Asset Forfeiture, Treasury's focal point for asset forfeiture matters.

FATF — Financial Action Task Force on Money Laundering, a multinational financial action task force devoted strictly to combating money laundering by harmonizing the financial and legal systems of its participants. The United States is a participant.

FATP — Federally Authorized Tax Practitioner Privilege under section 7525 of the Code.

FBAR — Report of Foreign Bank and Financial Accounts, FinCEN Form 114, for use by U.S. persons having a financial interest in or signature authority over any financial account outside the U.S. when the aggregate value of such accounts exceeds $10,000 at any time during the year. This form is referred to in shorthand as the Foreign Bank Account Report, hence the acronym FBAR.

FBI — Federal Bureau of Investigation, Department of Justice.

FDIC — Federal Deposit Insurance Corporation.

FinCEN — Financial Crimes Enforcement Network, Department of Treasury.

FOIA — Freedom of Information Act, 5 U.S.C. § 552.

FOPA — Firearm Owners' Protection Act of 1986.

FRCP — Federal Rules of Civil Procedure.

Fed. R. Crim. P. — Federal Rules of Criminal Procedure (also FRCrP).

Fed. R. Evid. — Federal Rules of Evidence (also FRE).

INL — Department of State's International Narcotics and Law Enforcement Affairs.

IRC — Internal Revenue Code of 1986, sometimes referred to in this book as the "Code."

IRM — Internal Revenue Manual.

IRS — Internal Revenue Service.

JDA — Joint Defense Agreement.

LGM — IRS Litigation Guideline Memorandum, a publication within the IRS to guide IRS lawyers and others as to matters involved in litigation.

MLAT — Mutual Legal Assistance Treaty, a type of treaty the U.S. enters into with other governments for mutual assistance in criminal and related information matters.

MSB — Money Service Business, subject to regulation akin to financial institutions.

OVCI — IRS's initiative as to voluntarily reporting offshore financial arrangements.

PSR — Presentence Investigation Report, the report prepared by the Probation Office addressing the various sentencing factors the sentencing judge should consider in setting sentence. Also sometimes identified with the acronym PSI.

RICO — Racketeer Influenced and Corrupt Organizations Act, 18 U.S.C. §§ 1961 *et seq.*

SAC — Special Agent in Charge.

SAR — Suspicious Activity Report, Form TD F 90-22.47, for use by depository institutions to report suspicious financial transactions. This acronym should not be confused with the same acronym for the Special Agent's Report.

SAR — Special Agent's Report. This report is prepared at the conclusion of an IRS administrative investigation or, as to a target of a grand jury investigation, when seeking DOJ Tax approval to seek an indictment.

SAUSA — Special Assistant United States Attorney, in this context usually meaning a DOJ Tax CES attorney assigned to prosecute or assist in a tax or tax-related prosecution in a local district.

SEC — Securities and Exchange Commission.

SOI — Summary of Investigation, the cognate in the grand jury context of the Special Agent's Report in the administrative investigation context.

SUA — Specified Unlawful Activity, a component of an element of a money-laundering crime.

TIEA — Tax Information Exchange Agreement, a type of treaty the U.S. enters into with other governments providing for tax information exchanges.

TIGTA — Treasury Inspector General for Tax Administration, which investigates administration by the IRS.

USAM — United States Attorneys Manual, a DOJ publication to provide guidance to DOJ personnel.

USAO — United States Attorney's Office, the DOJ local office for a federal judicial district.

U.S.S.C. — United States Sentencing Commission.

U.S.S.G. — United States Sentencing Guidelines.

Appendix B

ADDITIONAL RESOURCES

I. TEXTS

Ian Comisky, Lawrence Feld & Steven Harris, a two volume work consisting of Tax Fraud & Evasion: Offenses, Trials, Civil Penalties [Vol. 1] and Tax Fraud & Evasion: Money Laundering, Asset Forfeiture, Sentencing [Vol. 2].

Robert S. Fink, Tax Controversies: Audits, Investigations. Trials (formerly Tax Fraud: Audits, Investigations, Prosecutions). This text previously was dedicated to tax crimes but now has been expanded to cover procedure generally.

Stephen A. Saltzburg & David A. Schlueter, Federal Criminal Procedure Litigation Manual (updated manually). This book covers criminal procedure generally. It is not tax specific.

Michael Saltzman (current author Leslie Book), Tax Practice and Procedure. This is a standard practitioner text dealing with tax procedure generally. Although part of it covers tax crimes, tax crimes are not treated in the detail of dedicated publications.

Steven R. Toscher, Dennis L. Perez, Charles P. Rettig & Edward M. Robbins, Jr., Tax Crimes (BNA Tax Management Portfolio # 636).

II. ARTICLES

Ray A. Knight & Lee G. Knight, *Criminal Tax Fraud: An Analytical Review*, 57 Mo. L. Rev. 175 (1992).

Suneel J. Nelson & Rollo C. Baker, *Tax Violations*, 46 Am. Crim. L. Rev. 1099 (2009).

III. WEB SITES AND BLOGS

John A. Townsend:

> One of the authors of this book, John A. Townsend, maintains a larger tax crimes text. It is available in PDF at www.tjtaxlaw.com.

Department of Justice:

> Tax Division Criminal Tax Manual, http://www.usdoj.gov/tax/readingroom/criminal/titlepg.htm
>
> U.S. Attorney's Manual, www.usdoj.gov/usao/eousa/foia_reading_room/usam/
>
> Criminal Resource Manual, www.usdoj.gov/usao/eousa/foia_reading_room/usam/title9/crm00000.htm

Government Accounting Office:

http://www.gao.gov/. GAO reports on various Government administration issues, including tax.

IRS:

http://www.irs.ustreas.gov/

Treasury:

General: http://www.treas.gov/

TIGTA: http://www.treas.gov/tigta/. TIGTA produces various tax administration reports.

Sentencing Law & Policy Blog:

http://sentencing.typepad.com/. An excellent website for current developments in sentencing.

Fifth Circuit Pattern Jury Instructions (with links to pattern jury instructions of other circuits):

http://www.lb5.uscourts.gov/juryinstructions

United States Sentencing Commission:

http://www.ussc.gov/. This site is the mother lode for materials related to the Sentencing Guidelines.

Alan Ellis:

General: www.alanellis.com. Particularly useful as to sentencing and other post-conviction matters.

Appendix C

INDICTMENT OF RICHARD HATCH

APPENDIX C

UNITED STATES OF AMERICA
DISTRICT OF RHODE ISLAND

CR 05 98 T

UNITED STATES OF AMERICA	:	Criminal No.
v.	:	26 U.S.C. §§ 7201 and 7206(1), 18 U.S.C. §§ 1341, 1343 and 1344.
RICHARD HATCH	:	

<u>INDICTMENT</u>

FILED
SEP - 8 2005
U.S. DISTRICT COURT
DISTRICT OF RHODE ISLAND

The Grand Jury charges that:

<u>COUNT 1</u>

1. At all times relevant to this Indictment the defendant, RICHARD HATCH, was a resident of Rhode Island.

2. On or about November 19, 2002, defendant RICHARD HATCH signed and caused to be filed with the Internal Revenue Service ("IRS"), a 2000 U.S. Individual Income Tax Return, Form 1040, on his behalf. That return declared defendant HATCH's total income in 2000 to be -$41,087 and sought a refund from the United States of $4,483 in taxes paid. In signing and filing his 2000 income tax return, defendant RICHARD HATCH knowingly and willfully failed to declare the following three sources of his income: (i) approximately $1,010,000 in taxable income that defendant HATCH received from Survivor Entertainment Group in August 2000, (ii) approximately $18,708.50 in rental income that defendant HATCH received from tenants of 21 Annandale Road, Newport, Rhode Island, from January 2000 through August 2000, and (iii) approximately

-1-

$25,000 in income that was paid by Chambers Communications Corporation to Horizon Bound in December 2000 and used by defendant HATCH for personal expenses.

A. SURVIVOR INCOME

3. On or about January 25, 2000, the defendant, RICHARD HATCH, applied to be a contestant on a television show called "Survivor," which was to be broadcast on the CBS television network. The "Survivor" television series featured sixteen individuals who competed against one another for a monetary prize of one million dollars ($1,000,000).

4. From on or about March 1, 2000, through on or about April 15, 2000, the "Survivor" show was filmed on location on the island of Pulau Tiga off the coast of Borneo.

5. On or about August 23, 2000, the finale of "Survivor" aired on CBS. It was agreed that defendant HATCH would be paid $10,000 by Survivor Entertainment Group for his appearance on this finale show. During the show, it was announced that defendant RICHARD HATCH had won the competition and the corresponding monetary prize of $1,000,000 (one million dollars).

6. On or about August 18, 2000, Survivor Entertainment Group prepared two checks payable to defendant RICHARD HATCH in the amounts of $1,000,000 and $10,000 respectively. On or about August 29, 2000, defendant RICHARD HATCH deposited the $1,000,000 check into his personal bank account located at Newport

Federal Savings Bank, Newport, Rhode Island. He endorsed the $10,000 check and provided it to Downes Construction, Inc. as partial payment for renovation work that Downes Construction, Inc. was conducting on property owned by defendant RICHARD HATCH.

7. During calendar year 2001, Survivor Entertainment Group sent to defendant RICHARD HATCH and filed with the IRS an IRS form 1099-MISC, in which it declared that defendant RICHARD HATCH had received $1,010,000 in income from Survivor Entertainment Group during calendar year 2000.

8. In or about March 2001, defendant RICHARD HATCH retained the services of an accounting firm (the "Firm") in Newport, Rhode Island, to complete his tax return for calendar year 2000. Along with numerous other documents, defendant RICHARD HATCH provided the Firm with a copy of the aforementioned IRS form 1099-MISC, which denoted that he had received $1,010,000 in income from Survivor Entertainment Group. The Firm prepared an individual tax return for defendant RICHARD HATCH for the calendar year 2000, which included the $1,010,000 in income that defendant HATCH received from Survivor Entertainment Group. The return prepared by the Firm concluded that defendant RICHARD HATCH owed the United States $441,501 in taxes for calendar year 2000, comprised of $374,831 in taxes owed, and $66,670 in interest and penalties.

9. On or about November 20, 2001, a member of the Firm met with defendant RICHARD HATCH and handed him the year 2000 income tax return that had been

prepared by the Firm, indicating that defendant HATCH owed the United States $441,501. Defendant RICHARD HATCH told a member of the Firm that he would file the return with the IRS. In fact, defendant HATCH never filed this 2000 individual tax return with the IRS.

10. In or about December 2001, defendant RICHARD HATCH hired another accountant, a self-employed accountant (the "Accountant") in Middletown, Rhode Island, to complete his individual tax return for calendar year 2000. Defendant HATCH provided the Accountant with a copy of the aforementioned IRS form 1099-MISC, which denoted that defendant HATCH had received $1,010,000 in income from Survivor Entertainment Group. Defendant RICHARD HATCH further advised the Accountant that he owned a piece of rental property that was located on 21 Annandale Road, Newport, Rhode Island, but stated that he had no rental income from this property during the year 2000.

11. On or about March 1, 2002, the Accountant handed defendant RICHARD HATCH a year 2000 individual tax return the Accountant prepared on defendant HATCH's behalf. This return, which included the "Survivor" winnings but did not include other sources of income that were listed on the 2000 return prepared by the Firm, determined that defendant RICHARD HATCH owed the IRS $234,807 in taxes on income he received during the year 2000. On or about March 1, 2002, defendant RICHARD HATCH told the Accountant that he would file with the IRS the year 2000

return the Accountant had prepared. In fact, defendant HATCH never filed this 2000 individual tax return with the IRS.

12. In or about the Fall of 2002, defendant RICHARD HATCH told the Accountant that he wanted to know what his tax liability would have been for the year 2000 had he not received the Survivor winnings. At defendant HATCH's request, the Accountant prepared an individual tax return for the year 2000 which did not include the $1,010,000 in income that defendant HATCH received from Survivor Entertainment Group. This return concluded that without the $1,010,000 in income, defendant HATCH would have been due a refund of $4,483 from the United States.

13. On or about November 19, 2002, the Accountant handed defendant HATCH the aforementioned year 2000 tax return that did not include his "Survivor" winnings and advised defendant HATCH, both orally and in writing, that this tax return was for informational purposes only and was not to be filed with the IRS. The Accountant did not sign this return. Defendant HATCH agreed orally and in writing that this return was for informational purposes only and was not to be filed with the IRS.

14. On or about November 19, 2002, defendant RICHARD HATCH took possession of the aforementioned 2000 individual tax return, which did not include any of his "Survivor" winnings. Defendant RICHARD HATCH then signed this return and filed it with the IRS.

B. RENTAL INCOME

15. At all times relevant to this Indictment, the defendant, RICHARD HATCH, was the owner of property located at 21 Annandale Road, Newport, Rhode Island.

16. From in or about January 2000 through in or about August 2000, defendant RICHARD HATCH rented the property located at 21 Annandale Road, Newport, Rhode Island, to a number of tenants and received a total of approximately $18,708.50 in rental payments. Defendant HATCH did not declare any of this rental income on his 2000 U.S. Individual Income Tax Return, Form 1040, that he filed with the IRS.

C. CHAMBERS COMMUNICATIONS INCOME

17. Chambers Communications Corporation ("Chambers Communications") was a production company located in Eugene, Oregon. In the Fall 2000, Chambers Communications and FOR GOODNESS SAKE! LLC. were involved in the production of a pilot for a television show called "FOR GOODNESS SAKE!."

18. In or around the Fall of 2000, defendant RICHARD HATCH met with a representative of FOR GOODNESS SAKE! LLC. concerning defendant HATCH's possible appearance on the pilot of the television show "FOR GOODNESS SAKE!." During this meeting, the representative told HATCH that the purposes of this show were to promote the good work charities do and to raise awareness and money for good causes.

19. On or about November 20, 2000, Chambers Communications, acting on behalf of FOR GOODNESS SAKE! LLC., sent to defendant RICHARD HATCH a proposed

agreement concerning the filming of the pilot for the show. According to the agreement, in exchange for defendant HATCH's appearance as a guest on the pilot episode, either FOR GOODNESS SAKE! LLC or Chambers Communications agreed to pay $25,000 to a 501(c)(3) non-profit charity of defendant HATCH's choice. Defendant HATCH elected that the $25,000 be paid to a purported 501(c)(3) non-profit charity called Horizon Bound. On or about November 27, 2000, defendant HATCH sent an executed version of this agreement back to Chambers Communications.

20. On or about December 12, 2000, defendant HATCH caused Articles of Incorporation to be filed with the Office of the Secretary of State for the State of Rhode Island to establish a non-profit corporation named Horizon Bound.

21. On or about December 6, 2000, defendant HATCH entered into a second agreement with FOR GOODNESS SAKE! LLC. This agreement also provided that, in exchange for HATCH's appearance on the show, a $25,000 charitable contribution would be made to Horizon Bound, a purported 501(c)(3) non-profit charity chosen by defendant HATCH.

22. On or about December 7, 2000, according the aforementioned agreements, defendant HATCH appeared as a guest in the production of the pilot of FOR GOODNESS SAKE!.

23. On or about December 8, 2000, Chambers Communications issued a $25,000 check payable to HORIZON BOUND. On or about December 11, 2000, this check was

mailed to defendant HATCH.

24. On or about December 18, 2000, defendant RICHARD HATCH endorsed this $25,000 check and deposited it into his personal bank account located at People's Credit Union, Newport, Rhode Island. Prior to depositing this check into his personal account, defendant HATCH altered the check so as to add the name "RICHARD HATCH" as an additional payee on the check.

25. From on or about December 26, 2000, through on or about February 9, 2001, defendant RICHARD HATCH proceeded to spend, on personal expenses, all of the $25,000 that had been paid by Chambers Communications to Horizon Bound. None of the $25,000 paid to Horizon Bound by Chambers Communications was spent by defendant RICHARD HATCH on any charitable purpose.

26. As of December 2000, Horizon Bound had not received tax-exempt status as a non-profit charitable organization under section 501(c)(3) of the Internal Revenue Code.

27. Despite the fact that defendant RICHARD HATCH received the aforementioned $25,000 from Chambers Communications and spent it on personal expenses, defendant HATCH did not declare this $25,000 on his 2000 U.S. Individual Income Tax Return, Form 1040, that he filed with the IRS.

28. On or about November 19, 2002, in the District of Rhode Island, defendant RICHARD HATCH, a resident of Rhode Island, did willfully attempt to evade and defeat a large part of the income tax due and owing by him to the United States of America for

the calendar year 2000, by preparing and causing to be prepared, and by signing and causing to be signed, a false and fraudulent U.S. Individual Income Tax Return, Form 1040, which was filed with the Internal Revenue Service, wherein he stated that his taxable income for the said calendar year was the sum of -$41,087, and sought a refund in the sum of $4,483, whereas, as he then and there well knew and believed, his taxable income for the said calendar year was substantially in excess of that heretofore stated and that upon said additional taxable income a substantial tax was due and owing to the United States of America.

All in violation of Title 26, United States Code, Section 7201.

COUNT 2

1. The grand jury realleges and incorporates by this reference paragraph 1 of Count One of this Indictment in its entirety as though fully set forth herein.

2. On or about October 9, 2002, defendant RICHARD HATCH signed and caused to be filed with the Internal Revenue Service ("IRS"), a 2001 U.S. Individual Tax Return, Form 1040, on his behalf. That return declared defendant HATCH's total income in 2001 to be $228,077 and sought a refund from the United States of $43,296 in taxes paid. In signing and filing his 2001 income tax return, defendant RICHARD HATCH knowingly and willfully failed to declare the following six sources of his income: (i) approximately $326,540 in income that was paid by Entercom, Boston, LLC.

("Entercom") to Tri-Whale Enterprises, Inc. between March and December 2001 as compensation for defendant HATCH's services as a radio personality, (ii) approximately $9,396.40 in rental income that defendant HATCH received from tenants of 21 Annandale Road, Newport, Rhode Island, from September 2001 through December 2001, (iii) approximately $27,074.40 in income, representing the value of a General Motors Pontiac Aztec vehicle that was given to defendant HATCH in February 2001 as part of defendant HATCH's prize for winning the "Survivor" show, (iv) approximately $1,000 in income that was paid by East Boston Savings Bank to Horizon Bound in April 2001 and used by defendant HATCH for his personal expenses, (v) approximately $500 in income that was paid by CAM Media and Graphics to Horizon Bound in April 2001 and used by defendant HATCH for his personal expenses, and (vi) approximately $10,000 in income that was paid by Weakest Link Productions, Inc. to Horizon Bound in August 2001 and used by defendant HATCH for his personal expenses.

A. RADIO STATION INCOME

3. On or about January 23, 2001, defendant RICHARD HATCH entered into an employment agreement with Entercom, which was doing business as WQSX-FM, a radio station broadcasting from Boston, Massachusetts. Pursuant to the terms of the employment agreement, Entercom agreed to employ defendant RICHARD HATCH as an on-air co-host of "The Wilde Show," and to pay him a semi-monthly salary of $20,833.33.

4. On or about March 8, 2001, defendant HATCH caused Articles of Incorporation to be filed with the Office of the Secretary of State for the State of Delaware to establish an S-Corporation named Tri-Whale Enterprises, Inc. An S-Corporation is a flow through corporation, which means that any profit or loss flows from the corporation to the shareholder(s). The shareholder(s) is the taxpayer who is required to pay the taxes on any profit earned by the S-Corporation. Defendant RICHARD HATCH was the sole shareholder in Tri-Whale Enterprises, Inc.

5. On or about April 10, 2001, defendant RICHARD HATCH, acting as an agent for Tri-Whale Enterprises, Inc., entered into a modified agreement with Entercom. Pursuant to the terms of this agreement, defendant RICHARD HATCH was to continue to serve as co-host of The Wilde Show. In exchange, Entercom agreed to pay Tri-Whale Enterprises, Inc. a total amount of $179,807.82 for the period from March 16, 2001, through July 25, 2001. In addition, barring termination of the agreement, Entercom further agreed to pay Tri-Whale Enterprises, Inc. semi-monthly compensation in the amount of $20,833.33 for the six month period from July 26, 2001 through January 25, 2002.

6. Between approximately January 26, 2001, and approximately December 2001, defendant RICHARD HATCH served as a co-host of the Wilde Show.

7. From on or about January 26, 2001, through on or about March 15, 2001, in payment for defendant HATCH's services as an on-air personality, Entercom paid defendant RICHARD HATCH approximately $70,232.68.

8. From on or about April 16, 2001, through on or about December 7, 2001, in payment for defendant HATCH's services as an on-air personality, Entercom paid Tri-Whale Enterprises, Inc. approximately $326,540.

9. The payments from Entercom to Tri-Whale Enterprises, Inc. were each deposited into a bank account in the name of Tri-Whale Enterprises, Inc. at Newport Federal Savings Bank, Newport, Rhode Island. Defendant RICHARD HATCH had sole signature authority over this bank account. Following the deposit of the payments from Entercom, most of the funds were transferred from the Tri-Whale Enterprises, Inc. bank account into defendant HATCH's personal bank account, also located at Newport Federal Savings Bank, Newport, Rhode Island.

10. Defendant RICHARD HATCH, as the sole shareholder of the S-Corporation Tri-Whale Enterprises, Inc., was obligated to report on his 2001 United States Individual Tax Return all of the ordinary income earned by Tri-Whale Enterprises, Inc. in 2001. In fact, defendant RICHARD HATCH did not report on his 2001 individual return the approximately $326,540 in income that was paid by Entercom to Tri-Whale Enterprises, Inc. between April and December 2001.

11. On or about October 1, 2002, defendant RICHARD HATCH signed and caused to be filed with the Internal Revenue Service, a 2001 U.S. Income Tax Return for an S-Corporation, Form 1120-S, on behalf of Tri-Whale Enterprises, Inc.. Defendant HATCH signed the return as President of Tri-Whale Enterprises, Inc.. That return declared Tri-Whale Enterprises, Inc.'s total income in 2001 to be $68,173. The return did not include the approximately $326,540 in income that was paid by Entercom to Tri-Whale Enterprises, Inc. between April and December 2001 as compensation for defendant HATCH's services as an on-air personality.

B. RENTAL INCOME

12. At all times relevant to this Indictment the defendant, RICHARD HATCH, was the owner of property located at 21 Annandale Road, Newport, Rhode Island.

13. From in or about September 2001 through in or about December 2001, defendant RICHARD HATCH rented the property located at 21 Annandale Road, Newport, Rhode Island, to tenants and received a total of approximately $9,396.40 in rental payments. Defendant HATCH did not declare any of this rental income on his 2001 U.S. Individual Income Tax Return, Form 1040, that he filed with the IRS.

C. GENERAL MOTORS PONTIAC AZTEC

14. In addition to the financial monetary prize, RICHARD HATCH's also received an automobile for winning the "Survivor" show.

15. On or about February 27, 2001, defendant RICHARD HATCH went to Barry Pontiac Buick GMC, a General Motors dealership located at 250 W. Main Road, Middletown, Rhode Island, and took title and possession of his automobile prize, a 2001 Pontiac Aztec valued at $27,074.40.

16. During calendar year 2002, General Motors sent to defendant RICHARD HATCH and filed with the IRS an IRS Form 1099-MISC, in which it declared that defendant RICHARD HATCH had received $27,074.40 in income from General Motors during calendar year 2001. The reported income represented the value of the Pontiac Aztec that General Motors supplied to defendant HATCH on or about February 27, 2001.

17. Defendant HATCH did not declare any of this income, represented by the $27,074.40 value of the Pontiac Aztec, on his 2001 U.S. Individual Income Tax Return, Form 1040, that he filed with the IRS.

D. CAM MEDIA and EAST BOSTON SAVINGS BANK INCOME

18. CAM Media and Graphics ("CAM Media") was an advertising company located in Lynnfield, Massachusetts. One of its clients was East Boston Savings Bank.

19. In Spring 2001, CAM Media arranged for defendant RICHARD HATCH to appear as a speaker at the annual meeting of East Boston Savings Bank, which took place on or about April 17, 2001.

20. Following defendant HATCH's appearance at the annual meeting, representatives of both CAM Media and East Boston Savings Bank decided to make charitable contributions to Horizon Bound.

21. On or about April 23, 2001, CAM Media issued a check in the amount of $500 payable to Horizon Bound. On or about April 25, 2001, defendant RICHARD HATCH deposited this check into a personal bank account which he maintained at People's Credit Union, located in Middletown, Rhode Island.

22. Following the deposit of the $500 from CAM Media into his personal bank account, defendant RICHARD HATCH spent these funds on personal expenses, and not for any charitable purpose.

23. On or about April 24, 2001, East Boston Savings Bank issued a check in the amount of $1,000 payable to Horizon Bound. On or about May 21, 2001, defendant RICHARD HATCH opened a bank account at Newport Federal Savings Bank in the name of Horizon Bound, and deposited this $1,000 check as the initial deposit into the

account.

24. Following the deposit of the $1,000 from East Boston Savings Bank into the Horizon Bound Bank account at Newport Federal Savings Bank, defendant RICHARD HATCH spent these funds on personal expenses, and not for any charitable purpose.

25. Despite the fact that defendant RICHARD HATCH received the aforementioned $1,500 from CAM Media and East Boston Savings Bank and spent the money on personal expenses, defendant HATCH did not declare this $1,500 on his 2001 U.S. Individual Income Tax Return, Form 1040, that he filed with the IRS.

E. WEAKEST LINK INCOME

26. Weakest Link Productions, Inc. ("Weakest Link Productions") was a company that produced a television show called "The Weakest Link." On or about April 12, 2001, defendant RICHARD HATCH executed a Celebrity Contestant Release Agreement with Weakest Link Productions. According to the terms of this agreement, defendant HATCH agreed to participate as a contestant in an episode of The Weakest Link, which was to be broadcast on the NBC television network. In exchange, Weakest Link Productions agreed to pay defendant HATCH a small fee and to make a donation of ten thousand dollars ($10,000) to a charity chosen by defendant HATCH. Defendant RICHARD HATCH selected Horizon Bound, Inc. as the charity to which the $10,000 payment would be made.

27. On or about April 14, 2001, an episode of The Weakest Link show was filmed, in which defendant RICHARD HATCH was one of the contestants.

28. On or about June 11, 2001, defendant RICHARD HATCH caused a facsimile transmission ("fax") to be sent from his home in Middletown, Rhode Island, to a representative of NBC located in Los Angeles, California, consisting of a W-9 Request for Taxpayer Identification Number and Certification. The faxed document bears the forged signature of Ralph Magee.

29. On or about July 30, 2001, the defendant RICHARD HATCH caused a faxed document to be sent from his home in Middletown, Rhode Island, to a representative of NBC located in Los Angeles, California, stating that Horizon Bound is still a nonprofit organization. The faxed document bears the forged signature of Ralph Magee.

30. On or about August 10, 2001, pursuant to the Celebrity Contestant Release Agreement, Weakest Link Productions, Inc. issued a check in the amount of $10,000 payable to Horizon Bound, Inc. On or about August 17, 2001, defendant RICHARD HATCH deposited this check into a bank account in the name of Horizon Bound that he had established at Newport Federal Savings Bank, Newport, Rhode Island.

31. On or about September 24, 2001, defendant RICHARD HATCH wrote a $10,000 check from the Horizon Bound account to a construction company that was providing construction services to defendant HATCH at his personal residence. None of the $10,000 paid to Horizon Bound by Weakest Link Productions was spent for any

charitable purpose.

32. Despite the fact that defendant RICHARD HATCH received the aforementioned $10,000 from Weakest Link Productions and spent it on personal expenses, defendant HATCH did not declare this $10,000 on his 2001 U.S. Individual Income Tax Return, Form 1040, that he filed with the IRS.

33. On or about October 9, 2002, in the District of Rhode Island, defendant RICHARD HATCH, a resident of Rhode Island, did willfully attempt to evade and defeat a large part of the income tax due and owing by him to the United States of America for the calendar year 2001, by preparing and causing to be prepared, and by signing and causing to be signed, a false and fraudulent U.S. Individual Income Tax Return, Form 1040, which was filed with the Internal Revenue Service (IRS), wherein he stated that his taxable income for the said calendar year was the sum of $228,077, and sought a refund in the sum of $43,296, whereas, as he then and there well knew and believed, his taxable income for the said calendar year was substantially in excess of that heretofore stated and that upon said additional taxable income a substantial additional tax was due and owing to the United States of America.

All in violation of Title 26, United States Code, Section 7201.

COUNT 3

1. The grand jury realleges and incorporates by this reference paragraph 1 of Count One of this Indictment in its entirety as though fully set forth herein.

2. The grand jury realleges and incorporates by this reference paragraphs 3 through 9 of Count Two of this Indictment in its entirety as though fully set forth herein.

3. As detailed in paragraphs 3 through 9 of Count Two of the Indictment, on or about March 8, 2001, defendant RICHARD HATCH established an S-Corporation named Tri-Whale Enterprises, Inc. From on or about April 16, 2001, through on or about December 7, 2001, in payment for defendant HATCH's services as an on-air personality, Entercom paid Tri-Whale Enterprises, Inc. approximately $326,540. On or about October 1, 2002, defendant RICHARD HATCH signed and caused to be filed with the Internal Revenue Service, a 2001 U.S. Income Tax Return for Tri-Whale Enterprises, Inc., which return did not include the approximately $326,540 in income that was paid by Entercom to Tri-Whale Enterprises, Inc.

4. On or about October 1, 2002, defendant RICHARD HATCH, in the District of Rhode Island, did willfully make and subscribe a false U.S. Income Tax Return for an S-Corporation, Form 1120-S, on behalf of Tri-Whale Enterprises, Inc. for the calendar year 2001, which was verified by a written declaration that it was made under the penalties of perjury and was filed with the Internal Revenue Service, which said income tax return he did not believe to be true and correct as to every material matter in that the

said return reported $68,173 in total income, on Form 1120-S, line item 6, whereas, defendant RICHARD HATCH, then and there well knew and believed that Tri-Whale Enterprises, Inc. earned income substantially in addition to the amount reported, in that it did not report the approximately $326,540 in income that was paid by Entercom to Tri-Whale Enterprises, Inc. between April 2001 and December 2001 as compensation for defendant HATCH's services as an on-air personality.

All in violation of 26 U.S.C. § 7206(1).

COUNTS 4 - 5

A. Introduction

1. The grand jury realleges and incorporates by this reference paragraph 1 of Count One of this Indictment in its entirety as though fully set forth herein.

B. The Scheme

2. Beginning in or about November 2000, and continuing until in or about September 2001, in the District of Rhode Island, and elsewhere, the defendant, RICHARD HATCH, knowingly devised and intended to devise a scheme and artifice to defraud, and for obtaining money and property from, donors of charitable contributions by means of false and fraudulent pretenses, representations and promises.

C. **Manner and Means**

Chambers Communications

3. The grand jury realleges and incorporates by this reference paragraphs 17 through 26 Count One of this Indictment in its entirety as though fully set forth herein.

4. As detailed in paragraphs 17 through 26 of Count One of the Indictment, on or about December 8, 2000, in exchange for defendant RICHARD HATCH's appearance on a pilot episode of a television show, Chambers Communications made a charitable contribution by issuing a $25,000 check payable to Horizon Bound. On or about December 18, 2000, defendant HATCH altered the name of the payee on the check and deposited it into his personal bank account at People's Credit Union. Defendant HATCH subsequently spent these funds on personal expenses, and not for any charitable purposes.

CAM Media & East Boston Savings Bank

5. The grand jury realleges and incorporates by this reference paragraphs 18 through 24 Count Two of this Indictment in its entirety as though fully set forth herein.

6. As detailed in paragraphs 18 through 24 of Count Two of the Indictment, on or about April 23, 2001, CAM Media made a charitable contribution by issuing a $500 check payable to Horizon Bound, which the defendant RICHARD HATCH subsequently deposited into his personal bank account at People's Credit Union. On or about April 24, 2001, East Boston Savings Bank made a charitable contribution by issuing a $1,000 check payable to Horizon Bound, which the defendant RICHARD HATCH subsequently

deposited into a bank account in the name of "Horizon Bound" at Newport Federal Savings Bank. After these funds were deposited into the respective bank accounts, defendant HATCH spent these funds on personal expenses, and not for any charitable purposes.

The Weakest Link

7. The grand jury realleges and incorporates by this reference paragraphs 26 through 31 Count Two of this Indictment in its entirety as though fully set forth herein.

8. As detailed in paragraphs 26 through 31 of Count Two of the Indictment, on or about August 10, 2001, Weakest Link Productions, Inc. made a charitable contribution by issuing a $10,000 check payable to Horizon Bound, in exchange for defendant RICHARD HATCH's appearance on an episode of the television show The Weakest Link. On or about August 17, 2001, defendant RICHARD HATCH deposited this check into a bank account in the name of "Horizon Bound" at Newport Federal Savings Bank. Defendant HATCH subsequently spent these funds on personal expenses, and not for any charitable purposes.

D. Execution of the Scheme

9. On or about the dates set forth below, in the District of Rhode Island, and elsewhere, for the purpose of executing the aforementioned scheme and artifice, and attempting to do so, the defendant, RICHARD HATCH, did knowingly cause to be transmitted in interstate and foreign commerce, writings, signs, signals, and sounds, according to the directions thereon, that is, by facsimile transmissions (fax), the material set forth below:

Count	**Date**	**Material**
4	June 11, 2001	Faxed document from the defendant, RICHARD HATCH, to a representative of NBC consisting of an IRS Form W-9, Request for Taxpayer Identification Number and Certification, for Horizon Bound, Inc. and bearing the forged signature of Ralph Magee.
5	July 30, 2001	Faxed document from the defendant, RICHARD HATCH, to a representative of NBC, stating that Horizon Bound is a nonprofit organization and bearing the forged signature of Ralph Magee.

Each in violation of 18 U.S.C. § 1343.

COUNTS 6 - 9

A. Introduction

1. The grand jury realleges and incorporates by this reference paragraph 1 of Count One of this Indictment in its entirety as though fully set forth herein.

B. The Scheme

2. Beginning in or about November 2000, and continuing until in or about September 2001, in the District of Rhode Island, and elsewhere, the defendant, RICHARD HATCH, knowingly devised and intended to devise a scheme and artifice to defraud, and for obtaining money and property from, donors of charitable contributions by means of false and fraudulent pretenses, representations and promises.

C. Manner and Means

Chambers Communications

3. The grand jury realleges and incorporates by this reference paragraphs 3 and 4 of Counts Four and Five of this Indictment in their entirety as though fully set forth herein.

CAM Media & East Boston Savings Bank

4. The grand jury realleges and incorporates by this reference paragraphs 5 and 6 of Counts Four and Five of this Indictment in their entirety as though fully set forth herein.

The Weakest Link

5. The grand jury realleges and incorporates by this reference paragraphs 7 and 8 of Counts Four and Five of this Indictment in their entirety as though fully set forth herein.

D. Execution of the Scheme

6. On or about the dates set forth below, in the District of Rhode Island, and elsewhere, for the purpose of executing the aforementioned scheme and artifice, and attempting to do so, the defendant, RICHARD HATCH, did knowingly cause to be delivered by United States mail or a private or commercial interstate carrier, according to the directions thereon, and did knowingly take and receive from the United States mail or a private or commercial interstate carrier, the material set forth below:

Count	Date	Material
6	December 11, 2000	A $25,000 check from Chambers Communications Corp. payable to Horizon Bound sent to 21 Annandale Rd., Newport, R.I.
7	April 23, 2001	A $500 check from CAM Media and Graphics payable to Horizon Bound sent to 102 Green End Ave., Middletown, R.I.
8	April 24, 2001	A $1,000 check from East Boston Savings Bank payable to Horizon Bound sent to 102 Green End Ave., Middletown, R.I.

9	August 10, 2001	A $10,000 check from Weakest Link Productions, Inc., payable to Horizon Bound, Inc. sent to 102 Green End Ave., Middletown, R.I.

Each in violation of 18 U.S.C. § 1341.

COUNT 10

Introduction

At all times relevant to this Indictment:

1. The defendant, RICHARD HATCH, was a resident of Rhode Island.

2. Defendant RICHARD HATCH maintained a personal checking account at People's Credit Union, account number 02-50-2747343.

3. People's Credit Union was a financial institution with its principal place of business located in Newport, Rhode Island, the deposits of which were federally insured.

Scheme and Artifice to Defraud

4. On or about December 18, 2000, in the District of Rhode Island and elsewhere, the defendant, RICHARD HATCH, devised a scheme and artifice to defraud People's Credit Union, and to obtain monies and funds in the total amount of $25,000, owned by and under the custody and control of People's Credit Union, by means of false and fraudulent pretenses, representations, and promises.

Object of the Scheme and Artifice

5. It was the object of the scheme and artifice to obtain approximately $25,000 from People's Credit Union by depositing a check from Chambers Communications Corporation into an account at People's Credit Union in which the payee was altered.

Manner and Means

6. Chambers Communications Corporation ("Chambers Communications") was a production company located in Eugene, Oregon. In the Fall 2000, Chambers Communications and FOR GOODNESS SAKE! LLC. were involved in the production of a pilot for a television show called "FOR GOODNESS SAKE!."

7. In or around the Fall of 2000, defendant RICHARD HATCH met with a representative of FOR GOODNESS SAKE! LLC. concerning defendant HATCH's possible appearance on the pilot of the television show "FOR GOODNESS SAKE!." During this meeting, the representative told HATCH that the purposes of this show were to promote the good work charities do and to raise awareness and money for good causes.

8. On or about November 20, 2000, Chambers Communications, acting on behalf of FOR GOODNESS SAKE! LLC., sent to defendant RICHARD HATCH a proposed agreement concerning the filming of the pilot for the show. According to the agreement, in exchange for defendant HATCH's appearance as a guest on the pilot episode, either FOR GOODNESS SAKE! LLC or Chambers Communications agreed to pay $25,000 to a 501(c)(3) non-profit charity of defendant HATCH's choice. Defendant HATCH elected

that the $25,000 be paid to a purported 501(c)(3) non-profit charity called Horizon Bound. On or about November 27, 2000, defendant HATCH sent an executed version of this agreement back to Chambers Communications.

9. On or about December 6, 2000, defendant HATCH entered into a second agreement with FOR GOODNESS SAKE! LLC. This agreement also provided that, in exchange for HATCH's appearance on the show, a $25,000 charitable contribution would be made to Horizon Bound, a purported 501(c)(3) non-profit charity chosen by defendant HATCH.

10. On or about December 7, 2000, according the aforementioned agreements, defendant HATCH appeared as a guest in the production of FOR GOODNESS SAKE!.

11. On or about December 8, 2000, Chambers Communications issued a $25,000 check payable to Horizon Bound. On or about December 11, 2000, this check was mailed to defendant HATCH.

12. On or about December 18, 2000, defendant RICHARD HATCH endorsed this $25,000 check and deposited it into his personal bank account located at People's Credit Union, Newport, Rhode Island. Prior to depositing this check into his personal account, defendant HATCH altered the check so as to add the name "RICHARD HATCH" as an additional payee on the check.

Execution of the Scheme

13. On or about December 18, 2000, in the District of Rhode Island, the defendant, RICHARD HATCH, did knowingly and intentionally execute and attempt to execute the aforesaid scheme and artifice to defraud and to fraudulently obtain monies and funds owned and under the custody and control of People's Credit Union, by depositing a $25,000 check from Chambers Communications Corporation, on which the payee was altered, into his personal checking account at People's Credit Union.

All in violation of Title 18, United States Code, Section 1344.

ROBERT CLARK CORRENTE
United States Attorney

By: ANDREW J. REICH
Assistant U.S. Attorney

LEE H. VILKER
Assistant U.S. Attorney

GERARD B. SULLIVAN
Chief, Criminal Division

Dated: 9/8/05

Appendix D

INDICTMENT OF WESLEY TRENT SNIPES, ET AL.

APPENDIX D

UNITED STATES DISTRICT COURT
MIDDLE DISTRICT OF FLORIDA
OCALA DIVISION

UNITED STATES OF AMERICA

v.

WESLEY TRENT SNIPES
EDDIE RAY KAHN
DOUGLAS P. ROSILE

CASE NO. 5:06-cr-22(S1)-Oc-10GRJ
Ct. 1: 18 U.S.C. § 371
Ct. 2: 18 U.S.C. §§ 287 & 2
Cts. 3-8: 26 U.S.C. § 7203

INDICTMENT

The Grand Jury charges:

COUNT ONE

A. Introduction

It is relevant to this Indictment that:

1. Defendant WESLEY TRENT SNIPES ("defendant SNIPES") was a movie actor. Defendant SNIPES resided in Windermere, in Orange County, Florida, among other places.

2. Defendant SNIPES conducted his movie business through a number of entities, some of which operated as loan-out companies. The loan-out companies contracted with movie studios to provide the services of defendant SNIPES to the studios, collected payments from the studios for the services rendered by defendant SNIPES, paid expenses related to defendant SNIPES' movie projects, and paid compensation to defendant SNIPES and others.

3. Defendant EDDIE RAY KAHN ("defendant KAHN") was the founder and leader of American Rights Litigators ("ARL") and its successor, Guiding Light of God Ministries ("GLGM"). Defendant KAHN resided in Sorrento, in Lake County, Florida.

4. ARL was formed in 1996 and conducted business from an office located in Mount Plymouth, in Lake County, Florida. In August 2003, ARL moved to an office located in Mount Dora, in Lake County, Florida, and began operating as GLGM. ARL held itself out as a "professional organization that utilizes aggressive CPAs and attorneys dedicated to legally representing and protecting the rights of American citizens." GLGM held itself out as a non-profit "Christian ministry and organization established to assist men and women in their pursuit of truth and freedom as Americans." In reality, ARL and GLGM were for-profit, commercial enterprises that promoted and sold fraudulent tax schemes that interfered with the administration of the internal revenue laws of the United States.

5. ARL and GLGM charged members a membership fee, in return for which ARL/GLGM sent power of attorney forms (Forms 2848) ("POAs") to the Internal Revenue Service ("IRS") on behalf of the members. The POAs generally listed an attorney and a certified public accountant ("CPA"), who were affiliated with ARL/GLGM, to act as the members' representatives in tax matters before the IRS. The POAs listed ARL/GLGM's address as the representatives' address. As a result, ARL/GLGM received copies of correspondence from the IRS to the members. Upon receipt of such correspondence, ARL/GLGM would contact the members to offer response letters to such correspondence, for an additional fee. These response letters, which were

authored and/or approved by defendant KAHN, made false and frivolous arguments, demands, and/or requests to the IRS.

6. Defendant DOUGLAS P. ROSILE ("defendant ROSILE") was a former CPA, who continued to work as an accountant after his CPA licenses in Ohio and Florida were revoked. Defendant ROSILE prepared fraudulent tax returns for ARL members based on the "861 argument" (described below). Defendant ROSILE resided in Venice, in Sarasota County, Florida.

7. The IRS was an agency of the United States Department of the Treasury. The IRS had responsibility for the ascertainment, computation, assessment, and collection of taxes, including individual income taxes.

8. The tax laws of the United States, including the Internal Revenue Code (Title 26 of the United States Code), required every citizen and resident of the United States who received gross income in excess of the minimum filing amount established by law for a particular tax year to annually make and file an income tax return for that tax year. Examples of the types of gross income that were required to be reported on an income tax return included: (a) compensation for services, including fees, commissions, fringe benefits, and similar items; (b) gross income derived from business; (c) gains derived from dealings in property; (d) interest; (e) rents; (f) royalties; (g) dividends; (h) alimony and separate maintenance payments; (i) annuities; (j) income from life insurance and endowment contracts; (k) pensions; (l) income from discharge of indebtedness; (m) distributive share of partnership gross income; (n) income in respect of a decedent; and (o) income from an interest in an estate or trust.

9. Defendants KAHN and ROSILE, operating through ARL, promoted a fraudulent tax scheme based on the so-called "861 argument." According to the "861 argument," United States citizens and residents were not subject to tax on their wages and other income derived within the United States based on the claim that the Internal Revenue Code imposed taxes only on income derived from certain foreign-based activities. This argument was an intentionally false, fictitious, and fraudulent misapplication of section 861 of the Internal Revenue Code and the regulations thereunder. This argument has no basis in law and has been consistently rejected by courts.

10. As part of the "861 argument" scheme promoted by defendants KAHN and ROSILE, defendant ROSILE prepared fraudulent federal income tax returns (Forms 1040) and amended federal income tax returns (Forms 1040X) for ARL members, which falsely claimed that the members were not subject to federal income tax, and thus were entitled to refunds of previously withheld and/or paid taxes, based on the "861 argument." For each such fraudulent tax return, ARL charged its members a fee, half of which it paid to defendant ROSILE. In addition, if any such fraudulent tax return generated a tax refund, ARL would collect 20% of the refund from the member and pay half of such amount to defendant ROSILE.

11. So-called "Bills of Exchange" were fictitious documents fraudulently purporting to be financial instruments issued under the authority of the United States. Such documents were falsely drawn and had no material financial value.

B. Conspiracy

12. From in or about 1999 through the date of this Indictment, in Lake and Orange Counties, in the Middle District of Florida, and elsewhere,

WESLEY TRENT SNIPES,
EDDIE RAY KAHN,
and
DOUGLAS P. ROSILE,

the defendants herein, did knowingly, willfully, and unlawfully combine, conspire, confederate, and agree with each other and with others, both known and unknown to the Grand Jury, to defraud the United States by impeding, impairing, obstructing, and defeating the lawful government functions of the IRS in the ascertainment, computation, assessment, and collection of the revenue: to wit, income taxes.

C. Manner and Means

13. It was part of the conspiracy that defendants SNIPES, KAHN, and ROSILE would and did attempt, through deceit, craft, trickery, and dishonest means, to make it appear as if defendant SNIPES had no liability for federal income taxes, when in fact defendant SNIPES had such liability.

14. It was further part of the conspiracy that defendants SNIPES, KAHN, and ROSILE would and did attempt to obtain refunds of income taxes previously paid by defendant SNIPES, to which he was not entitled, through the filing of fraudulent amended federal income tax returns (Forms 1040X) based on the "861 argument."

15. It was further part of the conspiracy that defendant SNIPES would and did willfully fail to file federal income tax returns, beginning with the tax year 1999 and continuing to the date of this Indictment.

16. It was further part of the conspiracy that defendants SNIPES and KAHN would and did fraudulently present and cause to be presented to the Secretary of the Treasury "Bills of Exchange" in alleged payment of defendant SNIPES' federal income tax obligations.

17. It was further part of the conspiracy that defendant SNIPES would and did direct that taxes not be withheld from the pay of his loan-out company's workers.

18. It was further part of the conspiracy that the defendants would and did perform acts and make statements to hide and conceal and cause to be hidden and concealed the purpose of the conspiracy and the acts committed in furtherance thereof.

D. Overt Acts

In furtherance of the conspiracy and to accomplish the objects thereof, the defendants committed the following overt acts, among others, in the Middle District of Florida, and elsewhere:

19. On or about January 8, 2000, defendant SNIPES paid defendant KAHN a consulting fee.

20. On or about March 2, 2000, defendant SNIPES joined ARL by submitting a membership application and paying a membership fee.

21. In or about March 2000, defendant SNIPES had a telephone conversation with his long-time tax advisors regarding tax positions promoted by defendant KAHN.

22. In or about March 2000, defendant KAHN had a telephone conversation with defendant SNIPES' tax advisors in which defendant KAHN asserted that defendant SNIPES was not subject to federal income tax based on the "861 argument."

23. On or about April 19, 2000, defendant SNIPES signed and caused to be sent to the IRS, a fraudulent amended federal income tax return (Form 1040X) for defendant SNIPES for the tax year 1996, wherein a false claim for an income tax refund in the amount of $4,032,806.00 was made based on the "861 argument."

24. In or about June 2000, defendant KAHN traveled to California and gave a private seminar at defendant SNIPES' house to defendant SNIPES and others regarding the "861 argument" and other fraudulent tax positions.

25. Sometime after the meeting in California, defendant SNIPES had a discussion with a worker of his loan-out company about not withholding taxes from the pay of loan-out company workers.

26. On or about June 28, 2000, defendant SNIPES had a telephone conversation with one of his tax advisors in which defendant SNIPES tried to persuade his tax advisor to handle his tax matters in accordance with the "861 argument," notwithstanding his tax advisor's unequivocal advice that there was no merit to the "861 argument," that he was subject to federal income tax, and that he was required to file federal income tax returns.

27. On or about June 29, 2000, one of defendant SNIPES' POA representatives ("Conspirator One") sent a letter on behalf of defendant SNIPES to an IRS employee who previously had issued a letter informing defendant SNIPES that his 1996 Form 1040X claim for refund had been rejected as frivolous; said letter threatened to seek the termination of the IRS employee and requested payment of the refund claim with interest.

28. On or about October 17, 2000, defendant SNIPES executed an "Affidavit of Incompetence" in which he falsely claimed, among other things, that he did not understand the tax laws and did not know if they applied to him.

29. On or about November 30, 2000, defendant SNIPES caused to be sent to the Secretary of the Treasury a fictitious "Bill of Exchange" signed by defendant SNIPES, fraudulently denominated in the amount of $1,000,000.00, together with an IRS Payment Voucher (Form 1040-ES) bearing defendant SNIPES' name and Social Security Number.

30. On or about January 18, 2001, defendant SNIPES caused to be sent to the Secretary of the Treasury a fictitious "Bill of Exchange" signed by defendant SNIPES, fraudulently denominated in the amount of $12,000,000.00, together with two IRS Payment Vouchers (Forms 1040-ES) bearing defendant SNIPES' name and Social Security Number.

31. On or about April 6, 2001, defendant KAHN caused to be sent to defendant SNIPES an electronic mail (e-mail) message: (a) informing him that the IRS had sent a letter requesting that defendant SNIPES file his 1999 income tax return; (b) offering a response letter that ARL could prepare for a fee, which would involve seeking a "determination letter" from the IRS regarding defendant SNIPES' status as a taxpayer; and (c) advising defendant SNIPES that, if he sought such a determination letter, he would not have to file any tax returns until he received the determination letter.

32. On or about April 11, 2001, defendant SNIPES renewed his ARL membership and paid for ARL to seek a determination letter.

33. On or about April 11, 2001, defendant ROSILE prepared and signed, and defendant SNIPES signed and caused to be sent to the IRS, a fraudulent amended federal income tax return (Form 1040X) for defendant SNIPES for the tax year 1997, wherein a false claim for an income tax refund in the amount of $7,360,755.00 was made based on the "861 argument."

34. On or about June 29, 2001, one of defendant SNIPES' POA representatives ("Conspirator Two") sent a letter on behalf of defendant SNIPES to the IRS requesting a determination letter regarding defendant SNIPES' status as a taxpayer.

35. On or about October 1, 2001, Conspirator Two sent a letter on behalf of defendant SNIPES to the IRS asserting that defendant SNIPES was not required to file tax returns.

36. On or about October 15, 2001, Conspirator Two sent a letter on behalf of defendant SNIPES to the IRS asserting that defendant SNIPES was not required to file any tax returns until he received a determination letter from the IRS.

37. On or about October 29, 2001, Conspirator Two sent another letter on behalf of defendant SNIPES to the IRS asserting that defendant SNIPES was not required to file any tax returns until he received a determination letter from the IRS.

38. On or about March 2, 2002, defendant SNIPES renewed his ARL membership.

39. On or about September 10, 2002, defendant SNIPES caused to be sent to the Secretary of the Treasury a fictitious "Bill of Exchange" signed by defendant SNIPES, fraudulently denominated in the amount of $1,000,000.00, together with an

IRS Payment Voucher (Form 1040-ES) bearing defendant SNIPES' name and Social Security Number.

40. On or about March 24, 2003, defendant SNIPES renewed his ARL membership.

41. On or about November 3, 2003, defendant SNIPES signed and caused to be sent to a Special Agent of the IRS who was investigating this case a letter in which defendant SNIPES challenged the agent's authority to engage in a criminal tax investigation of defendant SNIPES.

42. On or about January 17, 2004, defendant SNIPES signed and caused to be sent to the same IRS Special Agent another letter in which defendant SNIPES again challenged the agent's authority to engage in a criminal tax investigation of defendant SNIPES.

All in violation of Title 18, United States Code, Section 371.

COUNT TWO

On or about April 11, 2001, in Lake County, in the Middle District of Florida, and elsewhere,

WESLEY TRENT SNIPES,
EDDIE RAY KAHN,
and
DOUGLAS P. ROSILE,

defendants herein, did knowingly make and present, cause to be made and presented, and aid and abet the making and presentation of, a materially false, fictitious, and fraudulent claim for payment upon and against the United States, presented to the United States Department of the Treasury, Internal Revenue Service ("IRS"), an agency of the United States, knowing that the claim was false, fictitious, and fraudulent; to wit, the defendants made and presented to the IRS, caused to be made and presented to the IRS, and aided and abetted the making and presentation to the IRS of, an amended federal income tax return (Form 1040X) for defendant WESLEY TRENT SNIPES for the tax year 1997, wherein a claim for an income tax refund in the amount of $7,360,755.00 was made, knowing such claim to be false, fictitious, and fraudulent.

In violation of Title 18, United States Code, Sections 287 and 2.

COUNTS THREE THROUGH EIGHT

1. During the calendar years listed below, in the Middle District of Florida and elsewhere,

WESLEY TRENT SNIPES,

the defendant herein, who was a resident of Windermere, in Orange County, Florida, had and received gross income substantially in excess of the minimum filing amounts established by law for each such year; by reason of such gross income defendant WESLEY TRENT SNIPES was required by law, following the close of such calendar years, and on or before the filing dates listed below, to make an income tax return to an authorized representative of the Internal Revenue Service in the Middle District of Florida, or to the Director of the Internal Revenue Service Center at Atlanta, Georgia, or to any other proper officer of the United States, stating specifically the items of his gross income and any deductions and credits to which he was entitled; however, well-knowing all of the foregoing, defendant WESLEY TRENT SNIPES did willfully fail to make an income tax return for such years to any such representative, said Director, or any other proper officer of the United States.

2. The allegations in paragraph one above are hereby realleged and incorporated by reference as though separately stated for each count.

COUNT	YEAR	FILING DATE
3	1999	10/16/2000
4	2000	4/16/2001
5	2001	4/15/2002
6	2002	4/15/2003
7	2003	4/15/2004
8	2004	4/15/2005

All in violation of Title 26, United States Code, Section 7203.

A TRUE BILL,

Foreperson

PAUL I. PEREZ
United States Attorney

By:
JAMES R. KLINDT
First Assistant United States Attorney

By:
ROBERT O'NEILL
Assistant United States Attorney
Chief, Criminal Division

By:
M. SCOTLAND MORRIS
Assistant United States Attorney

By:
JEFFREY A. McLELLAN
Trial Attorney
U.S. Department of Justice Tax Division

Appendix E

INDICTMENT OF JEFFREY STEIN, ET AL.

APPENDIX E

UNITED STATES DISTRICT COURT
SOUTHERN DISTRICT OF NEW YORK

\- X

UNITED STATES OF AMERICA	:	**SUPERSEDING INDICTMENT**
- against -	:	
		S1 05 Cr. 888 (LAK)
JEFFREY STEIN, JOHN LANNING, RICHARD SMITH, JEFFREY EISCHEID, PHILIP WIESNER, JOHN LARSON, ROBERT PFAFF, DAVID AMIR MAKOV, LARRY DELAP, STEVEN GREMMINGER, RAYMOND J. RUBLE, also known as "R.J. Ruble," GREGG RITCHIE, RANDY BICKHAM, MARK WATSON, CAROL WARLEY, DAVID RIVKIN, CARL HASTING, RICHARD ROSENTHAL, and DAVID GREENBERG,	:	
Defendants.	:	

\- X

COUNT ONE
(Conspiracy)

The Grand Jury charges:

Background

1

Pertinent Entities

1. At all times relevant to this Indictment, KPMG LLP ("KPMG"), a co-conspirator not named as a defendant herein, was a limited liability partnership headquartered in New York, New York, and with more than 90 offices nationwide. KPMG LLP is and was a member firm of KPMG International, a Swiss cooperative of which all KPMG firms worldwide are members. At all times relevant to this Indictment, KPMG was one of the largest auditing firms in the world, providing audit services to many of the largest corporations in the United States and elsewhere. Sixteen of the defendants are former KPMG partners, and one defendant is a former KPMG senior manager.

2. In addition, KPMG was in the business of providing tax services to corporate and individual clients, including some of the wealthiest individuals in the United States. These tax services included, but were not limited to, preparing tax returns, providing tax planning and tax advice, and representing clients in Internal Revenue Service ("IRS") audits and Tax Court litigation with the IRS. The portion of KPMG's tax practice that specialized in providing tax advice to individuals, including wealthy individuals, was known as Personal Financial Planning, or "PFP." The KPMG group focused on designing, marketing, and implementing tax shelters for individual clients was known at different times as CaTS ("Capital Transaction Strategies"), and IS ("Innovative Strategies"). The KPMG group focused on designing, marketing, and

implementing tax shelters for corporate clients was known as Stratecon. KPMG also had a department within the tax practice known as Washington National Tax, which was designed to provide expert tax advice to KPMG professionals in the field, and which participated in designing tax shelters and drafting opinion letters relating to those shelters.

3. At all times relevant to this Indictment, "Bank A" was a foreign bank with its principal United States branch located in New York, New York, and an audit client of KPMG. As described below, Bank A participated in FLIP, OPIS, BLIPS, and SOS tax shelter transactions

4. At all times relevant to this Indictment, "Bank B" was a foreign bank with its principal United States branch located in New York, New York and an audit client of KPMG. As described below, Bank B participated in BLIPS tax shelter transactions.

5. At all times relevant to this Indictment, "Bank C" was a foreign bank and an audit client of KPMG. As described below, Bank C participated in BLIPS tax shelter transactions.

6. At all times relevant to this Indictment, "Bank D" was a foreign bank with its principal United States branch located in New York, New York. As described below, Bank D participated in FLIP and OPIS tax shelter transactions.

7. At all times relevant to this Indictment, "Bank E" was a foreign

bank with its principal United States branch located in New York, New York. As described below, Bank E participated in a set of BLIPS tax shelter transaction.

The Defendants

8. Defendant JEFFREY STEIN, a lawyer with a Master's in tax law, was a tax partner at KPMG from at least in or about 1987 through in or about January 2004. In or about 1996, STEIN became the Partner-in-Charge of KPMG's international tax group; in or about March 1998, STEIN became Vice Chairman -Tax Operations; in or about 2000, STEIN became Vice Chairman of Tax Services; and in or about April 2002, STEIN became Deputy Chairman of KPMG.

9. Defendant JOHN LANNING, a certified public accountant ("CPA"), was a tax partner at KPMG from at least in or about 1982 through in or about 2000. In or about October 1996, LANNING became Vice Chairman -Tax Operations, and in or about March 1998, LANNING became Vice Chairman of Tax Services.

10. Defendant RICHARD SMITH, a lawyer, was a tax partner at KPMG from at least in or about 1995 through in or about 2004. He worked in Washington National Tax, became a leader of Washington National Tax, became Area Managing Partner for the Western Region of KPMG's tax practice in January 2002, and then in May 2002 became a Vice Chairman of KPMG in charge of tax.

11. Defendant JEFFREY EISCHEID, a CPA, was a tax partner in KPMG's Atlanta office from at least 1997 through in or about 2004. During that period

of time, he served as head of KPMG's Innovative Strategies group and Partner-in-Charge of KPMG's Personal Financial Planning group.

12. Defendant PHILIP WIESNER, a lawyer with a Master's in tax law and a CPA, was a tax partner at KPMG from at least in or about 1984 through in or about June 2004, and served as Partner-in-Charge of Washington National Tax during 1998 and a portion of 1999.

13. Defendant JOHN LARSON, a lawyer and a CPA, was a KPMG senior tax manager based in KPMG's San Francisco, California, office prior to 1997, and defendant ROBERT PFAFF, a lawyer and a CPA, was a KPMG tax partner based in KPMG's Denver, Colorado, office prior to 1997. In or about 1997, LARSON and PFAFF resigned their positions at KPMG and formed a limited liability company with its principal office located in San Francisco and a satellite office located in Denver. In or about 1999, LARSON, PFAFF, and the defendant DAVID AMIR MAKOV formed another limited liability company with its principal office located in San Francisco and a satellite office located in Denver. As detailed more fully below, LARSON, PFAFF, MAKOV and others, used the two limited liability companies described in this paragraph, and certain related entities (collectively referred to herein as the "Larson/Pfaff Entities") to participate in certain tax shelter transactions as, among other things, the purported investment advisor.

14. Defendant LARRY DELAP, a CPA, was a KPMG tax partner from

at least in or about 1974 through in or about September 2002. DELAP was the Partner-in-Charge of KPMG's Department of Professional Practice - Tax from the creation of that position by the defendant JOHN LANNING in or about 1997 through in or about September 2002.

15. Defendant STEVEN GREMMINGER, a lawyer, was a partner at KPMG and an associate general counsel in KPMG's Office of General Counsel from at least in or about 1998 through in or about 2005. GREMMINGER was the primary Office of General Counsel contact for KPMG's tax practice.

16. Defendant RAYMOND J. RUBLE, also known as "R.J. Ruble," a lawyer, was a tax partner in the New York, New York office of a prominent national law firm (the "RUBLE Law Firm").

17. Defendant GREGG RITCHIE, a CPA, was a KPMG tax partner from at least in or about 1987 through in or about September 1998. During his time at KPMG, RITCHIE was head of KPMG's CaTs group. In or about September 1998, RITCHIE left KPMG to work as chief financial officer of a company controlled by a businessman from Beverly Hills, California (the "Beverly Hills Businessman"), a KPMG client. RITCHIE worked in this capacity for the Beverly Hills Businessman's company through the date of this Indictment. While working for the Beverly Hills Businessman, RITCHIE acted as the liaison between the Beverly Hills Businessman and KPMG with respect to BLIPS and other tax shelter transactions.

18. Defendant RANDY BICKHAM, a CPA, was senior manager in KPMG's tax practice prior to July 2000, and from in or about July 2000 through in or about April 2002, was a KPMG tax partner. BICKHAM was a member of the Innovative Strategies group, and worked in KPMG's San Francisco, CA office.

19. Defendant MARK WATSON, a CPA, was a KPMG tax partner and the Partner-in-Charge of the PFP division of Washington National Tax from at least June 1998 through July 2000. In or about August 2000, WATSON was transferred to a KPMG affiliate partnership located in Amsterdam.

20. Defendant CAROL WARLEY, a CPA, was a KPMG tax partner from in or about 1993 through in or about December 2004. WARLEY worked in KPMG's Houston, TX office, and was a member of the Innovative Strategies group.

21. Defendant DAVID RIVKIN, a CPA, was a KPMG tax partner from in or about July 1999 through in or about April 2004. RIVKIN worked in KPMG's San Diego, CA office, and was a member of the Innovative Strategies group.

22. Defendant CARL HASTING, a lawyer and a CPA, was a KPMG tax partner from in or about July 1998 through in or about November 2003. HASTING worked in KPMG's Woodland Hills, CA office and was a member of the Innovative Strategies group.

23. Defendant RICHARD ROSENTHAL, a CPA, was a KPMG tax partner from at least in or about 1987 through in or about 2004. From in or about 1998

through in or about July 2000, ROSENTHAL was Area Managing Partner of KPMG's western region, from in or about July 2000 through in or about May 2002, ROSENTHAL was Vice Chairman - Tax Operations, and from in or about October 2002 through in or about 2004 ROSENTHAL was Chief Financial Officer of KPMG.

24. Defendant DAVID GREENBERG, a CPA, was hired by KPMG as a direct entry tax partner in or about May 1999. GREENBERG was a KPMG tax partner from in or about May 1999 through in or about August 2003. GREENBERG was a member of the Stratecon group and worked in KPMG's Los Angeles, CA office.

Tax Shelter Fraud

25. During the period from at least in or about 1996 through at least in or about 2005, the defendants JEFFREY STEIN, JOHN LANNING, RICHARD SMITH, JEFFREY EISCHEID, PHILIP WIESNER, JOHN LARSON, ROBERT PFAFF, DAVID AMIR MAKOV, LARRY DELAP, STEVEN GREMMINGER, RAYMOND J. RUBLE, also known as "R.J. Ruble," GREGG RITCHIE, RANDY BICKHAM, MARK WATSON, CAROL WARLEY, DAVID RIVKIN, CARL HASTING, RICHARD ROSENTHAL, and DAVID GREENBERG, and others known and unknown to the Grand Jury (hereinafter their "co-conspirators") participated in a scheme to defraud the IRS by devising, marketing, and implementing fraudulent tax shelters, by preparing and causing to be prepared, and filing and causing to be filed with the IRS false and fraudulent U.S. individual income tax returns containing the fraudulent

tax shelter losses, and by fraudulently concealing from the IRS those shelters.

26. The conspirators designed and marketed these shelters as a means for wealthy individuals with taxable income or gains generally in excess of $10 million in 1997 and of $20 million in 1998-2000 fraudulently to eliminate or reduce their individual income taxes to the IRS on that income or gains. As marketed and implemented, instead of the wealthy clients paying U.S. individual income taxes that were legally owed, generally 20% to 35% of their income or gains, the client could choose the amount of tax loss desired, and pay certain of the conspirators and others an all-in cost generally equal to approximately 5 to 7% of the desired tax loss. This "all-in" cost included the fees of KPMG, the Larson/Pfaff Entities, the various law firms that supplied opinion letters, including RUBLE and the RUBLE Law Firm, the bank participants, and others, as well as a small portion that would be used to execute purported "investments" that were designed to conceal the tax shelters. The size of the purported "investments," the timing of the transactions, and the amount of the fees to certain conspirators and participants were all determined based on the tax loss to be generated.

27. In order to conceal the true nature of the tax shelter from the IRS, to attempt to evade the wealthy clients' U.S. individual income taxes, and to shield the clients from IRS penalties for underpayment of income taxes, KPMG and/or a law firm provided the clients with opinion letters containing false and fraudulent representations

and statements and claiming that the tax shelter losses were "more likely than not" to survive IRS challenge. The law in effect from at least in or about August 1997 provided that if a taxpayer claimed a tax benefit that was later disallowed, the IRS could impose substantial penalties, ranging from 20%-40% of the underpayment of tax attributable to the shelter, unless the tax benefit was supported by an independent opinion relied on by the taxpayer in good faith that the tax benefit was "more likely than not" to survive IRS challenge. Thus, the conspirators issued false and fraudulent opinion letters with the intent that the clients would claim the fraudulent tax shelter losses on tax returns and provide the opinion letter and other false and fraudulent transactional documents and/or the false and fraudulent representations and statements contained therein to the IRS if and when the client was audited.

28. Among the fraudulent tax shelter transactions designed, marketed, and implemented by the defendants JEFFREY STEIN, JOHN LANNING, RICHARD SMITH, JEFFREY EISCHEID, PHILIP WIESNER, JOHN LARSON, ROBERT PFAFF, DAVID AMIR MAKOV, LARRY DELAP, STEVEN GREMMINGER, RAYMOND J. RUBLE, also known as "R.J. Ruble," GREGG RITCHIE, RANDY BICKHAM, MARK WATSON, CAROL WARLEY, DAVID RIVKIN, CARL HASTING, RICHARD ROSENTHAL, and DAVID GREENBERG and their co-conspirators were FLIP ("Foreign Leveraged Investment Program"), OPIS ("Offshore Portfolio Investment Strategy"), BLIPS ("Bond Linked Issue Premium Structure"), SOS

("Short Option Strategy") and their variants.

29. FLIP was marketed and sold from at least in or about 1996 through at least in or about 1999 to at least 80 wealthy individuals and generated at least $1.9 billion in phony tax losses; KPMG's gross fees from FLIP transactions were at least $17 million; the RUBLE Law Firm's gross fees from FLIP transactions were at least $3 million; the Larson/Pfaff Entities' gross fees from FLIP transactions were at least $3 million.

30. OPIS was marketed and sold from at least in or about 1998 through at least in or about 1999 to at least 170 wealthy individuals, and generated at least $2.3 billion in phony tax losses; KPMG's gross fees from OPIS transactions were at least $28 million; the RUBLE Law Firm's gross fees from OPIS transactions were at least $7 million; the Larson/Pfaff Entities' gross fees from OPIS transactions were at least $12 million.

31. BLIPS was marketed and sold from at least in or about 1999 through at least in or about 2000 to at least 186 wealthy individuals, and generated at least $5.1 billion in phony tax losses; KPMG's gross fees from BLIPS transactions were at least $53 million; the RUBLE Law Firm's gross fees from BLIPS transactions were at least $13 million; the Larson/Pfaff Entities' gross fees from BLIPS transactions were at least $134 million.

32. SOS was marketed and sold from at least in or about 1998 through

at least in or about 2002 to at least 165 wealthy individuals, and generated at least $1.9 billion in phony tax losses; KPMG's gross fees from SOS transactions were at least $17 million.

33. Among the individuals who used BLIPS and SOS-type shelters to evade their own taxes were the defendants JOHN LARSON, ROBERT PFAFF, DAVID AMIR MAKOV, GREGG RITCHIE, RICHARD ROSENTHAL, and DAVID GREENBERG, at least 14 KPMG partners, and other co-conspirators.

The Fraudulent FLIP and OPIS Shelters

34. In all material respects, FLIP and OPIS were the same. FLIP and OPIS were generally marketed only to people who had capital gains in excess of $10 million for FLIP and $20 million for OPIS. These shelters were designed to generate substantial phony capital losses (i.e., in excess of $10 million for FLIP and in excess of $20 million for OPIS) through the use of an entity created in the Cayman Islands (a tax haven). The client purportedly entered into an "investment" transaction with the Cayman Islands entity by purchasing a purported warrant or entering into a purported swap. The Cayman Islands entity purportedly made a pre-arranged series of purported investments, including the purchase from either Bank A (which at the time was a KPMG audit client) or Bank D of either Bank A or Bank D stock using money purportedly loaned by Bank A or Bank D, followed by a repurchase of that stock by the pertinent bank at a prearranged price. For the FLIP and OPIS tax shelter transactions in which the Larson/Pfaff entities

participated, the defendant JOHN LARSON directed the transactions purportedly executed by the Cayman Islands entity. The purported investments were devised to eliminate economic risk to the client beyond the all-in cost and minimize the portion of the client's all-in cost used for the investment component. The purported investments also were devised to eliminate economic risk to the bank and to guarantee the fees of KPMG, the defendant RAYMOND J. RUBLE, also known as "R.J. Ruble" and the RUBLE Law Firm, and others. The tax shelter transactions were devised to last for only approximately 16 to approximately 60 days, and the minimum duration of the shelter was determined by KPMG and the RUBLE Law Firm, rather than by investment performance or strategy.

35. In return for fees totaling approximately 7% of the desired tax loss, including a fee to KPMG equal to approximately 1.25% of the desired tax loss, the defendants JEFFREY STEIN, JOHN LANNING, JEFFREY EISCHEID, JOHN LARSON, ROBERT PFAFF, LARRY DELAP, STEVEN GREMMINGER, GREGG RITCHIE, RANDY BICKHAM, MARK WATSON, CAROL WARLEY, DAVID RIVKIN, CARL HASTING, and RICHARD ROSENTHAL, and their co-conspirators implemented and caused to be implemented FLIP and OPIS transactions and generated and caused to be generated false and fraudulent documentation to support the transactions, including but not limited to KPMG opinion letters claiming that the purported tax losses generated by the shelters were more likely than not to withstand

challenge by the IRS. The defendant RAYMOND J. RUBLE, also known as "R.J. Ruble" also issued "more likely than not" opinion letters in return for fees typically of approximately $50,000 per opinion, which opinions tracked, sometimes verbatim, the KPMG opinion letter. In general, all of these opinion letters were identical, except for the names of the clients, the names of the entities, the dates, and the dollar amounts involved in the transactions.

36. The defendants JEFFREY STEIN, JOHN LANNING, JEFFREY EISCHEID, JOHN LARSON, ROBERT PFAFF, LARRY DELAP, STEVEN GREMMINGER, RAYMOND J. RUBLE, also known as "R.J. Ruble," GREGG RITCHIE, RANDY BICKHAM, MARK WATSON, CAROL WARLEY, DAVID RIVKIN, CARL HASTING, and RICHARD ROSENTHAL, and their co-conspirators issued and caused to be issued opinion letters although, as they well knew, (i) the tax positions taken were *not* more likely than not to prevail against an IRS challenge if the true facts regarding those transactions were known to the IRS, and (ii) opinion letters and other documents used to implement FLIP and OPIS were false and fraudulent in a number of ways, including but not limited to the following:

a. FLIP and OPIS were falsely and misleadingly described as investment programs, when in truth and in fact, FLIP and OPIS were designed, marketed, and implemented to generate phony tax losses in order to evade income taxes for wealthy clients and garner substantial fees and income for KPMG, the

Larson/Pfaff Entities, the RUBLE Law Firm, the defendants JEFFREY STEIN, JOHN LANNING, JEFFREY EISCHEID, JOHN LARSON, ROBERT PFAFF, LARRY DELAP, STEVEN GREMMINGER, RAYMOND J. RUBLE, also known as "R.J. Ruble," GREGG RITCHIE, RANDY BICKHAM, MARK WATSON, CAROL WARLEY, DAVID RIVKIN, CARL HASTING, RICHARD ROSENTHAL, certain co-conspirators, and others.

b. Opinion letters began by falsely stating that the client requested KPMG's opinion "regarding the U.S. federal income tax consequences of certain investment portfolio transactions," when in truth and in fact, the conspirators targeted wealthy clients based on the clients' large taxable gains and in return for substantial fees to KPMG, the Larson/Pfaff Entities, RUBLE and the RUBLE Law Firm, certain co-conspirators, and others, offered to generate phony tax losses to eliminate income tax on that gain, and offered to provide a "more likely than not" opinion letter.

c. Opinion letters continued by falsely stating that the "investment strategy was based on the expectation that a leveraged position in the Foreign Bank securities would provide investor with the opportunity for capital appreciation," when in truth and in fact the clients executed the strategy to obtain the expected phony tax benefits promised by certain conspirators.

d. Opinion letters also falsely claimed that the clients "reviewed the economics underlying the investment strategy and believed it had a reasonable opportunity to earn a reasonable profit from each of the transactions . . . in excess of all associated fees and costs and not including any tax benefits that may occur" when in truth and in fact, there was no such opportunity.

e. Opinion letters falsely claimed that one of the participants in the transaction (an owner of the Cayman Islands entity) was a foreign person unrelated to the other participants, when in truth and in fact these foreign persons were simply nominees controlled by the defendants JOHN LARSON and ROBERT PFAFF. In fact, one of the foreign persons involved was an owner of Larson/Pfaff entities.

f. Opinion letters falsely stated that money was paid by the FLIP and OPIS clients for an "investment" component of the transactions (a warrant or a swap), when in truth and in fact that money constituted fees paid to KPMG, the Larson/Pfaff entities, the RUBLE Law Firm, the bank participant, and the nominee foreign person, and other participants, as well as money that was temporarily parked in the deal but ultimately returned to the client.

g. Opinion letters also falsely claimed that there was no evidence of a "firm and fixed" plan to complete the steps making up the shelter in a particular manner, when in truth and in fact, there was such a plan, and the transactions in fact were completed in the particular manner designed to generate the tax loss.

h. Opinion letters stated that the clients were "more likely than not" to survive an IRS challenge to the transactions based on the "step transaction doctrine" — a legal doctrine permitting the IRS to disregard certain transactions having no economic substance or business purpose and the purported tax effects of those disregarded transactions. This assertion was false, as the conspirators well knew. Indeed, the defendant GREGG RITCHIE, who at the time was in charge of CaTS, instructed KPMG partners involved in marketing OPIS, including the defendants JEFFREY EISCHEID, RANDY BICKHAM, and MARK WATSON, not to permit KPMG clients who were pitched OPIS to retain a copy of KPMG's powerpoint presentation describing the transaction "under any circumstances" because to do so would "DESTROY any chance the client may have to avoid the step transaction doctrine."

37. The defendants created and caused to be created this false and fraudulent documentation in order to assist clients in claiming the phony tax shelter losses on tax returns and in evading taxes.

The Fraudulent BLIPS Shelter

38. BLIPS was designed to generate any amount of capital and ordinary tax losses through a series of pre-arranged transactions that involved the client purportedly borrowing money from one of four banks — Bank A, Bank B, Bank C, or Bank E, three of which were audit clients of KPMG at the time — in order to make

purported foreign currency investments including currencies that were "pegged" to the United States dollar. The bank involved in the purported loan also served as the counterparty on all of the purported currency and other transactions involved in BLIPS. The transaction was designed by the defendants RICHARD SMITH, JEFFREY EISCHEID, PHILIP WIESNER, JOHN LARSON, ROBERT PFAFF, DAVID AMIR MAKOV, LARRY DELAP, RAYMOND J. RUBLE, also known as "R.J. Ruble," RANDY BICKHAM, MARK WATSON, under the supervision of defendants JEFFREY STEIN and JOHN LANNING, and their co-conspirators, and others, so that after a short period of time (virtually always approximately 67 days), the client would exit the purported BLIPS transaction and trigger the desired tax loss. BLIPS also included a nominal investment component that used only cash contributed by the client and that was not funded or secured by the purported loan.

39. In return for fees totaling approximately 7% of the desired tax loss, including a fee to KPMG equal to approximately 1.25% of the desired tax loss, a fee to the Larson/Pfaff Entities equal to approximately 2.75% of the desired tax loss, and a fee to RUBLE and the RUBLE Law Firm generally equal to approximately $50,000 per transaction, the defendants JEFFREY STEIN, JOHN LANNING, RICHARD SMITH, JEFFREY EISCHEID, PHILIP WIESNER, JOHN LARSON, ROBERT PFAFF, DAVID AMIR MAKOV, LARRY DELAP, STEVEN GREMMINGER, RAYMOND J. RUBLE, also known as "R.J. Ruble," GREGG RITCHIE, RANDY BICKHAM, MARK

WATSON, CAROL WARLEY, DAVID RIVKIN, CARL HASTING, and RICHARD ROSENTHAL, and their co-conspirators, and others, marketed and caused to be marketed, and implemented and caused to be implemented the transactions and generated and caused to be generated false and fraudulent documentation to support the transactions, including but not limited to opinion letters of KPMG and the RUBLE Law Firm that claimed that the purported tax losses generated by the shelters were more likely than not to withstand challenge by the IRS. In general, all of these opinion letters were identical, except for the names of the clients and entities involved, the dates, and the dollar amounts involved in the transactions.

40. The defendants JEFFREY STEIN, JOHN LANNING, RICHARD SMITH, JEFFREY EISCHEID, PHILIP WIESNER, JOHN LARSON, ROBERT PFAFF, DAVID AMIR MAKOV, LARRY DELAP, STEVEN GREMMINGER, RAYMOND J. RUBLE, also known as "R.J. Ruble," GREGG RITCHIE, RANDY BICKHAM, MARK WATSON, CAROL WARLEY, DAVID RIVKIN, CARL HASTING, and RICHARD ROSENTHAL, and their co-conspirators issued and caused to be issued the opinion letters although, as they well knew, (i) the tax positions taken were *not* more likely than not to prevail against an IRS challenge if the true facts regarding those transactions were known to the IRS, and (ii) the opinion letters and other documents used to implement BLIPS were false and fraudulent in a number of ways, including but not limited to the following:

a. BLIPS was falsely and misleadingly described as an investment program, when in truth and in fact, BLIPS was designed, marketed, and implemented to generate phony tax losses in order to eliminate income taxes for wealthy clients and garner substantial fees and income for KPMG, the Larson/Pfaff Entities, the RUBLE Law Firm, the defendants JEFFREY STEIN, JOHN LANNING, RICHARD SMITH, JEFFREY EISCHEID, PHILIP WIESNER, JOHN LARSON, ROBERT PFAFF, DAVID AMIR MAKOV, LARRY DELAP, STEVEN GREMMINGER, RAYMOND J. RUBLE, also known as "R.J. Ruble," GREGG RITCHIE, RANDY BICKHAM, MARK WATSON, CAROL WARLEY, DAVID RIVKIN, CARL HASTING, and RICHARD ROSENTHAL, certain co-conspirators, and others.

b. BLIPS was falsely described as a three-stage, seven-year investment program, when in truth and in fact, all participants were expected to withdraw at the earliest opportunity and within the same tax year in order to obtain their tax losses. Indeed, the defendants JEFFREY STEIN, JOHN LANNING, RICHARD SMITH, JEFFREY EISCHEID, PHILIP WIESNER, JOHN LARSON, ROBERT PFAFF, DAVID AMIR MAKOV, LARRY DELAP, RAYMOND J. RUBLE, also known as "R.J. Ruble," RANDY BICKHAM, and MARK WATSON, caused the opinion letters to contain a false representation (which was adopted by BLIPS clients, including the defendant GREGG RITCHIE and clients to whom the defendants CAROL WARLEY, DAVID RIVKIN, and CARL HASTING sold BLIPS) that the duration of the client's participation in the three-phase, seven-year investment program was dependent upon the performance of the program relative to alternative investments, when in truth and in fact, the duration of the client's participation was dependant on the client's desire to obtain the phony tax losses to be generated.

c. BLIPS was falsely described as a "leveraged" investment program, when in truth and in fact, the purported loan transactions that were part of BLIPS (and were the aspect of BLIPS that purported to generate the tax loss) were shams — no money ever left the bank and none of the banks assigned any capital cost to these purported BLIPS loans. Indeed, at least two of the banks did not fund the loans at all — they neither set aside from their own funds nor obtained from the market any money to cover these purported "loans" and "loan premiums." In addition, the sham loans were not in any way used in the purported "investment" program involving trades relating to pegged currencies but, instead, were used only to generate a phony tax loss. The only money used in making and securing the trades involving pegged currencies as part of BLIPS was money contributed by the client as part of the 7% all-in cost.

d. The BLIPS opinion letters falsely stated that the client (based on the client's purported "independent review") as well as the Larson/Pfaff Entities "believed there was a reasonable opportunity to earn a reasonable pre-tax profit from the [BLIPS] transactions," when in truth and in fact, there was no "reasonable likelihood of earning a reasonable pre-tax profit" from BLIPS, and instead the "investment" component of BLIPS was negligible, unrelated to the large sham "loans" that were the key elements of the purported tax benefits of BLIPS, and was simply window dressing for the BLIPS tax shelter fraud. Indeed, the defendant MARK WATSON, calculated that because none of the purported "loan" proceeds were used in any investments, the small "investment" component funded with a portion of the 7% all-in cost would have to generate a 240% annual return in order to cover a portion of the large fees paid to the bank, and would require an even higher return to cover fees paid to KPMG and other conspirators and participants, just to break even. WATSON performed this calculation and distributed it to others involved in designing, reviewing, and approving BLIPS prior to the implementation of any BLIPS transaction and prior to the issuance of any KPMG BLIPS opinion letters.

e. The opinion letters and other documents were misleadingly drafted to create the false impression that KPMG, the Larson/Pfaff Entities, the RUBLE Law Firm, and the banks were all independent service providers and advisors, when in truth and in fact they jointly developed and marketed the BLIPS shelter. Thus, for example, the KPMG BLIPS opinion letter misleadingly claimed that the client "requested our opinion regarding the U.S. federal income tax consequences of certain investment transactions that have been concluded" but the opinion letters, which falsely described a purported seven-year investment program and a withdrawal from that program based on the purported investment performance of the program, were drafted prior to the commencement of any BLIPS transaction.

f. Similarly, the KPMG engagement letter used for BLIPS contained the following false and fraudulent statements, among others, (i) that the client had engaged KPMG "to provide tax consulting services . . . with respect to participation in an investment program involving investments in foreign currency positions," when in truth and in fact KPMG marketed a tax shelter to the clients, and the clients engaged KPMG to assist the clients in generating phony tax losses using the tax shelter; (ii) that KPMG "understands that Client intends to engage" the Larson/Pfaff Entities "to provide Client with investment advisory services and trading strategies," when in truth and in fact, the Larson/Pfaff Entities were engaged to assist the clients in generating phony tax losses using a tax shelter; (iii) that the Larson/Pfaff Entities "had advised the Client that the utilization of a high degree of leverage is integral to the Investment Program," when in truth and in fact, the purported "leverage" was a sham loan designed only to support the creation of phony tax losses; and (iv) that KPMG's fees would not be dependent on "the amount of any tax savings projected," when in truth and in fact the amount of KPMG's fee, as well as the size of the nominal investment made as part of the fraudulent tax shelter, and fees for the Larson/Pfaff Entities and other participants in the transaction were all determined by the amount of phony tax losses desired by the client to offset income or gain received from other sources.

41. The defendants created and caused to be created this false and fraudulent documentation in order to assist clients in claiming the phony tax shelter losses on tax returns and in evading taxes.

42. At various points during the development of BLIPS, the defendants RICHARD SMITH, PHILIP WIESNER, LARRY DELAP, and MARK WATSON, their co-conspirators, and others, identified various significant defects of BLIPS, including that the description of BLIPS and the factual representations contained in the BLIPS opinion letter and in other documents were false, but nevertheless in 1999, SMITH, WIESNER, DELAP, and WATSON, and their co-conspirators, approved the marketing of BLIPS. When Washington National Tax approved the BLIPS documentation in August 1999, the defendant RANDY BICKHAM, who helped devise BLIPS wrote to the defendant RAYMOND J. RUBLE, also known as "R.J. Ruble": "We have received our 'get out of jail free card' from [Washington National Tax]."

43. On or about February 11, 2000, a law firm representing certain prospective BLIPS clients ("Law Firm 2") sent a memorandum (the "Law Firm 2 Memo") to defendant DAVID RIVKIN stating, in substance and in part, that the draft

BLIPS opinion letters to be issued by KPMG and the RUBLE Law Firm (i) omitted material facts, and (ii) contained false and misleading factual statements and representations. At the time, Law Firm 2 had an ongoing and long-standing attorney-client relationship with KPMG, although not with respect to the BLIPS transaction. The Law Firm 2 Memo was forwarded at least to the defendants JEFFREY EISCHEID, STEVEN GREMMINGER, RAYMOND J. RUBLE, also known as "R.J. Ruble," RANDY BICKHAM, and MARK WATSON.

44. In or about February 24, 2000, the defendant PHILIP WIESNER wrote to the defendants JEFFREY STEIN, JOHN LANNING, LARRY DELAP, MARK WATSON, and others that (a) of the BLIPS transactions implemented in 1999, all clients terminated the transaction at their earliest opportunity and prior to year-end 1999, and (b) questioned whether the factual representations in future BLIPS transactions would be credible, but nevertheless recommended that BLIPS opinion letters for the 1999 transactions be issued without revision.

45. In addition, in or about March 2000, and prior to the issuance of any BLIPS opinion letters to clients, during a meeting attended by the defendants JEFFREY STEIN, JOHN LANNING, RICHARD SMITH, JEFFREY EISCHEID, LARRY DELAP, and STEVEN GREMMINGER, and others, DELAP told the other participants in substance and in part that if the IRS litigates BLIPS in court, the client would "lose." In addition, another member of KPMG's tax leadership informed the participants at the

meeting, in substance and in part, that the tax position taken in BLIPS was "close to frivolous." During that meeting, the participants also discussed the risks of proceeding with tax shelter transactions like BLIPS, including the risk of criminal investigation, civil penalties, civil liability for fraud, action by the IRS's Director of Professional Practice, and action by state Boards of Accountancy. Nevertheless, and despite the obviously fraudulent nature of BLIPS and the warnings conveyed, the defendants JEFFREY STEIN and JOHN LANNING, and others, decided not to refund BLIPS fees and to proceed (i) with the issuance of "more likely than not" opinion letters on all of the 1999 transactions with the intent that BLIPS clients would claim the phony BLIPS losses on 1999 tax returns, and (ii) continued to implement more BLIPS tax shelter transactions in 2000 and, in 2001, to issue opinions to support those transactions and the claiming of those BLIPS losses.

46. In addition, in or about March 2000, the defendant STEVEN GREMMINGER telephoned KPMG's relationship partner at Law Firm 2 about the Law Firm 2 Memo and stated that Law Firm 2 was interfering with a KPMG tax transaction and that senior tax partners at KPMG were irate.

The Fraudulent SOS Shelters

47. These shelters were designed to generate substantial capital and ordinary tax losses through a series of pre-arranged transactions that involved the clients entering into virtually offsetting foreign currency option positions with a bank, including

but not limited to Bank A, sometimes transferring the offsetting positions to a partnership or other entity, and then withdrawing from the transaction, claiming a loss in the desired amount. These shelters were referred to by various names, including Short Option Strategy, Spread Option Strategy, Split Option Strategy, SOS, Binary Option, Digital Option, Gain Mitigator, Loss Generator, COINS, BEST, FX Transaction (hereinafter "SOS"). KPMG's Washington National Tax office and the defendant RICHARD SMITH considered whether KPMG could issue "more likely than not" opinions regarding SOS transactions, and they concluded that the phony losses generated by those transactions were *not* more likely than not to withstand IRS challenge. Moreover, KPMG's Washington National Tax office and the defendant RICHARD SMITH reviewed draft "more likely than not" SOS opinion letters prepared by the defendant RAYMOND J. RUBLE, also known as "R.J. Ruble," and other firms, and determined that the transactions described therein were not more likely than not to withstand IRS challenge. Nevertheless, between 1998 and 2002, the defendants JEFFREY STEIN, RICHARD SMITH, JEFFREY EISCHEID, LARRY DELAP, STEVEN GREMMINGER, RAYMOND J. RUBLE, also known as "R.J. Ruble," RANDY BICKHAM, CAROL WARLEY, CARL HASTING, and RICHARD ROSENTHAL, and their co-conspirators, assisted in marketing and implementing SOS transactions for KPMG clients for a fee to KPMG generally not less than 1% of the tax losses to be generated, and prepared and caused to be prepared tax returns based on the phony SOS tax losses. For many of these SOS transactions, KPMG did not issue an opinion letter, but instead certain lawyers, including RUBLE, issued "more likely than not" opinion letters with respect to those transactions so that clients would claim the fraudulent SOS losses and evade taxes.

48. In addition, from at least in or about 1999 through at least in or about 2002, the defendant DAVID GREENBERG, with the approval of members of KPMG's tax leadership, including the defendants JEFFREY STEIN, RICHARD SMITH, and RICHARD ROSENTHAL, marketed and implemented dozens of SOS transactions to KPMG clients, often charging fees well in excess of 1% of the phony tax loss to be generated. GREENBERG also arranged SOS transactions for at least 14 KPMG partners, including for the defendant RICHARD ROSENTHAL. In connection with the SOS transactions arranged by GREENBERG, GREENBERG issued KPMG opinion letters or caused others to issue opinion letters that falsely claimed that the tax losses purportedly generated by SOS were more likely than not to withstand IRS challenge, so that KPMG partners and GREENBERG's other clients would claim the fraudulent SOS losses and evade taxes.

49. SOS opinion letters, and other associated documents, were false and fraudulent in a number of ways well known to the conspirators, including the following:

a. They falsely and misleadingly describe SOS as an investment, when in truth and in fact, it was a tax shelter designed and marketed to generate tax losses in order to eliminate income taxes for wealthy clients and garner substantial fees and income for KPMG, the RUBLE Law Firm, certain co-conspirators, and others.

b. They falsely claimed that the client would have entered into the option positions independent of the other steps that made up SOS, when in truth and in fact, the clients would not have entered into those positions absent the anticipated tax loss to be generated.

c. They falsely claim that the option positions were contributed to a partnership or other entity to "diversify" the client's "investment" when in truth and in fact, the contribution was simply a necessary step in the tax shelter, was executed for the purpose of generating the tax loss, and was not executed to "diversify" any "investment."

d. They falsely claim that the offsetting option positions were entered into for "substantial non-tax business reasons," and were contributed to the partnership or other entity for "substantial non-tax business reasons," when in truth and in fact, the transactions were undertaken in order to generate the phony tax losses SOS purported to generate and not for any "substantial non-tax business reason."

50. The defendants created and caused to be created this false and fraudulent documentation in order to assist clients in claiming the phony tax shelter

losses on tax returns and in evading taxes.

51. Many of the SOS transactions marketed by the defendants CAROL WARLEY, CARL HASTING, DAVID GREENBERG and others at KPMG to KPMG clients were arranged and implemented by a tax shelter firm located in New York, New York (the "Shelter Boutique"). In addition, the defendant RICHARD ROSENTHAL's SOS transaction was arranged with the Shelter Boutique. The principal of the Shelter Boutique is a co-conspirator not named as a defendant herein ("CC 10").

Side Payments to RUBLE

52. In addition to the fees collected by the RUBLE Law Firm for the issuance of opinion letters on SOS and other tax shelter transactions, RUBLE accepted side payments for his benefit from the Shelter Boutique and other entities controlled by CC 10. The CC-10-related side payments to RUBLE totalled over $3 million. The CC-10-related side payments were not reported to the IRS by CC 10 or any entity controlled by CC 10, and RUBLE failed to report to the IRS over $700,000 of these side payments. In addition, the defendants JOHN LARSON and ROBERT PFAFF caused nominee entities to make side payments to RUBLE for his participation in tax shelter transactions. The LARSON and PFAFF side payments to RUBLE totalled approximately $500,000, and they were not reported to the IRS by LARSON, PFAFF, or RUBLE, or by any entities controlled by LARSON, PFAFF, or RUBLE.

53. Although, during the period 2001 through 2003, RUBLE received

millions of dollars in side payments relating to his participation in devising, marketing, and implementing tax shelters, RUBLE falsely stated to the RUBLE Law Firm that he had no outside income.

Fraudulent Concealment of Tax Shelters

54. In addition to preparing and causing to be prepared false and fraudulent documentation relating to and implementing the shelter transactions, and in addition to preparing and causing to be prepared tax returns that fraudulently incorporated the phony tax shelter losses, the defendants JEFFREY STEIN, JOHN LANNING, RICHARD SMITH, JEFFREY EISCHEID, PHILIP WIESNER, JOHN LARSON, ROBERT PFAFF, DAVID AMIR MAKOV, LARRY DELAP, STEVEN GREMMINGER, RAYMOND J. RUBLE, also known as "R.J. Ruble," GREGG RITCHIE, RANDY BICKHAM, MARK WATSON, CAROL WARLEY, DAVID RIVKIN, CARL HASTING, RICHARD ROSENTHAL, and DAVID GREENBERG and their co-conspirators employed various means fraudulently to conceal from the IRS the fraudulent tax shelters they designed, marketed and implemented, including but not limited to the following: (i) not registering the tax shelters with the IRS as required by law; (ii) preparing and causing to be prepared tax returns that fraudulently concealed the phony losses from the IRS; (iii) attempting to conceal from the IRS the tax shelter losses and transactions with sham attorney-client privilege claims; and (iv) obstructing IRS and Senate investigations into their tax shelter activities.

Failing to Register Tax Shelters

55. Under the law in effect at all times relevant to this Indictment, an organizer of a tax shelter was required to "register" the shelter by filing a form with the IRS describing the transaction. The IRS in turn would issue a number to the shelter, and all individuals or entities claiming a benefit from the shelter were required to include with their income tax returns a form disclosing that they had participated in a registered tax shelter, and disclosing the assigned registration number. Notwithstanding these legal requirements, the defendants JEFFREY STEIN, JOHN LANNING, JEFFREY EISCHEID, JOHN LARSON, ROBERT PFAFF, DAVID AMIR MAKOV, LARRY DELAP, STEVEN GREMMINGER, RAYMOND J. RUBLE, also known as "R.J. Ruble," GREGG RITCHIE, RANDY BICKHAM, and DAVID GREENBERG and their co-conspirators caused the entities with which they were associated not to register as required any of the tax shelters they devised, marketed and implemented, and thereby ensured that registration numbers would not be included on returns relating to unregistered shelters.

56. The defendants JOHN LANNING and JEFFREY STEIN and their co-conspirators decided not to register FLIP, OPIS, or BLIPS based on a "business decision" that to register the shelters would hamper KPMG's ability to sell them, and that the IRS penalties applicable to a failure to register would be dwarfed by the lucrative fees KPMG stood to collect from selling unregistered tax shelters. Indeed, the defendant

GREGG RITCHIE, the head of the CaTS practice, wrote a memorandum to the defendant JEFFREY STEIN arguing that, assuming OPIS was required to be registered, KPMG should make a "business decision" not to register OPIS because (i) registering the shelters would put KPMG at a competitive disadvantage as compared to other accounting firms, law firms, and other firms that were promoting tax shelters; and (ii) selling unregistered shelters would be so lucrative that the benefits outweighed the risk of civil penalties that might be imposed. Moreover, the defendant STEVEN GREMMINGER, among others, advised that by deciding not to register tax shelters, KPMG risked criminal prosecution, but advised that KPMG's tax leadership could nevertheless "make a business decision to not register the activity as a tax shelter." The defendant LARRY DELAP concurred in this advice.

Fraudulently Concealing Shelter Losses and Income on Tax Returns

57. The conspirators would and did prepare and cause to be prepared tax returns that were false and misleading and were intended fraudulently to conceal the fraudulent tax shelters from the IRS in a number of ways, including but not limited to the following:

a. Although the law requires that an individual's items of income, gain, and loss be reported on an individual income tax return, the defendants JEFFREY EISCHEID, JOHN LARSON, DAVID AMIR MAKOV, GREGG RITCHIE, and CARL HASTING, and their co-conspirators advised certain clients that the phony tax shelter losses and the income or gains that were to be sheltered should not be reported on the client's individual income tax return, and instead only the net of those two figures should be reported on the return. One method of "netting" pursued by the conspirators in order fraudulently to hide the tax shelter transactions from the IRS involved using a "grantor trust." A grantor trust is a trust that, because of certain features enumerated in the tax code, is disregarded as an entity for federal income tax purposes. RITCHIE and his co-conspirators devised a scheme to insert a grantor trust into a tax shelter transaction, and then, rather than disregarding the grantor trust as required by the tax code, reporting the large phony tax shelter loss and the taxable gain or income those losses were used to offset only on the grantor trust information return, while reporting only the small net of those numbers on the client's individual income tax return. Although the defendant MARK WATSON notified other members of the Innovative Strategies group, including the defendants JEFFREY EISCHEID, RANDY BICKHAM, DAVID RIVKIN, and CARL HASTING, as well as the defendant LARRY DELAP, that to pursue this "grantor trust netting" scheme was *not* a proper reporting position, and in fact would result in the filing of false income tax returns, EISCHEID instructed KPMG partners that each could decide for himself or herself whether to engage in grantor trust netting. As a result, dozens of tax returns for FLIP, OPIS, and BLIPS clients used grantor trusts fraudulently to hide the tax shelter losses (and the gains they were designed to shelter) on the clients' individual income tax returns.

b. In order to conceal tax shelter losses from the IRS, the defendants CAROL WARLEY, DAVID AMIR MAKOV and others, advised at least one client that phony tax shelter losses could be concealed and made to look like losses from the sale of a number of publicly traded stocks. In order to so conceal the losses, the Larson/Pfaff Entities purchased publicly traded stock on behalf of the shelter client, and then distributed those stocks to the client upon the client's withdrawal from the transaction. WARLEY and others then advised that the shelter could be concealed on the client's tax return and instead reported as losses resulting from the sale of the stock so distributed. In order to further conceal the phony tax shelter losses from the IRS, in some instances WARLEY, the defendant GREGG RITCHIE and others selected stocks that had already suffered large losses during the year as the stocks to which the shelter losses would be attached, in order to mislead the IRS into believing that the losses resulted from those stocks' poor performance, rather than from the fraudulent tax shelters.

Concealing Shelters with Sham Attorney-Client Privilege Claims

58. The conspirators also attempted to conceal their fraudulent tax shelter activities by attempting to cloak communications regarding those activities and certain of the activities themselves with the attorney-client privilege, although the

communications in question were not privileged. For example, the defendant DAVID GREENBERG, with the knowledge and approval of the defendant RICHARD ROSENTHAL, attempted to conceal his activities in this manner by purporting to have KPMG clients engage a law firm (the "Orange County Law Firm") to provide legal advice, which law firm would then purport to engage KPMG to work under the direction of the Orange County Law Firm. Under *United States v. Kovel*, communications by non-lawyer professionals such as accountants are protected under the attorney-client privilege when the accountant is in fact working under the direction of an attorney. Numerous *Kovel* arrangements purportedly established by GREENBERG and the Orange County Law Firm were sham arrangements because the clients did not directly engage the law firm, in many instances never even spoke to anyone at the Orange County Law Firm, and GREENBERG's work was done outside of the purported lawyer-client privilege. The purpose of this fraudulent conduct was to enable the client, with the assistance of GREENBERG and the Orange County Law Firm, to conceal the fraudulent tax shelter from the IRS by attempting to cloak all of the work for the shelter in the attorney-client privilege. The defendants GREENBERG and ROSENTHAL set up such a phony *Kovel* relationship with the Orange County Law Firm in an attempt to hide ROSENTHAL's fraudulent tax shelter transaction from the IRS.

Obstruction of IRS and Senate Investigations

59. In or about October 2001 the IRS initiated an examination of KPMG

for its failure to register the transactions with the IRS. As part of this examination, in early 2002 the IRS issued 25 summonses to KPMG calling for information relating to numerous tax shelters with which KPMG may have been involved. In addition, the IRS summonses required KPMG to designate a knowledgeable person to testify under oath at the IRS. KPMG designated the defendant JEFFREY EISCHEID, who at the time was the Partner-in-Charge of KPMG's Personal Financial Planning group, to testify. EISCHEID's testimony was false, misleading, and evasive. Among other things, EISCHEID falsely denied that KPMG's fees were based on anticipated tax benefits and misrepresented KPMG's role in devising, marketing, and implementing tax shelters. Indeed, after one day of testimony, another KPMG partner who attended the testimony reported in an email to the defendant RICHARD ROSENTHAL that KPMG's Office of General Counsel and outside counsel "determined that the best strategy was 'the less said the better,'" and that EISCHEID "felt that he had no choice but to be 'forgetful.' And so the record will reflect repeated 'I don't knows', 'I don't recalls,' and 'I was out of the loops' — the rope-a-dope/Enron defense."

60. IRS summonses called for production of documents relating to SOS tax shelters, among other things. The defendants RICHARD SMITH and STEVEN GREMMINGER were among the KPMG personnel directing KPMG's response to the IRS summonses and SMITH and GREMMINGER were aware of KPMG's involvement in marketing and implementing SOS transactions. Nevertheless, none of the SOS tax

shelters marketed or implemented by KPMG, or in which KPMG personnel participated, were disclosed to the IRS and on a number of occasions, SMITH, GREMMINGER and others caused KPMG falsely to claim to the IRS that the production of documents and information relating to the summonses was substantially complete.

61. In addition, when the IRS in May 2003 specifically inquired about KPMG's failure to produce SOS information, the defendants JEFFREY EISCHEID and STEVEN GREMMINGER intentionally caused KPMG's representatives to falsely respond that KPMG was not involved in SOS, but may have prepared a couple of tax returns containing SOS losses.

62. In January 2003, a Subcommittee of the United States Senate issued a subpoena to KPMG calling for documents and information relating to its tax shelter activities, including a specific request for documents relating to tax shelters used by KPMG partners to evade their own taxes. The subpoena specifically named the defendant DAVID GREENBERG as well as certain KPMG partners who, in fact, had used SOS transactions to evade their own taxes, including the defendant RICHARD ROSENTHAL. The defendants RICHARD SMITH and STEVEN GREMMINGER were among the KPMG personnel supervising and directing KPMG's response to the Senate investigation. In addition, SMITH and GREMMINGER were aware of ROSENTHAL's and other KPMG partners' use of GREENBERG shelters to offset those partners' own income or gain, and were aware of related documents responsive to the

Senate subpoena. However, the defendants SMITH and GREMMINGER and their co-conspirators caused KPMG's representatives falsely to respond to the subpoena as follows: "to the best of its knowledge and belief, after reasonable inquiry to date, the firm has not yet identified any documents that are responsive to this request."

63. In or about November 2003, the defendants RICHARD SMITH, JEFFREY EISCHEID, PHILIP WIESNER, JOHN LARSON, LARRY DELAP, and MARK WATSON, certain co-conspirators, and others testified before the Senate Subcommittee investigating tax shelter activities of KPMG and others. The defendants EISCHEID, WIESNER, and DELAP testified together in panel format. During this testimony, among other things, EISCHEID falsely denied that KPMG's fee was a percentage of the tax loss to be generated by the shelters. In addition, when asked by a Senator whether FLIP, OPIS and BLIPS were "designed and marketed primarily as tax reduction strategies," EISCHEID falsely stated "Senator, I would not agree with that characterization." In addition, among other false and misleading testimony presented at the hearing, SMITH gave evasive testimony regarding KPMG's involvement in designing, marketing, and implementing tax shelters. LARSON also provided false and misleading testimony by, among other things, falsely denying that BLIPS was designed so that investors would exit on day 60 of the transaction regardless of the purported 7-year structure of the purported loan, and falsely denying that FLIP was designed primarily for tax deductions.

RITCHIE's Obstruction of IRS Audit of the Beverly Hills Businessman

64. In 1999, the Beverly Hills Businessman participated in a BLIPS transaction that generated $300 million of phony tax losses, a portion of which was attached to various publicly-traded stocks. The Beverly Hills Businessman sold these stocks to trigger the losses. The Beverly Hills Businessman triggered and claimed a $225 million BLIPS-related loss on 1999 tax returns, and claimed the remaining BLIPS loss on 2000 tax returns. In or about early 2002, the IRS's Los Angeles office commenced a civil audit of the Beverly Hills Businessman and certain entities controlled by him with respect to the 1999 tax year.

65. During the course of, and in connection with, the IRS audit, defendant GREGG RITCHIE, who represented the Beverly Hills Businessman and the entities in connection with the audit, made a number of false and misleading statements to the IRS Revenue Agent conducting the audit in order to avoid disclosing to the IRS that the $225 million loss claimed by the Beverly Hills Businessman and related entities for 1999 was attributable to a BLIPS tax shelter transaction sold to the Beverly Hills Businessman by KPMG. Those false and misleading statements included that the alleged $225 million "loss" incurred by the Beverly Hills Businessman and ultimately claimed on tax returns was attributable to regular business activities of the Beverly Hills Businessman's companies. In addition to making false and misleading statements, RITCHIE (a) provided the IRS Revenue Agent with a false and misleading document

that purported to represent the organizational structure of the Beverly Hills Businessman's companies but which, in truth and fact, omitted a description of or reference to the entities through which the Beverly Hills Businessman participated in BLIPS and created the phony $225 million loss for the 1999 tax year, and (b) failed to provide the IRS Agent with the BLIPS power point, notwithstanding the fact that RITCHIE had been provided the power point by KPMG and used it to provide the Beverly Hills Businessman with an understanding of BLIPS.

66. After realizing during the audit that the IRS Agent conducting the audit had not uncovered the true nature of the $225 million loss, GREGG RITCHIE sought to expand the audit to cover the year 2000, and sought to have the IRS enter into a settlement, or "closing", agreement, which agreement would finally determine the Beverly Hills Businessman's tax liabilities for the 1999 and 2000 tax years. In order to create a false sense of urgency with respect to the execution of that agreement, GREGG RITCHIE falsely represented to the IRS that the closing agreement had to be finalized by April 15, 2002 because the Beverly Hills Businessman had to comply with certain IRS return filing deadlines.

67. On or about April 23, 2002, GREGG RITCHIE realized that the closing agreement relating to the IRS's audit of the Beverly Hills Businessman would not be completed prior to the expiration of the April 23, 2002 deadline set by the IRS for taxpayers to disclose to the IRS's Office of Tax Shelter Analysis in Washington, D.C.

their participation in tax shelters likes BLIPS, which disclosures would allow tax shelter participants to avoid certain civil (but not criminal) penalties. In order to comply with the disclosure filing deadline without alerting the Los Angeles IRS Revenue Agent about the filing, GREGG RITCHIE prepared and caused to be sent to the Office of Tax Shelter Analysis, in Washington, D.C., a disclosure form with respect to the Beverly Hills Businessman's 1999 BLIPS transaction. In that disclosure, RITCHIE falsely represented that he had provided a copy of the disclosure form to the Los Angeles IRS Revenue Agent who was conducting the audit of the Beverly Hills Businessman. In truth and fact, as RITCHIE well knew, he never provided the disclosure form to the Los Angeles IRS Revenue Agent the Los Angeles IRS Revenue Agent did not learn of the disclosure filing until after the execution of the closing agreement in or about May 2002.

Evasion of Defendants' Taxes

68. As noted above, the Larson/Pfaff entities collected at least $140 million in fees relating to FLIP, OPIS, and BLIPS. Between July and September 1999, the defendants JOHN LARSON and ROBERT PFAFF engaged in a BLIPS transaction through Bank E and claimed on tax returns approximately $24 million in purported losses as a result. LARSON and PFAFF used these fraudulent losses to evade their own taxes and taxes relating to an entity they owned and controlled ("Larson/Pfaff entity 1"). The defendants LARSON, PFAFF, and DAVID AMIR MAKOV engaged in a set of two BLIPS transactions from March through May 2000 through Bank C that purported to

generate a total of $75 million of losses. LARSON, PFAFF, and MAKOV generated these losses using a variety of entities and trusts controlled by them, and used them to evade individual income taxes and taxes relating to entities they owned and controlled ("Larson/Pfaff entity 2" and "Larson/Pfaff entity 3"). The defendants LARSON, PFAFF, and MAKOV exited the BLIPS transactions approximately 67 days after commencing the transaction; they did not remain in for later stages or seven years, and did not exit the transaction based on the performance of the nominal investment component of BLIPS.

69. In 1999, the defendant GREGG RITCHIE engaged in a BLIPS transaction that purported to generate tax losses of approximately $10 million. RITCHIE exited BLIPS at the earliest opportunity and before year-end 1999. RITCHIE's BLIPS transaction was conducted concurrent with the $300 million BLIPS transaction conducted by the Beverly Hills Businessman. The Beverly Hills Businessman also exited BLIPS at the earliest opportunity. However, the Beverly Hills Businessman triggered approximately $225 million in tax losses in 1999, attaching a substantial portion of the remaining losses to stocks and triggering them in 2000. Both RITCHIE and the Beverly Hills Businessman attached a portion of the phony BLIPS losses to a number of publicly traded stocks that had already suffered large losses during the year, in order to mislead the IRS into believing that the losses resulted from those stocks' poor performance, rather than from the fraudulent tax shelters. RITCHIE prepared and caused to be

prepared tax returns for himself and the Beverly Hills Businessman that reported the BLIPS losses as if they had resulted from the sale of these various stocks. In addition, although the Larson/Pfaff entities purchased these stocks on behalf of RITCHIE and the Beverly Hills Businessman on or about December 6, 1999, RITCHIE falsely reported that these stocks had been purchased on "various" dates to further conceal the BLIPS shelter and to mislead the IRS into thinking that the losses resulted from the poor performance of these stocks during the year.

70. The defendant RICHARD ROSENTHAL conducted an SOS transaction in 1999. ROSENTHAL used approximately $248,000 in tax losses from this transaction to evade 1999 taxes, and approximately $248,000 in tax losses from this transaction to evade 2000 taxes.

71. The defendant DAVID GREENBERG received approximately $1.6 million in income from KPMG in 1999, 2000, and 2001. On his tax returns for those years, he claimed losses of approximately $1.6 million with the notation "nominee," and therefore fraudulently understated his taxable income and paid virtually no tax on the money he received from KPMG. GREENBERG reported this money as income on the tax returns for an entity controlled by GREENBERG and a co-conspirator not named as a defendant herein ("CC 11"), but that entity conducted tax shelter transactions to generate phony losses that offset virtually all of that income. GREENBERG only reported on his individual income tax returns a total of $185,000 in income from this entity.

Statutory Allegations

72. From at least in or about 1996 through at least in or about 2005, JEFFREY STEIN, JOHN LANNING, RICHARD SMITH, JEFFREY EISCHEID, PHILIP WIESNER, JOHN LARSON, ROBERT PFAFF, DAVID AMIR MAKOV, LARRY DELAP, STEVEN GREMMINGER, RAYMOND J. RUBLE, also known as "R.J. Ruble," GREGG RITCHIE, RANDY BICKHAM, MARK WATSON, CAROL WARLEY, DAVID RIVKIN, CARL HASTING, RICHARD ROSENTHAL, and DAVID GREENBERG, the defendants, and their co-conspirators, including co-conspirators not named as defendants herein KPMG and Dominick DeGiorgio, unlawfully, willfully and knowingly, did combine, conspire, confederate and agree together and with each other to defraud the United States and an agency thereof, to wit, the Internal Revenue Service ("IRS") of the United States Department of Treasury, and to commit offenses against the United States, to wit, violations of Title 26, United States Code, Sections 7201, 7206(1), and 7206(2).

Objects of the Conspiracy

73. It was a part and an object of the conspiracy that JEFFREY STEIN, JOHN LANNING, RICHARD SMITH, JEFFREY EISCHEID, PHILIP WIESNER, JOHN LARSON, ROBERT PFAFF, DAVID AMIR MAKOV, LARRY DELAP, STEVEN GREMMINGER, RAYMOND J. RUBLE, also known as "R.J. Ruble," GREGG RITCHIE, RANDY BICKHAM, MARK WATSON, CAROL WARLEY,

DAVID RIVKIN, CARL HASTING, RICHARD ROSENTHAL, and DAVID GREENBERG, the defendants, and their co-conspirators, including co-conspirators not named as defendants herein KPMG and Dominick DeGiorgio, unlawfully, willfully and knowingly would and did defraud the United States of America and the IRS by impeding, impairing, defeating and obstructing the lawful governmental functions of the IRS in the ascertainment, evaluation, assessment, and collection of income taxes.

74. It was further a part and an object of the conspiracy that JEFFREY STEIN, JOHN LANNING, RICHARD SMITH, JEFFREY EISCHEID, PHILIP WIESNER, JOHN LARSON, ROBERT PFAFF, DAVID AMIR MAKOV, LARRY DELAP, STEVEN GREMMINGER, RAYMOND J. RUBLE, also known as "R.J. Ruble," GREGG RITCHIE, RANDY BICKHAM, MARK WATSON, CAROL WARLEY, DAVID RIVKIN, CARL HASTING, RICHARD ROSENTHAL, and DAVID GREENBERG, the defendants, and their co-conspirators, including co-conspirators not named as defendants herein KPMG and Dominick DeGiorgio, unlawfully, willfully and knowingly would and did attempt to evade and defeat a substantial part of the income taxes due and owing to the United States by tax shelter clients and others, in violation of Title 26, United States Code, Section 7201.

75. It was further a part and an object of the conspiracy that JEFFREY STEIN, JOHN LANNING, RICHARD SMITH, JEFFREY EISCHEID, PHILIP WIESNER, JOHN LARSON, ROBERT PFAFF, DAVID AMIR MAKOV, LARRY

DELAP, STEVEN GREMMINGER, RAYMOND J. RUBLE, also known as "R.J. Ruble," GREGG RITCHIE, RANDY BICKHAM, MARK WATSON, CAROL WARLEY, DAVID RIVKIN, CARL HASTING, RICHARD ROSENTHAL, and DAVID GREENBERG, the defendants, and their co-conspirators, including co-conspirators not named as defendants herein KPMG and Dominick DeGiorgio, unlawfully, wilfully and knowingly would and did make and subscribe and cause others to make and subscribe United States individual, corporation, and partnership income tax returns, which returns contained and were verified by written declarations that they were made under the penalties of perjury, and that the defendants and their co-conspirators did not believe to be true and correct as to every material matter, in violation of Title 26, United States Code, Section 7206(l).

76. It was further a part and an object of the conspiracy that JEFFREY STEIN, JOHN LANNING, RICHARD SMITH, JEFFREY EISCHEID, PHILIP WIESNER, JOHN LARSON, ROBERT PFAFF, DAVID AMIR MAKOV, LARRY DELAP, STEVEN GREMMINGER, RAYMOND J. RUBLE, also known as "R.J. Ruble," GREGG RITCHIE, RANDY BICKHAM, MARK WATSON, CAROL WARLEY, DAVID RIVKIN, CARL HASTING, RICHARD ROSENTHAL, and DAVID GREENBERG, the defendants, and their co-conspirators, including co-conspirators not named as defendants herein KPMG and Dominick DeGiorgio, unlawfully, wilfully and knowingly would and did aid and assist in, and procure, counsel,

and advise the preparation and presentation under, the internal revenue laws, of certain United States individual, corporation, and partnership income tax returns which were fraudulent and false as to material matters, in violation of Title 26, United States Code, Section 7206(2).

Means and Methods of the Conspiracy

77. Among the means and methods by which JEFFREY STEIN, JOHN LANNING, RICHARD SMITH, JEFFREY EISCHEID, PHILIP WIESNER, JOHN LARSON, ROBERT PFAFF, DAVID AMIR MAKOV, LARRY DELAP, STEVEN GREMMINGER, RAYMOND J. RUBLE, also known as "R.J. Ruble," GREGG RITCHIE, RANDY BICKHAM, MARK WATSON, CAROL WARLEY, DAVID RIVKIN, CARL HASTING, RICHARD ROSENTHAL, and DAVID GREENBERG, the defendants, and their co-conspirators, including co-conspirators not named as defendants herein KPMG and Dominick DeGiorgio, would and did carry out the conspiracy were the following:

a. They would and did concoct tax shelter transactions and false and fraudulent factual scenarios to support them so that wealthy United States citizens would pay certain of the conspirators and other participants in the transactions approximately 5 to 7% of income or gain instead of paying federal and state taxes on that income or gain.

b. They would and did prepare false and fraudulent documents to deceive the IRS, including but not limited to, engagement letters, transactional documents, representation letters, and opinion letters.

c. They would and did conceal the contents of tax shelter sales presentations in order to prevent the IRS from discovering the true facts regarding those shelter transactions.

d. They would and did prepare and provide to their clients false and fraudulent representations that the clients were required to make in order to obtain opinion letters that purported to justify using the phony tax shelter losses to offset income or gain. At times, the conspirators presented to their clients these false and fraudulent client representations after the all-in costs of approximately 5 to 7% of the desired tax loss were collected from the tax shelter clients.

e. They would and did prepare and cause to be prepared tax returns that were false and fraudulent because, among other things, they incorporated the phony tax losses and therefore substantially understated the tax due and owing by the shelter clients.

f. They would and did (i) fail to report on certain tax returns the losses and the gain or income they sheltered and thus fraudulently understate gross amounts of income and gain; and (ii) disguise the shelter losses on certain tax returns in a manner intended to deceive the IRS.

g. They would and did take various steps to prevent the creation and retention of documents that might reveal to the IRS the true facts regarding the fraudulent tax shelters as well as certain conspirators' role in designing, marketing, and implementing them, including but not limited to concealing from the IRS that the opinion letters provided by KPMG, the RUBLE Law Firm, and other firms were not independent and were instead prepared by entities involved in the design, marketing, and implementation of the tax shelters.

h. They would and did take various additional steps to conceal from the IRS the existence of the shelters, their true facts, and certain conspirators' role in designing, marketing, and implementing the shelters, including, but not limited to, failing to register the shelters, using sham attorney-client privilege claims, and concealing documents and providing false and misleading information in response to IRS and Senate investigations.

Overt Acts

78. In furtherance of the conspiracy and to effect the illegal objects thereof, JEFFREY STEIN, JOHN LANNING, RICHARD SMITH, JEFFREY EISCHEID, PHILIP WIESNER, JOHN LARSON, ROBERT PFAFF, DAVID AMIR MAKOV, LARRY DELAP, STEVEN GREMMINGER, RAYMOND J. RUBLE, also known as "R.J. Ruble," GREGG RITCHIE, RANDY BICKHAM, MARK WATSON, CAROL WARLEY, DAVID RIVKIN, CARL HASTING, RICHARD ROSENTHAL, and DAVID GREENBERG, the defendants, and their co-conspirators, including co-

conspirators not named as defendants herein KPMG and Dominick DeGiorgio, committed the following overt acts, among others, in the Southern District of New York and elsewhere:

a. On or about January 30, 1997, defendants JEFFREY EISCHEID and JOHN LARSON advised a FLIP client and his return preparer to create a grantor trust for the purposes of concealing on the client's tax return the FLIP tax loss to be generated and the client's gain from other sources.

b. On or about July 18, 1997, the defendant ROBERT PFAFF prepared a memorandum to the defendants JOHN LANNING and JEFFREY STEIN discussing how KPMG and the Larson/Pfaff Entities should jointly devise, market, and implement tax shelter transactions and how their fees should be divided.

c. On or about August 16, 1997, the defendant JOHN LANNING sent an email to the defendants JEFFREY STEIN, JEFFREY EISCHEID, JOHN LARSON, ROBERT PFAFF, GREGG RITCHIE, and others regarding a meeting focusing on successfully completing LARSON and PFAFF engagements, continuing to grow and expand the "Tax Advantaged Transactions" practice that LARSON and PFAFF had been overseeing, and endeavoring to forge an ongoing and successful relationship with the "Pfaff/Larson firm."

d. In or about September 1997, the defendant GREGG RITCHIE on behalf of KPMG and the defendant JOHN LARSON on behalf of the Larson/Pfaff Entities signed an "operating agreement" regarding joint marketing and implementation of FLIP transactions.

e. On or about December 15, 1997, the defendant RAYMOND J. RUBLE, also known as "R.J. Ruble," told the defendant RANDY BICKHAM, who in turn told the defendant GREGG RITCHIE that RUBLE's managing partner had approved his working with KPMG on a joint basis to develop and market tax products and jointly to share in the fees.

f. On or about March 14, 1998, the defendant JEFFREY STEIN sent an email to the defendant JOHN LANNING and others recommending, in substance and in part, that revenue credit for OPIS transactions be divided among KPMG practice groups in a particular manner based on the similarities between FLIP and OPIS.

g. On or about May 26, 1998, the defendant GREGG RITCHIE advised the defendant JEFFREY STEIN and others that KPMG should not register OPIS because to do so would put KPMG at a severe competitive disadvantage in marketing tax shelters.

h. On or about June 8, 1998, the defendant GREGG RITCHIE advised the KPMG team marketing OPIS not to leave the OPIS PowerPoint presentation "with clients or targets under any circumstances" because doing so "will

DESTROY any chance the client may have to avoid the step transaction doctrine."

i. On or about September 10, 1998, the defendant JEFFREY EISCHEID sent an email to defendant JOHN LANNING and others proposing an "alliance" with a competitor of the Larson/Pfaff Entities to implement OPIS transactions and noting that "we have very little time to work with if we are going to execute trades such that our clients can generate the desired benefits in calendar 1998."

j. On or about December 3, 1998, the defendant RAYMOND J. RUBLE, also known as "R.J. Ruble," prepared a memorandum to the defendant RANDY BICKHAM and another co-conspirator not named as a defendant herein proposing structuring BLIPS with a fixed-rate loan for purposes of avoiding a rule that would block the generation of BLIPS phony tax losses.

k. On or about December 15, 1998, the defendant RAYMOND J. RUBLE, also known as "R.J. Ruble," sent an email to his management stating that he had worked closely with KPMG in developing tax products and had agreed to issue "concurring" "more likely than not" opinion letters for those products in return for a fee from KPMG of $50,000 per deal for 1997, and a fee for 1998 based on deal size.

l. On or about January 22, 1999, the defendant JEFFREY EISCHEID instructed KPMG partners that each partner should decide for himself or herself whether to attempt to conceal losses from the IRS using a grantor trust.

m. On or about April 30, 1999 and May 1, 1999, the defendants JEFFREY EISCHEID, MARK WATSON, JOHN LARSON, DAVID AMIR MAKOV, RANDY BICKHAM, CAROL WARLEY, DAVID RIVKIN, and CARL HASTING, and certain co-conspirators met in Dallas, Texas for a BLIPS task force meeting.

n. On or about May 9, 1999, the defendant MARK WATSON sent an email to the defendants JEFFREY EISCHEID, PHILIP WIESNER, LARRY DELAP, and RANDY BICKHAM proposing false representations to be included in the BLIPS opinion letter.

o. On or about May 10, 1999, the defendant MARK WATSON sent an email to the defendants RICHARD SMITH, JEFFREY EISCHEID, PHILIP WIESNER, LARRY DELAP, and RANDY BICKHAM proposing a false representation to be included in the BLIPS opinion letter.

p. On or about May 10, 1999, the defendant JEFFREY STEIN sent an email to others in which he recommended that KPMG market and implement BLIPS.

q. On or about May 18, 1999, the defendant LARRY DELAP sent an email stating that marketing of BLIPS was approved.

r. On or about August 4, 1999, the defendant PHILIP WIESNER

announced that BLIPS was approved for marketing by KPMG personnel.

s. On or about August 5, 1999, the defendant RANDY BICKHAM sent an email to the defendant RAYMOND J. RUBLE, also known as "R.J. Ruble," in the Southern District of New York stating that he and the attorney had received a "get out of jail free card" as a result of obtaining permission from Washington National Tax to proceed with BLIPS.

t. On or about August 30, 1999, the defendant RANDY BICKHAM sent the defendant GREGG RITCHIE a BLIPS powerpoint presentation for the Beverly Hills Businessman.

u. In or about September or October 1999, Domenick DeGiorgio, a co-conspirator not named as a defendant herein, met at the offices of Bank B in the Southern District of New York with the defendant ROBERT PFAFF, and on another occasion, with JOHN LARSON and DAVID AMIR MAKOV and others.

v. In or about 1999, in the Southern District of New York and elsewhere, Banks A, B and C, prepared and caused to be prepared transactional documents relating to BLIPS tax shelter transactions.

w. On or about September 24, 1999, a co-conspirator not named as a defendant herein ("KPMG Partner 1") instructed the Innovative Strategies group that because banks were unwilling to execute as many BLIPS deals as had been sold to clients, the Innovative Strategies group should consult with DAVID

GREENBERG regarding a tax shelter transaction that BLIPS clients could use instead of BLIPS to shelter their income and gain.

x. On or about September 24, 1999, the defendant RICHARD ROSENTHAL advised defendant DAVID GREENBERG that defendant MARK WATSON would contact GREENBERG to arrange tax shelter transactions for clients to whom KPMG had offered BLIPS, but for whom KPMG could not arrange BLIPS transactions.

y. On or about September 27, 1999, the defendant DAVID AMIR MAKOV prepared a "loan premium rationale" designed to falsely make it appear that there were legitimate business and economic purposes for structuring the BLIPS purported loan in the manner it was structured.

z. On or about October 1, 1999, the defendant LARRY DELAP approved the sale of OPIS transactions to clients who were promised BLIPS but for whom KPMG could not arrange BLIPS transactions.

aa. In or about October 1999, the defendant DAVID AMIR MAKOV requested a treasury official of Bank B in the Southern District of New York to execute a swap transaction involving a BLIPS "loan" by employing two separate trade tickets rather than a single swap transaction ticket.

bb. In or about mid-October 1999, a co-conspirator not named as a defendant herein, caused KPMG professionals to be deployed to the New York,

New York offices of Bank B to aid in processing various BLIPS transactions in order to allow the transactions to be initiated and terminated by the end of the calendar year.

cc. On or about October 18, 1999, the defendant RICHARD ROSENTHAL instructed a co-conspirator not named as a defendant herein ("KPMG Partner 2") to send no further emails regarding a tax shelter client who had been pitched BLIPS, but then had been sold an SOS tax shelter transaction by DAVID GREENBERG ("DAVID GREENBERG Client 1"), resulting in a fee triple the fee that would have resulted from BLIPS.

dd. On or about December 1999, the defendant CARL HASTING sent an email to the defendant RICHARD ROSENTHAL reporting $437,500 revenue from a BLIPS transaction arranged for the husband of a KPMG partner and assigning to the KPMG partner "Teamwork Revenue" credit for this transaction.

ee. On or about November 30, 1999, the defendant CAROL WARLEY advised a BLIPS client to divide the phony tax shelter losses among 10 stocks that have been losers.

ff. On or about December 3, 1999, the defendant CARL HASTING sent an email to the defendant JEFFREY EISCHEID in which he itemized SOS transactions and $700,000 in fees due to KPMG. EISCHEID wrote "just a word of caution . . . DPP has mandated that we receive no value added fees from the client and no payment from [CC 10]. At $350 per hour, your $700,000 is 2,000 hours."

gg. On or about December 8, 1999, the defendant MARK WATSON advised others involved in marketing and implementing BLIPS that a document on which the client selected how much of the BLIPS loss should be ordinary and how much should be capital should not be kept in the file because "if the IRS were to discover such a document it could look very bad for the client."

hh. On or about January 9, 2000, the defendant CARL HASTING sent an email to the defendant RICHARD ROSENTHAL reporting $470,000 revenue from two SOS transactions arranged by HASTING and assigning to ROSENTHAL "Teamwork Revenue" credit for these transactions.

ii. On or about March 7, 2000, the defendants JEFFREY STEIN, JOHN LANNING, RICHARD SMITH, JEFFREY EISCHEID, LARRY DELAP, and STEVEN GREMMINGER, and others met in the Southern District of New York to discuss the risks of civil penalties and criminal investigation associated with completing the implementation of 1999 OPIS and BLIPS transactions.

jj. On or about March 21, 2000, a co-conspirator not named as a defendant herein advised others involved in marketing BLIPS that they should "NOT put a copy of" an email in their BLIPS file because "it is a roadmap for the taxing authorities to all the other listed transactions."

kk. In or about March 2000, the defendant STEVEN GREMMINGER called KPMG's relationship partner at Law Firm 2 about the Law Firm 2 Memo and stated that Law Firm 2 was interfering with a KPMG tax transaction and that senior tax partners at KPMG were irate. BLIPS was the KPMG tax transaction referred to by GREMMINGER.

ll. On or about March 29, 2000, the defendant DAVID GREENBERG issued to defendant RICHARD ROSENTHAL an opinion letter relating to ROSENTHAL's SOS tax shelter transaction. GREENBERG issued the opinion letter with the name of a nominee as the purported author in order to conceal GREENBERG's involvement in implementing the transaction, and with CC 11 as the purported addressee in order falsely to make it appear that the opinion letter was covered by the attorney-client privilege.

mm. In or about March and April 2000, in the Southern District of New York, the defendant RAYMOND J. RUBLE, also known as "R.J. Ruble," prepared and caused to be prepared dozens of BLIPS opinion letters.

nn. On or about November 9, 2000, defendant DAVID GREENBERG sent an email to CC 11 instructing CC 11 to establish entities and bank accounts to be used to execute SOS transactions for five KPMG partners and one KPMG former partner.

oo. In or about 1998, 1999, and 2000, the defendant RAYMOND J.

RUBLE, also known as "R.J. Ruble," caused dozens of invoices and opinion letters relating to fraudulent tax shelter transactions to be sent by overnight carrier from the RUBLE Law Firm in New York, New York to KPMG's Atlanta office.

pp. In or about 1998, 1999, and 2000, in the Southern District of New York and elsewhere, certain conspirators, including KPMG personnel and clients, and others involved in FLIP and OPIS tax shelter transactions prepared, signed and filed tax returns that falsely and fraudulently claimed over $4.2 billion in phony tax losses generated by FLIP and OPIS transactions.

qq. In or about 2000 and 2001, in the Southern District of New York and elsewhere, certain conspirators, including KPMG personnel and clients, and others involved in BLIPS tax shelter transactions prepared, signed and filed tax returns that falsely and fraudulently claimed over $5.1 billion in phony tax losses generated by BLIPS transactions.

rr. In or about 1999, 2000, and 2001, in the Southern District of New York and elsewhere, certain conspirators, including KPMG personnel and clients, and others involved in SOS tax shelter transactions prepared, signed and filed tax returns that falsely and fraudulently claimed over $1.9 billion in phony tax losses generated by SOS.

ss. In or about March 2001, defendants JEFFREY EISCHEID and STEVEN GREMMINGER attempted to procure an additional law firm to author a favorable opinion letter for a BLIPS client who had previously demanded that KPMG return all of his fees to him.

tt. On or about February 12 and 27, 2002, the defendant JEFFREY EISCHEID provided false and misleading testimony under oath to the IRS.

uu. On or about October 2, 2002, the defendant RICHARD SMITH sent a letter to the IRS in the Southern District of New York falsely claiming that "KPMG has at this time virtually completed its compliance with the summonses" although as SMITH well knew, KPMG had produced no documents or information regarding its involvement in marketing and implementing SOS transactions.

vv. On or about February 19, 2003, the defendants RICHARD SMITH and STEVEN GREMMINGER and others caused KPMG's outside counsel to falsely represent to the Senate that "after reasonable inquiry to date, the firm has not yet identified any documents" relating to shelter transactions used by KPMG partners to shelter their own income or gains, although SMITH and GREMMINGER well knew that KPMG had various documents responsive to this subpoena request.

ww. On or about November 18, 2003, the defendant JEFFREY EISCHEID provided false and misleading testimony under oath to a Subcommittee of the United States Senate.

xx. On or about November 18, 2003, the defendant RICHARD SMITH provided evasive testimony under oath to a Subcommittee of the United States Senate.

yy. On or about November 20, 2003, the defendant JOHN LARSON provided false and misleading testimony under oath to a Subcommittee of the United States Senate.

zz. On or about January 22, 2004, a BLIPS client ("CAROL WARLEY Client 2") provided false and misleading testimony under oath to the IRS.

(Title 18, United States Code, Section 371.)

COUNTS TWO THROUGH FORTY
(Tax Evasion)

The Grand Jury further charges:

79. The allegations set forth in paragraphs 1-71 are repeated and realleged as if fully set forth herein.

80. From on or about January 1 of each of the calendar years set forth below, through at least on or about the filing dates set forth below for each said calendar year, in the Southern District of New York and elsewhere, JEFFREY STEIN, JOHN LANNING, RICHARD SMITH, JEFFREY EISCHEID, PHILIP WIESNER, JOHN LARSON, ROBERT PFAFF, DAVID AMIR MAKOV, LARRY DELAP, STEVEN GREMMINGER, RAYMOND J. RUBLE, also known as "R.J. Ruble," GREGG RITCHIE, RANDY BICKHAM, MARK WATSON, CAROL WARLEY, DAVID

RIVKIN, CARL HASTING, RICHARD ROSENTHAL, and DAVID GREENBERG, the defendants, along with their co-conspirators, unlawfully, wilfully and knowingly did attempt to evade and defeat a substantial part of the income tax due and owing by the tax shelter clients and by certain defendants and entities controlled by defendants set forth below to the United States of America for the calendar years set forth below, by committing and causing to be committed the following acts, among others:

a. preparing and executing false and fraudulent documents to deceive the IRS, including but not limited to, engagement letters, transactional documents, representation letters, and opinion letters;

b. creating entities to be used in executing tax shelter transactions;

c. executing financial transactions to implement the fraudulent tax shelters;

d. preparing and filing false and fraudulent tax returns; and

e. taking various steps to conceal from the IRS the existence of the shelters, their true facts, and certain conspirators' role in designing, marketing, and implementing the shelters, including, but not limited to, failing to register the shelters, using sham attorney-client privilege claims, and concealing documents and providing false and misleading information in response to IRS and Senate investigations.

[illegible]	[illegible] Defendant	[illegible]	[illegible] Shelter Loss	[illegible]
2	Beverly Hills Businessman	1999 1040	$120 million	08/23/2000
3	Beverly Hills Businessman	2000 1040	$41 million	10/15/2001
4	GREGG RITCHIE	1999 1040	$2.7 million	10/14/2000
5	GREGG RITCHIE	2000 1040	$2.3 million	10/01/2001
6	RICHARD ROSENTHAL	1999 1040	$248,000	10/15/2000
7	RICHARD ROSENTHAL	2000 1040	$248,000	10/15/2001
8	CAROL WARLEY Client 1	1999 1040	$136 million	04/15/2000
9	CAROL WARLEY Client 1	2000 1040	$74 million	10/09/2001
10	CAROL WARLEY Client 1	2001 1040	$76 million	10/15/2001
11	CAROL WARLEY Client 2	1999 1040	$36 million	04/15/2000
12	CAROL WARLEY Client 3	1999 1040	$10 million	04/15/2000
13	CAROL WARLEY Client 4	1999 1040	$6 million	04/15/2000
14	JOHN LARSON Client 1	1999 1040	$10 million	05/10/2000
15	JOHN LARSON Client 1	2000 1040	$47 million	04/15/2001

[illegible]	[illegible]	[illegible]	[illegible]	[illegible]
16	JOHN LARSON Client 1 Trust	1999 1041	$20 million	05/10/2000
17	JOHN LARSON Client 1 Trust	2000 1041	$47 million	04/15/2001
18	Hedge Fund Manager 1	1999 1040	$52 million	08/01/2000
19	DAVID RIVKIN Client 1	1999 1040	$25 million	04/15/2000
20	DAVID RIVKIN Client 2	1999 1040	$59 million	04/15/2000
21	DAVID RIVKIN Client 3	1999 1040	$20 million	04/15/2000
22	DAVID RIVKIN Client 4	2000 1040	$30 million	10/15/2001
23	DAVID RIVKIN Client 5	1999 1040	$9 million	10/19/2000
24	DAVID RIVKIN Client 5	2000 1040	$17 million	06/18/2001
25	CARL HASTING Client 1	1999 1040	$36 million	04/15/2000
26	CARL HASTING Client 2	1999 1040	$50 million	10/15/2000
27	CARL HASTING Client 3	1999 1040	$7 million	09/19/2000
28	KPMG Partner 2	2000 1040	$590,000	10/10/2001
29	Venture Capital Fund Manager 1	1999 1040	$68 million	10/16/2000

[illegible]	[illegible]	[illegible]	[illegible]	[illegible]
30	Other Client 1	1999 1040	$81 million	04/15/2000
31	Other Client 2	1999 1040	$8 million	04/15/2000
32	JOHN LARSON	1999 1040	$8 million	10/13/2000
33	ROBERT PFAFF	1999 1040	$8 million	10/15/2000
34	Larson/Pfaff entity 1	1999 1040	$8 million	06/19/2000
35	Larson/Pfaff entity 2	1999 1120	$25 million	02/21/2001
36	Larson/Pfaff entity 2	2000 1120	$25 million	12/03/2001
37	Larson/Pfaff entity 3	2000 1120	$25 million	09/27/2001
38	DAVID GREENBERG Client 1	1999 1040	$19 million	10/15/2000
39	DAVID GREENBERG Client 2	1999 1040	$1.4 million	10/15/2000
40	DAVID GREENBERG Client 3	2000 1120	$119 million	09/30/2001

(Title 26, United States Code, Section 7201, Title 18, United States Code, Section 2.)

COUNTS FORTY-ONE THROUGH FORTY-FOUR
(Evasion of RUBLE's Income Taxes)

The Grand Jury further charges:

81. The allegations set forth in paragraphs in 52-53 are repeated and realleged as if fully set forth herein.

82. For the tax years 1997-2001, RUBLE knowingly omitted from his U.S. Individual Income Tax Returns over $1,482,000 in income in the form of side payments paid to him by the CC-10-related entities and by the LARSON and PFAFF nominee entities.

83. From on or about January 1 of each of the calendar years set forth below, through at least on or about the filing dates set forth below for each said calendar year, in the Southern District of New York and elsewhere, the defendants listed below, unlawfully, wilfully, and knowingly, did attempt to evade and defeat a substantial part of the income taxes due and owing by RUBLE to the United States of America for the calendar years 1998-2001 by various means, including, among others (a) opening and causing to be opened in New York, New York a bank account in the name of a trust controlled by RUBLE; (b) depositing and causing to be deposited in this trust bank account in New York, New York and another bank account certain side payments he received from tax shelter promoters; (c) falsely informing the RUBLE Law Firm that he had no outside income; (d) causing the issuance by the RUBLE Law Firm of IRS Forms K-1 that under-reported RUBLE's income for the calendar years 1998-2001; and (e) preparing and causing to be prepared, signing and causing to be signed, and filing and causing to be filed with the IRS, false and fraudulent U. S. Individual Income Tax Returns, Forms 1040, for the calendar years 1998-2001, which returns falsely omitted income in the amounts set forth below, which falsities caused RAYMOND J. RUBLE to

substantially understate his taxable income and tax due and owing each year, as set forth below:

Count	Defendant	[illegible]	[illegible]	[illegible]	[illegible]
41	RAYMOND J. RUBLE, JOHN LARSON, ROBERT PFAFF	1998	10/15/99	$350,000	$148,089
42	RAYMOND J. RUBLE	1999	09/30/00	$175,000	$71,379
43	RAYMOND J. RUBLE, JOHN LARSON, ROBERT PFAFF	2000	10/15/01	$250,000	$107,299
44	RAYMOND J. RUBLE	2001	10/15/02	$500,000	$201,365

(Title 26, United States Code, Section 7201, Title 18, United States Code, Section 2.)

COUNTS FORTY-FIVE AND FORTY-SIX
(Obstruction of the IRS)

The Grand Jury further charges:

84. The allegations set forth in paragraphs 1-71 are repeated and realleged as if fully set forth herein.

85. On or about the dates set forth below, in the Southern District of New York and elsewhere, the defendants listed below unlawfully, wilfully, and knowingly did corruptly obstruct and impede and endeavor to obstruct and impede the due administration of the Internal Revenue laws by committing or causing to be committed the acts set forth below:

45	10/02/2002	RICHARD SMITH, STEVEN GREMMINGER	False statement to the IRS in the SDNY that "KPMG has at this time virtually completed its compliance with the summonses"
46	05/28/2003	JEFFREY EISCHEID, STEVEN GREMMINGER	Telephone call by KPMG representative to IRS representatives in the SDNY and Washington, D.C. falsely claiming that KPMG did not promote or market SOS, but KPMG prepared at least 2 tax returns relating to SOS.

(Title 26, United States Code, Section 7212, Title 18, United States Code, Section 2.)

FOREPERSON

MICHAEL J. GARCIA
United States Attorney

Form No. USA-33s-274 (Ed. 9-25-58)

UNITED STATES DISTRICT COURT
SOUTHERN DISTRICT OF NEW YORK

UNITED STATES OF AMERICA

- v -

JEFFREY STEIN,
JOHN LANNING,
RICHARD SMITH,
JEFFREY EISCHEID,
PHILIP WIESNER,
JOHN LARSON,
ROBERT PFAFF,
DAVID AMIR MAKOV,
LARRY DELAP,
STEVEN GREMMINGER,
RAYMOND J. RUBLE,
also known as "R.J. Ruble,"
GREGG RITCHIE,
RANDY BICKHAM,
MARK WATSON,
CAROL WARLEY,
DAVID RIVKIN,
CARL HASTING,
RICHARD ROSENTHAL, and
DAVID GREENBERG,

Defendants.

SUPERSEDING INDICTMENT

S1 05 Cr. 888 (LAK)

18 U.S.C. § 371, 26 U.S.C. §§ 7201, 7212,
18 U.S.C. § 2

MICHAEL J. GARCIA
United States Attorney.

A TRUE BILL

Foreperson.

Appendix F

JURY INSTRUCTIONS RE WESLEY TRENT SNIPES

UNITED STATES DISTRICT COURT
MIDDLE DISTRICT OF FLORIDA
OCALA DIVISION

FILED IN OPEN COURT
OCALA, FLORIDA
FEB -1 2008
U. S. DISTRICT COURT
MIDDLE DISTRICT OF FLORIDA

UNITED STATES OF AMERICA

-vs-

CASE NO. 5:06-cr-22-Oc-10GRJ

WESLEY TRENT SNIPES
EDDIE RAY KAHN
DOUGLAS P. ROSILE

COURT'S INSTRUCTIONS TO THE JURY

Members of the Jury:

It is now my duty to instruct you on the rules of law that you must follow and apply in deciding this case. When I have finished you will go to the jury room and begin your discussions — what we call your deliberations.

It will be your duty to decide whether the Government has proved beyond a reasonable doubt the specific facts necessary to find the Defendant guilty of the crime charged in the indictment.

You must make your decision only on the basis of the testimony and other evidence presented here during the trial; and you must not be influenced in any way by either sympathy or prejudice for or against the Defendant or the Government.

You must also follow the law as I explain it to you whether you agree with that law or not; and you must follow all of my instructions as a whole. You may not single out, or disregard, any of the Court's instructions on the law.

The indictment or formal charge against any Defendant is not evidence of guilt. Indeed, every Defendant is presumed by the law to be innocent. The law does not require a Defendant to prove innocence or to produce any evidence at all; and if a Defendant elects not to testify, you cannot consider that in any way during your deliberations. The Government has the burden of proving a Defendant guilty beyond a reasonable doubt, and if it fails to do so you must find that Defendant not guilty.

Thus, while the Government's burden of proof is a strict or heavy burden, it is not necessary that a Defendant's guilt be proved beyond all possible doubt. It is only required that the Government's proof exclude any "reasonable doubt" concerning the Defendant's guilt.

A "reasonable doubt" is a real doubt, based upon reason and common sense after careful and impartial consideration of all the evidence in the case.

Proof beyond a reasonable doubt, therefore, is proof of such a convincing character that you would be willing to rely and act upon it without hesitation in the most important of your own affairs. If you are convinced that the Defendant has been proved guilty beyond a reasonable doubt, say so. If you are not convinced, say so.

As I said earlier, you must consider only the evidence that I have admitted in the case. The term "evidence" includes the testimony of the witnesses and the exhibits admitted in the record. Remember that anything the lawyers say is not evidence in the case. It is your own recollection and interpretation of the evidence that controls. What the lawyers say is not binding upon you. Also, you should not assume from anything I may have said that I have any opinion concerning any of the issues in this case. Except for my instructions to you on the law, you should disregard anything I may have said during the trial in arriving at your own decision concerning the facts.

In considering the evidence you may make deductions and reach conclusions which reason and common sense lead you to make; and you should not be concerned about whether the evidence is direct or circumstantial. "Direct evidence" is the testimony of one who asserts actual knowledge of a fact, such as an eye witness. "Circumstantial evidence" is proof of a chain of facts and circumstances tending to prove, or disprove, any fact in dispute. The law makes no distinction between the weight you may give to either direct or circumstantial evidence.

Now, in saying that you must consider all of the evidence, I do not mean that you must accept all of the evidence as true or accurate. You should decide whether you believe what each witness had to say, and how important that testimony was. In making that decision you may believe or disbelieve any witness, in whole or in part. Also, the number of witnesses testifying concerning any particular dispute is not controlling.

In deciding whether you believe or do not believe any witness I suggest that you ask yourself a few questions: Did the witness impress you as one who was telling the truth? Did the witness have any particular reason not to tell the truth? Did the witness have a personal interest in the outcome of the case? Did the witness seem to have a good memory? Did the witness have the opportunity and ability to observe accurately the things he or she testified about? Did the witness appear to understand the questions clearly and answer them directly? Did the witness's testimony differ from other testimony or other evidence?

You should also ask yourself whether there was evidence tending to prove that a witness testified falsely concerning some important fact; or, whether there was evidence that at some other time a witness said or did something, or failed to say or do something, which was different from the testimony the witness gave before you during the trial.

You should keep in mind, of course, that a simple mistake by a witness does not necessarily mean that the witness was not telling the truth as he or she remembers it, because people naturally tend to forget some things or remember other things inaccurately. So, if a witness has made a misstatement, you need to consider whether it was simply an innocent lapse of memory or an intentional falsehood; and the significance of that may depend on whether it has to do with an important fact or with only an unimportant detail.

When knowledge of a technical subject matter might be helpful to the jury, a person having special training or experience in that technical field is permitted to state an opinion concerning those technical matters.

Merely because such a witness has expressed an opinion, however, does not mean that you must accept that opinion. The same as with any other witness, it is up to you to decide whether to rely upon it.

In this case you have been permitted to take notes during the course of the trial, and most of you — perhaps all of you — have taken advantage of that opportunity and have made notes from time to time.

You will have your notes available to you during your deliberations, but you should make use of them only as an aid to your memory. In other words, you should not give your notes any precedence over your independent recollection of the evidence or the lack of evidence; and neither should you be unduly influenced by the notes of other jurors.

I emphasize that notes are not entitled to any greater weight than the memory or impression of each juror as to what the testimony may have been.

As you know, the Indictment charges eight separate offenses called "Counts." I will not read it to you at length because you will be given a full copy of the Indictment for reference during your deliberations.

As you will see, Count One of the Indictment — the alleged conspiracy offense — contains allegations that were not included in the abbreviated form of the Indictment contained in your jury books at the beginning of the trial.

With regard to the conspiracy offense charged in Count One, it is alleged that the Defendants knowingly and willfully conspired together to defraud the United States by impeding, impairing, obstructing, or defeating the lawful government functions of the IRS in the ascertainment, computation, assessment and collection of the revenue. Included in Count One are allegations of Overt Acts that one or more of the alleged conspirators are charged to have committed in furtherance of the conspiracy. I will explain that more fully in just a moment.

Count Two of the Indictment charges each of the Defendants with the commission of what is known as a substantive offense, namely, the knowing and willful presentation of a materially false, fictitious or fraudulent claim for payment against the United States in the form of an amended federal income tax return (Form 1040X) for the Defendant Snipes for the tax year 1997.

Counts Three through Eight of the Indictment, respectively, charge the Defendant Snipes alone with the offense of willfully failing to file an income tax return for each of the tax years 1999 through 2004.

I will explain the law governing each of the alleged substantive offenses in a moment. First, however, as to Count One, you will note that the Defendants are not charged in that Count with committing a substantive offense; rather, they are charged with having conspired to do so.

Title 18, United States Code, Section 371, makes it a Federal crime or offense for anyone to conspire or agree with someone else to defraud the United States or any of its agencies. To "defraud" the United States means to interfere with or obstruct one of its lawful governmental functions by deceit, craft or trickery.

A "conspiracy" is simply an agreement or a kind of "partnership" in criminal purposes in which each member becomes the agent or partner of every other member.

In order to establish a conspiracy offense it is <u>not</u> necessary for the Government to prove that all of the people named in the indictment were members of the scheme; <u>or</u> that those who <u>were</u> members had entered into any formal type of agreement; or that the members had planned together all of the details of the scheme or the "overt acts" that the indictment charges would be carried out in an effort to commit the intended crime.

Also, because the essence of a conspiracy offense is the making of the agreement itself (followed by the commission of any overt act), it is not necessary for the Government to prove that the conspirators actually succeeded in accomplishing their unlawful plan.

What the evidence in the case <u>must</u> show beyond a reasonable doubt is:

<u>First</u>: That two or more persons, in some way or manner, came to a mutual understanding to try to accomplish a common and unlawful plan, as charged in the indictment;

<u>Second</u>: That the Defendant, knowing the unlawful purpose of the plan, willfully joined in it;

<u>Third</u>: That one of the conspirators during the existence of the conspiracy knowingly committed at least one of the methods (or "overt acts") described in the indictment; and

<u>Fourth</u>: That such "overt act" was knowingly committed at or about the time alleged in an effort to carry out or accomplish some object of the conspiracy.

An "overt act" is any transaction or event, even one which may be entirely innocent when considered alone, but which is knowingly committed by a conspirator in an effort to accomplish some object of the conspiracy.

A person may become a member of a conspiracy without knowing all of the details of the unlawful scheme, and without knowing who all of the other members are. So, if a Defendant has a general understanding of the unlawful purpose of the plan and knowingly and willfully joins in that plan on one occasion, that is sufficient to convict that Defendant for conspiracy even though the Defendant did not participate before, and even though the Defendant played only a minor part.

Of course, mere presence at the scene of a transaction or event, or the mere fact that certain persons may have associated with each other, and may have assembled together and discussed common aims and interests, does not, standing alone, establish proof of a conspiracy. Also, a person who has no knowledge of a conspiracy, but who happens to act in a way which advances some purpose of one, does not thereby become a conspirator.

You are instructed that documents characterized as returns but which contain no financial information are not returns within the meaning of 26 U.S.C. § 7203.

Also, there is no legal merit to the "U. S. Sources argument" or the "Section 861 argument" claiming that the Internal Revenue Code only imposes taxes on certain foreign-based activities.

Title 18, United States Code, Section 287, makes it a Federal crime or offense for anyone to knowingly make a false claim against any department or agency of the United States.

You are instructed that the Internal Revenue Service is a department or agency of the United States within the meaning of that law.

The Defendant can be found guilty of the offense of making a false claim against the Government only if all of the following facts are proved beyond a reasonable doubt:

First:	That the Defendant knowingly presented to an agency of the United States a false or fraudulent claim against the United States, as charged in the indictment;
Second:	That the false or fraudulent aspect of the claim related to a material fact; and
Third:	That the Defendant acted willfully and with knowledge of the false or fraudulent nature of the claim.

A claim is "false" or "fraudulent" if it is untrue at the time it is made and is then known to be untrue by the person making it. It is not necessary to show, however, that the Government agency was in fact deceived or misled.

The making of a false or fraudulent claim is not an offense unless the falsity or fraudulent aspect of the claim relates to a "material" fact. A misrepresentation is "material" if it relates to an important fact, as distinguished from some unimportant or trivial detail, and has a natural tendency to influence, or was capable of influencing, the decision of the department or agency in making a determination required to be made.

The guilt of a Defendant in a criminal case may be proved without evidence that the Defendant personally did every act involved in the commission of the crime charged. The law recognizes that, ordinarily, anything a person can do for one's self may also be accomplished through direction of another person as an agent, or by acting together with, or under the direction of, another person or persons in a joint effort.

So, if the acts or conduct of an agent, employee or other associate of the Defendant are willfully directed or authorized by the Defendant, or if the Defendant aids and abets another person by willfully joining together with that person in the commission of a crime, then the law holds the Defendant responsible for the conduct of that other person just as though the Defendant had personally engaged in such conduct.

However, before any Defendant can be held criminally responsible for the conduct of others it is necessary that the Defendant willfully associate in some way with the crime, and willfully participate in it. Mere presence at the scene of a crime and even knowledge that a crime is being committed are not sufficient to establish that a Defendant either directed or aided and abetted the crime. You must find beyond a reasonable doubt that the Defendant was a willful participant and not merely a knowing spectator.

Title 26, United States Code, Section 7203, makes it a Federal crime or offense for anyone to willfully fail to file a federal income tax return when required to do so by the Internal Revenue laws or regulations.

The Defendant Snipes can be found guilty of that offense as charged in Counts Three through Eight, respectively, only if all of the following facts are proved beyond a reasonable doubt:

<u>First</u>: That the Defendant was required by law or regulation to make a return of his income for the taxable year charged;

<u>Second</u>: That the Defendant failed to file a return at the time required by law; and

<u>Third</u>: That the Defendant's failure to file the return was willful.

A single person under sixty-five years old was required to file a federal income tax return for the years 1999, 2000, 2001, and 2002 if he had gross income in excess of:

$7,050 for 1999;
$7,200 for 2000;
$7,450 for 2001;
$7,700 for 2002.

A married individual was required to file a federal income tax return for the year 2003 if he had a separate gross income in excess of $3,050, and total gross income, when combined with that of his or her spouse in excess of $15,600 where both were under sixty-five years old.

A married individual was required to file a federal income tax return for the year 2004 if he had a separate gross income in excess of $3,100, and a total gross income, when combined with that of his or her spouse, in excess of $15,900 where both were under sixty-five years old.

"Gross income" includes compensation for services, including fees, commissions and similar items; gains derived from dealing in property; and income derived from business including interest; rents; royalties; and dividends.

The Defendant is a person required to file a return if the Defendant's gross income for any calendar year exceeds the amounts given above even though the Defendant may be entitled to deductions from that income in a sufficient amount so that no tax is due. So, the Government is not required to prove that a tax was due and owing, or that the Defendant intended to evade or defeat payment of taxes, only that the Defendant willfully failed to file the return.

There is an issue in this case as to whether the Government has established what is known as proper "venue" in this court with respect to Counts Three through Eight of the indictment — the failure to file charges against Defendant Snipes.

The Sixth Amendment to the Constitution of the United States protects certain fundamental rights of any Defendant in a criminal case. One of the things it says is that "the accused shall enjoy the right to a . . . trial . . . in the state and district wherein the crime shall have been committed." This creates what is called a proper venue for the charging of any criminal offense, and it requires the Government to prove, as alleged in the indictment, that the charged offense or offenses were committed in the Middle District of Florida.

In that respect, you are instructed that both Lake and Orange Counties, among others, are within the Middle District of Florida.

You are further instructed that proper venue with respect to Counts Three through Eight, respectively, lies in the district of the Defendant Snipes' legal residence; and the term "legal residence" means the permanent fixed place of abode which one intends to be his residence and to return to it despite absences or temporary residence elsewhere.

On this issue of proper venue, and on that issue alone, you are instructed that the Government's burden of proof is somewhat less stringent than it is with respect to all of the other matters the Government must prove beyond a reasonable doubt as I have previously explained to you. Specifically, the Government must prove proper venue — that the alleged crime was committed within this district — by a "preponderance of the evidence." A preponderance of the evidence means evidence that is enough to persuade you that it is more likely than not or more probable than not that the alleged crime was committed within this district as charged. If the Government has failed to establish proper venue as to any of Counts Three through Eight by a preponderance of the evidence, you must acquit the Defendant as to that Count or those Counts.

Good faith is a complete defense to the charges in the indictment since good faith on the part of the Defendant is inconsistent with intent to defraud or willfulness which is an essential part of the charges. The burden of proof is not on the Defendant to prove good faith, of course, since the Defendant has no burden to prove anything. The Government must establish beyond a reasonable doubt that the Defendant acted with specific intent to defraud or willfulness as charged in the indictment.

So, with regard to the issue of willfulness, a Defendant would not be "willfully" doing wrong if, before taking any action with regard to the alleged offense, the Defendant consulted in good faith an attorney whom the Defendant considered competent, made a full and accurate report to that attorney of all material facts of which the Defendant had the means of knowledge, and then acted strictly in accordance with the advice given by that attorney.

Whether the Defendant acted in good faith for the purpose of seeking advice concerning questions about which the Defendant was in doubt and whether the Defendant made a full and complete report to the attorney, and whether the Defendant acted strictly in accordance with the advice received, are all questions for you to determine.

Similarly, with regard to the issue of fraudulent intent, one who expresses an honestly held opinion, or an honestly formed belief, is not chargeable with fraudulent intent even though the opinion is erroneous or the belief is mistaken; and, similarly, evidence with [*sic*: which] establishes only that a person made a mistake in judgment or an error in management, or was careless, does not establish fraudulent intent.

On the other hand, an honest belief on the part of the Defendant that a particular transaction was sound and would ultimately succeed would not, in and of itself, constitute "good faith" as that term is used in these instructions if, in carrying out that venture, the Defendant knowingly made false or fraudulent representations to others with the specific intent to deceive them.

You will note that the indictment charges that the offense was committed "on or about" a certain date. The Government does not have to prove with certainty the exact date of the alleged offense. It is sufficient if the Government proves beyond a reasonable doubt that the offense was committed on a date reasonably near the date alleged.

The word "knowingly," as that term is used in the indictment or in these instructions, means that the act was done voluntarily and intentionally and not because of mistake or accident.

The word "willfully," as that term is used in the indictment or in these instructions, means that the act was committed voluntarily and purposely, with the specific intent to do something the law forbids; that is with bad purpose either to disobey or disregard the law.

A separate crime or offense is charged against one or more of the Defendants in each count of the indictment. Each charge, and the evidence pertaining to it, should be considered separately. Also, the case of each Defendant should be considered separately and individually. The fact that you may find any one or more of the Defendants guilty or not guilty of any of the offenses charged should not affect your verdict as to any other offense or any other Defendant.

I caution you, members of the Jury, that you are here to determine from the evidence in this case whether each Defendant is guilty or not guilty. Each Defendant is on trial only for the specific offense alleged in the indictment.

Also, the question of punishment should never be considered by the jury in any way in deciding the case. If a Defendant is convicted the matter of punishment is for the Judge alone to determine later.

Any verdict you reach in the jury room, whether guilty or not guilty, must be unanimous. In other words, to return a verdict you must all agree. Your deliberations will be secret; you will never have to explain your verdict to anyone.

It is your duty as jurors to discuss the case with one another in an effort to reach agreement if you can do so. Each of you must decide the case for yourself, but only after full consideration of the evidence with the other members of the jury. While you are discussing the case do not hesitate to reexamine your own opinion and change your mind if you become convinced that you were wrong. But do not give up your honest beliefs solely because the others think differently or merely to get the case over with.

Remember, that in a very real way you are judges — judges of the facts. Your only interest is to seek the truth from the evidence in the case.

When you go to the jury room you should first select one of your members to act as your foreperson. The foreperson will preside over your deliberations and will speak for you here in court.

A form of verdict has been prepared for your convenience.

[Explain verdict]

You will take the verdict form to the jury room and when you have reached unanimous agreement you will have your foreperson fill in the verdict form, date and sign it, and then return to the courtroom.

If you should desire to communicate with me at any time, please write down your message or question and pass the note to the marshal who will bring it to my attention. I will then respond as promptly as possible, either in writing or by having you returned to the courtroom so that I can address you orally. I caution you, however, with regard to any message or question you might send, that you should not tell me your numerical division at the time.

Appendix G

JUDGMENT RE WESLEY TRENT SNIPES

UNITED STATES DISTRICT COURT
MIDDLE DISTRICT OF FLORIDA
OCALA DIVISION

UNITED STATES OF AMERICA

-vs-

Case Number: 5:06-cr-22-Oc-10GRJ

WESLEY TRENT SNIPES

USM Number: 43355-018

Daniel R. Meachum, Retained
1995 North Park Place, Suite 250
Atlanta, Georgia 30339

JUDGMENT IN A CRIMINAL CASE

The defendant was found guilty by jury verdict on Counts Three, Four, and Five of the Superseding Indictment. Accordingly, the court has adjudicated that the defendant is guilty of the following offenses:

Title & Section	Nature of Offense	Date Offense Concluded	Count Numbers
26 U.S.C. §7203	Wilful Failure to File Tax Return	October 12, 2006	Three, Four, and Five

The defendant is sentenced as provided in the following pages of this judgment. The sentence is imposed pursuant to the Sentencing Reform Act of 1984.

The defendant has been found not guilty by jury verdict on Counts One, Two, Six, Seven, and Eight of the Superseding Indictment.

Original Indictment dismissed on the motion of the United States.

IT IS ORDERED that the defendant shall notify the United States attorney for this district within 30 days of any change of name, residence, or mailing address until all fines, restitution, costs and special assessments imposed by this judgment are fully paid. If ordered to pay restitution, the defendant shall notify the court and United States attorney of any material change in the defendant's economic circumstances.

Date of Imposition of Sentence: April 24, 2008

UNITED STATES DISTRICT JUDGE

May 1, 2008

WESLEY TRENT SNIPES
5:06-cr-22-Oc-10GRJ

IMPRISONMENT

The defendant is hereby committed to the custody of the United States Bureau of Prisons to be imprisoned for a total term of **twelve (12) months as to Count Three, twelve (12) months as to Count Four, and twelve (12) months as to Count Five, respectively, to be served consecutively for a total, aggregate term of commitment of thirty-six (36) months.**

The Court recommends to the Bureau of Prisons: that the defendant be designated to a place of confinement as near as possible to his home in New Jersey.

The defendant shall surrender for service of sentence at the institution designated by the Bureau of Prisons as notified by the United States Marshal.

RETURN

I have executed this judgment as follows:

____

____

____

____

Defendant delivered on ________________ to ______________________

at ______________________________, with a certified copy of this judgment.

____
UNITED STATES MARSHAL

By:________________________
Deputy U.S. Marshal

WESLEY TRENT SNIPES
5:06-cr-22-Oc-10GRJ

SUPERVISED RELEASE

Upon release from imprisonment, the defendant shall be on supervised release for a term of **one (1) year**. The defendant shall report to the probation office in the district to which the defendant is released within 72 hours of release from custody of the Bureau of Prisons.

The defendant shall not commit another federal, state or local crime.

The defendant shall not illegally possess a controlled substance.

For offenses committed on or after September 13, 1994:

The mandatory drug testing requirements of the Violent Crime Control Act are imposed. The Court authorizes random drug testing not to exceed 104 tests per year.

The defendant shall not possess a firearm, destructive device, or any other dangerous weapon.

If this judgment imposes a fine or a restitution obligation, it shall be a condition of supervision that the defendant pay any such fine or restitution that remains unpaid at the commencement of the term of supervision in accordance with the Schedule of Payments set forth in the Criminal Monetary Penalties sheet of this judgment.

The defendant shall comply with the standard conditions that have been adopted by this court (set forth below). The defendant shall also comply with the additional conditions on the attached page.

STANDARD CONDITIONS OF SUPERVISION

1. The defendant shall not leave the judicial district without the permission of the court or probation officer;
2. The defendant shall report to the probation officer and shall submit a truthful and complete written report within the first five days of each month;
3. The defendant shall answer truthfully all inquiries by the probation officer and follow the instructions of the probation officer;
4. The defendant shall support his or her dependents and meet other family responsibilities;
5. The defendant shall work regularly at a lawful occupation, unless excused by the probation officer for schooling, training, or other acceptable reasons;
6. The defendant shall notify the probation officer **at least ten (10) days prior** to any change in residence or employment;
7. The defendant shall refrain from excessive use of alcohol and shall not purchase, possess, use, distribute, or administer any controlled substance or any paraphernalia related to any controlled substances, except as prescribed by a physician;
8. The defendant shall not frequent places where controlled substances are illegally sold, used, distributed, or administered;
9. The defendant shall not associate with any persons engaged in criminal activity and shall not associate with any person convicted of a felony, unless granted permission to do so by the probation officer;
10. The defendant shall permit a probation officer to visit him or her at any time at home or elsewhere and shall permit confiscation of any contraband observed in plain view by the probation officer;
11. The defendant shall notify the probation officer within **seventy-two (72) hours** of being arrested or questioned by a law enforcement officer;

WESLEY TRENT SNIPES
5:06-cr-22-Oc-10GRJ

12. The defendant shall not enter into any agreement to act as an informer or a special agent of a law enforcement agency without the permission of the court;

13. As directed by the probation officer, the defendant shall notify third parties of risks that may be occasioned by the defendant's criminal record or personal history or characteristics, and shall permit the probation officer to make such notifications and to confirm the defendant's compliance with such notification requirement.

ADDITIONAL CONDITIONS OF SUPERVISED RELEASE

The defendant shall also comply with the following additional conditions of supervised release:

1. The defendant shall comply with all tax laws of the United States;

2. The defendant shall settle any outstanding federal tax obligations, including any such obligations which he may have incurred during his term of imprisonment, within six months of the commencement of the supervised release term;

3. The defendant is required to disclose to his supervising Probation Officer any requested financial information;

4. The defendant shall be barred from promoting any unlawful scheme, the purpose of which is the evasion of taxes, and

5. The defendant shall cooperate in the collection of DNA, as directed by the Probation Officer.

CRIMINAL MONETARY PENALTIES

The defendant shall pay the following total criminal monetary penalties in accordance with the schedule of payments set forth in the Schedule of Payments.

Total Assessment	Total Fine	Total Restitution
$75.00	$0.00	$0.00

The defendant shall pay interest on any fine or restitution of more than $2,500, unless the fine or restitution is paid in full before the fifteenth day after the date of the judgment, pursuant to 18 U.S.C. § 3612(f). All of the payment options on the Schedule of Payments may be subject to penalties for delinquency and default, pursuant to 18 U.S.C. § 3612(g).

*Findings for the total amount of losses are required under Chapters 109A, 110, 110A, and 113A of Title 18, United States Code, for offenses committed on or after September 13, 1994 but before April 23, 1996.

SCHEDULE OF PAYMENTS

Having assessed the defendant's ability to pay, payment of the total criminal monetary penalties shall be due as follows:

Unless the court has expressly ordered otherwise in the special instructions above, if this judgment imposes a period of imprisonment, payment of criminal monetary penalties shall be due during the period of imprisonment. All criminal monetary penalties, except those payments made through the Federal Bureau of Prisons' Inmate Financial Responsibility Program, are made to the clerk of the court, unless otherwise directed by the court, the probation officer, or the United States attorney.

The defendant shall receive credit for all payments previously made toward any criminal monetary penalties imposed.

Appendix H

CRIMINAL COMPLAINT

UNITED STATES DISTRICT COURT
MIDDLE DISTRICT OF FLORIDA
TAMPA DIVISION

UNITED STATES OF AMERICA

vs.

RANDY NOWAK

CRIMINAL COMPLAINT

CASE NUMBER: 8:08-m-
8:08MJ1362TBM

I, the undersigned complainant, being duly sworn, state the following is true and correct to the best of my knowledge and belief. On or about June 24, 2008, in Polk County, in the Middle District of Florida, the defendant did,

attempt to kill an officer or employee of the United States while such officer or employee is engaged in or on account of the performance of official duties

in violation of Title 18, United States Code, Section 1114. I further state that I am a Special Agent with U.S. Treasury Inspector General for Tax Administration, and that this Complaint is based on the following facts:

SEE ATTACHED AFFIDAVIT

Continued on the attached sheet and made a part hereof: ☒ Yes ☐ No

Signature of Complainant
Robert W. Courtenay

Sworn to before me and subscribed in my presence,

July 30, 2008 at Tampa, Florida

THOMAS B. MCCOUN, III
United States Magistrate Judge
Name & Title of Judicial Officer

Signature of Judicial Officer

AFFIDAVIT

I, Robert W. Courtenay, being duly sworn, depose and state the following:

Introduction

1. I am a Special Agent (SA) with the United States Treasury Inspector General for Tax Administration (TIGTA) and have been so for over eighteen (18) years. I am currently assigned to the Atlanta Field Division (AFD), Tampa, Florida office. I have investigated matters involving threats and assaults committed against employees of the Internal Revenue Service (IRS), particularly in relation to violations of 18 U.S.C. § 111 (assaulting, resisting or impeding certain officers or employees) and 26 U.S.C. § 7212 (attempts to interfere with administration of Internal Revenue laws). I have also received training in investigating and making arrests in cases involving threats to and assaults on IRS employees.

2. Your affiant has developed probable cause to believe that Randy Nowak, owner of RJ Nowak Enterprises, Inc. has taken substantial steps to hire an individual to have IRS Revenue Officer Christine Brandt killed in a "murder for hire" plot, in violation of Title 18, United States Code, Section 1114. Specifically, your affiant has been able to confirm that Nowak has agreed to pay an undercover FBI agent (UC) posing as a hit man $20,000 to have IRS employee Brandt murdered, and in fact has already paid the UC $10,000 as a down payment.

3. The statements contained in this affidavit are based in part upon information gathered by myself, Special Agents of the Federal Bureau of Investigation (FBI), conversations held with other agents and officers from state and local law enforcement agencies, information obtained from a confidential source (CS), the

statements of Nowak consensually recorded during telephone and in person conversations, and your affiant's experience and background as a law enforcement officer. This affidavit does not set forth every fact resulting from the investigation; rather, it sets forth facts sufficient to establish probable cause.

Statutes and Definitions

4. Title 18, United States Code, Section 1114 prohibits a person from killing or attempting to kill any officer or employee of the United States or of any agency in any branch of the United States government while such officer or employee is engaged in or on account of the performance of official duties.

Background of the Investigation

5. On or about June 24, 2008, Detective [redacted] of the Polk County Sheriff's Office (PCSO) reported to the FBI that he had received information from a CS that Randy Nowak, an individual who lives in and has a business in Polk County, had been asking around to find someone to kill a female IRS employee. According to the information provided to the PCSO, Nowak sought to kill the IRS employee because she was auditing Nowak and Nowak stood to lose $4,000,000 that he had hidden offshore. The CS also told Detective Bellamy that Nowak was willing to pay $75,000 to have this IRS employee "deleted," that Nowak wanted to meet with the CS to discuss this further, and that he was ready to contact someone else if the CS could not find anyone to do the job. That same day, Detective Bellamy alerted the FBI's Lakeland, FL Resident Agency concerning this matter.

6. Your affiant has learned that Nowak had, at the time of the PCSO report, an outstanding liability to the IRS of approximately $300,000 related to his personal

income tax obligations. In addition, your affiant believes, based on Nowak's statements, that Nowak has approximately $4,000,000 hidden offshore in a Jamaican bank account that he is concerned the IRS will locate. Finally, at the time of the report to the PCSO, Nowak had four years of outstanding corporate tax returns for his business RJ Nowak Enterprises, Inc. that he had not filed. Your affiant has also confirmed that IRS Revenue Officer Christine Brandt was the Revenue Officer assigned to Nowak's case.

7. On or about June 24, 2008, your affiant, along with FBI SA Vincent Jones, interviewed the CS who corroborated the information reported to the PCSO. The CS further reported Nowak must have felt comfortable asking the CS to find someone to kill the IRS employee because although the CS was never a member, the CS used to ride motorcycles with the Outlaws Motorcycle Gang. The CS stated that based upon this information, Nowak believed the CS could find someone to perform a "hit." The CS reported to your affiant that Nowak told him of his intentions during a meeting between them on June 23, 2008, while Nowak was riding in the CS' vehicle with the CS. The CS said that Nowak told him that the IRS employee had all of his paperwork, and if he had her "bumped off," that would end the paper trail. Nowak told the CS he had already called someone who told him he could perform the hit for $75,000, but that was "too steep." On or about June 24, 2008, the CS agreed to begin recording telephone and in person conversations between himself and Nowak and to aid your affiant and the FBI with their investigations.

8. Pursuant to his cooperation and in consultation with your affiant and the FBI, the CS informed Nowak that he could put him in touch with someone to perform the

murder for hire and that the cost would be $20,000. Nowak agreed to this course of action.

9. On or about June 26, 2008, at approximately 8:47 am, Nowak called the CS. During the consensually monitored telephone call, Nowak asked if the CS was doing alright and if this "thing," i.e. the hiring of the hit man, would cause any distance between them. During the recorded call, Nowak further advised the CS that he would come by the CS's place of business later that day.

10. Later that same day, on or about Thursday, June 26, 2008, at approximately 10:34 a.m., Nowak met with the CS at the CS's place of business. The CS consensually recorded the conversation. During their meeting, Nowak said that he intended to meet with his attorney and she would meet with the tax expert to see where Nowak stood with respect to his tax obligations. Nowak elaborated that he would know Monday after talking with his tax attorney what direction he would have to go. Nowak asked if the CS had spoken to his "guy." The CS advised Nowak that his guy would trust Nowak so long as the CS trusted Nowak. The CS also told Nowak that the guy, a/k/a the hit man, would meet with Nowak if Nowak wanted. Nowak then asked, "Is the less I know, the better off I am or what?" The CS replied, "Yes." Nowak stated, "Because there's nothing tying me to it, and there's nothing tying me to him, nothing tying him to me, but it's pretty much a guaranteed thing." Nowak also stated, "Once you start it, you can't stop it." The CS replied, "Make sure it's what you want to do." Nowak explained that he owed the IRS thousands of dollars and told the CS, "I'm going broke on fucking gas and they don't do shit for me. This fucking lady, she has absolutely no personality at all, she's not demeaning, she's not degrading, she's like a fucking

machine, methodical, going down the line." Nowak also stated, "The government has been talking about doing something to regulate the IRS because they are out of control." Nowak continued, "So just 10 up, and 10 when it's done," referring to the price he would have to pay the hit man. The CS replied, "yeah, $10,000 I was told down, and $10,000 when it's done." Nowak then asked, "It's not like I am going to lose my 10 grand?" Nowak also stated, "It's a crime just talking about it." The CS stated that was why he told him to make sure it's what he wanted to do before he did it. Nowak then questioned if the hit man was affiliated with the Outlaws, and the CS replied, "yeah." Nowak observed, "They [the Outlaws] are pretty thorough" and that "They [the Outlaws] are pretty loyal to one another." Nowak also told the CS he felt someone "ratted" him out to the IRS. Finally, Nowak asked the CS, "This won't change anything between you and I would it?"

11. On or about July 1, 2008, at approximately 1:33 p.m., during a consensually monitored telephone call, the CS told Nowak that the CS had spoken to the hit man, whose name was "Reaper," and that the CS had known "Reaper" for a long time. The CS told Nowak that Nowak did not have to worry about "Reaper" and that the CS had given Nowak's cell phone number to "Reaper." The CS then stated to Nowak, "If you don't want to talk to him that's fine -- just hang up on him." Nowak asked, "You've known him a long time so it's all good right?" The CS replied in the affirmative. Nowak also said that he did not want something to happen during the meeting with "Reaper" that would cause him (Nowak) to get "nailed." Nowak said, "My big worry is I don't want to get nailed either way. I'm trying to avoid a situation not getting myself pulled into another one."

12. On or about July 7, 2008, during a consensually monitored telephone call between Nowak and the CS, Nowak told the CS that he (Nowak) did not see any other way to resolve his situation with the IRS and that he was getting what he needed together (i.e. the money) in order to go forward with the plan to hire Reaper to kill the IRS employee. Nowak also told the CS that "Reaper" had yet to contact him.

13. On or about July 10, 2008, the CS reported to SA Jones of the FBI that during a meeting that day with Nowak at approximately 9:00 a.m., Nowak asked the CS how "Reaper" was going to kill the IRS employee and asked whether the employee would be shot or would she just disappear. The CS replied that he did not know and directed Nowak to discuss the matter with "Reaper." During that same meeting, Nowak told the CS that he could get $20,000 from a friend as a loan because his bank accounts were frozen by the IRS. Nowak further explained that he was prepared to pay "Reaper" $10,000 one week and $10,000 a week to a week and a half later in exchange for murdering IRS employee Brandt. Nowak also told the CS that he was in possession of the IRS employee's name and that he (Nowak) was 90% sure that he knew her home address.

14. On or about July 12, 2008, at approximately 5:06 p.m., the UC, posing as "Reaper," telephoned Nowak on Nowak's cellular telephone. An unidentified male answered. The UC asked, "Is this Randy," and the male responded, "yes." The UC/"Reaper" then stated that the CS had advised him (the UC) to call Nowak regarding a personal matter. Nowak replied, "Yes, but I have my wife and kids here. I am unable to talk." The UC told Nowak that the number he (the UC) had called on was a good

number for Nowak to call him back. They agreed that they would speak in a few days. Nowak concluded the conversation by stating, "looking forward to it."

15. On or about July 15, 2008, at approximately 10:20 a.m., during a consensually monitored telephone call, Nowak told the CS that he (Nowak) was going to call "Reaper" and try to meet with "Reaper" on that Thursday, July 17, 2008.

16. On or about Thursday, July 17, 2008, at approximately 12:45 p.m., the UC, "Reaper," viewed his cellular telephone and saw a missed call from "call withheld." Assuming this was Nowak attempting to contact him, the UC/"Reaper" called Nowak and left him a voicemail message asking Nowak to call him (UC/"Reaper") back.

17. On or about Thursday, July 17, 2008, at approximately 2:44 p.m., Nowak called the UC/"Reaper" and said he (Nowak) had spoken to the CS and had been putting his affairs in order. Nowak thanked the UC/"Reaper" for his patience and stated that they would meet next week.

18. On or about July 22, 2008, Nowak called the UC/"Reaper" and told the UC/"Reaper" that he wanted to meet with him at the Harley Davidson shop in Brandon, in the Middle District of Florida. Nowak explained that there was a BBQ restaurant behind the Harley Davidson shop and that Nowak would like to meet at 11:30 a.m. the next day, July 23, 2008. During the call, Nowak described himself as a big guy with a goatee and blond hair so that the UC/"Reaper" could recognize him for the meeting. The UC/"Reaper" described what he looked like to Nowak.

19. On or about July 23, 2008, at approximately 11:20 a.m., Nowak met with the UC/ "Reaper" at the BBQ restaurant in Brandon. Nowak, who arrived first and 15 minutes early for the meeting, discovered that the restaurant was temporarily closed.

When the UC/"Reaper" arrived, he ("Reaper") suggested they talk at a covered picnic table nearby. This meeting was recorded by means of video and audio.

20. During the meeting between Nowak and the UC/"Reaper" on or about July 23, 2008, Nowak identified the IRS employee he wanted killed as Christine Brandt. Nowak went so far as to write the following on a piece of paper that he handed to the UC/"Reaper:" "Christine Brandt / IRS on Harden Blvd / in Lakeland / Old Polk Road." Nowak explained that Old Polk Road was a possible address for the IRS employee's residence. Nowak also told the UC/"Reaper" that he (Nowak) was going to work on finding the specific home address for IRS Employee Brandt and would call the UC back with that information once he found it. Nowak explained that because of his construction business, he (Nowak) had access to databases that listed residences and their owners and that no one could tell he (Nowak) was looking up her residence because it was a public computer. The UC/"Reaper" told Nowak that Nowak would have to pay him $10,000 up front. Nowak replied, "understood." The UC/"Reaper" then told Nowak that he (the UC) would find IRS Employee Brandt and take pictures of her to show Nowak and confirm with Nowak that she was the intended victim. The UC/"Reaper" then stated to Nowak that once Nowak confirmed her identity, he (the UC) would kill her and she would no longer be Nowak's problem. Nowak replied, "mmm hmmm." Then the UC/"Reaper" said he and Nowak would meet again and Nowak would pay the remaining $10,000. Nowak agreed to this plan of action.

21. On or about Thursday, July 24, 2008, Nowak called the UC/"Reaper" and provided the UC/"Reaper" with IRS employee Brandt's complete residential address.

The UC/"Reaper" told Nowak that he would call him in a few days – on Sunday or Monday - to set up the next meeting.

22. On or about Monday, July 28, 2008, at approximately 9:30 p.m., the UC/"Reaper" called Nowak and said he had tracked down the IRS employee and was ready to meet. Nowak and the UC/"Reaper" agreed to meet the next day, July 29, 2008, in Lakeland in the parking lot of the Home Depot.

23. On or about July 29, 2008, at approximately 11:00 a.m., Nowak met the UC/"Reaper" in the Home Depot parking lot in Lakeland, in the Middle District of Florida. This meeting was recorded by means of audio and video. At the meeting, the UC/"Reaper" handed Nowak two photographs each of two women (one of Brandt, the other of a co-worker) that generally matched the description of IRS employee Brandt. In these photos, the female employees were walking in to or out of the employee entrance of the Lakeland IRS office. Nowak reviewed the photos and identified the picture of Brandt as the intended victim.

23. Also during the meeting that occurred on or about July 29, 2008, Nowak handed the UC/"Reaper" an envelope containing $10,000 in cash. The UC/"Reaper" told Nowak he would give him a call when it was done and that he expected to kill IRS employee Brandt by the end of the week. Nowak shook his head yes and said "OK" in acknowledgment. Nowak also asked the UC/"Reaper" whether he, Nowak, could ask some questions. The UC/"Reaper" replied in the affirmative. Nowak then asked, "So it's not like she's going to be found any time soon?" The UC/"Reaper" replied "No, not at all," to which Nowak shook his head in the affirmative and said "OK." The UC/"Reaper" said, "She and her vehicle will be gone," to which Nowak again shook his

head in the affirmative and said "OK." With respect to the UC/"Reaper's" plans to murder IRS employee Brandt," Nowak further stated, "OK, cool." The UC/"Reaper" indicated that he was going to remove a few pieces of IRS employee Brandt's body, burn the body in the car, and "you [Nowak] will have no problems," to which Nowak replied, "OK, that's fine. That's perfect."

24. Also during the meeting on or about July 29, 2008, Nowak asked the UC/"Reaper," "How much more would it cost me to have that building severely damaged?" The UC/"Reaper" replied, "the IRS building?" Nowak stated, "yes.... Or do you not want to get into that? That's federal." The UC/"Reaper" said that would cost "a big chunk." The UC/"Reaper" asked whether Nowak was talking about taking some action in the middle of the night when nobody "was home," "like 3:00 in the morning....," at which time, Nowak interrupted the UC/"Reaper" and said "yeah, yeah, that's what I'm talking about." Then Nowak elaborated, "Yeah, cause all that's in there is a couple of law firms. I'm been through there a bazillion times. There's no fucking cameras. There's a mobile home park to the back and to the front so access.... I was just sitting here thinking about fucking nitrate and black powder over by the electrical system...." The UC/"Reaper" replied, "Well, anything's doable, brother." Then Nowak stated, "Yeah, well, I want to cover all of my bases... I want it to go away go away." The UC/"Reaper" then proposed that he take care of "job number 1 first," i.e. killing IRS employee Brandt, and then they could talk about "job 2," meaning burning down the IRS office. Nowak replied by nodding his head in the affirmative and stating, "perfect... sounds good." The UC/"Reaper" then reiterated that he would do the job by the end of the week and Nowak reached out to shake his hand before they departed.

CONCLUSION

Based upon the foregoing, your affiant believes there is probable cause to establish that Randy Nowak has attempted to kill an officer or employee of the United States or any agency in any branch of the United States government while such officer or employee is engaged in or on account of the performance of official duties, in violation of Title 18, United States Code, Section 1114.

Special Agent Robert W. Courtenay
United States Treasury Inspector
General for Tax Administration (TIGTA)

Sworn to and subscribed before me
this 30 day of July, 2008.

THOMAS B. MCCOUN, III
UNITED STATES MAGISTRATE JUDGE

TABLE OF CASES

[References are to pages.]

[References are to pages.]

C

D

E

[References are to pages.]

F

G

H

[References are to pages.]

[References are to pages.]

[References are to pages.]

O

P

Q

R

S

[References are to pages.]

T

U

V

W

[References are to pages.]

Y

TABLE OF STATUTES

[References are to pages.]

FEDERAL STATUTES, RULES, AND REGULATIONS

United States Constitution

United States Code

United States Code—Cont.

[References are to pages.]

United States Code—Cont.

Code of Federal Regulations

[References are to pages.]

Code of Federal Regulations—Cont.

Internal Revenue Code

Internal Revenue Code—Cont.

[References are to pages.]

Internal Revenue Code—Cont.

Federal Rules of Appellate Procedure

Federal Rules of Civil Procedure

Federal Rules of Criminal Procedure

Federal Rules of Criminal Procedure —Cont.

Federal Rules of Evidence

Treasury Regulations

[References are to pages.]

Treasury Regulations—Cont.

UNIFORM MODEL CODES

Uniform Commercial Code

TABLE OF SECONDARY AUTHORITIES

[References are to page numbers.]

ABA MODEL RULES, FORMAL OPINIONS, COMMITTEES, ETC.

ASS'N OF THE BAR OF THE CITY OF N.Y. COMM. ON PROFESSIONAL ETHICS

CCA

CHIEF COUNSEL DIRECTIVE MANUAL

CONGRESSIONAL RECORDS

CRIMINAL RESOURCE MANUAL

CRIMINAL TAX MANUAL

[References are to page numbers.]

DEPARTMENT OF JUSTICE (DOJ) TAX DIV. MANUAL

INDIANA STATE BAR ASSOCIATION LEGAL ETHICS COMMITTEE OPINION

INTERNAL REVENUE MANUAL

[References are to page numbers.]

I.R.S. LEGAL MEMORANDA

I.R.S. NOTICES

LAW REVIEWS, JOURNALS, ARTICLES, BOOKS & TREATISES

[References are to page numbers.]

[References are to page numbers.]

[References are to page numbers.]

[References are to page numbers.]

REVENUE PROCEDURES

REVENUE RULINGS

TAX COURT RULES

TAX DIVISION DIRECTIVES

TREASURY CIRCULARS

[References are to page numbers.]

UNITED STATES ATTORNEY'S MANUAL

UNITED STATES SENTENCING GUIDLINES

[References are to page numbers.]

WASHINGTON FORMAL OPINIONS

WISCONSIN ETHICS OPINIONS

INDEX

[References are to sections.]

[References are to sections.]

D

E

[References are to sections.]

[References are to sections.]

S

[References are to sections.]

T

V

W